Creative Thinking and Arts-Based Learning

Preschool Through Fourth Grade

FOURTH EDITION

Joan Packer Isenberg
George Mason University

Mary Renck Jalongo
Indiana University of Pennsylvania

PEARSON

Merrill
Prentice Hall

Upper Saddle River, New Jersey
Columbus, Ohio

THIS BOOK IS THE PROPERTY OF
THE NATIONAL CITY PUBLIC LIBRARY
1401 NATIONAL CITY BLVD
NATIONAL CITY CA 91950-4401

Library of Congress Cataloging-in-Publication Data

Isenberg, Joan P.
    Creative thinking and arts-based learning : preschool through fourth grade / Joan Packer
Isenberg, Mary Renck Jalongo.--4th ed.
       p. cm.
    Rev. ed. of: Creative expression and play in early childhood. c2001.
    Includes bibliographical references and index.
    ISBN 0-13-118831-3
    1. Early childhood education--Activity programs. 2. Creative activities and seat work. I.
Jalongo, Mary Renck. II. Isenberg, Joan P., Creative expression and play in early
childhood. III. Title.

LB1139.35.A37186 2006
372.13--dc22

2005043306

Vice President and Executive Publisher: Jeffery W. Johnston
Publisher: Kevin M. Davis
Editor: Julie Peters
Editorial Assistant: Michelle Girgis
Production Editor: Sheryl Glicker Langner
Production Coordination: Ann Mohan, WordCrafters
  Editorial Services, Inc.

Design Coordinator: Diane C. Lorenzo
Cover Design: Terry Rohrback
Cover Image: Corbis
Production Manager: Laura Messerly
Director of Marketing: Ann Castel Davis
Marketing Manager: Amy Judd
Marketing Coordinator: Brian Mounts

This book was set in Palatino by Carlisle Communications, Ltd. It was printed and bound by
R. R. Donnelley & Sons Company. The cover was printed by R. R. Donnelley & Sons Company.

Photo Credits: David Mager/Pearson Learning Photo Studio, p. 2; Joan Isenberg, pp. 16, 51, 62, 145, 284, 303,
327, 335, 373; Ann Peterson, pp. 21, 60, 116, 181, 243; Anne Vega/Merrill, pp. 22, 29, 58, 105, 124, 135, 158, 191,
220, 239, 277, 297, 332, 350, 365, 372, 400; Marilyn Deppe, pp. 34, 253; Andy Brunk/Merrill, p. 38; Janet Brown
McCracken/Subjects & Predicates, pp. 43, 59, 109, 176; Library of Congress, p. 44 (left); The Filson Club
Historical Society, Louisville, KY, p. 44 (right); Jamie Marlies Reynolds, p. 80; V.C.L./Getty Images, Inc.–Taxi,
p. 84; Charles Thatcher/Getty Images, Inc.–Stone Allstock, p. 121; Scott Cunningham/Merrill, pp. 132, 146; Todd
Yarrington/Merrill, p. 163; Barbara Schwartz/Merrill, pp. 185, 254, 289, 324, 410; Lloyd Lemmerman/Merrill,
p. 199; Elyse Lewin/Getty Images, Inc.–Image Bank, p. 203; Anthony Magnacca/Merrill, pp. 207, 272, 314, 420;
Jennifer Isenberg, p. 224; Nancy P. Alexander, pp. 268, 401; Tracy Phillips, p. 353; Jyotsna Pattnaik, p. 357; Dan
Floss/Merrill, p. 396; Mel Yates/Getty Images, Inc.–Photodisc, p. 417.

**Copyright © 2006, 2001, 1997, 1993 by Pearson Education, Inc., Upper Saddle River, New Jersey
07458.** Pearson Prentice Hall. All rights reserved. Printed in the United States of America. This publication is
protected by Copyright and permission should be obtained from the publisher prior to any prohibited
reproduction, storage in a retrieval system, or transmission in any form or by any means, electronic,
mechanical, photocopying, recording, or likewise. For information regarding permission(s), write to: Rights
and Permissions Department.

Pearson Prentice Hall™ is a trademark of Pearson Education, Inc.
Pearson® is a registered trademark of Pearson plc
Prentice Hall® is a registered trademark of Pearson Education, Inc.
Merrill® is a registered trademark of Pearson Education, Inc.

Pearson Education Ltd.
Pearson Education Singapore Pte. Ltd.
Pearson Education Canada, Ltd.
Pearson Education—Japan

Pearson Education Australia Pty. Limited
Pearson Education North Asia Ltd.
Pearson Educación de Mexico, S.A. de C.V.
Pearson Education Malaysia Pte. Ltd.

10 9 8 7 6 5 4 3 2 1
ISBN: 0-13-118831-3

*For Jacob and Sara Pearlstein, Alyssa and Alexander Muck,
and Jacob and Noah Bradshaw, who fill my life with love, joy,
and creative endeavors. May your childlike qualities
flourish inside each and every one of us.*

Joan Packer Isenberg
George Mason University

*For educators worldwide
who nurture every child's creativity and artistic expression.*

Mary Renck Jalongo
Indiana University of Pennsylvania

# Preface

Creative thought and artistic expression: what is the value of these processes and the resulting products for children and families, communities, and society at large? Why should educators be concerned about such things at a time when tough talk about academic standards, teacher accountability, and international ranking on tests dominates the educational scene? As this book will argue, the ability to think in innovative and productive ways is a survival skill in a world where we are inundated daily with information. In the past, the educated person took pride in knowing something about many things and knowing a few things reasonably well. Today, knowing no longer suffices. Instant access to information has made it relatively easy for us to know, or at least to quickly find out, about virtually any topic. In fact, if the information explosion continues and artificial-intelligence technology advances, the children we work with today will have even less need for the rote memorization of basic content that has characterized traditional early and elementary education.

The audience for this book needs only to look around to see that expectations for children, teachers, and teacher educators have changed dramatically. Contemporary children are immersed in a world of fleeting images and multiple symbol systems; their challenge is to negotiate the complexities of that increasingly chaotic context. Contemporary teachers are expected to teach for understanding to an increasing number of local, state, and national benchmarks and to improve their respective country's reputation for academic excellence. Today's college and university faculty are being challenged to demonstrate that their teacher candidates have attained not only knowledge of pedagogy but also the practical/professional abilities of an effective early childhood or elementary teacher. Across all of these groups, the message is consistent: aim higher, achieve more, and contribute further to society. When the pressure is on, there is a tendency to discredit, disregard, or completely overlook the very thing that is most necessary in the preparation of students and their teachers. We contend that creative thinking is necessary to survive and thrive in an uncertain future.

Why have so many others failed to arrive at a similar conclusion? Individuals and groups define, recognize, and support creativity in distinctive ways. Creativity and the arts are aspects of human functioning that are sometimes perplexing, often controversial, and challenging to assess.

Even within the same person, ideas about creative thought can be contradictory. The age of the person who creates a product can affect recognition of its value. An adult who is awestruck by the inventiveness reflected in the latest piece of technology, for example, may disregard the imaginative life of a child as the wellspring for the ingenuity. In other cases, the domain in which creative thought is expressed can influence perceptions of its relative merits. As a result, a teacher who delights in young children's drawings and writings may fail to recognize opportunities for creative thought in mathematics or science, treating them as "one right answer" subjects. In still other cases, the social organization in which creative thinking operates can unduly influence point of view. As a result, a political leader who extols the virtues of innovative thought and entrepreneurship in business also may be a shrill voice for "back to basics" in the public schools.

Few people possess an understanding of creative thought and artistic expression that is not woefully outdated. They are uninformed or misinformed about decades of research in cognitive psychology, on the human brain, and on the contributions of the arts to cognitive functioning. Their ideas about creativity and the arts emphasize natural talent, inspiration, and art as a curricular "frill," when the research supports instead the importance of training and practice, materials and opportunities, and the arts as a genuine basic (Jalongo, 2003).

Our vision for this book is that it will equip practitioners in the fields of early childhood and elementary education to counteract stereotypes that run rampant about the contributions of children's creative thinking; to educate professional colleagues and the general public about creativity and the arts; and to influence schools and communities to regard the creative processes and artistic products of children's minds with new appreciation and respect.

Challenges to Misconceptions About Children's Creativity

Although many college-level textbooks use the word *creativity* or *art* in their titles, many of these "creative activities" books make minimal contributions to teachers' creative growth, much less children's. Any book that claims to center on children's creative thinking must begin with respect for the child's intellect. Effective teachers acknowledge children's ability to construct their own understandings about their world and to express their ideas in original, inventive ways. We resent the condescending message of materials that presume to give young children patterns to copy, lines to color inside, and activities that are completely initiated and directed by adults. That is why we decided to write a book that would challenge popular misconceptions about children's creativity and do a better job of enabling teachers and caregivers to articulate this more enlightened view to families, colleagues, and administrative personnel.

Purpose

Above all, in this fourth edition we want to orient both preservice and inservice teachers to the profound and lifelong contributions of an emphasis on children's creative thinking and arts-based learning. There is little question that most educators' backgrounds in nurturing children's creativity and promoting learning through the arts are inadequate. For many teachers, preparation for educating students to become creative, critical thinkers and communicate through the arts consists of a single college course. In this text, the fourth edition of a successful college-level textbook on creativity and the arts, we have attempted to distill the essential research-based perspectives that can guide nonspecialist classroom teachers in promoting creativity, play, art, music, dance, and drama. *Creative Thinking and Arts-Based Learning: Preschool Through Fourth Grade* also delineates the teacher's role from a philosophical, pedagogical, and curricular stance by addressing key components, including the classroom environment, materials and resources, behavior management, assessment, and culturally responsive teaching.

Audience

This book is an outgrowth of our combined more than 50 years of teaching college courses on children's creativity and the arts. *Creative Thinking and Arts-Based Learning: Preschool Through Fourth Grade* is equally appropriate to early childhood and elementary students at various stages in their careers. Because the book is firmly grounded in theory and research, it is well suited for students seeking initial licensure or certification, whether they are enrolled in a community college, a four-year teacher-preparation program, or a fifth-year program for practicing professionals who are pursuing certification or a master's degree in early childhood or elementary education. The book's universal message of fostering creative and artistic expression is important to professionals who work with children throughout the world.

Description of the Book's Contents

The book begins with two chapters that form the foundation for the remaining chapters. Chapter 1 discusses creative thought: how it is defined, how it develops, and what adults can do to foster its growth. Chapter 2 examines children's play, games, and inventions and how these modes of inquiry support children's learning across the disciplines.

After establishing this base, Chapters 3 through 5 cover the topics that are traditionally associated with the fine arts (art, music, dance, dramatic arts), and Chapters 6 through 9 discuss topics that are foundational to teaching for creativity (planning and managing the environment, using materials and resources effectively, fostering children's creative thought and expression, and assessing creative processes and products). Chapter 10 is completely new and covers the influence of cultural contexts on creative thought and artistic expression, how to use brain research to foster creative thought, and strategies for fostering creative thought in teachers.

Each chapter begins with three classroom scenarios gleaned from observations in preschool, early primary, and third- and fourth-grade classrooms. These "Classroom Perspectives" can serve as the basis for a class discussion. Next, a theoretical framework forms the foundation for the chapter content, followed by "Reflections" from new and experienced teachers on the chapter content. Discussion questions conclude each chapter.

New to the Fourth Edition

The first edition of this book was published more than 10 years ago, in 1993. It was the first co-authored textbook for both of us, and, as is the case with many textbooks, we wrote it because we could not find a suitable book for the classes we were teaching in creative expression and play. It began as an early childhood book and continued as one through the second and third editions. As we have talked with college faculty at various institutions, however, we discovered that the book often is used in college-level courses that include both early childhood educators and elementary teachers. Thus, our fourth-edition challenge was to simultaneously preserve what had made the book successful—its early childhood emphasis—yet **broaden the book's scope** to make it more useful to adopters who were already using it with elementary teachers. Additionally, the reviewers urged us to incorporate more material on the **influence of culture on creative thinking and products.** In order to accomplish all of this, we have significantly revised both the book's content and its title to reflect this new focus.

Some new features that were developed and added to this edition include:

Classroom Perspectives are scenarios from three age groups—preschool, K–1 or K–2, and older primary—presented at the beginning of each chapter to serve as the basis for class discussion.

Frequently Asked Questions features in each chapter dispel misconceptions about creativity in the arts. Common questions and research-based and experience-based responses are provided.

Meeting Standards, a feature at the end of chapters, lists standards from various organizations and states to show teachers how learning experiences in the creative arts and play can align with standards.

Chapter 10—This chapter has been completely rewritten to discuss the cultural contents that affect what individuals, cultural groups, and nations accept and endorse where creative thought and artistic expression are concerned.

The fourth edition includes an **expanded ancillary package.** Please note that material from the third edition Website designed specifically to accompany the text has been moved to the *Instructor's Manual/Test Bank,* which is now available online. The *Instructor's Manual/Test Bank* includes test questions with responses, lists of outstanding children's literature to accompany the content-area chapters, as well as a suggested Interview and a Write-to-Learn activity. Another technology-based support for the instructor is a complete set of color PowerPoint slideshows that highlight key concepts from the chapters. Faculty can visit the Instructor's Resource Center at **www.prenhall.com** and download both ancillaries. PowerPoint slides can be used as provided in an onscreen show using a computer and projector. Or, instructors can make them into overhead transparencies. Additionally, instructors can duplicate the notes page version of the slides in PowerPoint and distribute them to students for use as a study aid.

Using This Book

Instructors will find that this exceptionally versatile book includes an array of text features that can be emphasized for different audiences. Those working with more advanced students may want to stress the theoretical framework and the Frequently Asked Questions in each chapter. Those working with early childhood and elementary educators who are at the beginning of their careers may want to place greater emphasis on the classroom scenarios and the Interviews and Write-to-Learn activities (available in the *Instructor's Manual/Test Bank*). All teachers will find that the new "Meeting Standards" feature, which appears at each chapter's end, is helpful in designing an integrated curriculum. By offering instructors various features that they can use as assignments and as in-class activities, *Creative Thinking and Arts-Based Learning: Preschool Through Fourth Grade* lends extensive support to instructors who are themselves at different levels of experience in working with future and current early childhood and elementary teachers.

Acknowledgments

We are deeply indebted to the many people who contributed to the development of this book. First and foremost, we would like to thank the colleagues and doctoral advisees who helped us expand the book's scope to include the elementary years. Their names are listed in the table of contents, but we also wish to acknowledge their contributions here. Laurie Nicholson Stamp, faculty member at Indiana University of Pennsylvania, co-authored Chapter 4 on music, movement, and dance. Marilyn J. Narey, an art teacher and doctoral candidate, collaborated on the art and assessment chapters. Shana Barr and Karen Curtis, doctoral candidates, assisted with the dramatic arts and environment chapters. We wish to acknowledge the graduate and undergraduate students at George Mason University and Indiana University of Pennsylvania for their cooperation in field-testing this book and for providing us with many of the rich classroom examples that appear throughout these chapters. Natalie K. Conrad and Norah Hooper, our former graduate assistants, merit special recognition for their work on the *Instructor's Manual/Test Bank* that accompanies the fourth edition of the text. We are also grateful to the many teachers, parents, and children whose photographs, art material, and stories are an integral part of this text. Thanks, too, to our many colleagues who helped us further clarify our thinking about children's creative thought and artistic expression.

We want to thank our editors for this edition, Kevin Davis and Julie Peters, who gave us a bit more time to complete this major revision and offered guidance and support. We are also grateful to the rest of the staff at Merrill/Prentice Hall who made the publication of this book possible, particularly our former editor, Ann Davis. They are a fine group of professionals and have been a pleasure to work with throughout the book's production. In addition, we appreciate the valuable input from those who reviewed the book: Linda Aiken, Southwestern Community College; Nancy Ratcliff, University of South Florida; Stan Wollock, William Paterson University; and Andrea Zarate, Hartnell College.

Finally, we wish to acknowledge the continuous and unwavering support of our families and close friends. We are especially grateful for their encouragement, understanding, and willingness to listen through each phase of the development of the book from the first to the fourth edition.

A Final Word

In education, there are three common misconceptions about teaching and learning—that it is all content, that it is all process, and that there is one best curriculum for all children (Eisner, 1990, 1998). Fortunately, any instructor who would choose our book for a course would also be likely to avoid these three errors. When it is approached with an open mind, the study of children's creative thought and artistic expression is a powerful reminder that neither coverage nor aimlessness is the answer and that, clearly, there are no panaceas. Rather, the teacher must create a classroom learning community that emphasizes quality over quantity of materials, balances freedom with control, and respects children as individuals while socializing them into an increasingly diverse society and global village. By bringing these perspectives to teaching, teachers and teacher educators not only avoid the pervasive pitfalls of which Eisner speaks, but also become more effective and reflective practitioners.

It has been gratifying to see the book that began as hopeful dreaming evolve into print. It has been humbling to realize, with each edition of the work, the amount of information we need to master in order to remain current in a rapidly changing field. It also has been encouraging to watch our collaborative efforts endure in the fiercely competitive college textbook market for more than a decade. As authors, we have been privileged to revisit our work and refashion it—each time, we trust, into a college-level text that better meets the needs of contemporary children, educators, and teacher educators.

Joan Packer Isenberg
Fairfax, Virginia

Mary Renck Jalongo
Indiana, Pennsylvania

Discover the Companion Website Accompanying This Book

The Prentice Hall Companion Website: A Virtual Learning Environment

Technology is a constantly growing and changing aspect of our field that is creating a need for content and resources. To address this emerging need, Prentice Hall has developed an online learning environment for students and professors alike—Companion Websites—to support our textbooks.

In creating a Companion Website, our goal is to build on and enhance what the textbook already offers. For this reason, the content for each user-friendly website is organized by topic and provides the professor and student with a variety of meaningful resources. Common features of a Companion Website include:

For the Professor—

Every Companion Website integrates **Syllabus Manager**™, an online syllabus creation and management utility.

- **Syllabus Manager**™ provides you, the instructor, with an easy, step-by-step process to create and revise syllabi, with direct links into Companion Website and other online content without having to learn HTML.
- Students may logon to your syllabus during any study session. All they need to know is the web address for the Companion Website and the password you've assigned to your syllabus.
- After you have created a syllabus using **Syllabus Manager**™, students may enter the syllabus for their course section from any point in the Companion Website.
- Clicking on a date, the student is shown the list of activities for the assignment. The activities for each assignment are linked directly to actual content, saving time for students.
- Adding assignments consists of clicking on the desired due date, then filling in the details of the assignment—name of the assignment, instructions, and whether or not it is a one-time or repeating assignment.
- In addition, links to other activities can be created easily. If the activity is online, a URL can be entered in the space provided, and it will be linked automatically in the final syllabus.

- Your completed syllabus is hosted on our servers, allowing convenient updates from any computer on the Internet. Changes you make to your syllabus are immediately available to your students at their next logon.

For the Student—

- *Introduction*—General information about the topic and how it will be covered in the website.
- *Web Links*—A variety of websites related to topic areas.
- *Timely Articles*—Links to online articles that enable you to become more aware of important issues in early childhood.
- *Learn by Doing*—Put concepts into action, participate in activities, examine strategies, and more.
- *Visit a School*—Visit a school's website to see concepts, theories, and strategies in action.
- *For Teachers/Practitioners*—Access information you will need to know as an educator, including information on materials, activities, and lessons.
- *Observation Tools*—A collection of checklists and forms to print and use when observing and assessing children's development.
- *Current Policies and Standards*—Find out the latest early childhood policies from the government and various organizations, and view state, federal, and curriculum standards.
- *Resources and Organizations*—Discover tools to help you plan your classroom or center and organizations to provide current information and standards for each topic.
- *Electronic Bluebook*—Paperless method of completing homework or essays assigned by a professor. Finished work can be sent to the professor via email.
- *Message Board*—Virtual bulletin board to post and respond to questions and comments from a national audience.

To take advantage of these resources, please visit Merrill Education's *Early Childhood Education Resources* Website. Go to **www.prenhall.com/isenberg**, click on the book cover, and then click on "Enter" at the bottom of the next screen.

Educator Learning Center:
An Invaluable Online Resource

Merrill Education and the Association for Supervision and Curriculum Development (ASCD) invite you to take advantage of a new online resource, one that provides access to the top research and proven strategies associated with ASCD and Merrill—the Educator Learning Center. At **www.educatorlearningcenter. com**, you will find resources that will enhance your students' understanding of course topics and of current educational issues, in addition to being invaluable for further research.

How the Educator Learning Center Will Help Your Students Become Better Teachers

With the combined resources of Merrill Education and ASCD, you and your students will find a wealth of tools and materials to better prepare them for the classroom.

Research
- More than 600 articles from the ASCD journal *Educational Leadership* discuss everyday issues faced by practicing teachers.
- A direct link on the site to Research Navigator™ gives students access to many of the leading education journals, as well as extensive content detailing the research process.
- Excerpts from Merrill Education texts give your students insights on important topics of instructional methods, diverse populations, assessment, classroom management, technology, and refining classroom practice.

Classroom Practice
- Hundreds of lesson plans and teaching strategies are categorized by content area and age range.
- Case studies and classroom video footage provide virtual field experience for student reflection.
- Computer simulations and other electronic tools keep your students abreast of today's classrooms and current technologies.

Look into the Value of Educator Learning Center Yourself

A four-month subscription to Educator Learning Center is $25 but is **FREE** when packaged with any Merrill Education text. In order for your students to have access to this site, you must use this special value-pack ISBN number **WHEN** placing your textbook order with the bookstore: 0-13-197200-6. Your students will then receive a copy of the text packaged with a free ASCD pincode. To preview the value of this website to you and your students, please go to **www.educatorlearningcenter.com** and click on "Demo."

Brief Contents

Contents

Part 3   Creative Teaching   219

NOTE: Every effort has been made to provide accurate and current Internet information in this book. However, the Internet and information posted on it are constantly changing, so it is inevitable that some of the Internet addresses in this textbook will change.

PART 1
FOUNDATIONS OF
CREATIVE THOUGHT

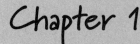

Chapter 1

Understanding Children's Creative Thought and Expression

The professional skill of the teacher is important in sustaining . . . creative effort, because creativity is easily extinguished. Creativity is an ability that is present within everyone, but the proper conditions are required for creativity to be expressed

Richard Peterson, 2001/2002, p. 8

CLASSROOM PERSPECTIVES ON CREATIVITY

Preschool–Kindergarten

Two 4-year-old boys put empty margarine tubs on their heads and move around the table where children are playing with puzzles. As they balance the tubs on their heads, they pretend to be band members who lift their knees up high and march while playing imaginary instruments and humming. The teacher tells them that the plastic tubs are for holding puzzle pieces and directs them to put everything away. They do; however, a few moments later, the boys disrupt play in the family living center and are reprimanded for their misbehavior.

First Grade–Second Grade

A group of kindergarten and first-grade children are playing house. Their teacher is rather surprised by some of the themes in their play—the stereotypic gender roles, an absent father, going to jail, viewing a movie that is rated PG, and a child who insists on being the baby. After listening in on the children's dialogue, the teacher asks herself, "Where do children's ideas for play come from?"

Girl 1: *(speaking to a boy while running a toy sweeper)* Get out, you're making a mess!
Boy: I didn't do anything wrong. I'm playing by myself.
Girl 2: Don't, honey. I already swept the floor, now I'll have to do it again. *(sweeps the floor, picks up a doll, and speaks to the boy)* You're her daddy. Our little girl needs to see you. You're her daddy.
Boy: No, I'm not. I have ten brothers and we are going to see a movie that's rated PG.
Girl 1: Daddy, dad, come here.
Boy: This is stupid. I didn't do anything bad. Let's play. *(moves a wooden ramp across the entrance to the housekeeping area)* Honey, pretend this is a jail and I can't get out. See, I got on handcuffs. *(puts wrists together)*
Girl 1: I can get you out. See, I just did.
Girl 2: Daddy, daddy. I want to be the baby.
Girl 1: No, you will not be the baby.
Girl 2: I am the baby—goo, goo, ga, ga. *(grabs baby bottle and crawls on the floor with it in her mouth)*

Girl 1:   Then who's going to be the father?
Boy: Not me, I'm going to work.

Third Grade–Fourth Grade

A school district offers summer school for children who are struggling with literacy skills. Rather than follow the customary approach of more drill and workbooks, the summer program has a community service emphasis. Today, the third and fourth graders are presented with a challenge: The local animal shelter is full to capacity with homeless dogs and cats. The director visits the children and asks them to help. The children form small groups to plan their strategy. One group will seek out creative ideas from other shelters across the country and throughout the world. Another group will design posters using the set of photographs and notes about each animal that the director provided, then go about gaining community support for displaying them in area businesses. A third group will plan and advertise an "adoptathon" at the pet supply store. As they work on these projects, the students use their research skills, artistic talent, interpersonal skills, and literacy skills to save the animals and contribute to their community.

These vignettes raise many questions about creativity, including what creative thought is, how children's creative thinking is distinct from that of adults, and what adults do to help or hinder children's creative growth. In this chapter, we explore the role of creative thought and expression in children's lives and its rightful place in education.

DEFINING CREATIVE THOUGHT

The word *create* comes from the Latin word *creare*, which means "to make a thing which has not been made before; to bring into being" (Barnhart & Barnhart, 1983). Based on these origins, the word *create* is used in contemporary society to mean to invent, or produce; to approach the realm of art (imaginative, artistic, literary); and to produce something useful or worthwhile (constructive, purposeful). In addition, because creative thought can be put to negative or destructive ends, positive intentions must underlie creativity.

Over the years, originality has been a constant factor in discussions of creative processes and products (Runco, 2004). What is too often overlooked, however, is that being different is not enough. It would surely be different for a college student to decide to dress in a gorilla costume and sit on the roof of the tallest building on campus to eat lunch; however, this is merely bizarre behavior. The creative response or product must also be effective, defined as relevant to the issue at stake and capable of offering some type of genuine solution (Cropley, 2001). E. Paul Torrance, one of the leading researchers in the field of creativity, defined creativity as "the process of sensing problems, forming ideas, and driving unprecedented solutions of unique problems with elaboration and embellishment" (cited in Tennent & Berhelsen, 1997, p. 91). An integrated concept of creativity includes the following:

- *Thinking,* which can be developed and measured
- *Sensing,* which results in the creation of new products or talent in a particular area
- *Feeling,* which generates emotional energy from the person who is engaged in creative behavior
- *Intuition,* which consists of heightened awareness and consciousness of elements in the environment (Clark, 1988)
- *Valuing,* which enables the person to select the most appropriate route and effective outcomes. Creative thought can be put to selfish or destructive purposes, and so the ethical dimension must be considered as well (Cropley, 2001)

A first step in clearing up the confusion about creativity is to use the word *creative* in combination with *thought* (Webster, 1990). Creativity is a key component in Sternberg's (1998) triarchic theory of intelligence, which combines three interrelated ways of thinking:

1. *Analytical thought,* which includes analyzing, comparing/contrasting, evaluating, explaining
2. *Creative thought,* which includes creating, designing, imagining, supposing
3. *Practical thought,* which includes using, applying, and implementing

Contrary to popular opinion, creative thought is not merely wild imaginings; rather, it relies on complex reasoning processes (Marzano, Pickering, & McTighe, 1993; Runco, 2004), such as "comparing, classifying, inducting, deducting, analyzing errors, constructing support, abstracting, analyzing perspectives, making decisions, investigating, inquiring, problem solving, and inventing" (Beattie, 1997, p. 5).

The children described in the vignettes that introduced this chapter connected with their previous experiences (an absent father), responded to objects (making margarine tubs into band hats), used symbols (hands joined to represent handcuffs), used ideas (a PG-rated movie), collaborated with other people (animal shelter personnel), and responded to situations (homeless animals). Creativity is both a cognitive (thinking) and affective (feeling) process (Feldhusen, 1995) that depends on a complex interplay of biological, psychological, and social factors (Craft, 1999; Dacey & Lennon, 1998). Figure 1.1 summarizes the cognitive and affective dimensions of creative thought.

From a psychologist's point of view, creativity is the ability to make something new out of available and stored information. With children, that "something new" may be old and familiar to adults but more than a copy to the child. When 3-year-old Ruiz paints a *mandala* (a circle shape with sunlike rays emanating from it), it is new to him even though adults have seen it many times in other children's drawings. Consider these activities of children at different ages and stages:

- Jessica, a 30-month-old, has wrapped a block in a blanket that she now refers to as "baby"; she is using an object to symbolize something else.

Four Cognitive Dimensions
Creativity as a Thinking Process
1. **Fluency**
   - Generating a large quantity of relevant responses
   - Following a train of thought
   - Building up collections of related ideas
2. **Flexibility**
   - Approaching things in alternative ways
   - Changing categories as appropriate
   - Viewing the problem from a different perspective
3. **Originality**
   - Producing unusual, novel, unique, or clever ideas
   - Combining known ideas into some new form and connecting the seemingly unconnected
4. **Elaboration**
   - Filling out ideas and adding interesting details
   - Stretching or expanding on an idea

Four Affective Dimensions
Creativity as a Feeling Process
1. **Curiosity**
   - Wondering, puzzling about something
   - Playing with ideas
   - Following intuition to see what happens
2. **Complexity**
   - Feeling challenged to do things in detailed ways
   - Seeking many different alternatives
   - Bringing order out of chaos
   - Seeing missing parts between what is and what could be
3. **Risk-Taking**
   - A willingness to express ideas to others
   - The courage to expose self to criticism or failure
   - The confidence to follow a hunch and "invest" in a humble idea
4. **Imagination and Fantasy**
   - The ability to form rich and varied mental images ("what if"/"as if")
   - The ability to put oneself in another place, time, or person's shoes
   - An intuitive sense of what might be or what something might become

Figure 1.1
Dimensions of Creativity
Note. Adapted from Guilford (1984) and Sternberg (1997).

- Arwen, age 5, is painting at the easel in response to a dream he had the night before in which he could fly; he is using his imagination.
- Miguel, a gifted third grader, is designing his own Web site; he is using his knowledge of the Web sites he has seen previously and applying his skills in technology to accomplish a goal.

In each situation, the dual criteria of originality and purpose are met (Cropley, 1999); creativity may be thought of as "purposeful novelty" (Peterson, 2001/2002). In addition, all of these children manifest the characteristics of creative, highly effective individuals: openness to experience, freedom from crippling restraints and impoverishing inhibitions, aesthetic sensitivity, independence in thoughts and actions, individuality, unquestioning commitment to creative endeavor, emotional stability or personal soundness, enthusiasm, determination, and industry (MacKinnon, 1978).

Creativity is interpreted many different ways. Nevertheless, everyday understandings of creativity are full of contradictions (Harrison, 1984). People may:

- Say that creativity is an asset, but have difficulty explaining it or believing that they have a right to participate in creativity and the arts (Kerka, 2002; McDaniel & Thorn, 1997).
- Extol the contributions of creativity to society, yet treat creativity as a threat to children's attainment of academic standards or to conformity and the social order (Horibe, 2001; Robinson, 2001).
- View creativity as impractical, yet treat it as if it were inspired in the case of inventions and technology (Peterson, 2001/2002).

THEORETICAL AND RESEARCH BASE: MULTIPLE INTELLIGENCES

Over the past decade, our view of human intelligence has expanded and enlarged. In the past, there was a tendency to think of intelligence as a singular trait—the general capacity of the human being for storing, retrieving, and processing information. Howard Gardner (1993a) defines intelligence as "the ability to solve problems, or to fashion products that are of consequence in a particular cultural setting or community" (p. 15) and he has proposed that there are nine—and possibly more—types of intelligence. (The ninth intelligence is newer and has not been researched as extensively as the other eight.) He argues that each way of thinking is sufficiently distinctive to warrant a special category. The nine types of intelligence are as follows:

1. *Verbal/linguistic*—intelligence with words and language, such as the skill possessed by a writer or a person who can speak several languages fluently.
2. *Logical/mathematical*—intelligence with sequential thinking and numerical reasoning ability, such as the abilities possessed by a mathematician or scientist.
3. *Bodily/kinesthetic*—wisdom about one's own body and its movements, such as the intelligence possessed by a figure skater or a wide receiver in football.

4. *Visual/spatial*—intelligence in using "the mind's eye" to work with images and see their interrelationships, such as the intelligence needed by an architect.

5. *Musical/rhythmic*—intelligence having to do with sound patterns, mastery of musical notation, and musical talent, such as the skills of a composer or performer.

6. *Interpersonal*—intelligence in dealing with human interaction and perceptivity about how to resolve social problems, such as the abilities of a skilled counselor or therapist.

7. *Intrapersonal*—wisdom about the self that leads to self-knowledge and personal growth, such as the intelligence of a person who fully understands how he or she learns.

8. *Environmental/naturalist*—intelligence having to do with adapting to and learning about the physical environment, both natural and human-made (Checkley, 1997). Examples of careers for naturalists are marine biologist, city planner, and forest ranger.

9. *Philosophical/moral*—Although research on this type of intelligence is not as well developed as it is for the previous eight, those who possess philosophical/moral intelligence are capable of seeing the big picture and getting to the heart of the matter. These individuals raise questions of significance and grapple with ethical considerations effectively. Examples of professions that would rely on this form of intelligence are judges and clergy.

Furthermore, Gardner argued that only the first two forms of intelligence—verbal/linguistic and logical/mathematical—were routinely emphasized in American schools and that, as a result, much human potential was being wasted. Many other educators agree that we need to plan programs that respect these different ways of knowing (Hatch, 1997; Reiff, 1997). To see what a teaching theme that provides for the eight main types of intelligence might look like, see the teaching themes for preschool, first grade, and third grade in Table 1.1.

Ideally all schools would (a) cultivate skills that are valued in community and society, (b) approach new concepts and subjects in a variety of ways, and (c) personalize instruction as much as possible (Latham, 1997). One reason for this is that creativity is, to some extent, field-specific. Different roles such as music video director, crime scene investigator, or vocalist on a nationally televised talent show obviously require different forms of creative thought.

 TEACHERS' REFLECTIONS ON CREATIVITY

Consider these preservice and inservice teachers' reflections as they completed a course on creativity:

Preservice Teachers

"My knowledge of creativity was really limited. I knew that it was beneficial, but I didn't really have any facts to back it up—just a vague feeling that it's basically good. Now I have reasons why creative thinking benefits the whole child in all areas of development."

Inservice Teachers

"I have always believed that creative expression was important to children's development, but I think I only considered the content—art, music, dance, etc. I think I viewed these subjects as something to be appreciated rather than in terms of ways they can support children's learning."

Your Reflections

- How do these teachers think about creativity in their students?

- What are your assumptions and understandings about creative thought?

- What role might creative thought play in learning and teaching?

TABLE 1.1 Teaching Themes Based on Multiple Intelligences			
The Eight Intelligences	**Preschool MI Theme on Colors**	**First-Grade MI Theme on Patterns**	**Third-Grade MI Theme on Pets**
Verbal/ Linguistic	Read concept books about colors (e.g., *Who Said Red?* [Serfozo, 1992]), produce class books about various colors (e.g., What Is Green? Our Favorite Colors), learn to recognize the names of the primary colors, conduct a simple survey to discover favorite colors of classmates and family members, invent a class version of a book that features colors, such as *Brown Bear, Brown Bear, What Do You See?* (Martin, 1967), learn color names in a different language, read *Naming Colors* (Dewey, 1995), learn the chant *My Crayons Talk* (Hubbard, 1996).	Define the concept of patterns by finding examples of patterns in the classroom, explore word patterns (e.g., chants, rhymes, and raps), write couplets, listen for patterns in story language (e.g., "but it was too small," "but it was too large," "and it was just right"), recite a poem with a refrain in unison, search for patterns in groups of words that rhyme (e.g., *mall, hall, fall, wall*), read and perform a story in rhyme such as *Chicka Chicka Boom Boom* (Martin & Archambault, 1989).	Identify animal sounds, discuss chapter books about pets, maintain a detailed observational log about a classroom pet, create group booklets with practical information about the care and feeding of pets, tape-record reports about a particular type of pet, read the classified section of the newspaper to see what pets are for sale, visit pet rescue Web sites to see what pets are available (e.g., mustangs, greyhounds), make a vocabulary book of words for groups of animals (e.g., *flock, herd*).

(continued)

TABLE 1.1 *(Continued)*

The Eight Intelligences	Preschool MI Theme on Colors	First-Grade MI Theme on Patterns	Third-Grade MI Theme on Pets
Logical/ Mathematical	Use paint samples to arrange hues from light to dark and produce color "families," develop a color chart after experimenting with food coloring (e.g., blue and red make _____), play sorting games with attribute blocks—flat, plastic blocks in three colors (red, yellow, and blue), three shapes (circle, triangle, square), and three sizes (small, medium, large), play a matching game with the color word on one side of a puzzle piece and a picture of a crayon that color on the matching piece.	Examine patterns in mathematical equations (e.g., adding 1 to a number), recognize the fact that subtraction problems can be checked by adding the two bottom numbers, produce pictorial patterns on the computer using various types of software, use a number line on the floor to count by ones, twos, and so forth, watch the video *How the Leopard Got Its Spots* and note the patterns in animals' fur (e.g., zebra stripes, giraffe spots), as well as the patterns in the soundtrack of African choir music.	Count the number of pets owned by everyone in the class, create a simple bar graph of the favorite pets owned by the class, list the common features of domesticated animals, rank-order pets from most to least popular, identify the most unusual pet owned by anyone in the group, match various pets to their preferred food choices, analyze the consequences of neglecting pets' care, figure out how much it would cost to raise a cat or dog for a year, make lists of pet-care tips after consulting reference materials.
Bodily/ Kinesthetic	Make finger and hand prints of different colors, use a simplified computer keyboard with keys in different colors, play a simple teacher-made color game on a plastic shower curtain or tablecloth on the floor, group children according to the color of their clothing for an activity, decorate plain cloth dolls for each child so that the doll's features can be made to match the child's hair color, eye color, etc., use hard candy to match colors to flavors (e.g., red for cherry, yellow for lemon), take a color walk after reading *Colors Everywhere* (Hoban, 1997).	Invent patterns of sound (e.g., clapping, tapping feet), create a product using a pattern (e.g., in and out for weaving), make pattern cards for others to follow using large wooden beads and string, give children a chance to arrange their bodies into letter patterns (e.g., a task card that asks three children to make their bodies into a capital letter A), make patterns using an ink pad and stamps constructed from Styrofoam, use wallpaper book samples to search for repeated patterns and sort them into groups on the floor, make rubbings of patterns (e.g., bottom of shoe).	Compare the relative sizes of pets to one another and oneself, invent a dance that characterizes a particular animal's style of moving, give a demonstration of how to groom a pet (e.g., a 4-H student showing how to care for a cow's feet), research and analyze how pets move (e.g., how a horse runs, a snake slithers).

The Eight Intelligences	Preschool MI Theme on Colors	First-Grade MI Theme on Patterns	Third-Grade MI Theme on Pets
Visual/ Spatial	Use word configuration (the outline or shape of the word) to match color words to the correct shape; use swatches of fabric to match colors, sort individual boxes of crayons into plastic containers of all the same color of crayon, identify the colors that typically go with various foods (e.g., apples as yellow, red, green or combinations of these), sort plastic fruits and vegetables by colors, discover the magic of mixing colors in *White Rabbit's Color Book* (Baker, 1995).	Create designs using parquetry blocks, design patterned borders for original picture books, make and follow cue cards to show the gestures that accompany an action song (e.g., "Little Cabin in the Woods"), print out common signs in various colors from the computer and make into a color-sorting game, look at a piece of landscaping software to see how patterns are used, take a virtual field trip to a museum to look for patterns in art, use architectural blocks to build a structure and make a diagram of the structure.	Make sculptures of various pets, examine a pet closely and create life-size silhouettes, identify animal tracks and match them to the animals that made them, design a poster to encourage responsible pet ownership, create diagrams of pets labeled with the proper terminology (e.g., *mane*, *withers*, and *fetlock* for a horse), take a video visit to a veterinarian's office, go on a virtual field trip to a pet supplies store online.
Musical/ Rhythmic	Sing color songs (e.g., "Jenny Jenkins" or "Mary Wore Her Red Dress"), learn a color song in another language (e.g., "De Colores"), use a toy xylophone with colored keys and a color-coded piece of music for a simple nursery tune and learn to play a song.	Participate in simple dances and musical games (e.g., square dance steps), move "in time" with music (e.g., swaying), lead a rhythm band, watch a musical video with a bouncing ball that shows the pattern for singing; recite a cumulative rhyme (e.g., "The House That Jack Built"), sing a song with a chorus or a refrain.	Find or invent an instrumental selection that captures the feelings associated with various pets, sing songs about animals, choose a rhythm that matches the characteristic movement of a pet, compose a song about a pet using music software.

(continued)

TABLE 1.1 *(Continued)*

The Eight Intelligences	Preschool MI Theme on Colors	First-Grade MI Theme on Patterns	Third-Grade MI Theme on Pets
Interpersonal	Work with a partner or a small group to develop a poster collage of colors, read a story about different skin tones, make a big poster-sized book on colors and share it with another class, use color paddles (wooden frames with tinted plastic inside) to look at things with a partner and discuss how a change in color changes the object.	Infer the steps in a process by observing others (e.g., how to operate a videotape, learn a jump rope game, play hopscotch), work with a partner to learn a rhyme with a clapping pattern ("Miss Lucy"), use coffee can drums to follow a tapping pattern, solve a simple secret code such as numbering the letters of the alphabet, learn about patterns and fabrics of different cultures in *Kente Colors* (Chocolate, 1996).	Participate in a class project designed to safeguard the welfare of pets in the community, interview a pet shop owner, arrange a classroom visit with an expert on animal care, correspond by e-mail with volunteers at the local animal shelter, put on a pet show with a wide variety of forms of recognition for pets (e.g., furriest, friendliest, etc.).
Intrapersonal	Think about the feelings associated with various colors (e.g., red as fiery, yellow as sunshine), choose dress-up clothes based on favorite colors, use the paint feature of a piece of art software to try out several colors for an object or a picture before deciding which one to save or print out.	Look for daily routines that are patterns of behavior (e.g., getting ready for school), identify patterns of sound that are pleasant (e.g., ticking of a clock), experiment with a piece of software to make patterns until a satisfying combination is produced.	Maintain a journal of activities enjoyed with a pet, describe reasons for choosing a particular pet as a favorite, prepare a statement of beliefs about animal rights, write a persuasive argument for choosing a mature animal rather than a baby animal or an animal without a home rather than a pedigreed pet.
Naturalist/ Environmental	Take a color walk, sort fallen leaves by color, search for animals who are hidden by their protective coloration in pictures, look at how different book illustrators use color and compare/contrast (e.g., Tomie de Paola and Ed Young), document how colors in nature change (e.g., watching an amaryllis bulb grow).	Look for repeated patterns in the environment (e.g., sunrise/sunset, a picket fence), listen for patterns of sound in nature (e.g., ocean waves) and patterns of sound from objects invented by people (e.g., train), make a collection of logos and look for patterns.	Research appropriate habitats for different kinds of pets, compare and contrast pet habitats with those of wild animals, investigate the illegal sale of exotic or endangered species pets, learn more about animals whose habitats are threatened by humans, investigate the Web site of the Humane Society.

Note. Based on Gardner (1993b) and Armstrong (1987).

✿ CREATIVE THINKING DURING CHILDHOOD

Creative thinking in children is both like and different from that of adults. It is alike in that children "have experiences that are similar in complexity, challenge, and creativity to those of creative experts" (Caine & Caine, 1996, p. 117). It is different in terms of experience and style. Mature individuals' creative processes and products emphasize expertise, which involves the technical skill, artistic ability, talent, or knowledge of useful information that they bring to whatever they produce, and work habits, which include work style, concentration and persistence, the ability to generate new possibilities, and openness to new ideas (Amabile, 1983; Kohn, 1987). Children obviously have less experience than adults and therefore less expertise, and their work styles are less well developed. But whatever children may lack in terms of expertise or style, they more than compensate for in their unique ways of thinking and approaching a task. Here is what Caitlin, a 3½-year-old, says out loud as she draws a picture. Notice Caitlin's vivid imagination as she describes the pictures she draws as well as her lack of inhibition about revealing her thoughts:

> I'm makin' a butterfly. This is grass, this green stuff is grass. I'm making a bridge this time. The butterfly's gonna go over the bridge—under the bridge, I mean . . . Now I'll make myself. I need some pink. Hmm, no pink. (she chooses a red crayon) I'll just have to color light if I want to make some pink. There, that's my honker (nose). This is my hair. I'm going to make some hair. There I am! (she smiles) I want black. Purple will do. I have some blush on—there! Ha-ha! I'll have to make a sidewalk here. Those are drainers (drains), like little logs. (in a singsong voice) I need a blue log log, blue log, blue log log. Can you make a flower, Caitlin? Blue will do it! Blue water. See, this is a log. I forgot to make the sunshine. I'll pretend this is Rudolph (the Red-Nosed Reindeer). Sunshine. There! Now I'm going to make an elephant . . .

As the preceding glimpse of Caitlin's thinking suggests, children excel at three characteristics thought to be related to creative genius: sensitivity to internal and external stimuli, lack of inhibition, and the ability to become completely absorbed in an activity (Holden, 1987). In other words, creative thought is simultaneously serious and playful (Rea, 2001).

Marina, a 3-year-old, is a good example of a child with *sensitivity to stimuli*. She was at a very important gathering where the bishop of her Greek Orthodox church was visiting the congregation. All of the adults were a bit intimidated and felt awkward; Marina "broke the ice" by walking up to the bishop and asking, "Do you know how to color? Would you like to draw pictures with me?" Marina seemed to sense that welcoming the bishop was important; she used her knowledge of how to make friends in a way that the entire congregation still remembers fondly.

Keiko, a 4-year-old, revealed his *spontaneity and lack of inhibition* during a testing situation. When the examiner asked him whether he was "very happy, happy, not very happy, a little sad, or very sad," Keiko said, "Happy!", whirled around, took the pen from the examiner, and circled the smiley face on the test form himself. Like Keiko, most children are less self-conscious and freer in their responses than adults would be in a similar situation.

Lauren exemplifies the child's *complete absorption in an activity.* She has created an imaginary friend named "Mousie," and before her family travels anywhere, she lifts the gas tank door and puts her hand, palm up, next to the opening so that Mousie can crawl inside. Lauren talks aloud to her imaginary pet and gives him instructions on how to behave, completely unconcerned that anyone might overhear her.

As the behavior of Marina, Keiko, and Lauren illustrates, children can become totally absorbed in pretending. They surprise us by their sensitivity, spontaneity, and playfulness. Because they are newer to the world, their sensory impressions are particularly keen. These characteristics lead us to seek careers working with young children and endear them to us as adults. Of all the characteristics that children manifest through behavior, perhaps none is more charming than their world of make-believe, the world of imagination and fantasy that we will explore next.

Imagination and Fantasy

In the estimation of both experts and lay people, imagination and fantasy are the great creative assets of early childhood. It is common to say that children have "active imaginations," meaning that the boundaries between reality and fantasy are not as clearly demarcated for children as they are for adults, and imaginative thought comes as readily to the child as literal thought comes to the adult. In fact, experts on creativity have long believed that, for most human beings, imagination peaks during early childhood.

What, exactly, is imagination and why might it be more active early in life? Imagination is defined as the ability to form rich and varied mental images or concepts of people, places, things, and situations that are not present. Kindergartner Mallory's drawings in Figure 1.2 offer a good example of the imagination at work. She has become intrigued by flowers—not just ordinary flowers, but flowers that exist only in her mind's eye. As she imagines what she calls "an acrobatic flower" and "a flower with pineapple teeth," Mallory uses both objective thought (what she knows) and intuitive thought (what she feels). In addition, Mallory considers how to communicate her thoughts and feelings to others. Imagination is an "as if" situation (Weininger, 1988, p. 142). Mallory has seen pineapple chunks before; now she draws "as if" they were in the flower's mouth as teeth. She has seen acrobats on television; now she draws her flower "as if" it had the physical skills of an acrobat. By examining how Mallory has combined apparently unrelated elements in her drawings to produce surprising new forms, we can glimpse her imagination at work.

Fantasy is a subset of imaginative thinking. Fantasy occurs when a person uses the imagination to create particularly vivid mental images or concepts that are make-believe, impossible, or at least not yet possible. Fantasy is a "what if" situation (Weininger, 1988, p. 144). Here is how one mother described her son's use of fantasy as he created a pretend companion:

> My son, who just turned 4, became fascinated by deer. This happened, I think, because while we were visiting friends out in the country, a doe and her fawn came into the yard. Now Scott has created a pretend friend named "Fawnbelly." His bedroom window faces the front porch, and that, according to my son, is where she sleeps. He feeds her by putting a plastic apple on the windowsill and, in return, she protects him at night. When he talks about Fawnbelly, I can picture this gentle, expectant doe with huge brown eyes keeping watch over our house.

Figure 1.2
Mallory's Flowers

This mother obviously values the vivid imagination and rich fantasy life of her child, and rightly so. Harvard psychologist Howard Gardner (1993a) has described how children are freer in their thinking: "The child is not bothered by inconsistencies, departures from convention, nonliteralness . . . which often results in unusual and appealing juxtapositions and associations" (p. 228). In fact, many adult artists report that they must struggle to get back in touch with those feelings and attitudes of early childhood in order to realize their creative potential. This nonliteral mode of thinking, so prevalent during early childhood, balances and complements literal thinking. As the next section describes, great ideas are produced by applying different modes of thought to a task or problem at various times.

Imagination and fantasy are the great creative assets of early childhood.

Modes of Thinking

Types of thinking may be broadly categorized as convergent or divergent. The creative process relies on both types in different measures at different times. Take, for instance, the invention of the Post-it note. When 3M employees invented a temporary adhesive, their colleagues—who had devoted their careers to striving for more permanent adhesives—simply could not wrap their minds around a use for it. Still, they approved the team to create some prototypes of the sticky notes and distribute them to the secretaries in the company. It was not until the secretaries were clamoring for more that the value of this item became apparent (Peters & Waterman, 1988). This illustrates the two modes of thinking—convergent ("dig the same hole deeper" and look for more permanent adhesives) and divergent ("dig in another place" and seek a use for a temporary adhesive) (DeBono, 1971).

Creative thought relies on both types of thought, employing them as the situation warrants, and orchestrating them appropriately. The blending of convergent and divergent thought is necessary for problem solving (De Bono, 1992).

Stages in the Creative Process

According to the classic theory of creativity, the creative process consists of four stages (Wallas, 1926). The stages are recursive, meaning that a person may move back and

---

✿ Preparation/Brainstorming (accessing information)

The thinker applies knowledge, skill, and understanding to materials, objects, problems, or combinations of these things. Creative individuals "engage" with the materials, objects, or problems with a playful or experimental attitude. Engagement with the ideas may be deliberate or accidental.

↓

⊡ Incubation (processing information internally)

The mind begins to formulate and work on a problem, often through images and associations.

↓

🕯 Illumination/Inspiration (arriving at a solution)

The thinker selects some ideas and rejects others; this is an evaluative phase.

↓

✓ Verification/Communication (evaluating the solution, communicating it to others, and validating its contributions)

The thinker tests the product of creative thought in terms of usefulness, completeness, and correctness. This testing may occur at three different levels (Glover, 1980): the individual level (a personal consideration of the work's originality and purpose), the peer level (soliciting the evaluation of peers), or the social level (assessing the contributions of the work to society at large).

Figure 1.3
Stages in the Creative Process
Note. Adapted from Cropley (1997), Glover (1980), Runco (1997), and Wallas (1926).

forth between and among them, rather than following them in an invariant sequence from first to last. These stages in the creative process are summarized in Figure 1.3.

IDENTIFYING CREATIVITY

The creative process has been studied in various ways (Runco & Pritzker, 1999). Isaksen (1992) refers to these approaches as "the four Ps of creativity":

1. Study of the *people* involved, including their traits, characteristics, or attributes (Sheldon, 1995)
2. Study of the creative *process,* including how a task is approached and performed (Runco, 1994)
3. Study of creative *products,* including the quality and usefulness of the final outcome (Simonton, 1996)

4. Study of the *press*—all the external, context-specific variables that exert an influence on people engaged in creative processes (Sternberg, 1997a)

But whether we study creative contexts, products, processes, or people, the basic question is: Why? Why do people create? Many experts have attempted to explain what urges people to think creatively (Simonton, 1996; Torrance, 1995). Generally speaking, theories that seek to explain why people create can be conceptualized as humanistic, psychoanalytic, and constructivist (Ebbeck, 1996). Figure 1.4 is an overview of the theoretical perspectives and theorists that have contributed to an understanding of creative thought.

✿ CHILDREN'S CREATIVE ABILITIES

Although childhood is the wellspring for later creative pursuits, adults frequently fail to develop the rich resources of imagination, creativity, curiosity, and

---

Classical Theories

Theory: Humanistic

- **Carl Rogers: The creative person is fully functioning.**

Implications: If the young child's natural curiosity, passion for learning, and active imagination are deadened by adults, the child becomes less rather than more capable from a creative standpoint over time.

- **Abraham Maslow: The creative person is self-actualized.**

Implications: When schedules are rigid and tasks are predetermined, children do not have an opportunity to make choices or solve interesting problems. Over time, they learn to depend on others for ideas rather than trusting their own ideas.

- **Rollo May: Being creative is courageous.**

Implications: Young children's ideas often seem outrageous or silly to adults who seek large amounts of predictability and control. Yet children need permission to pursue their unorthodox ideas so that they can "dare to be different" throughout life.

Theory: Psychoanalytic

- **Alfred Adler: Creativity is a way of compensating for perceived physical or psychological inferiority.**

Implications: Rather than having a "talent scout" mentality, in which only those children with potential to become great artists or inventors are afforded opportunities for creative expression, teachers need to cultivate creativity in all children.

Figure 1.4
Theories of Creativity

- **Carl Jung: Creative ideas emanate from a deeper source, from the "collective unconscious."**

Implications: It is essential that children become familiar with the creative processes and products of other times, cultures, ethnic groups, and races so that they can make personal connections with the sum of human creativity.

Theory: Constructivist

- **Jean Piaget: Creativity is a type of problem solving that depends on the child's thinking processes.**

Implications: Developing the young child's problem-solving processes gives children the time and opportunity to explore materials and use hands-on approaches in pursuing interesting challenges.

Contemporary Theories

Multiple Intelligences Theory

- **Howard Gardner: Creativity consists of a constellation of nine different intelligences.**

Implications: Every young child possesses at least nine distinctive ways of knowing that must be considered and valued when planning any curriculum that claims to meet individual needs.

Triarchic Theory of Creativity

- **Robert J. Sternberg: Creativity is a cluster of three types of abilities; synthesizing, analyzing, and practicing.**

Implications: Children need to have role models of creativity, raise questions, have time to use trial-and-error, take sensible risks, define and pursue their own problems, puzzle over ideas, overcome obstacles, earn support for their ideas, and be evaluated in ways that respect creativity.

Optimal Experience or "Flow" Theory

- **Mihalyi Csikzentmihalyi: Creative individuals acquire competence in a domain of interest and pursue that interest with passion and enjoyment.**

Implications: Throughout the world, young children will play spontaneously and persist at their play even though no one is directing it or reinforcing them. In studies of eminently creative adults, one consistent finding is that the lines between play and work are blurred and they tend to approach their work playfully.

playfulness that characterize childhood (Cobb, 1977; Martindale, 2001). All children have creative potential. In programs in which teachers and parents believe this, children's creativity flourishes (Duffy, 1998). Based on a review of the research, when children are using their creative abilities, they demonstrate the behaviors in Figure 1.5.

Note that each of these clusters of behavior might also be interpreted in a negative way by uninformed or insensitive adults. The child who is playful, energetic, and intrinsically motivated could be labeled as "hyperactive," the child who is independent, perceptive, and confident as a "smart aleck," and the child who is original, nonconforming, and adventuresome as "strange" or "stubborn." Similarly, adults may prefer children who are subdued, compliant, quiet, neat, and polite and who fit in easily wit h peers. This is one reason why it is so important for teachers to be well informed about children's creativity. Errors in teachers' judgment can damage children's self-esteem and thwart creative growth. Does this mean that everyone is creative to some extent? Yes. While there are different dimensions and levels of creativity, every child is creative if given the chance to be; "everyone has

- Playful, persistent, and intrinsically motivated
- Become intensely absorbed in activities, persist at work or play, and concentrate on a single task for a relatively long period of time
- Explore, experiment, manipulate, play, ask questions, make guesses, and discuss findings
- Use imaginative role play, language play, storytelling, and artwork to solve problems and make sense out of their world
- Curious, intuitive, and resourceful
- Ask many questions
- Are capable of tolerating ambiguity as they explore alternatives
- Are strongly intuitive and perceptive
- Enjoy thinking and working independently
- Resourceful, nonconforming, and adventuresome
- Tend to challenge assumptions or authorities based on well-reasoned differences of opinion
- Formulate hypotheses and conduct trials to test their ideas
- Try to bring order out of chaos by organizing their environment
- Do something new with the old and familiar and display interest in new ideas
- Use repetition as an opportunity to learn more from an experience rather than becoming bored with it

Figure 1.5
Observable Characteristics of Children's Creative Thought Processes
Note. Adapted from Davis and Rimm (1994), McAlpine (1996), Healy (1996), and Maxim (1989).

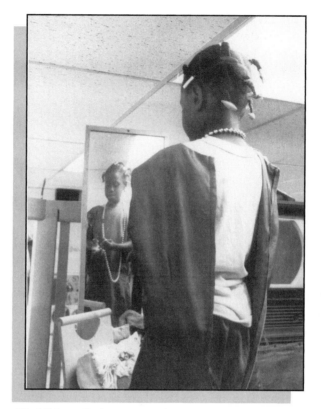

All children display creative behaviors at various times or in particular situations.

creative potential but developing it requires a balance between skill and control and the freedom to experiment and take risks" (Robinson, 2001, p. 445). This does not mean that everyone will invent something, perform on stage, or see his or her art displayed in a gallery. A teacher who invents a new learning activity is being creative. A mother who provides nutritious, tasty meals on a very limited food budget is being creative. A child who fashions an imaginary dinosaur out of clay is being creative. When we meet life's challenges and resolve problems, we are being creative (Ripple, 1989; Runco, 1996). In the next section, we look at the conditions that enable creativity to flourish.

UNLOCKING CREATIVE POTENTIAL

A story is told about a visiting efficiency expert who reported that one of the Ford Motor Company's well-paid employees sat with his feet propped up on the desk and appeared to be daydreaming most of the time. Henry Ford reputedly replied that that was exactly how the employee looked when he had an idea that saved the company more than enough money to cover his salary in the years to come.

Every child needs the opportunity to be creative.

Valuing creative thought as Ford apparently did is a prerequisite to understanding it. Warnock (1977) says that being more creative is analogous to being more healthy. We do not ask, "Why become more healthy?" because being healthy is simply good. The same holds true for creativity: Once we understand it, we know that it is an end in itself, just like being healthy.

Unlocking creative potential largely depends on two sets of internal psychological conditions: psychological safety and psychological freedom (Rogers, 1991).

Psychological Safety

Psychological safety is external; it depends on a low-risk environment. Children feel psychologically safe when significant others accept them as having unconditional worth, avoid external evaluation, and identify and empathize with the child. Consider how this mother provides psychological safety for her preschool son Lance's behavior:

> Lance [age 5] loves farming and he inherited a lot of toy farm equipment that
> used to belong to his dad and big brothers. One day he was playing farmer and
> took his toy manure spreader into the kitchen, filled it up with coffee grounds,
> and began spreading "manure" on his land, which just happens to be the
> kitchen floor!

Lance's mother knew that he was completely wrapped up in his farm fantasy and that his intentions were good, even if the outcomes were messy. She did insist that Lance help her clean up the coffee grounds, yet she did not punish him or make him feel ashamed of his desire to really "test out" his farm equipment. When adults respond sensitively to children's behavior, they contribute to the child's feelings of psychological safety.

Psychological Freedom

Psychological freedom is internal. It emanates from within the child. When children feel free to play with ideas, they have developed an inner state of psychological freedom. According to Rogerian theory, one person becomes more creative than the next because he or she has learned to play, to be open to experience and receptive to ideas, and to rely more on self-evaluation than the evaluations of others. Contemporary psychologists sometimes use the term *ego strength* for psychological freedom. In the absence of ego strength, "individuals are likely to conform to others' interpretations and fear or mistrust their own insights" (Runco, 2004, p. 22). The concept of ego strength as it relates to creativity is particularly important for teachers because educators can build children's ego strength in ways that will allow them "to stand up to peer pressure and to express themselves as individuals, even if it means being different" (Runco, 2004, p. 22).

Social Support

Lev Vygotsky (1933), a Russian theorist, has argued that learning is fundamentally a social activity: that children learn and grow with and from "the company they keep" (Smith, 1992). One of the basic precepts of Vygotsky's theory is the *zone of proximal development,* or ZPD, the level at which the child feels reasonably confident in pursuing an activity, yet not bored by it; the level at which the child feels challenged intellectually, yet not frustrated. Vygotsky argued that real learning takes place when the child is functioning at this level. Children need to pursue activities that urge them to move to higher levels of functioning. This is one reason why giving children printed pictures to color and/or cut out while sitting quietly at their seats—a common activity in American schools—is not recommended. True, this activity keeps children occupied, but it does nothing to challenge them intellectually, undermines creative thought, and offers no social support. Such an activity creates no feeling of functioning in a community of learners; it is simply busywork that is frequently performed in quiet isolation.

Vygotsky further argued that learning is fundamentally social and interactive in nature. Through social interaction, children internalize the cultural tools that the world of others presents to them (Davis & Gardner, 1992). For example, if we examine the drawings by a Japanese child or a Navajo child, we will see that their early representational drawings resemble the art from the culture they know; their style has been influenced by the art that they have experienced in their societies. As we have seen, psychological safety, psychological freedom, and social support are essential to promote optimal creative growth in children. How well are the schools meeting these requirements?

CREATIVITY AND EDUCATION

One way of thinking about creative thought and artistic expression is to consider what occurs to it across the lifespan. Most experts argue that it tends to decline over time as people begin to accept themselves as "ordinary" and therefore inferior or inadequate in creative thinking and artistic expression (Jones, McConnell, & Normie, 1996; Egan & Nadaner, 1988; Westby & Dawson, 1995). In response to social values, cultural attitudes, and educational practices, many adults start to see innovation and artistic expression as avenues open only to those who are officially recognized as having exceptional talent (Kerka, 2002). Although it is sad to think that education would be responsible in any way for thwarting the child's creative potential, there is considerable support for this point of view:

> Schools suppress creativity. How can this be stated so categorically? The reasoning goes as follows: most children are naturally curious and highly imaginative. Then, after they have attended school for a while, something happens. They become more cautious and less innovative. Worst of all, they tend to change from being participators to being spectators. Unfortunately, it is necessary to conclude from the investigations of many researchers (most of whom have been professional educators) that our schools are the major culprit. (Dacey, 1989, p. 200)

Are school personnel deliberately suppressing children's creativity? Actually, it is more often the case that adults have misconceptions about creativity and act on those erroneous beliefs (Williams, Brigockas, & Sternberg, 1997). For example, in a study that compared the results of a thorough assessment of preschoolers' creativity with their teachers' ratings of the children's creativity, Nicholson and Moran (1986) concluded that teachers are not very good judges of creativity. The three mistakes most commonly made by teachers are as follows:

1. *Confusing measures of intelligence with measures of creativity.* In the real world, apart from testing, creativity and intelligence apparently interact rather than function as separate entities (Runco, 1986). Creativity is a form of intelligence, but it is not the form usually assessed by tests and grades. Furthermore, a person who is an expert or even a creative genius in one domain, such as composing music, may not be particularly creative in another domain, and schools tend to focus on verbal/linguistic and logical/mathematical domains to the virtual exclusion of other areas. Nevertheless, teachers may assume that students who receive the highest grades are automatically the most creative students in their classes.

2. *Being overly influenced by socially desirable behavior.* Academic environments are not always accepting of children who "dare to be different." History is full of examples of people who were called "daydreamers," "underachievers," or "troublemakers" during childhood only to become highly creative or even creative geniuses in later life, such as the politician Winston Churchill, the actress Sara Bernhardt, the scientist Albert Einstein, the inventor Alexander Graham Bell, and the dancer Isadora Duncan. Teachers and administrators can become intolerant of children who do not "go along with the program" (Sternberg, 1997; Sternberg & Lubart, 1995).

3. *Being overly influenced by the child's rate of development.* Adults react more readily and more favorably to children's uncommon (advanced) behavior than to children's unconventional (creative) behavior (Nicholson & Moran, 1986). Compare the behavior of Aaron and Matt, both preschoolers. At age 3, Aaron can identify several words printed on flashcards. His parents think that he is exceptionally creative. But even though Aaron has been pushed into recognizing a few written symbols before his peers (advanced for his age), this is not an indicator of extraordinary creativity. Contrast this with the experiences of Matt, another 3-year-old. His parents try to encourage independence and creative problem solving. In fact, one of Matt's favorite expressions is "I have an idea. We could. . . ." Of the two children, Matt is getting more support in developing creativity. Aaron, on the other hand, is being conditioned to imitate adult behavior as rapidly as possible. He may be precocious, but his creativity is being compromised in the process.

How does acting on these common misconceptions about creativity influence teachers' behavior? Suppose a teacher is presenting a unit on basic shapes—circles, triangles, squares, and rectangles. When introducing a review lesson, she asks children to suggest the names of shapes that they know. Robert suggests, "There's an egg shape, only it's called an ellipse." How would you as a teacher handle this response? A teacher who is overly concerned about confusing the other children might say, "Robert, that isn't one of the shapes we learned." If you do, what will happen to Robert? He will feel rejected. Over time, Robert will probably begin to "play the game" and tell teachers what they want to hear. He may even quit contributing in class.

Situations such as these, repeated day after day, not only undermine children's creativity but also distort teachers' perspectives on what constitutes creative behavior. In a study of more than 1,000 teachers' attitudes toward creativity, conducted by Fryer and Collings (1991), only about half of the teachers realized that divergent thinking—thinking "outside the box"—is a key element of creative thought. Many teachers associate creativity with economic privilege and fail to notice it in students who are not engaged in the fine arts. Clasen, Middleton, and Connell (1994) found that African American students tended to outperform their peers in fluency and flexibility of thought, yet these abilities often are overlooked or actively discouraged by teachers. Similarly, a review of 62 studies concluded that arts education has particular advantages for students from economically disadvantaged backgrounds, yet this population is least likely to have extensive opportunities and a wide variety of materials (Manzo, 2002). The goal of studying children's creativity and play is to change teachers' perspectives—to prepare a new generation of teachers who will do a better job of meeting children on their own terms rather than trying to mold them prematurely into performing adult behaviors.

SCHOOLS THAT NURTURE CREATIVITY

Creativity is a complex developmental system that is shaped by at least seven influences: (1) cognitive processes; (2) social and emotional processes; (3) family aspects, both while growing up and current; (4) education and preparation, both informal and formal; (5) characteristics of the domain and field; (6) sociocultural contextual aspects; and (7) historical forces, events, and trends (Feldman, 1999, pp. 171–172). When schools do succeed in nurturing children's creativity and artistic expression, at least seven conditions exist:

1. *Positive emotional climate.* School personnel strive to reduce stress and anxiety in children and in themselves. Adults recognize the importance of positive affect— feeling good about being in school, treating one another with respect, and building self-esteem among children and colleagues (Isen, Daubman, & Nowicki, 1987).

2. *Process valued as well as product.* This means that children are encouraged to play with ideas and explore solutions rather than being pushed into premature conclusions. Creativity and productivity may actually be inversely related. When children are pressured to dash something off to meet someone else's schedule, they are not afforded the "luxury" of seeking many alternatives and refining the most promising ones. Rather, they are taught to value the quantity of work produced over the quality of the finished product (Amabile, 1989).

3. *Flexible schedules.* Time limits are removed from activities in which children are deeply involved. Children are free to become absorbed in what they are doing. In a school committed to creative expression, children follow their interests and enjoy what they are doing along with their peers, teachers, and other school personnel. This condition of being able to pursue an idea is the "labor of love" aspect of creative processes (Amabile, 1986).

4. *Support for creative thought and artistic expression.* A free, open atmosphere is established where self-expression is encouraged and valued. Teachers support children's creativity by providing a wide variety of interesting materials and keeping activities open-ended; they give help when needed, but they do not interfere with children's creative processes. Figure 1.6 provides an overview of the things that teachers do to foster creative thought and expression in their students.

5. *Mechanisms for peer support.* Children are encouraged to share ideas, not only with the teacher but also with one another. One of the ways that children begin to regard themselves as creative is in their reflected selves—in others' responses to them and their ideas. Therefore, it is important for children to give and receive supportive feedback, not only from adults but also from peers.

6. *Minimized competition and external rewards.* Creativity is fostered when teachers enjoy experiences along with children rather than singling out particular products for praise or rewards. When children are informed that there will be a contest, that some will win a tangible reward and others will lose, three things happen. First, they become more cautious and tend to "play it safe"; second, they feel pressured to please someone else and lose their intrinsic motivation; and third, they tend to rush to get the reward. All of these things result in less spontaneous, less complex, and less varied products; in other words, less creative responses.

7. *Adults who value children's creative thought and artistic expression.* Teachers often fear a loss of control and disapprove of children's departures from what is predictable and routine. Children's creative expression is supported in programs where teachers are inclined to notice and accept evidence of children's active imaginations at work.

A first-grade teacher helps illustrate how these six features of schools that nurture creativity are put into practice.

Classroom Environment, Materials, and Climate

- Create organizational and structural conditions that allow open and flexible distribution of roles, themes, problems, and activities
- Provide challenging and stimulating learning materials
- Offer opportunities to work with varied materials under different conditions
- Establish a classroom climate that permits alternative solutions

Professional Attitudes and Values

- Provide support and positive feedback for problem finding, not just problem solving
- Serve as a model of creative thought
- Tolerate ambiguity, accept alternative solutions
- Allow for humor and playfulness

Social Support for Creativity

- Have a cooperative, socially integrative style of teaching
- Enable children to participate in joint projects with self-selected partners
- Surprise students with recognition for creative processes and products
- Extend mastery of factual knowledge through collaboration

Recognition of and Respect for Children's Creativity

- Enable self-directed work that allows for a high degree of initiative, spontaneity, and experimentation
- Encourage and accept constructive nonconformist behavior
- Take children's questions seriously and tolerate "sensible" or bold errors
- Help students learn to cope with frustration and failure
- Reward courage as much as being right
- Actively teach creative strategies
- Foster intense concentration and task commitment through high motivation and interest in self-selected topics
- Increase autonomy of learning by recognition and self-evaluation of progress

Figure 1.6

What Teachers Do to Foster Creativity in Students

Note. Adapted from Clark (1996), Cropley (2001), and Urban (1996).

Ms. Kastenbaum uses a four-phase strategy that begins with awareness, then moves to exploration, next to inquiry, and finally to utilization (National Association for the Education of Young Children, 1991). She builds the children's awareness by asking, "What is a robot? How are robots made? What is special about robots? What robots have you seen?" Krish says that robots are "sort of like people, only they're machines." Taro mentions R2-D2 from *Star Wars,* and Joelle expresses a wish for a toy robot. Exploration begins as the children share and discuss a collection of robot pictures and the teacher summarizes by asking, "What have you learned about robots? What questions do you still have about robots?" Now Ms. Kastenbaum moves the group into inquiry as she invites them to examine a wide array of recycled materials and invent a robot puppet. One child begins with an old sock, another with a cardboard box; one child uses Styrofoam egg carton cups for "buggy eyes," while another chooses aluminum foil and cardboard tubes for arms. All of the children experiment with different fixatives such as glue, staples, tape, and sewing. The activity turns to utilization as the children's finished robot puppets move to electronic music.

TEACHERS' ROLES AND RESPONSIBILITIES IN PROMOTING CREATIVE EXPRESSION

Research suggests that either too much or too little *structure* can interfere with the development of creative expression (McLeod, 1997). If a classroom is regimented, there is too much structure. On the other hand, if a classroom is "anything goes," there is too little structure to provide proper guidance. How do teachers arrive at the right mixtures and balances?

Risk taking is yet another feature of the creative classroom. Too many teachers subscribe to what Paulo Freire (1973) calls the "banking model," in which they approach teaching as the task of making regular "deposits" of information in the students' brains. But children cannot simply absorb someone else's ready-made answers; children must build their own understandings about the world, and that path to understanding is littered with "errors." If we make learners self-conscious about mistakes, their progress will be slowed or even halted because they are afraid to be risk takers.

A third key responsibility for teachers is to fully *understand creative activities.* Too many teachers assume that "creative activities" are all focused on the teacher, when the value of creative activities is actually determined by the quality of the children's responses. Creative activities are not something that teachers *do for* children, such as designing "cute" games for them to play. Although it is fine for a teacher to make a beautiful visual aid to use during a lesson, this does not constitute "creative teaching." Teaching for creativity results in enriching and enlarging the child's capacity for creative thought and artistic expression. This should be good news for teachers who worry about their singing voices, their inability to draw, their clumsiness at dance, their inexperience with drama, or the fact that they never learned to play a musical instrument. The outcomes of creative teaching are to set children's creativity free and support the conditions for them to create, not to put on a polished performance for them.

Teachers build understanding and acceptance when they focus on each child's abilities and emphasize cooperation.

Another important role for teachers is to *encourage rather than praise.* What is the difference? In praise, the teacher passes judgment on the quality of the child's work ("You did a very good job on your story"); encouragement acknowledges the child's efforts ("I noticed that you worked very hard to revise your story until it was ready to be published online"). Effusive praise can actually suppress children's creativity. Suppose that a child paints an orange pumpkin with black triangle eyes and nose and a toothy grin. If adults shower the child with praise, saying, "Oh, that's so wonderful! It's just the cutest little pumpkin!" the child may get "stalled" at this stage because he or she is trying to please the adult. It is better to show genuine, personal interest than to overdo it with generalized praise. You can show interest in children's work by commenting specifically on the child's work ("Carla, that pumpkin looks really happy") or by asking questions about it ("How did you make the stem?"). Figure 1.7 suggests appropriate comments about children's creative work.

MEETING STANDARDS

Criteria for Creativity

For a behavior to be creative, it must meet four basic criteria (Guilford, 1984; Jackson & Messick, 1965). These criteria are described next using examples of young children's behavior.

How did you get the idea for this work?

This makes me feel . . .

I like the way you used _____ because . . .

This reminds me of . . .

What were you trying to do?

Maybe you could combine . . .

This interests me because . . .

How does this work compare with other work you have created?

I wonder what would happen if . . .

I like the part where . . .

I'd like to know more about . . .

You used some powerful ideas such as . . .

The part where you explained . . .

This is like your . . .

You are really good at . . .

Figure 1.7
Responses to Children's Work.
Note. Adapted from Cecil and Lauritzen (1994).

1. *Criterion 1: Creative behavior is original; it has a low probability of occurrence.*
Two-year-old Adam attended a college hockey game with his father, and the toddler now wants to be a hockey player. When Adam asked for hockey equipment, his parents told him he was too little and that it was too expensive, so Adam invented his own. He used a wooden spoon for a hockey stick, his sister's empty lip gloss container for a puck, socks for hockey gloves, and the open door to a closet as the goal net. Now "playing goalie" while his dad or older brother do the sports commentary is Adam's favorite game. Adam's behavior is unusual and surprising rather than typical and predictable. Thus it has a low probability of occurrence, and it is original.

2. *Criterion 2: Creative behavior is appropriate and relevant.* Six-year-old twins Becky and Belinda both love Hans Christian Andersen's story "The Little Mermaid." They want to look like mermaids and need to create long, flowing hair, so Becky suggests using scarves attached with bobby pins. To create a tail, Belinda has the idea of using a sock. Their mother helps out and gives them an old pair of socks to use. Belinda cuts off the foot portion and stretches the ankle part over both of her ankles, turning her feet outward to represent "fins." The twins' behavior is a good illustration of appropriateness. In order for behavior to be creative, it needs to be relevant to the goals of the person who produced it.

3. *Criterion 3: Creative behavior is fluent; it results in many new, meaningful forms.* Six-year-old Louie likes to invent things and does so frequently. One day he "invented a wind tunnel" with his dad's help. Louie attached a small sheet to the sides of a large box fan with duct tape. Then his dad plugged in and turned on the fan and the fabric billowed out. Louie could sit inside and read. Fluency in creativity is comparable to fluency in language; it means that the child can generate one idea after another with apparent ease.

   4. *Criterion 4: Creative behavior is flexible; it explores and uses nontraditional approaches to problem solving.* Lucia is seated next to Tomas, a fellow first grader who is disassembling a grease pencil. He pulls the string and unwraps the paper coiled around the lead. Lucia watches as Tomas throws the curls of paper in the trash can, and then she retrieves them. She cuts two pieces of curled paper, glues them on her drawing, and attaches a piece of string to each one. "There," she says aloud. "The windows of my house have shades just like this." The teacher comments on Lucia's picture, saying, "And the shades on the windows you drew really roll up and down, too! This looks like a very special picture—will you choose it for your portfolio?" Lucia's behavior is a good example of flexibility. She wanted to make her drawing three-dimensional, and she used a different method that involved materials that others considered useless.

   As the behaviors of these children suggest, children's thinking is creative when it is original, appropriate, fluent, and flexible.

   Researchers in the field of creativity have argued that the creative individual engages, to a considerable extent, not merely in problem solving but in problem *finding*. "Problem-finding behaviors suggest that creative thinkers search more extensively for problems worth solving and show greater flexibility in defining problems" (Dorn, Madeja, & Sabol, 2004, p. 77). Problem-finding patterns of thinking forge connections between creative thought (such as "outside the box" thinking), values (such as decisions about what is effective, elegant, ethical), and intrinsic motivation (that is, self-directed to pursue a goal). Hope (1991) contends that three basic intellectual functions support creative expression and the arts: finding out how existing things work, finding out what has happened, and producing new or unique things (Dorn, Madeja, & Sabol, 2003). As you review the following examples, refer to Figure 1.8.

Preschool: Finding Out How Existing Things Work

In a classroom for 3- to 5-year-olds, the food preparation gadgets in the cooking center have captured the children's imaginations. Among the children's favorites are the hard-boiled egg slicer, the melon baller, a manual orange juicer, an ice cream scoop, and an apple corer.

Primary: Finding Out What Has Happened

The essence of meeting children's needs is being alert to opportunities for them to excel. A second-grade teacher's observations of her second graders on the playground reveal that many of the students from low-income homes are much more adept at inventing games and playing cooperatively than the children who come from economically advantaged homes. Rather than allowing this important strength to go unnoticed, the teacher asks the children to show the class some of their games, which involve syncopated hand clapping and original jump rope chants. When the other children try to participate in the games these students

Activities stimulate creative thought and problem solving when they:

- Are relevant to the learner, meaning that they are developmentally appropriate, understandable to the learner, and have "real world" applications
- Meet the needs of children at different levels of development because the challenges have multiple answers (rather than one right answer)
- Enable students to engage in long-term, open-ended projects and pursue a narrower range of ideas and materials in greater depth
- Capitalize on children's interests, curiosities, and passions and allow the child to set the pace and take the lead
- Support children as they use the processes of exploring, selecting, combining, and refining a form
- Are framed by teachers and students, with teachers structuring or limiting as necessary
- Give the students something practical and worthwhile to do that engages thoughts and feelings, mind and body
- Encourage children to look for models and make connections, emphasizing the influence and the works of others
- Use a variety of perspectives (such as critic, philosopher, inventor)
- Help students develop a set of standards for evaluating their performance and peers' performance that goes beyond "good" or "bad" and carefully analyzes the dimensions of a work
- Expand opportunities for learning and lead to new, interesting challenges

Figure 1.8
Features of Creative Experiences and Activities
Note. Adapted from Felton and Stoessiger (1987), Jalongo and Stamp (1997), and Lindstrom (1997).

have created, they gain a new appreciation for their classmates' skills. The teacher further supports and extends the children's activity by sharing several books of jump rope jingles, by inviting each child to discuss favorite childhood games with various family members, by giving children the opportunity to share what they learned from their interviews, by inviting parents to come in to demonstrate favorite childhood games, and by teaching the children new games from other eras and lands. Some picture books that are particularly intriguing to the children are *Hopscotch Around the World* and *Jumprope Around the World.* As a result of this second-grade teacher's interest and encouragement, all of the students now recognize what has happened: Some children's outdoor play is remarkable for its resourcefulness, reliance on cooperation, and reflection of the children's culture and community.

Intermediate: Producing New or Unique Things

A wide array of strategies to promote creative thinking have been designed and implemented over the years (see Cropley [2001] for a review). What follows are some of the most well-known strategies that are used to facilitate creative thinking in older children and a description of how teachers might put them to use in a classroom. Brainstorming is a technique that is used to capitalize on the creative-thought and problem-solving capacities of a group. Feldhusen (2001) offers the following guidelines for brainstorming:

1. Make sure that students understand the task dimensions.
2. Indicate that generating many ideas or responses is the goal.
3. State that there will be no evaluation or judgment of responses while ideas are being produced.
4. Assure students that they should feel free to proffer unusual and original ideas.
5. Urge students to strive to connect, relate, or alter their own and others' ideas.
6. Suggest that students be brief in responding; lengthy statements should be avoided (Feldhusen, 2001, p. 12).

A creative-thinking technique that is used to stimulate "out of the box" type thinking uses the acronym SCAMPER. Barnes (2002) elaborates on the SCAMPER strategy originally developed by Osborn (1972) by using a series of questions to coax thinking out of routine and taken for granted ways.

S SUBSTITUTE To have a person or thing act or serve in the place of another.
Question: Can you think of a new way of using this?

C COMBINE To bring together or unite.
Question: What do you think might happen if you try to put these together?

A ADAPT To adjust for the purpose of suiting a condition or purpose.
Question: What else is like this?

M MODIFY To alter, change the form or quality.
MAGNIFY To enlarge, make greater in form or quality.
MINIFY To make smaller, lighter, slower, less frequent.
Question: Can you imagine this bigger? Smaller?

P PUT TO OTHER USES To use for purposes other than originally intended.
Question: Do you think we might use this for . . . ?

E ELIMINATE To remove, omit, or get rid of a quality, part, or whole.
Question: What might this be like if you got rid of . . . ?

R REVERSE To place opposite or contrary, to turn around.
REARRANGE To change the order, plan, layout, or scheme.
Question: What happens if you turn it backward . . . or upside down?

(Barnes, 2002, pp. 53–54)

Part of the creative process is exploring materials and finding out how existing things work.

CONCLUSION

As you consider children's creativity, keep in mind that "Children live ferociously. Their senses—taste, touch, vision, hearing, smell—are turbocharged, in overdrive at all times except during sleep . . . They sing, paint, play with imaginary friends, animate inanimate objects and tell richly woven, epic-length falsehoods. They fulminate with creative intensity" (Barasch, 1997, p. 54). Effective teachers capitalize on the creative propensities of childhood in three basic ways: (1) by teaching the skills and attitudes of creative thinking to students, (2) by orienting students to the creative methods of various disciplines, and (3) by creating a "problem friendly" classroom in which lines of inquiry with relevance for learners can be pursued through multidisciplinary methods (Starko, 1999). A classroom that promotes creative thinking takes a "problem finding" approach, differentiating between superficial mental exercises in which the teacher knows the answer in advance and genuine inquiry. In order to function at full creative capacity, children need the freedom to pursue questions that captivate them and work in learning environments that offer a blend of high support and high expectations (Rea, 2001). It is no

Frequently Asked Questions About Creativity

Is it true that children have active imaginations?

Studies of the brain activity of preadolescent children offer empirical evidence that children do indeed have active imaginations (Diamond, 1999). Even when wide awake, children experience more frequent theta wave activity, a daydreamlike state that mature adults experience primarily as their minds hover between being awake and falling asleep. Theta wave brain activity is more relaxed, freewheeling, and receptive to fleeting mental images. Eminent creative individuals in various fields report a host of techniques to capture theta wave activity (Goleman & Kaufman, 1992; Runco & Pritzker, 1999). Evidently, children are adept at forming varied and unusual images while adults tend to have the advantage when it comes to storing and retrieving information, drawing upon experience, and making judgments about what is appropriate and effective. So children may not be "more" imaginative, but they certainly do have active imaginations.

Are children more or less creative than adults?

Children are differently creative than adults. Children have unique ideas but may not yet have the ability to execute them well or communicate them clearly to others (Fishkin, 1998). Originality in children "reflects their lack of inhibitions rather than their intentional and metacognitive efforts . . . " (Runco, 2004, p. 22). Evidently the creative assets of childhood include a tolerance for ambiguity, a propensity for nonlinear thinking, and receptivity to ideas that might be quickly discarded by an adult as too fanciful to merit further consideration. The line of demarcation between fantasy and reality is not as firmly drawn for children as it is for adults, so ideas from one realm slip through easily into another. This may enable children to respond in ways that are nonstereotypic, a trait that many adults, particularly those in the arts, find enviable (Kincade, 2002).

Is being creative valued mainly because it provides an emotional release?

Creativity is more than "letting off steam." There is a difference between making noise and making music and between jumping around and dancing, for example. The artist's behaviors are planned, controlled, and practiced. This tendency to treat the arts as emotional outlets distances creative work not only from the cognitive and physical processes used to attain excellence, but also from the cultural contexts in which creative works are produced. Creativity is much more than an emotional outlet; it is an expression of values, a source of national pride, and, for those outside the culture, a way of communicating intercultural understanding.

How can teachers support the creative expression of children with special needs?

The key to unlocking the creative potential in children with disabilities is the search for opportunities for every child to experience success. This typically involves focusing on children's strengths and adapting the environment to enable them to express those abilities. For example, a child with a visual disability may not be able to use crayons to produce a drawing that is pleasing to the eye, but the child can use fabrics to create a fabric collage that is pleasing to the touch. Likewise, the child whose physical condition prohibits the requisite fine motor skills for sculpting or painting at an easel may be able to mold large objects with clay or use hand and arm movements to finger-paint.

mistake that Amabile's (1986) "creativity killers" include such things as inflexible schedules, intense competition, reliance on extrinsic rewards, and lack of free time. Educators bear major responsibility as advocates for children's creative thought and expression. Fulfilling this important role often involves unlearning common assumptions and replacing them with more enlightened perspectives.

CHAPTER SUMMARY

1. Creativity is a behavior characterized by originality, relevance, fluency, and flexibility.
2. Children's thinking is different from adults' thinking because, generally speaking, children are highly sensitive to stimuli, are less inhibited, and can become completely absorbed in imagination ("as if") and pretend ("what if").
3. If teachers regard the dimensions of children's creative behavior—originality, appropriateness, relevance, fluency, and flexibility—they can further develop children's creative potential.
4. Creativity, imagination, and fantasy are all interrelated types of thinking that largely depend on the ability to use symbols in inventive ways. Literal thought and imaginative thought are distinctive, yet complementary.
5. Theories that attempt to explain the desire to create may be categorized as humanistic, psychoanalytic, and constructivist.
6. The creative process can be described in four stages: preparation, incubation, illumination, and verification/communication.
7. Some ways that classroom environments support creativity include providing psychological safety by reducing stress and anxiety, valuing process over product, removing time limits, valuing self-expression, encouraging peer interaction, and minimizing competition and external rewards.
8. Active, child-initiated experiences give the child authentic opportunities for creative expression and build the child's inner sense of psychological freedom or ego strength. When teachers provide a classroom environment in which children feel safe to experiment, to take the risks associated with learning something new, and to learn from their mistakes as an accepted part of the learning process, the condition of psychological safety has been met.
9. Teachers and parents play a crucial role in fostering the creative process in children. One recommended teaching strategy is to begin by building children's awareness, then move next to exploration, then to inquiry, and finally to utilization.
10. All children are creative. If all children are to develop their creative potential to the fullest extent, every classroom must provide a wide range of opportunities for creative expression. This means that teachers will need to respect children's ethnic and cultural diversity, acknowledge the role of multiple intelligences, adapt materials to each child's needs, and encourage authentic self-expression.

Discuss: Perspectives on Creative Expression

1. Teachers are often advised to "work to children's strengths." How does an understanding of children's creativity enable you to do this more effectively?

2. Do you agree that schools in the United States sometimes actively discourage creativity? Why or why not?

3. Sometimes children's creativity is mistaken for misbehavior. Baldwin (2001) contends that many traits commonly displayed by African American children, such as low tolerance for boredom and excitement and involvement with novelty of design, music, or ideas; language rich in imagery, humor, symbolism, and persuasion; and high divergent thinking ability are associated with creative thinking in Clark's (1988) list of creative characteristics. Unfortunately, these traits are also often considered unacceptable behavior in a classroom. Were you ever punished as a child for thinking "outside the box"? Have you seen this happen to children in schools? How do you plan to avoid squelching children's creativity when you are teaching?

4. Cite several current examples of imagination and creativity at work in various fields (medical research, business, new inventions, film, music). How would an education that fosters creativity and artistic expression prepare children for the workplace of the future?

Chapter 2

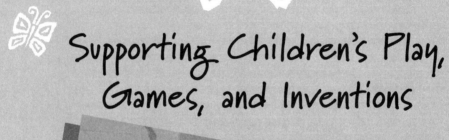

Supporting Children's Play, Games, and Inventions

Everything a child is, does, and becomes may at one time or another be demonstrated through play.

Garry Landreth and Linda Homeyer, 1998, p. 193

CLASSROOM PERSPECTIVES ON PLAY, GAMES, AND INVENTIONS

Preschool–Kindergarten

Jonah, Dylan, and Sarena are preschoolers who are playing in the dramatic play center. Their teacher recently read the book *Today Is Monday* by Eric Carle (1993), and the children are re-creating their own version of it. During their play, the children pretend to be different restaurant workers; talk extensively about their roles as cook, server, and cashier; and spontaneously develop and role-play a familiar restaurant theme. At one point, Jonah announces, "I think we should make this a restaurant," and initiates the restaurant play sequence with Sarena and Dylan. Dylan becomes the cook, who makes alphabet soup. The children also make connections to the Eric Carle book they recently heard. They check their own imaginative play against the reality of restaurants when they decide to "make alphabet soup . . . lock up the store . . . clean up the kitchen . . . and put the dishes away." Their words, actions, and gestures reflect their understanding of what is needed for a restaurant based on their actual experiences, the media, and the context in which the play occurs.

First Grade–Second Grade

In Ms. Lee's first-grade class, the children have been reading the Dr. Seuss book *Bartholomew and the Oobleck* (1949). Some of the children ask Ms. Lee if they can make oobleck, so she prepares some cornstarch, water, and red food coloring for the children to explore. The children explore the cornstarch—feeling, smelling, and tasting the white powder—and then mix it with water and red food coloring to produce red goo. The children explore the mixture, squeeze it, talk about it, shape it into balls, describe it as soft and gushy, and call it such names as "mushy mess." They laugh when they hold it in their hands to make it drip. Some add more water to see what happens; others add more cornstarch to see what happens.

Third Grade–Fourth Grade

Fourth graders Eli and Maya are playing chess in the game area of their classroom. During the game, you hear them using such terms as *jeopardy, capture, check,* and *checkmate* as well as reminding each other of the appropriate directions in which the different pieces can move. Their faces and body language reveal their intense thinking about the strategies they are using to protect their king piece.

Each of these perspectives reveals important information on children's play. What kinds of information can you gather about these children's knowledge and ways of thinking as they play, create, imagine, invent, figure things out, and make things work? This chapter explores the essential role of play as an important childhood activity that helps all children master their individual learning, developmental needs, and creative thought.

THEORETICAL AND RESEARCH BASE: WHAT IS PLAY?

Over the years, theorists, researchers, and educators have documented that play is the optimal vehicle for learning and development. They also suggest that the *absence of play* is often an obstacle to the development of happy, healthy, and creative individuals. Although experts who study play disagree on some of its aspects, there is genuine agreement on the characteristics that distinguish play from other types of human behavior (Fromberg, 1998, 1999, 2002).

Characteristics of Play

At least five essential elements characterize play. Each element was illustrated in at least one of the opening scenarios.

   1. *Play is voluntary and intrinsically motivated.* In play, children are free to choose the content and direction of their activity. The play is self-satisfying because it does not respond to external demands or expectations. In their self-chosen roles as cook and restaurant workers, Jonah, Dylan, and Sarena controlled how to play them out.

   2. *Play is symbolic, meaningful, and transformational.* Play enables children to connect their past experiences to their current world. It empowers them to transform themselves into others' roles as they switch back and forth and in and out of different situations. By pretending to be others, they assume a "what if" or "as if" attitude. When Dylan imagined himself as a cook making alphabet soup, he assumed a "what if" attitude by imagining what a cook might say or do. When he pretended to be a cook, he transformed himself into a cook by imagining cooking, stirring, and serving soup, like a cook. This "as if" attitude (the play) is the behavior that facilitates the further generation of ideas.

   3. *Play actively involves the players.* In play, children explore, experiment, investigate, and inquire with people, objects, or events. Notice how the first graders making oobleck explored what different proportions and combinations of cornstarch, water, and food coloring would do to it—making it drier, wetter, or mushier, depending on the amounts used. They also used language such as "mushy mess," to describe their experiences. Active play experiences increase children's awareness of what materials can do and what children can do with materials while at the same time increasing their skills of observation and description.

4. *Play is rule-bound.* Children are governed by either explicit or implicit rules during play. Younger children both create and change rules in play that apply to appropriate role behavior and object use. Older children accept predetermined rules that guide the play. In the restaurant scenario, the preschoolers created their own rules about paying, cooking, and cleaning up; in the chess scenario, the children focused on the appropriate language and moves for the individual pieces.

5. *Play is pleasurable.* When children play, they pursue an activity for the intrinsic pleasure it brings—not for an extrinsic reward. That is, all of these children were playing because they chose to play as they wished and played with total concentration on what they were doing (Fromberg & Bergen, 1998; Johnson, Christie, & Yawkey, 1999). Clearly, these children were pursuing their play because it made sense to them.

Play enables children to construct understandings of their world from their own experiences and strongly influences all aspects of their growth, development, and learning. In play, children become empowered to do things for themselves, to feel in control, to test out and practice their skills, and to affirm confidence in themselves. The play context is an important one for children's developing sense of competence (Wassermann, 2000).

These five characteristics of play explain what play is. While it is important to understand what play is, it is equally important to consider what play *is not.* Table 2.1 lists a continuum of behavior from play to work that differentiates between play and nonplay behaviors and also relate them to the type of learning that each generates.

Controversies Surrounding Play

With agreed-upon characteristics of play, why would there be any controversy about its definition and purposes? First, theorists and researchers have differed in their assumptions about play and its primary purpose, yet all have attested to its significance in children's physical, social/emotional, language, and intellectual growth and development. Freud (1958) and Erikson (1963) emphasized the emotional significance of play, the way children use play to express and release powerful emotions; Piaget (1962), on the other hand, emphasized play's cognitive significance, the way individual children use play to practice known information and construct understanding. Vygotsky (1967, 1978) emphasized the way children use play as a vehicle for social and cultural learning and the development of the social tool called language.

Second, our own culture makes a clear distinction between play and work (Johnson, Christie, et al., 1999; Fromberg, 1998, 1999, 2002). Children are pressured more and more to participate in high-stakes, fast-paced, teacher-directed, formal lessons leaving little, if any, time to learn through play. Many teachers believe that play experiences should be the centerpiece of their curricula. Yet they feel pressured to justify the use of play with the phrase "Play is children's work," which implies that work is serious and play is trivial. This misconception equates "real" school with rote learning and paper-and-pencil activities. Yet if we look at the best practices in each area of the curriculum, such as hands-on science, math manipulatives,

TABLE 2.1 Continuum of Behavior from Play to Nonplay and Types of Learning

	Child-Initiated Play, Freely Chosen	Facilitative Play	Directed Play	Work Disguised as Play	Work (Nonplay)
Focus of play	Child has greatest degree of control over situation, event, or other players. Can freely interact.	Child plays within a flexible environment of social rules, requiring players to attend to externally imposed control. Adults monitor play more closely than free play and often redirect, challenge, and add materials.	Adults impose play elements and often lead the play. Players do not usually choose whether, what, how, or when to play.	Task oriented activities that are not inherently playful but can be transformed into directed or guided play activities if the potential for internal control, motivation, and reality can be tapped.	An activity designed to reach an externally defined goal and for which motivation is external. No opportunity to bend reality. Adult's expectations are central and often evaluated.
Example	Child freely chooses when, how, what, and with whom to play. High levels of social and pretend play occur during free play.	Players may have a limited number of choices or be expected to engage in a specified number of play activities within a particular time period.	Group games, finger plays, directed story reenactment.	Rote memory activities such as singing ABC songs, spelling games, addition facts races.	Adults decide when, how, where, or on what to work. Goal-oriented tasks, such as worksheets and other drill-and-practice activities.
Type of learning	Discovery learning	Guided, discovery learning	Reception learning (acquiring a large amount of information)	Rote learning	Repetitive learning

Note. Adapted from Bergen (1987), Christie (2001), and Wing (1995).

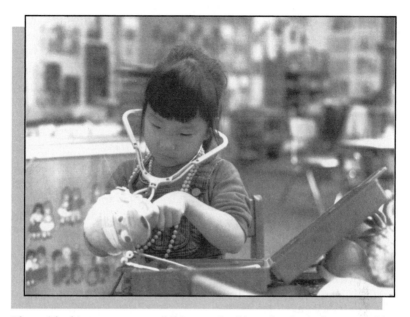

Play with objects empowers children to do things for themselves, to feel in control, to test and practice skills, and to develop a sense of competence.

music laboratories, and writers' workshops, it is easy to see that all of these approaches are play-based.

An illustration of how teachers' orientations to play affect the classroom comes from the following two very different second-grade classrooms. In Ms. McGill's room, children plan their daily schedules with their teacher during their morning meeting. Then, during a 90-minute uninterrupted block of learning experiences, the second graders complete some teacher-selected learning stations related to the current unit of study and then choose freely among a wide variety of accessible and well-organized materials; they play games, paint, construct with manipulatives, write in their math or writing journals, or investigate science ideas. There is a quiet buzz from the children's interactions with these carefully planned but diverse activities. They also have daily opportunities for outdoor play.

Mr. Sampson's second graders, on the other hand, sit in desks in neat rows. He directs his 7-year-olds to work in whole-group experiences to complete teacher-prepared activities, such as completing worksheets and making an art project by copying the sample Mr. Sampson made. His second graders are reminded to do their own work, with little time to talk with one another about what they are doing, thinking, or making. Outdoors, children play organized ball games or practice motor skills on the climbing equipment. How do these classrooms reflect each teacher's assumptions about play?

In a classroom like Mr. Sampson's, little attention is given to the powerful relationship of play to learning and development. His classroom experiences deny children the opportunity to work on challenging tasks in a playful context. Historically, early childhood educators have valued and supported the centrality of play experiences in the early childhood classroom (Johnson, Christie, et al., 1999; Isen-berg & Quisenberry, 2002). However, recent educational developments have em-phasized a more academic, structured orientation and have undermined the role of play in the curriculum. Classroom practices such as the use of stations, centers, problem-solving activities, and cooperative learning groups in today's curriculum offer one way of including play-based experiences in the curriculum.

The Educational Role of Play

If we could travel back in time and interview three educational leaders about the value of play, what would they say? John Dewey, Patty Smith Hill, and Susan Isaacs were all strong advocates of play in the classroom. Dewey (1916, 1938) ad-vocated that play was a major way all children learn about themselves and their world. While children build on what they know in their play, their play is continu-ally changed by their ongoing experiences. For Dewey, play becomes a recurring cycle of learning that is essential to what children know and can do. Through meaningful, firsthand experiences with concrete materials coupled with opportu-nities to think and talk about these experiences, children build new understand-ings. Through peer interaction and the negotiations that inevitably occur during play, they enhance their social growth. Dewey's ideas about **active learning** con-tinue to permeate today's curriculum.

Patty Smith Hill (1923), strongly influenced by Dewey's ideas, recognized the importance of play for children's learning. She invented the large hollow blocks

John Dewey believed that children learn about themselves and their world through their play.

Patty Smith Hill invented the large hollow blocks that are an integral part of today's early childhood classrooms.

that are still an integral part of most early childhood classrooms and believed that large classroom spaces enhance children's learning through play. In her work-play period, her kindergarten children freely explored the objects and materials in their environment, initiated and carried out their own ideas, and engaged in cooperative learning groups with their peers.

Susan Isaacs (1933) is another historical figure who believed that play contributes to all aspects of children's growth and development. Her work was especially helpful to teachers as they observed children's developing mastery of their emotions. Isaacs ardently defended children's right to play and challenged parents to support play, which she regarded as children's natural resource for learning.

Prior to the large-scale societal and educational reforms beginning in the 1960s, most early childhood practitioners recognized the importance of play. They believed that play reflects children's experiences, is meaningful and relevant, and is a rich resource for learning. The translation of Piaget's (1962) work in the 1960s began to find support for the idea that children of all ages are active learners.

At the same time, other researchers documented the importance of the early years for influencing intellectual development (Bloom, 1964; Bruner, 1966; Hunt, 1961). Educators soon began putting these research ideas into practice with the growing numbers of disadvantaged children, but did so in inappropriate ways. Classrooms at all levels became more academic and rigorous. As curriculum designers became driven by the belief that earlier is better, academic skills replaced play as central to the curriculum, to the grave concern of many early childhood educators.

But the educational climate is once again changing. New research on brain development supports children's need for many opportunities to learn spontaneously, to engage in constructive social relationships, and to think about the consequences of their actions (Jensen, 2000; Santrock, 2003). Teachers who work with children of all ages should be informed of the impact of the new brain research on children's learning. As educational leaders look to the skills and abilities future workers will need, they are raising questions about rote learning. Schools and curricula at all levels are being refashioned to invite children's initiative, inventiveness, and planning and focus on developing their problem-solving ability, divergent thinking, and social skills. Play provides the vehicle for children to develop such competencies. Thus, all teachers must understand the crucial role of play in the lives of all children. As the next section details, play is what childhood is all about. First, read what teachers have to say about play and then think about your own reflections.

TEACHERS' REFLECTIONS ON PLAY, GAMES, AND INVENTIONS

Preservice Teachers

"I never realized that there was so much to learn about play and games. I was surprised that a whole course could be designed on this topic. I've learned some reasons why so many people do not believe that play is important."

"I never really thought of play and games as learning tools. Rather, I thought of them as things to take up time with the children. Now I realize that play and games benefit children in many ways. They are excellent tools for learning, not just something children do to keep busy."

Inservice Teachers

"I realized I needed play in my classroom when the children began complaining of headaches and I was having no fun. I haven't changed any of my curriculum objectives; I've just looked for better ways to teach the children and for better ways for them to be learners."

"I never thought that the absence of play could be detrimental to children's development. As an experienced elementary school teacher, I am now struggling with my own philosophy of teaching that keeps swinging back and forth between play-centered learning experiences and teacher-directed ones."

Your Reflections

- What role do you think play, games, and inventions have in the curriculum?

- Can you envision different types of play in the curriculum?

- How might your beliefs about play enhance or inhibit children's learning and development?

WHY IS PLAY IMPORTANT?

Guidelines from the Association for Childhood Education International (ACEI) and the National Association for the Education of Young Children (NAEYC), two respected professional associations, affirm that play is essential for all children's healthy development and learning across all ages, domains, and cultures. Play does the following:

- Enables children to make sense of their world
- Develops social and cultural understandings
- Allows children to express their thoughts and feelings
- Fosters flexible and divergent thinking
- Provides opportunities to meet and solve real problems
- Develops language and literacy skills and concepts (Bredekamp & Copple, 1997; Gronlund, 2001; Isenberg & Quisenberry, 2002)

In the following play vignettes, consider how play contributes to children's cognitive, language, literacy, social/emotional, and creative development.

Cognitive Development

Ellen, Taralyn, and Jasmine are first graders. On this day early in the school year, they come into their classroom, hang up their backpacks, and then choose to play school at the chalkboard. Ellen decides that Jasmine and Taralyn should get a chair and bring it up to the board. They each also find a yardstick.

Ellen: We better have two chairs.

Taralyn: (*writing on the chalkboard*) Today is . . .

Jasmine: I need to check the size. (*using the yardstick, begins to measure herself while sitting down*) I am the big teacher. My size is up to here. (*pointing to where she measured herself*)

Ellen: (*gets up from the chair, ready to be the teacher*) I will write it. You sit down.

Jasmine: Today is what? (*gets up*) I want to be the teacher.

Ellen: It's my turn first. You can be the teacher next.

(*As Ellen looks at the calendar to find the words she wants to use, Taralyn measures herself with the yardstick.*)

Taralyn: Today is October 7, 2004.

Jasmine: Ellen, can I write, too?

Ellen: After I am finished. (*Taralyn and Jasmine begin giving Ellen weather words to write.*)

Taralyn: Read the calendar sentence. Hey, you forgot the 7.

Ellen: Yeah. (*She goes back and inserts the number 7. Then she writes* Tody *and* wet.)

Taralyn: What is the weather? It's my turn.

Ellen: Raise your hand for the weather.

Taralyn: Today the weather is sunny.

Ellen: (*Writing on the board, she asks Taralyn for help.*) What comes after *s-u-n*?

Taralyn: *N-n-y.*

The first graders in this scenario are using play as a tool for cognitive development. When we talk about cognitive development, we refer to how children make sense of their world. They do this by building on what they already know to interpret new experiences. In their play, Ellen, Taralyn, and Jasmine demonstrate the following four essential elements of cognitive development (Perkins, 1984):

1. *Problem solving.* Using the yardstick to measure herself sitting down and standing up, Jasmine figures out the concept of size.
2. *Mental planning.* When Ellen comes to the chalkboard area, tells Taralyn and Jasmine to get two chairs, sits down in front, and stands at the chalkboard to write, she clearly plans to play school. Mental planning also occurs when Ellen states she will be the teacher first.
3. *Self-monitoring.* We see Ellen checking her own spelling skills when she asks Taralyn for help spelling the rest of the word *sunny*.
4. *Evaluation.* When Taralyn is reading the calendar sentence and notices that Ellen forgot the 7, she demonstrates her understanding of writing the date.

Much of the research on play shows its relationship to the development of children's thinking and more sophisticated classification skills (Frost, Wortham, & Reifel, 2001; Perkins, 1984; Santrock, 2003) and the ability to use what they already know to construct new knowledge. In this case, these first graders are building on what they already know (the routines of school, specific teacher behaviors, and basic literacy concepts and skills) and extending it through playful interactions. They play with words and letters as they test the spelling of weather words and the way to record the day and date.

The cognitive skills children use in pretend play are essential for their success in school (Smilansky, 1968; Smilansky & Shefatya, 1990). All subjects and problems include cognitive skills children use to pretend, yet many subjects (such as social studies) are those with which children have limited experience. To illustrate, after a teacher shares books about the Chinese New Year, such as *Lion Dancer* (Waters & Slovenz-Low, 1990) or *China's Bravest Girl* (Chin, 1997), children's imaginations are stimulated. During play we might notice the children imagining a Chinese New Year celebration with its special dances to ward off evil spirits, colorful dragons and decorations, and special Chinese festival foods, because they are using their make-believe ability to play. In this way, real and pretend become complementary as children use make-believe to enhance their cognitive understanding (Berk, 2005; Johnson, Christie, et al., 1999; Smilansky & Shefatya, 1990).

Language Development

Evan and Anna are preparing a birthday celebration for their mother in the housekeeping area of their Head Start classroom. When they realize they need a present, Anna says, "Let's ask Mr. Bear." This is a reference to the book *Ask Mr. Bear* by Marjorie Flack (1932), in which Danny tries to find the perfect birthday present for his mother by asking several different animals for suggestions. After locating the book in the library corner, Evan and Anna become the goose, the goat, the cow, the hen, and the bear as they search for the perfect present. The book becomes the content for their play as they assume the roles of the animals, experiment with the intonations and inflections of the different animals, and use language to guide their own behavior and direct the behavior of others. Evan and Anna's play is contributing to their language growth and vice versa.

Proficiency in oral language is essential for all children's success in school. Studies of how children learn both their first and second language describe language use as a major influence on language development (Han, Benavides, & Christie, 2001; Morrow, 2001). In the previous scenario, we see at least four ways in which Anna and Evan's play of a birthday celebration enables them to practice important language skills:

1. *Communication.* In pretend play, children use role-appropriate statements and metacommunication, or language used to maintain the play episode; plan a story line; and assign roles. Pretending to be someone else enables children to use voice inflections and language in situations they may or may not have encountered.

Play helps children internalize the many rule systems associated with the language they are speaking. It also helps them generate multiple ways of expressing their thinking (Santrock, 2003).

2. *Forms and functions.* During play, children learn to use language for different purposes in a variety of settings and with different people. Michael Halliday (1975) calls this process "learning how to mean," as children discover that what they say translates to what can be done. Talking in play settings allows children to practice the necessary forms and functions of language (Halliday, 1975) and helps them think about ways to communicate. Moreover, for children whose native language is not English, play offers children opportunities to build on and practice fluency in their home language in safe and informal settings (Han et al., 2001; Owocki, 1999). Table 2.2 describes these functions, provides a language example, and identifies play contexts that support these language forms and functions.

TABLE 2.2   Halliday's Functions of Language with Samples from Three Kindergarten Girls Building with Blocks

Function	Language Usage and Sample	Play Experiences
Instrumental (get things done)	"I want . . ." "Let me have all the orange ones for turrets."	Choosing materials; entering a play situation
Regulatory (control others' behavior)	"Do this . . ." "Only three people can play here; don't knock that over."	Dramatic play; games; story retellings
Personal (tell about self)	"I like this . . ." "Oh no, this is hard to build. I really like castles."	Role playing; choosing roles
Interactional (maintain relationships with others)	"Let's do this . . ." "Let's build a moat around the castle and a bridge to go across it."	Play with language; puppetry; cooperative play; sociodramatic play
Heuristic (find out information)	"How come this is . . . ?" "How come this castle doesn't have a moat?"	Questioning games; investigations; TV shows
Imaginative (use pretend language)	"Pretend we are . . ." "Let's pretend there are snakes in the moat and we need to escape."	Role play; dramatic play; constructive play
Informative (provide information to others)	"This is how I made . . ." "You have to have one turret for each part on the wall. There are lots of castles in fairy tales."	Projects; investigations

Note. Adapted from Halliday (1975, pp. 19–21). Language samples courtesy of Kim Rose.

3. *Purposeful verbal interaction.* In play with others, children often use language to ask for materials, ask a question, seek out information and provide information to others, express ideas, explore language, and establish and maintain the play. For younger children, verbal give-and-take during sociodramatic play needs to be highly developed because children plan, manage, problem-solve, and maintain the play by verbal explanations, discussions, or commands (Smilansky & Shefatya, 1990). For older children, the ability to use a reflective and analytical approach to language is related to their level of linguistic awareness and achievements, which are essential to all forms of play.

4. *Play with language.* Children of all ages enjoy playing with language because, in doing so, they feel in control of it. Play is their arena for experimenting with and coming to understand words, syllables, sounds, and grammatical structure. Language play for elementary school children manifests itself in the jokes, riddles, jump rope rhymes, and games they use. Elementary school children are intrigued by the sound and meaning ambiguity of "knock-knock" jokes as well as by the humor of enacting scripts that include dialogue involving multiple meanings and rhymes. These forms of language play require the transformational ability to explore the phonological, syntactic, and semantic rules of language (Bergen, 2002; Clawson, 2002, Isenberg & Quisenberry, 2002).

Literacy Development

A growing body of evidence shows how children's play contributes explicitly to their literacy development. We know that children's literacy development—their reading and writing abilities—occurs from infancy along with their oral language development. By the time they come to school, they already possess a well-developed spoken language in their native language (Christie, Enz, & Vukelich, 2003). We also know that children learn to read and write in meaningful, functional social settings that involve both social and cognitive abilities (Morrow, 2001). Elementary children become proficient readers when they view reading as an enjoyable way of learning and an important means of communication. Proficient readers demonstrate some of the same characteristics of good players; they are strategic, engaged, fluent, and independent (Bromley, 1998).

Children at play can reveal the following literacy understandings:

1. *Interest in stories, knowledge of story elements, and story comprehension.* Evan and Anna demonstrated an interest in stories (choosing to retell *Ask Mr. Bear*), displayed knowledge of story elements (character, plot, setting, goal, and conflict), and exhibited story comprehension in their pretend dramatization of preparing for a birthday. Children's first attempts at reading and writing often occur during dramatic play as they read environmental print, make shopping lists, or play school. Most beginning readers rely on their oral language to gain meaning from books as they internalize the structure and meaning of language. More proficient readers have a more complex and developed concept of the interrelatedness of story elements. Dramatic play develops improved story comprehension and an increased understanding of story elements (Christie et al., 2003).

Children's first attempts at reading and writing often occur during dramatic play.

2. *Understanding fantasy in books.* In dramatic play, children enter the play world "as if" they were another character or thing. The ability to transform oneself in play enables children to enter the world often created in books featuring talking animals (such as *Ask Mr. Bear* or *Charlotte's Web* [White, 1952]) or to write stories in which they create hypothetical characters. Elementary children's ability to play with reality is necessary to understand science fiction as well as other types of fantasy books (Bromley, 1998; Christie et al., 2003).

3. *Use of symbols to represent their world.* As children reinvent or construct their own versions of stories, they naturally come to understand their world and make it their own by representing their understandings symbolically. Younger children's language, role enactment, or use of props provide evidence of children's competence in representing what they know (Johnson, Christie, et al., 1999; Owocki, 1999). Similarly, older children's story retellings, writing, wordplay, and the Internet provide evidence of their competence in representing the literacy behaviors they know. It is important for classroom teachers to understand the many ways children's play, games, and inventions contribute to their language and literacy development. Figure 2.1 is a checklist for documenting children's literacy development through play.

Child's Name: _____

Demonstrates "readinglike," literate behaviors

✓ Looks at books and other print materials

✓ Does pretend writing

✓ Shares reading/writing ideas with friends

✓ Uses sound spelling to write notes

✓ Practices reading familiar stories

✓ Chooses books and magazines that reflect their interests

✓ Other: _____

Shows understanding of stories and narrative language

✓ Acts out pretend stories

✓ Tells a story through drawing or other media

✓ Uses puppets to retell a story dramatically

✓ Engages in dramatic retellings that include _____ characters, _____ setting, _____ conflict, _____ plot, and _____ solution

✓ Dramatic retellings use story structure (e.g., beginning, middle, and end)

✓ Other: _____

Explores conventions of print

✓ Writes messages in dramatic play center

✓ Copies letters and words from other print materials

✓ Reads messages to others during dramatic play or story retellings

✓ Other: _____

Investigates book knowledge and the language of books

✓ Holds book right side up

✓ Turns pages left to right

✓ Pretends to read while turning pages

✓ Distinguishes between pictures and print

✓ Makes up words and stories to match pictures

✓ Reads books with familiar patterns or repetitive language

✓ Names some print while reading

✓ Other: _____

Figure 2.1
Documenting Children's Literacy Learning Through Play

Experiments with a variety of forms of written language

✓ Announcements	✓ Library cards
✓ Calendars	✓ Notes/Recipes
✓ Money/cash registers	✓ Signs
✓ Coupons	✓ Tickets
✓ Labels	✓ Other: _____
✓ Invitations	

Statement of literacy behaviors demonstrated:

Ideas for furthering literacy development:

Suggestions for parents:

Note. Adapted from Owocki (1999).

Social and Emotional Development

During play, children also increase their social competence and emotional maturity. Smilansky and Shefatya (1990) contend that school success largely depends on children's ability to interact positively with their peers and adults. Play is vital to children's social development. It enables children to do the following:

- Practice both verbal and nonverbal communication skills by negotiating roles, trying to gain access to ongoing play, and appreciating the feelings of others (Spodek & Saracho, 1998).
- Respond to their peers' feelings while waiting for their turn and sharing materials and experiences (Sapon-Shevin, Dobbelgere, Carrigan, Goodman, & Mastin, 1998; Wheeler, 2004).
- Experiment with roles of the people in their home, school, and community by coming into contact with the needs and wishes of others (Creasey, Jarvis, & Berk, 1998; Wheeler, 2004).
- Experience others' points of view by working through conflicts about space, materials, or rules positively (Smilansky & Shefatya, 1990; Spodek & Saracho, 1998).

Play supports emotional development by providing a way to express and cope with feelings. Pretend play helps children express feelings in the following four ways (Piaget, 1962):

1. *Simplifying events* by creating an imaginary character, plot, or setting to match their emotional state. A child afraid of the dark, for example, might eliminate darkness or night from the play episode.

2. *Compensating for situations* by adding forbidden acts to pretend play. A child may, for example, eat cookies and ice cream for breakfast in play, whereas in reality this would not be permitted.

3. *Controlling emotional expression* by repeatedly reenacting unpleasant or frightening experiences. For example, a child might pretend to have an accident after seeing a real traffic accident on the highway.

4. *Avoiding adverse consequences* by pretending that another character, real or imaginary, commits inappropriate acts and suffers the consequences. Children whose television viewing is monitored at home, for instance, can pretend to allow the doll to watch indiscriminately and then reprimand the "bad child" for unacceptable TV viewing habits.

In addition to expressing feelings, children also learn to cope with their feelings as they act out being angry, sad, or worried in a situation they control (Erikson, 1963). Pretend play allows them to think out loud about experiences charged with both pleasant and unpleasant feelings. A good example is Alexander, a 4-year-old whose dog was recently hit by a car. In his dramatic play in the pet hospital, his teacher heard him say to another child, "I'm sad because the car hurt my dog." Here he was trying to cope with unpleasant feelings from a frightening situation. Play enabled Alexander to express his feelings so that he could cope with his worry about his dog (Landreth & Homeyer, 1998). So, too, do older children learn valuable emotional skills, such as increasingly realistic self-perceptions, the ability to manage their emotions, and self-control that improves over time through games and inventions. As older children engage in spontaneous and structured play activities, they come to see themselves as good in some areas and less good in others. These opportunities to monitor and discriminate among feelings and emotions contribute to children's beliefs about their own capacity.

Physical Development

Play contributes to children's fine and gross motor development and body awareness as they actively use their bodies. Learning to use a writing tool, such as a marker, is an example of fine motor development through play. The natural progression in small motor development is from scribbles to shapes and forms to representational pictures. Playing with writing tools helps children refine their fine motor skills. Gross motor development, such as hopping and skipping, develops in a similar fashion. When children first learn to hop, they practice hopping on different feet or just for the pure joy of hopping. As elementary children, they integrate their hopping skill into many games, such as hopscotch and jump rope games. Using their bodies during play also enables them to feel physically confident, secure, and self-assured (Isenberg & Quisenberry, 2002).

Recess in schools has traditionally been the time for children to "take a break" from the sedentary academic activities of the classroom and engage in active, free play. Today, that part of the school day is in jeopardy. As a result, the National Association of Early Childhood Specialists in State Departments of Education (NAEC-SSDE) and the National Association for Sport and Physical Education (NASPE) have recommended that elementary children get at least 1 hour of exercise each day, preferably in 15-minute blocks without the structure of a physical education class.

While all children need active play for healthy physical development, the physical benefits are particularly valuable for children with joint or muscular illnesses, such as juvenile rheumatoid arthritis and multiple sclerosis. These children cannot engage in repeated strenuous exercise; they can, however, engage in active play. Active play helps them build or maintain energy, joint flexibility, and muscular strength (Majure, 1995). Side benefits of active play for these children include the development of social skills and an increasing ability to endure stressful situations.

Creative Development

In Chapter One, we talked about the important role of creative thought and expression in children's development and learning. Nearly 50 years ago, Sigmund Freud (1958) suggested that every child at play "behaves like a creative writer, in that he creates a world of his own, or, rather, rearranges the things of his world in a new way which pleases him. . . . The creative writer does the same as the child at play. He creates a world of phantasy which he takes very seriously—that is, which he invests with large amounts of emotion" (pp. 143–144).

The play context is ideal for supporting children's creative and imaginative thought because it offers a risk-free environment. Research supports the notion that play and creative thought are related behaviors because they both rely on children's ability to use symbols (Johnson, Christie, et al., 1999; Singer & Singer, 1998; Spodek & Saracho, 1998). Jerome and Dorothy Singer (1985, 1998) describe the ability to engage in make-believe as essential to children's developing the ability to create internal imagery, stimulate curiosity, and experiment with alternative responses to different situations. This capacity, practiced in play settings, enhances children's ability to engage successfully in new situations.

Creative thought can also be viewed as an aspect of problem solving, which has its roots in play. When young children use their imaginations in play, they are more creative, perform better at school tasks, and develop a problem-solving approach to learning (Dansky, 1980; Dansky & Silverman, 1973; Frost et al., 2001; Fromberg & Bergen, 1998; Pepler & Ross, 1981; Singer, 1973; Sutton-Smith, 1986).

The importance of play in children's lives is well documented. As children grow and change, play develops with them according to a developmental sequence.

HOW DOES PLAY DEVELOP?

Meet Jessie, a fourth grader. If you could go back through her play life and catch glimpses of her behavior, this is what you would see:

> As a 10-month-old, Jessie plays pat-a-cake with Grandma Marji. At age 2, Jessie pours sand back and forth into different-sized plastic containers. When Jessie is 4, she pretends to make pizzas and take delivery orders over the telephone with her friends, Lara and Michelle. At age 6, Jessie and two friends pretend to eat space food in a spaceship they have constructed. At age 8, Jessie plays a card game, I Doubt It, and is becoming quite adept at rummy. And now, at age 10, Jessie invents a memory game that matches ten inventors' names with their inventions.

As Jessie's experiences illustrate, play occurs in a sequence. The development of play at all ages has been studied from two major perspectives, cognitive and social. Both parallel and strengthen children's overall development and learning. Think about the following questions as you read the next section: What types of play do children demonstrate at different ages? Do these types of play reappear at later ages? How does play reflect and promote children's cognitive and social development?

Developmental Stages of Cognitive Play

Cognitive play reflects children's age, conceptual understandings, and experiential background. The ideas of Piaget (1962), Smilansky (1968), and Smilansky and Shefatya (1990) describe the following cognitive stages of play: functional play, symbolic play, constructive play, and games with rules. Although each of these types of play peaks at a particular age, they all continue in some form throughout life, have unique characteristics, and contribute to children's growing understanding of themselves, others, and their world. Table 2.3 provides an overview of the four categories of cognitive play, their typical behaviors, and an age-appropriate example.

Functional Play

Functional play (birth to age 2) is characterized by simple, pleasurable, repeated movements with objects, people, and language to learn new skills or to gain mastery of a physical or mental skill. It is also referred to as sensorimotor, practice, or exercise play (Piaget, 1962; Smilansky & Shefatya, 1990). Functional play dominates the first 2 years of development, about one-third of the play of preschoolers, and less than one-sixth of the play of elementary school children (Rubin, Fein, & Vandenberg, 1983), and continues in some form through adulthood.

Through functional or practice play, children develop coordinated motor skills and begin to feel confident and competent with their bodies, as in the following examples:

The 1-year-old who stacks and unstacks rings on a pole

The 4-year-old who incessantly repeats "I'm the king of the castle"

TABLE 2.3   Types, Characteristics, and Examples of Cognitive Play

Types	Characteristics	Examples
Functional play	Repetition of movements when new skills are being learned, with or without objects.	*Infants and toddlers:* grasping and pulling a mobile
		Preschoolers and kindergartners: repeating a pattern on a pegboard
		School-aged children: practicing throwing, catching, or doing acrobatics
Symbolic play	Use of imagination and role play to transform the self and objects and to satisfy needs.	*Infants and toddlers:* pretending to drink from a baby bottle
	Early symbolic play: mental representation that transforms one object for another.	*Preschoolers and kindergartners:* pretending a block is a broken car and pretending to fix it
	Later symbolic play: mental representation that transforms self and objects.	*School-aged children:* using secret codes or made-up languages to communicate
Constructive play	Manipulation of objects or materials to make something. Combines functional play repetitive activity with symbolic representation of ideas. Occurs when children regulate their own creations or constructions.	*Preschoolers and kindergartners:* constructing a hospital room for a sick animal
		School-aged children: creating an exhibit of a project just studied or designing virtual games and figures with electronic icons
Games with rules	Activities with predetermined rules that are goal-oriented and often competitive with one or more individual.	*Infants and toddlers:* playing pat-a-cake with an adult
		Preschoolers and kindergartners: playing simple singing and circle games
		School-aged children: tag, marbles, hopscotch, or contests such as relay races

Note. Adapted from Piaget (1962) and Smilansky & Shefatya (1990).

The 5-year-old who deliberately places pegs in a pattern on a pegboard

The 7-year-old who practices bicycling skills on a two-wheeler at every available minute

The 9-year-old who does variations on jump rope movements

Symbolic Play
Symbolic play (age 2 to 7), also called pretend, dramatic or sociodramatic, fantasy, or make-believe play, emerges during the second year and continues in different

Using their bodies during play enables children to feel competent and confident.

forms throughout adulthood. It arises when children are able to transform their world into symbols and usually contains three elements: props, plot, and roles. Symbolic play reflects children's growing mental ability to make objects, actions, gestures, or words stand for something or someone else (Van Hoorn, Monighan-Nourot, Scales, & Alward, 2003; Piaget, 1962). Play at this stage is called symbolic because it focuses on social roles and interactions (Smilansky & Shefatya, 1990) and reveals children's ability to play with ideas or symbols. In symbolic play, children make mental and verbal plans of action, assume roles, and transform objects or actions to express their feelings and ideas (Van Hoorn et al., 2003).

Infants and toddlers imitate actions associated with a particular prop in symbolic play, learn to substitute one thing for another, and act as if they were someone else who is familiar to them. For example, as a young toddler, Naomi picks up her toy cup and pretends to drink from it. As an older toddler, she may offer her doll a drink from the cup. Her symbolic play shifts from pretense about herself to pretense about others.

Preschool and kindergarten children's symbolic play is more complex. They pretend alone or with others, use nonrealistic objects, assume roles, and use objects as symbols in addition to what they stand for (Van Hoorn et al., 2003). Three-year-old Miriam uses her hand as a pretend hairbrush for the baby's hair. Five-year-olds Jimbo and Celeste become firefighters as they collaborate to rescue people from a burning building. These transformations are essential for symbolic play to occur. Symbolic play peaks during the preschool years, the golden age of make-believe,

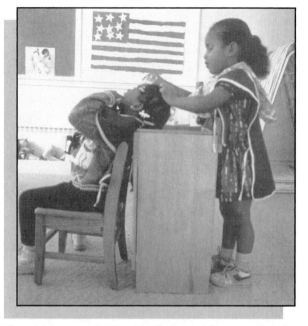

These girls are transforming their world into symbols by using props, creating a story, and assuming new roles as they reenact a "beauty shop."

but reappears later in the form of daydreaming, hypothetical thinking, and private fantasies from the middle grades through adulthood.

School-age children's symbolic play differs from the play of children at other ages because now their thinking is less public. They can integrate their symbols into age-appropriate, socially acceptable mental games and language play. Riddles, number games, secret codes, and daydreaming form the structure of symbolic play for school-age children (Elias & Berk, 2002; Johnson, Christie, et al., 1999). It is not uncommon to find 7-year-olds delighting in the use of secret code, a form of symbolic and language play, or to find 9-year-olds daydreaming. For school-age students, participating in simulations and games provides an opportunity to participate in situations that they cannot actually experience, thus increasing their interest and intrinsic motivation. The elements of fantasy and pretense make what otherwise would be a boring activity more meaningful (Pintrich & Schunk, 2002). Research shows that symbolic play increases children's memory (Newman, 1990), enriches language and expands vocabulary (Christie, 2001; Holmes & Geiger, 2002), enhances children's ability to reason with contradictory facts (Fromberg & Bergen, 1998), and fosters flexible and inventive thinking (Pepler & Ross, 1981).

Sociodramatic Play

When symbolic play involves two or more children who communicate verbally about the play episode, it is called **sociodramatic play**. Because it is person-oriented rather than object-oriented, sociodramatic play is considered a higher level of symbolic play behavior. Here children exchange information and ideas during a jointly elaborated play sequence or theme; they can also simultaneously be actors,

*In sociodramatic play, children imitate familiar roles
and develop social skills.*

interactors, and observers (Smilansky & Shefatya, 1990). Repeated opportunities to engage in this type of play offer children a rich arena for developing and refining concepts, solving problems, feeling in control by making things happen, enhancing peer relationships, and learning self-regulation (Elias & Berk, 2002). Sociodramatic play correlates highly with children's intellectual and social abilities (Smilansky & Shefatya, 1990). Table 2.4 describes Smilansky's six criteria for determining dramatic and sociodramatic play. Note that the last two characteristics (interaction and verbal communication) define symbolic play as sociodramatic. A discussion of the Smilansky scale for assessing sociodramatic play elements can be found in Chapter Nine.

Constructive Play

In **constructive play**, children create something or engage in problem-solving behavior according to a preconceived plan. Constructive play often combines functional and symbolic play and predominates during the preschool years (Forman, 1998). The following example occurred during center time in Ms. Mitsoff's multiage kindergarten and first-grade classroom.

Emily, Porsche, and Elizabeth chose to play in the block center. They had just visited the Washington, D.C., memorials and decided to build the Jefferson Memorial. To do this, they negotiated and discussed which blocks would be appropriate

TABLE 2.4 Smilansky's Characteristics of Dramatic and Sociodramatic Play

Play Behavior	Characteristics	Examples	Levels
Imitative role play	Child assumes a make-believe role of a person or object and expresses it in imitation and/or verbalization	"Let's pretend that I am the baby."	Beginning: Role relates to the familiar world, (e.g., mommy, daddy, baby) Advanced: Role relates to world outside the family (e.g., doctor, teacher, police)
Make-believe with regard to objects	Child substitutes movements, verbal declarations, and/or materials or toys that are not replicas of the object itself or real objects	Uses Lincoln Logs to make a house for the baby and uses chimneys from Lincoln Logs to make beds for the dogs.	Beginning: Real objects or replicas used (e.g., real toy car) Advanced: Uses prop as part of play scenario (e.g., stirs soup with a block)
Verbal make-believe with regard to actions and situations	Child substitutes verbal descriptions or declarations for actions and situations	Uses Lincoln Logs to outline a square for the house and says "This is a house for the baby."	Beginning: Imitates simple actions of adult (e.g., holds vacuum and moves back and forth) Advanced: Child's actions are integral to the play episode (e.g., "I'm vacuuming this floor so the baby can crawl around and not hurt herself")
Persistence in role play	Child stays within a role or play theme for at least 10 minutes	Plays role of baby, mother, and daughter within a family play theme for 10 minutes.	Beginning: Short, sporadic involvement (e.g., child enters area, picks up the baby, and leaves) Advanced: Child stays involved in area and the theme for more than 10 minutes
Interaction	At least two players interact within the context of a play episode		Beginning: Plays alone with no obvious awareness of others nearby Advanced: Cooperative effort to work together around a common theme
Verbal communication	There is some verbal interaction related to the play episode		Beginning: Simple dialogue around the use of toys (e.g., "Give me the bottle") Advanced: Dialogue about the roles, props, plot of the play scenario

Note. Adapted from Smilansky (1968) and Dodge, Colker, & Heroman (2002).

*In constructive play, the child becomes absorbed in
the process of creating a lasting end product.*

for the entrances, where to place them, how to make the river, and who would be
the statue. After they built their structure, which resembled the real Jefferson
Memorial, they engaged in symbolic play. In this play episode, the girls combined
constructive play (building a memorial) with symbolic play (visiting the memorial) by representing their ideas with the materials (blocks) and elaborating on
them in symbolic play (playing house inside the memorial). In constructive play,
the child focuses on a lasting end product (Forman, 1998).

School-age children engage in some constructive play in the school setting
because it is easily accommodated in work-oriented settings (Christie, 2001; Forman, 1998; Bergen, 1988). Typical constructive play might include creating a play
around a social studies topic (such as occupations), writing a story, creating an
interactive exhibit, using invented spelling, building virtual systems on a computer screen, or making a mobile out of recycled materials. In order for the play to
qualify as constructive, however, children must maintain a playful attitude (for instance, keeping the focus on "What if I do this?" rather than "Why won't it do
that?"), must become absorbed in the process, and must find it pleasurable. In that
way, the child keeps the goal in mind, but it does not dominate the play.

Games with Rules

Games with rules rely on prearranged rules that guide acceptable play behavior of
reciprocity and turn taking. Games with rules such as board games (such as Clue),
card games (such as rummy), and outdoor games (such as kickball) are the most

prominent form of play among elementary school children. Their more logical ways of thinking and advanced social skills make it possible for older elementary school children to follow a set of rules and negotiate with peers. Games with rules (see Chapter Seven for detailed discussion) enhance children's physical coordination, refine their social and language skills, build conceptual understandings, and increase children's understanding of cooperation and competition (Johnson, Christie, et al., 1999; DeVries, 1998).

In the following example of the card game Addition War, think about the rules fourth graders Tom and Chang use and how they reason their way through problems. The boys are sitting side by side so they can see each other's addition facts and lay their cards down like a vertical math problem.

> **Tom:** I have 18. How many do you have?
> **Chang:** I have 17.
> *(Tom picks up all four cards and places them face down at the bottom of his stack. They each put down two more cards.)*
> **Tom:** I win.
> **Chang:** I have 9 and 8. You know what that is? That equals 17 so I win this time.
> **Tom:** We haven't had a war yet.
> **Chang:** I have 18; what do you have?
> **Tom:** I have 11 and 8.
> **Chang:** 11 and 8 is 19.
> **Tom:** How much is an ace worth?
> **Chang:** 11. Oooh, you win! *(They lay down more cards.)* A jack and king equal 20. I have 20. Let me see. You have 16 and I have 20. I win. *(When the game ends, Chang quickly counts his cards)*. I have 39 cards and that means I win because it's more than half the deck.

In this card game, Tom and Chang use their knowledge of addition facts to play a rule-based game. They demonstrate understanding of prearranged rules (acknowledging the winner of each round and assigning a numerical value to the ace), conceptual understanding (the winner holding 39 cards has more than half the deck), and turn taking (knowing who goes next after each pair is placed on the table).

In sum, children use all types of cognitive play at different ages and for a variety of purposes. The unique nature of each type of cognitive play reflects what children know and are able to do. Because much of children's play occurs with or around others, the next section describes how play contributes to children's social competence.

Developmental Stages of Social Play

Social play, the ability of children to interact with their peers, also develops in age-related stages. This kind of play often develops rapidly during the preschool years and continues to be refined over the years. The now-classic ideas of Mildred Parten (1932) have focused attention on the social aspects of play during early childhood. Parten identified six types of play, beginning with the least socially mature (solitary play) and moving toward the most socially mature (cooperative play). Today,

TABLE 2.5   Levels of Social Play

Type of Play	Characteristics of the Child
Unoccupied behavior	Is not engaged in play and does not seem to have a goal. Plays with body, gets on and off chairs, walks about aimlessly.
Onlooker behavior	Observes, asks questions, and talks to other children but does not enter play itself. Stands within speaking distance to see and hear. More active interest and involvement than unoccupied behavior.
Solitary play	Plays independently and is not involved with other children. Playing with own toys is the primary goal. Most typical of 2- and 3-year-old children. Older children use solitary play for needed privacy and for elaborate individual dramatic play.
Parallel play	Plays alongside or nearby, but not with, others. Uses shared toys but plays independently. Does not share toys. Typical of young preschool children. Often considered the beginnings of group play.
Associative play	Plays with others in a similar, loosely organized activity. Conversation involves asking questions, using one another's toys. Some attempts made to control who may join the group. Is often the transition from parallel to cooperative play.
Cooperative play	Involves complex social organization with shared common goals. Uses negotiation, division of labor, differential role taking, and organization of play themes. Reciprocal role taking (such as turn taking) and a strong sense of belonging to the group. Organizes group for the purpose of making a product, dramatizing a situation, or playing a formal game.

Note. Adapted from Parten (1932).

most researchers consider Parten's "levels" as descriptive of styles of play rather than social maturity because as children grow older, they cycle back and forth between the types of social play (Van Hoorn et al., 2003). Table 2.5 describes the characteristics of Parten's six levels of social play.

Knowledge of the stages of play helps teachers provide appropriate, supportive learning environments for children. It also enables them to enjoy, encourage, and appreciate age-appropriate play behavior. Play is children's natural resource for developing social and cognitive skills that affect their present and future interactions. To appreciate the essential role of play in children's lives, it is important to understand the different theories of why children play and how these theories influence teachers' views of play.

WHY DO CHILDREN PLAY?

For more than 150 years, theories of play have been proposed, yet none adequately explains why children play. Some suggest that children play because they feel physically safe in the play setting (the house is not really burning, so they can escape); others suggest that children play because they feel safe emotionally (playing out events in a war-torn country provides a way for children to confront the realities of their environment). Still others suggest that play enables children to assimilate new information and make it their own, such as creating a new flying machine as part of a unit on space and flight or using invented spelling to write a message. Collectively, however, these theories represent a vision for the powerful role of play in children's development, which has greatly influenced teachers' thinking about its importance. These theories can be categorized as **classical theories** (those that were prominent in the nineteenth century through World War I) and **modern theories** (those that were prominent after World War I) (Johnson, Christie, et al., 1999).

Classical Theories

Classical theorists sought to explain the causes and purposes of play through surplus energy, recreation/relaxation, practice, and recapitulation (Ellis, 1973). We can see evidence of these theories in the way teachers currently view children's behaviors in the classroom.

Surplus-energy theory suggests that human beings have a certain amount of energy to be used for survival. Energy not used for survival is spent on play and becomes surplus energy. When children have limited opportunities to move around, they seem to have bursts of energy that relieve stress and tension so they can settle down again. Teachers' views about "getting rid of excess energy on the playground" support this theoretical perspective.

Recreation/relaxation theory, in contrast to surplus-energy theory, suggests that play replenishes energy used in work. The influence of this theory is evident in early childhood classrooms where children alternate between quiet and active activities and in elementary classrooms where children have daily opportunities for recess to provide balance in their daily lives.

Practice theory, also known as instinct theory, proposes that play prepares children for the future roles and responsibilities needed to survive in their culture. When young children pretend to be a mother, father, or teacher and invent ways to use materials to represent adult tools, they are practicing the behaviors and characteristics of significant adults in their lives. Even when no play materials are available, children will use available objects to create play episodes. When elementary children play board games, they practice strategic thinking and reasoning—essential life skills.

Recapitulation theory also focuses on innate instincts. In contrast to practice theory, it posits that play enables children to revisit developmental stages observed in their ancestors and shed any negative behaviors. Play is seen as a way of preparing children for living in today's world. Popular games of chase and pursuit can be categorized within recapitulation theory for all ages.

Modern Theories

The major difference between classical and modern theories of play is that modern theories emphasize the consequences of play for the child rather than focusing on the consequences for the culture at large. Three major modern theoretical orientations are psychoanalytic, supporting emotional development; cognitive-developmental, supporting mental development; and sociocultural, focusing on social development.

Psychoanalytic theory views play as an important vehicle for emotional release (Freud, 1958) and for developing self-esteem as children gain mastery of their thoughts, bodies, objects, and social behaviors (Erikson, 1963). Play enables children to enact feelings, without pressure, by actively reliving experiences and mastering them in reality. Moreover, it provides the teacher or caregiver with clues to children's individual needs. After the birth of a new baby, it is not uncommon to hear a preschool brother or sister at play saying to a doll, "I'm taking you back to the hospital." Expressing resentment through play enables children to gain control of it in real situations.

Cognitive-developmental theory examines play as a mirror of children's emerging mental abilities (Bruner, 1966; Piaget, 1962; Sutton-Smith, 1986). Piaget proposes that children individually create their own knowledge about the world through their interactions with people and materials. They practice using known information while consolidating new information and skills, test new ideas against their experiences, and construct new knowledge about people, objects, and situations.

Bruner (1966) and Sutton-Smith (1986) interpret play as flexible thinking and creative problem solving in action. Because children focus on the process of play, they engage in multiple combinations of ideas and solutions that they use to solve relevant life problems. For Bruner, play allows children to discover ideas for themselves and to view children as "knowers" even before we explicitly teach them.

Sociocultural theory, suggested by Vygotsky (1967, 1978) emphasizes the centrality of the social and cultural contexts in development. Vygotsky, (1978), believes that pretend play is a "leading factor in development" (p. 101) and that "in play a child behaves beyond his average, above his daily behavior; in play it is as though he were a head taller than himself" (p. 102). Because children first encounter knowledge in their social world that later becomes the origin of their conceptual understandings, play acts as a mental support that enables children to think through and solve problems in new ways. This "zone of proximal development" (Vygotsky, 1978) provides children with the freedom to negotiate reality and do things in play that they are often unable to do on their own outside the play setting. For example, in Ms. Rodriques's fourth-grade class, there is a weekly time for playing games children have constructed. The fourth graders work in pairs or small groups to create games that have all the elements of games (such as clear goals and rules, a variety of game pieces, a colorful design, and challenges). Children create variations of common board games such as bingo or Clue that often contain the content children were studying, such as questions about the properties of liquids, constants and variables, and vocabulary words such as *volume, weight,* and *graduated cylinder.* Notice that Ms. Rodriques provides the context for her fourth graders to understand these properties first in a social setting (pairs or small groups) and then as individuals in constructing their knowledge.

Each of these theorists supports the essential role of play in children's developing abilities. They help illustrate the many ways play can support children's

TABLE 2.6   Theoretical Perspectives of Children's Play

Theories	Theorists	Purpose of Play
Classical		
Surplus-energy	Schiller and Spencer	Expend excess energy to survive
Recreation/relaxation	Lazarus	Restore energy used in work
Practice/instinct	Groos	Practice future survival skills
Recapitulation	Hall	Reenact ancient activities
Modern		
Psychoanalytic	Freud	Master unpleasant experiences
	Erikson	Master physical and social skills to build self-esteem; express wishes and needs

Cognitive	Piaget	Practice and consolidate known information and skills through different types of play:
		  Functional play (repeated motions)
		  Symbolic play (make-believe)
		  Games with rules (predetermined rules)

	Bruner and Sutton-Smith	Promote flexibility and creative problem-solving through symbolic transformations
Sociocultural	Vygotsky	Foster abstract thinking and self-regulation through symbolic play. Contribute to potential development (performance with a more capable peer or an adult or the zone of proximal development). Enable child to grapple with unrealizable desires.
Other	Bateson	Operate on two levels at the same time. On one level, children are engrossed in pretending; on another level, they are aware of their true identities.

learning in meaningful and authentic ways. Table 2.6 lists the major theories, theorists, and purposes of play. Collectively, these theories provide teachers with a research base that guides the specific roles they assume in promoting the development of children's play and play skills in the classroom.

 # TEACHERS' ROLES AND RESPONSIBILITIES

One question that teachers often ask is, "Should I intervene in children's play?" When adults support children's play, everything they do can be considered a kind of intervention. Whether, how, and when teachers intervene determines whether play is enriched or disrupted.

Research tells us that children's play becomes more elaborate, richer, and more complex when adults support children in their play (Reifel, 2001; Smilansky & Shefatya, 1990; Vygotsky, 1978). A good blend of intervention strategies means that teachers are neither too directive nor too unaware about their role in children's play. When teachers are too controlling, children lose the opportunity to regulate their behavior. On the other hand, when teachers intervene in situations where children can already perform a task, they discourage children's self-regulatory behavior by fostering dependence on adults.

Why Should Teachers Intervene in Children's Play?

Guidance in answering this question comes naturally from the theories of Lev Vygotsky (1978), who suggested that play is a critical scaffold that helps children advance to higher ability levels in all domains. Scaffolding is particularly important as we examine the range of teachers' roles in play settings. Often there are tasks that a child cannot accomplish independently but can accomplish with the assistance of an adult or a more capable peer. This "zone of proximal development" is the optimum time for teachers to assist children in their learning.

When Should Teachers Intervene in Children's Play?

Although there are times when teachers are most likely to want to intervene explicitly in children's play, under no conditions should teachers assume a role that dominates the direction of children's play, nor should teachers participate in play when children clearly do not want them there. Usually, teachers intervene in the following situations:

1. When play is absent from children's behavior (for example, aimless wandering and inability to engage with another child, material, or activity)
2. When a child finds a task far too difficult (for example, being unable to make a bridge out of blocks)
3. When a child needs assistance to get something done (such as playing a board game or creating an invention for the science fair)
4. When a child has limited knowledge of the role, object, or situation (such as reenacting a scene from a literature selection)
5. When children ask them to participate (for example, teachers may assume the role of ticket taker at an imaginary airport or ask questions) (Trawick-Smith, 1998)

As you read each of the different roles teachers assume, think about when and how to use each role as an intervention.

What Are Teachers' Roles in Children's Play?

The following seven roles describe the various kinds of interventions teachers can use.

Teachers as Observers

Teachers must be good observers of children's play so that they can determine whether children need help with a problem; whether toys or materials are adequately stimulating; and how play situations are contributing to children's developing social, motor, and cognitive skills. Skilled observers note which child plays what role, which child chooses particular themes, how children enter and exit a play setting, which children seem to "get stuck" in a play theme and can't move forward with it, who needs one-to-one interaction, and which children are developing the ability to participate in group activity. Skilled observers also note when not to intervene, such as when children are already engaging in cooperative play or when they do not seem interested in adult participation. Careful observation and interpretation are the bedrock of all the other roles teachers assume in facilitating the play process (Trawick-Smith, 1998). For an extended discussion of informal observation measures to study play, see Chapter Nine.

Teachers as Collaborators

Sometimes children continuously repeat actions and cannot move forward with a role, theme, or idea. Teachers can extend their play by adding a new toy or prop or by asking a question that elaborates on but does not change the theme. One kindergarten teacher had a fast-food restaurant in her theme corner. After a week of play, she added a "Drive Thru" sign and a cardboard window that the children used to add a new dimension to their play. She also suggested adding the role of "cashier." In doing so, she extended the children's thought processes and imagination without undermining their original intentions (Fromberg & Bergen, 1998; Stooke, 1998). A teacher of fourth graders provided many opportunities for children to collaborate with others to compose stories out of a set of random words that had been a part of the children's content-area lessons in social studies and then watch as other children in the class added to the story. Occasionally, children would enact the final story. This teacher understood the importance of her role as a collaborator or in children's exploratory play with words.

Teachers as Planners

Teachers must also plan for children's play. An environment conducive to play provides enough time to develop and carry out a play theme; enough space for children to enact a theme or to construct something; a variety of materials that encourage all forms of play; common and familiar experiences so that children can enact roles they understand; and an appropriate ratio of children to adults who respond sensitively and knowledgeably to children's needs (Johnson, Christie, et al., 1999).

Selma Wassermann (2000) describes a K–2 multi-age classroom that shows a teacher's careful attention to planning for play. She writes about "breathing out," the first 45 minutes of the day when children transition from home to a school environment that absorbs their interest and prepares them for a day of learning. This environment includes plenty of space for learning stations including blocks, construction materials, dramatic play, and art; investigative play centers that operate later in the day where children explore explicit content; and a choosing board where children select how they will spend their time at centers. As children become absorbed in their play activities, teachers work individually with children on particular skills. Orchestrating this kind of play activity requires considerable skill.

Teachers as Responders

When teachers verbally describe children's actions and words or ask questions about the role or theme, they provide feedback on what the children are doing and saying. Making statements such as "I see you have bought a large bag of groceries" or "I noticed the tower is as tall as you are" gives children an opportunity to elaborate on that behavior if they choose. Asking questions, making suggestions, and helping children make contact with others are all ways in which teachers can respond to children's play (Trawick-Smith, 1998; Smilansky & Shefatya, 1990). These interventions, however, must address the role of the child and not the child. In this way, the intervention validates that playing is a valued activity. For elementary children, providing feedback to their playful learning requires that you have in mind the major concepts and skills that children can demonstrate through their play. Your questions and responses serve as pathways for children's further examination of a particular idea. Further, your way of responding, through either paraphrasing, further questioning, or making statements about what you see, contributes to children's ability to further explore an idea (Wassermann, 2000).

Teachers as Models

Sometimes teachers actively join the play and model a particular behavior or role relevant to the ongoing play theme. In this way, they can teach individuals or groups of children a needed play skill or behavior. Consider the following example. In Ms. Blum's preschool special-needs class, two 4-year-old girls are playing house in the housekeeping area. Ms. Blum notices that one child rocks with a doll while the other repeatedly opens and closes the oven door. She enters the play, sits at the table, and announces: "It is time for lunch." She asks, "What smells so good in the oven?" and later asks, "Could I help set the table?" Ms. Blum's modeling of family roles and behaviors encourages children to practice some of those skills, which children will then be able to transfer to other settings on their own.

Teachers as Mediators

The teacher's role as **mediator** is critical in helping children construct meaning from their play experiences by serving as a bridge between children's initial understanding of a concept or event and their deeper understanding as a result of direct experience with that concept or event. For example, teachers of young children frequently encounter children's conflicts and disputes in play situations. Very young children often have disputes about toys or space for play, while older preschool children may have disputes about role play or rules. Elementary children often argue over rules of the game, participation, and friends. Teachers who mediate young children's disputes use strategies that help children develop peaceful resolutions. These can include being aware of children's intentions; helping children use words to express their needs and feelings; making play spaces accessible and providing enough materials to share; and giving children enough time to negotiate their own solutions to problems (Wheeler, 2004). Teachers of older children mediate their learning by helping children elaborate on their ideas and make sense out of them. For example, in a basic science unit on matter, children explore ideas of weight and mass through exploring, asking questions, and testing solutions in response to the teacher's organizing, conceptual question that provokes their thinking (such as "How will you do this?") and invites them to explore, experiment, and test their ideas but does not tell them what to do or what to think. Finding the right balance as a bridge between ideas is a powerful role for the teacher as mediator.

Teachers as Monitors of Children's Safety

Teachers are responsible for creating and maintaining safe environments for children both inside and outside the classroom. The following checklist will help you analyze the environment for safety:

1. Check the environment for such hazards as exposed outlets and cords, dangerous plants, and nonchildproof gates.
2. Make sure the equipment and materials are in good repair and free of sharp edges, protrusions, or broken parts that toddlers could swallow or put in their ears or noses. Discard any materials that are worn out or damaged.
3. Store toys and materials on shelves that children can easily reach. If you have materials that you do not wish children to use, store them in locked cabinets or on high shelves that are not accessible.
4. Periodically disinfect materials and equipment to keep things sanitary. Use warm, soapy water followed by a disinfectant solution of 2 tablespoons chlorine bleach to 1 gallon of water. (Store the bleach in a locked cupboard where children cannot reach it.)
5. Supervise all children's play to ensure that materials are being used as expected and that the materials hold their interest and are appropriate to their needs.
6. Practice emergency procedures and encourage children to enact them or talk about them in "what if" situations in their play.

When teachers attend to their roles as monitors of children's safety, they exert a positive influence on early childhood curriculum and wean themselves away from a skills-based curriculum. As Fromberg (1998) so aptly stated, "The teacher's most useful direct intervention is maintaining a playful attitude and accepting and encouraging children's independent problem-solving and connection-making."

MEETING STANDARDS

Integrating Play Experiences Across Ages and Content Areas in Inquiry-Based Units on "Change"

Standards are statements that guide what children should know and be able to do in a given content area at a given time. They are used as a means to assess student learning and *promote accountability*. While there are no specific standards in the area of play, play-based learning provides an important means for teachers to teach to standards in each curriculum area, using an inquiry approach to learning while gaining important knowledge about children's thinking. Play-based experiences also meet national teacher education standards.

The four forms of cognitive play discussed in this chapter—functional play, symbolic play, constructive play, and games with rules—provide a framework for an inquiry-based approach to learning because they give children many opportunities to explore and clarify ideas, describe, internalize, and synthesize information as they come to understand their world. For example:

> In *functional play,* children explore objects with all of their senses, which involves experimenting and tinkering with materials.

> In *symbolic play,* children transform their world into symbols, which involves brainstorming, role-playing, and teamwork.

> In *constructive play,* children create something or engage in problem-solving behavior according to a preconceived plan, which involves problem solving and "thinking out of the box."

> In *games with rules,* children rely on prearranged rules that guide acceptable play behavior of reciprocity and turn taking, which involves strategic thinking and teamwork.

Youngquist and Pataray-Ching (2004) suggest that play-based experiences be viewed as acts of inquiry, a term that "connotes creative and reflective thought and promotes the attainment as intellectual capacity of every learner" (p. 171). When viewed as a form of inquiry, play-based learning experiences become a powerful vehicle for children to express what they know. The thinking abilities humans develop through play are mental characteristics critical to successful school-based learning—curiosity, persistence, imagination, and inventiveness. Many teachers find that the concepts students have to learn in the content areas lend themselves naturally through play-based learning.

What follows are examples of how teachers can incorporate play-based experiences across grade levels and content areas in different inquiry-based units on the broad concept of change. First is a list of key content-area standards for students. Next is a brief description of an appropriate unit followed by examples of play-based, age-appropriate learning experiences. Each example identifies the types of play used and the content area standard it addresses. Following the content area student standards are the teacher education standards that can be met through the incorporation of play in the PK-4 curriculum.

Content-Area Standards Related to the Concept of Change

> *Social Studies Standard: Time, Continuity, and Change:* Students should study the ways human beings view themselves in and over time.

> *Mathematics: Patterns, Functions, and Algebra:* Students should be able to analyze change in various contexts.

> *Science Standard: Science as Inquiry:* Students develop abilities necessary to do scientific inquiry and understandings about scientific inquiry.

Language Arts Standard: Students should use language appropriately in daily use as well as use new vocabulary to describe feelings, thoughts, experiences, and observations.

Teacher Education Standards

National Association for the Education of Young Children (NAEYC): Standard 4b Teaching and Learning: Teachers use effective approaches to positively influence child development and learning.

INTASC Standard 2: Student Development: Teachers understand how children learn and develop and can provide learning opportunities that support children's intellectual, social, and personal development.

Examples for Preschool/Kindergarten

As part of a unit on change, preschool and kindergartners are studying about themselves and their personal pasts. Their earliest understandings of history begin with learning about themselves and their own changing characteristics. They are learning about the changes in the way they look, what they eat, what they play with, what they wear, what they can do, and what they know.

Appropriate Play-Based Learning Experiences

Functional Play

- Explore with senses different tastes of baby food compared with real food. Graph with pictures favorite tastes of baby food and food they like now. (Math)

Symbolic Play

- Role-play in the housekeeping area the roles of baby, toddler, and adult. Include diapers, baby clothes, a variety of dolls, infant and toddler toys, sippy cups, booster seats, and a variety of adult clothing. Children can enact what they use today and compare with what they used when they were babies and what they might use when they are grown up. (Language Arts/Social Studies)

Constructive Play

- Construct a picture-rebus timeline of children's lives. Use photos and drawings to chronicle children's lives and changing abilities from birth to present, such as changes in height, number of teeth, amount of hair, how many letters they know, or how much they weigh. Be sure to use drawings for every child to be sensitive to children who do not have access to photos of their childhood. (Math/Social Studies)

Games with Rules

- Play "Guess Who I Am?" or a Name Chant. (Language Arts/Social Studies)

Now, add to these examples using one or more of the content-area standards.

Examples for First Grade–Second Grade

As part of their unit on change, first and second graders often study the water cycle, which involves learning about evaporation, condensation, precipitation, and collection. They learn that water moves in a continuous cycle between the air, the ground, and plants and animals. Because these children are naturally curious, they are motivated to use the following kinds of play-based inquiry experiences to find out how the water cycle works.

Appropriate Play-Based Learning Experiences

Functional Play

- Explore and examine the changes that water causes in the soil. Using soil, pebbles, and containers, children can explore soil changes when adding different amounts of water and what happens to water when they make a channel. Explore also samples of muddy water to observe the sediment when it settles. Describe patterns. (Math/Science)

Constructive Play

- Collaborate with others to build a model of the water cycle using clear plastic containers, sand, pebbles, a small amount of water, and leaves. (Science/Math/Language Arts)

Games with Rules

- Create a game that includes "water facts." (Science/Language Arts)
- Create a word search using different water cycle terms, such as *water, fresh, gallons, safe, clean.*
- Make a puppet and some rain sticks and tell the story of *It Rained on the Desert Today* (Buchanan, 1994) or *Peter Spier's Rain* (Spier, 1997). What happens to the dry desert or your backyard when it rains? (Science/Language Arts).

Symbolic Play

- Role-play different parts of the water cycle. (Science)

Now, add to these examples using one or more of the content-area standards.

Examples for Third Grade–Fourth Grade

As part of their historical study of the colonial period, third and fourth graders study about the founding and expansion of the 13 original colonies. Through research and interpretation of daily life in the colonial period, the children learn about such things as the types of homes, transportation, activities, games, recipes, clothing, and tools that were used in colonial days. They also learn about people and places.

Appropriate Play-Based Learning Experiences

Constructive Play

- Construct a three-dimensional or salt dough map that illustrates different features of colonial times and colonial communities. (Social Studies/Math/Language Arts)
- Visualize a timeline starting with colonial games and toys and compare them to the kinds of toys and games we use today. Select, organize, and sequence information about the toy's functional role in the historical era. Brainstorm reasons why and how some of these toys were used. (Math)
- Construct scale models of a colonial ship of choice. (Math)

Games with Rules

- Construct a game on the chronology of toys using various sources of information such as pictures, charts, inventors, and photographs to show an understanding of the past. (Social Studies/Language Arts)
- Create colonial word problems using metrics. (Math/Language Arts)

Symbolic Play

- Write a skit to communicate to younger children the different toys, clothing, and foods used long ago and why they were appropriate. Enact that skit for children of different ages. (Language Arts/Social Studies)
- Role-play the different occupations, such as blacksmith, cooper, miller, cobbler, silversmith, tinsmith, and town crier, that were common in colonial days. (Language Arts/Social Studies)

Frequently Asked Questions About Play, Games, and Inventions

Why are play and games so essential to children's learning and creative thought?

Play is a dynamic process that develops and changes as it becomes increasingly more varied and complex. Findings from research on the brain and learning delineate the importance of play (Bergen & Coscia, 2000; Jensen, 2000; Santrock, 2003). We know that active brains make permanent neurological connections critical to learning; we also know that inactive brains do not make those necessary permanent neurological connections. Research on the brain demonstrates that play is a scaffold for development, a vehicle for increasing neural structures, and a means by which all children practice skills they will need later in life. This research raises new questions for those who view play as a trivial, purposeless behavior and challenges them to recognize play for what it is—a serious behavior that

has a powerful influence on learning (Christie, 2001; Isenberg & Quisenberry, 2002; Wassermann, 2000).

I want to teach older children. Why do I need to know about play when most principals and parents oppose the use of play in elementary schools?

While some consider play trivial and simple, and even a waste of time, play is not wasted time but rather time spent building new knowledge from previous experience (Piaget, 1962; Fromberg, 2002; McCune & Zanes, 2001). Information about typical age-related play behaviors provides a useful framework for understanding the different forms and functions of children's play. Play is a major way children take ownership of new information by playing with it. Learning requires an interactive balance of gaining skills and knowledge and making them one's own.

Active play fosters personal meaning. When children perceive learning as relevant, it becomes part of their long-term memory; when children perceive learning as irrelevant, such as a continuous series of memorizing isolated facts and meaningless concepts, it typically will not become part of long-term memory.

How does play support children from culturally, ethnically, and linguistically diverse backgrounds?

With greater frequency, today's classrooms include children whose native language is not English and children who have different cultural and ethnic backgrounds. Children's play provides information about who they are and enables them to better understand others. Teachers can help realize play's potential for children from different cultures, races, and ethnic backgrounds in a variety of ways (Banks, 2001; Jalongo, 1991; Tiedt & Tiedt, 2000). First, teachers must recognize and respect ethnic and cultural differences by asking themselves some difficult questions to discover their basic attitude toward others, such as the following: *Am I aware of my own biases toward different populations? Do I recognize that different child-rearing practices affect a child's play?* Second, teachers can help children explore their cultural backgrounds through appropriate play-based experiences. A curriculum sensitive to diversity helps children appreciate their personal histories. As a teacher, you need to know enough about children and their families to make informed curriculum decisions, such as learning the background and culture of the children, finding out how long families have been in this country, what toys and materials children use at home, and what experiences have the children had

outside the home (such as eating in a certain kind of restaurant or observing cars being repaired at a gas station). This information is critical to providing relevant and familiar play experiences. Third, teachers need to be particularly sensitive to gender and racial issues as children enact familiar roles. Play is a powerful vehicle for understanding gender and racial issues. How teachers communicate messages about what girls, boys, and people of color can do affects how children view themselves and their competencies. In preparing children for today's and tomorrow's world, be sure to use culturally diverse materials and experiences, such as puppets, dolls, puzzles, music, art, and books in the room; that they provide enough novelty and challenge for all; and that all children are free to enact different roles.

I teach in an inclusive classroom. How can I use play with children with disabilities?

As classrooms become more inclusive, teachers are wondering how they can adapt their curriculum to include all children in meaningful play-based experiences. Research shows that play supports the developmental needs of children with language, motor, cognitive, or social disabilities (Deiner, 2005; Mindes, 1998; Rappaport & Schulz, 1999). Teachers can support inclusion by providing opportunities for children to practice specific skills, providing time for active and guided practice, assisting children with language development, and reducing the effects of stress in children's lives. The more opportunity for social interaction, the more likely that children will be able to overcome language delay, acquire developmental skills, and increase the complexity of their play. Teachers may want to contact the National Lekotek Center (http://www.lekotek.org), which provides services to foster the play-related abilities of students with disabilities, including a toy resource helpline (800-366-PLAY) and a toy-lending program. It also disseminates *The Toy Guide for Differently-Abled Kids.*

CHAPTER SUMMARY

1. Play has been studied from different perspectives, yet experts have not arrived at a consensus about its definition or primary purpose. There are, however, accepted identifiable characteristics.

2. Both classical and modern theories have influenced how play is viewed in the early childhood curriculum. These theories are essential to

understanding why children play and must be used as a basis of curriculum planning.

3. Play contributes to all areas of children's development. It is the primary vehicle through which their cognitive, language, literacy, social/emotional, and creative development occurs. Play has been studied primarily as an aspect of social and cognitive development.

4. Teachers have at least seven clear roles and responsibilities in children's play— observer, collaborator, planner, responder, role model, mediator, and monitor of children's safety. Each of these roles and responsibilities must be fulfilled in order to support children's learning and development through play.

5. Teachers must adapt their curriculum so that children of all ages can benefit from the power of play, games, and inventions. Each can be utilized to enhance the diversity of their classrooms, to challenge the imagination of all learners, and to integrate children with disabilities into the mainstream.

Discuss: Perspectives on Play, Games, and Inventions

1. This chapter has described the difficulty surrounding the study of play and games. Explain to your colleagues how assumptions about play and the play/work distinction have contributed to this confusion. Describe how you used to think about play and games before reading this chapter and the questions you now have after reading this chapter. How can you begin to find answers to these questions?

2. Your role as a classroom teacher is crucial in supporting play. Review the seven roles of the teacher discussed in this chapter. Of what significance is it to assume these different roles? Cite some examples from your personal or field experience that illustrate these roles. Were these the most useful roles to assume? Why or why not?

3. Reread the "Teachers' Reflections on Play, Games, and Inventions" early in this chapter. In what ways are these teachers' reflections similar in their thinking about play? What differences did you notice? Talk about which of these teachers' reflections made an impression on how you think about play after reading this chapter. Of what importance are teacher reflections?

4. An appropriate play environment is essential for children to grow and think creatively. What principles and practices would you adopt to ensure children's healthy development?

5. With the increasing emphasis on test scores and high standards, can you envision the play context as fundamental to learning? How do you think the play context can help children develop the knowledge and skills they need to be successful in school and in the workplace of the future? What do you believe about the importance of play? Why do you believe so?

PART 2
THE FINE ARTS

Chapter 3

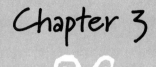

Promoting Children's Art

Mary Renck Jalongo
and Marilyn J. Narey

Educators have always recognized that the arts provide children with cultural advantages that contribute to their creativity. Now it is clear that they contribute to children's overall development as well. . . . [The arts] provide children with many opportunities to succeed, thereby helping them to develop positive attitudes toward themselves and learning. Through interactive experiences with the arts, children engage in the learning processes of exploring ideas, creating meaning, constructing knowledge, and communicating concepts, thoughts, and feelings.

Dolores Varnon, 1997, p. 325

CLASSROOM PERSPECTIVES ON ART

Preschool–Kindergarten

As is typical at this stage, when the 4- and 5-year-olds in Ms. Lin's preschool class draw themselves, the artwork often consists of a circular shape with a face and lines radiating out to represent legs and/or arms. The teacher's goal is to draw children's attention to various body parts so that they might begin to incorporate them into their scribbles and drawings. She starts a discussion of shoes with the book *Whose Shoes?* (Hines, 2001). Then she poses questions such as, What kinds of shoes do people wear? Look at your own shoes; what do you see? Do your shoes have ties, buckles, or Velcro? Next, the preschoolers draw a picture of themselves wearing their favorite shoes. As a result of the discussion, some children now scribble or draw shapes that represent shoes. For the children who do not do this, Ms. Lin accepts it as normal and does not point out the omission. Rather, she reads *Drawing Lessons from a Bear* (McPhail, 2000) to encourage them to practice. Over the course of the year, she gives many new artistic challenges, such as "I am smelling a flower" (nose), "I am holding a flag" (hands and arms), "I am combing my hair" (hands and hair), and "I am pushing a cart in the store" (arms and legs). By the end of the school year, the children's drawings are considerably more detailed and Ms. Lin has persuaded several of her colleagues to abandon coloring pages in favor of genuine support for children's art (see Golomb, 2004).

First Grade–Second Grade

Mr. Pena makes the most of the fact that the three first grades at his school take an annual field trip to an art museum. He knows that young children often will (1) respond to the sensory qualities of artwork (for example, responding to bright, intense colors), (2) relate the subject matter in art reproductions to their experiences, (3) invent stories about the shapes, colors, and images found in works of art, and (4) respond more to what is pictured (subject or theme) than to the artist's style

(Kerlavage, 1995). Mr. Pena's preparation for the museum visit begins with *Visiting the Art Museum* (Brown & Brown, 1990) and *Squeaking of Art* (Wellington, 2002), a picture book about an imaginary art museum tour by ten mice. The next day, Mr. Pena displays fine art reproductions throughout the room. He begins with a familiar print by Bruegel that depicts children of the Renaissance engaged in many different types of play and teaches children how to connect these works of art with their experiences (see Finnegan, 2001), then shares *The Fantastic Journey of Pieter Bruegel* (Shafer, 2003), and visits a Social Studies Development Center with artlinks at (http://www.indiana.edu/~ssdc/artlinks.htm) for curriculum ideas. Additionally, Mr. Pena leads children to discover themes in works of visual art (fantasy, realism, multiculturalism, caricature, still life, land/city/seascapes, and so forth). To further prepare for the museum visit, Mr. Pena invites the children to participate in an art version of show and tell. Each student selects an artwork from prints and postcards to "show" the class and "tell" the meaning ("This picture is about _____ because _____.") Each day includes a brief discussion (3–5 minutes) with different examples of art criticism questions, such as, "Do you like this artwork? Why or why not?" "What shapes, lines, colors, etc. do you see?" He also includes a bit of information that would be of interest to children about the artist, the culture, or the time period and poses questions such as, "When was this work of art made? Is it old? New? How can you tell? What did the artist use to make this? How do you know?" By the time the field trip is scheduled, the students are ready to play a search game in which they will identify one example of a piece of sculpture, a painting, a drawing, architecture, furniture design, costume, and so forth. Prior to the trip to the art museum, all of the students responded both through drawing and writing to the question, "What is art?" After the trip, the students revisit the assignment and discuss whether and how their definitions have changed.

Third Grade–Fourth Grade

The fourth-grade curriculum includes a mental health unit in which creative expression plays a key role. The classroom teachers and school counselor collaborate with the art, music, and physical education teachers to make the unit more interesting and effective. Today's lesson is about coping with difficult emotions and the culminating activity is being directed by the art teacher. She begins by projecting many different artworks and photographs that depict people's faces and emotional responses. Next is the students' turn to participate in "reading" faces. They are supplied with many different types of magazines that include celebrities, people from other cultures, and advertisements. Working in small groups, the students study collage in picture books (Prudhoe, 2003) and create poster-sized collages with the unifying theme of a particular emotion (joy, sorrow, surprise, confusion, anger, etc.). As a follow-up to the collage construction, the students compose a group essay about the kinds of experiences that prompt the various emotions. Students then work individually to write a personal story about a situation that they found difficult to cope with emotionally. They use a mirror to study their facial expressions and create a drawing, painting, or sculpture of that emotion to accompany their drawings. Their teacher uses a variety of books from the Adventures in

Art and Architecture Series (http://www.prestel.com) to stimulate the fourth graders' thinking about art.

DEFINING CHILDREN'S ART AND AESTHETIC EXPERIENCES

Test your assumptions about children's art and aesthetic experiences. Indicate whether you think each of the following statements is true or false.

Test Your Assumptions About Children and Art

1. Artistic ability unfolds naturally and children are best left to follow their own inclinations.
2. Producing art is an emotional process rather than a cognitive one.
3. Any sensory experience, such as playing with shaving cream, is an art experience.
4. Artworks need to be produced in a solitary fashion; otherwise, children will "copy" the work of their peers.
5. The primary purpose of art projects in school is and should be to make gifts or holiday ornaments.

You may be surprised to learn that all five of these statements are false. Here's why:

Question 1. False. It is not enough to throw children together with some art materials and hope for the best. Children need to learn techniques, such as preschoolers learning how to use just a bit of white glue so that wooden items will hold together and dry quickly or third graders learning how to sketch or build a scale model of a display of their work before actually constructing the display.

Question 2. False. Contrary to popular opinion, art is every bit as much a cognitive (thinking) process as it is an affective (emotional) one. When a group of children plans a display of their work, they are engaging in problem solving (Where will we place our display? How will we organize it?) as well as responding to affective responses (How does this look?). Realize too that art can be a source of frustration, such as when a weaving unravels or a clay sculpture breaks after it is fired in a kiln. So even though the arts are an outlet for creative expression, they can be a source of emotional stress when the work is not going well. The arts can teach children how to respond to complex challenges with tenacity and grace.

Question 3. False. There is a useful distinction between "messing about" with materials and art experiences. A baby who plays with his food is not having an art experience, because the behavior serves no purpose related to the arts. Likewise, a preschooler who plays with soap bubbles in a dishpan is not having "an aesthetic experience," because the activity is not elevated above the ordinary by being linked with creative expression.

Question 4. False. Art is a social activity, not merely a means of talent testing or promoting individual accomplishment. Children often are inspired by their peers to try new things in art, just as real artists are influenced by the works of artists they admire. Children should be allowed to interact with their peers during art activities.

Question 5. False. Art is not a commodity. When children paste cotton ball beards on a preprinted copy of a Santa face, it is not art, it is an assembly task. Likewise, children who color predrawn pictures are not producing art any more than an adult whitewashing a fence is producing art. In all cases, it is simply a task to be dashed off to schedule and there is little opportunity for creative expression or problem solving (adapted from Kindler, 1996).

If all of these assumptions about children's art are false, what is true? Actually, it is easy to avoid some of the worst activities masquerading as art by asking a few simple questions (Jalongo & Stamp, 1997):

Are the children's responses predetermined? If so, it is not art. A teacher who distributes patterns to color, trace, copy, or cut out in some designated way

Children often are inspired by their peers to try new things in art.

is not providing an art activity, no matter how clever it might be. It is an exercise in following directions.

Will one child's work look nearly identical to another's? If so, it is not art. When you can view a display of children's work and see nothing original or surprising, it is not really children's work and is not art.

Who is the activity for? If it is simply to convince parents that their child is keeping busy at school, it is not art. For example, the teacher who "fixes" children's cut-and-paste pictures by rearranging them to look more presentable for display not only has selected an inappropriate activity but also is undermining children's confidence in their ability to be makers of art.

Will the child's efforts lead to the creation of a new form that is satisfying to the child at his or her level of development? If a child is being pushed, it is not art. An adult who grasps a 3- or 4-year-old's hand and forces the child to produce a stick figure is not "teaching" the child to draw! Most young children will strongly resist such impositions, and understandably so. When a child is at the scribbling stage, scribbles are satisfying because they are something new and interesting. If adults have to do an activity for the child, it is not art.

Consider this example from Mr. Ortiz's first-grade class. His students have been collecting what he calls "beautiful junk" for several weeks. Included in these materials are items such as bits of fabric, yarn, buttons, lace, felt, boxes, and plastic bottles of various sizes and shapes. The children have been listening to stories about amiable monsters, including *Where the Wild Things Are* (Sendak, 1963), *The Very Worst Monster* (Hutchins, 1985), *There's a Nightmare in My Closet* (Mayer, 1968), and *Harry and the Terrible Whatzit* (Gackenbach, 1977). Mr. Ortiz's challenge to his students is simply this: "Using any of the materials we have collected here or others you may have at home, create your own monster. Think about questions like these: What is a monster? What is special about your monster? What does it eat? Are people afraid of it? Why? Where does it live now? What makes it happy? What makes it sad? What does it like to do? After you have created your monster, you will tell the class all about it. Then you will make up a story about your monster." Is this art? Use the four preceding questions and the information in Table 3.1 to arrive at your answer.

If you decided that the monster-inventing activity was art, you were correct.

🦋 THEORETICAL AND RESEARCH BASE: ART AS A LANGUAGE AND THE SCHOOLS OF REGGIO EMILIA

Art is a set of processes that uses symbols and tools to communicate meaning. Art is also a language through which the child can communicate understanding (Davila & Koenig, 1998). Participation in art activities enables children to elaborate

TABLE 3.1 Is It Art? How to Decide	
Not Art	
Category	**Examples**
Assembly Tasks	Gluing a magnet on a clothespin, collections of craft store items that are assembled at school, making houses out of Popsicle sticks
	Why isn't this art? There is no creativity involved. Each child's work will appear very similar. The emphasis is on following directions.
Using Food as Art	Macaroni necklaces, "painting" with pudding, making a "house" out of graham crackers and icing, "painting" on bread with food coloring, gluing beans, rice, and other food items onto paper
	Why isn't this art? Real artists do not use these materials. These projects waste good food and may be perplexing or offensive, particularly to people from communities where food is in short supply.
Copy Work	Coloring pictures from coloring books, follow-the-dots drawing, using clip art, tracing patterns or using templates, painting by the numbers
	Why isn't this art? These activities emphasize conformity and fine motor control rather than resourcefulness and originality.
Art	
Category	**Examples**
Creative Problem Solving	Designing an original picture book, sculpting a dinosaur from clay, constructing a well-balanced mobile
	Why is this art? Each child's work will be a one-of-a-kind original. Children are choosing their own artistic challenges, making decisions about the medium, and determining ways to share and display their work.
Aesthetic Responses	Pairs of children examining art postcards and notecards and discussing them, describing/comparing/contrasting the artistic style of picture books, responding to beauty outdoors or in nature photographs
	Why is this art? Children are developing emergent skills in art criticism and insights about style.

on their ideas, interests, and experiences (Korn-Bursztyn, 2002). For children who are just learning to communicate their thoughts and feelings through words, art takes on even greater importance as a language (Danko-McGhee & Slutsky, 2003). Year after year, the majority of children report that art is one of their favorite subjects in school. It is not difficult to understand why, when we consider how art typically is taught in elementary school. In art, children have a greater opportunity to make meaningful choices, to work at their own pace, to spontaneously seek new challenges. There is no right or wrong answer, but there is satisfaction in work well done and the chance to develop skill in self-evaluation. Through art, children learn that pride in craft is essential, that details are important (Eisner, 1992b).

Of all the early childhood programs in the world today, those in a municipality of Italy called Reggio Emilia are recognized as some of the very finest, particularly where the art curriculum is concerned. Providing opportunities for children's creative expression is a cornerstone of the early childhood programs in Reggio Emilia, and educators from around the globe travel there to marvel at the creative genius of children that is expressed through their work. The first question that this raises is, Why? What occurs in these programs that supports children's creative expression? Surely no one would argue that Italian children are innately more creative than other children! So what is the teaching philosophy, what is the curriculum, and what are the conditions that lead to such impressive work from children? Review Figure 3.1, then read the description of the Reggio schools written by Frankie DeGeorge that follows.

The Reggio Emilia approach to early childhood involves a system of interrelationships among children, parents, teachers, and the environment. Central to the approach is the view of the child as an active seeker and builder of knowledge (Edwards, Gandini, & Forman, 1993).

Children's interests determine what will be investigated, experienced, and interpreted. This display of interest can be initiated in various ways: by a book, a local happening, or a problem that presents itself within the group. Children's interest in these projects may last only a few days, be sustained over several weeks, or appear intermittently over a number of months.

The teachers play an important role in these projects—as inquirers to encourage thinking, as co-learners who construct knowledge along with the children,

---

Prior experience with art materials: Do children have access to materials and art tools? Is the range, supply, or quality of materials limited?

Cultural opportunities: Do children have the opportunity to see various types of art in their environment? For instance, do they visit studios or museums, examine different types of architecture, or appreciate the folk art traditions of their culture and other cultures?

Family discipline: How do parents react to the child's artistic efforts? Is a child severely punished for drawing on the wall, for instance? Are boys actively discouraged from artistic pursuits?

Visual skills, mental capacity, and motor coordination: What strengths and abilities does the child bring to the art activity? Can the activity be adapted to challenges or special strengths of the child?

Figure 3.1
Variables Affecting Children's Artistic Expression
Note. Based on Henkes (1989).

as projectors of the possible directions of a project and as resources for equipment or experiences to support the children's initiatives. It is important to mention here the role of the *atelierista,* or arts educator, who assists the children and the teachers in providing the appropriate art medium for the children's use in expressing and creating, thereby documenting their own work as the project unfolds.

This idea of documentation is another essential element in the Reggio Emilia approach. It begins in the *asili nido* (infant center) for children approximately 1 to 3 years of age. Each child has an album filled with photographs, teacher descriptions of events, developmental milestones, and children's scribbles. Seeing these albums gives visitors, and surely parents, an overwhelming sense of the respect and value that teachers have for children. Quotations from parents were seen over each crib in one center. They had been gathered from interviews and conversations with parents. These words, held to be so special by the teachers, conveyed this same feeling for the parents.

Documentation for ages 3 to 5 involves the display of children's artwork, which remains at school. It comprises photographs, questions, and comments of the children as they investigate, experience, and create, all beautifully displayed on classroom walls. Seeing this documentation contributes to the children's understanding that their words and work are valued by the adults around them. This knowledge engenders a continued interest in creating and participating by the children. Indeed, this documentation has a positive effect on parents, who can see the whole scope of a project and their child's development through it. This knowledge fuels interest in their child's work and furthers parental participation in the school.

Displays of children's artwork and photograph panels also play an important part in the interior decor of Reggio Emilia schools. The children's artwork is displayed with all the attention and care given to the work of professional artists. Mobiles hang from the ceiling, translucent works are attached to glass, some works are framed on a wall-mounted light box, and many sculptures are neatly arranged on shelves. The effect is delightful.

The environments draw the children, as well as the adults, into a world of light, reflection, and involvement. Mirrors are seen everywhere—at entrances, along stairwells, under blocks, and particularly in the totally mirrored, small triangular houses where a child can see multiple reflections. All the schools visited included a large, tiled central square or piazza, where gatherings take place and special play centers are available. These areas were lovely with plants, artifacts, and equipment neatly and artistically arranged.

Each of the schools also provided a puppet stage frequently used by the municipal puppeteer, who entertains and intrigues the children with issues of reality versus fantasy—"It is and it isn't." This recurring theme is also played out in the dress-up centers where, to quote a teacher, "A child goes in one person and comes out another." A large shadow screen where children can create settings and dramatize is also provided.

Other materials found in the schools include blocks with many props, table games, comfortable book corners, housekeeping areas, water play activities, music rooms for listening and creating, and indoor climbing equipment.

The dining rooms were especially inviting with decorative items that added a homelike touch. Small tables were covered with cloths. Each table was graced with a centerpiece; at one school, it was an African violet, at others, children's creations.

In the art rooms varieties of paper, art supplies, and other materials were neatly stored on open shelves for everyone's use. The tops of the storage units held divided trays of bits and pieces, beads, seeds, buttons, sequins, and marvelous collections of items to be used creatively. Wire and other metal fencing materials were available for shaping and weaving. Also in supply were translucent papers for painting and transparent material for encasing three-dimensional works of art. One display of clay sculptures created by children showed adults, each holding a child in a different way. One adult held a child's hand, one carried a child on his back, one held a child in her arms, and one bounced a child on his extended leg. The pieces were individually designed, detailed, well proportioned, and expressed sensitivity to feelings.

The *atelierista* (art teacher) explained that the children are encouraged to be attentive to the details of the object they are representing. The teachers may point out the shape, curve, or other specifics to the children. In addition, the children are given the opportunity to "revisit" their previous works in the same area and improve on them, since the work remains at school. This practice allows children to see mistakes or missed details as their knowledge of the subject matter improves and their project continues. Learning and creativity are purposely intertwined in the program. As this description suggests, creative expression and play are at the heart of practice in the exemplary schools of Reggio Emilia.

Figure 3.2 highlights key principles of developmental theory and their implications for the child's growth in art. As you review these principles, consider not only how they are reflected in the schools of Reggio Emilia but also how you will incorporate these understandings into the art experiences that you provide for children.

TEACHERS' REFLECTIONS ON ART

Preservice Teachers

"After we talked about children's art in class, I decided to use what I am learning to plan the activities for my volunteer work at the Community Center program. It was a theme that I had used with success before, during my first prestudent teaching experience. In it, I recited a poem about the gingerbread man prior to making gingerbread cookies. That part still seemed good, so I kept it. But the art activity I had chosen to do while we were waiting for the gingerbread to bake seemed inappropriate after taking this class. Originally, I had planned to make copies of a gingerbread person that I found in a book. It had decorations to cut out and paste on the pattern. Instead of doing this, I decided to let the children create their own drawings and decorations. I was so impressed by what they produced on their own!"

Principle 1: Children think about art in ways that are different from that of most adults.

Children have their own ways of thinking and representing their worlds (Gardner, 2000). When a typical adult judges a drawing, it is based on how much it "looks like" the original. Not so for the young child who uses drawing more like a language, as a way to organize thoughts and construct meaning (Goodenough, 1954; Kellogg, 1979). Young children draw patterns rather than events or objects; they do not approach art as many adults do—as mere decoration (Vygotsky, 1925).

Principle 2: Growth in art is indicated by sequential stages of development that cannot be forced.

It is foolish for adults to push children to draw in a particular way long before they are sufficiently mature to accomplish such tasks (Vygotsky, 1986). Illustrating this point, Lowenfeld and Brittain (1982) describe a study in which researchers attempted to teach nursery school children the task of copying a square. Despite "saturating" the children with square-making instruction, square-making ability did not improve. Furthermore, when the children who had been pressured to copy squares reached age 4, their skill level did not differ from that of peers without direct instruction. The ability to draw people and animals in a variety of poses develops slowly in the child (Vygotsky, 1925). For example, kindergartners often draw the body first, then draw the clothes, making the clothes appear "transparent." Elementary school-aged children draw people primarily from frontal view and find it challenging to depict a body in motion—jumping to play basketball, eating food, or walking the dog. Development in art centers on the representation of space and understanding of spatial-geometrical constructs (Kindler, 1997). For instance, children who have not yet reached Piaget's stage of concrete operations (age 7 to 11) find it difficult to consider the way objects look when viewed from different angles (Cox & Ralph, 1996; Li, 1996). This understanding of space can be observed in children's drawings of trees growing on a hillside, a chimney on a roof, or a path leading up to the front door of a building: in each case, a child who has not yet reached a level of spatial understanding will draw these objects perpendicular to the surface.

Principle 3: Children learn to express themselves through art by interacting with their environments.

Learning takes place in the context of what is known (Lowenfeld & Brittain, 1982). The brain assimilates new information only by understanding it in relation to information that it has already processed. The drawings of young children, for example, seldom have a baseline; rather, figures appear to float on the page. As children gain experience with representational drawing, however, their works begin to show the ground, often with grass or flowers or asphalt—whatever the child has experienced or can imagine. Most first-grade students are not cognitively or conceptually ready to deal with space in terms of linear perspective or to learn body proportion. It is more important that they spend time developing their own schema

Figure 3.2
Developmental Principles and Children's Art

for the world that surrounds them, investigating and interpreting their environment. As the students begin to realize that their technical skills do not allow them to communicate their environment in the representational way that older children tend to prefer, it is then appropriate to provide instruction in linear perspective and human proportion.

Principle 4: With competent assistance, a child can reach a higher level in art development than what could be reached alone.

There is a middle ground between, at one extreme, leaving children entirely to their own devices and, at the other extreme, giving children a predetermined model to imitate. In art, that middle ground is Vygotsky's (1986) ZPD or zone of proximal development. It is the place where a teacher or more competent peer can provide assistance so that a child can move beyond the level that could be reached on her or his own (Gilbert, 1996). Vygotsky calls this support a "scaffold" and, like a house painter's scaffold, it provides the support needed to accomplish a task.

Inservice Teachers

"Because I graduated in elementary education two years ago and have been substitute teaching while I work on a second certification in early childhood, I have done many of the things that were criticized in this chapter. Usually, I have to follow plans left by the teacher, and most things are 'product art' that results in exactly the same thing from each student—a cut-and-paste Christmas stocking, an Easter egg picture to color, a Valentine's Day heart to trace. But, to be honest, even if I didn't have the plans, I probably would have done 'art' activities like those anyway because they are so common and accepted. Now I feel encouraged to break away from teacher-dominated approaches and really support children's creative expression."

"Teaching the fourth grade, I always felt that we have to focus on the core subjects. I didn't realize that art is really a core subject, too! I have begun to integrate the arts into my entire curriculum and the students are not only more engaged in their learning but they seem to be developing a greater understanding in all areas. When they are involved in the art experience, they have to think more broadly and deeply. They are not just taking in information, they must synthesize it, evaluate it and restructure it."

Your Reflections

- What is a creative art activity in early childhood? In elementary school? What criteria can be used to differentiate between art activities and other types of classroom activities?

- What contributions does art make to every child's overall development?

- What concerns do you have about making art an integral part of your curriculum?

HOW CHILDREN LEARN THROUGH ART

Generally speaking, four types of learning are promoted through the arts. Figure 3.3 provides an overview of the four major types of learning (Katz, 1988) promoted through the arts.

Through art, children learn to do the following:

- Observe carefully and record their observations
- Organize ideas and express their feelings
- Work with purpose and maintain a focus
- Solve unstructured problems through trial and error
- Respect themselves and their achievements
- Communicate feelings and ideas with others
- Discover their own points of view while appreciating different points of view
- Appreciate the contributions of different cultural groups
- Create changes in their environments using a wide range of media
- Make aesthetic discoveries and render evaluative judgments (Cohen & Gainer, 1995; Jalongo & Stamp, 1997).

Making decisions about children's art education involves a balance among three components: the needs of the learner, the goals of society, and an understanding of the subject. Each time a teacher decides to provide an art experience for children, three questions are raised (Stankiewicz, 2000):

1. *Who do we teach?* The "who" are the children in our classrooms: the 2-year-old in our Head Start program who is just beginning to make marks, the kindergartner who recognizes a reproduction of a Renoir painting on television, or the fifth grader who is struggling to compose her science poster.

2. *Why do we teach?* The "why" in a broad sense is our current culture, which increasingly bombards us with visual images, multidimensional communication, paradox and metaphor, abstraction, fragmentation, synthesis, complexity, and evaluation (Hicks, 2001). The "why" in a more individual context is the culture that the learner inhabits: the urban, suburban, or rural; the particular family structure; the religious, ethnic, and social framework that constructs the child's world.

3. *What do we teach?* The "what" is the knowledge and the processes of inquiry involved in art, which include instruction in the production of art, aesthetics, art criticism, and art history (Walling, 2001).

The "who," the "why," and the "what" of art are dynamic components that continuously interact and affect one another (Stankiewicz, 2000). Teachers must be aware of the integral relationship among the learner, society, and the subject in order to design effective learner-centered art experiences.

Understanding children's artistic development, the role of art in promoting meaningful self-expression, and the basic principles of a high-quality art education

1. **Knowledge about the arts** *is developed by:*

Sensory experiences and the exploration of materials.

Meeting real, live artists and watching them at work.

Thoughtful examination and discussion of works of art.

What practitioners can do:

Select high-quality art materials that children will want to return to again and again.

Teach children to respect and care for art materials (e.g., cleaning up, proper storage).

Use community resources to provide role models of craftspersonship.

Use the library, the media center, the Internet, and museum-quality reprints and reproductions to stimulate children's thinking about art.

Extend children's vocabulary by using descriptive words when talking about art.

2. **Skills in the arts** *are developed by:*

Experimenting with arts materials, tools, and processes in a low-risk environment.

Gentle guidance from others who have already acquired the skills.

A certain amount of trial and error; making mistakes and learning from them.

What practitioners can do:

Provide a wide variety of high-quality art materials.

Make time for art experiences every day.

Experiment yourself with the materials that you provide for children.

Emphasize the process that children use to create art products.

3. **Dispositions toward the arts** *are developed by:*

Interaction with role models—more competent peers, teachers, and professional artists.

Experiencing the arts alongside enthusiastic arts advocates.

Participating successfully in the arts.

What practitioners can do:

Encourage children to use their own imaginations and ideas in their work and to find their own ways of responding to lesson objectives.

Teach children to be observant and aware of the visual arts in their surroundings.

(Continued)

Figure 3.3
Four Types of Learning Promoted Through the Arts

Invite children to select their best work and display artwork created by every child.

4. Feelings about the arts *are developed by:*

A sense of belonging to a community and feeling support from the group.

Opportunities to respond to works of art created by others.

The sense of efficacy that results when a child's artistic efforts evoke a positive response from others.

What practitioners can do:

Teach children to respect the work created by peers.

Model for children ways to respond thoughtfully to the works of professional artists.

Invite children to consider why their work evoked particular responses from others.

Figure 3.3   (*Continued*)

Note. Based on Cohen & Gainer (1995), Jalongo & Stamp (1997), and State of Florida Department of State (1990).

is essential to a well-balanced curriculum (Wright, 1997). Skillful teachers have learned to use the arts not as an afterthought or add-on, but as a key to the elementary curriculum (Rasmussen, 1998).

Developmental Sequence for Children's Art

When we speak about art, we are talking about something that is perceptual, cognitive, developmental, graphic, and affected by the context and culture. Consider Figure 3.4, an original picture book by Vickie, a first grader whose mother is expecting a baby. Vickie's original picture book reveals her understandings and feelings about this important event.

Art is perceptual. Artists of any age must be keenly aware of sensory input. It is clear from Vickie's story that she is aware of the changes in her mother's body.

Art is cognitive. When Vickie forms symbols, she must know the material (in this case, the media of paper and crayons), know the referent (in this case, the mother and baby), and use that material/medium to express something about that referent (in this case, original drawing and writing) (Smith, 1982).

Vickie's *art is developmental,* meaning that as she matures and gains experience, her art changes along with her. Drawings created by 6-year-olds are distinctively different from the scribbles produced by toddlers, for example. A drawing by a primary-grade child typically resembles what it represents and includes many details—a reflection of an emerging sense of realism. This is not to say that a drawing is inherently "better" than a scribble, only that drawings are more characteristic of older children.

My mom is fat because She's haveing a Baby

She's not fat yet

by vickie RYan

a.

b.

She's geting fat

I Love my moM

c.

d.

now it's ready to be born

We went to the hasRtal to wate for it to be born

e.

f.

and it was born

it was so tiny

g.

h.

Figure 3.4
Vickie's Book

95

Vickie's *art is graphic,* meaning that it is a representation and an interpretation of her reality. Her depiction of the hospital, her pregnant mother, and the new baby show that she is learning the art techniques necessary to give form to her feelings, ideas, and experiences. These techniques include color, line, arrangement, proportion, and placement.

Finally, Vickie's *art is affected by culture and the context.* Because the birth of a new child is celebrated as an important life event in her family, she has chosen it as a worthy subject for her art.

Figure 3.5 illustrates the stages in children's drawings from age 2 through 9.

TEACHERS' ROLES AND RESPONSIBILITIES

Phyllis is a 5-year-old who has just started kindergarten. One day she comes home from school looking distraught. She bursts into tears, reaches into her pocket, and takes out a tissue with a broken crayon wrapped inside. It seems that the teacher had been especially harsh in cautioning children about taking care of school supplies and not breaking the crayons. Phyllis knew she had committed the unpardonable sin—"pressing too hard." To avoid punishment, she had resorted to concealing her "crime." Phyllis's experience illustrates how important it is for classroom teachers to understand their role in providing a balanced art program (see Table 3.2).

As you work to support children's growth in art, keep in mind the recommendations that follow.

Emphasize process as well as product. When children are pushed to make their work represent the superficial aspects of an object or experience, product is being

---

Art-Making Activities

Art-making activities in the visual arts typically include such things as:

Painting, drawing, printmaking, collage

Sculpture, including mobiles, assemblages, and light

Photography, films, television, theater design, videography, and digital imagery

Crafts—ceramics, fiber arts, jewelry, metalwork, enameling; works in wood, paper, plastic, and other materials

Environmental arts—architecture, urban design, landscaping, interior design, product design, clothing design, and graphic communication in both personal and public environments

Technology—computer-generated graphics, multimedia design, and use of the Internet as a resource (National Art Education Association, 1999)

Figure 3.5
Developmental Sequence for the Making of Art

Approximate Age: 2 years
Art Skills: Explores media through all the senses
Makes random marks on paper
Begins scribbling

Figure 3.5 *(Continued)*

Approximate Age: 3 years
Art Skills: Explores and manipulates materials   Scribbles are more controlled
             Makes scribbles one on top of the other   May cover paper with layers of color
                                                            Process, not product, is important to child

Figure 3.5 *(Continued)*

Infants and Toddlers

Developmental Profile: The child communicates directly through body movements, such as enjoying the medium of finger paint and observing the effects of different hand movements on the patterns on the paper. For the very young, visual artworks are more of a happening, more of an experience and an event than a means of communicating with others. An infant's attempt at drawing tends to be random. If the drawing implement makes contact with the paper, that is what is produced.

Typical Art Activities: Infants tend to engage in sensory experiences—touching, tasting, smelling, and mouthing objects. During early infancy, they begin to focus their gaze and then track objects with their eyes. Young infants have a definite preference for high-contrast pictures (such as black-and-white patterns) and the human face. During later infancy, they study objects intently and manipulate toys and objects that interest them. They frequently are fascinated by variation in what they see (a mobile over the crib, a blinking light). Toddlers begin to explore simple art materials in ways that do not demand high levels of manual dexterity, such as finger paints, play dough, scribbling with a fat crayon on paper, and so forth.

Preschool and Kindergarten

Developmental Profile: The child begins to learn how to communicate through symbols and to use one thing to represent another. The drawings typically produced by 3-year-olds are **controlled scribbles**, because the child is better able to deliberately make marks on paper. Although a young preschooler's scribble in response to a cat may not look anything like a cat, that scribble might represent all of the child's sensory impressions of an experience with a cat—sandpapery tongue, beautiful fur, the sound of its purr, and its playfulness. The child may announce, "That's kitty", hence this stage is referred to as naming of scribbles. As control of drawing increases, typically developing 3- and 4-year-olds often begin to produce repeated small shapes, almost like geometric designs. By the time most children are in kindergarten, they recognize that art has the power to communicate. They often use artwork as a "narrative prop"—as a way of telling a story. Their drawings and play-dough creations begin to resemble the objects that they have in mind. This is referred to as **representational art**.

Typical Art Activities: Basic art materials and techniques are used, such as crayons and paper; finger paints and wet paper; large paintbrushes, tempera paints and easels; modeling dough or clay; white glue and wood; torn-paper constructions; simple collages; crayon rubbings of objects (leaves, shoe sole); painting with objects (for example, marbles dipped in paint and rolled around in a box on paper); learning to use scissors; and simple printmaking with Styrofoam shapes dipped in paint. At this stage, children learn to use crayons, scissors, paste, and paint to design, cut, arrange, and paste various items, such as child-made books, murals, simple masks, and replicas of objects (for example, a large cardboard box transformed into a house), and consider ways of displaying art.

(Continued)

Figure 3.5 *(Continued)*

Approximate Age: 3—4 years
Art Skills: Scribbling stage continues
Perceives shapes in work
Attempts to make shapes
Often names scribbles

Figure 3.5 *(Continued)*

EMERGING REPRESENTATIONAL

Approximate Age: 4—5 years
Art Skills: Combines two shapes, often a circle and a cross, to make mandalas
Draws suns
Represents humans as a circle with arms and legs, a tadpole person
Figures appear to oat on the page
Art is used to represent feelings and ideas
Represents what has made an impression, rather than everything that is
seen or known

Figure 3.5 (*Continued*)

REPRESENTATIONAL

Approximate Age: 6–8 years

Art Skills: Child's art clearly resembles whatever it represents
Baseline begins to appear in drawings
More planning and inclusion of details
Child strives to master various art skills and begins to evaluate own work
Work tends to be more realistic in terms of proportion and arrangement

Figure 3.5 (*Continued*)

First Grade

Developmental Profile: The child becomes more confident as a symbol maker. With greater mastery of language, the child frequently chooses to weave symbols together (as when making a picture book).

Typical Art Activities: New and more involved techniques such as papier-mâché, paper weaving, and collage construction are introduced. Materials and techniques involving yarns, fabrics, and stencils are experienced. More sophisticated clay construction techniques (such as using coils of clay to construct items, or planning constructions that will stand and stay together) are used. Children create simple stitchery (for example, yarn and plastic needle on burlap) and puppets (such as rod and sock puppets).

Second and Third Grade

Developmental Profile: This stage corresponds to the industry-versus-inferiority stage of Erikson's psychosocial theory. The child seeks to build competence by undertaking a wide variety of art activities. Crafts such as toymaking, painting with acrylics, fashioning items from fabric, and making ceramic items or holiday decorative items are all common during this stage that Davis and Gardner (1992) refer to as "youth as craftsperson."

Typical Art Activities: Students learn more complex uses of art tools (for example, the clay sculpting tools used by artists). They develop more manual control and ability (as when exploring watercolors and fine brushes). Children begin to explore stitchery (by making a class quilt or a simple stuffed toy), create more elaborate props (such as by painting on fabric to create a scenery backdrop), investigate design problems (as in creating posters for an event), and explore multistep group projects that are fashioned to scale (such as using chicken wire and papier-mâché to construct a dinosaur).

Figure 3.5   (*Continued*)

Note. Adapted from Feeney, Christensen, & Moravcik (1991).

emphasized. The most common type of product requires children to color pictures neatly in designated areas, cut out predetermined shapes on the lines, paste them onto paper in some preordained way, and take the result home to decorate a refrigerator door. Activities such as these communicate the message that children's original artwork is inferior to that of adults.

Value originality rather than conformity. Stan overheard his second-grade teacher saying that she wanted to do an art activity in February. Stan thought about President's Day, Flag Day, and Valentine's Day and invented a new kind of flag. Instead of using stars to represent the states, Stan used red hearts on a white background. For this 8-year-old, creating the flag was an original activity. But if the teacher requires every child in the class to copy Stan's idea, she is demanding conformity

TABLE 3.2   The Teacher's Role in a Balanced Art Curriculum

Component	Group Structure	Teacher's Role	Recommended Activity
Voluntary art activity	Individual	To observe and respond to children's work	Sketchbook drawing
Teacher-guided demonstration	Large group	To initiate a theme, select appropriate materials, and guide children in discussing and mastering specific techniques for producing art	Teacher shares/discusses a picture book about art and/or art reproductions, then demonstrates a technique for achieving the effect in the book or art reproduction. This is not a model to copy!
Art projects	Small group	To set up the art centers, facilitate children's responses to the various projects, and guide them in moving to the next activity when ready	Art projects—students go to a center to use the materials and techniques discussed during the large-group session.

Note. Adapted from Bae (2004), Bresler (1993), and Epstein (2001).

rather than encouraging originality. The goal of art is to break stereotypes rather than to perpetuate them. Art is not coloring pages and following the dots; art is not a hand-traced turkey for Thanksgiving, a tree that looks like a lollipop, or a square-plus-triangle house. If it isn't original, it isn't art.

Allow children to retain ownership. Children retain ownership of their artwork when they (1) choose their own ideas or subject matter, (2) have the freedom to express their ideas in their own way, and (3) have the right to organize their art in their own way (Jefferson, 1963). Children need the latitude to use many different art media. The goal is not to compete and make comparisons between and among children by using the teacher's model as the standard for all to follow.

Develop the child's appreciation for mixtures and balances. Think about how different your life would be without the visual art of film. Now think about a favorite film that you have watched many times or own. What was it about the style of the film that captured your imagination? Are there other films by this same director that you also like? Answers to questions such as these illustrate the importance of a concept in aesthetics called mixtures and balances. Clearly, many films can be made, but it is the particular combination of ingredients and the interplay of those elements that creates a satisfying whole. Skillful mixtures and balances transform the ordinary into the extraordinary, the mundane into a work of art. Working with mixtures and balances is something that children need to experience for themselves in order to recognize and appreciate it in others. Asking children questions such as,

Authentic art experiences emphasize the process, value originality, and allow children to retain ownership of their artwork.

"Why did you choose this painting for your portfolio?" or "How is the mural going?" helps children reflect on mixtures and balances.

Provide a safe and healthy environment. Teachers are often unaware of the potential hazards of art materials and activities. Figure 3.6 provides a checklist that you can use to assess your knowledge about safety issues in working with art materials.

Establish rules and limits. Effective teachers should establish rules and limits that enable children to get the most from their art experiences. Figure 3.7 is a suggested list of classroom management considerations in art (Schirrmacher, 1988).

Select appropriate materials and demonstrate skills effectively. When children first begin using paints, a teacher might present the basic concepts of using protective clothing, putting the brush back in the same color, and cleaning up after painting. As they gain some experience, the teacher could present the strategy of wiping each side of the brush on the rim of the paint container to avoid drips and grasping the brush with the fingers (rather than the fist) above the metal rim, which increases the child's control over the brush. Next, the teacher could show children how to avoid smearing by letting one color dry before putting wet paint over or very close to it, how to use different-sized brushes for different purposes (narrow/pointed for details, wide/flat for large areas), and how to rinse brushes in cool water and store them with bristles up. As children gain experience with paints in the primary grades, they can learn different brush strokes, learn how to sketch before

	Yes	No
The Environment		
Is the area free of dirt, debris, and dust?	☐	☐
Is the floor clean and dry to avoid slipping and falling?	☐	☐
Is equipment arranged to avoid tripping, falling, and pulling items down (e.g., electrical cord taped to baseboard)?	☐	☐
Is ventilation (e.g., fresh air, open window, fan) adequate?	☐	☐
Is the lighting adequate?	☐	☐
Is protective gear (e.g., dust masks, plastic gloves, eye protection) in use?	☐	☐
Are safety rules posted (e.g., no running, no using art tools as weapons)?	☐	☐
Are emergency procedures posted and is the Poison Control Center number displayed?	☐	☐
Supplies and Storage		
Are the items to which children need independent access stored so that children can obtain them readily?	☐	☐
Are materials that require teacher supervision stored in a locked cabinet?	☐	☐
Health and Safety Practices		
Are health and safety considerations part of the planning of activities?	☐	☐
Are health and safety issues part of the explanation of activities to children?	☐	☐
Is there evidence that children have been taught safe and healthy practices (e.g., pictorial warning signs, a poster about washing hands)?	☐	☐
Are the art materials and equipment that children use maintained and inspected regularly?	☐	☐
Instructional Practices		
Does the teacher use good sense in selecting activities that are both age-appropriate and individually appropriate (e.g., "painting" with shaving cream is *not* appropriate for toddlers, who may attempt to taste it or accidentally rub their eyes)?	☐	☐
Are children taught the way to use tools properly?	☐	☐
Is the teacher aware of environmental toxins and their effects?	☐	☐
Does the teacher know about the ratings of art supplies (e.g., nontoxic, AP/Approved Product or CP/Certified Product of the Art and Craft Materials Institute) and avoid using inexpensive imported products that may be hazardous?	☐	☐

Figure 3.6
Health and Safety Issues in Art: A Checklist

106

	Yes	No
Are policies and procedures clear (e.g., handling scissors, distributing or collecting tools, no horseplay with art materials)?	☐	☐
Is the teacher aware of potential hazards due to ingestion, inhalation, or absorption through the skin?	☐	☐

Special Needs

	Yes	No
Does the teacher have detailed information about which children have allergies, chemical sensitivities, respiratory problems, fine or large motor impairments, etc.?	☐	☐
Has the teacher carefully considered the characteristics of students, such as their manual dexterity or familiarity with the tools, when planning art activities?	☐	☐
Is there evidence of low-tech and high-tech adaptations that will enable young children with special needs to participate in art activities?	☐	☐

Teacher Knowledge

Did you know that . . .

	Yes	No
Clay is 60% silica, and if clay dust becomes airborne, it can aggravate respiratory problems or even cause lung disease with prolonged exposure?	☐	☐
Powders and mixtures that are often used to make art materials (e.g., flour, cornstarch, plaster of paris) can be inhaled and precipitate an asthma attack in children with this disease?	☐	☐
Even if children do not deliberately eat art supplies, they can accidentally ingest them by touching their mouths, biting their fingernails, or putting an art tool in their mouths?	☐	☐
Food dyes once believed to be completely harmless are now considered carcinogenic (cancer-causing)?	☐	☐
Real clay, dug from the earth, can contain molds and bacteria that may trigger allergies or cause infections?	☐	☐
Children may rub their eyes and accidentally get dyes, paints, ink from markers, and other substances in their eyes, causing swelling and irritation?	☐	☐
The main ingredient in play dough and paste is wheat flour, and the main ingredient in white glue is milk. Therefore, if children with an allergy to wheat (celiac condition) or milk products (lactose intolerance) ingest these substances, they can become very ill?	☐	☐

Note. Based on Qualley (1986) and Center for Safety in the Arts, http://artswire.org; National Safety Council, www.nsc.org/ehc/airqual.htm.

1. Decide on a few important general rules rather than many insignificant specific rules.

2. Limit the number of children at a center at any one time. This avoids disputes over materials and accidental damage to a child's work caused by overcrowding.

3. Impress on children the need to wear protective clothing. Provide smocks, aprons, or simply a man's old shirt worn backward with sleeves rolled up.

4. Teach children how to use and care for art tools, such as rinsing paintbrushes, putting the lid on paste, and returning materials to their original location when finished.

5. Model for children the importance of conserving materials and using only what is needed. You could give them a dab of white glue on an old margarine tub lid, for example, rather than the whole bottle.

6. Teach children to share supplies and respect others. Model for children, asking rather than grabbing ("May I use the stapler next?" "Are you finished with the pink Play-Doh?"). Discuss with children the importance of accepting the art activities of other children.

7. Rather than simply announcing, "Time to clean up," demonstrate how children are supposed to clean up after each art activity.

Figure 3.7
Establishing Rules and Limits in Early Childhood Art Programs
Note. Adapted from Schirrmacher (1988).

painting, or experiment with paints that are more difficult to control, such as watercolors.

Evaluate materials and experiences. Walk down the hall of an elementary school, look at children's artwork, and you will notice a definite trend. In kindergarten and first grade, there is a freshness and spontaneity to children's work. Most kindergartners and first graders will tackle nearly any illustration challenge—a suspension bridge, a giraffe, or a trailer court. By second or third grade, however, many children have begun to trace and copy rather than create their own drawings.

You will know that you are providing quality art materials and experiences when:

*   Children use and request specific art materials.
*   Children confidently accept new challenges in art.
*   Children pursue art activities during free time at home and at school.
*   Children express positive attitudes toward art and artistic abilities during class discussions.

Responding Appropriately to Children's Art

Two-year-old Katie likes to curl up with Kirstie, a border collie, while she is looking at books and produces a scribble that she names Kirstie. Young children do not separate their sensory impressions from one another, nor do they dichotomize feelings and ideas as adults are prone to do. Maybe Katie's scribble goes beyond the visual image that she has of the dog and represents the softness of the animal's fur or the pleasurable feeling of being surrounded by warmth and closeness. The adult who remarks, "Very good, but what happened to the dog's tail?" or demands, "What is it?" fails to appreciate young children's early forms of artistic expression. Davis and Gardner (1992) reported that when they asked a young preschooler to draw "a scary house," the child obliged by drawing a regular-looking house, but growled all the while he drew it! Sometimes, children are simply exploring an artistic medium—for example, the sensory pleasure of squishing clay into different shapes or gliding a crayon across the page.

As you respond to children's artwork, keep the following guiding principles in mind:

- *Treat child artists and their work with respect.* Let children know that their work is valued by displaying it proudly, helping them transport it home safely, and finding something positive to say about their work (Rankin, 1995).
- *Emphasize feelings and responses.* Rather than treating art as an assembly task or an exercise in following directions, encourage children to explore emotions via the arts.
- *Suggest alternatives when children seem stalled or frustrated.* Ask questions that will help children to take a different approach or perspective rather than falling into a rut or quitting in frustration. Encourage children to persist when tasks are challenging rather than becoming discouraged if the way to proceed is not clear or obvious.

Sensory experiences are the foundation for later artistic understanding and appreciation.

- *Help children sort out what is essential from what is unnecessary.* Teach them the skill of emphasizing what is most important in their creative products and help them understand that many times "less is more" and aesthetic experiences are improved by the elimination of extraneous details.
- *Guide children in doing their best.* Do not encourage or accept slapdash work. When it is clear that children did not produce their best work, try to find out why and give them an opportunity to revise and excel.
- *Recognize children's efforts.* Encourage self-evaluation and avoid a contest mentality. It is better to encourage all children than to single out a few for prizes (adapted from Cohen & Gainer, 1995).

Generally speaking, it is best to rely on artistic elements when discussing art with very young children. You could comment on color ("Look at all that yellow, Ishaka!"), on arrangement ("Lester, you covered the whole page with paint"), texture ("This clay feels smooth now that you rolled it out"), line ("I see the interesting patterns you made with the toothpick and paint on your paper, Claudia"), or shape ("Stevie and Alexei made lots of small round bubbles. Kerri and Man-Li made one big long bubble"). For older children who are creating representational art, it is best to follow the children's lead. You might begin by saying, "Tell me about your picture," and then follow the child's lead in the discussion. It is best to really notice what children are working to accomplish through art and remark on it rather than pass judgment on the quality of the work.

Locating Resources and Storing Materials

Few teachers have the luxury of purchasing whatever art materials they please. More often, it is a matter of making choices among many possible alternatives. Materials such as paints, paper, crayons, clay, and wood are usually referred to as consumable because they need to be replenished constantly. When budgets are tight, the focus is often on nonconsumables, materials that need replacement less often. Many times, adults are not particularly unhappy to see messy materials go. But these art materials are a basic means of self-expression and something that children should have access to every day. Rather than eliminating them altogether, teachers need to be creative problem solvers and seek out art materials wherever they can find them. An added bonus to this approach is that it teaches children the value of responsible recycling.

Art materials should do the following:

1. *Extend children's experience.* Figure 3.8 highlights ways that children's picture books can be used to extend the children's art experience. See also *Talking with Artists I* and *Talking with Artists II* (Cummings, 1992, 1993) and, for older students, *Side by Side: Five Favorite Picture-Book Teams Go to Work* (Marcus, 2001).

2. *Be plentiful.* Recycling is a way to acquire an ample supply of free paper. Newspaper printers sometimes give away the ends of paper rolls, and wrapping paper from gifts can be saved by everyone in the class. For special papers, make contact with a printer that prints stationery and invitations or get in touch with a frame shop. Another way to achieve greater variety in classroom resources is to

A story guide is a set of activities designed to accompany and extend a particular children's book. A good story guide integrates content areas and invites children to respond to the book in meaningful ways. Below are two story guides that emphasize the arts, play, creativity, and imagination.

Story Guide for *Tar Beach*

Book *Tar Beach,* by Faith Ringgold (1996)

Summary City apartment dwellers pretend that their apartment building roof is a beautiful beach. On their "tar beach," they have a picnic and enjoy one another's company. Then the narrator, a young African American girl, and her younger brother go on a flight of fancy through the neighborhood before returning safely home. Illustrations for the book come from a quilt created by the author.

Introduction Today we are going to hear a story about pretending. What are some make-believe games that you play? Look at the cover of this book by Faith Ringgold. It is about a girl and her brother who like to pretend. The pictures in this book are very special. Instead of drawing the pictures, Faith Ringgold sewed them. Then she put them all together into a quilt.

Questions

1. What are some things that you like to pretend?

2. Why did the people in the story pretend to have a beach?

3. If you could fly, what would you choose to fly over? Why?

4. Who would you choose to go with you?

Props A real quilt or a book of quilts with picture patterns.

Follow-Up

- Look at other books with unusual illustrations—the plasticine illustrations in *Have You Seen Birds?* by Joanne Oppenheim and Barbara Reid (1988); the collage in *The Snowy Day,* by Ezra Jack Keats (1962); or the moving parts in *The Wheels on the Bus,* by Paul O. Zelinsky (1990).

- Try sewing some pictures of your own with burlap, large plastic needles, and yarn.

- Look at a book or calendar or magazine pictures of prize-winning quilts. Take a survey on which quilt each member of the class likes best and why.

- Ask someone who makes quilts to visit the class and bring several quilts in different stages of completion.

- Read some other books about quilts that tell a story, such as Patricia Polacco's *The Keeping Quilt (1988),* Tony Johnston's *The Quilt Story (1984),* and Lauren Mills's *The Rag Coat* (1991).

(Continued)

Figure 3.8
Using Children's Picture Books to Develop Arts Awareness

- Read another book about another flight of fancy, such as *Abuela,* by Arthur Dorros (1991), or watch a video of Raymond Briggs's *The Snowman* (1978).
- Watch the movie *Peter Pan.* Then read *Amazing Grace,* a story by Mary Hoffman (1991) about an African American girl who wants to play Peter Pan in the school play.

Story Guide for *Seven Blind Mice*

Book *Seven Blind Mice,* by Ed Young (1992)

Summary In this variant of the Indian tale "The Blind Men and the Elephant," each mouse examines one small portion of the elephant's anatomy (ear, tusk, tail, etc.) and draws an incorrect conclusion about the total object. It is only after the seventh mouse examines the entire elephant and puts all of their observations together that they realize what the object really is!

Introduction Make a pair of old sunglasses into a blindfold by gluing black paper over the lenses. Let children wear the "blindfold" while attempting to guess what various objects are by touch alone.

Questions

1. Why were six of the mice wrong in their guesses about what the object was?
2. What did the last mouse do that was different from the other six mice? How did that help him make a good guess?
3. Did your eyes ever play a trick on you? Did you ever see one thing and think it was something else?

Props Create a large silhouette of an elephant and seven felt finger puppets or paper stick puppets of mice.

Follow-Up After you read the story, have children retell the story using the elephant silhouette and mouse puppets they have created.

- Create a "Guess What?" class book using children's drawings or photographs cut out from magazines. Cover each picture with a piece of cardstock and create small, numbered flaps to lift. Children should try to guess what is pictured by seeing only a small portion of the total picture. After guessing what the picture is, they can lift the entire sheet to see the total picture. Bind each child's page into a large class book.
- Try using bright acrylic paints on a black background to create some of the same effects that the artist used in the book.
- Read other stories with surprises, including *Boo! Who?* by Colin and Jacqui Hawkins (1984) or the *I Spy* picture riddle books series by Jean Marzollo.
- Look at several optical illusions. (Psychology books or reference books about vision are good sources.) Also look at some books that show how animals hide using various types of camouflage.

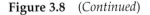

Figure 3.8 (*Continued*)

Exploring Art Media Through Picture Books

(Amann, 1993; Kiefer, 1995)

Watercolor Transparent paint mixed with water. It is usually painted on a white background, giving it a luminous quality.

Examples of watercolor illustrations from children's books

Sue Williams/Julie Vivas, *I Went Walking* (1992)

Uri Shulevitz, *Dawn* (1988)

Allen Say, *Grandfather's Journey* (1993)

Experiencing watercolor with children Teach children how to control the color intensity by the amount of water that they use to mix with the paints; teach them to rinse the brush out thoroughly when switching from one color to another.

Pastel chalk A stick of color made from powdered pigment in soft hues.

Examples of pastel chalk illustrations from picture books

Judith Hendershot/Thomas Allen, *In Coal Country* (1987)

Experiencing chalk with children Use sidewalk chalk to create a life-size board game, to draw a hopscotch board, to advertise an upcoming event in the classroom, to guide a walk around the playground, to draw oversized pictures, or to make giant scribbles.

Pen and ink Pigment (usually black) applied with a pen to paper (usually white).

Examples of pen-and-ink illustrations from picture books

Chris Van Allsburg, *Two Bad Ants* (1988)

Mercer Mayer, *Frog Goes to Dinner* (1977)

Experiencing pen and ink with children Give children white shelf paper or shirt or hosiery cardboard and an assortment of black ballpoint pens and black felt-tip pens so that they can create pictures in black and white; look at sketches done by artists in black and white.

Acrylic paints Pigments bound with vinyl that resemble oil paint but are faster drying.

Examples of acrylics from picture books

Donald Hall and Barbara Cooney, *Ox-cart Man* (1984)

Experiencing acrylics with children Visit an artist's studio or a display of art at a local bank, museum, or university. If you have access to some acrylics, allow the children to experiment with them on a small scale (these paints are rather expensive), but be sure to protect the children's clothing (these paints will not wash out).

Airbrush A mechanical tool used by commercial artists that looks like a pen. An airbrush takes a small amount of paint and sprays it very evenly on a surface using a small compressor.

(Continued)

Examples of airbrush techniques from picture books

Donald Crews, *Freight Train* (1978)

Leo and Diane Dillon, *Why Mosquitoes Buzz in People's Ears* (1983)

Experiencing an airbrush with children To see an airbrush in use, watch *A Video Visit with Donald Crews,* published by Trumpet Book Club. Invite a commercial artist to demonstrate the use of the airbrush and let children use it. Try mixing thin tempera and using a pump spray (like the ones used for hairspray) to create outlines of shapes created by the children.

Collage The use of an assemblage or collection of materials and textures to create a picture.

Examples of collage illustrations from picture books

Eric Carle, *The Very Hungry Caterpillar* (1969)

Ezra Jack Keats, *The Snowy Day* (1962)

Experiencing collage with children Invite children to create books using collage illustrations; to create a collage that represents a feeling or characterizes a person; or to make a nature collage of leaves, seed pods, branches, dried flowers, etc.

Resist The technique of masking a surface so that it repels paint, dye, or ink. Batik uses this process with fabric.

Examples of batik illustrations from picture books

Roni Schotter and Marcia Sewall, *Captain Snap and the Children of Vinegar Lane* (1988)

Margaret Mahy and Patricia MacCarthy, *Seventeen Kings and Forty-Three Elephants* (1993)

Experiencing resist with children Use crayon resist and paste batik.

Linoleum or block prints A pattern or picture is cut into metal, wood, or linoleum so that raised lines and shapes are created. Then paint or ink is applied to the surface of the block and the pattern is printed on paper.

Examples of prints from picture books

Gail Haley, *A Story, A Story* (1988)

Ashley Wolff, *A Year of Birds* (1984)

Experiencing prints with children Use a cut-out piece of Styrofoam glued onto a block of Styrofoam to create a stamp, use a small screwdriver to create a shape on the Styrofoam, and make a print.

Photography The technique of using film to record a picture of something.

Examples of photography in picture books

Tana Hoban, *A Children's Zoo* (1985)

Dav Pilkey, *Dogzilla* (1993)

Figure 3.8 *(Continued)*

Experiencing photography with children Get children involved in using inexpensive, durable cameras to take pictures during a special event; ask children to bring in family snapshots.

Oil paint Paint that uses oil as a base for the pigment.

Examples of oil paintings in picture books

Hans Christian Andersen and Thomas Locker, *The Ugly Duckling* (1985)

Paul O. Zelinsky, *Rumpelstiltskin* (1986)

Experiencing oil paints with children Collect scraps of canvas board so that children can paint on the same surface that real artists use. Use a plastic lid from a small jar as a palette and place a small daub of various colored oil paints inside. Invite children to comment on the texture and rich colors oil paints produce.

Plasticine A modeling material similar to clay that does not harden when exposed to air.

Examples of plasticine in picture books

Joanne Oppenheim and Barbara Reid, *Have You Seen Birds?* (1988)

Barbara Reid, *Two by Two* (1993)

Experiencing plasticine with children Use various types of modeling material, including plastic clay. Invite children to study the illustrations and invent some pictures with bits of brightly colored clay.

Children's picture books about art experiences

Carle, E. (1992). *Draw me a star.* New York: Philomel.

Cohen, M. (1980). *No good in art.* New York: Greenwillow.

de Paola, T. (1988). *The art lesson.* New York: Putnam.

Lionni, L. (1991). *Matthew's dream.* New York: Knopf.

Rylant, C. (1988). *All I see.* New York: Orchard.

Velthuijs, M. (1992). *Crocodile's masterpiece.* New York: Farrar, Straus & Giroux.

Wolkstein, D. (1992). *Little mouse's painting.* New York: Morrow.

---

send home a list at the beginning of the year asking for such things as sewing and craft materials (buttons, trim, pieces of fabric, yarn, and ribbon) and throwaway materials that can be put to another use (plastic bottle caps, detergent bottles, food containers, six-pack holder rings, and foil canisters of various sizes).

3. *Be accessible.* It is important for children to use materials when they wish, rather than being completely dependent on adults for access to materials. Be alert to inexpensive alternatives. An old microwave cart, divided trays, or a lazy Susan can all help provide children access to many different materials, keep the materials organized, and make the collection more mobile.

4. *Be age-appropriate.* When a mother volunteered to work in her preschool son's Head Start classroom, both she and the teacher were surprised to see him take the paper off the easel and put it on newspaper on the floor to paint. Apparently, the child's only experience with painting was on a horizontal rather than a vertical surface. Gradually, the teacher was able to extend his experience to painting at an easel.

5. *Be of high quality.* Adults sometimes insist that children use crayons rather than markers, because markers are expensive and can easily be ruined by leaving the caps off or pressing too hard. But rather than avoiding markers, teachers need to demonstrate how to use and care for them.

Displaying Children's Art

Some general guidelines for displaying children's art include placing the work at children's eye level where they can enjoy it, rotating art regularly, and utilizing a variety of spaces—not just walls or bulletin boards, but also cardboard box panels, doors, windows, shelves, and display cases. Consider also how you will deal with works in progress as opposed to finished projects. Usually, the works in progress need to be placed where children can return to them again easily. A part of displaying children's art that is often neglected is the finishing touch, such as a frame for a picture. Frames for children's art can be colored paper, Styrofoam

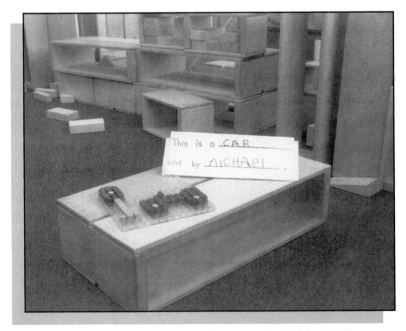

Displaying children's art is one way of encouraging children's efforts.

meat trays, plastic microwave food trays, plastic coffee can lids, or boxes and lids of every description. With older children, you may want to develop an art gallery of their framed art, tape-record children's descriptions of their art, or even make a walking-tour tape similar to that used in a museum.

Remember, displaying art is for everybody, not just the small percentage of children who might become professional artists someday. Rather than singling out only a few pieces of artwork to be displayed, teachers should recognize every child's efforts at self-expression. Children should be permitted to take their work home within a reasonable time period if they wish or to leave it on display at school. Teachers who care about children's art make sure that the paint is dry before rolling up the picture or, if the art is three-dimensional, plan a way for the child to transport the item home safely. Clean, recycled milk cartons with the tops cut off are good carriers for clay creations, for example.

Talking About Art

Children need a wide range of opportunities to look at art and talk about it (Burton, 2001). When children talk about the meaning of works of art, it encourages them to express meaning through the artworks that they produce (Barrett, 1997; Walsh, 1993). Verbalization occurs naturally during the child's image-making process as children think out loud when problems are confronted or observations are made (Thompson, 1997). Sharing and discussing art in social settings helps children become critical, enthusiastic, and supportive audiences for each other's work (Thompson, 1997). Figure 3.9 provides an overview of discussion strategies to be used in discussing works of art and art reproductions.

Developing a child's vocabulary of art involves three things:

1. *Encouraging children to discuss the artwork first in ordinary language.* If children discuss art in their own words first, it permits an equal sharing of adult and child perceptions. Five-year-old children who examined a large, colorful book of American artist Mary Cassatt's paintings made interesting observations such as "She must like little kids" and "The pictures look soft." By allowing children to make these observations first, the teacher can follow their lead, explaining briefly about the artist's life ("Deidra was right, Mary Cassatt did love little children. Sometimes she used her own family as models for her paintings"). Teachers might pose interesting challenges such as, "What could an artist do to lines to make the picture 'look soft,' like Harrold said? Let's try to make some pictures that way, pictures without dark lines, pictures that look softer."

2. *Introducing the vocabulary in context.* If children use new words in conjunction with direct experience, they are more likely to incorporate new words such as *texture, etching,* or *symmetry* into their vocabularies.

3. *Using accurate, appropriate vocabulary.* Teachers need to provide new vocabulary words readily and unobtrusively so that they underscore the child's experience. Building a vocabulary of art is important because it enables children to participate in the world of art both in and out of school throughout their lives.

Types of Questions

Questions on aesthetics—Look at the lines on your paper. On the ceiling. Can you find other lines? Thin lines? Thick lines?

Questions on art criticism—Here are pictures of some famous buildings in the world. If you could choose one to be built in our town, which one would it be? Why?

Questions about art history—Which of these sculptures was made a long time ago? Why do you think so?

Questions on art production—What are some ways artists can make their pictures look smooth? Rough?

1. *Who made it?*

Situation: Looking at a UNICEF calendar of children's artwork.

Question: "Do you think these drawings were made by adults or children? What are you seeing right now that can give you a clue?"

2. *How was it made?*

Situation: Looking at a large metal sculpture

Question: "Does anyone know how pieces of metal are joined together?"

3. *When was it made?*

Situation: Looking at an ancient piece of sculpture

Question: "If you look at this carefully, you will notice that some of the pieces are broken off. Do you think this sculpture is new or old? Why?"

4. *For whom was it made?*

Situation: Looking at a wooden toy

Question: "One of my neighbors makes toys out of wood like the ones I brought today for you to play with. Who do you think he makes the toys for?"

5. *What is the message or meaning, if any?*

Situation: Looking at a heritage quilt

Question: "Do you know anyone who makes their clothes by sewing them instead of buying them already made at the store? The owner of this quilt said that her great-grandmother made it from scraps of fabric that were left over from the sewing she did for her family. Why would their grandmother do all of this work to make a quilt?"

6. *What is its style?*

Situation: Looking at the art in picture book illustrations

Question: "On this table, we have several books written and illustrated by the same person. These three are by Rosemary Wells, these by Keith Baker, these by Jerry Pinkney, and these by Diane Goode. What can you say that explains what each artist's work is like? How are these drawings by Rosemary Wells alike? How are they different from all the others?"

Figure 3.9
Questions about a Work of Art

118

7. *What is the quality of experience it affords?*

Situation: After viewing a film

Question: "You all know the book *Frog Goes to Dinner* by Mercer Mayer (1975). Which did you like better, the movie or the book?"

8. *What was its place in the culture in which it was made?*

Situation: Watching a Navajo sand painter at work from the video on sight by Diane Ackerman from the PBS series *Mystery of the Senses*

Question: "Were you surprised to see that someone could paint with sand? Why are these sand paintings made?"

9. *What is its place in the culture or society of today?*

Situation: Visit to an art museum

Question: "How do you decide which of your art projects or paintings to keep and which ones to throw away? One of the people we will be meeting has a special job in taking care of these paintings. The paintings need to be cleaned, and sometimes they need to be fixed. Can you think of some reasons why people think these paintings are important enough to keep?"

10. *What peculiar problems does it present to understanding and appreciation?*

Situation: Looking at an art print that uses pointillism

Question: "Some of you were wondering why this picture looks so different close up than it does from a distance. If you look very closely, you will see that the picture is made up of hundreds of dots. Did any of you ever experiment with dots as a way to make pictures? When you work at the computer to make a picture, the computer actually makes the dots for you. Use this magnifying glass to look at one of the pictures you made last week. Now look at this piece of a newspaper. You can see that the print is made of dots too."

Additional Questions about a Work of Art

What is this work of art?

What is it made from?

What is the most interesting thing about this work of art?

What is the artist trying to tell us?

Is there a story here? What is it?

Does the artist suggest new ways of seeing things?

How does the work make you feel? Why?

What does it make you think of?

What did the artist use (medium, techniques, tools, ways of organization, effects, composition)?

How is this the same (or different) from other pieces you have seen by this artist? By other artists?

(Continued)

What makes a work of art great?

What makes an artist great?

Do you like this work of art? Why or why not?

Sources for Art and Art Reproductions

Children's picture books, prints of famous works of art borrowed from the library, picture postcards of art, walls of a local gallery, an artist's studio, a display of children's work at a public building, a museum exhibit, a university, slides, art history books, encyclopedias, film. Specific sources include:

Full-size (approximately 22" × 28")
Metropolitan Museum of Art
New York, NY 10028

Modern Learning Press
P.O. Box 9067
Cambridge, MA 02139-9067
(800) 627-5867

Miniature (such as postcard size)

Art Visuals	Parent Child Press	University Prints
P.O. Box 925	P.O. Box 675	21 East Street
Orem, UT 84059	Hollidaysburg, PA 16648	Winchester, MA 02138

Figure 3.9 *(Continued)*

Note. Adapted from Amann (1993), Heberholz (1974), Jalongo & Stamp (1997), and Rowe (1987).

MEETING STANDARDS

Interdisciplinary Curriculum and Key Experiences in the Arts

Sadly, some teachers miss out on the rich contributions of art to the curriculum by relying entirely on work disguised as art or by delegating all of the responsibility for teaching art to the art teacher. As a result art is further segregated from the child's total life experience. Treating art as a second-class subject is a contradiction of what we know: that all knowledge is interconnected.

Increasingly teachers have begun to integrate two or more subject areas to capitalize on the insights and techniques from various disciplines. This approach, referred to as interdisciplinary curriculum, has much to recommend it. It is not only more efficient (that is, it avoids duplication) but also a better way to develop a depth of understanding. Additionally, because it provides different avenues for students to demonstrate what they have learned, interdisciplinary curriculum is a better way of meeting the needs of diverse groups of learners. As you think about creating new interdisciplinary units or evaluating the ones planned by others, refer to the guidelines in Figure 3.10.

The point of interdisciplinary instruction is not the number of disciplines integrated, but rather how the unit meets the needs of diverse learners by offering opportunities to attempt difficult tasks and learn new skills in an exciting context (Barab & Landa, 1997; Gardner, 2000). Students who are frustrated by typical school assignments are often motivated by an integrated unit that incorporates art and allows them to use their strong visual and spatial intelligences.

The National Art Education Association (1999) has identified nine key opportunities that teachers should provide to students through art.

1. **Examining extensively both natural and human-made objects from many sources.**

A group of second graders has been examining both real items and representations of things. Taking her lead from Japanese schools, their teacher has created a special classroom space called a "beauty area" where interesting and lovely items are displayed. In September, it was an assortment of fall leaves; in March, a spray of forsythia in a vase; and in early June, several different varieties of peonies. During their unit on animals, the teacher shared books about elephants and invited a collector to share her assortment of elephants. Included in the collection were ceramic, wood, metal, plastic, and fabric elephants. The children saw a hand-carved wooden elephant from India, a stuffed toy, and a green elephant sculpted from malachite. The children were able to examine these objects closely and compare/contrast them with photographs and drawings. Afterward, the elephant

Art gives diverse learners opportunities to attempt difficult tasks.

General Criteria

When the arts are combined appropriately with other subject areas,

- Each area of the curriculum is genuinely enhanced by the other and new understandings are developed through the connections made.
- Content and instruction is organized thematically and focuses on important social issues.
- The integrated curriculum has personal relevance for students.
- The theme explores a wide variety of resources to achieve contextual understanding.
- Instruction effectively underscores art's unique perspective rather than treating it as an afterthought.
- The study is collaborative for students and their teachers.

Evaluation Questions for Curriculum

In this interdisciplinary unit of study,

_____ Are meaningful connections made between or among the disciplines?

_____ Is in-depth learning promoted?

_____ Are high quality examples from the arts and the other discipline(s) used?

_____ Is appropriate technology used?

_____ Are the artistic processes of creating, performing, and responding incorporated?

_____ Is the assessment ongoing throughout the project?

_____ Is there a final evaluation of student learning?

Evaluation Questions for School Personnel

In this educational setting,

_____ Is there planning time and ongoing professional development for teachers?

_____ Are sufficient resources available?

_____ Is the schedule sufficiently flexible?

_____ Is there administrative support and involvement?

Figure 3.10

Criteria for Evaluating the Interdisciplinary Curriculum and Including Art

Note. Adapted from Ulbricht (1998) and Consortium of National Arts Education Associations (2002).

items were on display so that children could vote for their favorites and give a reason for each choice that was written on a sentence strip and placed next to each one. During math class, the children learned how to make a simple bar graph that summarized their choices by using self-stick notes labeled with their names arranged next to a digital photo of each item.

   2. **Expressing individual perceptions, ideas, and feelings through a variety of art media suited to the manipulative abilities and expressive needs of the student.**

Teachers of preschoolers will find that young children's art often evolves from daily events and "news" that children bring with them to the classroom. The drawings of young children frequently focus on "I" and "my" experiences. ("I am eating a Popsicle." "I am jumping in a puddle." "My toy is broken.")

As children move into the primary grades, it is helpful to provide new challenges such as "jumping rope with my friends," "lying on the grass and looking at the clouds," or "the day we got caught in a thunderstorm". Asking directed questions such as, "How does the grass feel? Soft? Tickly? Prickly? How can we show that in your picture (or sculpture)? What happens when it storms? Is it windy? Can you see the wind? How can you show that the wind is blowing hard in your artwork?" will help children learn to select the most effective media to communicate their ideas.

   3. **Experimenting with art materials and processes to understand their potentials for personal expression.**

Demonstrations of how to use art materials—paint, finger paint, clay, and so forth—can be followed by student experimentation with the material. Students can also work with different implements (thin and thick markers, chalk and crayons, bingo markers, colored pencils) on paper of different sizes (3-by-3-inch squares, long narrow strips, large rolls of paper) or paper with different surfaces (construction paper, corrugated paper, sandpaper). At first, children may seem as if they are reverting to an earlier stage of development as they just "try out" the medium. A child who is drawing representationally, for instance, might make scribbles with the new medium as a way of exploring it. The teacher's main role is to relate the new materials and processes to the child's expressive needs. If, for instance, a child is fortunate to have 166 different colors of crayons at home and just 16 colors at school and is disappointed to see that the color he uses for his hair is not available, the teacher might suggest some color-mixing experiments.

   4. **Working with tools appropriate to the students' abilities to develop manipulative skills needed for satisfying aesthetic expression.**

Beginning teachers are sometimes surprised to encounter preschoolers who do not know how to cut with scissors. Rather than insisting that all children begin using scissors immediately, skilled teachers give children options such as tearing paper, cutting pieces of modeling dough rolled thin, tearing at the paper with scissors, resting the scissors on the desk while cutting, and making simple cuts (such as paper fringe) (Schirrmacher, 1988). When introducing simple cutting exercises to the young child, break down the task into simple steps. First teach the child how to hold the scissors and open and close them. Then demonstrate how to cut through half-inch-wide strips of stiff construction paper (cheaper paper often bends in the blades and does not result in a successful cut, which can frustrate the child). When the child has mastered cutting through the strips with one cut, demonstrate how to make cuts (fringe) along the sides of a small sheet of paper (approximately 3 by 6 inches). Later, a straight line from one edge of a small rectangle of paper to the other can be drawn. The child can be shown how to make a cut and then open the scissors without removing them from the cut to take another "bite."

A skilled teacher also knows that it is too difficult for young children to cut out small interior spaces (such as the eye holes for a mask), partly because they lack the fine motor control needed for such a task, and partly because they need sharp, pointed scissors to do the job, which can result in injury. Teachers also wait until children have gained experience with scissors before expecting them to cut on lines or to use special equipment such as pinking shears, which must be kept at a right angle to the fabric in order to function properly.

In order to make art accessible to all children, teachers also need to make appropriate adaptations for students with special needs. Some recommended ways of adapting the art curriculum for inclusive settings are listed in Figure 3.11.

5.   **Organizing, evaluating, and reorganizing works in progress to gain an understanding of the formal structuring and expressive potential of line, form, color, and texture in space.**

One way of glimpsing young children's thinking about art is to encourage them to talk as they work with materials and listen to what they have to say. Lynn, a 4-year-old, is drawing a picture for her sister. She explains her selection of materials as follows: "Crayons make fat lines I do not want; colored pencils are 'thins' that

Skillful teachers adapt art activities to children's developmental levels. These children with Down syndrome are preparing crafts for a parade.

Children with Learning Disabilities or Attentional Difficulties

Provide encouragement.

Establish and maintain routines.

Give directions one step at a time.

Provide quiet areas for children who are easily distracted.

Offer a choice of media for exploring techniques or skills.

Help the child deal with frustration productively.

Let the child work with a partner but do not let the partner do the work for the child.

Children with Orthopedic (Physical) Impairments

Make materials easily accessible.

Use low-tech adaptive devices to increase independence (e.g., rubber grip for paintbrush).

Use high-tech adaptive devices as available and appropriate (e.g., special foot switch for a computer).

Ask if the child needs help before giving it.

Ensure that facilities do not pose obstacles to wheelchairs, crutches, or other equipment.

Allow more time for movement.

Children with Emotional Disabilities

Provide lessons that are structured yet flexible.

Plan activities that enable the child to capitalize on positive energy.

Promote confidence by building on small successes.

Keep only those supplies that are necessary within reach.

Encourage the child to express emotions in socially appropriate ways.

Defend each child's right to personal space where the student feels safe and protected.

Establish a few simple rules and expectations and follow them consistently.

Children with Visual Impairments

Help children achieve greater mobility by standing next to and a little ahead of the child. Bend your arm at the elbow and ask the child to place his or her hand on your forearm. Walk slowly, giving verbal cues and advance warnings about any obstacles. Teach aides and peers this procedure.

Get in the habit of identifying yourself and letting the child know you are talking to him or her.

Announce that you are leaving before you walk away.

(Continued)

Figure 3.11
Making Art Activities Accessible to Young Children with Special Needs

Speak in a normal tone of voice.

Invite children to touch objects as well as to listen to very detailed, concrete description.

When describing sizes, relate it to something with which the child is very familiar (e.g., "It's about as tall as your chair").

Children with Hearing Impairments

Avoid changing your message suddenly.

If the child reads lips, make sure he or she can see and avoid turning away or covering your mouth.

Use simple, basic language, speaking clearly and at an even pace.

Emphasize nonverbal communication, such as facial expressions and gestures, to communicate your thoughts.

Keep paper and pencil handy to quickly sketch a picture or write a word that might help the child understand.

If the child speaks, listen carefully and strive to get the gist of the message. If you cannot understand the child, ask him or her to repeat it slowly. If there is a chance that the group may not understand, repeat what the child said.

Try to avoid coming up suddenly or making quick movements. You may startle the child or make him or her dizzy.

Give the child ample opportunity to view and handle objects before explaining. Remember that many children with hearing impairments cannot listen and look at the object at the same time because they need to watch a person talking.

Children with Mental Retardation

Keep directions simple, break the task into sequential steps, and demonstrate each task.

Offer frequent praise and encouragement.

Be patient and allow the child extra time to observe and think.

Repeat directions and identify all materials verbally.

Deal in concrete ideas and familiar terminology.

Use multisensory approaches.

Use the child's ability range as a guide in planning lessons rather than basing them on chronological age.

When giving verbal instructions, establish eye contact first.

Guide a child through the motions of the task.

Encourage cooperation among students.

Figure 3.11 (*Continued*)

Note. Adapted from Pappatardo (1990).

make pretty pictures." By listening to Lynn, we can better understand how she is thinking about her work in progress and how she will select art materials and art elements that express her ideas.

6. **Reading about, looking at, and discussing works of art and design from contemporary and past cultures using a variety of educational media and community resources.**
7. **Seeing artists and designers at work in their studios and in the classroom through the use of technology.**

Consider these examples of classroom teachers incorporating fine art into their elementary curriculum. A kindergarten teacher included fine art in a unit on shapes and colors. For example, the children searched for circles in Vincent van Gogh's painting *Starry Night,* and afterward, one mother reported that her daughter commented that the bubbles in her bath water looked like the circles in van Gogh's painting. Meanwhile, a group of first graders searched for triangles in Winslow Homer's *Croquet Scene.* Their work with shapes is more challenging than that of the 5-year-olds because they have to identify some "hidden" triangles—in background space, in negative space, or in the "dot to dot" arrangement of the players' heads. At this same school, the fourth graders are studying the style of Japanese artist Hokusai (Ray, 2001; http://www.prestel.com) and making a list of characteristics that define his style. Their teacher uses Mike Venezia's series *Getting to Know the World's Greatest Artists* and the *Smart about Art* series to expand students' understanding of style and to familiarize them with artists such as Edgar Degas (Cocca-Leffler, 2001), Claude Monet (Kelley, 2001), Jackson Pollock (Greenberg & Jordan, 2002), Leonardo da Vinci (Stanley, 1996), Benjamin West (Brenner, 2003), and Andy Warhol (Warhola, 2003).

One teacher invited women from the senior center to talk with the children. Before they arrived, he shared the picture book *The Seasons Sewn: A Year in Patchwork* (Paul, 2000) and drew the children's attention to classic quilt patterns and their names through a matching game made from the pictures of a calendar. On the first visit, the ladies developed the concept that a quilt can tell a story. They showed the children several actual quilts as well as examples in quilt pattern books. Next, the ladies shared their plans and pattern for the quilt and gave each child a small scrap of fabric to keep. The students read several picture books about quilts—*The Quilt* (Jonas, 1989b), *Quilt Story* (Johnston, 1984), and *The Patchwork Quilt* (Flournoy, 1985)—and watched excerpts from a movie about quilting borrowed from the library. On the second visit, the ladies demonstrated how a quilt is put together. The children learned about stitching, appliqués, polyester fiberfill, and a quilting frame. On the third visit, a portion of the quilt was finished and a piece was added while the children observed, and on the last visit, the quilt was finished. Through this simple project, children looked at, discussed, and directly experienced folk art using educational media and community resources.

8. **Evaluating art of both students and mature artists, industrial products, and home and community design.**

Schiller (1995) describes how to set up a rich environment based on art experiences for preschoolers. She used art prints of flowers by Georgia O'Keeffe and Vincent van Gogh in response to the children's fascination with flowers on the playground. Interest in the flower prints led to a discussion about the other artworks in the room. This expanded to looking at books and talking about the work of other artists. The children participated in a "Which picture is my favorite?" game in which children's art selections were placed on the floor in the middle of the circle and children explained why each was their favorite (Schiller, 1995).

As part of a unit on consumer education, a group of fourth graders decided to compare/contrast the features of three comparable pieces of computer software. The students established a rating sheet for the product, tried each program, compiled their data and then, using published software reviews as a guide, wrote a critique for each. In this way, children gained firsthand experience in the evaluation of industrial/technical products.

9. **Engaging in activities that provide opportunities to apply art knowledge and aesthetic judgment to personal life, the home, and the workplace.**

Aesthetic judgment is a process that develops over time. Therefore, it is important to teach children to observe closely and consider what makes an object beautiful and worthy of appreciation.

One third-grade teacher involved her students in reorganizing their classroom space. She used the room arrangement grid and shapes in a school furniture catalog; the children experimented with many different room arrangements by shifting the items around at the overhead projector until they decided on the best classroom layout.

Frequently Asked Questions About Art in the Curriculum

How will I know if an activity truly is art?

The three most common errors in teaching art are as follows: (1) advocating formulas and requiring conformity, (2) mistaking lack of guidance for freedom, and (3) unduly emphasizing copying and neatness (Gaitskell, Hurwitz, & Day, 1982). Surprisingly many, if not most, of the "art" activities that adults do with young children are not art at all (Szyba, 1999). More often than not, they are exercises in following directions.

Shouldn't art be mainly about process?

Creativity is not all process. Although it is true that the process needs to be valued, the creative cycle typically culminates in the evaluation of a product. Take, for example, written composition. Although the child's writing process needs to be valued and supported, the writer also needs opportunities to share writing with others. When children are urged to languish at the process stage based on some adult's misguided ideas about process, the child is robbed of bringing work to a

satisfying conclusion, which is surely one of creativity's great rewards.

If an elementary teacher provides the materials and just trusts the children's natural creativity, won't that be sufficient?

Creativity, like any other ability, needs active encouragement, gentle guidance, and appropriate instruction in techniques. Too often, a belief in natural unfolding leads teachers to see themselves as distributors of art materials. Children need to be apprenticed into understanding the repertoire of skills necessary to attain excellence and be given the opportunity to practice those skills alongside helpful, observant professionals and peers. As Fritz (2002) argues, teachers must have the determination to "find the balance between stifling the students within a limited set of skills and letting them loose with endless horizons but ill equipped with skills and knowledge to realize their ideas" (Critical Judgment section, para. 2).

How can teachers recognize children's gifts in the arts?

Research on young gifted children suggests that they may (a) strive for realistic portrayals, many details, and complete accuracy in what they represent, (b) become intensely interested in particular topics not routinely of interest to peers (such as meteors or sea creatures), (c) go beyond what is immediately observable and explore the subject in greater depth (for example, making a cross-section drawing of the *Titanic*), (d) display exceptional sensitivity to emotion and ways of expressing it (for example, choosing to explore the subtleties and complexities of humor), or (e) produce works of visual art that display types of perception not commonly found in young children's work (such as light and shade or near/far perspective) and that require advanced development in the physical domain (Harrison, 1999).

How can work in the visual arts support the goals of multicultural education?

In order for all children to flourish as artists, they must communicate about a wide range of artistic styles and forms, see those styles and forms accepted by others, freely experiment with art media, and learn to accept one another's art. Art offers a way of communicating and accepting other cultures. Mexican piñatas, African masks, and Ukrainian decorated eggs each give children insight into the history, values, and aesthetic sensibilities of others. The newly immigrated child who is an English-language learner can express ideas, thoughts, and feelings nonverbally through paper, sculpture, pottery, and fabric.

What can teachers do to support the artistic expression of children with special needs?

Creative teachers adapt art activities to accommodate children with physical disabilities. It might mean a "low-tech" solution, such as putting clay on a wheelchair tray rather than at the table, or giving a child larger or longer paintbrush handles or crayons that can be held in the palm of the hand. It could also mean a high-tech solution such as equipping a computer software program with a Touch Window, a Big Red switch, or kidDraw so that children with physical limitations can

operate the program. If access to materials is limited due to a family's financial circumstances, teachers may want to use an ARTtache as described by Hutinger (1997). These were take-home bags of expressive art materials accompanied by notes inviting families to work with their children on projects at home that could then be brought to school and shared. Also included in the ARTtache kits were a comment page for children to draw or write about what they liked best and a family questionnaire to evaluate the kits. In every case, the key is sensitivity to the child, knowledge about the child's abilities, and creative problem-solving techniques.

How important are the materials in art?

All children need the challenge and excitement of working with new art media. It is thrilling to draw with brand-new, sharply pointed, soft-leaded colored pencils or to draw and color a picture with watercolor markers that include unusual colors such as silver or gold. Unusual papers are appealing too. Paper that is heavy, embossed, glossy, or foil, such as that used in greeting cards and wrapping paper, can often be recycled for a lasting supply of high-quality material. Many children do not have access to art materials (other than crayons and paper) at home. Materials such as oil pastels, colored chalk, washable acrylic paints, and clay are generally unavailable because parents cannot afford them, do not recognize their value, or are concerned about the mess. Even fewer children have access at home to artist's tools such as an easel, woodworking tools, or crafts materials. Consider supplying some of the real tools used by artists, demonstrating how they are used, and making them available to children.

How do children connect the symbol system of art with the symbols of language?

When children age 5 to 9 were interviewed about the connection between their drawing and writing, their responses fell into four basic categories. The children used drawings (a) as objects to label, (b) as catalysts for generating ideas, (c) as ways of making the abstract concrete, and (d) as aids to their thinking (DuCharme, 1991). Many young children who draw representationally use narrative art, pictures that tell a

story. Sometimes their storytelling depends entirely on the pictures; sometimes the pictures are combined with captions. Five-year-old Isabell explained the advantage of drawing over writing this way: "I'll draw you what I would write, but drawing is funner." Even before children are writing alphabetically, teachers can develop the concept of pictures accompanied by print—squiggles, letterlike forms, or letters and numbers that the child happens to know. An activity that is very appropriate for linking art with literacy is creating a web for a work of art. At the center of the web might be a print or photograph of the work. Radiating out from the center might be categories such as works of similar type (such as other sculptures), works with a similar subject or theme (such as animals), works by the same artist (such as Winslow Homer), works of similar style (such as picture books that use collage), and so forth. In this way, children are using literacy and art together.

CONCLUSION

Eisner (1976) has defined the personal inclinations for the arts as those abilities that enable us to "play with images, ideas and feelings, to be able to recognize and construct the multiple meanings of events, to perceive and conceive of things from various perspectives, to be able to be a clown, a dreamer, a taker of risks" (p. vii). As educators, we need to build these attributes in ourselves, in our colleagues, and, most important, in our students. Art is a way of building, understanding, and communicating ideas and meeting new challenges.

CHAPTER SUMMARY

1. In order for a classroom activity to qualify as art, it must value process as well as product, emphasize originality rather than conformity, allow children to retain ownership of their work, and develop an appreciation of mixtures and balances.
2. Understanding children's art depends on an appreciation of the child as artist, knowledge of the developmental sequence in children's art, an understanding of the principles of art education, and a recognition of the many contributions art makes to children's overall development.
3. In a quality art program, children learn not only to become artists but also to appreciate the artwork of others.
4. To support the goals of art education, teachers should locate quality art and art reproductions from many sources and discuss these works skillfully with children. Critical issues in art programs for young children include

health and safety considerations as well as the selection, presentation, evaluation, storage, and display of art and art materials.

5. Teachers in child-centered classrooms believe that quality art experiences with a variety of materials build every child's artistic sensibilities and skills.

6. Art is a true curricular basic, a way of knowing that is just as valuable in the real world as other types of know-how.

7. Art must be integrated into different subject areas so that it receives the attention that it merits.

Discuss: Supporting Children's Art

1. Use Allen Say's (2003) book *Emma's Rug* to spark a discussion about how artists get ideas for their work. Work in groups to plan how you would introduce and discuss this book with preschoolers, children in the primary grades, and older students.

2. A friend asks you how to tell if her child is artistic. How would you respond, based on what you have read in this chapter?

3. Reread the quotation that introduced this chapter. How has your understanding of it been enriched?

4. Suppose that a parent volunteers to work in your classroom and you observe the parent with his or her hand on top of a child's hand and paintbrush, forcibly showing the child how to paint a flower. After the children leave, the parent tells you that the child was rude and unappreciative. How would you respond?

5. Collect some of the following children's picture books about art and artists. In small groups, discuss how you could build a lesson around each book.

Brenner, B. (2003). *The boy who loved to draw: Benjamin West.* Boston: Houghton Mifflin.

Brown, L. K., & Brown, M. (1990). *Visiting the art museum.* New York: Puffin.

Catalanotto, P. (2001). *Emily's art.* New York: Simon & Schuster.

McPhail, D. (2000). *Drawing lessons from a bear.* Boston: Little, Brown.

Shafer, A. C. (2003). *The fantastic journey of Pieter Bruegel.* New York: Dutton.

Stanley, D. (1996). *Leonardo da Vinci.* New York: HarperCollins.

Weitzman, J. P., & Glasser, R. P. (2002). *You can't take a balloon into the Museum of Fine Arts.* New York: Dial.

Williams, V. B. (1986). *Cherries and cherry pits.* New York: Greenwillow.

Chapter 4

Engaging Children in
Music, Movement, and Dance

Mary Renck Jalongo and
Laurie Nicholson Stamp

Dancing is every child's cultural birthright . . . Music, too, is the memory of our people brought to life . . . [In music and dance] our children can awaken to a knowledge of themselves—their community and their country—in ways that cannot be duplicated.

Jacques D'Amboise, 1991, p. 5

CLASSROOM PERSPECTIVES ON MUSIC, MOVEMENT, AND DANCE

Preschool–Kindergarten

It is summertime and, at the community park, a concert band consisting of high school students, local music teachers, and retired professors from the local college is playing a weekday concert. Children from the toddler class at the university child-care center have arrived in their multiseat wagons and strain to see where the music is coming from. As they are lifted up from their seats, 2-year-old Marcus puts his chubby fists to his mouth and blows, imitating the trumpet players featured in the patriotic tune being played. Jasmine claps her hands almost in time to the music, and Shenay takes the hands of her teacher and sways from side to side. Then a group of 4-year-olds arrives, walking hand in hand with their partners. The preschoolers excitedly begin to point out and identify the instruments that their teacher displayed in the classroom as preparation for the walking field trip. Curtis and Lexie imitate the snare drummer and cymbal player, Maurice sits down to watch, and Jennica finds a stick on the ground that she uses to mimic the conductor's animated gestures. All of these young children have responded to a live musical performance by spontaneously connecting music with movement.

First Grade–Second Grade

Since the first week of school Mr. Torrez's second graders have arrived to find music playing each morning as they arrive. "First Circle," a jazz tune by Pat Metheny, is today's selection. Davis taps his eraser lightly in time as he visits his mailbox and reads a message from Mr. Torrez regarding yesterday's math assignment. Kayla reads the liner notes from the CD that her teacher has displayed, and Matthias, a recently immigrated child from Kenya, looks at the percussion instruments Mr. Torrez has on display that are being played in today's recording. Mr. Torrez consulted with Mrs. Kephart, the music specialist in their elementary building, before choosing musical selections for his classroom. Because the second graders meet with Mrs. Kephart for just thirty minutes once a week, Mr. Torrez works to reinforce the concepts and integrate the ideas that the children explored during music class.

Third Grade–Fourth Grade

Renee and Enrique rush back from the media center to join their fourth-grade class. Mrs. Arnett's room is filled with a variety of activities. As a part of the social studies unit on World War II, children are seated at tables and on the floor in small groups working with replicas of posters, books, and note cards from the era. Renee and Enrique are working with their group to plan a demonstration of the popular dances of the 1940s and the pair has just downloaded audio clips of the Andrews Sisters and a video clip of 1940s dances. Kyle, Leslie, and Desiree listen to Martin's findings about swing orchestras, while David, Ornate, and Ashley prepare their presentation on patriotic music of the time. Around the room, reproductions of work by photographers and painters of the 1940s are displayed. Mrs. Arnett has invited veterans from the community to their culminating activity, and in doing so, found that elderly twin sisters from her church worked as USO hostesses in San Diego during the war. Emma and Francine, both widows now, will enrich the children's understanding of the period by sharing scrapbooks, recordings, and song sheets from their volunteer days.

These vignettes point out the variety of roles that music, movement, and dance can and should play in the classroom life of the developing child.

UNDERSTANDING MUSIC, MOVEMENT, AND DANCE

Music, movement, and dance are rich and natural teaching resources for educators. Music is not merely a content area; it is also a unique way of communicating and a unique language. It is also a domain of intelligence. Musical/rhythmic intelligence refers to sensitivity to sounds and patterns of sound that results in the ability to appreciate, participate in, and perform music. In the classroom, music can include every child because enjoying music does not depend on specific skills or competence. "It offers varying levels of engagement ranging from simply listening or observing to joining in as an active participant" (Humpal & Wolf, 2003, p. 103). Throughout the world, softly sung lullabies are used to calm fussy infants. Parents and caregivers instinctively communicate with infants in a musical fashion because, although infants don't understand words, melodic stimulation always gets their attention (Weinberger, 1998). Similarly, action songs are used to entertain toddlers or preschoolers, and older students are taught to sing and play musical instruments. Adults have long operated on the assumption that musical activities were good for children by noticing children's positive responses—the baby being lulled to sleep, the toddler or preschooler laughing delightedly and asking for more, or the elementary school child proudly playing a musical instrument during a concert at school.

Consider the case of 3-year-old Mira, a recent immigrant from Russia. Mira speaks only Russian, and she has been quiet and withdrawn during her 2 weeks in the preschool class. The children are learning an action song that involves a variety of hand and body motions and, as their teacher demonstrates the song, she exaggerates the movements, encouraging the children to join in. Mira creeps closer to the circle and bobs her head animatedly in time to the music, and her teacher wonders if Mira knows the song. Later that day, the teacher overhears singing and is delighted to turn the corner and find Mira standing on a stepstool at the sink and singing in a mixture of English, Russian, and tuneful syllables while looking in the mirror and perfectly executing the accompanying motions.

As Mira's behavior suggests, movement is quite often part of a child's initial response to music. The terms *creative movement, movement,* and *creative dance* are used interchangeably to refer to the child's natural physical response to music. Teachers of young children often speak of creative movement rather than dance to differentiate movement from formal lessons and on-stage performances (see Werner, Timms & Almond, 1996). Children's creative movement "begins with an awareness of the movement of the body and its creative potential. During early childhood, children become engaged in body awareness and movement exploration that promote a recognition and appreciation of self and others" (Consortium of National Arts Education Associations, 1994, p. 23). For young children, the connection between movement and understanding is particularly strong. One team of researchers found, for example, that it was not until after children were asked to physically rotate their bodies that they were then able to understand the mental

For young children, the connection between movement
and understanding is very strong.

concept of rotation (Wohlschlaeger & Wohlschlaeger, 1998). Both movement and dance rely on kinesthetic intelligence, which is the ability to coordinate the body and orchestrate one's physical movements in space and time. Physical/spatial/temporal or kinesthetic intelligence is possessed and cultivated to a high degree by dancers and athletes.

Dance is distinctive from movement in that it is a more formal and structured type of movement; it is a kinetic art form, a physical language that speaks the integrated response from the mind and the body (Ross, 1994). Unlike creative movement, dance tends to denote an organized and discrete set of steps or body movements that have a right and wrong manner of performance. Dance depends on cultural and symbolic resources to make meaning and express creativity using the human body (Johnson, 2003). Children's kinesthetic intelligence grows when adults provide (1) a supportive physical and emotional environment, (2) opportunities for social interaction, and (3) role models to emulate.

Obviously, music, movement, and dance are interconnected. Everyone has seen young children spontaneously "walk, run, rock, or twist as they sing or speak in rhythm" (Tarnowski, 1999, p. 28). Ideally, musical and kinesthetic intelligence also are integrated with other areas of the curriculum. One Massachusetts school district's experience with integrating music, literature, and movement illustrates how this can occur. Creative and innovative classroom teachers and music specialists decided to explore the fairy tale and ballet called *Firebird* with kindergarten children. Repeated readings of the story, opportunities to listen to the music, and a virtual treasure trove of props allowed these kindergartners to retell the enchanting story of the Firebird through in their own words and make observations such as: "The music helped our ears hear the story. There is another way to tell a story—with feet. Dancers can dance a story. A dancing story is called a ballet" (Roebuck, 1999, p. 34).

HISTORICAL INFLUENCES ON MUSIC, MOVEMENT, AND DANCE FOR CHILDREN

The history of music, movement, and dance education is distinguished and exceptionally international in scope. Table 4.1 highlights educators who have had a major influence on music education for children.

Contemporary educators often take an eclectic approach to music that draws on the best features of each tradition. We recognize the importance of early experience as Rousseau did, we help children understand movement through time and space as Dalcroze did, we prepare a musical environment as Montessori did, we attend to the developmental levels of children as Kodaly did, we emphasize spontaneity and originality as Orff did, and we appreciate the importance of parental involvement as Suzuki did. Even though there are many published music curriculum guides (Andress, 1998; Snyder, 1995), teachers use music throughout the day and incorporate a wide variety of musical experiences, rather than slavishly following a particular program. Look in on any high-quality program for children

TABLE 4.1 Leaders in Music Education

Educator and Country of Origin	Background and Philosophy	Major Contributions to Music Education
Jean Jacques Rousseau (1712–1778) *France*	Rousseau's mother died when he was born, his father abandoned him, and the boy endured a variety of difficult foster-care situations. Rousseau became a highly controversial figure of his day. His contention that people are born free and equal was revolutionary. He advocated respect for the natural ways of children, which was at odds with most of his contemporaries who favored harsh punishment.	In his book about an imaginary "everychild" named *Emile,* Rousseau argued that music and movement go hand in hand. He emphasized the importance of singing to children and recommended that mothers should sing simple, interesting songs suitable for children. Rousseau believed that singing to and with children would make the child's voice accurate, uniform, flexible, and sonorous as well as make the child's ear sensitive to meter and harmony.
Emile Jacques-Dalcroze (1865–1950) *Switzerland*	An accomplished composer appointed to the Conservatory of Music at age 27, Jacques-Dalcroze challenged the prevailing views of musical training that relied on imitation, repetition, and harsh criticism. He argued for an approach that considered time, space, and energy.	The Dalcroze method emphasizes coordination of the eye, ear, mind, and body. Components of the method are (1) eurhythmics (expression of physical and mental rhythms and the laws affecting their performance), (2) solfege (training the ear, eye, and voice in pitch, melody, and harmony), and (3) improvisation (use of musical, physical, and verbal rhythms for spontaneous personal expression). The Dalcroze method continues to be popular today.
Maria Montessori (1870–1952) *Italy*	Montessori was the first woman in Italy to qualify as a physician. She was assigned to working with children living in poverty who were considered "ineducable." The general educational principle of her method was *first the education of the senses, then the education of the intellect.*	Montessori argued for sound exploration activities for young children. She invented a set of mushroom-shaped bells that helped children discover musical concepts. Montessori-method schools were established throughout the world and continue to exist today.

(continued) |

TABLE 4.1 *(Continued)*

Zoltan Kodaly (1882–1967) *Hungary*	An active composer, Kodaly wrote a great deal of choral, vocal, and orchestral music.	Kodaly proposed that musical literacy be developed through a carefully sequenced program of folk music that began with 3-year-olds. Kodaly's method revolutionized approaches to listening and ear training. It also inspired music educators worldwide to preserve the folk and traditional music of their respective countries and cultures.
Carl Orff (1895–1982) *Germany*	Orff was a composer of music, primarily stage pageants. As a teacher, Orff founded a school for gymnastics, music, and dance that influenced his thinking about early musical training. He developed creative musicianship in children by engaging them in spontaneously producing and creating their own music, rhythmic responses, and imaginative actions.	Orff's approach was child-centered and focused on activities that children do naturally and with pleasure. He provided children with ways to make music using their voices and simple percussion instruments. Carl Orff schools were established throughout the world to educate children using his methods.
Shinichi Suzuki (1898–1998) *Japan*	Suzuki was one of 12 children and his father owned a violin factory. Although he initially regarded these instruments as toys, Suzuki taught himself to play the violin, inspired by a stunning performer. He later took lessons and began to teach young children. Suzuki believed that all children have talent if they are taught well by loving parents and teachers. When the young children Suzuki had trained performed, people worldwide were amazed by their level of proficiency at such a young age. Thousands of parents enrolled their children in Suzuki training.	Suzuki originated a program that taught very young children to play the violin and cello using child-sized instruments. The success of the program, which took a musical literacy approach, relied on extensive parent involvement. Suzuki's mission was unique in that it did not have the production of more concert violinists or cellists as its major mission; rather, his goal was to introduce children to a world of beauty and appreciation through music. Suzuki contended that hearing and playing beautiful music helped children mature into people with good hearts.

from toddlerhood through the elementary grades and you will see children chanting, singing, clapping, swinging, tapping, marching, skipping, doing simple dances, and fully engaging in all kinds of music and movement activities. Effective teachers have learned to make the most of children's natural propensity to move and make music rather than searching for ways to keep children still and silent.

THEORETICAL AND RESEARCH BASE: BRAIN RESEARCH, MUSIC, AND DANCE

Research on the human brain from the fields of neuroscience and cognitive science supports the importance of music and dance in children's development. The connections that are formed between the cells of the brain, called synapses, are strengthened through use, and music and dance represent a unique form of cognitive stimulation (Gromko & Poorman, 1998; Lang, 1999; Wilcox, 2000). Music evidently affects the "circuitry" of the brain, and we now know that the human brain contains building blocks that enable human beings to perceive and respond to music (Weinberger, 1998). With advanced technology it is actually possible to determine which areas of the human brain are stimulated by certain activities. There is evidence to support the contention that early musical experiences provide a unique form of cognitive stimulation in the early years (Caulfield, 1999). Additionally, learning to play an instrument enables children to "develop strong pattern extraction and develop abilities that are essential to higher brain functions in logic, math, and problem solving" (Jensen, 1998a, p. 2), thereby enhancing overall cognitive growth.

The brain appears to be more malleable during the first 10 years of life than in adulthood (Flohr, Miller, & Debeus, 2000). Thus, the absence of the particular forms of cognitive stimulation provided via music and dance can have long-term adverse consequences for cognitive development. A culture of increasing pressure on teachers to meet academic standards and raise children's test scores often leads to the neglect of music during early childhood and elementary years, which diminishes musical potential throughout life. While many school districts employ music specialists, few districts have the luxury of enough musical instruction time, and educational settings that include children younger than kindergarten age may have no specialist at all. It is generally accepted, for example, that the singing voice of the "average" adult does not develop much beyond that acquired by age 7 or 8 when no training or additional opportunities are provided. A lack of access to music education would seem to widen the deficit that already exists for some children in other academic areas, and may adversely affect children's artistic and aesthetic development.

From a cognitive development perspective, children's abilities in the musical and kinesthetic domains tend to progress through three stages identified by Jerome Bruner (1968): (1) enactive, (2) iconic, and (3) symbolic. At the *enactive stage*, physical activity and music are intertwined. Consider all of the rhythmic games that adults play with infants and toddlers, and how they combine physical activity with music. We rock babies to sleep with a lullaby such as "Rock-a-Bye Baby," tickle a child's toes to the chant of "This Little Piggy," or begin sharing simple action songs such as "Eensy Weensy Spider" with toddlers. Bruner's enactive stage relates to Piaget's (1952) sensorimotor stage and Erikson's (1950) trust-building stage. When we think about the enactive music stage of babies and toddlers, it is clear that the activities adults select not only stimulate the child's senses and foster cognitive development, but also build social relationships by communicating warmth and acceptance.

During the *iconic stage*, which is typical of preschoolers, children use tangible items (real objects and pictorial representations of objects, such as photographs and drawings) to represent their experiences. At this stage, children are highly imaginative (Piaget, 1962) and assert their autonomy, yet want to be accepted by the group (Erikson, 1950). Musical experiences that are appropriate for this stage recognize all of these characteristics of preschoolers. Consider, for example, a teacher who extends the musical game "The Farmer in the Dell" by providing toys to represent each character in the game. Such an activity gives children a chance to connect music and dance with words, actions, and objects and paves the way for understanding symbols.

At the *symbolic stage*, children begin to use abstract symbols, primarily language, to represent ideas. By the time most children are in elementary school, they rely less on icons (pictures) and learn to use multiple-symbol systems that are more abstract, including words, musical notation, and the movement and gesture of dance. School-age children think more logically and realistically (Piaget, 1952). They also have a sense of industry, which is manifested in their drive to master many different skills (Erikson, 1950). Intellectual development from birth through the school years runs the course of the enactive, iconic, and symbolic systems "until the human being is able to command all three" (Bruner, 1968, p. 12). Throughout the early childhood and elementary years, music, movement, and dance are important ways for children to demonstrate their intelligence. Figure 4.1 presents an overview of musical development and activities suitable for each stage.

Infants

Music

Sensitive to dynamics, the loudness or softness of a sound; startle at loud sounds and are comforted by soft, rhythmic, melodious sounds (e.g., musical toys, lullabies). Respond to the human voice, especially the primary caregiver's voice; respond in more lively ways to action songs and more subdued ways to lullabies.

Movement

Tend to respond to music with the entire body. "Lap babies" will bounce to lively music; babies who are standing may rock from side to side, sway back and forth, or bounce up and down by flexing their knees.

Toddlers

Music

Discriminate among sounds and may attempt to imitate sound or to approximate pitches; listen to music and respond more enthusiastically to certain songs. Explore sound making with household objects (e.g., hitting a pan with a wooden spoon), musical toys, (e.g., a toy xylophone), or musical instruments; express greater interest in recordings. Can demonstrate knowledge of sounds and music by

---

Figure 4.1
Developmental Sequence for Music, Movement, and Dance

identifying familiar sounds or instruments played on a tape or outside their view. Experiment with songs and voice and gain some control of the singing voice; occasionally match melody and may join in on certain phrases of familiar songs; sing or hum improvisationally during play.

Movement

Use primarily arms and legs and can move in response to the tempo (fast/slow) of a rhythm instrument (e.g., run, walk, "freeze"). Will often "dance" on request while music is playing and show more control over physical responses. Respond well to large and small motor musical activities that emphasize repetition and rhyme—simple finger plays and action songs.

Recommended Picture Books for Infants and Toddlers

The Baby Dances (Henderson, 1999); *Old MacDonald Had a Farm* (Carter, 2001); *If You're Happy and You Know It, Clap Your Hands* (Carter, 2001); *Hanukkah, Oh Hanukkah* (Roth, 2003); *Baby Danced the Polka* (Beaumont, 2004); *Knick-Knack Paddy Whack!* (Zelinsky, 1992); *God Bless the Child* (Pinkney, 2003).

Three-Year-Olds

Music

Have better voice control, rhythmic responses, and mastery of song; most have names for their favorite tunes, can recognize familiar tunes, and can sing portions of them with a fair degree of accuracy (Day, 1988). With experience, most can play a simple rhythm instrument in ways that reveal an emerging awareness of beat, tempo, and pitch in response to songs with simple, definite rhythm patterns.

Movement

Move in a more coordinated way to music (usually running) and may experiment with different types of body movements, such as walking on tiptoe; movements tend to be more graceful than previously. Usually try to participate in action songs and finger plays by performing the gestures; often combine creative drama with song.

Four-Year-Olds

Music

Capable of learning some basic musical concepts such as pitch (high/low), duration (long/short), tempo (fast/slow), and loudness (soft/loud) and can use language to express these ideas; can classify musical instruments by sound, shape, size, pitch, and quality. Sing complete songs from memory with greater pitch control and rhythmic accuracy; sing both original songs and structured songs spontaneously. Vocal range, rhythmic ability, and vocabulary expand rapidly; can sing an average of five notes. Usually enjoy group singing games and more complex songs. Longer attention span in guided listening to records.

Movement

Movements suggesting rhythm (e.g., swinging on a swing) are likely to be accompanied by spontaneous song. Master new movements and can switch rapidly

(Continued)

141

from one type of movement to another when the word is substituted (e.g., "Hop, hop, hop to my Lou").

Five-Year-Olds

Music

Sense of pitch, rhythm, and melody emerge; usually understand some melodic contours and intervals (skips and steps in a melody); can demonstrate some musical concepts (e.g., fast/slow, high/low, short/long duration) on a small keyboard. Enjoy longer songs with predictable structures (e.g., colors, numbers, repetition, rhyme). Can reproduce the melody in an echo song and have a vocal range of five to six notes.

Movement

Movements have a more rhythmic quality than previously. Can march around in a circle while playing in a rhythm band and participate in a variety of group singing games with simple dance movements to songs such as "Looby Lou."

Recommended Picture Books for Preschoolers

Dancin' in the Kitchen (Gelsanliter & Christian, 1993); *Song and Dance Man* (Ackerman, 1988); *I Know an Old Lady Who Swallowed a Fly* (Gulbis, 2001); *Ah, Music!* (Aliki, 2002); *The Ants Go Marching* (Manning, 2003); *Mole Music* (McPhail, 1999); *The Philharmonic Gets Dressed* (Kuskin, 1982); *Giraffes Can't Dance* (Andreae, 2001); *Violet's Music* (Johnson & Huliska-Beith, 2004); *Ty's One-Man Band* (Walter, 1987); *Max Found Two Sticks* (Pinkney, 1994); *Dance!* (Cooper, 2002); *Presenting Tanya, the Ugly Duckling* (Gauch, 1999); *Zin! Zin! Zin! A Violin* (Moss & Priceman, 1995); *My Mama Had a Dancing Heart* (Gray, 1996); *The Moon Jumpers* (Udry, 2002); *From Miss Ida's Porch* (Belton, 1993); *There Was an Old Lady Who Swallowed a Fly* (Taback, 2002); *That Dancin' Dolly* (Merz, 2004); *What Charlie Heard* (Gerstein, 2002); *The Jazz Fly* (Gollub, 2000); *Hip Cat* (London, 1996); *Music Is* (Moss & Petit-Roulet, 2003); *Our Marching Band* (Moss, 2001); *The Musical Life of Gustav Mole* (Meyrick, 1990).

Six-, Seven-, and Eight-Year-Olds

Music

Singing voice is at nearly mature level. Sing "in tune," with a vocal range of approximately eight to ten notes; are aware of a song being pitched at a comfortable singing level. Sense of harmony is emerging. By second or third grade, can sing a round and may master a simple two-part harmony if given adult direction. Enjoy silliness and begin to understand wordplay in song lyrics; learn to read song lyrics; able to master songs that place greater demands on memory and sequencing skills. Greater awareness of printed music and its relationship to the way that music is sung or played; usually able to conceptualize musical notes as "stairsteps." Musical preferences are fairly well established; may express an interest in learning to play a musical instrument.

Figure 4.1 *(Continued)*

Movement and Dance

Able to improvise movements and match movements to the beat of the music (i.e., clapping "in time," playing a rhythm instrument "to the beat"). Capable of following more complex instructions and can learn simple folk dances with adult direction.

Recommended Picture Books for Children in the Primary Grades

Lion Dancer: Ernie Wan's Chinese New Year (Waters & Slovenz-Low, 1990); *Meet the Orchestra* (Hayes & Thompson, 1995); *Here's Bojangles: Think of That!* (Dillon & Dillon, 2002); *Handel, Who Knew What He Liked* (Anderson, 2002); *Strange Mr. Satie* (Anderson, 2003); *My Country 'Tis of Thee* (Smith, 2004); *Horace and Morris Join the Chorus (But What about Dolores?)* (Jave, 2002); *The Story of the Incredible Orchestra: An Introduction to Musical Instruments and the Symphony Orchestra* (Koscielniak, 2000); *Lives of the Musicians: Good Times, Bad Times (and What the Neighbors Thought)* (Krull, 1993); *Raggin': A Story about Scott Joplin* (Mitchell, 1992); *If Only I Had a Horn: Young Louis Armstrong* (Orgill, 1997); *Duke Ellington: The Piano Prince and His Orchestra* (Pinkney, 1998); *Ella Fitzgerald: The Tale of a Vocal Virtuosa* (Pinkney, 2002); *John Coltrane's Giant Steps* (Raschka, 2002); *Ragtime Tumpie* (Schroeder, 1989); *Charlie Parker Played Be Bop* (Raschka, 1997); *Music for Alice* (Say, 2004); *Snow Music* (Say, 2003); *When Marian Sang* (Ryan, 2002); *Aaron Copland* (Venezia, 1995); *John Philip Sousa* (Venezia, 1999).

ESSENTIAL UNDERSTANDINGS ABOUT MUSIC, MOVEMENT, AND DANCE

As children participate in music, movement, and dance at the enactive, iconic, and symbolic stages, they acquire the following attitudes (adapted from Hall, 1989):

• *I can listen to music and watch dance.* Children recognize different ways of using their senses to experience, appreciate, and differentiate among various types of music and dance. To achieve this, they need adults who model appreciation and respect for music, movement, and dance. Many studies, of both exceptionally talented musicians and adults in general, suggest that early experiences that were relaxed, informal, and enjoyed in the company of supportive adults contributed to the child's early attachment to music (Wilson & Roehmann, 1990). Interestingly, a team of researchers who studied infant musical development concluded that the parents' own singing might be the single most important influence on an infant's musical activity (Kelly & Sutton-Smith, 1987). On the other hand, when significant others express disdain for music and dance, these negative pronouncements tend to narrow children's range of interests. If, for example, a child hears others ridicule males who are interested in dance or music, the child often learns to devalue these activities too. Contrary to popular opinion, music and dance education is not limited to the few individuals who are sufficiently talented to make their living at it. Practically everyone is capable of enjoying music and dance performed by others.

- *I can join in music and movement.* Think about the continuum of participation in music and dance reflected in 9-year-old Colleen's history. When she was a toddler, her version of the traditional singing game "Ring Around the Rosy" was simply "rindaround . . . pocketful . . . boom," and she delighted in holding her mother's hands, moving in a circle, and dropping to the floor at the song's end. As a 3-year-old in nursery school, Colleen mastered all of the words (substituting "Ashes, ashes, we all fall down" for "boom") and learned how to move together with the other children around the circle. Now that she is in elementary school, Colleen takes dance lessons and has learned to coordinate her movements with those of her dance group. She also sings in her church choir and is inspired by the religious music and camaraderie. Colleen has learned that she can participate in music and dance composed and choreographed by others.

- *I can create music, movement, and dance.* Children need to feel free to explore sound and motion in response to music and dance. Consider the response of Owen, a 3-year-old who is waiting for his mother at the hairstylist's shop. After he hears a lively Sheryl Crow song on the radio, he begins to move his head back and forth. Owen's mother smiles and the stylist turns to see the small boy responding to the music. When the stylist asks him if he feels like getting up and dancing, Owen replies, "Well, my feet don't want to, but my head sure does." Education should help a child like Owen acquire the confidence to translate his feelings into dance and music compositions.

- *I can understand the language of music and dance.* A basic goal for children is for them to learn to use the vocabulary of music and dance. One preschool teacher encouraged her students to pick up and put away work and play materials while listening to music. She worked alongside them, stooping, reaching, and stretching, all the while modeling how cleanup could be done "in time" to the distinctive rhythms of a Sousa march, a portion of Benjamin Britten's *Young Person's Guide to the Orchestra,* and an excerpt from Edward Elgar's *Enigma Variations.* The teacher did not stop there, however. She also used terminology that would prepare her students to talk about music in more precise and satisfying ways, and words such as *tempo, style,* and *rhythm* were seamlessly integrated into daily classroom routines. The companion Web site for this chapter provides a list of orchestral music suitable for classroom listening.

- *I can compose music and choreograph movements.* Naturally, the selection of both music and movement activities depends on the developmental levels of the children. Toddlers can rock a teddy bear to a lullaby, preschoolers can make "dancing dolls" (empty detergent bottles and fabric skirts) and swirl them about in response to a Strauss waltz, and primary-grade children can lope along to a cowboy song as they hold the reins of their horse (a length of ribbon or yarn encircling the waist of a partner). Children spontaneously create and sing original songs, invent dances to accompany musical selections, or think of ways to use streamers, scarves,

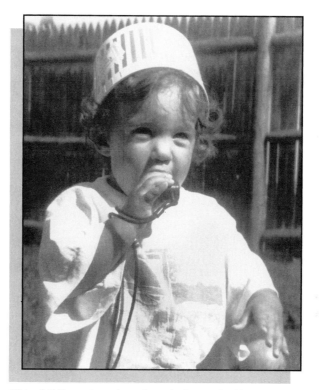

*This child's exploration of musical sounds illustrates
her emerging understandings about music.*

paper fans, or feathers to accompany a musical selection. With older children, a
task such as composing a simple melody using the pentatonic scale (C-D-E-G-A)
to accompany various three-line haiku poems might pose an interesting musical
challenge (Burns, 2002). When children record their compositions in some way and
lead others in performing them, they are learning the rudiments of composing.

• *I can perform music and dance.* "Musical activities should give pleasure to
all who are participating, and if they don't, they are probably worse than useless"
(Boyd, 1989, p. 8). It is not enough to simply "bathe" children in music or let children race around aimlessly to expend surplus energy because, to the young child,
music is both active (something that you do) and interactive (something that you
share with others). Even young children can perform music and movement at
some basic level, such as using "sleigh bells" to accompany a winter song. As
school-age children begin to acquire performance skills, they also learn another lesson—that performances in music and dance often demand a level of excellence that
exceeds those in other fields. Professional musicians and dancers continue to practice until even a single wrong note or missed step is avoided.

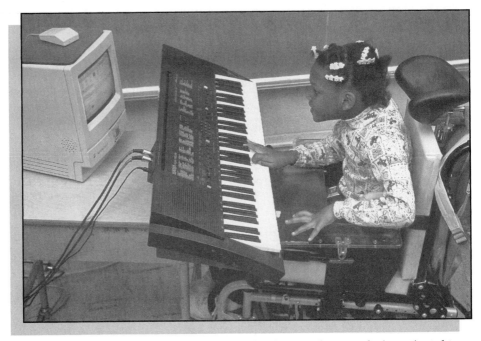

Music contributes to this child's psychomotor development because she is motivated to play a song on the electronic keyboard.

CONTRIBUTIONS OF MUSIC, MOVEMENT, AND DANCE TO CHILDREN'S LEARNING

Music contributes to the child's total development: psychomotor, perceptual, affective, cognitive, social, cultural, and aesthetic. Figure 4.2 highlights ways that teachers can use music and dance more effectively in the classroom.

Psychomotor Development

As children participate in music, movement, and dance, it contributes to their psychomotor development. Babies who have not yet learned to crawl usually will raise their arms and legs up off the floor and make rapid swimming motions in response to lively music. Preschoolers learn to coordinate the small muscles of their hands and arms, or fine motor skills, when they strike the keys on a toy xylophone or tap lightly on a tambourine; they use the large muscles of their bodies when they invent actions to go along with a song or interpret the mood of a musical selection through creative dance. Elementary students coordinate their voices and body movements with those of their classmates in order to perform at a musical event at their school. In all of these situations, music, movement, and dance offer physical benefits to children. Failure to develop competence in fundamental skills of movement

- To begin the day and greet one another
- To create a warm, positive atmosphere
- To establish a particular mood
- To ease transitions from one activity to another
- To link the arts with other subject areas
- To focus children's attention
- To make special events even more special
- To celebrate diversity
- To establish social solidarity
- To refresh and relax
- To sharpen thinking skills
- To promote creative expression
- To bring the day or an event to a satisfying conclusion

Figure 4.2
How Teachers Use Music and Dance in the Curriculum
Note. Adapted from Hildebrandt (1992).

may result in a poor body image (Green, 2001), and may deter children from participating in any organized sport or physical endeavor (Garcia, Garcia, Floyd, & Lawson, 2002). Thus, the need for children to develop competence and confidence in their own abilities to move and use their bodies is critical. Figure 4.3 provides recommendations on ways to incorporate music and dance in your classroom.

Perceptual Skills

Children are accustomed to hearing music—at shopping malls, on television programs, on Web sites, or from windup musical toys—but these experiences do not really teach children to listen thoughtfully to music. Children may hear others attempt to sing along with a CD, mimicking a particular vocal style, but this does not make them aware of the voice and breath control that go into singing. Likewise, children often see others jumping around as if they were dancing or may attempt to imitate real dancers they see, such as walking on tiptoe after watching ballet—but these experiences do not make children aware of the control and precision necessary in order to dance. Appreciation of and participation in the arts demands heightened perceptual skills.

From the earliest days of life, children show that they are capable of perceiving music and movement. A baby who recognizes her mother's voice is differentiating between it and all the other voices in her environment. Toddlers' sensory perceptions of music may be so striking that they do not expect them to be perceived by hearing alone. A teacher might play a note on the piano and realize that a toddler is running around to search for that note, expecting to see and touch as well as hear it. Likewise, a kindergartner who remarks that "The Flight of the Bumblebee"

General Principles

- Base the program on four elements: listening (e.g., playing the music of different cultures in the background), moving (e.g., inviting children to experiment with dance steps that accompany musical selections with distinctive beats), playing (e.g., teaching children a story song and inviting them to dramatize it), singing (e.g., encouraging joyful, spontaneous singing in response to activities such as swinging on a swing).

- Provide a balance of large-group, small-group, partner, and individual music and movement activities. Adapt the environment and materials to give children with special needs opportunities to participate. Also provide a balance of teacher-facilitated and child-initiated activities.

- Expect children's responses to vary and invite children to respond in their own ways to music and dance rather than requiring everyone to do the same thing. For instance, balance the use of songs that have the motions predetermined (like "Eensy Weensy Spider") with opportunities for children to invent their own actions to accompany songs.

- Build the children's self-confidence as people who can enjoy, participate in, and respond to music and dance. Invite children to share their ideas, but do not force them to perform or ask the group to critique their performance.

- Avoid generic praise ("That's great, everyone!") and use personalized encouragement instead ("I notice that you are using your whole body, Jason," and "I see that Chelsea decided to use mostly her arms.").

- Actively seek to build the children's vocabularies related to music and movement. While toddlers may focus on simpler concepts (e.g., fast/slow, turning around), older children can learn the terminology used by artists (e.g., dynamics, pirouette).

- Encourage and support the children's spontaneous songs and dances by observing and documenting what they have created on audio or videotape. Invite the child to teach his or her song or dance to you.

- Join in as appropriate, by offering to sing with a child or accompany the child's song or dance on whatever instrument you can play (e.g., a drum, a kazoo, a guitar, a keyboard).

- For children who seem reluctant to express themselves through music and movement, model joyful responses and invite the child to sing or move with you in response to music.

- Avoid a talent-scout mentality, in which you focus on a few children who appear to be precocious in music or dance. Give all children opportunities to engage in music and movement to the best of their abilities.

Figure 4.3
How to Incorporate Music and Dance in Your Classroom

Preparation

- For safety's sake, when children are engaged in movement activities, make sure that they are wearing shoes with nonslip soles. Make certain also that children are not being asked to sing during snack or meal times, as food may get caught in their throats and cause them to choke.

- Select a space that will accommodate the activity. During creative movement activities, use a large, open, uncluttered area and tell children to behave like peanut butter and s-p-r-e-a-d out! Even if space is more limited, ask children to extend their arms and turn slowly about to be sure that they will not bump into anyone else. You will need a large group area for playing circle games (e.g., "Ring Around the Rosy"), and a listening center equipped with high-quality sound equipment and musical selections from throughout the world. Remember to include outdoor musical experiences, such as galloping to music with stick horses.

- When you set up learning centers, provide music and movement opportunities every day (e.g., a listening center, a music center) as well as centers that change periodically (e.g., a musical prop-making center, materials for making sandpaper blocks at the woodworking center). Have a center that includes scarves, ropes, balls, streamers, and other materials that encourage movement and dance. Consider a special dramatic play area for conducting music that includes a music stand, baton, and podium. Plan a music laboratory where children can invent their own music, equipping it with a set of bells, a keyboard, xylophone, drums, and rhythm band set. Add music to the home-life center by including a cassette or CD player, musical stuffed toys, a music box, or some musical instruments.

- At various times, combine music and movement with all other subject areas and centers in the classroom (e.g, a work song playing in the woodworking area for preschoolers, or a group of second graders who invent a song parody about energy in science, or a third-grade class that composes and performs a musical puppet play on sets and subsets for the first grade).

Materials and Resources

- Don't choose a book, recording, or piece of software simply because it is "popular"—much of the "children's music" in wide use is of inferior quality and simply well marketed. Strive to provide the very best. Choose high-quality materials and sound equipment. You might be able to use the CD player on a computer to provide better sound quality than that provided by old records or cassette tapes, for example.

- Song lyrics should be matched to the interests and developmental levels of *children* (e.g., romantic songs are not appropriate). Songs need to be pitched at the child's singing range.

- When young children sing or move to music, they should be responding sincerely and genuinely rather than mimicking adults. Strive for a neat, clean appearance and avoid makeup, suggestive song lyrics or risqué costumes.

(Continued)

- Teach children to respect and care for props, instruments, equipment, and software. Organize your classroom so that it is easy for children to see where things belong and how they are to be put away.

- Give children independent access to musical experiences by providing a listening center, a place to record music, a center or cart with homemade and real musical instruments, and computer software about music and dance. Teach children how to operate the equipment and provide posters with illustrated instructions.

- Expand children's appreciation for different types and styles of music and dance by introducing the music and dance of many eras, ethnic groups, and cultures throughout the entire year.

- Use community resources to provide a wide array of recorded and live performances in music and dance. Collaborate with families, colleagues, and professionals in other fields. Send out a request to those who have skill in music, asking them to share their talent and level of accomplishment with children.

- Begin a file of online and print resources for parents/families about young children's music and dance. When parents turn to you for advice about lessons in music or dance, have authoritative answers ready.

Presentation

- Don't reserve music and movement activities for one specific time block. Rather, use music and creative movement throughout the day, particularly during transition times such as arrival/departure at the school or center; as children move in and out of free play; before, during or after a story session; or as children move inside and outside for outdoor play.

- Remember that young children enjoy repeating familiar songs and dance movements. Feel free to revisit the familiar as well as introduce something that is new.

- When young children are moving to music, the emphasis should be on developing techniques rather than on displays of athleticism or stunts. Incorrect technique can cause physical damage to the young child's body.

- Pay attention to variety and pacing. Even a brief music or creative dance time period will require several different activities. Stop an activity before the children grow tired of it and save some of that enthusiasm for next time.

Evaluation

- Quality music and movement programs help all children develop positive attitudes and emotional responses. Early musical experiences should inaugurate a lifelong love of music and dance.

- Closely observe how children respond to particular music and movement activities. Make some brief notes about what was particularly well received and what was not.

- Realize that a lukewarm response to a song or a movement experience may mean that it was not developmentally suited to the children at that time. Perhaps if it is introduced later on, children will respond more favorably.

Figure 4.3 (*Continued*)

- Don't allow yourself to get caught up in high-pressure, on-stage performances for large audiences. Even people who have extensive musical training may not understand the needs of young children very well and you will need to advocate for the children's needs. Remember, you aren't selling tickets, you are teaching children.

- Exercise good judgment about how formal a music or dance experience should be for children. Help parents and community members to understand that when children are acting tense and anxious, rather than enjoying the activity, it is time to reconsider.

- Remain current with the recommendations of leading organizations in music and movement, such as Music Educators National Conference, and use their guidelines as a basis for ongoing self-evaluation.

- You will know that your music and movement program is achieving its goals when children learn to listen and observe appreciatively, sing tunefully, move expressively and rhythmically, play classroom instruments, develop age-appropriate musical concepts, create self-satisfying responses, and value music and dance as part of everyday life.

Note. Based on Bennett, Wood, & Rogers (1997), Gold & Cuming (1999), Greenberg (1979), Persellin (1998), and Turner (1999).

sounds "buzzy" demonstrates that he is making a connection between music and his prior experience. As children mature, their ability to perceive the mood of music and articulate that mood in words increases. After some third graders heard the mournful tune "Ashokan Farewell," the theme song for Ken Burns's *The Civil War* series on PBS, one child remarked, "It's kind of slow and sad and makes you feel the way you feel if your friend moves away." Music, movement, and dance are an effective way of heightening the perceptual development of children.

Emotional and Social Development

Darren, a kindergarten teacher, shared this story from his classroom: "The other day, I wanted to introduce the children to the song 'Old Brass Wagon.' We've been working on right and left and I thought that would be a great reinforcement for the concept. So I invited the children to the carpeted area of the classroom to join me for a game. Many came over at once, but Keisha and a little knot of her chums stayed in their places. 'Come on' . . . I invited, 'we need you, too.' Then Keisha asked, 'Mr. Martin . . . is this a fun game or a WINNING game?'" Keisha's question points out another contribution of musical games and movement activities: They can be adapted to allow everyone to feel competent, successful, and accomplished, without having to declare a winner.

In fact, many music and movement activities encourage participation, sharing, and cooperation and, in most cultures throughout the world, music and dance are part of the bonding process across the generations. "Musical ability is developed in a relationship, in a succession of relationships—musical self in relation to musical selves" (Bernstein, 1990, p. 401). A classroom activity such as the group singing game "London Bridge," for example, teaches children learn to subordinate their individual wishes to the goals of the group—the essence of cooperation.

Cognitive Skills

Musical intelligence involves children's ability to process mentally the tonal aspects of rhythm and melody. The child who learns to sing "This Old Man," for instance, has learned to focus on a task, sequence material, and link words with actions. Musical experiences, such as creating a tune at a keyboard, can develop all the higher-level thinking skills of application, analysis, synthesis, and evaluation. There are cognitive connections between learning music and learning to do mathematics or learning to read, since all of these tasks depend on mastering a language.

Multicultural Development

Music familiarizes children with the musical heritage of various geographic regions, cultures, and ethnic groups. A group of second graders who heard the Grammy award–winning African music group Ladysmith Black Mambazo were captivated by their majestic Zulu harmonies. The children with African roots felt renewed pride in their ethnic heritage, while children with a different cultural heritage felt admiration for the music of a culture different from their own. Likewise, when a Lakota Sioux group performed their breathtaking ceremonial dances at a university and a beautifully synchronized troupe of Greek folk dancers demonstrated the power of their art at an ethnic festival, their audiences were not only enthralled, but also filled with admiration. Many compilations feature the music and songs of various groups, such as *Fiestas: A Year of Latin American Songs of Celebration* (Orozco, 2004) and *Dance, Sing, Remember: A Celebration of Jewish Holidays* (Kimmelman, 2000). Another good resource for recordings of multicultural music and across-the-curriculum ideas is Putumayo World Music.

Aesthetic Awareness

Lead children to reflect on questions such as the following:

*   What do we hear in the music and notice in the dance?
*   Why do we respond the way that we do to what we hear and see?
*   What is beautiful in music and dance?
*   How might we show appreciation for music and dance?
*   What are some ways that each of us might participate in music and dance?

Invite children to develop their aesthetic sensibilities with the following questions:

*   Can you show me with your body that the music is getting louder? Softer? Higher? Lower? Can you show me with just your hands? Can you show me with your whole body that it is getting faster? With just your head? With just your feet?

- Can you show me giant steps as you move around the circle? Baby steps? Can you imagine how an elephant might dance to this music? How about a mouse?

- Show me *happy*. How would your face look if you just opened the best present ever? Now add your arms. Next, show your whole body being happy. Show me how *happy* moves around the room. Now choose a prop that makes you look even happier, joyful.

- Show me how a leaf flutters down from the tree using your whole body. Can you show me with a paper streamer? With just your arms?

Note that the teacher is not performing music, movement, or dance *for* the children; rather, the teacher is urging children to think and respond aesthetically.

 ## TEACHERS' REFLECTIONS ON MUSIC, MOVEMENT, AND DANCE

Preservice Teachers

"After reading this chapter and contrasting it with what happened in the name of music at the child-care center where I worked last summer, I can see that we were really missing the whole point. We basically used music as a 'cheap filler' or tried to drill children on some skill through music, like 'The Alphabet Song.' Now I see how much more we could have been doing in terms of selecting, presenting, and simply enjoying music together."

"You haven't really enjoyed 'The Hokey Pokey' until you've heard Sharon, Lois, and Bram's rock version and compared it to Michael Doucet's zydeco version! And you have forgotten how 'Skip to My Lou' is supposed to be sung until you've listened to John McCutcheon's lively version!"

Inservice Teachers

"After *Riverdance* was on PBS and the talent show *Star Search* came on with a 'Young Dancer' category, several of my fourth graders became interested in dance. I think that watching these programs helped the children to appreciate the energy, strength, control, and hours of practice that go into these performances."

"Our school never has enough instruments so we sponsored an instrument donation drive. It was amazing how many people were willing to sponsor a child by providing an instrument that was useable but no longer in use. The donators were our special guests at the elementary school concert."

Your Reflections

- How would you characterize your current thoughts about how music, movement, and dance activities contribute to children's lives and their overall development?

- What types of musical experiences, artists, and resource materials, both traditional and contemporary, would you choose for young children? Why?

- What concerns do you have about your own abilities to foster young children's creative expression through music, movement, and dance?

TEACHERS' ROLES AND RESPONSIBILITIES

You may discover that there is limited support for music, creative movement, and dance at your school or center. At one time, teachers were required to complete as many as 15 credits in the arts prior to teaching. Now it is commonplace for teachers to have just one or two classes and hope that a music and art specialist will be available. Yet even when these services are available, each group of children typically gets just 20–30 minutes per week of the specialist teacher's time. Therefore, no matter what your training or setting, you will have responsibility for providing quality music and movement experiences for young children.

Teachers often operate under the mistaken impression that they must be able to sing beautifully and accompany themselves on an instrument or have professional training in dance in order to integrate these subjects into the curriculum. Actually, very few adults possess such performance skills. It is important to remember that the major focus is on the children's expression through music and dance rather than on appraisals of your talent. Some ways of supporting children's development in music and dance without possessing performance skills yourself are highlighted in Figure 4.4.

Teachers fulfill their musical roles and responsibilities effectively when they function as motivators, planners, facilitators, and observers.

Teachers as Motivators

It is not sufficient for teachers to set up a music center and a listening station and sing a few songs. Children need to be introduced to music and dance experiences in an engaging way, just as with a story or lesson. The motivation for a music activity should include a concrete object, thought-provoking questions, and active participation. Mrs. O'Malley introduced a new song to her kindergarten class by placing a four-sided wooden object with one pointed end and a stem in the center of the circle. The children were not really sure what it was or why it had unusual markings on it. When she gave the object a twirl and it began to spin around, they called out delightedly, "A top!" Mrs. O'Malley then explained that it was a very special type of top, a dreidel; that it was a traditional toy of Jewish children; and that the markings on the top were Hebrew letters. Then the children learned to sing "My Dreidel" while each child took a turn spinning the top. Additional motivational ideas include introducing "The Teddybears' Picnic" with a picnic basket and arranging chairs in bus seat formation to sing the action song *The Wheels on the Bus* (Zelinsky, 1990). Older students are often captivated by popular music and, with careful screening for

Even teachers who are relatively untrained in music and movement and feel they have very little ability in music or dance can, with the right attitude and resources, provide a high-quality musical program for children.

1. **Identify the source of your inhibitions.** Did someone tell you that you couldn't carry a tune? Are you concerned that the children will judge you? First, keep in mind that you are teaching children, not a contestant on *American Idol!* Judge your voice by the ability to sing children's songs, not by your ability to imitate famous vocalists. The great majority of songs for preschoolers have a range of about five notes. An ordinary singing voice coupled with extraordinary enthusiasm is perfectly adequate to sing most songs for young children. You probably know many of the songs already or can quickly learn them by singing along with a tape or record.

2. **Use recorded materials and live performances.** Teachers can obtain many excellent CDs, tapes, and children's concert videotapes through their public library. To avoid fumbling around to find a particular selection on a tape or CD, make copies on tape with just the songs you will be using that day, or use the counter on the videotape machine and write down the exact location of each song. This will enable you to move smoothly from one selection to another. What if you find the sheet music to a song in a book but cannot find a recorded version? Find a person who plays an instrument well to make a tape for you. You might ask the person to sing the song the first time so that you can learn it, then play just the background music the second time. Videotapes of skilled children's musicians in action are not only for children's viewing, but are also useful self-teaching tools for early childhood educators. Tapes such as *A Young Children's Concert with Raffi* (Raffi, 1984) model the enthusiasm and ways of presenting material that achieve maximum audience participation. Children often are inspired to try music and dance after watching performances. Show videos or CDs of great performances and work within your community to bring dancers and professional musicians to the school or center.

3. **Start out right.** Singing requires breath control. Before you start singing, be certain that you stand or sit up straight. Determine your range, the low and high of what you can sing comfortably. Consult with someone who knows music about your range. To get off to a good start, consider playing a note and matching your voice to it; with older children, you might ask a child to start the song and then join in. What about dance? Are you fearful that you will be clumsy or undignified during creative movement or dance? Remember the African adage, "If you can talk, you can sing. If you can walk, you can dance." Actually, it isn't necessary to be a dancer yourself, only to guide children's expression through creative movement or dance. Children might understand the concept of rhythm better if it is related to a concrete experience many of them already have, such as the ticking of a clock. A teacher might pass around a clock, tell children to listen, and then ask, "How can we make our rhythm sticks sound like a clock?" Alternatively, the children might listen to the song "My Grandfather's Clock" or the music of the

(Continued)

Figure 4.4
What If I Can't Sing? What If I Can't Dance?

"Syncopated Clock" and move their heads, hands, or feet to the sounds of the clock. If a group of school-age children want to present a story such as "Coppelia" by Leo Delibes (1986) with musical sound effects, the teacher can relate it to their picture-symbol knowledge with questions such as, "How could you help the players remember when to play?" Children may decide to provide the director with pictorial cue cards of each instrument, to make a large story chart coded with the symbols, or to provide each player with the text of the story coded with the instrument symbols. It is appropriate to teach them dances that they will have the opportunity to enjoy throughout life as they attend celebrations—a waltz, a polka, a folk dance. Above all, avoid perpetuating the inhibitions you feel in your students. (See Moore, 2002, and Neelly, 2002, for further suggestions).

4. **Accomplish curriculum goals through music, movement, and dance.** Is your goal to teach rhythm? If so, you could use a simple chant such as the Big Book version of *Peanut Butter and Jelly* (Wescott, 1987) to emphasize the rhythmic patterns of language. To pose a rhythmic challenge to third graders, you could select a complicated rap such as "The Little Shekere" on Sweet Honey in the Rock's *All for Freedom* album (1989). If your goal is to improve children's memory, you might select a song with several verses, such as Peter Spier's *The Fox Went Out on a Chilly Night* (1961) for first or second graders, or something simpler such as "If You're Happy and You Know It" for preschoolers.

5. **Use the simplest accompaniments.** You may have decided that, unless you can play the piano or guitar, you cannot lead children in song. But what about the simplest instruments, such as a tom-tom, a tambourine, or maracas? One simple instrument that children (and teachers) can learn to play is the chorded zither called an autoharp. Instead of having to learn the chords by positioning the fingers (as with a guitar), you simply press a button corresponding to that chord and strum down with your thumb and up with your finger in time to the music. The major drawback to the autoharp is that it must be tuned. The best way for nonmusicians to tune it is to ask a musician to do it for you or, better yet, learn to do it for yourself by matching each string's sound to those on a CD or tape (Peterson, 1979). Another alternative is the Omnichord, an electronic version of the autoharp that requires no tuning—you need only to push a button and stroke a pressure-sensitive keyboard. There are many different models of the Omnichord, and the smaller ones are reasonably priced.

6. **Seek opportunities for professional development.** When teachers are not specialists in music and dance, they need to rely on high-quality resources. Use the library. Many of the most popular children's musicians have concert tapes that you can borrow. Weston Woods has several song picture books on video, including Pete Seeger's *The Foolish Frog,* Aliki's *Hush Little Baby,* and Maurice Sendak's *Really Rosie.* Another source for musical and dance performances is public television or live musical events in your area. When you attend professional conferences, seek out sessions on music, movement, and dance

Figure 4.4 *(Continued)*

and visit booths where you can review materials. One shortcut to high-quality materials is to find materials that have earned positive reviews from professional organizations and have earned awards (e.g., Parent's Choice Award and the American Library Association's Notable Recording). Consult professional journal and magazine articles about music, movement, and dance activities. Finally, talk with teachers, both music specialists and regular classroom teachers, about the materials and experiences in music and dance that that they have found particularly effective with children.

appropriateness, some of this music can be used for listening enjoyment, for curriculum tie-ins, and to motivate students to complete academic tasks.

Teachers as Planners

Planning a musical experience involves preparation, pacing, and variety. Preparation includes identifying your purpose, deciding what to include, and assembling all of your materials. If you are using recording equipment, ensure that it is in working order. Careful preparation will enable you to keep your attention on the children rather than on the book, musical instrument, or recording equipment. Another aspect of preparation is getting the children assembled and ready. Teach the children some basic signals that are useful when transitioning into music or dance, such as shaking a tambourine to announce singing together or using the "freeze" command to calm them down if movement and dance get too rambunctious. Strive to reduce background noise and other distractions before beginning.

Pacing is important too. Do not drag out an activity or race through it. It is generally best to alternate "mostly listening" activities with "mostly movement," to limit the amount of unfamiliar material at any one session, and to conclude with a quiet song or a song that leads into the next activity planned. If children ask to sing a song again honor their request but stop before interest wanes.

Variety is another consideration. Give children a variety of opportunities to participate by listening, singing, moving, dancing, and playing simple instruments. Think of adaptations that will allow all children to participate in some way (see the Frequently Asked Questions for this chapter, p. 173). Remember that the goal is to extend and balance children's musical experiences, so include many different types of musical selections (see Figure 4.5), not only during music time, but also throughout the day.

It is also important to develop a variety of strategies for achieving learning goals. If you want to teach children a new song, for example, you could:

- Play the song in the background for several days so children will be familiar with it when it is introduced.
- Teach children the chorus while you sing the verses (at first).
- Sing along with a recording and tell children to join in singing with whatever portions of the song they feel comfortable with.

In high-quality early childhood settings, the emphasis is on children's musical activity. These primary grade children are playing simple instruments and singing with a partner.

Lullabies—Traditional and Original, American and Multicultural
Examples: *Baby's Morning Time* (Judy Collins), *Lullaby Berceuse* (Connie Kaldor & Carmen Campagne), *Star Dreamer* (Priscilla Herdman), *Earthmother Lullabies I and Earthmother Lullabies II* (Pamala Ballingham), *Lullabies for Little Dreamers* (Kevin Roth), *Nitey-Night* (Patti Ballas & Laura Baron), *Nightsongs and Lullabies* (Jim Chappell)

American Folk Songs—Children's Chants, Play Songs, and Singing Games
Examples: *Let's Sing Fingerplays* and *Activity and Game Songs* (Tom Glazer), *Circle Time* (Lisa Monet), *Family Tree* (Tom Chapin), *Doc Watson Sings Songs for Little Pickers* (Doc Watson), *Stories and Songs for Little Children* and *American Folk Songs for Children* (Pete Seeger), *The Best of Burl's for Boys and Girls* (Burl Ives), *Come On In* and *Fiddle Up a Tune* (Eric Nagler), *This a Way, That a Way* (Ella Jenkins), *Stay Tuned* (Sharon, Lois, & Bram), *American Children* (various artists), *Peter, Paul, & Mommy* (Peter, Paul, & Mary)

Figure 4.5
Types of Music

Nursery Tunes and Songs for the Very Young
Examples: *Mainly Mother Goose* (Sharon, Lois, & Bram), *Singable Songs for the Very Young* and *More Singable Songs for the Very Young* (Raffi), *Baby Songs and More Baby Songs* (Hap Palmer), *The Baby Record* (Bob McGrath & Katherine Smithrim), *Lullabies and Laughter* (Pat Carfra), *Shake It to the One You Love the Best: Play Songs and Lullabies from Black Musical Traditions* (Cheryl Warren Mattox)

Multicultural Music from Around the World and Music of the Child's Ethnic Heritage
Examples: *Children's Songs of Latin America* and *Cloud Journey* (Marcia Berman), *All for Freedom* (African-American) (Sweet Honey in the Rock), *Family Folk Festival: A Multicultural Sing-Along* (various artists), *Mi Casa Es Su Casa* (Michele Valeri), *Beyond Boundaries: The Earthbeat! Sampler* (various artists), *Miss Luba and Kenyan Folk Melodies* (Muungano National Choir of Kenya), *Shake Shugaree* (various cultures) (Taj Mahal), *Le Hoogie Boogie: Louisiana French Music for Children* (Michael Doucet)

Holiday, Religious, and Seasonal Music
Examples: *Leprechauns and Unicorns* and *Oscar Brand and His Singing Friends Celebrate Holidays* (Oscar Brand), *Holiday Songs and Rhythms* (Hap Palmer), *Songs for the Holiday Season* (Nancy Rover), *Just in Time for Chanukah* (Rosenthal & Safyan), Mormon Tabernacle Choir, Vienna Boys Choir, Gregorian Chant (Benedictine Monks), Reverend James Cleveland, Mighty Clouds of Joy

Contemporary Children's Music
Examples: *Evergreen, Everblue* (Raffi), *Rosenshontz* (Gary Rosen & Bill Shontz), *Sillytime Magic* (Joanie Bartels), *All of Us Will Shine, Hug the Earth,* and *Circle Around* (Tickle Tune Typhoon), *1-2-3 for Kids* (The Chenille Sisters), *Little Friends for Little Folks* (Janice Buckner), *Singin' and Swingin'* (Sharon, Lois, & Bram), *Collections* (Fred Penner), *Take Me with You* (Peter Alsop)

Popular Music—Rock, Jazz, New Age, Pop, Electronic, Movie Music, Show Music
Examples: *Sebastian the Crab* (from *The Little Mermaid*) (various artists), *Peter and the Wolf Play Jazz* (Dave Van Ronk), *Star Wars Trilogy Soundtrack* (London Philharmonic), *Electronic Music II* (Jacob Druckman), *Really Rosie* (children's musical) (Carole King/Maurice Sendak), *Baby Road* (Floyd Domino), *Fresh Aire I and Fresh Aire II* (Manheim Steamroller), *The Lion King* (Elton John)

Chants, Rhymes, and Rap
Examples: "The Little Shekere" from *All for Freedom* (Sweet Honey in the Rock), "Fiesta Musical" from *Music for Little People Sampler* (Maria Medina Serafin), various playground chants and African chants from *Where I Come From!* (Cockburn & Steinbergh)

Classical Music
Examples: *Peter and the Wolf* (Sergei Prokofiev), *Sorcerer's Apprentice* (Dukas), *Carnival of the Animals* (Camille Saint-Saens), *Sleeping Beauty* (Peter Ilyich

(Continued)

Tchaikovsky), *The Firebird* (Igor Stravinsky), *Fiedler's Favorites for Children* and *More Fiedler Favorites* (Arthur Fiedler and the Boston Pops Orchestra), *G'morning, Johann: Classical Piano Solos* (Ric Louchard), *Nutcracker Suite* (Peter Ilyich Tchaikovsky), *Symphonie Fantastique* (Hector Berlioz), *La Mer* (Claude Debussy), *Mr. Bach Comes to Call* (Toronto Boys Choir and Studio Arts Orchestra)

Music for Dancing, Patriotic Songs, and Marching Songs
Examples: *Play Your Instruments* (Ella Jenkins), Sousa marches, Strauss waltzes, *Swan Lake* (Peter Ilyich Tchaikovsky)

Music from Various Historical Periods
Examples: *Dance of the Renaissance* (Richard Searles & Gilbert Yslas), *Shake It to the One You Love the Best: Play Songs and Lullabies from Black Musical Traditions* (various artists), *Harpsichord Music* (Jean-Philippe Rameau)

Music by Contemporary Artists
Examples: *Who's Afraid of Opera* video (Joan Sutherland), Beverly Sills, Stevie Wonder, Luciano Pavarotti, *Songbird* (Kenny G)

Story Songs for Quiet Listening
Examples: "The Ugly Duckling" from *A Child's Celebration of Song* (Danny Kaye), "Puff the Magic Dragon" from *Peter, Paul, & Mommy* (Peter, Paul, & Mary), "My Grandfather's Clock" from *Family Folk Festival: A Multicultural Sing-Along* (Doc Watson), "Mail Myself to You" from *Special Delivery* (John McCutcheon), "The Circus Song" from *Family Folk Festival: A Multicultural Sing-Along* (Maria Muldaur)

Sources for Children's Recordings

Children's Circle	Music for Little People
Weston, CT 06883	Post Office Box 1460
(800) KIDS-VID	1144 Redway Drive
	Redway, CA 95560
	(800) 346-4445
Educational Record Center	Redleaf Press
Building 400, Suite 400	450 North Syndicate Suite 5
1575 Northside Drive	St. Paul, MN 55104-4125
Atlanta, GA 30318-4298	(800) 423-8309
(800) 438-1637	

Figure 4.5   *(Continued)*

- Use lined poster paper to create a song chart that older students can read.
- Create a rebus (words and pictures) song sheet for children to use so that picture cues remind them of the content of each verse.
- Teach children the song one phrase or sentence at a time, then combine the phrases.
- Teach children the actions to an action song first, then teach them to sing the words (or vice versa).

Variety, both in your music/movement teaching strategies and in the materials you select, will help maintain children's interest and encourage participation.

In the role of planner you will no doubt want to develop thematic units. Figure 4.6 is a thematic unit on African rhythms and harmonies.

What Is a Teaching Theme?

A teaching theme begins with the concepts that children are expected to acquire as a result of the theme. Using those concepts as a foundation, the teacher identifies a variety of activities that will further develop those concepts. Other concepts suggested by the experiences can also be identified and elaborated on as they emerge from the experiences and the children's interests.

Concepts to Be Developed

Concept #1: Rhythm is the pattern that we hear in music; rhythm is what some people call the beat.

Introduction to Concept #1: Use a drum to demonstrate a clear, steady rhythm and a random bunch of sounds. Then play a song with a strong, steady beat that children can easily pick out and replicate on their drums. Ask children to invent rhythms on coffee can or oatmeal box drums. Share the picture book *To Be a Drum* (Coleman, 2000).

Concept #2: Harmony is what makes music blend together well; harmony makes music pleasing to the ear.

Introduction to Concept #2: Use a simple musical instrument, such as a toy xylophone, to illustrate two notes played simultaneously. After each combination of notes, ask children whether the two sounded good together or not so good. Explain that when the notes complement one another and sound good together, it is called harmony.

Activities

Pulling Together Tie a rope around a relatively heavy object, such as a small desk, and ask several of the children to pull it across the floor. Listen to "Harambe," an African chant that means "Let's all pull together," from the album *The Evolution of Gospel* by The Sounds of Blackness (1991). Point out to the children that this is a work song, one that will enable them to work more effectively because they can tug in rhythm to the song. Play the song again and tap the rhythm on a drum or sticks. Tell the children to coordinate their pulling and to tug only when they hear the beat. Compare the progress that they made in moving the object in an uncoordinated way with the progress they made when they synchronized their pulling and worked together. Measure the distance that the object moved each time and contrast the two.

Talking Drums Tell the children that you are going to answer their questions yes or no by playing a drum. Invite them to guess whether your answer is yes or no by listening alone. Demonstrate with a simple question (e.g., "Can a dog fly?"). Hit the drum sharply once for no. Then demonstrate with another question (e.g., "Can a

(Continued)

Figure 4.6
Sample Teaching Theme on African Rhythms and Harmonies

cow moo?") and play a light roll of the drum with your fingertips to mimic the sound of the word *yes.* Use the *All for Freedom* recording by Sweet Honey in the Rock (1989) to explain why drums are so important to the African culture. For older children, invite them to generate a list of other nonverbal methods of communication (e.g., smoke signals, the flash of a mirror, a telegraph, or signal flags). Then ask them to make a list of devices we use to amplify, transmit, and enhance verbal communication (e.g., a cellular phone, microphones, walkie-talkies, letters, or a paper-cup-and-string telephone). Look at a chart of the universal symbol codes for *school crossing, danger, stop,* etc. and/or look at books that combine pictures with words to communicate, such as Marc Brown's *Hand Rhymes* (1985), *If You're Happy and You Know It* (Weiss, 1987), or *"I Can't," Said the Ant* (Cameron, 1961). Ask children if they are aware of any other cultures that used pictures to communicate (e.g., Egyptian hieroglyphics, Native Americans).

Sets and Subsets Make a list of activities and ask the children to classify them into two groups: things they can do all by themselves (e.g., roller skating, riding a bike, reading a book, or putting together a puzzle) and things that they cannot do without others (e.g., playing a lotto game, playing in a rhythm band, or using a seesaw). For older children, introduce the concept of the intersection of sets using hula hoops or circles of yarn as Venn diagrams. Include a list of things that lend themselves to individual and group participation, such as jumping rope.

Chants and Rap Listen to a recorded chant on an album by the Grammy award–winning Zulu a capella choral group Ladysmith Black Mambazo, or watch their performance on Paul Simon's *Graceland* video. Then teach the children to sing the African nonsense chant "Che Che Koolay" and compare/contrast it with American children's playground chants on the album *Where I Come From! Poems and Songs from Many Cultures* (Cockburn & Steinbergh, 1991). Use the work chant/song "There Come Our Mothers" by Ladysmith Black Mambazo and a children's chorus (1994) to sing a song in two languages. Use "Fiesta Musical" (Serafin, 1994), a Latino rap song, as an introduction to rap.

Life in Africa Develop children's understanding of African culture by reading books such as *A is for Africa* by Ifeoma Oneyefulu (1997), *A Country Far Away* by Nigel Gray (1998), *The Village of Round and Square Houses* and *Darkness and the Butterfly* by Ann Grifalconi (1986, 1987), and *Galimoto* and *When Africa Was Home* by Karen Williams (1990, 1994).

Figure 4.6   *(Continued)*

Teachers as Facilitators

Teachers have a responsibility to facilitate children's ideas about music and movement. Ms. Kelly, a preschool teacher, notices that Kai, Andre, and Tyler are working together in the block area. "Let's make a video," Tyler says, taking two of the oblong blocks and placing them together in front of one of her eyes. "You guys be the band." Kai picks up a long block, placing his left hand near the top of it and propping the other end on the waistband of his jeans. Making a metallic sound, he draws his other hand in a strumming motion across the block and begins to move as he has seen MTV and VH1 performers do. Meanwhile, Andre picks up a cylindrical block and holds it in front of his mouth. "This is my microphone thing," he announces. Ms. Kelly, observing from nearby, asks if the children would like some music to use. She brings over a small CD player and pops in James Taylor and Carly Simon's recording of "Mockingbird," which the children have heard and sung before. Tyler "videotapes" with her block cameras from every angle, and Andre and Kai perform their folk song variation.

Teachers as Observers

In the role of observer, teachers notice how children are making music, movement, and dance a part of their daily lives. Three-year-old Tracy is playing in the housekeeping area. She has the baby doll propped on her hip as she stirs the soup at the stove. Clearly, Tracy has observed the multitasking of homemaking and child care. When she is satisfied that the soup is "enough peppery," she moves to the rocking chair, where she wraps the doll in a blanket, begins to rock, and softly sings an invented lullaby. Observing Tracy's play provides her teacher with important information concerning this young child's increasing knowledge of music; she notices that Tracy understands the use of soft dynamics, a slow melodic line, and a less lively rhythmic pattern for a soothing song.

Participating in a rhythm band teaches both musical skills and cooperation.

When sharing music with young children, watch for these behaviors (Jalongo & Collins, 1985):

1. *What parts of the activity generate the most response?* Without prompting, children may clap, sway from side to side, bounce up and down, or associate specific words with actions. When singing, children do not usually sing every word. They may join in by singing just one word, a phrase, the first word of a verse, or the chorus.

2. *When do children follow along best?* Experiment with different methods of presenting concepts to children and note which are most effective. Try to relate explanations to something that the children have all experienced—asking, for example, "Can you make the halves of your coconut shells sound like the clip-clop of a horse's feet?"

3. *How do children use music spontaneously?* Note when and where children burst into song, dance around, or use musical instruments. If talk with a parent reveals that a child who never sings at circle time is singing away as she rides home in the car, an audiotape of the class singing might be sent home to build the child's confidence. If children seek a quiet corner in the classroom to play their instruments, a new music center and better room arrangement might be the answer. If a field trip is planned, including music and song in those plans might make it more successful as children and adults learn new camp songs and share favorites. By keeping in mind that the purpose is to support children's growth, teachers can provide the best possible experiences for their students. Figure 4.7 provides a listing of some typical classroom instruments.

A well-balanced program contains many different types of music. Research suggests that children generally prefer music and songs that have dominant rhythm patterns, repetition, and nonsense syllables; evoke a mood (such as calm or lively); emphasize enjoyment; suggest enactment and movement; and tell a story (Bayless & Ramsey, 1990).

MEETING STANDARDS

Music Educators National Conference and National Dance Standards

In general, appropriate music activities for children include singing songs together, playing and listening to records and tapes, learning the names and uses of musical instruments, discovering ways of making sounds, experiencing the different ways that music makes us feel, learning to participate with music through physical action and song, discovering rhythms in everyday life, observing different instruments being played, and playing simple musical instruments (Taylor, 1999). What principles should guide teachers as they strive to incorporate music, movement, and dance into the curriculum? Music Educators National Conference (MENC) and the National Dance Association (NDA) are the major organizations that have set the standards for pre-K through high school in music, movement, and dance. They offer detailed recommendations concerning opportunities to learn as well as criteria for appropriate facilities, curriculum and scheduling, staffing, materials,

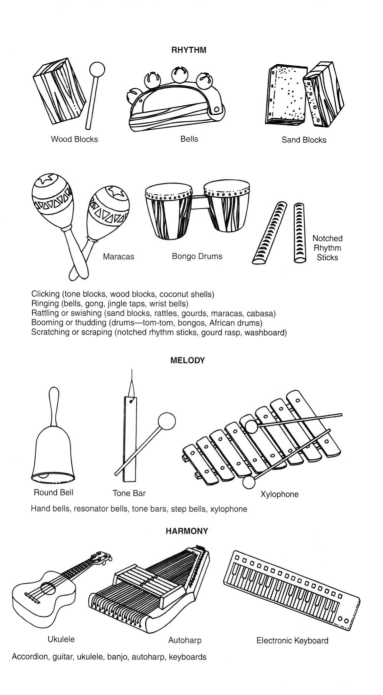

RHYTHM

Wood Blocks

Bells

Sand Blocks

Maracas

Bongo Drums

Notched Rhythm Sticks

Clicking (tone blocks, wood blocks, coconut shells)
Ringing (bells, gong, jingle taps, wrist bells)
Rattling or swishing (sand blocks, rattles, gourds, maracas, cabasa)
Booming or thudding (drums—tom-tom, bongos, African drums)
Scratching or scraping (notched rhythm sticks, gourd rasp, washboard)

MELODY

Round Bell

Tone Bar

Xylophone

Hand bells, resonator bells, tone bars, step bells, xylophone

HARMONY

Ukulele

Autoharp

Electronic Keyboard

Accordion, guitar, ukulele, banjo, autoharp, keyboards

Figure 4.7
Simple Musical Instruments
Sources for classroom instruments: *Suzuki, Rhythm Band, Inc., and Music for Little People.*

and equipment. Figure 4.8 offers a general framework of beliefs governing music, movement, and dance that is based on the recommendations of MENC and NDA.

The following section identifies key standards from Music Educators National Conference (Consortium of the National Arts Education Associations, 1994) that guide music education and offers examples of classroom activities that support each standard.

Singing, Alone and with Others, a Varied Repertoire of Music

Even for the very young child, singing can be a part of the day-to-day curriculum. MENC guidelines suggest that 12 percent of every day be spent in activities that

---

- All children have potential in music and movement.
- All children bring their own unique interests and abilities to the music and movement learning environment.
- Very young children are capable of developing critical thinking skills through musical ideas and movement activities.
- Children come to early childhood music and movement experiences with diverse backgrounds.
- Children should experience exemplary musical sounds, activities, and materials.
- Young children should not be pressured to perform on stage with an audience.
- Children's music and movement activities should be enjoyable and inaugurate a lifelong appreciation for music and movement.
- Children learn best in safe, pleasant physical and social environments.
- Diverse learning environments and varied opportunities are essential in order to serve the developmental needs of many children.
- Children need effective, enthusiastic adult models.

The National Dance Association believes that all children should acquire the following abilities in dance:

1. *Movement mechanics.* Students can do the movement they choreographed with attention to transitions, flow through phrases, and correct techniques.
2. *Spatial awareness.* Students demonstrate appropriate diagonal, circular, level, or zigzag motion in relation to other persons and space.
3. *Timing and rhythm.* Students dance with correct phrasing and counts per measure of music.
4. *Dynamics.* Students demonstrate contrasts between fast and slow, sharp and flowing motions.
5. *Performance.* Students demonstrate appropriate stage presence and facial expressions and don't let mistakes keep them from completing the dance.

Figure 4.8

A Framework of Beliefs about Young Children, Music, Movement, and Dance

Note. Adapted from Palmer & Sims (1993), Blizard (1996).

involve music. Choose songs that encourage active involvement; relate to children's interests; engage the whole child; have repetitive, easy-to-learn phrases; and emphasize rhyme, rhythm, and alliteration. One excellent resource for teachers that supports both music education and literacy with print is the song picture book (Jalongo & Ribblett, 1997). A song picture book is an illustrated version of a song's lyrics (Jalongo, 2004). Often these books bring a familiar song to life and provide the music, such as *That Dancin' Dolly*, a version of the folk song "Buffalo Gals"; sometimes the books are accompanied by a recording, such as *Over in the Meadow* (Keats, 1965); and sometimes they tell the history of the song, such as *Follow the Drinking Gourd* (Winter, 1988). Of course, teachers and/or children can also design original illustrations to accompany song charts or books. A teacher might invite children to invent new verses for a song, beginning with simple substitutions such as "If you're happy and you know it, _____," or older children can experiment with writing and illustrating song parodies such as *On Top of Spaghetti* (Glazer, 1982), a parody of "On Top of Old Smokey," or *Old MacDonald Had a Woodshop* (Shulman, 2004), a parody of "Old MacDonald Had a Farm." It is easy to locate these books at the library by conducting a search that uses the categories of "picture book" and "song."

Performing on Instruments, Alone and with Others, a Varied Repertoire of Music

Having high-quality recorded music in the classroom is much easier today than ever before. Why not have the children play rhythm sticks along with Hap Palmer, shake bell bracelets along to Leroy Anderson's "Sleigh Ride," or use guiros, hand drums, and tambourines to accompany Carlos Santana? Taggart (2000) states, "Children must be immersed in a playful musical environment in which their musical utterances are nurtured and treasured" (p. 24). Providing simple rhythm band instruments for children to play is naturally motivating. Even if resources are limited, rhythm sticks can be made from dowel rods, sandpaper blocks from scraps of wood and sandpaper, and drums from pieces of inner tube stretched over coffee cans. For many ideas on making simple instruments, see *Listen!* (Wilt & Watson, 1977). Other inexpensive instruments such as kazoos, tuned bells, or toy electric keyboards are another resource for making music. Additionally, try organizing a musical instrument drive in your neighborhood where unused instruments stored away are put back into service in the classroom. Elementary school children often begin their music education by learning to play plastic flutes called recorders with the music specialist. Selecting a song that the whole class can play will allow for "half the group singing while the other half plays" types of performances. Another way to provide varied opportunities for performing music is to designate a child who is learning to play an instrument in band or orchestra to play along on his or her instrument to the morning's patriotic or opening song.

Another way of performing music relies on children's voices. Older students can learn to sing the parts of songs individually and then blend their voices together during a multi-age grouping rehearsal. One teacher involved the second-, third-, and fourth-grade classes in learning different parts of a song and recording them. That way, when each class came in to rehearse, they could practice blending their voices together even if schedules did not permit a total group rehearsal. The result was a stirring performance at the school's spring concert.

Improvising Melodies, Variations, and Accompaniments

Improvisation is often neglected because it requires materials and time as well as thoughtful planning and guidance. The Suzuki String Method, for example, introduces children to improvisation in a gradual way. Young Suzuki violinists learn a very simple version of "Twinkle, Twinkle Little Star" that begins with a simple back-and-forth bow stroke. After that is mastered, new challenges are posed, such as the "Mississippi hot dog" bow stroke, which can be identified by the rhythm of its four short strokes followed by two longer strokes.

Another opportunity for improvisation is in inventing musical accompaniment for stories read aloud. "Jack and the Beanstalk" can be accompanied by a slide whistle to represent characters' ascent and descent on the stalk, with drums of different sizes to represent Jack's and the giant's footsteps, or with a catchy melody to accompany "Fee fi fo fum. . . ." Most high-quality recordings for young children contain at least one story with sound effects and music, such as "Bear Hunt" (Bayes, 1983), that can be used to illustrate the idea. Older students might use a story about a journey, such as *Frog Odyssey* (Snape & Snape, 1991) or *How Many Days to America: A Thanksgiving Story* (Bunting, 1990), to develop a corresponding musical journey (Mantione & Smead, 2003).

Composing and Arranging Music Within Specified Guidelines
Reading and Notating Music

One of the best ways of leading children to music is to provide an environment where they have the materials, time, and opportunity to discover and build their own knowledge about music (Fox, 1989; Upitis, 1990). A music laboratory is one way of achieving this. It functions much like a scientist's laboratory—it emphasizes active involvement and gives students a chance to explore and experiment with music. Work in the music laboratory is supported by teachers who observe, model, facilitate, encourage, comment on, and ask questions about the child's activities. In the music laboratory, children can compose, arrange, read, and notate music, depending on their interests and developmental levels.

Listening to, Analyzing, and Describing Music

Asking children to listen quietly to music provides a learning opportunity. One first-grade teacher broadened her students' listening opportunities by playing music every morning when the children arrived and creating a listening center with a variety of high-quality recordings. The teacher obtained, free of charge, recordings produced by different U.S. military bands and colleges' and universities' CDs of wind ensembles, concert bands, marching bands, orchestras, vocal groups, and jazz bands. Additionally, she borrowed CDs from the public library on a regular basis. As a result of her efforts to encourage children to listen to, analyze, and describe music, her first graders not only identified the mood that a particular piece evoked but also became adept at describing the emotion in music to others. Figure 4.9 suggests strategies for building concepts in music and dance.

Musical Element: Dynamics (Soft/Loud)

Reception

Even before birth, during the last months of pregnancy, infants have a hearing ability comparable to that of an adult, although the sounds they can hear while immersed in amniotic fluid are muffled. They startle to loud, sudden noises and are comforted by soft sounds, such as quiet music or a lullaby. Newborns and young infants benefit from listening to music of different types, including classical music, traditional lullabies, and music of many different types and cultures.

Imitation

Toddlers and young preschoolers can be helped to understand the distinction between loud and soft if these concepts are made sufficiently concrete. Allow children to directly experience what happens when the volume is turned down low and then turned up high on a piece of listening equipment. Try tapping a drum very softly, then loudly. Invite them to slap their thighs very softly, then louder, or tap their feet softly, then stomp their feet loudly. Get them to use the words *loud* and *soft* to refer to their experiences (e.g., the thunderstorm was loud, the sound of rain falling was soft).

Production

Most preschoolers are capable of demonstrating their understandings of dynamics by producing sounds. You might construct a large, cardboard dial that the children can see and ask them to begin singing, then allow children to operate the dial and "turn up" or "turn down" their voices.

Musical Element: Tempo (Fast/Slow)

Reception

While still in the hospital nursery, infants respond differentially to slow music, such as lullabies, and lively music, such as action songs. Babies become more active when lively music is played (Wilcox, 1994).

Imitation

Make the fast/slow aspect concrete by looking at things in nature. Look at animals that move quickly, others that move slowly. Ask children to show how they move slowly and quickly by walking/running or by making the wheels of their wheelchair move faster. Get children moving around the circle and ask them to change how they move in response to the music. Then play slow songs followed by fast songs.

Production

Invite children to work at the music center to create fast and slow songs using the props provided there. Children may, for example, create a lively chant or cheer to go along with pom-poms and create a slow song to accompany scarves or paper fans.

(Continued)

Figure 4.9
Strategies for Building Concepts in Music and Dance

Musical Element: Pitch (High/Low)

Reception

Even young infants are apparently able to distinguish between high and low pitches. If the same pitch is played repeatedly, the infant grows accustomed to it. But when a new pitch is introduced, babies will often begin to suck on a pacifier vigorously, indicating that they detect the difference and are interested again.

Imitation

Differences in pitch are often introduced to preschoolers as stair steps because this gives them a concrete way of relating to high and low pitches. Try using a wooden rocking boat set upside down and a set of tonal bells or a toy xylophone as a prop. Begin with very dramatic differences between pitches. After several demonstrations of moving up on top of the boat when the music goes higher, give children a chance to play this high/low game. The game can be made more challenging by choosing notes on the scale that are closer in pitch or by adding steps.

Production

Using a pitch pipe, keyboard, bells, or xylophone, play each note on the scale and ask children to "match" it with their voices. Teach children the song "Do Re Mi."

Musical Element: Rhythm (The Patterns of Sounds)

Reception

Even before birth, infants grow accustomed to rhythmic sounds of the mother's heartbeat and respiration. Hospital nurseries sometimes have toys or sound equipment that plays similar sounds to comfort newborns. Babies frequently relax and drift off to sleep from the rhythmic motion of a caregiver's gentle rocking, a car, a stroller, or a swing.

Imitation

Rocking and gently bouncing babies and toddlers as a part of playful games and nursery tunes teaches them the rudiments of rhythm. A child who learns to play "Pat a Cake" is imitating the rhythm.

Production

Even preschoolers can begin to move their bodies "in time" to the rhythm of the music if it is modeled for them. A good rhythm song for kindergarten and primary is "Horsey, Horsey" by Sharon, Lois, and Bram. The entire song follows the clip-clop of the horse's hooves, which can be produced by using rhythm sticks or tapping together the shells of an empty coconut.

Musical Element: Harmony (The Blending of Complementary Sounds)

Reception

From the earliest days of life, children are immersed in the harmonies of their cultures. There is ample evidence to suggest that an understanding of harmony is accelerated by early exposure and atrophies with disuse.

Figure 4.9 (*Continued*)

Imitation

An understanding of harmony is generally considered the last to develop. Make the complementarity of sounds concrete by playing two musical notes together on a keyboard. Ask children whether the notes sound better together or not. Consider watching a video of an African choir or inviting musicians whose work relies on close harmony, such as a barbershop quartet or folksingers, to perform for the class.

Production

It is not until elementary school that most children are taught to sing a song in two or three parts and harmonize their voices. A good recording is the Chenille Sisters.

Evaluating Music and Music Performances

Just as we compare and contrast versions of favorite pieces of children's literature, we can offer students the opportunity to hear several versions of musical works performed by different singers or instrumentalists. In doing so, we build skills of listening, discernment, and musical preference. Exposing children to the very best quality in music and musical experiences is essential. Provide high-quality recorded music, but also invite young performers from the upper grades in the district to be a part of the musical culture of the classroom. Sarah, the 9-year-old cellist from the fourth grade, cannot be expected to play like the celebrated artist Yo-Yo Ma, but kindergarten children will meet a child to whom they can relate doing something that is interesting and engaging musically.

Understanding Relationships Between Music, the Other Arts, and Disciplines Outside the Arts

Musical intelligence and bodily/kinesthetic intelligence are two distinctive "kinds of smart." As a result, children who perform well in academic subjects may or may not be gifted musically or kinesthetically. In a special project involving elementary school students that was designed to identify talent in the performing arts, 62 percent to 82 percent of those identified as gifted in dance had reading levels in the bottom half of the class, and 34 percent were below grade level in mathematics (Kay & Subotnik, 1994). Just imagine what might happen to these students if no educational opportunities in music and dance—a chance for them to shine—were available. They probably would exit the educational system early, disillusioned and defeated. If all children are at least given the opportunity to try various kinds of music and movement activities, they can begin to appreciate more fully the rich diversity among their classmates and to recognize that each person has unique strengths and talents. They also can begin to see the relationships among the various disciplines when teachers make those connections more explicit. A teacher of young children might connect music and movement with literacy learning by asking questions such as the following:

- Can you show me how Baby Bear might go for his walk as you move around the circle? Now let's see Papa Bear's walk. Now Mama Bear's.
- Which rhythm instrument will you choose for each billy goat in the story? Who can show me how the little billy goat would cross our balance beam bridge to this music?
- In the book *Color Dance* (Jonas, 1989a), the dancers made colors with their scarves. Can you mix the colors while you dance, too?

Understanding Music in Relation to History and Culture

Music and movement provide a common vehicle for children to know about, understand, appreciate, and preserve cultural traditions. Children can respond to dances from other cultures through recordings. Simple dances from the Far East, India, Africa, the Americas, and continental Europe can be taught using the Nonesuch Explorer series (Numbers 7–11) as a guide. Songs in picture book format such as *Tortillitas para Mama* (Griego, 1980), a Spanish work song, or *Moonsong Lullaby* (Highwater, 1981), a Native American lullaby, expose children to the language and music of other cultures. Music is also ideal for fostering multicultural appreciation as children listen to a collection of songs, chants, and poems from a wide array of ethnic and cultural groups through a musical collection such as *Where I Come From! Poems and Songs from Many Cultures* (Cockburn & Steinbergh, 1991). Music for Little People has a series of recordings that are collections of various types of music such as opera, show tunes, soul, lullabies, and dance music.

CONCLUSION

In a democratic society, the goal of teaching music is not to single out those who are gifted in music. Rather, the goal is to maximize the musical abilities of every child. All children need opportunities to develop their musical/rhythmic and bodily/kinesthetic intelligences; such opportunities should not be restricted to the privileged children whose parents and families can afford private lessons in settings outside of school. All adults who care about children need to ask themselves, "Do we value children's music, creative dance, and dance only for its imitation of adults' music and dance, or do we appreciate it in its own right?" Identifying young children as musicians or dancers should not be based on the expectation that they will demonstrate precocious musical behavior (Fox, 1991) or on the hope that they will become concert pianists, successful rock singers, or ballet prima donnas someday. Rather, the focus should be on music and dance for today and every day, music and dance for everyone.

There are music and movement activities suitable for every child, regardless of age, talent, or physical limitations. Leading children to music and movement is

Frequently Asked Questions About Music and Dance

Do parents and families really support music and dance in schools?

Participation in the arts is clouded by stereotypes, gender bias, and prejudice. In a qualitative study of parental attitudes toward arts education for children, most parents considered the arts feminine, frivolous, and nonessential to getting ahead in the "real world," other than occasionally teaching discipline (for example, practicing a musical instrument). They were conflicted about ways in which the arts affected social status, and even families that strongly supported arts education sometimes wanted it to be an extracurricular activity to preserve the exclusivity of their child's training (Gainer, 1997). Educators need to encourage parents, families, and communities to challenge the prevailing assumptions about creativity and talent (Kemple & Nissenberg, 2000; Kindler, 1997; Rotigel, 2003).

Isn't the purpose of a school music program to identify the children who have the talent to benefit from instruction?

Creative expression depends not on talent alone, but also on motivation, interest, effort, and opportunity. Contemporary psychologists are downplaying the role of innate talent and emphasizing instead deliberate practice (Ericcson & Charness, 1994). If it is talent we seek, then we must actively develop it rather than merely take notice of it after it has emerged. The appropriate role of education is to provide all children with a host of thoughtfully designed experiences in creative representation, beginning in early childhood (Brickman, 1999; Chenfeld, 2002) and continuing throughout school (Torff, 2000).

What kinds of adaptations are made for children with special needs to enable them to participate in music and movement?

Many accommodations can enable a child to enjoy and participate more fully in music and movement. Take, for example, a child with a physical challenge such as cystic fibrosis, which can cause a deterioration in breath control and affect singing. You may find that a child with physical limitations can participate in singing if given an opportunity to rest for a moment, or you might invite the child to sing just one part of the song. A child's cognitive limitations can make it difficult for him or her to recall words and melodies, focus on the music activity, or follow directions to an action song (Darrow, 1985). You could help such a child by using visual, verbal, and physical cues; providing more repetition; reducing distractions and background noise; breaking tasks into smaller segments; and ritualizing procedures (Darrow, 1985). Cerebral palsy affects a child's motor skills and may prevent participation in certain movement activities. Yet teachers who are alert to each child's capabilities might discover that the child with cerebral palsy sometimes has more motor control on one side of the body than on the other and can therefore participate to some extent in motor activities. That child might enjoy clapping along with the music by using one hand to tap on the table or slap his or her knee, for example.

Hearing impairments of various types obviously affect listening capacities and pose another challenge to the child (Darrow & Loomis, 1999). But you may find, for instance, that a child with hearing loss has enough residual hearing to perceive a song played on earphones, or has low-frequency acuity and can hear low-pitched sounds, such as a bass drum. Even a child who is deaf can feel the rhythm of the vibrations by gently touching the speakers of the record player. For the child with attention disorders, creative dance is a way to concentrate because "dancing involves making movement significant in and of itself. The first step in making movement dance is to pay attention to it" (Stinson, 1990, p. 35). Often, children with special needs are so motivated to participate in music that they function at the highest possible level.

also for all early childhood educators, regardless of their performance skills in music or dance. When teachers make music, movement, and dance an integral part of the school day, children's development in all areas—cognitive, physical, emotional, social, and aesthetic—is supported and enriched.

CHAPTER SUMMARY

1. Each child develops musical/rhythmic and bodily/kinesthetic intelligences through interaction with others, and enjoyment of a wide variety of music and movement suited to his or her developmental level.
2. The goal of music, movement, and dance activities is to support every child's growth in these domains and develop skills in each area beginning in the earliest days of life.
3. Research on the human brain suggests that experiences with music, movement, and dance exert an enduring influence on the way that the brain responds, functions, and ultimately is organized.
4. From a cognitive perspective, children proceed through the enactive, iconic, and symbolic modes in their understandings about music.
5. A supportive physical and emotional environment, positive adult and peer interaction, and varied opportunities to enjoy and create music, movement, and dance contribute to the child's overall development.
6. Teachers fulfill their roles and responsibilities in music education when they select, present, and evaluate musical experiences effectively; when they function as motivators, planners, facilitators, and observers; and when they integrate music, movement, and dance throughout the school day and across various subject areas.

Discuss: Your Ideas About Music

1. Compare and contrast the beliefs, values, and attitudes that underlie a program to maximize every child's musical talent with those that seek to identify precocity in music. Use your readings to support the philosophy of building every child's abilities.
2. A parent tells you, "I don't sing to my child because I never learned to play an instrument, but I play his song tape for him at night." How would you respond? Why?
3. An administrator observes the children briefly during your lesson, then asks, "Why are they having music during social studies?" How would you support your decision without becoming defensive?
4. If money were available through the budget, a donation, or a small grant, what music, movement, and dance materials would you purchase for students at various ages and stages? Why?

Chapter 5

Inviting Children's
Participation in the Dramatic Arts

Of all of the arts, drama involves the participant most fully: intellectually, emotionally, physically, verbally, and socially. As players, children assume the roles of others, where they learn and become sensitive to the problems and values of persons different from themselves. As spectators, children become involved vicariously in the adventures of the characters on stage.

Nellie McCaslin, 2000, p. 4

CLASSROOM PERSPECTIVES ON CHILDREN'S PARTICIPATION IN THE DRAMATIC ARTS

Preschool–Kindergarten

In Mrs. Paitsel's preschool class, the children have been reading *Brown Bear, Brown Bear, What Do You See?* (Martin, 1967) and are now ready to enact it. The children choose a headband that resembles one of the animals in the book. As Mrs. Paitsel reads the book aloud, the children pantomime how the animal moves when they hear their animal's name read. Mrs. Paitsel rereads the story until all the children, including Andrew, a young boy who uses a wheelchair, have an opportunity to participate. Through this dramatic arts experience, the children warm up their bodies and use their imagination in a low-risk environment that promotes successful participation for all children.

First Grade–Second Grade

In Ms. Clark's first-grade class, five children have asked to enact "The Little Red Hen." Florence, a nonreader, has volunteered to be the narrator. Jesse, a shy, obese African American boy, has asked to play the role of the hen. Ms. Clark knows how important child-initiated activity is for children. Her first graders thought of dramatizing a favorite, familiar story. They also selected and negotiated roles, jointly planned costumes, and chose their audience, and Ms. Clark capitalized on their interests. A simple enactment activity like this one helps children learn about themselves and others, develop a sense of belonging in a community of learners, gain self-confidence, and master skills and concepts in meaningful situations. Analyzing the children's behavior reveals how important these goals are in every classroom.

Jesse usually speaks softly and does not enunciate clearly, but because he wants to be the Little Red Hen, he practices and refines his speaking skills. Florence is not yet reading, but her role as narrator has prompted her to listen to a tape recording over and over again until she can rely on familiarity with the story to read the book aloud.

Third Grade–Fourth Grade

Mr. Carson's fourth graders are reviewing for their social studies test on the Boston Tea Party. An essential part of their review is the preparation and videotaping of a news broadcast of the actual events prior to and on December 17, 1773. The children, representing different characters, assemble in corners of the classroom depicting the settings of England, Boston, and Washington, DC. Newscasters Dana, Brandon, and Emma are "Live on the Scene" at their different locations ready to interview people about their role in the historic event. Their researching, writing, rehearsing, and teamwork involved them in a meaningful learning experience that clearly reflects the knowledge and understanding of this historic event.

In each of these scenarios, the teachers engaged the children in purposeful and meaningful activities and supported their learning through dramatization. The activities supported many curriculum goals and standards while engaging the children in creative problem solving. Why should teachers devote so much time to drama? This chapter explores the role of the dramatic arts as an important instructional strategy that makes learning real and meaningful to children.

THEORETICAL AND RESEARCH BASE: WHAT DO WE MEAN BY DRAMATIC ARTS?

Drama, often called *enactment*, emerges from the spontaneous play of children and uses the art of theater to enhance the participants' awareness of self, others, and the world in which they live. In drama, children act "as if" their imagined world were an actual world and represent familiar feelings, thoughts, and actions for themselves rather than memorizing a script for an audience (Gelineau, 2004; McCaslin, 2000; Wilhelm & Edmiston, 1998). Drama not only provides children with a meaningful form of communication and an opportunity to imagine possibilities, but also is a useful learning resource for higher-order thinking, problem solving, feelings, and reflection as children show what they know through oral communication. Drama also provides a strong foundation for literacy development, because it supports all four of the language arts—listening, speaking, reading, and writing (Cecil & Lauritzen, 1994; Furman, 2000b; Heller, 1996; Hennings, 2003; McMaster, 1998; Wilhelm & Edmiston, 1998).

Drama experiences tap into four kinds of intelligences that capitalize on children's learning potential: (1) bodily/kinesthetic, (2) verbal/linguistic, (3) interpersonal, and (4) intrapersonal intelligence (Gardner, 1993a, 1993b). Gardner's work suggests that people develop and learn in many ways and that neither children nor adults possess intelligence that is "fixed" in one area. Children, like adults, depend on different areas of their brain in different situations, at different times, and for different reasons. As children act out stories, situations, and ideas, they use their bodily/kinesthetic and/or verbal/linguistic intelligence to express themselves through gesture, voice, or movement. They also use their interpersonal intelligence to work cooperatively to determine how to dramatize a favorite story or interact with an audience, and they use their intrapersonal intelligence to access their own

TABLE 5.1   Multiple Intelligences Most Related to Enactment

Type	Definition	Relation to Enactment	Enactment Examples
Bodily/Kinesthetic	The ability to use the body to express feelings and thoughts and solve problems; to use hands to handle objects skillfully.	Offers children a concrete, specific, and personal way to develop abstract thought and represent their knowledge through "hands-on" experiences.	• Role play • Story re-enactments • Pantomime • Dramatic play • Dance and movement
Interpersonal	The ability to distinguish among the intentions, moods, and feelings of others by being sensitive to voice, gesture, and facial expressions, and to respond sensitively to others' feelings and moods.	Enables children to explore feelings, moods, and points of view of others and to respond sensitively to them.	• Improvisation • Pantomime • Role play • Pretend • Puppets
Intrapersonal	The ability to detect one's own moods, needs, desires, and to look both inward and outward.	Enables children to reflect on and explore their own feelings and moods in socially acceptable ways and to test out their own feelings and emotions as well as their responses to others.	• Dramatic play • Pantomime • Improvisation • Readers' theater • Puppets
Verbal/Linguistic	The ability to use words and language to express one's own thoughts and to understand others.	Enables children to create dialogue, solve problems, and express feelings, thoughts, and ideas.	• Dramatic play • Improvisation • Readers' theater • Puppets • Role play • Pretend • Story re-enactments

feelings through different forms of role play and pantomime. These ways of expression offer a window into children's understandings. Table 5.1 lists and defines these four types of intelligences, relates them to enactment, and supplies some enactment examples.

Experiences with enactment help all children succeed in school by uncovering their hidden strengths or by challenging undeveloped areas of learning. Consequently, opportunities for drama belong everywhere in the curriculum (Heller, 1996; Hennings, 2003; Bromley, 1998).

TEACHERS' REFLECTIONS ON THE DRAMATIC ARTS

Preservice Teachers

"I now know there is an important role for an audience when using some forms of drama in the classroom. The children will always have some special involvement."

"I learned how drama helps make language arts more concrete because the child can actually interpret the character."

Inservice Teachers

"I used story drama in my fourth-grade class for the first time this year. I noticed that the children were empowered by either retelling or re-creating versions of their own, and that they had a much clearer understanding of sequential story events. Their retellings grew increasingly more accurate."

"I learned to address the role of the child rather than the child when intervening in dramatic play. For instance, if John is playing the role of the wolf, I say, 'Wolf, what are you going to do now that . . . '"

Your Reflections

- What role do you think the dramatic arts have in the curriculum?

- How would you integrate drama activities and experiences in your curriculum?

- How might your knowledge and beliefs about drama enhance or inhibit children's self-expression and creative thinking?

The Meaning of Enactment

Five-year-old Haley was captivated by the story of *Perfect the Pig* (Jeschke, 1985). In this story, a homeless, flying piglet is found, loved, and cared for by a young woman who decides to name the pig Perfect. Perfect is stolen and abused by a man who operates a carnival sideshow, then is happily reunited with the woman when a judge awards her custody. After hearing this story, Haley pretends to be Perfect, experiencing the feelings and thoughts of the pig. She also decides which props ("I'll need wings") and behaviors ("This is how he oinks when he needs help") she needs to enact that role.

Enactment occurs when children adopt the actions, feelings, thoughts, and behaviors of people in particular situations. This ability emerges at about age 3 and signals the child's developing imagination. Enactment is potentially the most powerful kind of learning because children can:

- Assume roles, create dialogue, feel emotions, use their bodies, and make decisions.

- Use their past and present experiences to talk about and solve problems.
- Develop knowledge of appropriate roles, actions, and behaviors.
- See others' points of view.
- Try out new and emerging skills.
- Explore the forms and functions of language (Shaftel & Shaftel, 1982; Gelineau, 2004; Wilhelm & Edmiston, 1998).

Children learn about their world not only from their interactions with it, but also from the way their world interacts with them. These concrete, personal experiences provide the basis for their developing abstract, interpersonal knowledge, which comprises much of the learning that goes on in schools today. Because drama is always concrete, specific, and personal, it helps children more easily understand how their physical and social worlds work and interact (Johnson, 1998; McCaslin, 2000). In other words, the dramatic mode is a powerful way of knowing.

Infants and toddlers enact events that they have directly experienced, such as diapering and feeding; preschool and kindergarten children add to these incidents with more imaginative and make-believe situations, such as preparing meals for a family or taking care of a baby. Children through fourth grade often

Enactment is a powerful kind of learning.

imagine themselves in real-life problem-solving situations, such as controlling a space shuttle in outer space or enacting their own or others' narrative stories and historical events like the Revolutionary War or Greek mythology. Enactment helps all children stretch their imaginations, share experiences in a low-risk setting, and explore feelings, emotions, and ideas in socially acceptable ways (Heinig, 1993; Heller, 1996; Roe, Smith, & Burns, 2005).

Forms of Enactment

Enactment occurs in three forms: (1) informal drama, (2) story or interpretive drama, and (3) formal or scripted drama. These drama forms can be differentiated according to their degree of spontaneity versus formality (Tompkins, 2002). Following are the characteristics and an example of each form.

1. **Informal drama** is the earliest and most spontaneous type of enactment. It includes dramatic and sociodramatic play as well as pantomime and some movement activities. In informal drama, young children spontaneously take on a role or behavior of someone else (such as pretending to direct traffic as a police officer), use an object to stand for something else (such as sitting on a block and driving an "imaginary tractor" around fields), and use make-believe to act out familiar events (such as enacting a trip to a fast-food restaurant). There is no audience and the teacher serves as an observer or facilitator. Older children who enact their own scripts base them on familiar life situations (such as family celebrations of holidays), literature (such as a play based on the dramatic story of a little fruit bat, *Stellaluna* [Cannon, 1993]), or media experiences (such as the film *Jumanji*).

2. **Story or interpretive drama** involves interpreting someone else's ideas and words rather than creating new ideas and words. Children through Grade 4 often enact favorite stories they have heard and read or they create original stories. Take, for example, the book *Amazing Grace* (Hoffman, 1991). Grace is an African American child with a flair for drama. She pretends to be a nurse whose patients' lives are in her hands, imagines that she is the African trickster Anansi the Spider, and pretends to be a peg-legged pirate. When the class decides to enact Peter Pan, her peers tell Grace that she cannot play the lead role because she is female and black. With her mother's and grandmother's support, Grace pursues her dream. This story really lends itself to interpretation because Grace is practicing some form of enactment on every page. Story drama is particularly valuable in stimulating children's oral language and literacy learning.

3. **Formal or scripted drama,** the most structured form of drama, involves a polished production of a prepared script before an audience (McCaslin, 2000). In scripted drama, the children memorize lines and someone directs. Because it is product-oriented, scripted drama focuses more on technique rather than spontaneous self-expression (Bolton, 1985) and is most appropriate for children in Grade 4 or beyond. These children often write and perform, and may even direct, their own formal dramatic productions. Current thinking in the field of early childhood education is against the use of formal or scripted drama for young children through the primary grades unless, of course, children choose to create and produce their own

plays (Tompkins, 2002). Table 5.2 arranges these types of enactment from least to most formal, compares the preparation time needed for each form, contrasts the role of the players and audience, analyzes materials needed, and examines implications for teachers.

Informal drama and story drama are the only forms of drama that belong in the early childhood curriculum. They offer purposeful ways to develop children's oral language, literacy understandings, imagination, thinking, nonverbal communication,

TABLE 5.2   Three Types of Drama Activities

Informal Drama/Dramatic Play	Story or Interpretive Drama	Formal/Scripted Drama
Least Formal ◄————————————————————————————————► Most Formal		
Characteristics		
Unrehearsed, spontaneous, invented enactment of roles and behaviors of familiar people or characters. Most characteristic of 3- to 8-year-olds.	Invented, improvised interpretation of ideas and stories using voices, gestures, and facial expressions; involves some rehearsal and is more formal.	Memorizing a written script; performing polished plays before an audience.
Preparation Time		
Minimal: children initiate roles, behaviors, actions, dialogue, and movements based on something familiar.	Moderate: children rehearse reading, interpret story, and enact roles.	Extensive: children memorize parts, dialogue, and gestures.
Roles of Players and Audience		
Active: children move freely from role of audience to that of player; not designed for an audience.	Active: children read parts individually or as members of a group.	Passive: roles must be rehearsed to play; audience watches.
Materials		
Simple, familiar props; some realistic.	Simple or no props.	Elaborate costumes, props, scenery.
Implications for the Classroom		
Exerts powerful influence on children's learning and development; can be used with children's favorite or original stories.	Increases children's confidence in using scripted drama; allows for cooperative work with peers.	Should be used only at the children's suggestion and be child-directed.

and self-confidence. All three types are appropriate for children in Grade 4. In the next section we will see how drama supports all children's learning.

✲ THE IMPORTANCE OF THE DRAMATIC ARTS IN THE CURRICULUM

For all children, the dramatic arts are a powerful vehicle for understanding difficult concepts through enacting ideas, engaging in genuine dialogue that is based upon shared meaning, and thinking and feeling about oneself and others (Fennessey, 1995; Furman, 2000a; Gelineau, 2004; Podlozny, 2000; Verriour, 1994; Wilhelm & Edmiston, 1998). This is a particularly important strategy for second-language learners. The dramatic arts develop understanding in four main ways.

1. *Dramatic arts value and respect children's individuality and creative expression.* Drama builds positive self-concepts in children as they participate in experiences that have no right or wrong answers (McCaslin, 2000). Each child's interpretation of a role is unique. One child might play the role of the wolf in "Little Red Riding Hood" as sly, another as mean, and still another as foolish. These possibilities help each child feel good about involvement in a group experience. Children's language and culture gain respect as children participate in drama activities both in their native language and in the majority language of the culture.

2. *Dramatic arts offer a means for cooperative learning and teamwork through shared experiences.* One group of fourth graders, for example, asked their teacher if they could make up a skit. With only 40 minutes to prepare, they decided on the theme of ancient Rome, a topic they were studying, and wrote a script about a chariot race and a slave who wins his freedom by defeating a gladiator. The group collected props such as jump ropes, construction paper, and rulers and invited their classmates to watch their skit and become improvised characters.

3. *Dramatic arts enable children to make abstract situations meaningful and personalize real-life situations.* After 4-year-old Mary's puppy died, she initiated an animal rescue theme play. In her dramas, unlike the real-life situation, Mary was always able to save the animal's life, enabling her to understand loss and cope with grief.

4. *Dramatic arts provide opportunities to be actors and spectators.* Whether children are enacting or watching others enact, they are simultaneously imagining the situations and problems of others. After hearing a story about a Kwanzaa celebration, a small group of kindergartners shared dances, poetry, songs, and food to celebrate the bounty of the earth. As a result, the children functioned as actors for their peers during some parts of the event and as spectators of their peers during others.

The dramatic arts explicitly contribute to each academic area and enhance children's ability to learn in school settings. In the following enactment of a restaurant theme, Kellie and Tammie, 4-year-old twins, and Brenda, a college student, are co-playing. Consider how this dramatic play episode contributes to the twins' developing imaginative thinking, problem-solving ability, language and listening skills, perspective-taking ability, and appreciation of drama as an art form.

Some creative drama experiences provide opportunities for children to be both actors and spectators.

Kellie: Oh, here's your table. *(she gestures toward the table)*
Brenda: Well, what should we eat, Tammie? What do you have here, Kellie?
Kellie: Well, we have pork chops, lima beans, and fish sticks.
Tammie: That sounds good. We'll take it. *(Kellie exits and returns with a "tray"—two parts of a plastic sweater-drying rack)*

The girls continue their play, name their restaurant "King's," order drinks, and then ask for a check.

Tammie: I want my check to be five dollars.
Kellie: Five dollars . . . and eighty-six cents.
Tammie: Okay.
Brenda: Do you have any money?
Tammie: Oh, yeah. I have a lot of money. Oh. I forgot. I don't have a lot of money. *(starts rummaging through her purse and begins to giggle)*

In this restaurant scene, Kellie and Tammie were using drama to develop their imaginative thinking. Both girls' strong mental images of a restaurant enabled them to create and enact the roles of customer and server as well as to embellish and ad-lib the scenario they created. When Kellie needed a tray to serve the food in the restaurant, she was problem-solving as she used two parts of a plastic sweater-drying rack for this prop. Through drama, children relive their experiences by creating their own worlds and experiment with solutions to real-life problems (McCaslin, 2000).

Drama also provides meaningful opportunities for children to practice literacy skills. It elicits more verbal play and richer language than in any other setting (Christie & Johnson, 1983; Furman, 2000b; Tompkins, 2002), develops narrative competence when children invent stories that contain essential story elements, displays children's knowledge of the functions of reading and writing (McMaster, 1998; Wiltz & Fein, 1996), and increases both children's confidence in their abilities to speak language and the value they place on communicating precisely (McMaster, 1998). Play episodes such as this one give children opportunities to use all of the various forms and functions of language (Halliday, 1975).

Role enactment also develops children's perspective-taking ability. When children actually become someone else, they not only learn the behaviors and feelings of that character or role but also see how people affect others. By becoming slaves and gladiators in their skit, the students gained a deeper understanding of the masters' treatment of slaves and gladiators in ancient Rome and of their effect on them. Even very young children may glimpse insights that help in understanding people and, therefore, in living. In the restaurant episode, Kellie and Tammie practiced appropriate behaviors for eating in a restaurant. They also watched Brenda, the college student, model the customer role by asking, "Well, what should we eat, Tammie? What do you have here, Kellie?"

Through early drama experiences, children learn to appreciate drama as an art form. Today's children are tomorrow's audiences and players. School is an important context for them to gain an understanding of what drama is and how it comes into being.

Drama, in its many forms, is an important stimulus for creative thinking and expression. It enables children to express their thoughts, feelings, and ideas in both verbal and nonverbal ways. As so poignantly stated by Gavin Bolton (1985), a recognized expert in drama education, "Drama allows children to experience the complexities of today's world and to be prepared to live in the twenty-first century" (p. 156). Therefore, the dramatic arts are not a "frill"—they are a curricular basic.

CRITERIA FOR INTEGRATING THE DRAMATIC ARTS INTO THE CURRICULUM

Teachers exert a powerful influence over children's dramatic expression. When teachers are open to children's creative efforts and establish a safe, supportive, learner-centered environment, they build the foundation for a meaningful curriculum. A meaningful curriculum contains a variety of opportunities for children to dramatize familiar experiences and to share enactments with both peers and adults.

Selecting and Presenting Appropriate Drama Experiences and Materials

Some considerations that enhance the dramatic arts and capitalize on children's multiple intelligences include space, materials, and an enthusiastic teacher (McCaslin,

2000; Gelineau, 2004). Here are five brief examples of how to release children's creative potential through drama.

1. *Define the space to be used.* How space is arranged sends strong messages about how to use that space for drama. Providing specific space for dramatic activity (such as a puppet stage), as well as clear pathways to enter and exit those spaces, is important.

2. *Use a large assortment of hands-on materials.* Materials influence the content of children's enactments and support their ability to initiate and sustain informal and story drama activities. A group of preschoolers were playing out a rescue operation in a medevac helicopter they had constructed with blocks. Using the accessible props of buttons, plastic cups, and a steering wheel, they took their helicopter into the air and onto the hospital landing platform while using their control panel to communicate with the hospital emergency room.

3. *Provide accessible and easily stored materials.* Three first-grade children were role-playing in their classroom grocery store and decided to make signs for the "weekly specials." Their teacher provided folders and table easels to save or reuse their work. Prop boxes, discussed in the section on dramatic play in this chapter, offer another type of accessible storage. Accessible and easily stored material gives children autonomy in pursuing dramatic interests.

4. *Allow adequate time.* Children need ample time to plan, carry out, and sustain their dramatic activity. Drama requires time to recruit players, locate materials and props, negotiate roles and plots, and carry out agreed-on ideas. To capitalize on this, we, as teachers, need to schedule ample blocks of time for dramatic arts (Johnson, Christie, & Yawkey, 1999).

5. *Arrange opportunities for cooperative learning.* When children engage in dramatic activities, they tap into their "interpersonal intelligence" (Gardner, 1993a). In a thematic unit on the Brazilian rain forest, for example, fourth graders shared key ideas and information about plant life and ecology as a basis for determining how to dramatize their final project. Opportunities like this one, whether with peers or in small groups, enable children to work cooperatively—an important life skill for functioning in social settings while maintaining a level of personal involvement.

Let's think about the five considerations for selecting and presenting drama experiences—space, "hands-on" materials, storage, time, and cooperative learning by looking at Mr. Sanchez's first grade, which is enacting a camping theme. As you read about the camping theme in Mr. Sanchez's classroom, consider how these variables affect the children's enactments.

Because camping is a relatively inexpensive family vacation, many children have had some direct experience with this activity. Mr. Sanchez began by reading several camping stories, including *Bailey Goes Camping* (Henkes, 1985), *Three Days on a River in a Red Canoe* (Williams, 1981), and *Stringbean's Trip to the Shining Sea* (Williams, 1988), to help children elaborate their dramatic play. Next, they brainstormed a list of ideas about camping and grouped their list into a concept map on poster board. They came up with categories of where you go (backyard, state park, campground, lake), how you get there (walk, car, trailer, truck with camper, motorhome), where you sleep (in a camper, in tents, in sleeping bags), what you eat (trail mix, food from cans, fish you catch, hot dogs, marshmallows), and things to do (swim, sing songs, bike, hike, explore, tell stories). In planning this theme, Mr. Sanchez cleared a corner of the classroom so that it could be left in place for as long as the children's interest allowed. Next, with Mr. Sanchez's support, the children used, made, or brought in various props to represent a campground with tents, a campfire, trees, a lake, trails, and wildlife. Following a few days of play, Mr. Sanchez observed the children repeatedly reenacting the same sequence of putting up and taking down their tents. After talking with them about other camping activities, such as how they were preparing their meals, he decided to add some cooking equipment and empty boxes of real food products for a camp store. Clearly, this episode illustrates the teacher's key role in dramatic arts in the classroom.

TEACHERS' ROLES AND RESPONSIBILITIES

Teachers often wonder how much, if at all, they should intervene in children's enactments. As facilitators who encourage drama and dramatic play, teachers assume an important role in the preparation and follow-up to children's dramatizations (Wilhelm & Edmiston, 1998). One common error is for teachers to become too intrusive, to act as "directors" who disrupt the children's spontaneity. A second common error is the reverse—to completely ignore the children's drama and work on other routine tasks such as putting out the paints or arranging a bulletin board display.

The following strategies will help you avoid both of these extremes and will allow you to infuse drama throughout your classroom. As you explore these strategies, remember that your role as a teacher strongly influences how children use drama.

1. *Address the roles of the participants and audience.* To be successful and engaging, discuss the roles of the participants and audience prior to the activity. All children, whether participating in an acting role or as an audience member, must agree to work in a pretend situation, agree to the wishes of the group over the wishes of an individual, participate without monopolizing the scene, and commit to work without making fun or provoking laughter among classmates (Flynn, 2000). For particular situations, specific rules, such as keeping one's hands to oneself, may be needed.

2. *Ask thoughtful questions that provoke creative thinking.* Before any drama activity, find out what children know or want to know about the content and roles. During the activity, be curious and be a good listener. When Mr. Sanchez's first graders were planning their camping theme corner, he asked them to talk about what they knew about camping. He also asked them questions such as "Where will you all sleep?" "How will you prepare your food?" and "What will you do for fun on your trip?" By understanding the experiences of the children in his class, Mr. Sanchez challenged their thinking, which helped them enact more complex camping themes.

3. *Model a behavior or attribute.* Modeling is one of the most effective strategies for empowering children through drama. Watch, however, for the appropriate moment to do this. In drama, teachers should not impose their ideas on children. Rather, they should encourage children to develop their own ideas, value their responses, support their improvisations, and encourage them to believe in themselves and their abilities. When Mr. Martinez's first graders wanted to enact a firefighting scene, they needed a prop to use as a fire hose. He invited them to problem-solve, asking, "What kind of object do you need?" Children suggested that it should be long, rounded, skinny, and sort of stretchy. They decided to use a plastic Slinky.

4. *Reflect with children.* Talking about specific roles and situations during and after the drama helps children clarify their thoughts and feelings. Ms. Wengel's second graders had created a shoe store as part of their unit on clothing. The shoe store contained a variety of styles of real shoes, such as slippers, boots, running shoes, and ballet shoes. It also contained shoe catalogs and photos of old-fashioned shoes and boots that the children used to sort, classify, measure, and make purchases. Ms. Wengel helped the children reflect on their roles in the shoe store by asking them to think about how the old-fashioned shoes differed from today's styles and to imagine how shoes might change in the future when they become adults. In their reflections, the children thought about shoes of the future, such as "jet shoes" that could help you take off and fly. They also listened to others' ideas and responses, which they then incorporated into future dramatizations in the shoe store.

Talking with children about their drama, assuming different roles, and providing time, space, and resources are the building blocks of the dramatic arts. This foundation provides children with the needed opportunities to explore appropriate dramatic arts activities and experiences.

APPROPRIATE DRAMATIC ARTS ACTIVITIES AND EXPERIENCES

Some of the most appropriate drama activities include dramatic and sociodramatic play, story play, pantomime, puppets, story drama, and readers' theater. These drama activities help children do the following:

1. Develop improved skills in reading, listening, speaking, and writing.
2. Develop skill in thinking analytically and acting decisively and responsibly.
3. Increase and sustain the ability to concentrate and follow directions.
4. Strengthen self-concept by cooperative interaction with others.
5. Increase motivation to learn.
6. Develop individual and group creativity (Hennings, 2003; Roe et al., 2005; Wilhelm & Edmiston, 1998).

Dramatic and Sociodramatic Play

Three-year-old Michelle dons a surgeon's cap, hangs a stethoscope around her neck, and examines "Spotty," a large teddy bear. She uses a spoon to give her patient a shot, scribbles a prescription on a scrap of paper from the play area, and hands it to her playmate, Jacob.

A group of kindergartners are being air traffic controllers and helping planes land during a blizzard. Their conversation includes negotiations and decisions about how many controllers can fit into the control tower and which planes belong to which controller. These children are engaged in dramatic and sociodramatic play.

Why Use Dramatic and Sociodramatic Play?

In dramatic and sociodramatic play, children can be both actors and directors. As actors, children actually experience the feelings, thoughts, and behaviors of the roles they are playing. As directors, they imagine the thoughts, feelings, and behaviors associated with a role and coach the actors. Playing both roles in dramatic and sociodramatic play helps children:

- Construct their own understanding of how the world works by stepping into the shoes of another person (Jalongo & Isenberg, 2004; Corbey-Scullen & Howell, 1997).
- Negotiate with players with different needs and views (Furman, 2000a).
- Express their inner feelings (Mayesky, 2002).
- Practice language skills as they assume different roles (Roe et al., 2005).
- Use printed words in play that later become sight words (Roe et al., 2005).
- Explore freely and imaginatively the more structured forms of drama (McCaslin, 2000).

Suggestions for the Classroom

Ms. Senack has set up a beach theme center that includes assorted related materials such as a large ocean poster, a child-sized beach chair, a small umbrella, a collection of shells, water toys, and cassette tapes for her 4-year-old class. Ari spreads his towel along the sand, then checks his bag for sunglasses and sand toys. Shayna locates her portable radio and skips over stations until she finds the appropriate music. "Hey, Ari!" Shayna asks, "do you like this song? Let's pretend we are teenagers!" Eventually, they use towels to bury themselves and call themselves "dancing sand people." At the sand table, they engage in the following dialogue:

> **Ari:**   Put all the shells you want in your pile. Don't get them mixed up. These are mine! *(gets a magnifying glass from the science table)* Look, this one is really dirty!
> **Shayna:**   Let me see! *(Ari hands her the magnifying glass, and Shayna examines the shell)* That's not dirt! That's the way the shell is. It comes like that! You just don't know 'cause only if you have a 'fying glass can you see what it looks like underneath.
> **Ari:**   My mom sometimes uses shells for plates. She has really big shells and puts our food on them.
> **Shayna:**   Here's some macaroni and cheese! *(hands Ari a shell with some sand on it)*

In dramatic play, children experience the actual
feelings, thoughts, and behaviors of the roles they enact.

This beach theme play illustrates the use of two strategies for enhancing role play—prop boxes, or dramatic play kits, and theme corners, or play centers.

Prop Boxes and Dramatic Play Kits.   **Prop boxes or dramatic play kits** contain a collection of real items that are related in some way, such as a picnic basket, plastic food, a tablecloth, and plastic ants. Using real items can stimulate children's imaginative play with particular concepts, situations, and roles. Prop boxes do the following:

- Promote experiences with real materials and tools related to a theme (a toolbox).
- Sustain children's interest in their theme play (books, posters, records, and tapes related to the theme).
- Increase opportunities for family involvement by contributing materials and using literature-based prop boxes from school in the home setting.
- Provide opportunities to enact familiar roles (deposit slips and checks for a banker or boots, a net, and a fishing pole for a fisher) (Barbour & Desjean-Perrotta, 2002; Edwards, 2002; Myhre, 1993).

Well-planned prop boxes enhance dramatic and sociodramatic play opportunities. Younger children need adequate props, space, and time to pursue dramatic play even though their roles and themes shift frequently. Older children, who are more sophisticated in their play, can plan their theme and often negotiate roles and responsibilities. At all ages, children use the props in many different ways. Be certain, however, that all of the items are safe to use and free of dangerous or loose parts.

The following guidelines will help you use prop boxes and dramatic play kits to extend units of study and to support children's enactments.

1. *Brainstorm themes that interest the children.* Choose some themes that are very familiar (such as a grocery store or a farm), others that are somewhat familiar (such as a gas station or a TV studio), and still others that are even less familiar to children (such as a travel agency or a construction project). Be certain to provide adequate background experiences that will support children's enactment.

2. *Collect storage containers.* Strong boxes with lids (such as those that contain photocopy paper) or clean, dry 5-quart ice cream tubs work well for this purpose. Label the outside of the container with the theme ("The Three Bears" or "Chinese New Year") and draw a picture or paste on a photo that will help children identify each container's contents. You might also invite the children to paint and decorate these boxes.

3. *Generate a list of possible items to include in the prop box.* Ask children, parents, colleagues, and local businesses to contribute items. Clothing, especially old uniforms and costumes, and recycled materials such as old toys and household articles are generally useful. Invite families to provide materials such as clothing, accessories, or props for a particular piece of literature to be studied in the classroom. Stories such as *The City Mouse and the Country Mouse* (Stevens, 1987), *Sylvester and the Magic Pebble* (Steig, 1969), and *Stone Soup* (Brown, 1975) lend themselves to family involvement.

4. *Think about your goals for the theme or unit.* What vocabulary could children use in their drama? How will you introduce the theme and related activities so that they capitalize on what children know? You may want to include some books that correspond to the theme or an audiotape of appropriate background music or sounds. Record these ideas and tape them inside the cover of the prop box to serve as a guide for parents, substitute or student teachers, or administrators. These ideas will help keep the dramatic play well connected to the goals of the unit. Figure 5.1 shows a properly labeled prop box. Figure 5.2 gives examples of what to include in a puppet prop box and a medical prop box. Appendix A shows how to use a dance prop box and contains ideas for additional prop boxes.

Theme Corners or Play Centers.   Theme corners or play centers contain materials focused on a topic familiar and interesting to a particular group of children. They encourage children's spontaneous play with a variety of roles (Howe, Moller, Chambers, & Petrakos, 1993; Woodward, 1985). Theme corners make a subject of study, such as nutrition or careers, more real to children, and build interest in the topic. Use the following four guidelines to encourage children's dramatizations with theme corners or play centers.

Information to be taped inside the lid or cover of the prop box	Theme: _____
	Goals for Center: _____
	Vocabulary: _____
	Introduction Procedure: _____
	Field Trips and Resource People: _____

Information on the outside of the prop box	Theme: _____
	Props (costumes, real things, objects): _____
	Materials in Box: _____
	Suggested Supplements: _____
	Child-Made Materials: _____

Suggestions for adults	Observer: Watch play.
	Collaborator: Add a new prop, ask a question, help children gain entry to play without intruding on the ongoing play of the others.
	Model: If invited, join the play and model a role or action and then leave.
	Mediator: Help children develop peaceful solutions to conflicts.
	Safety Monitor: Check for hazards, worn or damaged materials, clutter.

Figure 5.1
Properly Labeled Prop Box

1. *Provide a variety of background experiences.* Use pictures, stories, and discussion about the theme to build background knowledge. Children need to be familiar with roles in order to enact them.

2. *Create an attractive physical setting.* Posters, books, and materials can transform an area of the classroom. The physical setting can invite children to enter the area and can stimulate their imaginations.

3. *Provide safe, simple, and durable props.* Select props and materials that are well suited to children's ages, interests, and abilities. Simple props such as a cape or a magic mirror inspire children to enact roles and behaviors. You will want to check periodically that your props are in good repair and are being used properly.

4. *Involve children in planning.* Encourage children to suggest ideas for themes and to develop new theme corners periodically. Children can make and collect the necessary props. When introducing a new theme corner, jointly establish

Puppet Prop Box:

Paper plates, paper bags, craft sticks, tongue depressors, buttons, sequin pieces, wallpaper pieces, cotton balls, construction paper, pipe cleaners, yarn, glue, scissors, markers, tape, books about puppetry and puppet making.

Medical Prop Box:

Dolls, stuffed animals, doll-sized furniture, doctor kit, stethoscope, plastic digital thermometer, plastic syringes, bandages, eye chart, white shirts for uniforms, pad, pencil, telephone, appointment book, shower cap, empty pill containers, scale, patient folders, coupons for medical supplies and products, magazines, books and posters about doctors and nurses.

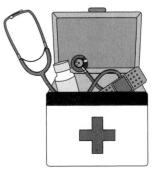

Figure 5.2
Materials for Puppet and Medical Prop Boxes

limits such as the number of children who can be there at any one time. Figure 5.3 shows a theme corner for a fast-food restaurant that incorporates goals, materials, and related activities. Figure 5.4 lists other ideas for theme corners and shows a doctor's office.

Story Play

Story play, also called *story dictation,* is a form of guided drama that uses children's own stories as the content for enactment (Paley, 1990b). In this kind of drama, children can be both writers and actors by dictating stories to an adult or by writing their own stories that later become plays to dramatize. As the authors, children choose which of their friends might play certain roles as the teacher reads the original stories. Story play in the preschool and kindergarten years is a natural transition to the journal writing and shared reading and writing typically encountered in the primary grades (Vukelich, Christie, & Enz, 2002). In Grades 1–4, story drama provides ways for young writers to compose meaning on multiple levels and facilitates children's ownership of their imaginative work within the drama world, which reappears in their writing (Crumpler and Schneider, 2002).

Goal	Vocabulary	Teacher-Provided Props
To increase children's ability to choose and enact roles	Restaurant Drive-through Cashier Cook Menu Food Customer Trash can Cash register Tables and chairs	Uniforms Play money Trash can, dishcloth, mop Stove Cups, straws, trays Assorted containers Cooking utensils Pencils Cards for taking orders Wall posters of food & prices

Child-Provided Props	Introducing the Theme Corner	Related Activities
Hats Aprons Menus Signs Decorated car made from box Price list Styrofoam containers	1. Discuss eating in a fast-food restaurant. 2. Discuss roles of workers and customers. 3. Introduce imprinted items from different restaurants and have children sort and classify them.	1. Take a field trip and eat in a fast-food restaurant. 2. Invite employees to talk with the children about their work. 3. Collect cups, napkins, hats, and other objects. 4. Cook and taste different kinds of potatoes.

Figure 5.3
Theme Corner for a Fast-Food Restaurant
Note. Adapted from Isbell (1995).

Why Use Story Play?

Vivian Paley (1990b) reports that children who see their own stories enacted are motivated to write other stories for dramatization so that they can become story players. Many teachers use children's own stories to dramatize in order to support children's language and literacy development and to build a strong sense of community in the classroom. In this way, enactment provides all children an opportunity to be "story tellers," to engage in both verbal and nonverbal expression of ideas, to increase their communicative competence, and to participate in a simple yet powerful dramatic experience. Story play is predicated on the idea that children can learn to read and write more easily if they are using their own words because they have more meaning for them. Story play is one way to include shy children, second-language learners, and children with special needs into classroom drama.

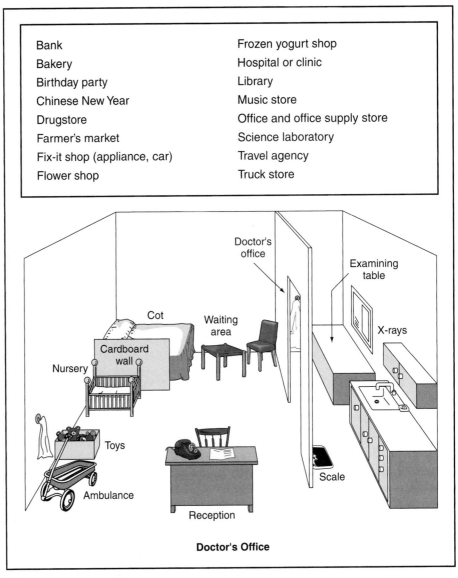

Bank   Frozen yogurt shop
Bakery   Hospital or clinic
Birthday party   Library
Chinese New Year   Music store
Drugstore   Office and office supply store
Farmer's market   Science laboratory
Fix-it shop (appliance, car) Travel agency
Flower shop   Truck store

Doctor's Office

Figure 5.4
Suggestions for Theme Corners

Suggestions for the Classroom

Story play begins by encouraging children to write their own stories or to dictate stories to an adult who writes them down. Older children can write their own stories for later enactment to a small group or to the whole class. One by one, each child author chooses a role to play from his or her story and selects classmates to play different roles. The child author may also serve as the director as the teacher reads the child's story aloud. Periodically, select an original story to keep in each child's portfolio so that you can see his or her storytelling abilities progress over time.

The story play procedure validates children's attempts at writing and telling stories. The more opportunities children have to elaborate their own ideas, the more complex their stories will become and the better insight they will have about the structure of narrative.

Pantomime

Pantomime, a type of informal drama sometimes referred to as charades, is a good starting point for the dramatic arts. In pantomime, children use gestures and movement to communicate ideas, feelings, and actions—all without words. As part of their unit on the circus, a group of second graders were pantomiming eating cotton candy. Some children held their hands in front of their faces and bit off chunks of the cotton candy; others pulled some candy off the cones with their hands and ate it; still others just licked their hands and fingers. The teacher encouraged responses from the onlookers by asking, "How did you know it was cotton candy?" or "What else might the mimers have done to show you it was cotton candy and not an ice cream cone?" In this way, the second graders and their teacher used pantomime to give form to their ideas.

Why Use Pantomime?

Pantomime helps children feel comfortable with their bodies while interpreting ideas, feelings, and actions. Because it begins with physical experience, it makes concepts more concrete. More specifically, it helps children:

1. Develop the confidence needed for later story dramatization.
2. Become aware of the importance of nonverbal communication.
3. Convey their actions, thoughts, and feelings through gesture and movement.
4. Develop skills in listening, language, remembering, acting, and audience awareness (Edwards, 2002; Hennings, 2003; McCaslin, 2000).

Because mime uses no words or dialogue, it is particularly valuable for children who are nonnative English speakers, who have speech or hearing problems, or who are very shy. It helps them develop confidence in their abilities to express themselves through body language. In pantomime, all children can be successful because they do not have to be concerned about verbal communication.

Suggestions for the Classroom

It is a good idea to introduce pantomime first as a whole-group activity. Once children feel comfortable using their bodies to act out situations, they can begin to explore simple characterizations and role-play common experiences. Children express themselves more freely when many children and the adults participate. Younger children need help getting started with pantomime. The less experienced children are, the more background and modeling they need to stimulate their imaginations before they can create their own interpretations. Children respond positively to teachers' suggestions, such as, "Show me with your body that it is cold outside" or "Let's pretend you are a stick floating down a quiet stream." Young children also like to interpret their actions and gestures to music or pantomime characters from a favorite story, such as "The Three Billy Goats Gruff."

School-age children enjoy making up original and humorous skits for group pantomime. They also can be encouraged to pantomime individuals currently in the news, such as politicians or sports figures. In this way, they explore sophisticated variations of actions or feelings and respond favorably to teachers acting as choreographers in changing their actions (Hennings, 2003). The more children observe nonverbal behaviors, the more able they are to add body language and gestures to their own nonverbal repertoire. One third-grade class, for example, was pantomiming ways of walking in response to these teacher's calls: "You are walking on slippery ice . . . through the muddy jungle . . . in the very hot desert . . . and in a very dark alley." As the context changed, the children interpreted and invented the appropriate movements, such as tiptoeing, sliding, staggering, or walking rapidly.

Because all children like to make and do things, miming actions interests them. Children will be most able to mime actions that they have experienced and that they can easily imagine. Some appropriate mime activities for young children are:

1. Acting out familiar nursery rhymes such as "Jack and Jill" or "One, Two, Buckle My Shoe."
2. Showing what it is like to do your favorite after-school activity, such as riding a bike or working in the family garden.
3. Being a character or an animal in favorite songs. Short songs, such as "I'm a Little Teapot," are good introductions to mime and song.
4. Modeling familiar actions such as brushing teeth, washing hands, riding on a crowded bus, or eating in the school cafeteria. Children also like to mime throwing balls of different sizes, eating a dripping ice cream cone, or washing dishes.
5. Imagining they are other creatures, such as a tiger stalking through the jungle looking for food, a kitten lapping some milk, or a wriggling worm.

Older children who have little experience with mime also need practice and modeling before they feel comfortable enough to mime. Group experiences of the same action convey the message of multiple interpretations with no right or wrong response.

Some appropriate mime activities for older children are as follows:

1. Showing the different stages in a life cycle such as a caterpillar or mealworm.
2. Imagining they are slaves traveling along the Underground Railroad.
3. Acting out historical events such as the Boston Tea Party, landing on the moon, or the "shot heard 'round the world" at Lexington, Massachusetts.

Puppets

Puppets make powerful teaching tools. Even though the word *puppet* comes from the Latin word for "doll," puppets are more than dolls. They invite children to explore their imaginations and share their imaginings with others. Puppets are the perfect props for all forms of drama!

Why Use Puppets?

Puppets add life to the classroom and are a natural vehicle for creativity, imagination, and arts-based learning. In today's product-oriented world, they help children convey feelings, emotions, values, and ideas. They are particularly motivating for the listener because they carry a bit of mystery with them.

For children, the process of creating and using puppets makes the learning valuable rather than focusing on the puppet as a finished product. Teachers can also use puppets to enhance their own creativity, view children in different roles, and nurture affective development.

A puppet can become a nonthreatening vehicle for the following:

*   Self-expression, storytelling, improvisation, and enactment (Mayesky, 2002; Vukelich et al., 2002).

Puppets are the perfect props for all forms of creative drama.

- Risk taking and building confidence in speaking abilities (Hennings, 2003).
- Social negotiation (McCaslin, 2000).
- Releasing emotions, distinguishing between reality and fantasy, and practicing life experiences (Hunt & Renfro, 1982).

Many puppets are simple, safe, and easy for children to create and use. A wooden spoon easily becomes a person when given a face; a mitten can be transformed into an animal by adding eyes and a nose. If puppets are to become real tools for unlocking children's creative potential, they must be easily accessible for children. Figure 5.5 lists ideas for making puppets.

Suggestions for the Classroom

Here are some suggestions for class work with puppets.

1. Provide opportunities for children to experiment with different puppets before they create their own. Have them hold the puppets in front of them or over their heads. Introduce a mirror so that they can explore the puppet's movements, voice, and gestures. Young children find it easiest to manipulate puppets with moving mouths so that they can use dialogue if they choose (Hunt & Renfro, 1982).

2. Create a puppet center with a box of puppet-making materials such as scraps of fabric, paper tubing and plates, recycled buttons, yarn, and popsicle sticks. Locate the center away from the normal traffic pattern so children can gather and use their puppets in informal enactments. Preschoolers enjoy using paper plates or other recycled materials to invent new types of puppets. Primary-grade children often use the puppet center to create silhouette stick puppets of favorite book characters to share informally with one another. Notice the confidence in first grader Brittany's comments while working with a friend in the puppet center:

> **Brittany:** Oh, I love puppets. They are so cute. Hmmm . . . what can I make? I think I'll make a girl. Can I make two? Okay, then I'll make a girl and a boy. We can do a little play then. I'll be the girl and you can be the boy.

3. Use puppets to help children express feelings with their voices. Children can be encouraged to use high- or low-pitched voices, or animal sounds such as squeaking, growling, or chirping (Bromley, 1998; Hunt & Renfro, 1982). For example, a kindergarten teacher uses paper plate puppets with happy, sad, surprised, and frightened faces on them. She tells a short story, stops, and asks a child to respond using one of the puppets and an appropriate voice.

4. For children who are planning a puppet show and have difficulty manipulating puppets and saying the words at the same time, suggest making an audiotape. Making a recording in advance gives them the chance to focus on the puppet's actions.

5. Children in third and fourth grades enjoy creating puppets that illustrate what they are learning. One teacher has her children create puppets dressed to represent the different social classes in ancient Rome. The children write their own scripts and perform puppet shows for younger children.

6. Provide guidelines for safety and management. To maximize the value of puppets in the classroom, be sure to involve children in establishing limits and

Finger, Glove, and Mitten Puppets

Draw characters on fingers with washable markers.

Cut fingers from old work gloves or rubber gloves.

Cut a hole in old Ping-Pong balls and draw a face.

Bottle lids that are large and deep may be painted or decorated.

Use commercial finger puppets.

Decorate cardboard tubes (e.g., old bandage tube).

Box Puppets

Assorted small boxes (e.g., small candy carton, pudding, or cereal boxes for hand and finger puppet)

Assorted large boxes (e.g., cereal) for larger puppets

Assorted envelopes of all colors and sizes

Paper Bag Puppets

Assorted brown and white bags to be decorated with materials for face puppets

Assorted brown and white bags to be decorated for the body and use the fingers through the flattened bottom as the face.

Grocery bags become body puppets (called humanettes: half people, half bag)

Stick Puppets

Draw faces on assorted sticks (e.g., tongue depressors, Popsicle sticks).

Draw faces on wooden clothespins to make storytelling puppets.

Draw faces on lightweight cardboard.

Use a tongue depressor attached to a paper plate for a paper plate puppet.

Make pipe cleaner and wooden spoon puppets.

Ball Puppets

Use a Styrofoam ball for the head.

Decorate old tennis balls.

(continued)

Figure 5.5
Ideas for Making Puppets

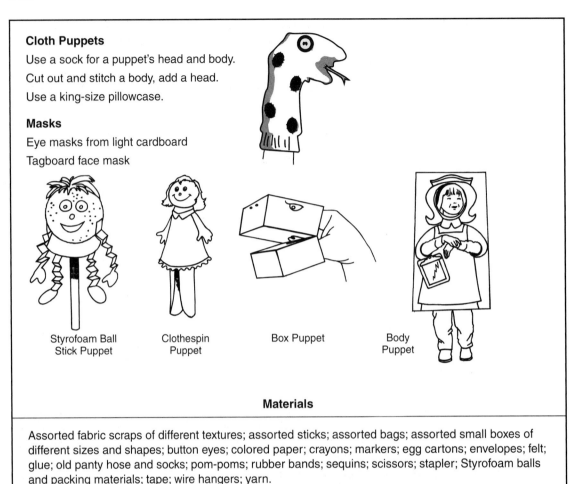

Cloth Puppets

Use a sock for a puppet's head and body.

Cut out and stitch a body, add a head.

Use a king-size pillowcase.

Masks

Eye masks from light cardboard

Tagboard face mask

Styrofoam Ball
Stick Puppet

Clothespin
Puppet

Box Puppet

Body
Puppet

Materials

Assorted fabric scraps of different textures; assorted sticks; assorted bags; assorted small boxes of different sizes and shapes; button eyes; colored paper; crayons; markers; egg cartons; envelopes; felt; glue; old panty hose and socks; pom-poms; rubber bands; sequins; scissors; stapler; Styrofoam balls and packing materials; tape; wire hangers; yarn.

Storage: Using common recyclable materials enhances children's play with puppets and makes storage attractive and accessible. Teachers and caregivers have successfully used the following items: aprons with pockets; cardboard six-packs; egg cartons; expanding hanging baskets; hat or wine rack; photocopy paper boxes; multiple skirt hangers; plastic gallon containers or 2-liter plastic bottles; shoe box, bag, or rack.

Figure 5.5   *(Continued)*

responsibilities in using puppets. For example, puppets can be used for talking with one another, creating a puppet show, or retelling a story. Teachers and caregivers should not allow puppets to be used as action figures in "hand-to-hand" combat.

Story Drama

Story drama, a type of interpretive drama, is based on the reenactment of familiar stories, poems, fables, or original stories. Sometimes referred to as story retelling, story drama often consists of a teacher-led group experience with children creating scenes from familiar literature that use both dialogue and movement (Morado, Koenig, & Wilson, 1999; Vukelich et al., 2002). Preschool and kindergarten children enjoy dramatizing cumulative tales such as *Henny Penny* (Galdone, 1968) or *Over in the Meadow* (Keats, 1971). Children in first and second grades enjoy dramatizing scenes from longer stories such as *Ramona the Brave* (Cleary, 1975), *Doctor De Soto* (Steig, 1982), or *Knots on a Counting Rope* (Martin & Archambault, 1987). Children in third and fourth grades enjoy dramatizing and debating character conflicts in longer stories such as *Number the Stars* (Lowry, 1989), *Shiloh* (Naylor, 1991), or *Holes* (Sachar, 1998).

Why Use Story Drama?

Story drama supports children's understanding of story structure, characterization, and language usage. For the teacher, it offers a natural and authentic form of literacy understanding. Research shows that enacting stories (1) improves reading comprehension by enabling readers to clarify concepts and gain a deeper understanding of the literature (Bromley, 1998; Dupont, 1992; Furman, 2000b; Jalongo, 2002); (2) promotes speaking, listening, critical, and creative reading skills by interpreting familiar material (Hennings, 2003); (3) heightens students' awareness of sequence of events, personalities, dialogue, and mood (Roe et al., 2005); (4) increases the ability to speak clearly and use appropriate vocabulary (Roe et al., 2005) and (5) enables children to experience the feelings and behaviors of others (McCaslin, 2000; Tompkins, 2002). Story drama meets the needs of children at all developmental levels because the children control the length and interpretation of the particular retelling.

Story drama supports children's understanding of story structure, characterization, and language usage.

Suggestions for the Classroom

When choosing and adapting stories to dramatize, think about the following characteristics.

1. *Choose stories with immediate action, a simple plot, few characters, and appealing dialogue that children can easily put into their own words.* Students must be familiar with the story and characters if they are to re-create the plot and the conversation. Folk tales such as *How Many Spots Does a Leopard Have?* (Lester, 1990) or *Fables* (Lobel, 1980) fit this criterion.

2. *Involve children actively in the selection of the story.* Allowing them to choose stories to enact builds interest in dramatization. Stories suitable for dramatization, such as *The Mixed-Up Chameleon* (Carle, 1984), *One Fine Day* (Hogrogrian, 1971), *The Doorbell Rang* (Hutchins, 1986), and *The Phantom Tollbooth* (Juster, 1988), should be readily available in the classroom library.

3. *Adapt familiar stories and enthusiastically support children's spontaneous interpretations.* Young children have simple and often loose interpretations; older children have more sophisticated understandings and a more coherent plot that follows the original story more closely. One effective technique is to use "yarn-tug stories," where children hold on to knotted pieces of yarn and sit in a semicircle around a child who starts the story. That child then tugs at the knot of another child, who continues the retelling. The process continues until all children have participated in the retelling and the story is complete.

4. *Be a facilitator.* Prepare questions in advance to help children focus on story elements and to gain distance from the story. For example, in reenacting the story of *Charlotte's Web* (White, 1952), you might ask, "I wonder how Wilbur felt being the new animal and the only pig on the farm. If you were an animal on Mr. Zuckerman's farm, what would you do to help Wilbur? What qualities do you look for in a friend? Why?"

5. *Provide ample time and space for children to plan the dramatization, decide which parts to read or enact, and explore the dimensions of their characters.* Each child must determine how a character feels and thinks before trying to act like that character. In one first-grade reenactment of *Caps for Sale* (Slobodkina, 1947) children asked one another these questions to help them better understand the character of the peddler: Where do you live? Where did you get your caps? How will you shake your fingers, shake both hands, stamp your feet, and throw your caps on the ground? How will you act like a monkey in the trees?

6. *Evaluate the reenactment.* By second grade, children can evaluate their story dramatizations. Always begin with the strengths of the drama. What did you see that you liked? Then ask questions that will help children reexamine the drama elements of voice, action, diction, and movement of the characters.

Readers' Theater

Readers' theater, another form of interpretive drama, is a presentation of a story or script by a group of readers. In selecting literature for readers' theater, choose stories with a simple plot; a clear ending; interesting characters; and clear, simple dialogue. Readers then assume a role, read aloud, and interpret the parts of the script that relate to their particular role. Props are not necessary. This form of drama enables children to use facial and vocal expressions, gestures, and their imaginations to interpret a play or story in a nonstaged performance to communicate shades of meaning. Sometimes a narrator sets the tone, but this is not necessary. Children in third and fourth grades often develop their own scripts from familiar stories, which involve making decisions on important dialogue and narration.

Because readers' theater incorporates practice before presentation, less-proficient readers can often be successful in oral reading and interpretation (Forsythe, 1995; Hennings, 2003; Walker, 2004). Although readers' theater was designed for older children, it is easily adaptable to primary-grade children and non-readers using a memorized big book on an easel (Jalongo & Stamp, 1997b), or by telling the story using a felt board.

Why Use Readers' Theater?

In readers' theater, children focus only on the oral interpretation of the material, facial expressions, and simple gestures. Unlike formal, scripted drama, they are not pressured to memorize lines or use elaborate props. During readers' theater, the audience receives information and responds to the participants. Readers' theater is a particularly useful form of drama for incorporating multicultural stories, such as *Abiyoyo* (Seeger, 1986) or *Tar Beach* (Ringgold, 1991); deepening children's language proficiency by finding and enacting words through such books as *Chicka Chicka Boom Boom* (Martin & Archambault, 1989) that begin with certain sounds, such as the *b* in *button;* practicing reading in a supportive environment, enabling less-able readers to experience fluency and comprehension in a low-anxiety setting; and providing a strategy for fostering language acquisition for second-language learners (Burke & O'Sullivan, 2002).

Suggestions for the Classroom

Teachers typically use the following procedure for readers' theater (Bromley, 1998):

1. Have readers sit on the floor or stand, with their books in front of them, while they read and follow along with the material.
2. Use material that children can read without help, such as predictable books children use as big books or stories from their reading program because children have memorized them from repeated readings.
3. Select material that is action based, exciting, and capable of interpretation in a dramatic fashion. Folktales such as "Chicken Little" and stories in verse such as *The Adventures of Taxi Dog* (Barracca & Barracca, 1990) meet these criteria.

The scenarios[1] provided here illustrate appropriate uses of readers' theater with preschool/kindergarten and school-aged children. A good resource for readers' theater is:

Readers Theater Script Service
P.O. Box 178333
San Diego, CA 92117
(619) 276-1948

---

[1]Scenarios on pages 205–206 and 209 are courtesy of Kelli Jo Kerry Moran, Indiana University of Pennsylvania.

READERS' THEATER FOR PRESCHOOL/KINDERGARTNERS

Margy Scalia's preschoolers are focusing on the folktale "The Three Little Pigs." She encouraged the children to explore the folktale through dramatic play by adding pig and wolf puppets to the puppetry center and simple costume pieces to the dramatic-play area to support dramatic retellings of the tale and to make up their own versions. When the children were familiar with the tale, Ms. Scalia extended her literacy activities through an informal variation of readers' theater.

To do this, Ms. Scalia created prompt cards with pictures and printed text for a few of the simple words that were repeated throughout the story that she reviewed with the children, giving them an opportunity to touch them and look at the words and pictures before using them in a story. Some children were fascinated by the cards while others quickly moved on to different activities. Ms. Scalia was used to the children's different interests and did not force anyone's participation. After a few practice tries of holding up a card and having the children say the printed and illustrated word aloud, they told the story with Ms. Scalia serving as the narrator and the children joining in with the prompt card words and other familiar phrases. Afterwards, Ms. Scalia added the cards to the classroom's literacy center for the children's own story making. A few of the children had so enjoyed the activity that they often pulled out cards so that the entire class could tell the story of "The Three Little Pigs."

READERS' THEATER FOR THIRD AND FOURTH GRADES

Josh Morales had just finished grading the readers' theater scripts his fourth-grade class had completed for the culminating activity of their civil rights unit. The quality of their work was impressive and Josh was finally glad that his cooperating teacher had insisted that he integrate language arts into his social studies unit. Readers' theater had been a good fit because it incorporated all the elements of language arts and helped Josh achieve an additional objective of helping the children develop a more empathetic understanding of the obstacles faced by civil rights leaders.

A few days later, Josh brought in a series of scripts about Martin Luther King, Jr., and taught the children some basic readers' theater conventions such as turning their back to the audience to indicate being "off stage." He modeled expressive reading and led the children in brainstorming additional ways to make readers' theater more effective. Then he divided the children into small groups, with each group given a different script. The groups negotiated their own roles, and the next day was devoted to practice. Not only were the subsequent performances great, but it was obvious that real social studies and language arts learning had taken place.

Appropriate drama activities and experiences develop children's understanding of the forms and functions of language, nonverbal communication, and possibilities in dealing with life, while simultaneously building self-esteem and self-confidence. These activities can be used to integrate the curriculum and reinforce learning in all subject areas for all types of learners.

INTEGRATING DRAMATIC ARTS INTO THE SUBJECT AREAS

Drama experts recommend that drama activities be infused into the subject areas (Bolton, 1985; Gelineau, 2004; McCaslin, 2000; Wilhelm & Edmiston, 1998). In this way, children come to understand abstract ideas by enacting them concretely. The activities that follow are grouped by subject area and may be adapted across ages and subject areas.

Mathematics, Science, and Technology

Children enjoy dramatic arts activities that focus on mathematics and science. Examples of these activities follow.

Props and other materials make it easy to integrate drama across the curriculum, adapting oral language experiences to the skills, abilities, and interests of all children.

Body Plays and Finger Plays

Young children are particularly fond of these activities. While studying animals, they enjoy inventing their own gestures and acting out rhymes, such as this one about an elephant:

> His name is Elmer elephant, *(point to self as elephant)*
>
> His lip and trunk are one. *(put two fists in front of mouth)*
>
> And when I went to pick him up, *(bend way down)*
>
> I knew he weighed a ton! *(lift up arms enclosed in a semicircle and make facial gestures)*

They also enjoy changing their bodies into shapes—shapes for objects (such as a bridge or a ball), shapes that change (such as an egg to a chicken), or shapes that move (such as a top) (Chenfeld, 2002).

Pantomime

Young children enjoy pantomiming seasonal changes with their bodies. They can show spring by miming planting seeds in a garden, summer by making sand castles, fall by imitating falling leaves blowing in the wind, and winter by pretending to be a skier or an ice hockey player. As part of their study of life cycles, first and second graders can cooperatively plan a pantomime of the life cycles, for example, of the caterpillar and the frog. Their classmates may provide feedback. Third and fourth graders can cooperatively pantomime the positions of the planets and how they rotate and revolve around the sun.

Theme Corners

As part of a grocery store theme corner, children's dramatic play can include counting items on the shelves, sorting and classifying empty boxes and containers of different foods, counting money and making change, and designing a recycling bin for clean, used grocery bags. Environmental awareness can be introduced through questions such as, "Do you want plastic or paper bags?" As part of a career theme corner, older children can begin to imagine a future career while researching famous scientists, engineers, and doctors.

Readers' Theater

In a unit on time, one third-grade class invented its own story of the future and presented it as readers' theater. They created third-grade characters in a school setting in the year 2100 along with dialogue that might be used in the next century and compared their story to what life was like for them today. Here is a longer scenario from a second-grade teacher.

READERS' THEATER FOR FIRST AND SECOND GRADES

Ms. Lee invited her second graders to volunteer to play Anansi, a trickster from the Ashanti culture of West Africa, as told in the African tale *Anansi the Spider* (Mc-Dermott, 1972) in the upcoming readers' theater. She had selected a play that fit the interests and developmental level of her second-grade classroom and had shared the story with the children before beginning the readers' theater activity so they were already familiar with the plot and characters.

Each child assumed a role, with most roles being shared by two or three children. One of Ms. Lee's greatest challenges in large-group activities was making the activity appropriate for all skill levels. This time she assigned each child's part at the appropriate reading level and used rebus scripts to support those children unable to read the entire text. After a week's worth of daily practice, Ms. Lee and the children felt ready to perform an in-class, informal performance with a few teachers as a supportive audience. Ms. Lee noticed especially how Jarom and Elsie had practiced and reread the script so many times that by the end of the week they were confident and able to read their parts with ease and expression. Ms. Lee had never seen them put forth so much effort.

Movement

One teacher had her children develop rhythmic patterns to different number bases in mathematics. Divided into different bases, the group rhythmically grouped and regrouped themselves according to their base. They enjoyed working with the concept on paper after they had interpreted it physically.

Ms. Green used body movements to teach the concept of shadows to her first graders. The children used their bodies to do "shadow dancing" and to show shadows at different times of the day.

Language, Literature, and Literacy

Try the following drama activities to enrich your language, literature, and literacy curriculum.

Pantomime

Toddlers like to act out action words. They choose an action picture from the teacher's shoebox collection and then do what they see in the picture. Some popular pictures include a child jumping, an airplane flying, a kitten lapping up milk, a horse galloping, and a mother cuddling a baby.

First and second grade children respond positively to pantomiming action words that relate to favorite books or book characters and feelings. They like unusual words such as *glide, hammer, inside out, jiggle, limp, nod,* and *quake.* Third and fourth grade children can do more complicated charades based on poetry, folktales, and fairytales such as "Hey Diddle Diddle," "Jack and the Beanstalk," and

"The Princess and the Pea." They enjoy working in groups to present a frozen picture of a significant event in a story. To bring a character to life, the teacher may touch the shoulder of a child in the frozen picture to hear the character's thoughts aloud (Flynn, 2000). During a frozen picture or shoulder touch activity, older children are challenged to use one of their vocabulary words correctly in a sentence.

Role Play and Dramatic Play

Young children can role-play an event, such as a trip to the farm, through drama that begins by sharing personal knowledge of what a farm is like, and is followed by enactment of such roles as a farmer, farm animals, and visitors. Teachers then discuss the enactment and may also read a book on the topic. Many teachers place real telephones in the theme or housekeeping area for children to converse freely with an imaginary person.

Older children can create situations in which they have to relay messages, such as taking a sick child to the doctor, asking for information about a movie, or making a reservation at a restaurant. These role plays in the early years successfully build children's prior knowledge, so critical to literacy development.

Body Plays

Vocabulary enacted through drama provides children with a strong mental image of the word that has been experienced visually, aurally, and kinesthetically. Children of all ages enjoy enacting parts of speech, such as antonyms, synonyms, or homonyms, and having someone else guess the opposite or provide a matching word. They also enjoy enacting the same words but with different characteristics. For example, several groups of primary children formed the word *dog*. There were *fat* dogs, *skinny* dogs, *scary* dogs, *short* dogs, *sad* dogs, and *little* dogs.

Storytelling

Primary children enjoy inventing beanbag stories. With children sitting in a circle, a child begins to tell a story. After a few sentences, the storyteller stops and throws a beanbag to another child, who continues the story. When no more ideas can be generated, another person starts a different story.

Characterization

With their favorite story in hand, third and fourth graders like to create a "Literature Talk Show" and become the talk show host. Some children call in and ask questions about the characters in the book, the characters' feelings and actions, or the resolution of the story. Other children make book characters come to life with sock puppets as they portray Frog and Toad, for example, from a favorite book, *Frog and Toad Are Friends* (Lobel, 1970).

Social Studies, Health, and Nutrition

Drama helps solidify important social studies, health, and nutrition concepts, such as the four food groups, community workers, valuing different cultures and traditions, geography, and maps.

Role Play

Using gestures, facial expressions, intonation, and movement, young children can communicate social studies concepts (such as enacting parenting behaviors), health and safety concepts (such as dramatizing safe and unsafe ways to cross the street), and nutrition concepts (such as preparing a puppet play about balanced meals and the four food groups). One first-grade class compared similarities and differences between Japanese and American families. After extensive background experiences, including reading *The Boy of the Three-Year Nap* (Snyder, 1988), their teacher, Mr. Arakaki, observed the children dramatizing scenes from each culture's home life and enacting different ways of sleeping, eating, and greeting people. Third and fourth graders can role-play different solutions to conflicts in a story. After reading the first three chapters of *Roll of Thunder, Hear My Cry* (Taylor, 2002), children may role-play a possible solution for the character Little Man, who is outraged at being given a book that is a castoff from a white school.

Finger Plays

Young children enjoy songs, finger plays, and poems related to nutrition. Try having children enact "I'm a Little Teapot," "Little Jack Horner," "The Muffin Man," or "To Market, to Market."

Identifying and Expressing Feelings

During a unit on families, preschool and primary children enjoy enacting how family members feel when they are hungry, hurt, afraid, lonely, or tired. Children of all ages can relate to the different emotions exhibited by the Seven Dwarves—bashful, grumpy, sneezy, sleepy, dopey, doc, and happy. Using a mood cube made from a box like the one in the following illustration also encourages the expression of feelings. Children roll the cube and enact a situation that elicits the emotion depicted on the cube.

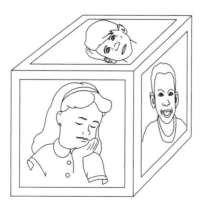

Prop Boxes

As part of her unit on the post office, Ms. Packer and her kindergarten children prepared a prop box. They located scales, stamps and stamp pads, mailers, wooden mailboxes, a mail carrier's bag, and a cap. The children used the props to enact the roles of the postal worker, mail carrier, and customer and wrote letters and cards to mail at the post office.

Body Movement and Nonverbal Communication
While studying maps, elementary children can use body movements to demonstrate map symbols and directions. One child becomes the hands of the compass pointing north; another lies down and faces east. They can also use their bodies to show such map symbols as mountains, roads, and railroads.

Puppetry
Following a unit on careers and vocations, elementary children can use puppets to interview one another about their careers. Use simple hand, finger, and face puppets to create a set of interview questions such as, "Why did you choose this career?" "What do you do in your job?" "How do you get to work?" "What do you like about your work?" "Is your boss nice?" "What is the hardest part of your work?"

Without an understanding of how the dramatic arts can be integrated into the subject areas, it is easy to see how many teachers overlook its possibilities. All children benefit from relevant, meaningful activities that focus on intensive oral language experience and use imagination to deal with abstract ideas. Drama, in particular, is easily adapted for all children's skills, abilities, and interests.

MEETING STANDARDS

Integrating Dramatic Arts Experiences Across Ages and Content Areas

The Goals 2000: Educate America Act (1996), named the arts as a core academic subject. The act calls for education standards that define what America's schoolchildren should know and be able to do in the arts by the time they complete high school. The standards, developed by the Consortium of National Arts Education Associations, address four arts disciplines—dance, music, theater, and visual arts—and are categorized in grade-level clusters.

What follows is a list of the national theater standards by grade cluster K–4 followed by examples of how teachers can incorporate these standards into typical grade-level themes. Each example illustrates one way to meet these national standards.

1. Improvisation

Standard #1 (K–8): Script writing by planning and recording improvisations based on personal experience and heritage, imagination, literature, and history

Standard #2 (K–4): Acting by assuming roles and interacting in improvisations

Preschool–kindergarten: Preschool children often study family life and role-play adults and children in a family. In the classroom's family living area, children decide who will be the parents and children. They gather props and assume different family roles, such as cooking breakfast, feeding the baby, getting ready for school, and going to work.

First grade–second grade: As part of a unit on "Families Around the World," children create their own passports and use them to visit families representing different countries and cultures. Each family plans and pantomimes a short skit to illustrate who is in the family, what each member does, what life is like in their country, how they get around, and how the climate influences their life. Children record their observations in their passports as they visit each family around the world.

Third grade–fourth grade: To prepare for an upcoming dramatic enactment, "The Boston Tea Party: Live on the Scene," children write 1-to-2-minute monologues of the character and role they are portraying. Children practice their monologues while standing up, bending over, sitting down, lying on their backs, running in place, and doing jumping jacks. After discussing how the movements affect their abilities to project their voices and use good diction, all children have an opportunity to enact their monologue, on which the children in the audience may provide feedback on the oral communication by raising a green piece of paper to show that the monologue was loud enough, with clear diction, and not too fast, or a red piece of paper to show that the monologue needed improvement in one or more of these areas.

2. Designing and Directing

Standard #3 (K–4): Designing by visualizing and arranging environments for classroom dramatizations

Standard #4 (K–4): Directing by planning classroom dramatizations

Preschool–kindergarten: During a unit on weather, preschool children learn how to dress appropriately for different environments. Seasonal clothing and toys in prop boxes give children the opportunity to enact how to dress appropriately during different seasons. For example, when asked to enact playing in the summer, children might choose a shovel and pail and put on sunglasses, sandals, and a hat while pretending to play in the sand.

First grade–second grade: As part of a unit on habitats and Native American environments, children participate in choral readings and discussions of Byrd Baylor's book *The Desert Is Theirs* (Baylor & Parnall, 1975). The culminating activity for the unit is an interactive museum, in which groups of children portray frozen picture scenes from the book.

The children decide who will enact the people and animals in the desert habitat, how they might look, and what props and scenery they will need. Teachers and children view the exhibits "coming to life" with the children enacting their scene in the story.

Third grade–fourth grade: After discussing historical information about the "the shot heard 'round the world" and the Boston Massacre, children design and enact a modern-day talk show of the historical event. The children decide who should be the show host, co-host, cue-card holder, and lighting and sound technicians, and which people to interview. The role of the talk show audience allows for open debates with the interviewees. The children work collaboratively and use their five senses to help visualize and create the appropriate scenery, lighting, and sound for the show's setting.

3. Researching, Comparing, and Analyzing Art Forms

Standard #5 (K–4): Researching by finding information to support classroom dramatizations

Standard #6 (K–4): Comparing and connecting art forms by describing theater, dramatic media (such as film, television, and electronic media), and other art forms

Preschool–kindergarten: After reading *The Cat in the Hat* (Seuss, 1957) and watching the animated video, children discuss the characteristics of both real and imaginary characters. With art supplies, they design their own imaginary puppets to act in an improvised puppet show. The teacher invites children to describe what they like to eat, wear, and do for fun.

First grade–second grade: For a unit on continents, children work in groups to research, design, write, and perform in commercials for a fictitious travel agency. Each commercial features pertinent information about the continent and reasons one would want to visit.

Third grade–fourth grade: As part of a unit on the Civil War, children research, design, write, and perform in a courtroom drama debating slavery from the perspectives of the abolitionists and the southern planters (Fennessey, 2000). The children look at courtroom debates in movies to find ways to add visuals, music, and movement to make their arguments more compelling.

4. Analyzing and Utilizing Forms of Media

Standard #7 (K–4): Analyzing and explaining personal preferences and constructing meanings from classroom dramatizations and from theater, film, television, and electronic media productions

Standard #8 (K–4): Understanding context by recognizing the role of theater, film, television, and electronic media in daily life

Preschool–kindergarten: As part of their unit on the zoo, preschool children discuss how animals communicate. They use movement and sounds to show their feelings and to convey their needs. The children enact different scenarios such as "a hungry lion," "a sleepy bear," or "an angry gorilla." During each enactment, the teacher and students discuss what movements and sounds gave them clues as to how the animal was feeling or what the animal needed.

First grade–second grade: After reading *The Daring Escape of Ellen Craft* (Moore & Young, 2002), children work in groups to reenact scenes from the suspenseful story of two slaves determined to escape to freedom. Each group develops one of the following story parts: exposition, rising action, conflict, crisis and resolution. One group reenacts what they think is necessary background information for the characters and setting. At the end of their enactment, the teacher calls out "Freeze," and the next group of children (rising action) take their place and begin their reenactment. The groups continue to enact their parts of the story until the story is complete. At the conclusion, the children discuss how reenacting a story helps in comprehending the parts of a story.

Third grade–fourth grade: Children studying citizenship education and democratic values hold real or mock elections for classroom delegates to the school's student council. Each class selects a candidate to support and designs a political campaign for that candidate. The children collaborate to help their candidate with press conferences, debates, campaign commercials, and public service announcements. After the election, the children analyze and discuss the most and least effective strategies in each candidate's campaign.

Frequently Asked Questions About the Dramatic Arts

How do I provide drama experiences for children who are English-language learners?

Drama's social nature provides opportunities for English language learners to initiate and engage in conversation with fluent English speakers, improve their oral language skills, and develop positive attitudes toward each other. Nellie McCaslin (2000), noted drama expert, says, "The most common error in dealing with [limited English–speaking] children is underestimating their ability and overestimating their verbal skill" (p. 339). Drama activities such as body movement, choral speaking, and pantomime utilize children's concentration without the pressure of verbalization; dramatic-play opportunities naturally immerse children in oral language where they can create and interpret familiar character roles, situations, and events (de León, 2002),

and read alouds that lend themselves to enactment are a powerful way to expand children's language and provide nonnative English speakers with opportunities to "connect the structure [of the language] with the underlying meaning because the drama in which they encountered the structure has supplied them with that context" (Burke and O'Sullivan, 2002, p. 3).

How do I include children with exceptionalities in drama activities?

Alicia, a third grader with a hearing impairment, used sign language to communicate outside school. Mr. Ubek, her teacher, invited Alicia to share her knowledge of sign language using pantomime. Her hearing peers acted as spectators as they interpreted the signs that Alicia shared. For the child with a hearing impairment, pantomime and movement are the easiest mediums for success (McCaslin, 2000). Children with other physical disabilities can participate in drama activities by taking the role of the narrator in a retelling, the puppeteer in a dramatization, or a group member in choral speaking. All children with disabilities can participate in and feel successful in drama activities. They, too, must experience the rewards from drama (Kirk, Gallagher, & Anastasiow, 2003).

How do I engage extremely shy children in drama activities?

Drama enables children to work together in groups or teams to create, direct, and interpret meaningful situations. However, for a shy student, drama activities can be very intimidating. Teachers need to resist the temptation to coax shy children into participation, because they often need additional time to observe others before participating in drama activities. Shy children may choose to watch their classmates or sit on the sidelines until they feel comfortable that their efforts will be accepted and encouraged before they actually participate. Teachers can use puppets, masks, or other props that children can either stand behind or use to take the attention away from them and feel more open to express themselves (Pearson, 2000). Additionally, teachers also need to practice the art of *side coaching,* a drama technique in which the leader gives suggestions or comments from the sidelines to heighten and advance as well as control the playing (Heinig, 1993).

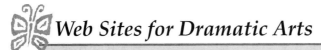

Web Sites for Dramatic Arts

http://aaronshep.com/rt/
Children's author Aaron Shepard provides many resources for readers' theater, including the acclaimed Reader's Theater Editions series of free
scripts. Each script includes the length of the play, description of the genre,
culture, theme, and number and ideal age of readers.

http://artsedge.kennedy-center.org/
ArtsEdge offers free, arts-integrated, standards-based teaching materials for
classroom use. It also provides student materials and guidelines for arts-
based instruction and assessment.

http://www.byu.edu/tma/arts-ed/
Provides many classroom drama activities for each of the National Standards
for Theatre Education. There are also lists of activities for improvisation
and theater games.

http://library.thinkquest.org/5291/
Children's Creative Theater, an Education World Reviewed Site, Graded A+,
includes the history of theater, a glossary of theater terms, theater games,
theater resources for all age levels, an original skit, and the opportunity to
visit a children's theater online.

CHAPTER SUMMARY

1. Drama contributes to every child's learning and is an essential part of a learner-centered classroom. Enactment enhances the development of children's imaginative thinking, problem solving, communication, perspective-taking abilities, and appreciation of drama as an art form.

2. Drama focuses on children's natural expression of thoughts, feelings, and ideas rather than on a polished theatrical performance.

3. Drama activities can be characterized on a continuum from least to most formal. Informal drama uses children's natural, pretend behavior to enact roles, behaviors, and actions in such activities as role-play or pantomime. Story or interpretive drama involves some rehearsal, and participants use voice, gestures, and facial features to interpret someone else's ideas and words. Scripted or formal drama uses a memorized script performed for an audience.

4. Teachers possess the most powerful influence over children's dramatic expression. How teachers select and present drama activities and experiences significantly influences how children will develop their creative potential.

5. Appropriate drama experiences and activities for children include sociodramatic and dramatic play, story dictation, pantomime, puppets, story drama, and readers' theater. All of these drama forms can be integrated with every subject area.

Discuss: Perspectives on the Dramatic Arts

1. Many educators believe that the answer to our educational problems is a "back to basics" philosophy. What arguments would you put forth to convince other educators that drama is basic to an early childhood curriculum?

2. Teachers have an important role in developing and sustaining the dramatic arts as an integral part of the curriculum. What teaching behaviors would you expect to see from a teacher who supports children's growth through drama?

3. Review the opening case study of first-grade children preparing to enact the story "The Little Red Hen." Why do you think Ms. Clark devoted one week to this activity? If a colleague of Ms. Clark's criticized her for "wasting time," how might Ms. Clark respond without being overly defensive?

4. Have you ever performed a scripted drama on stage in front of an audience? Describe your feelings. How do you think children feel when engaged in this kind of activity?

5. As a beginning teacher, how much experience with drama do you need to have? What are the minimum skills and values you will need to incorporate drama successfully into your curriculum?

6. Research describes the positive effects of dramatization on children's reading comprehension. Choose some appropriate stories or picture books for children at different age levels to reenact. Why did you select these particular stories? How can teachers encourage story drama in their classrooms?

PART 3
CREATIVE TEACHING

Chapter 6

Planning and Managing the Classroom Environment

Students need a learning environment they can trust. An environment that constantly changes, particularly without warning, can make students feel insecure and undermine a sense of group ownership.

From Marylynn Clayton (2001), *Classroom Spaces That Work*, p. 55

CLASSROOM PERSPECTIVES ON THE CLASSROOM ENVIRONMENT

Preschool–Kindergarten

When Ms. Ring had surgery, she missed two weeks of school and a substitute taught her class. On the day Ms. Ring returns to her classroom, she is shocked by what she sees. There may be a place for everything, but nothing is in its place. Puzzle pieces are in the toy box, on the floor, and buried in the sand table. Dolls and stuffed toys are sticky with glue, raisins are squashed into the carpet, and crayons are mixed in with the woodworking tools. The substitute had brought in sieves, sifters, and soil so that the children could categorize and label the soil as rocks, gravel, or sand. Now those materials are everywhere. Before Ms. Ring took sick leave, she conferred with the substitute and felt confident in her creative and appropriate classroom. Now Ms. Ring has doubts. Her classroom is no longer a quality learning environment. It is, in her words, a "disaster area"—unsupervised, unstructured, and unplanned.

First Grade–Second Grade

Mrs. Rapoza's second-grade classroom is always in disarray. Mrs. Rapoza keeps her materials in several areas throughout the classroom so students have access to learning tools. Unfortunately, it is difficult for Mrs. Rapoza to keep materials stored in an orderly and accessible way because the children tend to start a project using supplies in one area and finish the project using the supplies in another area, often not returning the materials to the original place. Mrs. Rapoza talks with her students about the importance of keeping materials stored appropriately so they are available for others to use; however, the students take little action to maintain order with classroom supplies.

Third Grade–Fourth Grade

Mr. Bell, a fourth-grade teacher, prides himself on teaching in a quiet, neat, and orderly classroom. He has designed his classroom for students to work primarily on individual tasks at their desks with little or no peer interaction. Mr. Bell closely guards classroom supplies to ensure that they are not misplaced and always has required learning assignments for the whole class. Although he says he sees the importance of an environment in which children have freedom of choice, he limits that option to Friday afternoons after all required work has been completed. During the rest of the week, he reserves playlike activities for physical education and recess.

These scenarios highlight how a classroom can become a poor classroom environment for learning. Teachers must design high-quality classroom environments and view them holistically, as "a planned arrangement of ideas, people, time, space, and resources" (McLean, 1995, p. 7) that is essential to the teaching and learning process. A carefully planned and managed classroom environment encourages children's creative processes, creates a sense of belonging and ownership, builds on children's natural curiosity and joy of learning, and allows personal initiative to flourish, yet develops respect for others and for learning.

The choices teachers make in planning and managing the classroom environment strongly affect children's interactions with one another, with adults, with materials, and with learning experiences. If we compare Ms. Ring's concept of a quality classroom environment with that of the substitute, it is easy to see how the environment can reveal our own beliefs about creativity and learning. Likewise, we can see how Mr. Bell's classroom can inhibit creative thought and intrinsic motivation to learn. Planning and managing the classroom is as important as planning for instruction. Each must harmonize with the goals of the program and/or curriculum.

To capitalize on children's creative thought, teachers need to create rich environments that are responsive to the needs of all learners. Quality classrooms should be filled with numerous resources, such as books, videos, and databases, to encourage self-directed learning and provide learning experiences that offer multiple opportunities for children to work with a variety of peers in collaborative small-group contexts (Edmiston & Fitzgerald, 2000). In the following section, we provide the theoretical and research foundation for quality classroom environments.

THEORETICAL AND RESEARCH BASE: FEATURES OF QUALITY CLASSROOM ENVIRONMENTS

Recall some of your own classroom environments in which you were comfortable, felt valued, and looked forward to learning as compared to those in which you were uncomfortable, felt devalued, and felt like learning was a chore. In the first case, the quality of your classroom environment was positive; in the latter case, the quality was negative. Quality classroom environments have three basic features: *climate, space,* and *time* (Frost, Shinn, & Jacobs, 1998; Garreau & Kennedy, 1991; Johnson, Christie, & Yawkey, 1999; Kauchak & Eggen, 2003; Jones, 1977). These features greatly influence children's capacity to think creatively, to engage in complex play, and to learn.

Climate

Climate refers to the emotional and academic feeling one gets from the environment and dictates to what extent children can be productive, engaged thinkers and learners. Classrooms that promote children's creative thought have the following:

- *Teachers* who are accepting and caring, have high expectations for all students' success, show genuine interest in children's activities, support children's efforts, and create positive classroom designs.
- *Children* who feel emotionally safe, are absorbed in learning, have choices, and make decisions about work to be done.
- *Materials* that capture and sustain children's interest and imagination and that are stored attractively and orderly on shelves.
- *Design features* that evoke a warm, homelike quality, such as carpeted surfaces; soft, light colors; and comfortable furniture in a safe and orderly environment.

On the other hand, classrooms that *hinder* children's creativity are product-oriented and have the following:

- *Teachers* who criticize creative thinking, interact minimally with children, do not believe that all students can be successful, and strive for control through numerous verbal commands.
- *Children* who are passive learners, worry about being criticized, have few choices, rarely make their own decisions, and are unlikely to be risk takers.
- *Materials* that elicit one correct answer, suggest a "hands-off" approach to learning, and are stored on crowded shelves.
- *Design features* that evoke an institutional feeling, such as neutral colors, unmovable furniture, or an abundance of uncoordinated patterns.

Consider these features as you think about the feeling emanating from two second-grade classrooms. In Mr. Kaminsky's class, desks are aligned in neat rows; children are quiet and work individually on the same tasks while the teacher reads with a reading group in the back of the room. Teacher-made bulletin boards, cartoon figures, and posters of classroom rules dominate the room. Mr. Kaminsky divides his daily schedule into five subject-area time blocks. When he rings the bell, the children move quietly to the next activity. The children worry about "being right" and often do only the minimum required.

In the class across the hall, Ms. Reiks plans a flexible schedule with long blocks of time and arranges her classroom into learning and interest centers, each identified by inviting and colorful hanging signs. Upon arrival each morning, the children talk with one another and plan their instructional day with selections on a planning and procedures board. They move easily and freely around the room, independently accessing materials and placing completed assignments and learning contracts in designated, labeled boxes. Active and quiet activities occur simultaneously. Some children read to one another in the classroom library; others construct scenery for a play they have created; still others work with Ms. Reiks on a three-dimensional community map. Displays of children's original work,

*Quality classrooms greatly influence children's capacity
to think creatively, to engage in complex play,
and to learn.*

mounted attractively and placed at the children's eye level, fill the room. At planned times during the day, the class gathers for group experiences, sharing, and additional planning.

Clearly, the climate in Ms. Reiks's classroom is safe, orderly, and conducive to creative thought. Her learner-centered environment is responsive to children's needs and interests, respectful of children's ability to participate in making decisions, challenging, safe, and secure for all learners.

Classroom climate is also greatly influenced by an environment's aesthetic appeal (Edwards, Gandini, & Forman, 1999; Sanoff, 1995). Classrooms for children should be beautiful places to learn. The schools in the Reggio Emilia section of Italy have learning environments that are explicitly created to appeal to children's aesthetic senses. A visitor to such a school might see environments full of light, color, plants, and mirrors selected for their aesthetic characteristics. Great care is taken to create a beautiful environment—detail is given even to such seemingly inconsequential considerations as how bathrooms are decorated, how materials are stored, and how lunches and snacks are presented. The environment in Reggio Emilia schools is warm and beautiful, and it is taken as seriously as planning instruction (Edwards et al., 1999).

Published rating scales and guidelines support teachers' design of appropriate classroom environments for children of all ages. These scales provide the salient criteria needed to establish quality classroom environments. Appendix B lists and describes several such scales.

Space

Space includes the degree to which the classroom environment is organized to develop active, creative thinkers and has a strong influence on how children function and learn. Children feel more connected to classrooms that have adequate space, anticipate their needs, and respect them as individuals. Young children need at least 25–30 square feet to play productively and to minimize disputes (Rettig, 1998; Smith & Connolly, 1980). Effective use of space involves flexible use of materials, defined space for quiet and noisy activities, private space, and accommodations for children with special needs.

- *Flexible use of materials.* Effective teachers use easels, movable cabinets, storage shelves, and tables to define areas so that children can work individually, in small groups, or in a whole group. The more flexible the materials and furnishings within a space, the more possible it is to maximize the potential of any room regardless of its size or shape. If, for example, children are in a school building that is undergoing renovations and want to reconstruct what they are seeing with blocks or other large materials, flexible furnishings allow for spaces to be increased and decreased in response to the children's current project needs.

- *Defined space for quiet and noisy activities.* Well-balanced classroom space separates quiet and boisterous activity and creates safe traffic patterns. It also provides small spaces necessary for young children to create imaginative playworlds in which they can engage for long periods of time. These arrangements give both children and teachers more control and choice over their learning experiences and their play (Clayton, 2001; Johnson, Christie, et al., 1999; Kritchevsky, Prescott, & Walling, 1977) and maximize the use of time available for play. Many teachers are quite inventive in using classroom space in creative and appropriate ways.

- *Private space.* Teachers sometimes underestimate the young child's need for private space. Some children need a periodic rest from the action and interaction of the classroom in a place to restore energy or to think quietly before resuming classroom activity. Certain activities, such as listening to a story tape, are enjoyed more fully in a secluded place. If classrooms lack such places, children often create their own, such as the first graders who found that the space underneath their teacher's seldom used desk was a favorite place to read. Figure 6.1 lists ways

---

- *Lofts*, which use both upper and lower spaces at the same time.
- *Alcoves*, which often occur between shelves.
- *Closets*, with the door removed, which can become learning centers.
- *Screens*, which create a cozy space and enable teachers to monitor children.
- *Appliance boxes*, which become another center or an imaginary place.

Figure 6.1
Suggestions for Creating Small Play Spaces
Note. Adapted from Wellhousen (1999).

of creating small spaces in your setting to increase the quality and length of children's play and creative thought.

- *Accommodations for children with special needs.* Adapting space for children with special needs helps them feel part of the classroom community. A child in a wheelchair, for example, will need additional space to maneuver or sit at a table. Children who are impulsive often need two distinct spaces—one space to work alone and one space to be in a group. Children with communication disorders need environments that minimize noise and promote language learning by having many opportunities to talk. How space is arranged and used influences how time will be used.

Time

Time clearly conveys the importance of an activity or experience and affects teachers' short-term and long-term planning. More than 200 years ago, Benjamin Franklin referred to time as "the stuff of life." The same could be said about time and teaching, for teachers seem to think there never is enough time to cover the material. Unfortunately, much classroom time is used inefficiently and inappropriately.

When children have long blocks of time, their thinking is more constructive, cooperative, and expressive than with short, interrupted time periods. In a full-day preschool or kindergarten, for example, 30 minutes per day of play is a minimum (Johnson, Christie, et al., 1999). Teachers who are sensitive to time factors must be able to decide when to extend or stop an activity or when to capitalize on a "teachable moment." Time exerts an important influence on three dimensions of creative thought—self-expression and self-regulation, attention span, and more complex thinking.

- *Time influences children's self-expression and self-regulation.* When children are continually interrupted, they can become disengaged in learning (Johnson, Christie, et al., 1999). In contrast, when children have enough time during the school day to choose some learning activities, they become more self-directed learners. Classroom environments that have ample time tend to foster children's imaginative spirit. Recall Ms. Reiks's flexible schedule that incorporated long blocks of time for learning.
- *Time affects children's attention span.* Many teachers erroneously believe that because children have short attention spans, activities must be changed constantly. When children are engaged in meaningful learning, they can concentrate for comparatively long periods of time. In the schools of Reggio Emilia, for example, very young children remain with a topic for as long as they show an interest in it. Often these topics last for several months (Edwards et al., 1993). In elementary schools, for example, children remain with inventions and investigations for long periods of time because the projects are highly interactive and engaging.
- *Time affects the complexity of children's creative processes and play.* When children have ample time, they can tap into the kinds of creative processes used by inventors—curiosity, persistence, imagination, communication, and problem

solving. Higher levels of play, such as sociodramatic play, require considerable amounts of time to plan and carry out an activity that is particularly engaging and meaningful to the child (Edwards et al., 1999; Garreau & Kennedy, 1991; Tegano, Moran, DeLong, Brickey, & Ramassini, 1996). Long blocks of time increase children's ability to move from exploration to more complex forms of investigative play with materials, people, and events. To illustrate, one primary-grade teacher helped her children observe and record changes of plant growth over time. The children classified that data by similarities and differences in types of plants, answered questions using scientific processes, and concluded their study with cooking, dramatizing, and illustrating the plant growth cycle. In this example, long blocks of time investigating a process (change in plant growth) helped children deepen their conceptual understanding (Wassermann, 2000).

The features of quality classroom environments—climate, space, and time—are critical foundations of classroom environments that can either enhance or hinder children's creative processes. Classrooms that allow time for children to explore, inquire, and utilize its contents within an emotionally safe and secure setting support children's creative processes and also support children's and teachers' changing needs, interests, and abilities. Classroom environments that are responsive to all children are a prerequisite to learning and should be modified periodically to meet these changing needs. Figure 6.2 contains key features of quality classroom environments that affect children's creative processes.

TEACHERS' REFLECTIONS ON CLASSROOM ENVIRONMENTS

Preservice Teachers

"During my student teaching, I noticed that because of the short blocks of time my cooperating teacher allotted for centers, the children often started cleaning up almost as soon as they initiated an activity. When I had responsibility for full-time teaching and planning, I extended the time blocks and saw its benefits on children's learning and creative thinking."

"I used to think that classrooms should be serious, 'no nonsense' places to learn. I now believe that warm, safe, and homey environments are more beneficial to fostering creative thinking because they help children feel comfortable."

Inservice Teachers

"The idea of the environment as the 'third teacher' has prompted joyful wanderings in my own head of the possibilities associated with this notion. How to make this happen in my kindergarten class is daunting to me now, but I am convinced of the need for it and am pursuing it."

"As a school board member, I was asked to examine the playground space at one of our elementary schools and hesitated at first. Playground space just did not shout out creative thinking or priority to me in this time of high accountability and

1. Softness

Describes the feeling of the environment.

	Hardness
Carpeted areas	Hard surfaces (wood or linoleum)
Soft, comfortable, and mobile furniture	Immobile furniture
Warm, soft vocal tones	Drab colors

2. Open

Closed

Describes how materials, storage patterns, and program structure enhance or restrict children's creative interactions with materials and with each other.

Open materials offer unlimited possibilities for use (e.g., collage and water)	Limited alternatives (e.g., puzzles and matching games)
Relatively open materials offer a number of possibilities (e.g., construction materials)	No visible or reachable storage
Visible and accessible storage	Materials to be used in one way

3. Simple

Complex

Describes the extent to which materials and equipment sustain children's interests. Simple materials do not hold children's attention very long; complex materials contribute to children's imagination.

Single use not fostering manipulation (e.g., slides, puzzles, swings)	Combine two different materials (e.g., art, dramatic play); supercomplex materials: combine three or more materials (e.g., sand, tools, and water)

4. High Mobility

Low Mobility

Concerns the degree of children's physical activity.

Gross motor, active physical activities (e.g., climbing, jumping)	Small motor, sedentary activities (e.g., drawing, writing)

5. Intrusion

Seclusion

Concerns boundaries and opportunities for privacy.

Adds new people and materials to the environment; children free to move about; cross-age grouping and teachable moments	Defined private sectors

6. Risk

Safety

Concerns opportunities for risk taking and environmental safety.

Opportunities to experiment with new materials, ideas, and ways of playing in careful ways	Protects children from hazards

7. Large Group

Individual

Addresses the balance between large- and small-group learning opportunities throughout the day.

Story time, musical experiences, group games, morning meeting	Lap reading, one-to-one reading, individual activities

Figure 6.2

Key Features of Quality Classroom Environments

Note. Adapted from Jones (1977) and Prescott (1984).

focus on test scores. Now, I realize how the playground can hold the key to hands-on extensions and expand children's view of their life, the world, and the future."

Your Reflections

- What do you think are the effects of the classroom environment on children's and teachers' behavior?

- How might your knowledge and beliefs about a quality environment influence children's self-expression and learning?

- Explain how you would go about planning and managing your own classroom environment and provide a rationale for your decisions.

PLANNING AND MANAGING THE INDOOR ENVIRONMENT

In enriched classroom environments, children experience a balance of self-selected, self-directed, and teacher-selected activities. Picture these two third-grade classrooms. In Mr. Lee's class, the day begins with centers containing activities and projects selected by the children as part of their unit of study on the solar system. Some children are constructing models of planets; others are researching the distances between each planet and the sun; still others are investigating moon shapes and illustrating the different phases; and others are publishing original books, plays, and poetry about what they see in the night sky. Following centers, the children gather in a circle for their morning whole-group meeting. Mr. Lee likes the group circle arrangement for whole group because it minimizes distractions and creates a sense of belonging. Mr. Lee places traditional, whole-group activities (such as problem solving, planning events of the day, sharing, and academic or social skill development) after centers to capitalize on children's high interest in starting to learn early in the day. Next door in Ms. Gorman's classroom, the children spend the first hour and a half of each day in a language arts block. They must remain seated at their desks as they begin their day with traditional openings, such as attendance, the calendar, the lunch count, and the weather. Ms. Gorman follows these opening activities with a group skill lesson and a lengthy period of teacher questions to individual children about the lesson. She constantly reminds the children to pay attention and often isolates several from the group by sending them to the "thinking chair" as punishment for becoming distracted.

Notice how the children in Mr. Lee's classroom are eager to learn, have choices of selected learning activities, and engage in dialogue with their teachers and peers. Mr. Lee's classroom has a flexible schedule and organization, contains a variety of interest centers, and has well-managed transitions and routines that meet children's needs. In Ms. Gorman's room, on the other hand, the room arrangement is invariant, there are no interest centers, one activity blurs into another, and routines are established for teacher convenience, dictated by the schedule. In this case,

Ms. Gorman's classroom environment does not provide rich opportunities for children to assume responsibility for their own learning, while Mr. Lee's arrangement supports a learner-centered focus. The following section describes two important aspects of quality indoor environments—*room arrangement* and *centers.*

✿ FEATURES OF QUALITY INDOOR ENVIRONMENTS

Room Arrangement

Room arrangement refers to the way space is organized for children's learning and movement. It can be planned, such as the art center and the area around it, or unplanned, such as a cubbyhole between two shelving units that attracts children. Space affects children's and teachers' behaviors and attitudes with one another and with materials (Clayton, 2001; McLean, 1995; Prescott, 1984).

When arranging the classroom environment, keep in mind the following principles:

1. *The environment communicates messages about appropriate behavior.* If you are invited to dinner, you would behave differently at a cookout with paper plates and plastic utensils than at a formal dinner party with china, silver, and crystal. Space works in the same way. It dictates how children may interact and use materials and affects their work pace. Well-organized space facilitates movement, creative expression, and learning. In contrast, poorly organized space invites ongoing interruptions, decreases children's attention spans, increases the likelihood of conflicts, and demands more teacher direction about rules and regulations (Jalongo & Isenberg, 2004; Johnson, Christie, et al., 1999).

2. *Space must be easy to supervise.* Carefully arranged space enables teachers to scan the room from all vantage points to observe and monitor children's behavior. In this way, teachers can facilitate behaviors that support learning goals and redirect those that do not. It is equally important to distinguish between the child's and the adult's environment. Teachers and children view their surroundings from different perspectives. Both usually attend to what is at their eye level (Bredekamp & Copple, 1997; Clayton, 2001).

3. *Materials must be accessible and easy to use.* Ms. Reich teaches a class of 2-year-olds and has arranged the manipulative toys such as large Tinkertoys and shape sorters along low, open shelves that face a carpeted area away from traffic flow. Because toddlers usually dump manipulatives on the floor to play with them, Ms. Reich provided the space for them to do so. From a developmental perspective, this teacher made her toys easy to use. Making materials accessible to children enhances children's sense of ownership of the classroom, encourages creative problem solving, and fosters exchanges of materials from one part of the classroom to another (Isbell & Exelby, 2001).

4. *Be alert to traffic patterns.* Well-arranged rooms provide clear pathways for a smooth and easy flow of traffic throughout the room. When centers are too close to one another and children cannot freely move among them, children interfere with each other. This usually causes conflict. To maintain freedom of movement that enables children to focus on their creative processes, paths should not be used for any other purpose. Unclear paths often distract children on their way to a space or disrupt activities by leading children to intrude in others' ongoing play or to accidentally knock over materials (Clayton, 2001).

Room arrangement is a powerful tool in a quality classroom environment. It requires knowledge of how space can affect behavior and creative thinking. Figure 6.3 shows room arrangements for three age groups: toddlers, preschoolers/ kindergartners, and children in Grades 1–4.

Centers

Most classrooms for children organize space into well-defined, thematic interest areas or centers. Centers are a valuable educational tool, enabling teachers to organize a flexible environment to meet such diverse learning needs as interests, rates of learning, attention, and creative thought. They also help teachers integrate the curriculum, overlap subject areas, develop multicultural awareness, teach to all

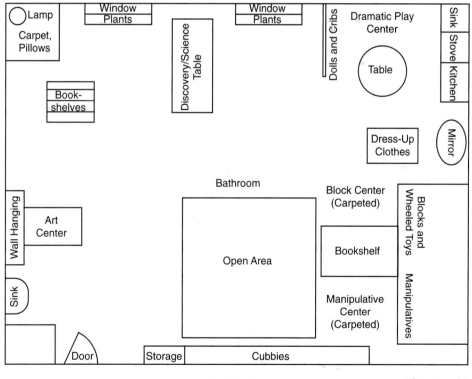

For Toddlers   (*Continued*)

Figure 6.3
Room Arrangements

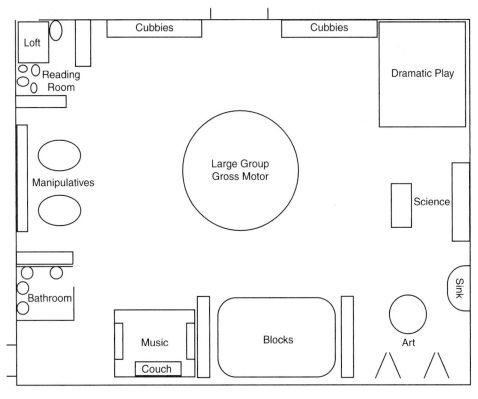

For Preschoolers/Kindergartners

Figure 6.3 *(Continued)*

of children's intelligences, and nurture children's spontaneity and originality (Christie et al., 2003; Isbell & Exelby, 2001; Roe, Smith, & Burns, 2005; Sloane, 1999). Carefully designed centers contain a variety of books and real and manipulative materials that do the following:

- Promote active learning, planning, decision making, problem solving, originality, and interaction throughout the subject areas.
- Increase social and verbal interaction and various forms of play among peers.
- Require children to choose how to spend and manage their time and when to move to another activity.
- Reflect children's interests and cultural backgrounds.

Organizing Centers for Different Age Levels

Organizing learning in centers focuses on the question, "What do the children need to learn and how will they learn it?" A center arrangement is appropriate for children of all ages. Centers not only integrate learning but also provide an organized system for teaching to children's multiple ways of learning and are

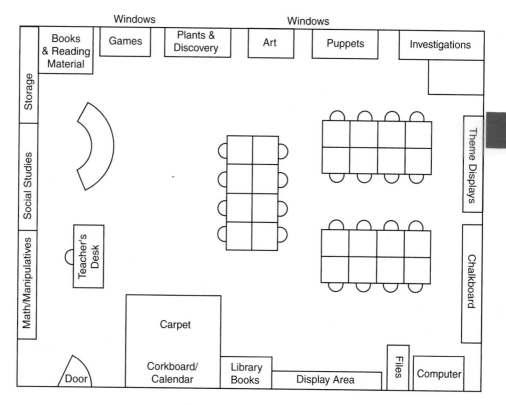

For Children in Grades 1–4

useful for taking into account individual needs, interests, and levels of learning. Some adaptations, however, must be made for children at different ages.

Toddlers need centers that contain a variety of play materials with different levels of complexity, as well as time for exploration (Bredekamp & Copple, 1997; Christie et al., 2003; Rettig, 1998). They must have low, open shelves to display and help the children find materials that reflect familiar people and places matched to the children's developmental level. Toddlers also need materials that encourage exploration and large motor development with climbing and push-pull toys, provide a private space to watch others play or to rest with a soft toy, and offer sensory and creative experiences with music, science, pretense, construction, manipulatives, and sand and water to encourage different types of play.

Preschoolers and kindergartners need centers that meet all of the requirements for toddlers and contain a variety of interesting materials and supplies that can be used to role-play pretend games (such as hats and shoes) and to construct (such as wood, glue, and blocks). The materials must reflect the expanding world of their community, their culture, and their increasing interest in all subject areas (Bredekamp & Copple, 1997).

First and second graders need centers that support their developing logical thinking skills, create an orderly environment, support belonging to a peer group, and help them demonstrate competence in a particular area. They need learning experiences that capitalize on their need to be active learners and that enable them to feel competent and successful. Children in third and fourth grades tend to like resources that include literacy materials, challenge cards, hands-on learning, and ongoing projects (Sloane, 1999). Chapter Seven details the variety of age-appropriate materials children can use in centers.

Teachers who organize their classrooms with centers need to consider the essential elements of space, special requirements, and supervision. *Space* includes planning to ensure visible, defined areas; clear pathways; private space; and arrangement by type of activity (such as large or small group, or active or quiet interaction). *Special requirements* include water, electricity, large floor space, and privacy. *Supervision* entails organizing materials close to their appropriate centers and maintaining a proper vantage point for observation (Isbell & Exelby, 2001; Petrakos & Howe, 1996; Sloane, 1999). The following section provides suggestions for managing centers in your classroom.

Managing Centers in a Learner-Centered Classroom

Centers require management to capitalize on children's natural need for self-directed behavior. Ideally, centers should contain all the materials needed to complete the activity, including instructions, checklists, progress sheets, and options for exploring the concepts and theme. The following techniques will help you organize and manage a center-based environment (Rybczynski & Troy, 1995; Sloane, 1999; Wassermann, 2000):

1. *Implement centers that are appropriate for a particular group of children.* Knowing the needs, interests, and background of your students is important for establishing a center that invites children's participation. You might ask, "What is appropriate for individual children to learn while using this center?" "How will the children who use this center be able to express what they know?" Managing centers involves assessing what students know and can do, soliciting children's ideas about units of study and help in collecting items for that unit, and involving children in planning procedures for its use. Consider, for example, Mr. Kennedy's second-grade classroom. There are two large child-created displays related to their unit on insects. One display contains a variety of three-dimensional imaginative insects created by the children at the art center. Another presents children's illustrated stories about their creations. These centers contain interesting and accessible materials that invite children's participation, are attractively stored in color-coded plastic baskets and tubs, and are clearly labeled to help children keep them properly organized.

2. *Introduce the center with guidelines for its use.* Some teachers provide mini "field trips" before using the centers. These excursions help children understand the boundaries of the center, highlight the materials and equipment available for use, and give children a sense of how much time they have for sustained play, exploration, and investigation. They also help individual children know what learning goals are expected. In Mr. Kennedy's second grade, he organizes children's work as well as materials. Children use individual mailboxes made from recycled 2-liter or gallon jugs with the tops cut off, egg cartons as scissors holders, and a clothesline to display their art. Organizing children's work provides children with a sense of order that fosters their ability to gain a sense of control over their environment, as illustrated here.

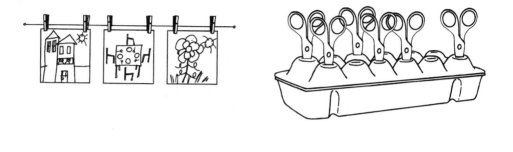

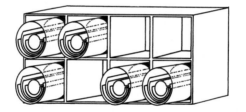

3. *Use planning boards, procedure charts, and learning contracts.* These tools encourage children to recognize the beginning and end of an activity, develop planning and organizational skills related to their own activities, manage their time, work independently and with others, assume responsibility for their own activities, and reflect on their decisions (Sloane, 1999; Wassermann, 2000). Planning boards also help teachers limit the number of children in a center or activity at any one time, evaluate and change centers as needed, and observe children's choices. Planning boards and procedure charts can be easily made from pegboard or tagboard, pictures or labels for centers, and name tags. Some teachers use a magnetic board with small magnets or magnetic tape strips on the board and paper clips glued on the back of cards. For children who are not yet readers, children's names and the names of the centers can be illustrated pictorially. Figure 6.4 illustrates a planning board and procedures chart used with preschoolers, kindergartners, and first graders; Figure 6.5 illustrates procedure charts used with primary-grade children.

Learning contracts are a simple organizational strategy to guide independent study and promote autonomy, facilitate instruction and monitor learning, and diversify learning for children (Tomlinson, 1999). Contracts allow children to choose what work to do, when to work, with whom to work, and where to work. For example, after studying the habits of different animals, some second graders

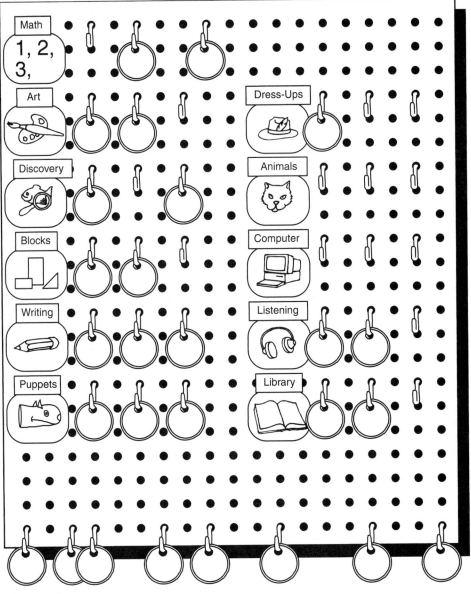

Figure 6.4
A Planning Board

236

Figure 6.5   (*Continued*)
Procedure Charts
Note. Courtesy of Gail V. Ritchie, Kings Park Elementary School, Fairfax, VA.

contracted to extend their knowledge through art by making drawings or models of their favorite animal; others wrote original stories; still others created original play scenarios, such as "Meet My Pet Boa Constrictor." Figure 6.6 illustrates learning contracts for preschoolers/kindergartners; Figure 6.7 illustrates learning contracts for first and second graders, and Figure 6.8 illustrates learning contracts for third and fourth graders.

4. *Assume specific teacher roles to facilitate learning.* Teachers play a critical role in the appropriate use of learning centers. They can use centers to observe and assess children for social or skill use and document children's progress. Teachers should also meet with individual children to guide their center choices that are related to specific learning goals. Moreover, teachers can use center time to model behavior for children who are reluctant to participate in the center project, support children's ideas and projects through listening or participating as a co-player where needed, or pose questions that will keep children engaged in their learning experiences.

5. *Document children's progress and evaluate center use.* Documentation helps teachers identify what children are learning through center activity. Because children are engaged in a variety of learning experiences at the same time, it is important to

Figure 6.5 (*Continued*)

have a system in place to show what children can do. (Refer to Figure 2.1 in Chapter Two for a checklist for documenting children's literacy learning through play.) It is equally important for teachers continually to ask themselves whether children are engaged in meaningful activity and whether the centers provide ongoing opportunities and challenges. Moreover, a key part of the evaluation is to watch for children's waning interest. They may need additional props or materials or may need to start brainstorming ideas for a new theme.

Types and Uses of Centers

Indoor centers can be permanent, temporary, or rotating and include some of the following commonly found materials to support children's creative processes. The best centers include a rich variety of materials that invite exploration and experimentation.

Art Center. The art center enables children to investigate and create using a wide variety of materials. Some teachers even display works from famous artists in or near the center to enhance aesthetic appreciation. The art center should be located near a water source. If not, use plastic sheeting to cover carpeted areas or tables when children are using messy materials.

Most art materials should be organized and accessible on low, open shelves. This arrangement enables children to use them in other centers as needed. For example, in one preschool classroom, two children were designing a menu and a

*A workbench and tools are an important part
of a center-based classroom.*

cover for their Mexican restaurant theme center. They used the menu to elaborate on their play. In a third-grade class, Horace used the art center to create a glove finger puppet as a prop for his story on dragons. Mrs. Ritchie's fourth graders created flyers advertising pets available for adoption to help the local animal shelter as a follow-up to reading *Shiloh* (Naylor, 1991). The students researched facts about the available pets and created an advertisement for one of them, which included a drawing of the animal, its age, and what it liked to eat and play with. In these rooms, the centers provided a vehicle for integrating the curriculum while supporting children's creative thought. Chapter Three contains a detailed list of appropriate uses of art materials.

Block and Construction Center.   Blocks and construction materials (such as Unifix cubes and Legos) help children develop essential classification and seriation skills and concepts, as well as increase their social and problem-solving skills. The block and construction center should be located away from busy traffic areas and in an area with ample space for construction. It should contain a wide assortment of blocks and accessories, such as human figures, road signs, and small-wheeled vehicles for young children and a variety of construction sets and materials for older children. Literacy materials and tools are also important so that children may sketch their "blueprints" on paper, label a building they've created, or write a story about their experience. Blocks should be accessible on open shelves marked with paper silhouettes of each block size and shape. Placing the center adjacent to the

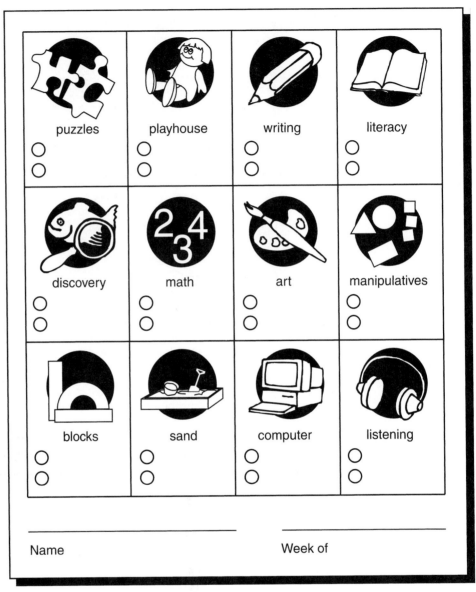

Figure 6.6
Learning Contract for Preschoolers/Kindergartners

dramatic play center for younger children increases the interchange among centers (Hirsch, 1996; Vergeront, 1996). Chapter Seven contains more detailed information on blocks and construction materials.

Discovery and Science Center.   In this "hands-on" center, children actively explore materials that help develop scientific and conceptual understandings, such as

I _____ agree to the following learning activities:

1. Complete _____ activity.
2. Choose _____
3. Read _____
4. Conference with _____

Name _____ Week of _____

Language Arts	Math
_____ ○	_____ ○
_____ ○	_____ ○
Social Studies	Science
_____ ○	_____ ○
_____ ○	_____ ○

Skill Group

Lunch 🍎📚		Story 📖	Recess ⚽	
Blocks	○ ○	Literacy	○ ○
Manipulatives	○ ○	Sand	○ ○
Listening	○ ○	Puzzles	○ ○
Projects	○ ○	Computer	○ ○

Figure 6.7
Learning Contract for First and Second Graders.

Biography of an Artist

1. Choose one of the following biographies to learn about an artist's life as a child and as an adult:

_____ *Sebastian: A Book about Bach* (Winter)

_____ *In Search of the Spirit: The Loving National Treasure of Japan* (Hamanaka)

_____ *When Miriam Sang* (Ryan)

_____ *Michaelangelo* (Stanley)

_____ *Alvin Ailey* (Pinkney)

_____ *Duke Ellington: The Piano Prince and His Orchestra* (Pinkney)

2. Find out about your artist's life and talent as an artist, musician, or dancer. What dreams did he or she have and how did he or she fulfill them?

3. Share your findings in one of the following ways:

    a. Illustrate an interesting incident about your artist and write about why you illustrated what you did.

    b. Write a skit about your favorite part of the biography.

    c. Make a model of the artist you read about.

    d. Interview a classmate who has read this book or another book about your artist.

    e. Use computer art to represent a big idea about your artist.

    f. Other—specify: _____.

I plan to read _____, share by _____, and complete my work by _____.

Student _____

Teacher _____

Date _____

Figure 6.8
Learning Contract for Third and Fourth Graders

shape, number, volume, or buoyancy. Children gain firsthand experiences with concepts about animals, vegetation, and minerals, as well as the equipment used to study them such as scales, magnets, and simple measurement tools. Materials for experiments may include boxes of collected items, such as shells or rocks, for sorting, classifying, comparing and contrasting, and literacy materials and tools that support reading and writing across the subject areas. Often children use these materials for ongoing projects in other centers. To illustrate, one kindergartner took the magnifying glass from the discovery center to examine sick animals she was tending in the dramatic-play area during a play theme on the veterinarian's office. A fourth grader added information about his plant's growth to the classroom graph. The discovery and science center also includes experiences with sand, rice, and water that offer many opportunities for teaching about safety issues with the materials being used.

Dramatic-Play Center.   The dramatic-play center offers a rich setting for extending children's exploration and expansion of roles, behaviors, social skills, and language. It also promotes career and cultural awareness as children explore various occupations and cultures. Dramatic-play centers are often transformed into thematic units of study, such as a bakery during a unit on economics, a shoe store during a unit on measurement, and an artist's studio during a unit on famous artists. Regardless of the theme, a dramatic-play center provides rich opportunities for building literacy skills and concepts. When pencils, pads, telephone books, literature books, and other print materials are added to this center, children's voluntary use of literacy is encouraged (Roe et al., 2005; Christie et al., 2003). Prop boxes, described in Chapter Five, are appropriate in this center and enhance children's play.

Library and Literacy Center.   This center invites children to read a variety of print materials and should be located in a quiet area of the classroom. It should be

Children can develop scientific understandings through exploration with a variety of plastic containers and tubing and a large water table.

attractive, inviting, stocked with books that match children's interests and their topics of study, and comfortable for browsing and reading. Some teachers have used a rocking chair, a seat removed from a car, or an old bathtub filled with pillows in their literacy centers. An ample supply of familiar and interesting books in different formats such as story and information books, wordless and predictable books, riddles, rhymes, and child-made books should be easily accessible and displayed on bookshelves. The center should also contain printed signs and questions that invite children to explore the book selections. Some teachers include the Sunday comics, old catalogues, puppets and prop boxes for retelling stories, recycled copies of children's magazines, and mobiles of information about a featured author. Interesting writing materials, such as recycled colored paper from a print shop and unusual pens and pencils, should be available. For younger children, this center encourages early literacy play—an important precursor to learning to read and write (Christie et al., 2003; Morrow, 2001; Roe et al., 2005). For older children, this center provides ample opportunities for self-selected books that range from easy-to-read materials (such as magazines) to a variety of high-quality literature (such as fiction and poetry) to match students' ability and interest levels as well as opportunities to discuss and share literature.

Manipulative and Math Center.   Manipulative materials, such as colored blocks, buttons, counting frames, and cubes, encourage children's growing mathematical understanding of numbers, classification, ordering, comparing, measuring, estimating, and counting. The center needs to be located near low, open shelves that contain an organized system for storing manipulatives and math games such as dominoes. Writing materials, a chalkboard, and a flannel board should also be available for children to create their own math stories and explore and practice mathematical skills and concepts. Chapter Seven contains an extensive list of appropriate manipulative materials for different ages.

Media and Music Center.   This center uses electronic media (such as CDs, computers, audio tapes, and videotapes) as vehicles for play and playful expression as well as opportunities to invent music with different material (such as PVC pipes for listening to and creating sounds, child- and teacher-created musical instruments, and music for listening and movement). The media and music center needs to be located away from extreme heat, cold, and glare but near an electrical outlet. Many teachers find that laminated posters with rebus-type instructions on operating and caring for the equipment are useful. Computers should be placed on tabletops at eye level and should be arranged so that two or three children may work together at any one time (Swaminathan & Wright, 2003). The media and music center should be as open and accessible as other centers so that children can use the equipment for play and investigation. It should also contain a variety of music for children to listen to, simple musical instruments for children to create their own music, music and instruments from other cultures that children can explore, and opportunities for recording (Kemple, Batey, & Hartle, 2004).

Technology Center.   Technology can be used to expand a child's understanding about a topic or reinforce concepts already learned in the classroom. Age-appropriate software maximizes children's learning by enhancing their inventive thinking, self-expression, teamwork, and creation of high-quality products, all of which are essential skills for the twenty-first century (Haugland, 2001; NAEYC, 1996). Selecting appropriate Web sites is also important. Whether it is an information site, which helps children gain new knowledge and answer questions; a communication site, which puts children in touch with others; or a publication site, which provides a place for children to post their work, all sites must be evaluated using stringent criteria and specific evauation tools (Swaminathan & Wright, 2003). Teachers will find that the award-winning developmentally appropriate software and Web sites posted at http://www.childrenandcomputers.com are useful resources for the technology center.

Writing Center.   In this center, often placed near the library center to prompt children to write about what they are reading, children experiment with writing and illustrating in many forms, from scribbling or drawing to composing poems and stories. Sometimes they come here from other centers to make signs or captions for their work. Good writing centers contain chalkboards, a stapler, glue, pencils, markers and crayons, and an assortment of papers in various sizes, shapes, and colors for writing and illustrating. Magazines, newspapers, old catalogues, scissors, and glue are also available for children to illustrate stories or add to their creations. Some teachers have children keep a box of children's drawings for others to use to create stories (Christie et al., 2003).

Centers offer children more than just good opportunities to engage in an activity; they offer children the chance to explore, investigate, and utilize their ideas in new and creative ways. It is unlikely that you will use all of these centers simultaneously. Most teachers use about six permanent centers that are aligned with their classroom, program, and school goals. Teachers periodically transform these centers to be aligned with ongoing themes and units the children are studying at a particular time. When using centers as a teaching and learning strategy, be sensitive to children's pace of learning and help them move comfortably from one activity to another by paying attention to transitions and routines.

Transitions and Routines

Transitions are times during the day when children move from one activity to the next. In a classroom with centers and choices, each transition requires children to make a decision (Kohn, 1993; Wood, 2001). Routines are regular and predictable activities that form the basis of the daily schedule; they help children sense the passage of time (for example, snack follows cleanup or math follows lunch) and anticipate events (such as by playing a musical selection at the end of each day).

Transitions and routines consume 20 to 35 percent of the preschooler's day and about 15 percent of an elementary child's day (Jalongo & Isenberg, 2004). Unless appropriately planned, they can be difficult and stressful periods for both children and teachers because children's sense of time and level of absorption differs with age and engagement. Failure to plan for transition times encourages inappropriate behaviors, boredom, and increased dependence on the teacher. Following are characteristics of appropriate transitions and routines.

1. *Facilitate children's control over the environment.* One beginning teacher was struggling with classroom management. Each time the children moved from one activity to the next, they playfully pushed one another, tripped or knocked over materials, and constantly asked what to do. What was happening in his teacher's classroom? Her daily schedule consisted of a series of whole-group activities requiring children to spend an inordinate amount of time waiting for a turn, and she paid little attention to transitions. The teacher's mentor suggested examining the organization of the day, starting with planning for routines and transitions. The teacher replied, "It never occurred to me that I should even think about those times in the day. I just assumed children knew what was expected of them when they finished. Now I realize that I must plan for transitions just as I plan for instruction."

2. *Help children make connections to their ongoing, thematic activities.* During a preschool unit on transportation, Ms. Plate sang the song "Riding in an Airplane," by Raffi, with the children. At the end of the song, she suggested that the children pretend to fly to the art tables equipped with paper, markers, and photographs of airplanes and make appropriate airplane noises along the way. This connected their study of transportation with music and art and assured a positive transition.

3. *Plan for smooth transitions from indoors to outdoors.* Some children may be engaged in an indoor activity and might be hesitant to leave; others may prefer indoor activities but need the opportunity to be outdoors. Giving a warning to prepare children for the next experience or location is essential. Planned transitions and routines that are developmentally appropriate are essential for children of all ages. They differ from other activities in purpose, length, and frequency and depend on the age of the children and the available physical facilities. Thoughtful planning provides a structured yet flexible environment that is predictable, minimizes chaos, and empowers children (Kohn, 1993). Figure 6.9 provides suggestions for appropriately managing transitions and routines for children.

Just as teachers regularly consider the design of the indoor environment, they also need to consider how the outdoor environment contributes to creative thought. An interactive and engaging outdoor environment motivates participation and stimulates innovative thinking, imagination, and other creative habits of mind. In the next section, we examine the outdoor environment.

PLANNING AND MANAGING THE OUTDOOR ENVIRONMENT

Many teachers view the purpose of outdoor play as a release of tension and excess energy. This narrow view perpetuates the neglect of the outdoor environment as an important setting for stimulating children's creative ways of thinking. Outdoor environments need the same systematic attention to space, materials, and equipment as indoor environments. The best outdoor environments are safe, are appropriately planned, and provide children opportunities to engage in all forms of

Routines are an integral part of learning and offer both children and teacher more control over their environment.

Arrival

- Prepare materials and activities before children arrive.
- Be available to greet children.
- Prepare engaging activities that attract children's attention and are easy to monitor.
- In extended-day settings, communicate any unusual behaviors or concerns to staff and teachers who follow you.
- Ask parents who want to talk to stay for a moment, if feasible, or call them later to arrange a time.
- Construct an attendance chart, center planning board, or procedure charts so that children can sign in and choose activities as they arrive.

Opening Group Time

- Begin this part of the day after children have had a chance to explore the environment.
- Introduce choices for the day and ask children to decide what they will do.
- Use this time to review or create any classroom rules related to using a particular center or piece of equipment. When children help set these limits, they are more likely to internalize them.
- Demonstrate the appropriate use of new materials.

Cleanup

- Give notice. Children need a 10-, a 5-, and then a 1-minute warning to begin cleanup.
- Play tape-recorded music and have children listen for something special as they put away materials.
- Use a song to announce that cleanup time is approaching and sing while cleaning up.
- Organize a precleanup circle. Decide how to divide the tasks so that each child picks up a certain number of objects or a particular kind of object (such as everything that is smaller than a shopping bag or everything that has a metal part) or use a cleanup helpers' board.
- Model the behaviors you want to see from the children.
- Follow cleanup with an interesting activity that children can anticipate with enthusiasm.
- Create rhymes to familiar tunes that refer to putting away materials or helping ("This is the way we clean our room . . . ").

(Continued)

Figure 6.9

Ideas for Managing Routines and Transitions

Note. Adapted from Clayton (2001) and Johnson, Christie, & Yawkey (1999).

Departure

- Establish a departure ritual such as hearing a story or enjoying a song together.
- Briefly preview some of the interesting things that will take place the next day or later that week.
- Encourage children to bring tote or paper bags for papers, newsletters, and other forms of communication.
- Be available to say good-bye.

Transitions from One Activity to Another

- Develop a repertoire of songs and finger plays to be used as children move from one place to another. Use a song or finger play (for example, "Two Little Blackbirds;" ask one child to name another by color of clothing, kinds of fasteners on shoes, or name card).
- Have books ready for children to read while others finish their activities and get ready to join the group.
- Use a mystery box, puppets, a riddle ("I see something red, white, and blue with stars on it"), finger plays, or quiet songs.

For Children in Grades 1–4:

- Review the day and talk about tomorrow.
- Plan ahead on how to move from one activity to another.
- Have materials ready for the next activity.
- Assign children responsibilities for transitions ("Katie, please gather the scissors").
- Allow children to move from one activity to another at their own pace, when possible.

Figure 6.9   *(Continued)*

play—exercise, dramatic and constructive play, and games with rules in an environment with natural features (Flynn & Kieff, 2002; Frost, 2004; Frost & Woods, 1998; McGinnis, 2002; Rivkin, 1995; Sutterby & Frost, 2002).

Think about Ms. Ogur's concerns about her preschoolers' outdoor environment. In her school, the playground equipment included three tricycles, two balls, and a combination swing set/climbing apparatus for 15 children to share. The children often squabbled over the materials. Ms. Ogur knew that these disputes were caused, in part, by not having enough challenging materials and equipment.

After talking with other colleagues and reading professional literature on outdoor play for preschoolers, she discovered that some materials have different levels of complexity. Kritchevsky et al. (1977) classify materials as follows:

- **Simple units** that have a single, obvious use, with no subparts for children to manipulate or create (such as swings and tricycles).

- **Complex units** that have subparts of two very different kinds of materials for children to manipulate or invent (such as water and plastic containers, or sand and digging tools). This category also includes single play materials that have many diverse possibilities (for example, art materials such as dough and paint, a box of books, or a jump rope).
- **Supercomplex units** that have three or more subparts that children can combine and juxtapose (such as sand, digging tools, and water). Supercomplex units hold children's attention and interest the longest because children have many opportunities to manipulate and juxtapose the parts and integrate them into their play themes.

Ms. Ogur then decided to expand children's play by adding some complexity to the environment. She brought out a wagon; created an obstacle course from old, worn tires; and made some simple traffic signs out of scrap lumber and paint. She also brought out the police officer's hat from the dramatic-play center and markers and scrap paper from the literacy center. From these simple additions, the children created elaborate play themes or scenarios about accidents, traffic, parking, and speeding. Some children even created and handed out parking tickets. On other occasions, the children used the wagon as an ambulance to transport an accident victim to the hospital, where another elaborate scenario was enacted. Ms. Ogur even used the traffic signs to reinforce bicycle safety practices.

Ms. Ogur illustrates what a resourceful teacher can do to make the outdoor environment more stimulating and challenging even with limited financial resources. She also demonstrates how well-planned outdoor environments have the potential to stimulate learning and be more inclusive. Teachers like Ms. Ogur, who view the outdoor environment as a support for children's learning and development, know that activities such as balancing, crawling, and playing games contribute to children's physical development; activities that involve personal care, risk taking, and role playing contribute to children's emotional development; activities that include cooperative games, verbal dialogue, and planning promote children's social growth; and activities that include listening, experimenting, imagining, and symbolizing promote children's cognitive growth (Frost et al., 1998; Frost & Woods, 1998).

Types of Playgrounds

Basically, there are three types of playgrounds: traditional, adventure, and creative (Frost, 2004; Rivkin, 1995). Each differs in origin, types of equipment and materials, targeted age groups, and purpose. Each also differs in promoting or constraining the amount of children's physical activity and social interaction.

Traditional playgrounds originated in the early part of the twentieth century and were designed for physical exercise to emphasize gross motor play. They contain large, steel, immovable equipment (such as climbing bars, slides, and swings)—mostly simple units—to be used for one single purpose: exercise. The lack of variety and challenge in this type of equipment often results in boredom. Traditional playgrounds are often not well maintained or supervised, are built on dangerously hard surfaces, and are not consistent with what we know about children's learning and development, yet they are prevalent in elementary school playgrounds

(Frost & Woods, 1998; Frost et al., 2001). Since the late 1970s, wooden superstructures with a variety of apparatuses have replaced some of this steel equipment and plastic has begun to replace wood. Traditional playgrounds favor physically able children who can take advantage of the play opportunities available. On the other hand, these playgrounds may constrain less physically able children who are reluctant to participate in these types of gross motor activities.

Adventure or "junk" playgrounds, originating in Denmark in the middle of the twentieth century and uniquely European, are designed to provide supervised, creative play opportunities for urban children. They contain unconnected tools and materials that enable children to build, create, and pretend with their own play structures using materials in a free and open atmosphere. Varying in size, they offer children options (such as building, gardening, using sand or water, and cooking). Each adventure playground contains a large hut filled with a variety of typical indoor materials such as art, dramatic-play materials, and music that children choose to use. Adults function as play leaders, support children's ideas, and act as facilitators. Adventure playgrounds support children's freedom to learn through discovery in an enriched environment. These types of playgrounds never were very popular in this country because of our concerns with safety, the unavailability of trained play leaders, and concerns that the adventure playground was not as aesthetically pleasing to adults' eyes.

Creative/contemporary playgrounds, adapted in the twentieth century from the adventure playground concept, are a way to integrate elements of adventure playgrounds into contemporary settings. They provide children with a more stimulating environment for play than that of a traditional playground. Creative playgrounds contain a superstructure with movable parts (such as boards, ramps, and wheels), are action-oriented, provide safe underneath surfaces, offer a variety of stimulating materials and equipment, and promote all forms of play (functional, constructive, dramatic, and games). In addition, they offer children numerous possibilities for social interaction (Barbour, 1999). Creative playgrounds are "developmentally pleasing and aesthetically rich" (Frost & Woods, 1998, p. 234).

Playgrounds that provide many possibilities for children are important learning environments. They stress integrated rather than isolated equipment and extend learning from the indoor to the outdoor environment. Their design has certain features that enhance all forms of children's play.

Features of Quality Outdoor Environments

Outdoor environments provide many benefits for all children and should be utilized year round (Frost, 2004; Frost et al., 2001; Rivkin, 1995). High-quality outdoor environments should focus on four primary features: equipment and materials, safety, supervision, and storage. Figure 6.10 is a checklist of criteria to use in planning and managing the outdoor environment.

Equipment and Materials

Equipment and materials in high-quality outdoor play environments hold children's interest over time and promote creative thought through all four forms of

Place an X under the appropriate response to see if your playground is safe for children.

Adequate Space

Does the environment   Y   N

- Stimulate all four types of play—exercise, constructive, dramatic, and games with rules—through appropriately arranged space and traffic patterns?   _____   _____

- Provide appropriate spaces for individuals and small groups of children according to their ages, physical sizes, interests, and abilities?   _____   _____

- Develop play areas (zones), so that activities such as tricycle riding and climbing do not occur in close proximity to one another?   _____   _____

- Ensure that movement from one zone to another will be safe and manageable?   _____   _____

- Offer a visually pleasing area in which the natural elements and fabricated structures complement each other?   _____   _____

- Provide overall cohesiveness rather than discrete, unconnected objects or structures?   _____   _____

- Foster a sense of flow from one activity to another?   _____   _____

- Provide varied ground surfaces such as hardtop for games and vehicles, grass, water, soft mulch or sand, hilly and flat areas, construction areas, sunlight, and shade?   _____   _____

- Offer easy access to coats, toilets, and drinking fountains?   _____   _____

- Provide protected storage for equipment?   _____   _____

- Contain space for walking, running, and skipping?   _____   _____

- Include a shaded area with tables and benches for art activities, table games, or snacks?   _____   _____

Materials

Does the environment   Y   N

- Offer ample opportunities for a child's physical, cognitive, and social development through a dynamic, challenging, age-appropriate environment with complex materials?   _____   _____

- Promote independent and creative uses of flexible materials such as sand, water, dramatic play, and superstructures with room for many children?   _____   _____

- Contain equipment for active and quiet play and for solitary, parallel, and cooperative play?   _____   _____

(Continued)

Figure 6.10

Checklist for Planning and Managing the Outdoor Environment

Note. Adapted from Frost (2004), Frost, Shinn, & Jacobs (1998), National Association for the Education of Young Children (1996a), and National Program for Playground Safety (1999).

- Contain materials for dramatic play (e.g., car, boat, house)? _____ _____
- Contain materials for constructive play and experimentation (e.g., boards, ramps, tires, tools, nails)? _____ _____
- Provide materials for gross motor development (e.g., climbers, wide slides)? _____ _____
- Provide a sand area located away from people, with proper covering to protect it from inclement weather and animals? _____ _____
- Include a water area located near an outdoor water supply with a variety of materials for experimentation, problem solving, and exploration? _____ _____
- Contain a variety of balls? _____ _____
- Contain nonlocomotor materials for stretching, carrying, and swinging? _____ _____
- Contain manipulative materials for throwing, kicking and catching? _____ _____

Activities and Experiences

Does the environment   Y   N

- Provide for children's interactions with materials, peers, and adults through proper storage, defined spaces, and interest areas? _____ _____
- Offer a range of activities, experiences, and equipment with "loose parts" that children can adapt to their own play schemes? _____ _____
- Provide large equipment for gross motor development; loose parts and natural materials for constructive play; enclosed structures for dramatic play; linked platforms for social play; semiprivate spaces for hiding; and nature areas for gardening? _____ _____

Safety   Y   N

- Are adults actively supervising the play area? _____ _____
- Is the equipment in good repair, in working order, and free of sharp edges? _____ _____
- Are there fences at least 5 feet high with lockable gates that work well? _____ _____
- Are there 8–10 inches of sand, mulch, or pea gravel under climbing and moving equipment? _____ _____
- Is there some type of edging (e.g., railroad ties) to contain the cushioning materials? _____ _____
- Is the area free of litter (e.g., broken glass)? _____ _____

Figure 6.10 *(Continued)*

play (Frost, 2004; National Association for the Education of Young Children [NAEYC], 1996a). Equipment should be sturdy, safe, and age-appropriate. Children who play on equipment that is not appropriate for their size, strength, and decision-making capabilities are exposed to the possibility of serious injury. High-quality equipment and materials feature movable parts; a combination of simple, complex, and supercomplex materials; a wide variety of experiences and activities; and well-defined spaces.

Movable parts are pieces that children can manipulate and use to improvise. Lightweight objects of different sizes, shapes, and textures; boards or ramps; and organic materials such as sand and water can be moved from place to place within the play area as children choose. They also add complexity to the environment. Movable parts provide for flexibility, diversity, novelty, and challenge, which are all important ingredients for creative thought, socialization, and learning.

Complexity refers to the number of possibilities the material offers children. The more possibilities the material has, the more likely it is to hold children's interest and attention because children can do more with it (Kritchevsky et al., 1977). If too much of the outdoor play equipment is designed to be used by one child at a time or to be used in just one way, it severely limits the outdoor environment's complexity. For example, a large tire swing that can hold two or more children offers more options than a swing on a swing set.

Diversity or variety refers to the number of ways materials can be used, regardless of their complexity. It influences how children get started in their play

Outdoor environments provide many benefits for all children and should be utilized year round.

(NAEYC, 1996a). A wide slide, for example, has more possibilities than a narrow slide. A variety of materials offer children necessary choices to create their own forms of play.

Well-defined spaces are those in which both the amount and the arrangement of space facilitate children's play patterns. Accreditation criteria of the National Association for the Education of Young Children (1996a) and the National Academy of Early Childhood Programs (2004) require a minimum of 75 square feet of play space outdoors per child. When the outdoor space is designed using these criteria, children retain ownership over their play, communicate thoughts and feelings, practice persistence, develop feelings of competence and engage in decision-making and problem-solving. Well-planned outdoor environments meet all of children's needs, including physical and mental flexibility. Figure 6.11 provides examples of props and play crates for use outdoors.

Safety

A safe outdoor environment is essential. Yet national survey data reveal that today's playgrounds are unsafe, causing a dramatic increase in childhood playground injuries over the past two decades (Frost, 2004; NAEYC, 1996a; National Program for Playground Safety [NPPS], 1999; Thomason & Thrash, 1999; Thompson, Hudson, & Mack, 2000). Unsafe playgrounds:

- Are poorly designed, antiquated, and inadequately maintained.
- Lack storage facilities, suitable surfacing materials, and accessibility.

Safety is an important issue in the design and construction of outdoor playground equipment.

Play crates help you organize your materials on the playground and extend children's interests from the classroom to the outdoors. Store your materials in durable wood or plastic storage containers that are easily transportable from indoors to outdoors.

Automobile Repair

Auto parts	Empty oil cans	Sparkplugs
Mat	Filters	Flashlight
Cable sets	Wiring	Gears
Windshield wipers	Pliers	Auto parts catalogue
Keys	Bicycle pump	Plastic spray bottles
Piece of hose	Wrench	Nuts and bolts

Fishing

Plastic boat	Stringer	Cane poles
Fishnet	Rod and reel	Play fish
Plastic worms	Rubber snakes	Spinner baits (no hooks)
Rubber lizards	Tackle box	Cricket box
Ice chest	Minnow bucket	Paddles
Small stool (optional)		

Gardening

Water cans	Seed packets
Small garden hoses	Gardening catalogue
Small rakes	Flowerpots
Garden tools	Labels for plantings
Child-sized garden gloves	Stakes

Beach

Sunglasses	Ice chest	Whistle
Seashells	Beach towel	Diving mask
Suntan lotion bottles	Snorkel	Paperback books
Life preserver	Air mattress	Swimming tube
Pail and shovel	Sun visor	

Camping

Knapsack	Sleeping bag	Canteen
Flashlight	Plastic dishes	Tent
Sticks for fire	Mosquito repellent	

Figure 6.11

Props and Play Crates for the Outdoor Environment

Note. Adapted from Odoy & Foster (1997).

255

- Neglect features children prefer, such as dramatic-play materials and nature areas.
- Focus entirely on motor activity.
- Are developmentally inappropriate.
- Are used without safety orientation for staff or children.

Supervision

It is estimated that about 40 percent of playground injuries are related to inadequate supervision. Thus, we suggest the following guidelines for better safety and supervision in outdoor settings:

1. Have the same ratio of adults in the outdoor environment as you do in the indoor environment. At no time should there be fewer than two adults supervising outdoor settings, and they should have knowledge of injury prevention and first aid.

2. Circulate around the area rather than standing in a group and talking.

3. Set clear, reasonable limits about what children may do, such as sitting down on the slide.

4. Decide on supervision of areas in advance. Give special attention to swings or climbers where there is a lot of activity and potential for injury.

5. Place 8–10 inches of fall-absorbing material, such as pea gravel or bark mulch, under and around all moving equipment (such as swings and rotating devices), because falls from high places are the number one cause of playground injuries to children (U.S. Consumer Product Safety Commission, 2002). Be certain to include a retaining border to hold the material and replenish it frequently. Figure 6.12 illustrates an acronym to help you recall the essential elements of playground safety.

Storage

Storage facilities are essential on playgrounds. They house the materials that children use to develop and extend their play. The location of the storage is critical. Storage that

---

Supervise carefully. Make sure that adults who monitor the playground have knowledge of injury prevention and first aid.

Age-appropriate equipment and materials. Ensure that the height, size, and complexity of the equipment is safe for the age and skill level of the children using it, such as having climbing equipment that is not taller than the children using it.

Falls. Have landing surfaces that are resilient, such as wood chips and rubber mats, which cushion falls.

Equipment. Periodically inspect the playground for open hooks, sharp edges, or missing parts. Also check for well-anchored equipment.

Figure 6.12
SAFE Playgrounds
Note. Adapted from NAEYC (1996a) and NPPS (1999).

is accessible to the immediate play area saves time in transporting toys and encourages responsibility in children. Think about storage fits the following criteria:

*   Is child-scaled to facilitate taking out and putting away equipment.
*   Is weathertight and vandalproof to protect the equipment.
*   Is multipurpose, contains space for teacher storage, and allows children to play on the structure.

These characteristics of high-quality outdoor environments apply to children of all ages. However, some adaptations need to be made to make them accessible for all children.

Outdoor Environments for Children of Different Ages and with Diverse Needs

Like indoor environments, outdoor environments must be adjusted to children's diverse developmental levels, needs, and abilities. Outdoor play environments support a range of learning and developmental goals, including a sense of competence and cooperation through vigorous physical activity.

Infant and Toddler Years

Playgrounds for infants and toddlers should meet their rapidly increasing motor and social development, their boundless energy and curiosity, and their clear need for autonomy. Infant and toddler playgrounds have unique safety issues (Frost et al., 2001; Frost & Woods, 1998; Stephenson, 2002). For this age group, give special attention to the following:

*   *Ground cover* that cannot be ingested, such as pea gravel and small wood chips.
*   *Hazardous material* that may have accumulated overnight, such as broken objects, sharp edges, or foreign objects. Teachers need to check the playground daily for such obstructions.
*   *Swing seats* that include a strap to prevent falling.
*   *Safety barriers* such as 4-foot-high fences with self-latching gates that protect infants and toddlers from traffic, fall hazards, and pools of water.
*   *Shade* for sun- and heat-sensitive infants.
*   *Monitoring* all *water play.* Infants and toddlers can drown in even very small amounts of water, such as a 5-gallon bucket (Frost et al., 2001).

Infants and toddlers also need opportunities for a wide range of sensory experimentation and exploration with a few simple, safe, age-appropriate choices. Adding materials of different textures, such as sticks, bugs, or tree bark, or clear pathways to walk on, touch, and explore, enhances their play. They need stimulating equipment close to the ground, such as tunnels or simple climbing structures; dramatic-play options; movable parts for stacking, gathering, and dumping; and natural experiences with living plants and animals (Frost et al., 2001; Rivkin, 1995; Stephenson, 2002).

Some interesting additions for toddler outdoor play include the following:

- Hanging inflatable objects from a tree and having children try to "catch one" with a cardboard tube.
- Painting the pathways, equipment, or fence with small buckets of water and large brushes.
- Washing dishes and furniture with pans of warm, soapy water, sponges, and scrub brushes.

Preschool/Kindergarten Years

Playgrounds for preschoolers and kindergartners should promote all four forms of play—functional, constructive, dramatic, and games with rules to support these children's need for vigorous gross motor play and increased interest in role playing and games. Play structures must develop a wide range of skills and abilities while emphasizing dramatic play. They should contain a convenient and accessible storage facility for portable materials, a grassy area for group games, a place for privacy to accommodate children's need for solitary and parallel play, and a variety of child-sized equipment for motor development (Debord, Hestenes, Moore, Cosco, & McGinnis, 2002; Frost et al., 2001). The best outdoor environments for preschool and kindergarten children include a complex superstructure with a combination of movable parts (for example, raw materials such as sand, water, and assorted lumber boards) and climbing structures with lots of moving parts, such as swings, bars, ladders, hanging ropes and structures with potential for dramatic-play activities.

Try some of these activities to add novelty and complexity to the outdoor environment:

- Turn wheeled vehicles into a fire engine, ambulance, or tractor by taping on a sign and adding appropriate props nearby to stimulate dramatic play.
- Use a large, empty carton and other appropriate props to create a service station area for wheeled vehicles, a bank drive-through, or a roadside produce stand.
- Have a car wash for the wheeled vehicles. Use large buckets of warm, soapy water and add other appropriate props to stimulate imaginative play outdoors.
- Mix bubbles from $1/4$ cup dishwashing detergent and 1 gallon of water. Use an assortment of recycled materials, such as berry baskets and straws, for bubble wands.
- Encourage children to paint along the fence by clipping easel paper on it; use cardboard six-packs to hold plastic paint containers. Leave the paintings up for an art show.
- Read *A Rose for Pinkerton* (Kellogg, 1981) and *Pet Show* (Keats, 1972) and then have a pet show with children's stuffed animals. Make judges' clipboards out of cardboard and clothespins, stands for the animals out of recycled ice-cream tubs, and prize ribbons out of used gift wrap.
- Create nature collages. Use shoebox lids and white glue to make collages of natural materials located on or near the playground, park, or nearby woods.

First Grade–Fourth Grade
Environments for children in Grades 1–4 should encourage natural investigation and challenge imagination. These children prefer structures with numerous physical challenges, such as climbers, equipment for social development, and safe places for group games. Following are some suggestions that challenge school-age children in outdoor areas.

- Plan and conduct a scavenger hunt. Use a variety of clues that incorporate riddles, listening, or writing. Tie the scavenger hunt into the unit of study where possible.
- Provide plenty of chalk so that children can make outdoor games, such as hopscotch or foursquare, or create shadow drawings.
- Do some tie-dyeing. Tie old T-shirts with rubber bands, dip them into fabric dyes, and dry them along the fence. Repeat the process with another color for more complex and symmetrical designs.
- Do a shadow play in the afternoon. Invite children to enact various roles and use cardboard silhouettes for props. Have the audience watch the show on the ground rather than the players themselves.
- Assign "fitness" homework, such as walking, hopping, jumping rope, counting steps, or stretching that improves fitness.

Accommodating Children with Exceptional Needs in the Outdoor Environment

With the 1991 passage of the Americans with Disabilities Act, many outdoor areas are being planned or modified to allow children with disabilities an opportunity to use play equipment with other children. Federal guidelines on accessibility and playground equipment (NPPS, 1999) specify the minimum level of accessibility required in the construction and alteration of play areas. Information is posted at http://www.access-board.gov.

Opportunities for outdoor play are equally necessary for children with special needs. Playing outdoors offers a change from the classroom environment and provides opportunities to develop gross motor, self-help, and social skills (Klein, Cook, & Richardson-Gibbs, 2001). The key to including all children, regardless of their abilities, is to adapt the environment to their diverse needs by providing challenges with differing degrees of difficulty, such as balance beams of different lengths, simple obstacle courses, or noncompetitive games (Wellhousen, 2002).

Outdoor environments usually require different adaptations from those indoors. For example, for children with physical challenges, playground equipment can be adapted by positioning it so that children can attain maximum range of reach, motion, muscle control, and visual contact. Adapting the outdoor environment for children in wheelchairs can be accomplished by placing equipment lower, or building a sand table at wheelchair height that is sturdy enough to withstand leaning.

Outdoor environments can also be adapted to meet the needs of children with visual or hearing disabilities by marking play areas with audible and visual cues (such as wind chimes or bells) or having a playmate wear a brightly colored vest to provide a visual clue (Wellhousen, 2002). Some teachers attach Braille labels to materials to help children with low vision. For children with diverse cognitive abilities, teachers can keep vocabulary simple, incorporate noncompetitive games, and shorten obstacle courses. Some children with autism need additional supervision for monitoring safety on equipment, limiting the number of materials available for choice, and communicating clear boundaries. To best meet the needs of all children with exceptional needs, consider access (for example, all entryways should be as level as possible) and surfaces (for example, people with mobility challenges need a smooth stable surface to walk on; children on the playground need something relatively soft to fall on).

Outdoor environments can be arranged to foster all children's creative thought through a variety of planned uses of space, activities, experiences, and materials. Teachers who believe in the power of the environment for learning must assume roles that guide children's creative processes.

TEACHERS' ROLES AND RESPONSIBILITIES

What we as teachers believe about creativity influences how we plan and manage the classroom environment. We would be wise to keep in mind the words of Danette Littleton (1989): "It is our own playfulness that links the child within each of us to the child we teach: the feeling child, the thinking and reasoning child, the creative child, the compassionate child. All of these are a whole fabric woven of the unending thread of play" (p. xiii).

The following suggestions foster a safe, secure, and accepting classroom environment that promotes creative habits of mind. The message emanating from the environment comes from how teachers create places that enable children and teachers to function comfortably, productively, and effectively together.

1. *View yourself as a creative teacher.* Ask yourself the following questions: In what ways do I support children's creativity and build a creative learning environment? Do I have original ideas? How do I solve problems and make decisions? Do I provide opportunities for children who respond in unusual ways to engage in creative development? Could I identify the most creative children in my class? Creative teachers exhibit spontaneity, sensitivity, open-mindedness, and a high tolerance for ambiguity. Their classroom environments maximize student participation and engagement, support learner-centered teaching, encourage children to "live the question," reward imaginative ideas, and encourage children's self-evaluation (Edwards, 2002; Jalongo & Isenberg, 2004).

2. *Maintain an orderly and safe environment.* An orderly environment gives children control over activity choices, helps them carry out their ideas, and builds responsibility for the care and storage of materials. Materials for children of all ages should be neatly arranged, pleasantly displayed, open-ended, and self-leveling so that they can be used in many different ways. When children have access to materials, they also must assume responsibility for returning them to their place when finished. This means that the materials must be organized so that children understand where they belong. Most teachers separate materials by type in simple, labeled containers.

3. *Consider the environment a powerful learning tool.* When teachers are knowledgeable about space and materials they can often anticipate how children will use them. Predicting behavior in this way promotes children's independence, active involvement, and sustained attention (McLean, 1995). The environment can also be used to manage tasks. A predictable schedule, for example, helps all children learn the rhythm of the day and feel able to participate. Carefully arranged and displayed materials invite children's participation in appropriate ways with a minimum of adult intervention. One preschool teacher uses children's photographs for taking attendance and rebus recipes for preparing snacks. Such tools reduce the amount of time teachers devote to routine administrative tasks, freeing them to focus on children's creativity and learning.

4. *Plan for diversity.* Just as individuals differ in developmental level, differences in abilities, cultural or language background, and interests also influence how teachers need to think about the classroom environment. It is important to have a variety of materials and subject areas to stimulate children's imagination and creative thought. Be innovative in your use of the classroom environment, but keep your purpose in mind. Sometimes you might use an area to stimulate aesthetic appreciation; other times you might change the area to provide use of complex, inquiry-oriented materials and projects. For children whose first language is not English, provide an environment in which they can use their language. Believing that second-language learners are capable and competent is critical to their success as learners in your classroom. Planning for diversity means providing a variety of materials that respond to children's cultural backgrounds, interests, and ability levels; a balance of teacher-directed/child-initiated activities; and flexible grouping (Elgas, Prendeville, Moomaw, & Kretchmer, 2002; Kemple et al., 2004).

MEETING STANDARDS

Classroom Environments

Professional organizations for teachers all have a set of standards for establishing high-quality classroom environments. These standards indicate that the classroom environment should support children's honest expression and thinking, and help children feel ownership in their learning by having some choice and input into their work and its completion, assessment, and display. All teachers are expected to be able to create, plan, and manage environments that contribute to the success of every learner. High-quality classroom environments reflect teachers' views of teaching and learning and also influence students' behavior and academic learning.

Figure 6.13 illustrates some indicators of quality classroom environments, guided by national standards. It includes examples that foster positive relationships, positive learning outcomes, a positive emotional climate, and a positive

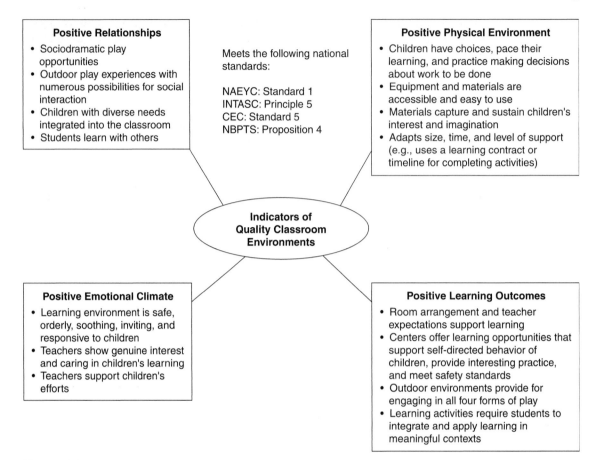

Positive Relationships
- Sociodramatic play opportunities
- Outdoor play experiences with numerous possibilities for social interaction
- Children with diverse needs integrated into the classroom
- Students learn with others

Meets the following national standards:

NAEYC: Standard 1
INTASC: Principle 5
CEC: Standard 5
NBPTS: Proposition 4

Positive Physical Environment
- Children have choices, pace their learning, and practice making decisions about work to be done
- Equipment and materials are accessible and easy to use
- Materials capture and sustain children's interest and imagination
- Adapts size, time, and level of support (e.g., uses a learning contract or timeline for completing activities)

Indicators of Quality Classroom Environments

Positive Emotional Climate
- Learning environment is safe, orderly, soothing, inviting, and responsive to children
- Teachers show genuine interest and caring in children's learning
- Teachers support children's efforts

Positive Learning Outcomes
- Room arrangement and teacher expectations support learning
- Centers offer learning opportunities that support self-directed behavior of children, provide interesting practice, and meet safety standards
- Outdoor environments provide for engaging in all four forms of play
- Learning activities require students to integrate and apply learning in meaningful contexts

Figure 6.13
Indicators of Quality Classroom Environments

physical environment. Use Figure 6.13 to discuss and identify other examples that contribute to these key indicators of quality classroom environments.

While the following four standards come from different professional organizations, each addresses the same essential elements of quality classroom environments. Read the standards and identify the common elements among them. Review the key elements in this chapter that are indicators of quality environments. Choose an age level (infants/toddlers, preschool/kindergarten, first through fourth grade) for which you will create a "state of the art" quality classroom environment. Now, write a scenario for one of the following that includes:

- all quality indicators for a particular age level
- some quality indicators for the same age level
- no quality indicators for the same age level

Compare and contrast your scenario with a peer and recommend three changes based on your conversation. Be willing to add other indicators and examples from the chapter that would provide evidence for your choices.

National Standards on Classroom Environments

National Association for the Education of Young Children (NAEYC)

Standard 1: Child Development and Learning.

Teachers use their understanding of young children and their needs and of multiple interacting influences on child development and learning to create environments that are healthy, respectful, supportive, and challenging for all children.

Council for Exceptional Children (CEC)

Standard 5: Learning Environments and Social Interactions

Special educators actively create learning environments for individuals with exceptional learning needs (ELN) that foster cultural understanding, safety and emotional well-being, positive social interactions, and active engagement of individuals with ELN. In addition, special educators foster environments in which diversity is valued and individuals are taught to live harmoniously and productively in a culturally diverse world. Special educators shape environments to encourage the independence, self-motivation, self-direction, personal empowerment, and self-advocacy of individuals with ELN. Special educators help their general-education colleagues integrate individuals with ELN in regular environments and engage them in meaningful learning activities and interactions.

Interstate New Teacher Assessment and Support Consortium (INTASC)

Principle 5:

The teacher uses an understanding of individual and group motivators and behaviors to create a learning environment that encourages positive social interaction, active engagement in learning, and self-motivation.

National Board for Professional Teaching Standards (NBPTS)

Proposition 4:

Teachers are responsible for managing and monitoring student learning. Accomplished teachers create, enrich, maintain, and alter instructional settings to capture and sustain the interest of their students. They make the most effective use of time in their instruction.

Frequently Asked Questions About Classroom Environments

Is recess necessary in today's classroom?

Nationally, 64 percent of children do not participate in any daily unstructured physical activity (Jensen, 1998b). A combination of long work hours for parents, scheduled after-school activities, and schools' increased focus on academics (National Association of Early Childhood Specialists in State Departments of Education [NAECSSDE], 2002) has jeopardized recess as an integral part of childhood. Recess is an essential component of the total educational experience for elementary-age children. It provides children with discretionary time and opportunities to engage in physical activity that helps to develop healthy bodies and enjoyment of movement (National Association for Sport and Physical Education, 2001). Unstructured physical play is a developmentally appropriate outlet for reducing stress in children's lives, improves children's attentiveness, and decreases restlessness (NAECSSDE, 2002). Eric Jensen (1998b) makes a strong case for movement and its connection to learning by describing how physical activity stimulates brain development by increasing neural connections. Play is an active form of learning that unites the mind, body, and spirit of children. Up until age 9, children's learning occurs best when the whole self is involved (NAECSSDE, 2002).

How can I ease newcomers into my classroom routines when they know little or no English?

Only when students feel comfortable with your classroom's social and academic routines will optimal second-language acquisition and academic learning occur. Using Maslow's (1970) hierarchy of human needs as a foundation, you will want to assure safety and security and a sense of belonging. To help second-language learners feel safer and more secure, you might assign a personal buddy, who speaks the child's language and follows the predictable routines in your classroom, to each newcomer. This plan creates a sense of security for all students but is especially

important for students who are new to the language and culture of the school. In fact, your predictable routines may be the first stable feature some students have experienced in a long time. To help second-language learners achieve a sense of belonging, you might seat new students in the middle or front of the room, integrating them early in cooperative groups, and help them follow predictable routines.

How can I design a quality classroom environment for students from diverse cultural backgrounds?

In their book *Multicultural Literacy: Mirroring the Reality of the Classroom* (1995), Barbara Diamond and Margaret Moore describe how to design culturally sensitive learning environments. First, they suggest creating culturally sensitive centers that portray both the visible and invisible aspects of the children's culture. For younger children, the media or literacy center might include recordings of favorite informational and narrative literature from different countries and cultures, such as *The Black Snowman* (Mendez, 1989), *Abuela* (Dorros, 1991), and *Chicken Sunday* (Polacco, 1990). For older children, centers are good places to display cultural artifacts, games, foods, maps, books, and clothing from a specific culture, and invite children to become aware of the unique features of the environments of different countries such as the people, animals, weather, workers, and modes of transportation. Second, Diamond and Moore (1995) suggest integrating play throughout the curriculum for children to have the opportunity to share power with their peers and other adults, which is integral to culturally responsive teaching (Stremmel, 1997). Some teachers develop classification activities and educational games using family pictures, children's artwork, or objects from home to infuse cultural content into the curriculum through play. When children bring artifacts and toys from their home culture into their classrooms, they portray information about themselves and their culture in a meaningful way (Johnson, Christie, et al., 1999).

Finally, they suggest infusing children's literature and all of the creative arts to encourage an appreciation of cultural diversity. Creech (1995) tells of 13-year-old Salamanca's quest to find her mother, which draws strength from her Native American ancestry and enables her to face the truth, in *Walk Two Moons*. In another example, Cass befriends Jemmie when they become neighbors in *Crossing Jordan* (Fogelin, 2000) and forge a strong friendship in spite of parental opposition. (See Chapters Three and Five for suggested materials.)

How can I adapt my environment to meet the needs of children with exceptional learning needs?

A classroom environment can often address the needs of children with various disabilities with some simple adjustments in equipment, materials, and room arrangement. The first step in adapting environments is to fully understand the nature and extent of each child's limitations. The next step is to adapt the environment so that each child can participate in a way that emphasizes abilities rather than disabilities (Hallahan & Kauffman, 2002; Hughes, 1999). For example, children with hearing difficulties often feel frustrated and socially isolated from other learners. As a result, they engage in less pretend play with others and are less likely to use objects symbolically. Teachers can adapt the environment for children with hearing difficulties by seating them away from noisy backgrounds such as windows, doors, and heating and cooling systems; allowing them to move freely about so that they can position themselves to hear better and see the faces of their peers; and reducing classroom noise with carpeting and corkboard walls. Children with visual impairments always require a physical orientation to the classroom including the location of materials, centers, and exits. Environments for these children include an orientation to the classroom from a single focal point such as their table or desk; an orientation to the school after they are familiar with the classroom, noting which play materials, equipment, activities, and playmates are available during playtime; providing a sensory-rich play environment with a variety of cues (such as tactile maps and tape-recorded directions placed in key areas of the room, which could be identified through the use of tactile material); information about any changes in the physical arrangement and the use of play materials so children can become familiar with them by touch; a designated sighted guide for special activities such as fire drills; lighting that does not cast shadows or glare on their work and allows them to move so they can comfortably see each activity; traffic patterns and pathways that are clear and free; simple room arrangements; and encouragement of their play. Children with limited motor abilities may have problems with either large or small muscles and have a slower reaction time than other children. The adaptations for them vary according to the severity and type of disability. Environments for these children should include modifications for writing such as computers, felt-tip rather than soft lead pencils, and pads rather than sheets of paper; playground designs that use smooth pathways and ramps to help them gain access to play areas; wheelchair-height tables and trays so that children can use water tables and manipulatives; and outdoor environments that have wide gates and pathways (44 inches) and ramps to provide access to all parts of the playground for children in wheelchairs or those with impaired walking ability.

All children need environments that foster self-directed learning and opportunities for play in which they can plan for their own learning, identify resources and materials, and interact with one another.

❀ CHAPTER SUMMARY

1. Planning and managing the classroom environment is as important as planning for instruction.

2. Quality classroom environments have three basic features: climate, space, and time. Climate refers to the emotional and academic tone one gets from the environment and dictates to what extent children can be productive learners; space includes the degree to which the classroom environment contributes to active, creative thought; and time encompasses how the classroom schedule affects children's expression, attention span, and self-directedness.

3. Room arrangement refers to the way space is organized for children's learning and movement. When arranging the classroom environment, consider what it communicates to children; how easily the space can be supervised; how accessible the materials are; how you feel about unpredictable behaviors, and why you feel that way. Teachers also need to distinguish between the child's and adult's environment and be alert to traffic patterns.

4. There are a variety of types and uses of centers. Centers organize space and promote active learning, planning and decision making, problem solving, originality, and interaction. All classrooms should have the following centers: art, blocks, discovery/science, dramatic play, library/literacy, manipulative/math, media/music, technology, and writing.

5. Transitions are times when children move from one activity to another. Routines are activities that occur regularly and form the basis of the daily schedule. Planned transitions and routines are essential to ensure predictability and a sense of security for all children.

6. What teachers believe about the creative process influences their classroom environment. Teachers need to be creative themselves, maintain a safe and orderly environment, use planning tools, and consider the environment as the third teacher.

7. Outdoor environments need the same systematic attention to space, materials, equipment, and safety as indoor environments. They need simple, complex, and supercomplex units to hold children's interest over time and challenge their imagination.

8. There are three types of playgrounds—traditional, adventure, and creative. Action-oriented playgrounds contain a superstructure with movable apparatuses, loose parts, and safe underneath surfaces.

9. Adapting the environment to meet the needs of all children means adjusting the basic characteristics of climate, space, and time for each child's particular abilities and background.

Discuss: Perspectives on Classroom Environments

1. Think about your most pleasurable play environment as a child. How does this relate to what you know about the importance of environments to support creative growth?
2. Visualize your ideal classroom, both indoors and outdoors. In what ways do you think your beliefs about creativity influence your mind's-eye view of the indoor and outdoor environment?
3. Refer to the case study at the beginning of the chapter. What were Ms. Ring's reactions to the state of her classroom when she returned from leave? Were her reactions justified? On what basis? How will she go about re-creating a creative environment? If Ms. Ring's substitute asked you how she could improve her classroom, what would you suggest? Why?
4. Some teachers admit that they never think much about children's outdoor play and treat it just as a way to have children expend energy. What do you think of this practice? Why?
5. In planning and managing your high-quality classroom environment, think about how you would respond to a parent or a colleague who said, "But they are just playing! When are they going to learn something?" What would you say and why?

Chapter 7

 Using Classroom Materials
and Resources Effectively

*When children have the chance to notice, collect, and sort materials, and
when teachers respond to their ideas, the children become artists,
designers, and engineers. When children are simply given materials to use
without the chance to explore and understand them, the materials do not
become part of their world.*

Walter Drew and Baji Rankin, 2004, p. 42

CLASSROOM PERSPECTIVES ON MATERIALS AND RESOURCES

Preschool–Kindergarten

In the block area, five boys and girls are constructing a pirate ship from hollow wooden blocks. In the absence of pirate garb, the children make do with cowboy boots, vests, and construction worker hard hats. One child, sitting in front, steers the ship while the "lookout" paces about. A child dashes from the block area to the housekeeping area, snatches the "jewelry case," then darts back to her fellow pirates. Suddenly, the cry goes up, "Jewels! We've found the treasure! We're rich! Jewels, jewels, jewels!" With great noise and excitement, the pirates display their necklaces, bracelets, and rings. In the days that follow, the children extend this pirate theme by adding a treasure map to assist with their forays and decorating boxes to use as treasure chests.

First Grade–Second Grade

Ms. Thomas begins her plant unit by inviting her first graders to suggest how they want to learn about plants. Following the children's brainstorming, they decide to study pumpkins because it is October and they want to make a class Big Book about pumpkins and build a giant pumpkin patch. So Ms. Thomas reads different pumpkin books to the class during the next few days and gathers a variety of different materials and resources for the children to investigate pumpkins. The children explore pumpkins by carving pumpkins of different sizes and shapes, counting pumpkin seeds, measuring different-sized pumpkins, estimating the number of objects that would fit inside the class plastic pumpkin, collecting and sorting pumpkins of different shades of orange, and determining whether pumpkins could sink and float. From their investigations, the children make their learning visible by creating a pumpkin patch made from giant paper pumpkins, illustrate stages of pumpkin growth on the computer and on paper, write books, enact the life cycle of the pumpkin, make pumpkin bread and muffins, and construct a model of the inside of the pumpkin.

Third Grade–Fourth Grade

In Ms. Wong's fourth-grade class, the children are studying a state-mandated unit on the California gold rush. To demonstrate their understanding, Ms. Wong invites the children to teach others about the gold rush. Some children create songs, raps, and poems; others create skits and games to express their knowledge. Their original products use materials that show people arriving from all over the world on horseback, by foot, on wagon trains, and by ship to see if they could find gold. Each of the representations includes references to facts and concepts such as panning for gold, using sluice boxes, and constructing tent towns. The children also use props and language that illustrate the clothing the miners wore (such as denim jeans), the food they ate (such as sourdough bread and pancakes), and the tools they used to pan for gold.

As these three episodes illustrate, the careful selection of materials and resources supports children's creative thinking, their play, and their artistic expression. In these classroom scenarios, 4-year-olds used objects symbolically to initiate and carry out their pirate play theme; first graders used writing and illustrating, enactment, and construction to demonstrate their understanding of pumpkins as a plant; and fourth graders used props, role play, and games to express their knowledge of the gold rush. The children's responses to materials revealed their original uses of common materials (using the jewels as a treasure), role playing (enacting the life cycle of a pumpkin), and games (showing people, tools, and food in the Gold Rush).

THEORETICAL AND RESEARCH BASE: THE IMPORTANCE OF MATERIALS AND RESOURCES

Materials are the concrete tools with which children explore, experiment, investigate, and understand their world. All children have the same need for carefully chosen materials to do their work well because materials are the vehicles used in classrooms to study and learn the knowledge, skills, and attributes associated with each of the curriculum areas. For teachers, then, three concepts are important to understanding the value of appropriate play materials and resources: (1) their historical development, (2) their convergent or divergent nature, and (3) their safety.

History of Toys and Playthings

Have you ever thought about how early toys and materials originated and what they were like? Children's toys and playthings have a long history in education. In fact, the materials we provide for children reflect social, political, and cultural issues. In colonial America, for example, boys played with simulated hunting and fishing materials, while girls played with corncob dolls. Near the turn of the century, construction toys were strictly for boys; homemaker toys were strictly for girls (Hewitt & Roomet, 1979; Mergen, 1982).

During the Industrial Revolution in the mid-1800s, toys specifically designed for children became industrialized as well. When wheeled toys, board games, dolls, and doll furniture first appeared, they were mass-produced on the assembly line. At the turn of the century, during the child-study movement, childhood was recognized as a distinct period of development and children were no longer viewed as miniature adults. As a reflection of this movement, toy manufacturers began producing educational toys. During this time, Dr. Maria Montessori also introduced an array of sensory materials for children with mental retardation. Lacing frames, knob puzzles, and graduated cylinders were just a few of Montessori's contributions to educational toys. She is also credited with originating the concept of "self-correcting" toys—toys that can be used in a particular sequence and a specified way. These materials slowly became part of some early childhood programs.

In the 1920s, toy manufacturers invited educators to help develop materials that would stimulate children's imagination and self-expression. Influenced by the ideas of child development specialists and educators such as John Dewey, early childhood educators provided firsthand experiences for children with concrete, imaginative materials such as blocks, clay, paint, and wood. Additionally, they encouraged children under age 6 to play with language and rhythms and to invent their own games (Monighan-Nourot, 1990). Today, the same child may play with an heirloom set of nesting dolls from her great-grandmother's era, a rag doll from her grandmother's day, a Barbie doll from her mother's era, and modern dolls for both boys and girls.

In today's world, technology has brought new dimensions to objects with which children can play. Children play with media-related figures that replicate what children see on television. These highly structured toys limit children's creativity and often increase the level of violence found in play (Levin, 1999). They also play with electronic figures that can communicate feelings and hold high appeal for young children. The advent of "digital dolls" that exist only inside a computer, and objects that children can animate once they have created them, have the potential for changing the world of play materials for children both at home and in the classroom. While play with digital materials is quite different from the modes of play envisioned more than 150 years ago by German educator Friedrich Froebel, the founder of the kindergarten movement, play with digital media and in virtual playgrounds can still have the features of make-believe and relate to children's experiences. As a stroll through a toy store or a look at a materials catalogue will attest, teachers need to make thousands of choices among materials for children. The following sections outline some basic considerations in selecting materials and resources for enhancing children's creative thinking.

Convergent and Divergent Play Materials

The materials children use influence their growing knowledge, their play possibilities, and their expression of ideas. Some materials lead to single or prescribed uses and encourage convergent thinking. Windup toys, talking dolls, and coloring books are generally considered **convergent** materials. These materials lead children to think about a single or correct way to use them. There is little opportunity to use such materials in novel ways.

Other materials lead to multiple uses and are more open-ended. Blocks, sand, and water encourage thinking about possibilities and are considered divergent materials. Divergent materials invite a variety of children's responses through exploration, experimentation, and original thinking that stimulates their problem-solving ability.

Think about Amy and Tony, 4-year-olds who watched with great interest as their caregiver was preparing to give away some materials. Among them was a baby carriage with wobbly wheels, prompting Amy to ask, "Could we have the wheels from the carriage to play with?" What appealed to them were the divergent properties of the wheels—the endless possibilities for creative play. In the weeks that ensued, the wheels became a steering wheel for a camper, a home for wooden animals, and a tray for food in the children's restaurant play.

Divergent or open-ended materials—blocks, carpentry tools, dress-up clothes, paints and markers, modeling dough, mud, sand, and water—are usually the most valuable (Bisgaier & Samaras, 2004; Drew & Rankin, 2004; Hendrick, 2001; Johnson, Christie, et al., 1999). These materials do the following:

1. *Enable children to use their imaginations in original and satisfying ways.* After 3-year-old Melissa had eye surgery, she used a spoon from the housekeeping area to operate on the eyes of a toy dog and wrapped the dog in bandages made from

The materials children use influence their growing knowledge, their play possibilities, and their expression of ideas.

paper towels. She created a new use for the spoon while practicing what she knew about surgeons and having an operation.

2. *Deepen children's understandings through connections to what they are learning.* When first grader Jamal painted subway stops on a class mural about different types of transportation, he investigated the properties of art—color, line, and form. When Jamal added a ticket booth, an engineer, and shapes for subway seats, he demonstrated what he knew about subways as a means of transportation.

3. *Encourage children to work cooperatively.* In Ms. Anderson's second-grade unit on the community, the children used blocks to build to build a city; sand to sculpt the terrain; paper, pencils, rulers, and protractors to make scale models of the buildings; and earth-moving toys to create roads. They learned more from their experience than Mr. Smith's second graders, who completed dot-to-dot papers and worksheets on community helpers.

4. *Have no right or wrong uses, are failure-proof, and build self-esteem.* When 5-year-old Taso carefully dressed up as a cook and proudly stood before a long mirror, he exuded a sense of self-confidence and competence. The dress-up gear enabled him to view himself in a role he could not directly experience.

5. *Are process-oriented rather than product-oriented.* After hearing the rhyming verse of *Jamberry* (Degen, 1983), a story about a bear who rejoices in finding all kinds of berries, a group of kindergartners repeatedly chanted, "One berry, two berry, pick me a blueberry." Their sheer delight in the rhythm and rhyme from this captivating piece of literature produced giggles and laughter as they elaborated and created other silly *Jamberry* rhymes. Here, play with language illustrates the children's interest in process over product.

Divergent materials offer children unlimited possibilities. To capitalize on this potential, children must have opportunities to explore, manipulate, investigate, and use all types of materials.

Selection and Use of Safe Materials

The materials children use can either enhance or hinder their creative thinking and artistic expression (Charney, 2002). Good materials are relevant to children's development and the curriculum and enable children to use their imagination to understand their world. Good materials can also be used for more than one topic or activity, and should be used regularly. Consider replacing or recycling materials used infrequently with another kind of material more likely to be used regularly. Choosing materials and selecting resources is an important task. What qualities should you look for in choosing age-appropriate materials and equipment? Are there special considerations for safety? Safe materials use appropriate dyes, are high-density, have no carcinogenic plastic parts, are flame retardant, and are in good condition. When choosing materials, remember it is the play, exploration, and experimentation itself that contributes to children's learning. Table 7.1 provides guidelines for selecting and using safe and appropriate materials that enhance children's creativity and imagination.

TABLE 7.1   Selecting and Using Safe and Appropriate Materials

Guideline	Example
Choose Materials That:	
• Hold children's interest and can be used in more than one way	Construction materials; modeling materials; generic toy figures
• Promote creativity and problem solving by enabling children to decide what to do	Building sets; board games; pretend materials
• Can be used with other materials for changing and more complex play	Blocks and housekeeping materials
• Add new dimensions to children's play	People and animal props; natural materials, dress-up clothes, and housewares; balls; medical kits
• Are safe, are durable, and work for children with disabilities	Read labels for age and safety recommendations; check toys periodically for wear and damage; supervise for proper use of toys; store toys on shelves or safe boxes
Avoid Materials That:	
• Can be used in only one way	Programmed or mechanical toys that limit children's imaginations
• Promote violent and stereotypical play behaviors	Action figures and props connected to television programs and movies
• Appeal to a single age or developmental stage	Materials with very small pieces for very young children or games that require considerable academic skill; puzzles with too many pieces
• Are unsafe, are not durable, and do not work for children with disabilities	Outdoor toys that cannot withstand different kinds of weather; materials with toxic paint; dolls whose heads and eyes can be easily removed

Note. Adapted from Bronson (1995), Johnson, Christie, & Yawkey (1999), Levin (1999), and Moyer (1995).

 TEACHERS' REFLECTIONS ON MATERIALS AND RESOURCES

Preservice Teachers

"After observing my preschoolers use blocks, I am amazed at what they can do. The children used geometric shapes for food, medicine, furniture, amusement parks, and counting. This helped me see the many possibilities in just one material."

"When I added board games such as Cootie and The Very Hungry Caterpillar to my limited second-grade centers as part of my student teaching, I watched the children practice social skills ('How many and who can play?'), problem-solve ('Since only six can play, we'll play next time'), think strategically ('I only need two more turns before . . . '), and practice school skills ('I rolled a six on the number cube . . . 1, 2, 3 . . . '). The children's responses to these games convinced me how appropriate these materials are."

Inservice Teachers

"My eyes are now open to a multitude of materials that promote convergent and divergent thinking. With a variety of found materials, I have created 'Imagination Boxes' that the children use to construct and invent objects. I now have to figure out appropriate storage for these boxes—but I know I can do that easily."

"In my third-grade classroom, my use of Lego blocks for a community-building experience introduced me to a whole new way of thinking about problem solving. My students used Legos as a vehicle to create a three-dimensional representation of the interests of one of their friends, which meant brainstorming possible ways to do this. The most meaningful moments of the project occurred when the students were figuring out how to construct something that was so abstract."

Your Reflections

*   What do you think are age-appropriate materials, resources, and games?

*   How do you think materials nurture children's creative thinking?

*   How might you learn about the value of different types of toys, play materials, and imaginative resources?

As you integrate play and the arts into your curriculum, you will want to consider the different types of materials that invite children's creative thought. The varying types of materials and their uses will be described in the next section.

TYPES OF MATERIALS

Two-year-old Allysun clutches a fat red crayon and vigorously scribbles on a large piece of paper. She is absorbed with her markings and the gliding movement of the crayon across the paper's smooth surface.

Four-year-olds Lourdes and Maria, children of migrant workers in a Head Start classroom, pack, unpack, and repack boxes with dishes and food and talk about where they will next live.

Six-year-old twins Caroline and Diana are building tunnels and bridges with blocks as part of their unit on transportation.

Eight-year-olds Kim and Brady are engrossed in a game of checkers. They carefully contemplate their next strategic move.

Ten-year-olds Jacob and Noah like to organize relay races during recess. They use balls, ropes, running, throwing, and jumping in different ways to vary the races that they organize and invent.

Each of these children is using a range of materials in age-appropriate ways. Materials can be categorized into six groups that serve as concrete learning tools. The following section describes these types of materials, which include skill/concept, gross motor, manipulative, construction, self-expressive, and natural, everyday materials (Isenberg & Quisenberry, 2002; Johnson, Christie, et al., 1999; Moyer, 1995).

Skill/Concept Materials

Skill and concept materials are prescriptive and product-oriented. Children commonly practice skills such as eye-hand coordination, sorting, classifying, and counting with them. Typical materials in this category consist of board games such as Lotto, card games such as Fish, all types of books, attribute blocks, Cuisenaire rods, and perception materials such as lacing beads and puzzles. These structured materials have limited possibilities for creative and divergent thinking.

Gross Motor Materials

Gross motor materials stress large muscle activity and skill development. Children use them primarily to explore and practice motor abilities and to develop strength in large muscle coordination. Typical gross motor materials for younger children include balls, climbers, pull toys, riding toys, and ropes. Older children tend to like team sports, throwing, catching, relay races, and rope courses. As motor development increases due to activity, these materials have the potential to encourage divergent and inventive thinking when used in supportive environments.

Manipulative Materials

Manipulative materials (sometimes called fine motor materials) develop small muscles in children's fingers and hands, basic concepts, imaginative thinking, and eye-hand coordination. Children's use of manipulative materials provides important opportunities for literacy and numeracy development; offers concrete experiences with basic attributes of color, size, and shape; provides opportunities for cooperative problem solving; and increases awareness of cultural diversity. Typical fine motor materials for children through the primary years include beads, building sets, crayons, dough, geoboards, markers, jigsaw puzzles, lacing and sewing frames, pegs, pencils, pop-up boxes, and scissors. Third and fourth graders enjoy practice with a variety of tools, such as protractors, rulers, templates, and brushes, and tasks such as weaving, carving, drawing, and cartooning.

Construction Materials

Construction materials have separate pieces that can be combined in different ways and encourage children to create different ways to do so. These materials include blocks (units, pattern, parquetry), building sets (Lincoln Logs, Tinkertoys), two-and-three dimensional shapes (triangles, cubes, cylinders) and woodworking materials (hammer, nails, wood scraps, white glue). Construction materials offer endless possibilities and support coordination and inventive thinking. The number of pieces influences how children choose to combine pieces and determine when their product is finished.

Self-Expressive Materials

Self-expressive materials encourage children to experiment with different roles, feelings, and behaviors and express them through drama, music, and art. Materials in this category include dolls, dress-up clothes, computer music and art, housekeeping toys, markers, miniature life toys such as Weebles or bendable people, musical instruments, literature of all types, puppets, and works of art. Children determine how the materials will be used, invent personalities and roles, and respond imaginatively. As a result, self-expressive materials promote a sense of pride and accomplishment in children.

Natural and Everyday Materials

Natural and everyday materials have specific, nonplay purposes. Children decide how to use them, employ imaginative and divergent thinking, and imitate and model adult roles with them. Everyday materials might include such household

Developmentally appropriate materials are concrete, real, and meaningful to children.

items as boxes, buttons, carpentry tools, and pots and pans. Natural materials include sticks, twigs, leaves, rocks, pinecones, sand, mud, and water. Use of natural and everyday materials brings life to the classroom and helps children make it their own, as in the program for preschoolers that used a majority of "found" materials such as palm branches, PVC pipes, and large cardboard tubes to provide children with challenging opportunities outside as well as inside (Yinger and Blaszka, 1995). Figure 7.1 suggests appropriate uses for recycled materials, and Table 7.2 describes the types of materials, their specific uses, lists the child's role and the potential creative possibilities within each category.

To make the most of each material, teachers and children need to consider possibilities. This might involve altering the object in some way or adding materials to it. For example, think of an empty detergent bottle. A toddler might fill and empty it; a preschooler might experiment with the number and location of holes punched in it and the rate of water flowing out; an elementary-school child might add plastic tubing and create a siphon. In this way, one recycled piece of plastic has become a challenging yet developmentally appropriate resource for each child.

DEVELOPMENTALLY APPROPRIATE MATERIALS

Developmentally appropriate materials are concrete, real, and meaningful to children (Bredekamp & Copple, 1997). They are basic because they support child-initiated learning and learner-centered teaching, stimulate the imagination, facilitate recall about meaningful experiences, and aid communication. Through extensive interactions with real materials and with others, children through fourth grade come to understand the people, events, and things in their world. Thus, developmentally appropriate materials should fill classrooms with things to do, things to touch, and things to learn. These kinds of materials foster self-directed learning, of which creativity is a natural by-product. In the following sections, we describe developmental characteristics and age-appropriate play materials for infants/toddlers, preschoolers/kindergartners, and first through fourth grade children. We also suggest how you can use these materials appropriately with children of different ages.

Infants and Toddlers

Infants and toddlers learn by feedback from sensory exploration and social interaction. As infants roll, reach, grasp, and crawl they need a variety of textured objects to view and to reach. Because infants repeat interesting, pleasant experiences, they need toys and objects that make pleasant sounds (such as mobiles and musical toys); are soft and squeezable (such as soft fabric toys with different textures and soft fabric-covered balls); and are simple and realistic (such as cloth picture books and bath toys).

Goals
<ul><li>To help children think creatively—"Let's see what we can make!"</li><li>To encourage children to work together—"Oh, no! We can't let it fall!"</li><li>To involve children in inventing patterns—"First red, then blue, then yellow, now red again."</li><li>To build children's problem-solving skills—"If I do this, I think it might . . . "</li><li>To allow children to explore ideas—"I wonder what would happen if . . . "</li><li>To support creating and inventing—"Teacher, look at what I made!"</li></ul>
Sources
<ul><li>Ask *families* to collect decorating items (wallpaper, fabric, paint chips, framing materials); craft and hobby items (yarn, wood scraps, lace, buttons); kitchen items (plastic containers, egg cartons, paper towel tubes, plastic caps, detergent bottles); machines and machine parts (old telephones, alarm clocks, typewriters, computer parts).</li><li>Gather materials from *businesses* too:<ul><li>Restaurants (bags, straws, cups, bowls, trays, spoons, corks, boxes, ice cream cartons)</li><li>Building supply and home centers (lumber, sawdust, wood curls, nails, wire, wallpaper books, linoleum tiles, plastic pipe pieces, carpet samples, ceramic tile pieces)</li><li>Cleaners and tailors (buttons, hangers, large spools, fabric scraps)</li><li>Camera stores and frame shops (usable expired film, plastic film cylinders, matboard pieces, frame scraps)</li><li>Factories (plastic injection molders, die cutters)</li><li>Packaging companies (plastic scraps and punch-outs in a wide variety of colors and shapes, gaskets, washers, sponge-type foam, and Styrofoam)</li><li>Newspaper plant or printer (card stock, newsprint, fancy papers of many types)</li><li>Grocery, drug, and department stores (boxes, divided cartons, countertop or floor displays)</li></ul></li></ul>
Storage Suggestions
1. Create a central storage "warehouse" for materials. 2. Label the storage bins and involve children in sorting materials. 3. Provide small plastic baskets for children to transport materials from the storage area to the work area. 4. Develop a collection schedule so that materials arrive at predetermined times. 5. Put labeled containers next to the door for collecting donated materials.

Figure 7.1

Appropriate Uses for Recycled Materials

Note. Based on Drew & Rankin (2004) and Jalongo & Stamp (1997b).

TABLE 7.2   Materials for Divergent Thinking

	Types of Material					
	Skill/Concept	Gross Motor	Manipulative	Construction	Self-Expressive	Natural and Everyday
Illustrative Examples	Card and board games; lacing, sorting, and stacking materials	Balls, indoor/outdoor climbers, pull and riding toys	Puzzles, interlocking plastic and wooden sets, nuts and bolts, table blocks	Blocks, interlocking building sets, markers, paper, scissors	Dolls, dress-up clothes, housekeeping toys, markers, musical instruments, puppets	Buttons, natural materials, pots and pans, carpentry tools
Intended Use	Teach skills and concepts. Structured and outcome-oriented.	Emphasize large muscle development.	Emphasize small muscle development and eye-hand coordination.	Contain materials with separate parts to make things.	Relate to child's role or identity and creative expression in art.	Have clear nonplay uses in the adult world.
Child's Role	Responds to materials with senses, both physically and intellectually.	Responds, explores, and practices gross motor skills.	Responds, explores, and practices fine motor and perception skills.	Creates with multiple pieces. Determines beginning and end of project.	Decides how to use material. Invents situations, personalities, and roles. Responds imaginatively to materials.	Determines use and incorporates into activity.
Potential for Divergent Thinking	Limited number of uses. Structure imposed by material. Little opportunity for creative expression.	Some opportunity for creative and imaginative input in language, depending upon the environmental conditions and the role of the teacher.		Multiple combinations possible, depending upon number of pieces available.	Multiple possibilities to respond and invent scenes and express language and ideas.	Self-motivating and versatile materials encourage children to imitate and model adult roles and behavior.

Toddlers actively struggle with issues of independence, show great interest in children their own age, and have a high energy level. They test out materials and are fascinated by finding new and different ways to use them. Both infants and toddlers need materials for looking, feeling, listening, grasping, and moving that are carefully matched to their abilities. Toddlers also prefer materials that do the following:

- Make sounds or movements, such as musical toys.
- Fit together, pull apart, and stack, such as fill-and-dump toys, sorting boxes, and blocks.
- Stimulate pretend play, such as pots and pans, simple dress-up clothes, and empty containers.
- Can be read and examined, such as board books and photo albums.
- Pull and push, such as large cartons and wagons.

Although a variety of toys is necessary, infants and toddlers need only a few at one time. Tables 7.3 and 7.4 provide examples of developmentally appropriate materials for infants (birth to age 1) and toddlers (ages 1–3).

TABLE 7.3   Developmentally Appropriate Materials for Infants (Birth–Age 1)

Type of Material	Appropriate Materials	Examples
Skill/concept	Books/records and tapes	Soft cloth and thick cardboard books; lullabies, voices of familiar caretakers
	Games	Peek-a-Boo, So Big, Where Is the Baby?" and other socially interactive games
Gross motor	Active play	Push/pull toys; large balls, infant bouncers
Manipulative	Fine motor	Simple rattles, teethers, sturdy cloth toys, squeeze and squeak toys, colorful mobiles, activity boxes for the crib; clutch and texture balls; stacking toys
Construction	Blocks	Soft rubber blocks
	Puzzles	Two-to-three-piece puzzles of familiar objects
Self-expressive	Dolls and soft toys	Soft baby dolls, plush animals
	Puppets	Soft hand puppets
	Dramatic play	Large, unbreakable mirrors attached to the crib or wall
	Sensory	Tactile toys; colorful visuals; auditory toys; suitable teethers
Natural and everyday	Household	Pots and pans; plastic containers

Note. For further information see Bronson (1995), Johnson, Christie, & Yawkey (1999), and Moyer (1995).

TABLE 7.4 Developmentally Appropriate Materials for Toddlers (Ages 1–3)

Type of Material	Appropriate Play Materials	Examples
Skill/concept	Books/records and tapes	Simple picture books and poems about familiar places and people; records and tapes of children's songs, folk songs, nursery rhymes, popular songs, songs from other cultures; movement and exercise music
	Games	Social interaction games with adults, such as Pop Goes the Weasel, Ring-a-Round-a-Rosy, and Round and Round the Garden
Gross motor	Active play	Toys to push and pull; toys with objects; ride-on toys
	Outdoor	Low slides and climbers, tunnels of oversized cardboard boxes for crawling, variety of balls, sand and water materials
Manipulative	Fine motor/perception	Colored paddles, dressing dolls, activity boxes, pop-up toys operated by pushing a button, nesting and stacking toys; toys to put together and take apart; large colored beads and spools, sewing and lacing cards, large shape sorters, pegboards, with a few large pegs, frames for zipping and snapping
	Puzzles and form boards	Simple two-to-three-piece puzzles and form boards with familiar shapes and objects; puzzles with books
Construction	Building sets	Small, lightweight sets of 15–25 pieces before 18 months; solid wooden unit blocks (20–40 pieces); wooden hollow blocks and accessories; interlocking building sets
	Carpentry	Assorted pounding toys with large wooden pegs or balls, plastic hammers, plastic pliers, thick Styrofoam boards
Self-expressive	Dolls and soft toys	Soft-bodied or rubber dolls; simple caretaking accessories
	Dramatic play	Toy telephone, full-length mirror; miniature dishes, pots and pans; dress-up clothes; shopping cart
	Sensory	Soft, cuddly, easy-to-hold, safe toys; modeling dough; visual and auditory stimuli; sensory games and boxes
	Art/music	Rhythm instruments, bells, large crayons, markers, unlined paper
Natural and everyday	Sand and water	Sponges, small shovel, pail, cups, plastic containers for dumping and filling, baster, molds
		Pots and pans, plastic containers, cooking utensils; real objects that are familiar to children

Note. For further information, see Bronson (1995), Johnson, Christie, & Yawkey (1999), McKee (1986), and Moyer (1995).

Your Role
The following guidelines will help you nurture infants' and toddlers' development and enhance their self-expression with materials.

1. *Use only toys that meet safety standards.* Avoid toys and materials that have sharp points or edges, as well as nails, wires, or pins that can be swallowed or have parts that can lodge in children's ears and throats. Be sure that toys are painted with nontoxic or lead-free paint, do not require electricity, can be easily cleaned, and cannot pinch fingers or catch hair.

2. *Provide a rich sensory environment with plenty of materials.* Infants and toddlers need to experience materials with all of their senses. Teachers who create a "crawling trail" made from scraps of distinctively different textures of fabrics, such as satin, lace, corduroy, and flannel, are providing a sensory environment that intrigues and involves infants and toddlers. Toddlers need plenty of materials and containers to collect, fill, dump, and stack objects. Simple, small, plastic containers of all sizes and shapes, cloth sacks, a variety of cardboard tubing, and empty wooden spools are necessary for water, sand, and manipulative play. Toddlers also enjoy attractive, everyday, safe objects and often use one object to represent another. Blocks, water, sand, and dress-up clothes appeal to toddlers' imaginations.

3. *Use appropriate social games.* Infants and toddlers respond positively to Peek-a-Boo, So Big, Trot, Trot to Boston and other familiar social routines. These highly repetitive games have simple rules through which infants and toddlers learn the beginning of turn taking, the rhythms of conversation, and the bonds of social relationships.

Preschoolers and Kindergartners

Preschoolers and kindergartners show an increasing social ability, a fascination with adult roles, a growing mastery over their small and large muscles, and a deep passion for make-believe play that peaks at about age 5. Their simple, unstructured play includes family roles, such as Mommy, Daddy, Grandma, and Baby, and roles of familiar people outside the family, such as a supermarket checker or truck driver. These children use both realistic and nonrealistic props and accessories.

Materials for preschoolers and kindergartners should support their developing social skills and interest in adult roles, growing imaginations, increasing motor skills, and rapidly expanding vocabularies. They need the following:

- Dramatic-play props such as discarded adult clothes, props from familiar adult roles, and literacy tools to write.
- Realistic replicas or models of useful objects such as telephones and cars.
- Construction materials, such as simple building sets, to create products.
- Sensory materials, such as sand and water, to explore.
- Manipulative materials, such as simple puzzles, to test ideas concretely.
- Wheeled vehicles to demonstrate gross motor skills and to facilitate social interaction.

Materials for preschoolers should support their developing social skills and increasing motor skills.

- Picture books that capitalize on familiar themes such as transportation, families, and communities that represent people and objects from other cultures.
- Everyday objects such as boxes, cardboard tubing, and an assortment of plastic caps.

Table 7.5 provides examples of developmentally appropriate materials for preschool and kindergarten children.

Your Role

Teachers need to keep in mind the following guidelines when providing materials for preschoolers and kindergartners:

1. *Include adequate props and materials both indoors and outdoors.* Younger children and less-skilled players need more-realistic props, such as miniature cars, people, or tools, to support and sustain their play and engage their thinking. Older children and more advanced players need less-realistic materials for variety and flexibility of play themes, although they still enjoy realistic props. One preschool teacher noticed, for example, that a bridal veil, a bouquet of plastic flowers, and an old tuxedo jacket that she found at a secondhand store stimulated considerable excitement and elaborated play in the dress-up corner. Be certain to include natural

TABLE 7.5 Developmentally Appropriate Materials for Preschool and Kindergarten Children (Ages 3–6)

Type of Material	Appropriate Materials	Examples
Skill/concept	Books/records	Picture books, simple and repetitive stories and rhymes, animal stories, pop-up books, simple information books, wide variety of musical recordings
	Games	Socially interactive games with adults, such as What If; matching and lotto games based on colors and pictures, such as picture bingo or dominoes; games of chance with a few pieces that require no reading, such as Chutes and Ladders; flannel board with pictures, letters, storybook characters
Gross motor	Active play	Push and pull toys; ride-on toys; balls of all kinds; indoor slide and climber; rocking boat
	Outdoor	Climbers, rope ladders, balls of all sizes, old tires, sand and water materials
Manipulative	Fine motor	Dressing frames; toys to put together and take apart; cookie cutters, stamp and printing materials, finger paint, modeling dough, small objects to sort and classify; bead stringing with long, thin string; pegs and small pegs; colored cubes, table blocks, magnetic board/letters/numbers and shapes; perception boards and mosaics

	Puzzles and form boards	Fit-in or framed puzzles
		    For 3-year-olds: from 4 to 20 pieces
		    For 4-year-olds: from 15 to 30 pieces
		    For 5-year-olds: from 15 to 50 pieces
		Large, simple jigsaws; number/letter/clock puzzles

	Investigative	Toys, globe flashlight, magnets, lock boxes, weather forecasting equipment, scales, balances, stethoscopes
Construction	Building sets	Small and large unit blocks; large hollow blocks; from age 4, interlocking plastic blocks with pieces of all sizes
	Carpentry	Workbench, hammer, preschool nails, saw, sandpaper, pounding benches, safety goggles
Self-expressive	Dolls and soft toys	Realistic dolls and accessories; play settings and play people (e.g., farm, hospital)
	Dramatic play	Dress-up clothes, realistic tools, toy camera, telephone, household furniture

(Continued)

Type of Material	Appropriate Materials	Examples
	Sensory	Tactile boxes; auditory and musical materials such as smelling and sound boxes; cooking experiences
	Art/music	All rhythm instruments, music boxes; large crayons, paint, paste, glue, chalkboard and chalk, sewing kits, collage materials, markers, modeling dough, blunt scissors
Natural and everyday	Sand and water	Sandbox tools, bubbles, water toys
		Old clocks, radios, cameras, telephones; telephone books; mirrors; doctor kits; typewriter; magazines; fabric scraps; computer; cash register and receipts; measuring cups and muffin tins

TABLE 7.5   *(Continued)*

Note. For further information see Bronson (1995), Johnson, Christie, & Yawkey (1999), and Moyer (1995).

and everyday objects that are likely to have personal significance for the child, such as a stuffed toy dog with a bowl, leash, brush, and bone.

2. *Model the use of open-ended materials when necessary.* As children use more highly developed make-believe skills, encourage them to use less-realistic props. One kindergarten teacher brought a square block to the post office theme corner and suggested: "Let's pretend this is a package that just came in the mail" or "Look what the UPS driver delivered today!" Be certain to leave the play once interactions are established.

3. *Develop your own imagination.* One of Mr. Phelps's kindergartners brought in a pith helmet and sombrero to add to the dress-up corner. Rather than simply leaving the gear on a hat rack, Mr. Phelps thought about the possibilities and created a game that the children loved called Expedition. He put a piece of blue cloth on the floor and put the balance beam over it with a rubber crocodile below. He strategically positioned other animals around the room too. Soon, the children's activity took on many new dimensions—sinking in the quicksand, swinging from a pretend vine, and getting lost in the jungle. Each time Mr. Phelps introduced a new picture book such as *Junglewalk* (Tafuri, 1988), the children introduced new themes.

4. *Use available resources to meet the needs of individual children.* One preschool teacher used resources as the vehicle for helping a preschool child who was having difficulty entering group play situations learn how to join a group of players. The teacher quietly suggested that the child offer a new prop for the group's play, which allowed the child to become a participant. This sensitive teacher used a simple resource to support a shy child's entrance into an ongoing play episode.

First- Through Fourth-Graders

First- through fourth-grade children are refining skills and talents that they prize, are relying more on support from their peer group, are becoming more organized and logical thinkers, and are enjoying problem solving and inventing. Each of these qualities is clearly reflected in their expressive thinking and play. Materials for these children should reflect their need for realistic, rule-oriented, and peer activities. They need the following:

- Organized educational or physical games with rules, such as card, board, computer, and outdoor games that help them practice school skills, strategic thinking, decision making, and problem solving.
- Construction materials and puzzles, such as building sets, markers and stampers, and puzzles that have 50 to 500 pieces.
- Songs, chants, word games, and rituals, such as Scrabble, Boggle, or Word Yahtzee, as well as jokes, riddles, tongue twisters, and hyperbole. Mastery of games with rules also teaches a child how to follow instructions and preserve moral order. Table 7.6 lists a variety of developmentally appropriate materials for first- through fourth-grade children.

Your Role

Teachers must carefully consider how to use developmentally appropriate materials and resources to foster first- through fourth-graders' creative thought. The following guidelines will help you think broadly about such uses.

1. *Use projects and investigative activities.* In their unit on ecosystems, a group of fourth graders created small habitats for their land snails. The children and their teacher collected gravel, moss, soil, rocks, bark, twigs, and plastic tanks and gallon jugs with air holes poked through the top. In pairs, the children observed, recorded, and researched their snail with magnifying glasses. They investigated their snail's reaction to a shining flashlight beam, a piece of wet lettuce, and some drops of water and compared their information with that of their classmates. They even compared the size of the snail to their own size and sought answers to their own questions about snails, such as what it means to be alive. To do this, they supplemented their observations with resources such as the Internet, information books, CD-ROMs, and interviews with friends who have pets. Some concluded their study with a group book about snails that contained illustrations from their own research; others created artistic displays of their work (Koch, 2005).

2. *Use developmentally appropriate materials.* Developmentally appropriate materials take into account children's ages, needs, interests, abilities, and cultural backgrounds. They also challenge children's creative thinking and artistic expression within familiar contexts. Younger children take pride in demonstrating developing motor and intellectual skills and are fascinated with language play, number games, riddles, and jokes. They are intrigued by the sound ambiguity of knock-knock jokes, enjoy manipulating song lyrics like Raffi's "I like to oat, oat, oat oaples and banonos" and enjoy the ambiguous language of such books as *The King Who Rained* (Gwynne, 1970), while older children are intently interested in enacting and inventing humorous scripts.

TABLE 7.6 Developmentally Appropriate Materials for First- Through Fourth-Grade Children (Ages 6–10)

Type of Material	Appropriate Materials	Examples
Skill/concept	Books/records	Books on different cultures, recipe books, Caldecott and Newbery Award books and tapes, folktales, fables, historical fiction books in a series, biographies, jokes, riddles, tall tales; music of all types
	Games	Strategy and memory games; more-complex board and card games for problem solving and decision making; sports games
Gross motor	Active play	Organized group games
	Outdoor	Jump ropes, flying disks, bicycles, rope ladders, wagons, beanbags, assorted balls, sports sets
Manipulative	Fine motor	Gardening equipment, canister of buttons to sort and classify, weaving looms, sewing kits, combination locks, pickup sticks, Spirographs
	Puzzles	More complex puzzles with 50–100 pieces; puzzles of reproductions of paintings; form boards by famous artists
	Investigation	Science materials and kits; printing sets; terrariums and aquariums to create and observe
Construction	Building sets	Sets with realistic models, additional unit blocks, shapes, and accessories; props for roads and towns
	Carpentry	Add screwdrivers, vises, and accessories
Self-expressive	Dolls and soft toys	Dolls from other cultures; more detailed, smaller dolls; varied play settings and action figures
	Dramatic play	Storybook masks and costumes, walkie-talkies
	Sensory	Collecting toys in sets; clay and clay tools
	Art/music	Small crayons, chalk, watercolors, hole punchers, staplers, all musical instruments, basket-making materials, pottery wheel, stencil and craft kits
Natural and everyday	Sand and water	Add food coloring, funnels, pumps, hoses, plastic tubing, and assorted containers and utensils Simple cameras and film; computers, paper and pencils; items for "collections"

Note. For further information see Bronson (1995), Johnson, Christie, & Yawkey (1999), and Moyer (1995).

3. *Arrange the classroom in interest centers.* As part of an integrated curriculum in one urban second-grade class, children used a sandbox as the centerpiece of the language arts center. Through their reading about knights and castles, they used the sand table to construct their own interpretation of elaborate sand castles. They also used materials in the art center to illustrate more detailed aspects of the medieval environments they were learning about (Barbour, Drosdeck & Webster, 1987).

TECHNOLOGY MATERIALS, CREATIVE THINKING, PLAY, AND THE ARTS

Technology is changing the availability of materials and resources for creative thinking, play, and the arts. It has given teachers and children access to works of art from all historical periods and across many cultures, opportunities to explore inventions, and information through searches and Web quests. The Internet, in particular, has made whole museum collections widely available to students and teachers (Arts Education Partnership, 2004a). Teachers today use various technologies such as CD-ROM encyclopedias, computers and calculators, digital sound and visual image recording, and the Internet to promote creative thought and to integrate play and the arts across disciplines (March, 2004). Technological materials can invite new ways of playing and expressing ideas. They are tools that enable children to create and control their own playful microworlds; they invite fantasy creations by the imaginative child and enable children to play with real-world

Computers are a part of daily life for children and can promote playful and imaginative experiences.

items, such as musical instruments, works of art, dolls, and story characters (Arts Education Partnership, 2004a; Swaminathan & Wright, 2003).

Technology materials that promote creative thought are appropriate for all children. Research (Haugland, 2001) shows that creativity is significantly diminished in children who use drill-and-practice software for just 45 minutes per week. All adults who work with children and computers, an example of one kind of technology, need to know how to choose and use software that facilitates children's creative and artistic expression as well as their own roles in facilitating children's learning with computers.

Appropriate Software

Certain features of software design promote children's playful and imaginative experiences. Some of these include a simple design that has many possibilities, clear instructions so that children can use the program with little adult involvement, and easy access to and exit from the program (NAEYC, 1996b). Software that meets the needs and interests of children and enhances their creative thought and artistic expression enables them to do the following:

1. *Discover, invent, and control their symbolic world.* When children play with technology, they have many opportunities to determine the outcome of their play through the use of various symbols. Computer drawing programs such as Color Me, Crayola Make a Masterpiece, and Delta Draw encourage discovery as children experiment with the fill features, change and overlay colors and backgrounds, and invent stories about their creations. And virtual reality programs such as I Can Be a Dinosaur Finder, in which children become paleontologists, can provide rich symbolic experiences (Haugland, 2001).

2. *Apply a range of skills and abilities.* Some software materials require children to use a very simple set of skills (such as matching and rhyming skills in Reader Rabbit) as opposed to the use of strategic thinking required in more open programs such as paint programs or Kid Works 2. Programs like Millie and Bailey's Preschool use trial-and-error testing to match the right shoes to different-sized feet of customers. More open-ended software encourages children's exploration and self-directed learning that helps them control the pace of their own learning. Software such as Thinkin' Things Collection 3 for older children, in which children draw a design on a two-dimensional rectangle that instantly appears in 3D as a spinning shape, focuses on the development of "visual thinking." The more time children have to explore possibilities with this program, the more intriguing the mental puzzles become to solve.

3. *Enhance children's social interactions.* Quality educational software is fun and easy to use, has several levels of difficulty, and encourages children to work together. In Ms. Hicks's preschool classroom, different animals fascinated the children, so she added the program Fantastic Animals to the computer center. In pairs or triads, the children playfully selected a body, head, tail, and legs to create an animal that danced across the screen. Ms. Hicks noticed that the children were also using Delta Draw to create their own fantastic, mixed-up animals. Some of the children even invented pretend scenarios for their animals. Other open-ended software for young children that fosters social interaction includes Millie's Math House, where children construct a mouse house together and take turns choosing shapes, and Facemaker, which enables children to create limitless kinds of faces.

4. *Foster inquiry learning and problem solving.* Computer materials that promote inquiry and problem solving provide children with possibilities for gathering information, making decisions, generating creative ideas and solutions, and testing their plans and solutions. Software that enables children to "build" their own stories by selecting particular backgrounds, icons, or characters is powerful for all children because it capitalizes on children's divergent thinking and brings a story to life. With a simple click of the mouse, children can change a story's preset animals, characters, or objects to those of their own inventions. In Wiggins in Storyland, for example, young children can explore Wiggins the bookworm's living room, play tic-tac-toe on Wiggins's windows, hear classic stories read aloud, and make a snack for Wiggins to drink. Older children enjoy creating their own different story endings for web stories by exploring software such as Create Your Own Adventure with Zeke (Swaminathan & Wright, 2003). In Oregon Trail, older children find themselves having to problem-solve survival issues by deciding how to equip their wagons with limited funds. Problem-solving software has limitless possibilities and fosters children's mental flexibility.

5. *Make connections to their thematic units.* During dental health week, one second-grade teacher introduced the software program Color Me for the children to create bright illustrations for their original stories about healthy teeth. The second graders created scenic backgrounds and characters to illustrate their texts about toothbrushes as part of their study. Other programs like Cubby Magic: Folk Tales Around the World use native adults to share stories, which can be read with and without rebus pictures. Children can also make their own illustrations or use rebus pictures to interpret multicultural ideas. The challenge for teachers is to choose software that enables children to explore possibilities within a technological world (Yelland, 1999).

The Internet

The Internet has already started to transform education through the emergence of e-learning. E-learning may help develop creativity and imagination, which are seen as essential skills for the twenty-first century (Thompson & Randall, 2001). One use of the Internet for elementary children is the use of Web quests, an inquiry-oriented technology activity in which some or all of the information for learners comes from resources on the Internet. Web quests, either short-term or long-term, should be designed to make the most of a learner's time and be real, relevant, and rich. The questions children seek to answer should be real, be meaningful, and lead to active learning (Swaminathan & Wright, 2003). For an extensive array of examples of Web quests, go to http://webquest.sdsu.edu/materials.htm and click on "Lesson Templates for Students and Teachers."

Your Role

Your primary responsibility with technology materials is to ensure that they are used as one of many powerful learning tools for all children. You can do this by providing (1) technology materials that are age-appropriate, individually appropriate, culturally sensitive, and free from stereotypes and violence and (2) equal access to computer use for all children. Select software that does the following:

1. *Enhances language skills*, such as Bailey's Book House, which enables very young children to create their own greeting cards and invitations; I Spy, where children select objects to search for in a microworld; or Storybook Weaver, which enables older children to create their own stories with a word processor and multicultural illustrations.

2. *Develops and refines subject-area skills*, such as Millie's Math House, which helps very young children learn about sizes, shapes, patterns, and seasons; Blue's Clues 1 2 3 Time Activities, in which children sort food items into categories, complete patterns on colorful floats, and categorize snacks. Older children tend to benefit from Thinkin' Things Collection 3, in which children create their own songs and games in a problem-solving environment, or Number Munchers, in which children match numbers that "fit the rule" and avoid those that do not, thereby promoting physical and mental dexterity.

3. *Encourages interpersonal and intrapersonal skills* that enable children to get along with others and to better understand their own desires and feelings. Very young children may do this with Richard Scarry's How Things Work in Busytown as they learn about cooperation through building roads and baking bread, while older children might respond favorably to SimCity 2000 by designing fantasy houses of the future. Moreover, Kid Desk! Internet Safe now makes the Web accessible to children without adult assistance.

4. *Promotes artistic and creative thought* that develops visual-spatial perception, such as Kid Pix 2 for very young children, who create stamped designs and artwork; or Crayola Make a Masterpiece for older children, who use animated traditional art tools (such as watercolor, oil, chalk, and markers), unusual art tools (such as popping corn), and magic effect tools for different styles (such as mosaics) to create computer art.

Whatever the software, girls and boys, children of color, and children with disabilities need equal access to this powerful technology. In the next section, we describe other specific divergent materials that should be available to all children in every classroom regardless of resources.

OTHER DIVERGENT MATERIALS AND RESOURCES

Certain divergent materials are basic for all children—blocks, modeling materials, sand, and water. These materials offer many possibilities for children to express their ideas and feelings, grow naturally with children, and can be used for more than one topic or activity.

Blocks

In his autobiography, Frank Lloyd Wright (1932) enthusiastically recalled his kindergarten experiences with blocks: "The smooth, shapely maple blocks with which to build, the sense of which never afterward left the fingers: so form became feeling" (p. 11). With blocks, children are free to create imaginative constructions and determine what to do with them, as can be seen in a glimpse of Ms. Mitsoff's first-grade classroom. Ms. Mitsoff rearranged her room to double the block-building space. Throughout the year, her first graders used the blocks as the focal point for their units of study. In their unit on the farm, for example, the children conceptualized, built, and played in a farm containing stalls for cows, a henhouse, a main farmhouse, and a barn. They also assumed different roles, including those of the farmer, milker, and egg collector. Ms. Mitsoff noticed her children practicing the following concepts:

- Science concepts as they observed, compared, and interpreted findings on ways to collect, store, and deliver milk.
- Math concepts as they estimated the distance between the farmhouse and the henhouse.
- Social studies concepts as they re-created the roles of the farm workers.
- Literacy concepts as they named and labeled their structures and considered books as references.
- Art concepts as they repeated patterns in their symmetrical buildings.

Types and Uses

There are many different types of blocks—hollow blocks, unit blocks, and table blocks. *Hollow blocks* are large wooden blocks that have an opening for carrying. Children often use these blocks to build large structures. *Unit blocks* should be made from hard wood, have smooth and rounded corners and edges, and be accurate so that children can build without frustration. To build structures, children need precisely measured unit blocks including units, double units, quadruple units, wedges, triangles, cylinders, and half-rounds. *Table blocks* are small, colored cubed blocks that children use alone or in pairs around a table. They often include unusual shapes that invite children's inventiveness. Figure 7.2 illustrates the various unit block shapes.

Children pass through the following seven stages in block building (Hirsch, 1996):

- Stage 1: Carrying—Very young children carry blocks around but do not use them to build.
- Stage 2: Building begins—Children make mostly rows, either horizontal (on the floor) or vertical (stacked). There is much repetition in this early building pattern.
- Stage 3: Bridging—Two blocks with a space between them, connected by a third block.
- Stage 4: Enclosures—Blocks placed in such a way that they enclose a space.
- Stage 5: Decorative patterns—When facility with blocks is acquired, much block symmetry can be observed. Buildings, generally, are not yet named.

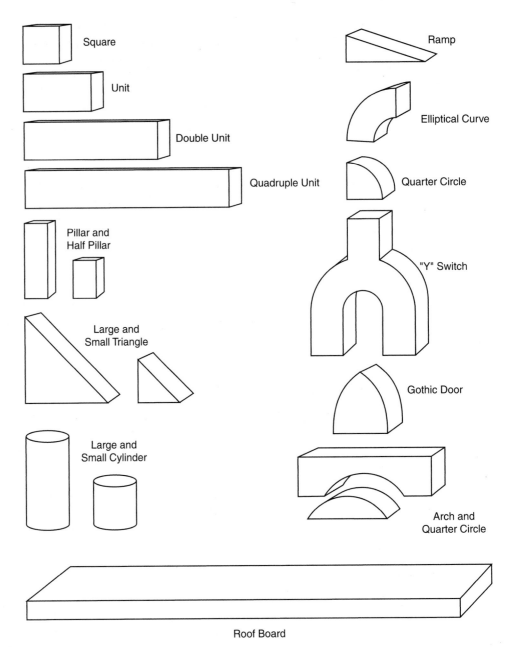

Square

Ramp

Unit

Elliptical Curve

Double Unit

Quarter Circle

Quadruple Unit

Pillar and
Half Pillar

"Y" Switch

Large and
Small Triangle

Gothic Door

Large and
Small Cylinder

Arch and
Quarter Circle

Roof Board

Figure 7.2
Illustrations of Block Shapes

294

- Stage 6: Naming structures for dramatic play—Before reaching this stage, children may also have named their structures, but the names were not necessarily related to the function of the building.
- Stage 7: Resembling reality—Children's buildings often reproduce or symbolize actual structures they know, and there is a strong impulse toward dramatic play around the block structures.

Your Role

Block play is central to children's learning in all areas. For example, block play contributes to children's literacy development as they gain experience with symbolic representation, a basic abstract aspect of the reading and writing process; it promotes visual discrimination as children select particular blocks for their constructions; it helps children develop the fine motor strength needed for writing; and it enables children to develop their oral language skills by communicating about their plans and needs for their structures. The following guidelines will help you maximize the potential learning in block play for children of all ages.

- Store blocks on low, open shelves for easy access.
- Provide an adequate supply of blocks—200 blocks for a group of ten 3-year-olds. A complete set of more than 750 blocks is not too many for an older group of 20 children.
- Allocate enough floor space for building out of the traffic patterns, next to the dramatic-play area, and away from a quiet activity area.
- Provide enough time for building (45 to 60 minutes).
- Provide props and accessories such as cars and animals.
- Maintain a periodic physical presence in the area to attract children to the block center.
- Label shelves with the shape of the long side of the block in view so children can locate materials quickly, perceive the relationships of the blocks to one another, practice classification skills, and assist with cleanup.
- Use blocks in ways other than building, such as a matching or measuring game with blocks of a specific size.
- Develop a genuine appreciation for block playing (Hirsch, 1996).

Modeling Materials

Dough and clay are three-dimensional, sensory materials that offer children possibilities for expressing knowledge, thoughts, and feelings. Young children enjoy pounding, squeezing, and rolling these materials. Older children do the same but also represent and/or create familiar objects or people. Where possible, consider letting the children mix the dough themselves. Figure 7.3 contains some simple recipes for modeling materials.

Modeling materials allow children to explore, manipulate, discover, create, and observe changes in physical properties. Children can learn the attributes of modeling materials through the changes they make involving consistency (from wet to dry), color (from primary to secondary), identity (from a ball to a snake), space (from small to large), and weight (from light to heavy).

Clay Substitute
1 cup flour
1/2 cup salt
1/3 cup water

Vegetable Dye
1 cup flour
1/2 cup salt
1 teaspoon powdered alum
1/2 cup water

Sawdust Dough
2 cups sawdust
3 cups flour
1 cup salt
Water as needed

Cornstarch Dough
1 cup cornstarch
2 cups baking soda
1/4 cup cold water
Food coloring

Play Dough
1 cup salt
1/2 cup cornstarch
1/2 cup boiling water

Peanut Butter Dough (edible)
1 cup honey
1 cup peanut butter
2 cups dried milk

Goop
1 cup cornstarch
1 cup water
Add food coloring and pour into
plastic tub
(Messy but unique!)

Soapy Clay
2 cups detergent flakes
2 tablespoons water
Food coloring, if desired

Figure 7.3
Recipes for Modeling Materials

These "hands-on" experiences with transformations help children begin to make connections between actions and events, a fundamental understanding for the development of logical thinking. Children need plenty of dough for modeling to be satisfying. Be certain to focus on the process of the material and avoid pushing children to create a product.

Sand and Water

Sand and water are readily available, inexpensive, satisfying resources that help children explore concepts and release tension. Children learn science concepts, such as the effects of objects dropped on water; math concepts such as volume, by guessing the number of cups of water needed to fill a larger container; and social interaction skills.

Sand and water are particularly absorbing and relaxing materials for children. Children can release tension as they pour water back and forth in containers or let sand gradually sift through their fingers. When children use sand and water, their social interactions are often quite calm and cooperative.

Play with sand and water should take place both indoors and outdoors. Some teachers place the sand or water in large plastic tubs or in specially prepared tables. Other teachers substitute rice, shelled corn, or birdseed for indoor sandboxes when sand is unavailable. The inside of an old truck tire laid flat makes a

Water is a particularly rewarding and relaxing material for children of all ages.

serviceable outdoor sandbox. Be certain to cover the sandbox when the children are not using it so that a stray animal does not foul it. Check outdoor sandboxes frequently for insect infestations too.

Your Role

When using sand and water, consider the following:

- Use sand and water together so children can mold the mixture.
- Vary the equipment so that children are continually challenged to think of new uses. Some common materials for sand and water play include various-sized molds, sponges, plastic bottles and containers of assorted sizes, flexible plastic tubing, measuring cups and spoons, and small replicas of cars, buildings, and boats. Plastic aprons are also useful.
- Ask open-ended questions such as, "Why do you think the water is coming out so slowly?" or "I wonder what would happen if you added water to your sand mound?"
- Decide in advance on simple rules so that water and sand do not get tracked around the classroom. Have materials available so that children take responsibility for cleanup.

Materials of all sorts need to be matched to individual abilities. They are children's tools for understanding their world. Teachers have a key role in ensuring a balance of appropriate materials and resources for the release of children's creative and artistic expression. They provide a different experience from games.

ORGANIZED GAMES

In the following scenario, think about triplets playing games at different ages. Rosa, Dolly, and Norman are now fourth graders. When they were toddlers, their caregiver played social games with them, such as This Little Piggy and Hide the Keys. In their Head Start program, they played running and chasing games and simple spinning games of chance, such as Hi-Ho Cherry-O. In these games, rules did not matter. Now Rosa plays on the school soccer team and practices soccer skills wherever she can. Dolly actively seeks friends to play strategy games such as Rummy and Clue. And Norman thrives on memory and word games such as Twenty Questions and Scrabble.

The games Rosa, Dolly, and Norman played are typical. Although games broaden the curriculum for children of all ages, many teachers believe games with rules foster a competitive rather than a cooperative spirit, question their value, and view them as frivolous.

What Is a Game?

A **game** is a form of play in which children follow an agreed-upon set of rules, predetermine an outcome, assign players specific roles, and assign sanctions for violations (DeVries, 1998; Hughes, 1999; Kamii & DeVries, 1980). Dictionary definitions usually include the elements of rules, competition, and winning.

Most children's games involve physical skill, chance, strategy, or some combination of these elements to determine the outcome. In games of physical skill such as jump rope or stickball, motor skill is essential. Games of chance, such as the simple board game Winnie the Pooh, rely on dice or a spinner. Games of strategy, such as checkers or Boggle, require decision-making skills and compel players to take turns, follow complex directions, and employ complicated strategies. Organized sports are often considered strategy games because they require a player to plan strategies and imagine oneself in the opponent's role.

The Value of Games

Games are one material that contributes to children's creative-thinking, decision-making, and problem-solving skills. Games themselves are motivating for many children because the desire to play them comes from within. For many children, games provide a means to learn new skills and to practice known skills. Some educators believe that organized games for young children are developmentally inappropriate, thwart creativity, and encourage competition. Others believe that they can be appropriate if teachers positively confront the competitive element (DeVries, 1998; 1999; Kamii & DeVries, 1980). Games for school-age children should capitalize on their increased coordination, desire to challenge themselves individually, interest in facts and how things work and why things happen, and genuine love of group games. When group games match children's developmental levels, children do the following:

- Develop *cooperative behaviors and strategic thinking* by experiencing others' thinking and relating it to their own. One third grader, for instance, talked about setting up a "double jump" in checkers, indicating her thinking in relation to her actions.
- Practice *autonomy* by choosing whether to play the game and to follow its rules. To illustrate, when Carmella's kindergarten friends wanted to play shadow tag, she chose another activity because she did not want to be "it."
- Engage in *problem solving* by deciding how to follow rules and play fairly. In one scenario, a group of first graders was trying to start a game of Go Fish but could not begin their play until they solved the problem of who was to go first.
- Practice *critical thinking* by monitoring each other's actions. In a game of dominoes, it is common to hear one child tell another, "That domino doesn't have the same number of dots. You can't use that one" (Johnson, Christie, et al., 1999).

Games suitable for young children have one or two simple rules, include all children who want to participate, encourage children to figure things out for themselves, and do not stress being first, winning, or losing. Young children like noncompetitive guessing games such as "I'm thinking of something in the room that is . . . ," simple sorting and matching games, simple board games (if they can change the rules), and basic running and chasing games.

Children in first through fourth grades need strategy games that develop problem-solving and decision-making abilities while encouraging them to think about others' thoughts and feelings. Board games and active outdoor group games are typical of this age for both boys and girls. With an emphasis on involvement, mutual enjoyment, and respect, group games can promote basic intellectual and social skills in children through fourth grade.

Competition Versus Cooperation

Games should be a positive experience for all children. All children should benefit from the physical challenge, exercise, problem solving, and strategic thinking while simultaneously enjoying a sense of belonging to the group, a commitment to goals, and enhanced cooperative skills, all of which contribute to academic success. If teachers make it clear that the goal of a game is doing as well as each child can, then games can enhance cooperation. To illustrate, Ms. Ake's second graders were involved in relay races. When she reminded them that the goal of these races was to do their very best, she noticed how they urged one another on in their three-legged races as they jointly figured out ways to get quickly to the other side of the room.

Cooperation means operating together. It involves negotiating to arrive at an agreement that is acceptable to all. As a result, some disputes and conflicts are inevitable. When children play games cooperatively, they construct rules for themselves as they begin to experience others' viewpoints. An emphasis on cooperative games encourages children to play together rather than against one another by focusing on group participation, sharing, giving each player an opportunity to play, and making rules that suit the players. Cooperative games help children develop a sense of teamwork, loyalty to the group, and knowledge of how to get along with others. Because Western culture is inherently competitive, it is a challenge for teachers to handle competition constructively in classrooms.

Your Role

Consider this group of elementary children playing Marble Run, a commercial game in which children combine small blocks with slides and intricate grooves into a course for the marble. As the children excitedly invent new courses, they exclaim, "Now, let's try this!" or "Look at it go!" Their teacher commented, "This is their favorite game because it has so many possibilities and combinations. When I say, 'It's game time,' I have to be sure to say 'Only four children can use Marble Run.' It is truly the favorite game in our classroom."

The teacher's role, in this case, was that of observer and manager as she freed the children to utilize the many available combinations. There was no correct way to play the game. The children constructed the rules in ways that made sense to them.

When using games in educational settings, teachers must provide opportunities for children to modify rules and create their own games. In that way, games such as Marble Run, as they are being played, become a powerful vehicle for developing intellectual and social autonomy. You can help children modify game rules by doing the following:

1. *Supporting their initiatives in games.* The children playing Marble Run were encouraged to play the game in many different ways. Sometimes the game involved races; at other times it became a maze. Each group of players could initiate the way to play the game and then negotiate rules for it.

2. *Focusing on noncompetitive games.* Children who compete can and do also cooperate in games as well as other activities. All children function best when they actively participate in most or all of the game instead of being excluded or eliminated by focusing on winning or losing. Appendix C describes appropriate, noncompetitive ball games, quiet games, singing games, running games, and partner games that can be introduced into the curriculum to enhance cooperation.

3. *Allowing them to modify rules during the game.* Even though the children usually started one of the Marble Run games with a race of some kind, they often decided to change it in midstream to a different game. Their teacher supported their thinking about all of the variations they invented by using positive language that empowered them to think about the many possibilities inherent in the game.

Games are useful for active and quiet times, for transitions from one activity to another, and for fostering specific learning outcomes. Therefore, you will need to develop a repertoire of games that foster a cooperative spirit that will last children through their lives.

CHILD-CONSTRUCTED GAMES

Child-constructed games promote children's understanding and acceptance of rules as well as their ability to cooperate, compete, and think flexibly. Unfortunately, children in today's world spend less time spontaneously inventing games and more time using prepared commercial games with predetermined instructions, rules, and outcomes or in organized team sports. This limits their opportunities to make, revise, and follow their own rules with their peers and to control their social interactions. In the next section, we describe the power of children's invented games on their divergent thinking, artistic expression, and overall development.

Invented Games

Inventing games makes rules meaningful and relevant for children (Castle, 1998). They help children do the following:

1. *Become autonomous learners.* Second grader Andy made a simple baseball game from oak tag, markers, and colored dots. When other children were excited about using it and helped him modify the game, Andy gained confidence in his ability as an independent yet collaborative learner.

2. *Practice ongoing basic skills.* Julia wanted to create her own version of hopscotch on the playground outdoors. She practiced her writing to label the asphalt with chalk and to write the game's rules; she used reading skills to read her rules to a friend; and she incorporated mathematics when figuring out the procedures and format of her hopscotch game.

3. *Develop organizational skills.* In invented games, children plan the game, construct it, play it with others, discover its problems, and make changes. Some of Ms. Spencer's fourth-grade girls invented a board game called Shopping. The object was to move along a path to purchase various department store items. While playing the game, they discovered that their rule of getting the exact number on the dice to move the number of spaces remaining on the game board left them sitting for many turns waiting to complete the game. So they agreed to change the rules.

Invented games encourage mutual self-interest in rules and rule making and differ greatly from teacher-imposed rules. They provide an appealing and satisfying vehicle for children to apply skills, increase their understanding of rules, see others' ideas and points of view, and improve their social interaction skills. Older children can make board games based on the content they are studying, while younger children might invent games based on stories they are reading. Think about the following second graders in Mr. Green's classroom. Paolo, Kristin, and Sarah are struggling readers and have some difficulty with basic arithmetic operations. For one hour every Wednesday afternoon, Mr. Green expects all of his second graders to invent their own games, either alone or with a partner, using assorted available materials. Let's look at the games of Kristin, Sarah, and Paolo.

Kristin made the "Go Here and There Game" alone and then taught it to her friend. Her simple path game included starting and finishing points, some obstacles along the way, a few game cards, and an individual card for rules. During play her friend asked, "Where are the place cards?" Kristin said, "Oops, I forgot them" and went back to make them.

Sarah's game reflects the solar system unit her class is studying. It includes all the planets, Saturn's rings, a darkened background indicating night, and the sun and stars. She made cards for the number of spaces to move forward and back, as well as outer-space instructions like "Tack a peas [take a piece] of the moon rock and stay." She used existing dice to designate turns and dried beans for markers. Her simple rules read as follows: "RULES: Start from the moon go to the Erath and the first person to get there wens." When she tried to teach the game to a friend the next week, she quickly discovered that she had no labels on the dots telling players when to choose a card. As a result, the game could not begin. Sarah then made the necessary modifications.

Paolo's game, Colorland, is also a simple path game containing a clear beginning and end, periodic spots to pick cards, a place labeled "card," and many cards sending players to jail or helping them escape from jail. Two of his cards read "brach owt of jail [break out of jail]" and "Go 5 steps forwerd." Paolo has played his game several times with his classmates. His final version evolved from the many questions his friends asked while playing.

Notice that in all three cases, children were refining the format or organization of their games, practicing skills in context, and collaborating with peers. Child-constructed games provide children with the opportunity to construct and use rules in relevant ways, to apply content they are studying, to see others' points of view, and to figure things out autonomously or cooperatively.

Making Games with Children

The following guidelines will help you include game making in your curriculum.

1. *Find information and collect facts.* Before making a game, the children need to determine what information they need. If children are studying environmental issues, for example, this is a good time to review the content learned during the unit and clarify what they still want to know. This is also the time for children to gather books and other informational resources to verify facts.

2. *Make a rough draft.* As in the writing process, making a rough draft of the game board, cards, content, and accessories frees children to plan. It provides an organizational framework for thinking and working together for a common outcome.

3. *Make the game.* Have a variety of free and inexpensive materials available, such as file folders, poster board of all sizes and colors, beans, markers, sticky dots, labels, plastic bread ties, old magazines, calendar numbers, and assorted plastic bottle caps. Expect children to decide the type of game to make (board, card, and motor) and invent it. Their games will usually look like games that are familiar to them, yet the content and the play of the game will vary.

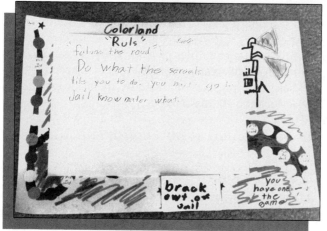

Three invented games.

4. *Play the game.* Playing the games helps children notice problems and pitfalls. Children "go back to the drawing board" willingly to produce a playable game.

5. *Revise the game to achieve more accuracy.* Revision means literally "to see again." As children revise their games, they re-see and re-think them until they achieve excellence in the finished product. The revision process provides multiple opportunities for creative expression, constructive conflict resolution, and practice in self-evaluation. By observing, recording, and comparing children's progress with invented games throughout the year, teachers have a powerful learning, teaching, and assessment tool that appeals to children of all ages (Castle, 1998; Surbeck & Glover, 1992).

MEETING STANDARDS

Using Classroom Materials and Resources Effectively

Teachers often find that providing materials and resources for creative thinking and artistic expression is challenging because they feel less prepared in creativity and the arts than in academic subjects. Materials and resources that promote creative thought and artistic expression are connected to standards across disciplines and require both "hands on" and "minds on" learning (Beeghly & Prudhoe, 2002; Wassermann, 2000). These materials invite children to tinker and experiment, visualize and model, brainstorm and role-play, inquire and problem-solve as well as to paint, draw, dramatize, act out, and dance their understanding. Using materials in this way parallels the types of play discussed in Chapter Two (functional play, dramatic play, sociodramatic play, and games with rules).

Many museums and arts organizations have fine Web sites that provide information, lesson plans, and activities for teachers to use materials and resources effectively. Still, teachers are responsible for selecting the most appropriate materials and resources; deciding when, where, and how to make them accessible; and answering the questions, "What classroom materials and resources promote standards-based teaching?" and "How do different teaching materials and resources affect learning?"

What follows are examples of ways teachers can incorporate materials and resources that promote creative thought and arts-based learning into ongoing instruction. These examples are followed by the appropriate national content, arts, and teacher-education standards.

Materials and Resources for English Language Arts

Example

Read the book *Dance with Me* (Esbensen, 1995), a collection of 15 poems about different kinds of dance steps illustrated in pastels. The poems portray everyday objects and events from the author's perspective, such as the tap-dance sounds of raindrops falling on the roof in a summer storm, a baby tapping a beat with her reflection in the mirror, and a woman dancing as she weeds her garden. Readers see ordinary subjects such as bubbles, waves, and dust and through different lenses.

Preschool/Kindergarten

Using the poem "Bubbles" from the book *Dance with Me* (Esbensen, 1995), invite children to become "bubbleologists" and study bubbles. With some bubble solution and a variety of wands, have them explore, investigate, and make bubbles. Encourage them to describe their bubbles—color, shape, size, number, length, and duration—and determine which wands work best.

Possible Activities:

- Use pastel colors to write and/or illustrate poems inspired by "Bubbles."
- Use rhythm instruments to make sound effects for the reading of "Bubbles."
- Create rebus picture words for bubbles of different shapes.
- Brainstorm ways to float like bubbles.

First Grade–Fourth Grade

Possible Activities:

- Redefine the ordinary: Create an interesting poem about something ordinary in your daily life (use movement, voice, action, person, place, and thing).
- Use the Internet to discover dance steps from around the world and apply them to ordinary objects.
- Construct a cardboard model of something ordinary and share your construction with a friend.

Connection to English/Language/Arts Standards

The Arts (Dance): Understanding choreographic principles, processes and structures

Applying and demonstrating critical and creative thinking skills in dance
Language Arts: Students apply a wide range of strategies to comprehend, evaluate, and appreciate texts. They draw upon their prior experiences, their interactions with other readers and writers, and their knowledge of word meaning and other texts.

Science (Physical Science): Students develop an understanding of the properties of objects and materials.

Teacher Education:

INTASC–Principle 1, Content Pedagogy

NAEYC–Standard 4, Teaching and Learning, and Substandard 4c, Understanding Content Knowledge in Early Education

Materials and Resources for Science

Materials and resources for science should promote sustained inquiry and understanding. Effective science teaching requires the availability and organization of a broad range of basic scientific materials, equipment, media, and technology as well as specific tools for particular topics and learning experiences. Teachers must balance safety, proper use, and availability with students' needs to participate actively in designing experiments, selecting tools, and constructing apparatus, all of which are critical to the development of an understanding of inquiry.

Science literacy also involves the use of materials and resources outside the school, such as science centers and museums. The school's indoor and outdoor physical environment can easily be used as a living laboratory for the study of natural phenomena and should be used as a resource for science study wherever the school may be located.

Example

Preschool/Kindergarten

Appropriate basic materials include aluminum foil and plastic wrap; basic rock, mineral, and shell collections; assortments of seeds, beans, and peas; egg cartons; food coloring; hand lenses; magnets of various sizes and shapes; measuring cups and spoons; rubber balls of various sizes; scales; shoe boxes; small plastic animals and trays; and trade books.

Possible Activities:

- Investigate color changes with food coloring and eyedroppers.
- Mix modeling dough and observe changes.
- Construct a model out of dough.
- Use found or recycled materials to create collages to compare and contrast changes.

First Grade–Fourth Grade

In addition to the preceding materials, use balloons, barometers, batteries, beakers, calculators, charts of regional birds, rocks, minerals, compasses, graduated cylinders, plastic containers, tubing, straws, prisms, pulleys, and safety goggles.

Possible Activities:

- Use an "invention sketchpad" to create an invented animal, food, game, or machine. Draw "ideas" on the sketchpad and then use some of the basic materials to create your invention.
- Write a story about your invention.
- Search the Internet to find out about your favorite inventor and what materials he or she used to create an invention.
- Take an invention walk around your school to identify all the things that have been invented.
- Make "junk bags" by filling lunch bags with items from your basic science materials and have the children invent something in teams.

Sources for Free and Inexpensive Materials:

Environmental Protection Agency Public Information Center and Library
401 M Street SW
Washington, DC 20460

National Aeronautics and Space Administration (NASA)
NASA Education Division
NASA Headquarters
300 E Street SW
Washington, DC 20546

National Science Foundation
Division of Pre-College Education
1800 G Street
Washington, DC 20550

Outstanding Science Trade Books for Students K–12
Recommended reading levels arranged by seven topical categories
http://www.nsta.org/ostbc

Connection to Science Standards

NSES Teaching Standard D: Teachers of science design and manage learning environments that provide students with the time, space, and resources needed for learning science. In doing this, teachers make available the science tools, materials, media, and technological resources accessible to students and identify and use resources outside the school.

Teacher Education:

INTASC–Principle 1, Content Pedagogy

NAEYC–Standard 4, Teaching and Learning, and Substandard 4c, Understanding Content Knowledge in Early Education

Materials and Resources for Social Studies

Example

In a study of author Gary Soto, children learn about the Hispanic culture through the author's works. For younger children, read *Chato's Kitchen* (1997), a story of five mice who move next door to a cat and who end up being friends and celebrating with an elaborate fiesta. For older children, read *Neighborhood Odes* (1992), a collection of 21 poems set in a Chicano neighborhood that offer new ways to think about common things such as the music of an ice cream vendor's truck, the top of a refrigerator where old bread lies in plastic, and dust released into the air when a boy strums a guitar, which is evoked by the form of the poems, which fall in long vertical columns with short lines. Woodcut illustrations capture the culture of the Chicano community. The odes celebrate fireworks, pets, grandparents, tortillas, and the library.

Preschool/Kindergarten

Possible Activities:

- Design a book of your favorite poems.
- Make quesadillas.
- Draw a self-portrait of characters and create a portrait gallery.
- Investigate local neighborhoods and explore Mexican and Mexican American culture.
- Create a collage picturing your favorite things in your house (toys, food, furniture).
- Create puppets to represent historical figures.
- Explore museum sites for contributions of Hispanic figures.
- Learn folk songs and singing games of the culture.

First Grade–Fourth Grade

Possible Activities:

- Create a new country with favorite food, sport, greeting, main form of transportation, flag, national anthem, name of country, and motto.
- Invent games (Memory, Concentration) that use the images in Soto's poems.
- Create an ode about a favorite person or object in your daily life.
- Play a game from one of the countries.
- Visit some key Web sites such as those of *National Geographic,* the Getty Museum, and Exploratorium to locate other links to the Hispanic culture and to explore Mexican American art.

Connection to Social Studies and Arts Standards

Social Studies (Culture): Students explore how cultures express themselves through the arts.

Social Studies (Global Connections): Students explore how exposure to diversity found in cultural universals (dancing, cooking, and hospitality) may lead to global understandings or misunderstandings.

Social Studies (Culture): Students investigate how different cultures, groups, and societies are similar and different across common situations.

The Arts (Visual Arts): Understanding and applying media, techniques, and processes

Understanding the visual arts in relation to history and cultures

Teacher Education:

INTASC—Principle 1, Content Pedagogy

NAEYC—Standard 4, Teaching and Learning, and Substandard 4c, Understanding Content Knowledge in Early Education

Frequently Asked Questions About Materials and Resources

I have so much English to teach to children who are English-language learners. Why should I use games with them?

Children in schools today speak more than 400 different languages. For all children, engaging in simulations; drama games; story, word, and writing games; and outdoor games can improve their learning, offer a different way to express knowledge, and create an atmosphere of ease, original thinking, and imaginative thought. Games create experiences with language and ideas, and "experience is the glue that makes learning stick" (Peregoy & Boyle, 2005, p. 131). For English-language learners at all levels, games encourage students to work on motivating projects; provide scaffolds for oral language, where evident; and focus on easy use of oral language, exploding the myth that games are not appropriate for nonnative language learners (Kindler, 2002).

I have children from many different countries in my classroom. How do I know what kinds of materials to choose, because I cannot teach about all of these different cultures?

The materials that children use are powerful vehicles for multicultural education because they are visual representations of others' feelings, behaviors, artifacts, and traditions. Using materials "rooted in cultural traditions may help children identify more deeply with their cultures and share their cultures with others. When integrated into the teaching of other subjects, the arts provide a vehicle for students to introduce their life experiences into the classroom in purposeful ways for their recognition of their peers and teachers" (Arts Education Partnership, 2004b, p. 26). Students from diverse backgrounds can also use art materials to engage with each other and to build understanding of race, culture, and socioeconomic status. Materials, therefore, should reflect the individuality of children and adults in that setting (Isenberg & Quisenberry, 2002; Ramsey, 1998; Wootton, 2004).

Materials and resources contribute to children's growing awareness of diversity when teachers provide interest centers that reflect not only the cultural backgrounds and customs represented in the classroom but also those of other cultures, such as a celebration of the Chinese New Year, Hanukkah, or Kwanzaa. Teachers should also provide literature to enrich children's understanding of cultural pluralism, such as *Knots on a Counting Rope* (Martin & Archambault, 1987) or *I Hate English!* (Levine, 1990), and multimedia that uses pictorial and visual information for learning about other cultures. To help children express themselves through materials, all teachers need to ensure that children from other cultures feel welcome and safe in their classrooms and experience many opportunities to use materials that are real, concrete, and culturally relevant.

I teach in an inclusive classroom. Is it true that the materials and resources affect children's creative thought and expression?

Children with special needs often have a disability (for example, cognitive, communication, physical, or sensory) that affects how they choose and use materials. They need materials that span various ranges of difficulty, that present individually appropriate challenges, and that can be modified as needed to meet individual needs. For example, children with sensory impairments need tactile and auditory materials, such as tactile maps for exploration, large-type print kits, Braille materials such as a Braille menu for the housekeeping area, and a rice table for sensory exploration. Children with communication disabilities need materials to help them communicate about familiar people, events, and objects such as a toy telephone, computer, or puppet. With technology materials, children with special needs may require assistive devices such as touch-sensitive screens, condensed keyboards, or speech synthesizers that promote their ability to express themselves to one another and to adults, giving them access to greater social and intellectual participation in classroom experiences, enhancing their interactions with peers, and facilitating the learning of particular skills and concepts (Haugland & Wright, 1997; Hull, Goldhaber, & Capone, 2002; Mitchell, 2004).

In my student teaching classroom, some children are gifted and also second-language learners. What kinds of materials and resources do these children need?

Many myths surround children who are gifted second-language learners. These children need a language-rich environment that integrates critical and higher-order thinking as well as the use of multiple intelligences. It is not true that these children are less capable, are unable to articulate, or do not work as well in groups or independent research projects (Castellano, 2003). Because of their often exceptional verbal ability, high-achieving preschool children need to use more language play, such as riddles, jokes, and poems, and more logical, rules-oriented games. Children who are academically talented enjoy playing or inventing computer games that are intellectually demanding, solving advanced problems in mathematics, exploring ideas, testing hypotheses, and judging the quality of their solutions. Investigations, learning centers, and contracts offer children many possibilities to use their gifts.

In every classroom, children need a variety of open-ended materials and resources that hold their fascination, challenge their thinking, keep them engaged, and support meaningful play and creative thought. See Appendix F for sources for free and inexpensive classroom materials and resources.

Web Sites to Visit

http://www.exploratorium.edu
Hands-on exhibits devoted to inquiry-based teaching and learning.

http://www.thegateway.org
Provides access to lesson plans, curriculum units, and other education resources.

http://www.puzzlemaker.com
Allows users to create puzzles and games for newsletters, flyers, handouts, or classroom assignments.

http://www.terra-quest.com
Includes information about ecology, travel, environments and wildlife, and history.

http://webquest.sdsu.edu
Provides an inquiry-oriented resource to those using the Web quest model to teach with the World Wide Web.

http://www.fieldguides.com/trips
Field trips for children of all ages in a variety of subject areas.

CHAPTER SUMMARY

1. Throughout history, children in all cultures have played with materials. The types of materials available are affected by economic, cultural, and political issues and strongly influence children's self-expression, inventiveness, and divergent thinking.
2. Materials that hold the most promise for creative thought and arts-based learning have multiple uses, encourage inventiveness and problem solving, and are process-oriented. Playing with these materials fosters children's inventiveness.
3. Children should experience a balance of materials including skill/concept, manipulative, construction, self-expressive, and natural and everyday materials.
4. Developmentally appropriate materials, which are concrete, real, meaningful, and stimulating to the imagination, should be available to children of all ages. Younger children need sensory materials to explore and investigate in dramatic play, art, music, construction, and manipulative play. Older children also need realistic, rule-oriented, and peer-related activities.
5. Technology materials are one of many classroom learning tools. They enable children to control their symbolic world, apply new and familiar skills, enhance their social interactions, foster self-directed learning, solve problems, and connect information to what they know and are studying.
6. Organized games can be a significant aspect of the curriculum if presented and played appropriately. They can encourage autonomy, decision making, cooperation, and use of rules.
7. Teachers should incorporate opportunities for children to invent, teach, and play their own games as part of the curriculum.
8. Using a variety of open-ended materials and resources is one of the best ways for teachers to adapt the curriculum to a wide range of children's abilities, interests, and cultural backgrounds.

Discuss: Perspectives on Play Materials

1. Select, investigate, and explore a child's play material from your current setting. Think about the possible ways children could use it. If you can, observe different children using the same material. Keep a list of the children's uses. Compare your list with those who selected a similar material. How did infants/toddlers, preschoolers/kindergartners, and children in Grades 1–4 use the material?
2. Reread the chapter's opening quotation. Describe how your thinking has changed since reading this chapter.
3. Incorporating invented games into the curriculum provides children many opportunities for learning. Discuss these opportunities and suggest ways to include them as part of a thematic unit.

4. Why should children use open-ended materials? List as many types of these materials as you can and briefly state a rationale for including each in the curriculum.

5. Refer to the chapter opening classroom scenarios. Why was it important for the children's teachers to provide these kinds of materials? What was their role? Defend your thinking.

6. Observe a child who is using a material for the first time. Refer to the discussion of the uses of materials in this chapter and describe his or her behaviors. How do the behaviors fit the progression?

Chapter 8

Fostering Creative Thought and Expression

We need to embrace a broader view of mind, by which I mean a broader view of the ways in which thinking occurs. By no means is thinking limited to what words alone can carry. The limits of our cognition are not defined by the limits of our language.

Elliot Eisner, 2003, p. 10

CLASSROOM PERSPECTIVES ON FOSTERING CREATIVE THOUGHT AND EXPRESSION

Preschool–Kindergarten

It is center time in Ms. Manning's kindergarten classroom. David and Ahmad are making puppets so that they can dramatize their original stories about farm animals. When their puppets are finished, they begin tugging on each other and wrestling with their puppets. The boys become increasingly boisterous, so Ms. Manning comes over.

Ms. Manning: Pardon me, David and Ahmad. Please talk with me over here. *(she goes to a quiet corner, kneels down, and talks to them at their eye level)* What was in your story that made you pull on each other so roughly? *(she listens intently to their responses)*

Ahmad: Playing pigs and robbers. The robbers were getting my pigs and we needed to catch them to get our pigs back. *(David nods in agreement)*

Ms. Manning: David, tell me in your own words about what you were doing.

David: Playing pigs and robbers. But I was done with the game and didn't want to be the robber anymore, and Ahmad kept pulling on me.

Ms. Manning: You were done playing with your puppets for your story. Do you think when you're playing like that, when you might be wrestling or pulling, that you need to tell each other when you stop playing? *(David nods)* David, did you tell Ahmad when you wanted to stop? *(shakes head no)* Look at my eyes, David. How will Ahmad know that you want to stop the game if you don't tell him? You know, next time you could say in your own words, "Ahmad, I don't want to play this game anymore." *(David looks down and shakes his head)* When you leave the game, tell the person you're playing with so they know. All right? Let's go back to finishing your puppet stories about the farm animals. *(all three get up and leave)*

First Grade–Second Grade

In Mr. Connor's second grade, the children are studying underwater mammals. During their language arts and music block, the children read the book *I'm a Manatee*

(Lithgow, 2003) in which a little boy dreams of becoming a manatee, sing the accompanying music, and write about their dreams of becoming a real or fictional underwater mammal. Knowing that children who have just read about a manatee would be predisposed to writing about one, Mr. Connor primes the children's thinking by leading them in a guided-imagery trip under the sea, encouraging divergent thinking to inspire their writing. He sets the mood using recorded sounds of the ocean and asks the children to close their eyes and picture the world around them. He asks, "What does your mammal look like? What do you see? Hear? Smell? Touch? Taste?" Through guided imagery, the children visualize and imagine almost simultaneously how they would live as an underwater mammal (Annarella, 1999).

Third Grade–Fourth Grade

As part of Mrs. Barr's social studies unit, she uses the book *Shiloh* (Naylor, 1991), in which 11-year-old Marty cares for a mistreated beagle pup as his own. When Marty discovers that the pup belongs to a neighbor, he faces many difficult questions. Should he return the dog to its owner? Should he tell his parents? Should he steal food to help the abused pup? Through small-group and whole-class discussions, Mrs. Barr invites children to respond to Marty's dilemmas and relate them to their own everyday occurrences at home and school. In a culminating activity, the children reenact scenes from the book that show how Marty's behavior affects the relationships of the people he cares for the most.

In each of these scenarios, the teachers use different strategies to foster children's creative thought and expression. Ms. Manning uses modeling and discussion to seek solutions to problems ("David, did you tell Ahmad when you wanted to stop?"), models how to communicate that need ("You know, next time you could say in your own words, 'Ahmad, I don't want to play this game anymore.'"), and expresses confidence in David's ability to take charge of his own behavior ("When you leave the game, tell the person you're playing with so they know. All right?"). Mr. Connor uses guided imagery to prompt creative thinking, and Mrs. Barr uses reenactment of a quality piece of literature to illustrate moral and ethical dilemmas. The teachers' underlying beliefs that children can guide their own behavior and become fully functioning individuals (Rogers, 1961) are an important part of fostering children's creative growth.

Fostering children's creative thought and expression can be accomplished both indirectly and directly. Indirectly, children's thought and expression are affected by the strategies teachers use to plan, arrange, and manage the people as well as the classroom space, materials, and schedule. These strategies were explained in detail in Chapters Six and Seven. Directly, children's thought and expression are affected by the physical, verbal, and affective strategies teachers use to shape children's behavior and ways of thinking. As teachers, we are responsible for offering children many opportunities to engage in creative endeavors that serve as an important bridge to learning (Gordon & Browne, 2004; Hearron & Hildebrand, 2005; Marion, 2003). This chapter explores the important role of creative growth in preparing children with real-life skills.

THEORETICAL AND RESEARCH BASE: FOSTERING CREATIVE THOUGHT

Teachers use three major developmental theories to foster children's creative thought: constructivism, humanism, and behaviorism/social-learning theory. Each theory provides a way for adults to understand how and why children think, act, and learn as they do as well as ways to guide their own and children's creative thinking and behavior.

Constructivism

Constructivists, like Piaget (1952) and Vygotsky (1976), view children as active agents in their own development. They study the mental process of creativity (how children think about their world, other people, and how to behave) and are interested primarily in how children come to understand their world and solve problems they face (Papalia, Olds, & Feldman, 2002). Constructivists assume the following:

- Creative growth refers to concept building and problem solving, which depend on a child's level of cognitive development.
- Children are doers—they actively construct or build understandings of their world.
- Children think differently from adults and gradually come to understand the viewpoints of others.

For constructivists, fostering creative thought and behavior would include the following adult-child interactions:

- Adapting to children's different ways of working together and solving problems.
- Providing many opportunities to communicate thoughts and feelings.
- Supporting children's investigations and experimentation with tasks and materials.
- Providing a respectful, comfortable, and accepting environment that has clear, consistent, and fair limits for all children.
- Understanding that children's emotions provide motivation for learning.
- Facilitating development of self-control and self-directed behavior (Bredekamp & Copple, 1997; Edwards, 2002; Gordon & Browne, 2004; Hyson & Christiansen, 1997).

Using constructivist theory to guide children's creative thinking is most effective when the adults working with children understand their social and intellectual development, encourage children's interaction with others to increase their perspective-taking and social interaction skills, and probe children's thinking and reasoning about ideas.

Humanism

Humanists such as Carl Rogers and Abraham Maslow believe that people are capable of controlling their lives if their basic needs are met. They do this positively through choice, creativity, and self-realization (Papalia et al., 2002). Thus, how children feel about themselves strongly influences their ability to be cooperative, curious, and creative learners. Maslow and Rogers propose that a creative person and a self-actualized person share similar personality traits and self-understanding that is linked with one's potential to be a creative human being.

From a humanistic perspective, human beings strive to become fully functioning individuals. Such an individual possesses four characteristics:

- Positive self-regard.
- Awareness of personal feelings and those of others.
- Acceptance of responsibility for decisions.
- Ability to solve problems (Rogers, 1961).

Children who interact with supportive, accepting adults learn to view themselves as competent and worthwhile. In contrast, children who are deprived of supportive, accepting adults do not develop such feelings and often seek approval in inappropriate ways. Teachers who draw on humanistic traditions foster children's creative growth by allowing them to think about and investigate problems, by encouraging them to express a range of feelings, and by accepting a range of solutions to problems. They also value qualities such as spontaneity, freshness of appreciation, and a sense of humor.

Supportive, accepting, resourceful teachers facilitate children's investigative capacity. They help children talk about feelings, especially during conflicts, and guide them toward self-regulation (Charney, 2002; Edwards, 2002).

Behaviorism and Social-Learning Theory

Behaviorists view the environment as the single most important variable in shaping behavior and focus on observable, measurable behaviors. From this perspective, children react to the forces in their environment. Consequently, behaviorist theory does not address feelings or emotional states. Behaviorists assume the following:

- All behavior is learned. Learned behavior is shaped by external influences and causes development by rewarding observable behaviors.
- All children gradually learn how to respond to environmental influences.
- Adults in the environment are the major catalysts in changing or shaping children's behavior (Papalia et al., 2002).

The behavioral perspective has provided the foundation for the extensive use of behavior modification programs currently used in educational settings. The danger, of course, is that overreliance on these intrusive methods may make children more dependent on adults to resolve problems and less independent in defining problems and seeking solutions to them. For example, using timeout repeatedly to allow children to regain control often does not achieve the desired behavior. Rather, children perceive it as an opportunity to gain additional attention.

Social-learning theorists view social interaction as the major influence on learning and development. Rather than relying on reinforcement to influence children's growth and behavior, social-learning theorists hold that children learn socially appropriate behavior by observing and imitating *models* in their world (Papalia et al., 2002). In this way, children are learning by example—a powerful teaching and parenting tool because children typically imitate role models in their world.

An Eclectic Approach

Most teachers rely on the assumptions and practices of several theoretical perspectives for techniques that foster creative thought and behavior, including Howard Gardner's view of multiple intelligences (see Chapter One). In other words, our philosophy of creative growth tends to be eclectic. An eclectic approach means applying a variety of theories that fit your beliefs and help you make the best educational decisions for children's creative thought and behavior. We need an eclectic approach because no one theory is ever comprehensive enough to foster children's creativity (Marion, 2003).

To understand how an eclectic philosophy operates, recall the three opening scenarios. Ms. Manning adopts a constructivist and behavioral/social-learning approach to guide David's understanding of appropriate behavior; Mr. Connors helps the children construct their own understanding of their underwater world through the use of guided imagery and guiding individual creative thought; and Mrs. Barr adopts a constructivist and humanistic approach by facilitating children's investigations in solving dilemmas.

A growing research base supports the importance of nurturing children's creative expression. Perhaps more than anything else, all children want to be competent learners. Teachers often underestimate the influence of their own upbringing and value system on guiding the creative behavior of others. To a considerable extent, our orientations derive from our experiences. We need to be aware of how the social context often determines the guidance strategy we select.

As teachers, we must avoid dealing with all children in exactly the same way. Each child brings a rich history of experiences, cultural backgrounds, and personality traits to the classroom. Consequently, we must be as flexible as possible in guiding their creative thought and behavior. Like an artist who selects particular paints, colors, and paper to convey an idea or image, teachers must select the most appropriate approaches and strategies to foster each child's creativity. The more that educators understand the different perspectives and their own beliefs and values about creativity, the more able they will be to respond appropriately to children's creative ideas and behaviors. Table 8.1 presents three theoretical perspectives that affect fostering creative thought and expression and provides examples of each. Consider which ones reflect your current views.

TABLE 8.1 Theoretical Perspectives on Creative Growth

Theory	Behavioral Outcome	Teacher Role	Strategies
Behaviorism and social learning	Increase desired behavior.	Direct the process.	• **Provide a cue:** Remind child before expected behavior (e.g., "Johnny, see if you can find your mailbox for your painting.") • **Ignore the behavior:** Do not acknowledge minor behavioral infractions (e.g., ignore child in circle who dominates others' conversations). • **Model appropriate behavior:** Demonstrate how to ask for a toy or to gain entry into an ongoing play situation.
Humanism	Develop a strong self-concept, which is the child's image of himself or herself.	Guide children's ability to control and direct their own behavior.	• **Own the problem:** If the problem is an adult's, say, "I have a problem, and I need your help." If the problem is the child's, say, "It seems as though there is a problem here; do you need my help?" • **Listen actively:** Listen to the message the child is conveying. Do not interrupt the child or make a judgment. • **Use I-messages:** Name the behavior causing the problem and your feelings, such as "I feel angry when I see you grab the block from Johnny."
Constructivism	Gain understanding and control of their world through development of problem-solving abilities and conceptual understanding.	Facilitate and guide children's investigations with materials and with one another.	• **Provide opportunities to learn:** Use circle or meeting times for children to tell their versions of the problem to solve, talk about appropriate behaviors, and suggest alternative solutions. • **Set clear and appropriate limits:** Focus the child's attention and set predictable limits. • **Redirect behavior:** Provide new options, introduce a new material or idea, or limit choices, if necessary. • **Take social conflicts seriously:** Be at eye level while listening to children; empathize with all children involved in the conflict.

Note. Adapted from Marion (2003), and Papalia, Olds, & Feldman (2002).

TEACHERS' REFLECTIONS ON FOSTERING CREATIVE THOUGHT

Preservice Teachers

"By observing the strategies my cooperating teacher used to support children's creativity, I am beginning to understand that I need to help children develop their creative thought, which is something that never occurred to me. I now own a poster of Albert Einstein with his quote, 'Creativity is more important than knowledge,' which I plan to hang in my own classroom as one way to remind me."

"In my student teaching, I saw the effects of strategies for encouraging creative thinking. In my culminating unit activity, the first graders in my classroom worked in cooperative groups to produce creative works of art, music, and drama to show what they learned about different shelters."

Inservice Teachers

"As a preschool home resource teacher, I look for ways to help families foster their children's play, creative thought, and behavior in their own homes. I have started to use home-school journals with my preschool parents as a place to share examples of divergent thinking, problem solving, and imagination instead of only reporting on behavior and achievement. Parents are responding with such positive statements as 'I am looking at my child in a whole new way.'"

"After our school completed a museum-in-progress project, one teacher told our principal that she wasn't sure she'd ever be able to go back to 'textbook only' teaching. Her comment not only indicates that the children showed her that they really learn by doing research for projects but also shows that the teacher is becoming more comfortable with children learning through projects."

Your Reflections

- What are some ways to support children's creative thought and problem-solving ability?

- How do you think a creative teacher would manage his or her classroom?

- What new awareness about creative thought and behavior comes to mind for you after reading these teachers' reflections?

YOUR ROLE IN FOSTERING CREATIVE GROWTH

Consider the different responses of these second graders to their teachers' challenge of using a blank piece of corrugated cardboard to make something. Each teacher gave the children an $8\frac{1}{2}$-by-11-inch piece of corrugated cardboard and asked them to think of a way to use it, design a creation, and then share how they made it. Becky quickly saw the possibility of folding the cardboard, making it into a bird feeder, and decorating it with birds, flowers, and seeds. Sam looked sadly at the blank cardboard with tears welling up in his eyes. When his teacher asked him what the problem was, he said, "I can't do this. I don't know what you want me to make." He refused to think of any way to use the cardboard. Andrea hastily folded her piece of cardboard into a "crayon box," but after a few unsuccessful attempts to figure out how to get it to stay closed, she left the project unfinished on the table.

Clearly, children respond to creative tasks in different ways. The adult's interactions with children exert a major influence on the way they express creative behavior. A teacher who tells Sam, "You're just not trying hard enough. Put on your thinking cap," may be providing choices and freedom, but without support. On the other hand, teachers who guide children in a sensitive and accepting way support their creative growth. A sensitive teacher realizes that Andrea needs encouragement and recognition of her efforts to persist at a task. She might encourage Andrea with a statement such as, "I like your idea of a crayon box. I wonder if this stapler would help you close those edges." On the other hand, teachers who are not accepting make it difficult for children to develop a creative, problem-solving approach to ideas and tasks.

STYLES OF ADULT-CHILD INTERACTIONS

There are three basic styles of adult-child interactions—autocratic, permissive, and democratic (Baumrind, 1967, 1993; Papalia et al., 2002). Each refers to how demanding or responsive teachers are with children; each also cultivates typical behaviors and mind-sets to creative thought and behavior.

Autocratic Interactions

Autocratic adults demand that children respond to an inflexible set of rules and standards. The autocratic teacher does the following:

- Maintains stern and formal interactions with students.
- Devalues adult-child verbal interactions in which there are disagreements.
- Emphasizes a "no-nonsense" classroom environment.
- Discourages individuality or autonomy in children.

When teachers are autocratic, children often become resentful and rebellious. Autocratic methods tend to develop children who have difficulty with peer relations, lack initiative, and tend to be anxious, withdrawn, and apprehensive. Because the autocratic adult is so controlling, children do not learn self-control or risk-taking; rather, they become dependent on the adults in their lives to control their behavior.

Permissive Interactions

Permissive adults have an "anything goes" orientation. They place few demands and controls on children's decision making and problem solving in a poorly organized environment with unclear and inconsistent standards for behavior. The permissive teacher does the following:

- Projects a laissez-faire, uninterested attitude.
- Presents an inconsistent, unpredictable environment.
- Fails to set clear, firm limits on behavior.

The methods of permissive teachers tend to develop children with little self-control, self-reliance, or exploratory or investigative behavior. Because the standards for behavior are so inconsistent and the environment is so unpredictable, children cannot anticipate that their rights will be protected, or even clearly determine what their rights are.

Democratic Interactions

Democratic adults believe that children need firm but reasonable limits for behavior as well as opportunities for choice, verbal negotiation, and decision making. The democratic teacher does the following:

- Exhibits confidence in his or her ability to guide children.
- Understands child development, limits, and potentials.
- Listens to children and respects their ideas and opinions.
- Has high expectations for all children.
- Responds to children's initiatives and suggestions.
- Prepares the environment with choices, age-appropriate activities and materials, and plenty of time for interaction.
- Expects students to be responsible for the consequences of their decisions.

Children who live and work with democratic teachers appear to feel secure, know what is expected of them, and be self-sufficient, self-controlled, and self-assertive. They also tend to be "self-starters" who are capable of initiating and completing projects independent of adults. Democratic teachers do more than cover material—they develop children's concepts and problem-solving skills by engaging them actively in learning and empowering children to accept responsibility for their own learning and actions. Democratic teachers embody the principles held

Democratic teachers and caregivers really listen to and respect children.

by teachers in Reggio Emilia—that teachers facilitate children's creative interpretations of their worlds and that children are competent decision makers about what they want to learn.

Teachers can look to guidelines from Reggio Emilia schools (Edwards, Gandini, & Forman, 1998), the National Association for the Education of Young Children (Bredekamp & Copple, 1997), and the Northeast Foundation for Children (Charney, 2002) to foster children's creative growth. These guidelines provide teachers with a framework for encouraging children to unlock their creative potential, to investigate their worlds through a variety of paths, and to promote their ability to communicate in multiple forms. They also make clear that the teacher's role is one of support, acceptance, and promotion of desirable behavior through prevention, redirection, and collaboration. Creative teachers guide children's expression through their active engagement in a variety of real, firsthand learning experiences, such as enactments, projects and thematic units, field trips, and community resources. They also use developmentally appropriate guidance techniques to foster children's creative expression. Figure 8.1 lists several guidelines for creative thought and expression.

All children need adults' respect and acceptance to nurture their creative thought and behavior. Teachers who care for them can use these guidelines to promote children's creative growth when and where appropriate.

1.   *Use positive guidance techniques,* such as setting clear limits for younger children and helping older children set their own limits, modeling appropriate behavior, and redirecting inappropriate behavior. Positive techniques enable children to imagine and *focus on what to do* rather than on what not to do and prompt children to control or regulate their behavior in age-appropriate ways.

   Example: Enlist children in creating and monitoring classroom rules. Introduce and model the "You can't say you can't play" rule (Paley, 1992) so that children know how to ask to join an ongoing play situation and to help children learn positive ways of communicating with one another.

2.   *Prepare interesting and challenging activities that promote prosocial behavior and independent thought.* Through projects, investigative play experiences, and divergent materials, children develop positive social skills such as cooperation, negotiation, problem finding, and perseverance.

   Example: Children can find out information for a science project, take responsibility for care of part of the room, or choose a topic of study that helps children consciously manage their unpredictable world with new solutions and reflects the conscious beliefs of the teachers and caregivers.

3.   *Model care and respect for all people in your setting.* Help children learn positive skills of sharing, cooperating, taking responsibility, showing concern, and demonstrating empathy. Care and respect for one another are created in social settings in which children talk, work, play, and solve problems together.

   Example: In constructions, children often share ideas in deciding what structure to build and support one another in finding the appropriate places and materials to build it.

4.   *Be a creative teacher.* Creative teachers view themselves as problem solvers, risk takers, and decision makers. They expect children to share responsibility for their own learning, value their ideas, and guide children's inquiry, exploration, and experimentation with materials and ideas. In this way, they act as facilitators and are more likely to create classrooms in which creativity can thrive.

   Example: To guide children's creative growth, you first need to determine what beliefs and values you bring to your classroom. It is the positive, confident teacher who understands and accepts himself or herself who can bring out the best in children.

5.   *Help children verbalize their feelings and emotions.* Children's ability to express, understand, and control their emotions and feelings takes a long time to develop. As a result, they need many opportunities to talk about and label their feelings, in order to gain control over them.

   Example: When a very shy child tries to enter ongoing doctor play and is "not allowed in," she sits alone in a corner looking sad and dejected. Teachers can help shy children by saying "I know you feel sad about not playing with the others. Let's see if they could use a pharmacist to get the sick baby's medicine."

6.   *Provide children with opportunities for choices and decisions.* All children should be given some choice about when to work on a particular task, how to determine what happens in their classes, what materials to use for art projects, how to solve their own classroom problems, whether to work alone or with another child, whether to use manipulatives or play in the dramatic-play area, or what message to write in a note to a sick classmate.

   Example: As a group, young children have less experience in making choices, so they need to begin with two or three alternatives so that they are not overwhelmed by the possibilities. The range of choices can be increased as children gain in self-confidence and experience with decision making.

Figure 8.1

Guidelines for Fostering Creative Thought and Expression

Note. Based on Bredekamp & Copple (1997), Hearron & Hildebrand (2005), and Marion (2003).

DEVELOPMENTALLY APPROPRIATE GUIDANCE

Three-year-old Hans uses a wheelchair, but he wants to participate in a movement activity. Justine suggests that he can be the engine when the group sings "Little Red Caboose." Five-year-old Sandy is trying to make her picture "look snowy" after the first snowfall. Ralph remembers that they used a mixture of soap flakes, water, and silver glitter in his Sunday school class. He asks the teacher if he and Sandy can try the recipe at after-school care. Eight-year-old Monica helps Jeffrey rig a pulley system to send messages across the room. Later, Jeffrey sends a note to Monica: It reads: "Thank you to Monica. Your friend, Jeff."

These children are demonstrating prosocial behavior—spontaneously sharing with or helping another. Prosocial behavior develops in children who live and work in supportive environments where adults model cooperative, helping behaviors. It is characteristic of children who have a high level of self-esteem, self-control, and emotional understanding. Teachers can facilitate the development of these attributes by positive guidance in the classroom community.

Fostering Prosocial Behavior

When children see adult models of prosocial behavior and feel accepted in a group, they not only develop cooperative, helping, and responsible behaviors themselves but also learn to respect themselves through their accomplishments (Charney, 2002; Marion, 2003; Papalia et al., 2002). In creative learning environments there is mutual respect among teachers and children.

Picture the following scenario in Ms. Payne's 4-year-old class. After a few days of playing in the camping center, Ms. Payne introduced the idea of fishing. She added a pup tent, a blue paper lake, and a small grill filled with crumpled black and orange paper inside to represent a glowing charcoal fire. She developed the fishing theme by including fishing licenses, some magnetic fishing poles, a bucket, and some paper fish shapes with paper clips attached to the ends. She stimulated the children's interest in the idea by relating that she noticed people fishing nearby, so that the pond was probably well stocked with fish. In the following play text, try to identify examples of *prosocial behavior* in the 4-year-olds (such as cooperative, helping, sharing, and respectful behaviors). What role did the teacher have in fostering such behavior? Look at the photos on page 327 to better understand the children's interactions.

> *(Katie, Steven, Melanie, and Harold fish excitedly at the pond)*
> **Katie:**   I need a fish. *(fishing)* Is this real water?
> **Ms. Payne:**   No, it is blue paper but we are pretending it is a lake.
> **Katie:**   *(at the lake)* Got the fish. One, two, three . . .
> **Steven:**   I need a fish. That one. *(points to the big one)* I caught a fish for myself. Look how big!

Harold: Here's a fish.

Katie: Pick it up. *(says to Harold)* Put it over here. *(points to the bowl)* I caught it for you.

Steven: *(cutting the fish and eating)* That was good. I need more.

Katie: Hey, all the fish are gone. *(everyone has caught all of the fish)*

Steven: We have to put some back.

Harold: We have to catch them all over again. *(they put some of the fish back; Katie catches one and starts to put it back in the water)*

Steven: Don't throw him back!

Harold: We have to put them back after we catch them.

(Ms. Payne passes by the center and adds ideas about baiting the hook to catch the fish, cleaning the fish before cooking and eating them, and throwing back those that are too small)

Katie: I am the mother and I am going to cook everything.

Melanie: No, I am the mother. I want to cook.

Katie: No, you can be the grandma and help me cook, but we can have only one mother.

Melanie: Okay. *(they both go over to the grill and start to cook fish)*

Katie: *(to the fish)* Hey, you! Don't burn! Are you done? I need a fork and a cup.

Melanie: I'll get one. *(returns with a long stick)* We have to turn the fish with a fork. I think I burned my finger. Ouch! Ouch! *(blows on finger)*

Katie: Come over here, Grandma. I can put a bandage on it, and it will make it feel real good. *(pretends to take out some bandages and fix the finger)*

Steven: I want pink fish. They taste better.

Harold: I have a pink one and I have a big fish.

Steven: Can I have the pink one?

Harold: I'll give you another one. You can have two and I'll have two.

Steven: Okay. Hey, Grandma, where are the fishies? Are they done yet?

Melanie: No, I burned them. So now I have to clean the grill because the fish are burnt on it. *(she takes the sponge and pretends to wipe it up)* All clean.

Katie: Dinner today will be fish, macaroni, and juice.

Steven: *(starts setting up for dinner and then goes back to fish with Melanie; they fish and put the fish in bowls for dinner)* Mom, can I help you with dinner?

Katie: Sure, just give everybody fish. Put two fishies on each plate.

Steven: I passed out the fish. *(the children all sit down for a fish dinner; other children come by to join the fish dinner feast)* Is everyone hungry? Boy, I sure am. Melanie, please pass the corn. *(Melanie passes the corn)* Harold, do you want some?

Harold: No, I want some fish. *(Katie passes Harold some fish)*

Steven: Pass me a napkin and cup, please. *(Harold passes them to him; all the others are eating, passing different containers around, and pretending to eat and drink)*

While this play scene may seem unimportant to the novice, it is actually rich with examples of creative and prosocial behavior. These children are not only drawing upon their experiences, but are also solving problems as they arise, practicing social skills, using their imaginations to engage in friendly interactions, and working as members of a cooperative group. From an experiential perspective, the children have shared a common episode—helping to prepare, cook, and eat food together with family and friends. They used their imaginations as they solved problems—how to cook fish on the grill and what to do when the fish were gone from the lake. They practiced social skills as they negotiated who was to play the mother when both Katie and Melanie wanted the role. And they engaged in friendly fantasy interactions as they caught fish and threw them back in the lake. In this 45-minute play episode, the children were responsible for the contents, roles, and sequence of events. After the play began, Ms. Payne intervened only once with a comment about catching, cleaning, and cooking the fish.

Using the preceding play text and the guidelines for creative growth in Figure 8.1, identify which specific episodes supported children's prosocial behavior. What was Ms. Payne's role in this scenario?

Although it is important to recognize and respect positive behaviors in children, teachers must also prepare children to cope with conflicts that inevitably arise. How teachers interact with children in conflict situations largely determines how children will approach problem solving; an essential attribute of creative thought (Edwards, 2002; Kohn, 1996; Marion, 2003; Wheeler, 2004).

UNDERSTANDING CHILDREN'S CONFLICTS

In Ms. Balboa's Head Start classroom, Juanita joins Erik at the play-dough table. Within a few minutes, she rolls out a large, thick pancake shape, and the following dialogue occurs:

Juanita: Look at my big thing! *(Points to a long, snakelike shape)*
Erik: Oh man! That's big!
Juanita: I'm gonna get it even bigger. *(She picks it up and shows Erik the thumbprint on the bottom)* See, on the back, Erik?
Erik: Whoa! *(Erik leans on his rolled-out play dough, making a "tummy print;" Juanita cuts biscuit shapes with a plastic cup)*
Erik: Hey! I need that cup!
Juanita: NO!
Erik: *(in increasingly loud, angry tones)* I need that cup! I need it. I need it. I'm gonna make balls and put the balls in it. So, gimme it. Gimme that. Teacher! Juanita won't let me have the cup.

A dispute over a toy is the number one cause of conflict among preschool children, whereas disputes over resources (such as school supplies and equipment) and preferences (such as what game to play or what activity to choose first) predominate for older children. Without a doubt, conflicts hold significance for the teacher. In fact, children's inappropriate behavior is a major concern of educators, both novice and expert. But, what about the children? What causes conflict? What are the consequences of various types of conflict resolution for their development of creative thought and behavior? And what are some guidelines for conflict resolution?

Causes of Conflict

Children's conflicts are a natural part of their lives. Conflict occurs when one person does something to which a second person objects. Underlying reasons for the conflict may be either intentional or unintentional. Whatever the cause, conflict is a powerful tool for creative growth because children must negotiate ideas and actions that lead to some outcome (Kohn, 1996; Wheeler, 2004; Woolfolk, 2005).

Conflicts tend to follow a developmental sequence. Toddlers often have conflicts over possessions or toys because sharing toys and materials is an essential part of group functioning in classrooms. Preschool children's conflicts continue to focus on play materials but also include struggles over playing roles; gaining access to an ongoing group, space, or number of players allowed in a space; and fitting into the ongoing play needs by gender, size, or dress (Isenberg & Raines, 1992). Children in first through fourth grades often disagree with their peers over rules for games, initiating interactions, and maintaining relationships as well as about resources and preferences. They tend to be inflexible in thinking about rules and, as a result, often find themselves involved in disputes over them.

Most teachers want to stop conflicts at all costs as soon as they arise or try to prevent them from occurring. Yet conflict has a positive side. It offers children the opportunity to deal with their thoughts and feelings in social situations. Successful conflict resolution helps children develop the skills and attitudes needed for group living, form friendships with peers, and perceive others' ways of thinking. As teachers, we need to guide conflict to enhance children's creative thought and behavior.

Types of Conflicts

Today, educators are spending as much time helping children learn nonviolent ways of solving problems as they spend on creating other ways of learning. Whether children are bickering over a plaything or calling one another names, conflicts are a fact of life. Your own comfort level with conflict, such as how quickly you look for solutions, how sensitive you are to hurt feelings, how much you choose to ignore a problem hoping it will go away, and how willing you are to find mutually agreeable solutions, influences greatly how you approach conflict and model conflict resolution in the classroom. Table 8.2 lists some typical conflicts children experience, describes those conflicts, and suggests strategies for prevention and intervention.

Helping Children Resolve Conflicts

The following guidelines will help children resolve conflicts peaceably and in ways that enrich their ability to solve problems, take another person's perspective, and enhance social skills (Charney, 2002; Marion, 2003; Wheeler, 2004). When families are also invited to use these guidelines, then children receive the same messages in both home and school.

1. *Allow children to find solutions to conflicts on their own, where possible, before intervening.* Teachers who nurture children to be responsive to the needs of others must provide opportunities that guide children toward caring about and helping others. You might remind older children to "look at the class suggestions about what to do when something is bothering you" or suggest that younger children "think about the problem and come back to it in a few minutes." In conflict situations, focus on what can be done rather than unraveling the complex causes of the dispute. Ask the children questions, such as, "What do you think we can do about this problem?" or "What are your ideas of how we can make this work?" Taking action will help children resume their activity, and this in itself is reinforcing. Eventually, children learn that making a few concessions can keep their play going instead

TABLE 8.2   Types of Children's Conflicts

Type	Description	Appropriate Strategies
Possession disputes	Occur when children argue over ownership of a toy or material.	• Ignore the dispute. • Ask children to share the material or toy. • Redirect the behavior by suggesting an alternative material or way to use that material. • Discourage the practice of bringing items to school from home that children will not or should not share.
Power struggle disputes	Occur when children want to be first or force other children to play "their way."	• Suggest different ways of playing the same role or using the same materials for different purposes. • Reassure children they will get a turn. • Keep track of turn taking to ensure that every child really does get a turn.
Group-entry disputes	Occur when children try to join the ongoing activity of another group.	• Use the "You can't say you can't play" rule to deal with problems of insiders and outsiders. • Be clear that all children are expected to get along with one another. • Model ways to approach an ongoing group of children already engaged in activity.
Aggressive play	Occurs when violent, boisterous play escalates in intensity and tempers flare and frustration rises.	• Set reasonable limits on play. • Temporarily disband the group and redirect the children to a different activity. • Establish a caring classroom where adults and children demonstrate cooperation, kindness, and respect for others. • Have conversations about what kindness, cooperation, and respect mean and how children can show those behaviors in the classroom.
Peer and adult disputes	Occurs when children have differences over rules, preferences for games or activities, or initiating or maintaining interactions.	• Provide opportunities for peer acceptance. • Provide opportunities to participate in rule-governed games. • Model constructive ways of dealing with conflict and problems.

Note. Adapted from Jalongo & Isenberg (2004), Marion (2003), and Wheeler (2004).

of bringing it to an abrupt halt. Classrooms that encourage children's cooperative conflict resolution promote children's prosocial understandings.

   2. *Teach specific social skills to children who are aggressive, unpopular, and rejected by their peers.* Children often suffer peer rejection because they lack the skills for gaining entry into existing play groups, rely overly on adults to solve problems for them, or dominate the play. Consider, for example, a kindergarten classroom where children have been assigned to small groups to reenact "The Three Little Pigs." Dana takes total control. She shoves the other children and berates them if

Teachers can help children resolve conflicts in ways that enrich their creative expression.

they deviate from her planned script. Just as the group is about to perform, a shy child named Rolando, who was completely excluded by Dana, says quietly to his teacher, "But I was supposed to be the narrator." Dana is desperately in need of guidance. She needs to see that she can experience success in the group without being overbearing. Rolando needs to have his rights protected as well. If the adults in this kindergarten classroom ignore this peer conflict, neither child's social skills will be enhanced.

3. *Use group meetings to discuss how to handle conflicts.* Group meetings provide a powerful opportunity for teaching the skills needed to manage conflicts positively, because the atmosphere is calm and children are not caught up in the immediacy of the dispute. Role playing, puppets, children's illustrations of their own conflicts, and children's literature dealing with conflict resolution provide rich opportunities for talking about conflicts, discussing ways to resolve them, and generating alternative solutions to the conflict. Younger children can generally describe the problem and give information, give their own opinions, and accept more than one possible solution to a problem. Older children can develop more than one solution, explore different points of view, and anticipate the pros and cons of different outcomes (Charney, 2002).

Children's conflicts hold important opportunities for developing positive social interaction skills and creative growth with both peers and adults. In all classrooms, the following three strategies are particularly well suited to fostering children's creative thought and behavior.

STRATEGIES FOR FOSTERING CREATIVE THOUGHT AND EXPRESSION

A major goal of any curriculum is to enable all children to become divergent thinkers. Strategies designed to meet this goal include inquiry- and problem-based learning groups (Johnson, Johnson, & Holubek, 1999; Tegano, Sawyers, & Moran, 1989; Woolfolk, 2005); investigative play (Wassermann, 2000); and project work (Katz & Chard, 2000).

Inquiry- and Problem-Based Learning Groups

Inquiry- and problem-based learning groups involve a major concept or big idea, a shared goal or interest, a difference of opinion, and an active exchange of ideas. In these groups the children and adult work together to solve essential questions in ways that emphasize positive interaction and individual responsibility to the group. This kind of group cooperation exposes children to different points of view, enhances their perspective-taking ability, and increases social interaction skills.

All children can inquire and solve problems. A child's incessant "why" questions show that motivation to inquire and wonder is fully alive. Teachers can help children become more skillful inquirers by using "big ideas" both as part of the daily classroom life and as a way of learning subject matter. Children who have developed their inquiry abilities can draw conclusions based on evidence and judge whether that evidence supports the conclusions drawn by others (Parker, 2001; Woolfolk, 2005).

Children solve problems regularly through their cooperative play and daily interactions as they decide how to bridge two blocks, fit two children on a swing, or paint a mural together. However, not all problems lead to inquiry or cooperative problem solving, which depends on good communication and positive relations in working through issues. Inquiry- and problem-based learning are enhanced when there are good problems to solve. Figure 8.2 describes the characteristics of good problems.

Fostering Inquiry- and Problem-Based Learning

Use the following guidelines for fostering inquiry- and problem-based learning that contributes to children's creative thought and behavior.

1. *Plan activities with a common goal.* A group of kindergartners were building a school bus to enact the song "The Wheels on the Bus." Before they began, their teacher encouraged them to discuss their ideas, to agree on how to build the bus, and to decide what to include on it (such as steering wheel, seats, horn, driver, steps, and a door). Many children find these kinds of groups a less intimidating setting to test ideas. Helping children work together on a common goal encourages cooperative problem-based learning.

2. *Encourage children's free exchange of ideas.* As part of a unit on environmental responsibility, a third-grade teacher invited children to collect clean, recyclable

- Are relevant and interesting to children.
- Involve real or simulated materials and/or people.
- Require the child to modify, move, or transform the materials.
- Elicit many possible solutions.
- Can be solved by the child, yet provide interesting challenges.
- Help the child believe in his or her own problem-solving abilities.
- Encourage children to share differing points of view.
- Occur spontaneously in children's play.
- Occur in open-ended, content-specific, planned activities.

Figure 8.2
Characteristics of Good Problems
Note. Based on Bredekamp & Copple (1997), Tudge and Caruso (1988), Wassermann (2000), and Woolfolk (2005).

materials and encouraged the children to use them as they wished. Nothing much came from her suggestion. Later, she decided to try the same activity with small groups and asked guiding open-ended questions that focused children's thinking on particular attributes. Most children responded more favorably to this activity, because they were able to build on one another's ideas as well as suggest their own.

3. *Provide children with specific roles and responsibilities.* To promote the necessary social, decision-making, and conflict management skills, children need to participate regularly in cooperative-learning groups. By designating and rotating group members' roles as leader, recorder, questioner, or reporter, children experience different group roles. Participation in cooperative-learning groups motivates second-language learners by giving them more face-to-face interactions, enriching their group relations and self-esteem, and improving their communication in both languages.

All children can engage in inquiry- and problem-based learning activities during spontaneous play, planned open-ended activities, or planned content-specific activities, such as science investigations. Through shared exchanges of ideas, children explore new possibilities together and enhance their creative thinking.

Investigative Play

Mr. Yoon's first graders are exploring the effect of different formulas on soap bubbles. Two groups of children are experimenting with different solutions of food colorings, liquid detergents, corn syrup, and glycerin. They are also using other materials—straws, lids, a plastic tennis racket, plastic tubing attached to a funnel, and the plastic rings from a six-pack of soda cans—to produce bubbles of various sizes. Mr. Yoon has given them an activity card with the following guidelines:

- Find out everything you can about bubbles.
- What did you observe about the different formulas? Colors?

- What solution made the biggest, strongest bubbles?
- What materials can be used to make many small bubbles? To make one huge bubble?
- Talk about what you noticed.

One group of children added glycerin to see if they could get stronger bubbles. They started with one teaspoon, and then increased to two, three, four, and five. Another group tried different ways of making different-sized bubbles. In both groups, all the children were involved in the tasks, either as investigators or as observers. Mr. Yoon served as a facilitator, encouraging and supporting children's investigations with such comments as, "I see you are now going to try a new color of bubbles."

This activity illustrates a three-step model for organizing instruction that challenges children's divergent thinking, called **play-debrief-replay** (Wassermann, 2000). Each step is explained next.

Play

During *play,* children investigate and explore materials to make predictions, observe and classify information, and make both individual and collaborative decisions. Investigative play builds children's concepts about materials and ideas and

All children want to be competent learners.

enables them to examine key curriculum concepts such as, "Plants are living things" and "The work different people do requires special abilities and talents." In play, teachers set the stage and challenge children's learning, while children control their own learning. Wassermann reports that teachers using this model "feel exhilarated, energized and empowered" (2000, p. 28). Mr. Yoon's first graders were testing hypotheses about the "perfect" soap bubble formula. They were learning about viscosity, pressure, velocity, colors, and light—all basic concepts of physics.

Debrief

In the second step, *debriefing* becomes the common base for children's reflections. In either small or large discussion groups following exploratory play, Mr. Yoon asks the children questions that encourage them to reflect on their experiences, such as, "What did you notice about the bubbles?" and "How did you figure that out?" Good questions cause children to think carefully and to add their understandings to others. In the hands of a skillful, knowledgeable teacher, debriefing play experiences empower children as thinkers, invite new ideas, build self-esteem, and provide a foundation for future play with new insights about the same concept (Wassermann, 2000).

Replay

Replay occurs after debriefing. Some replay may involve the same materials; other replay may involve some new materials to move the inquiry along. A teacher might invite children to figure out the best way to transfer a bubble from one person to another without breaking it or ask children to introduce some new ways of blowing into the bubble makers. Replay provides additional practice with the concept or skill and an opportunity to replicate and verify findings. As a result, replay gradually builds children's conceptual understandings. Children's creative thought is enhanced when they can investigate objects, ideas, and events. Investigations encourage children to ask questions, explore ideas, and reflect on their thinking to make learning meaningful and powerful. They enable children to participate with their own learning styles and to begin to assess their own ways of thinking through reflection and debriefing. Play-debrief-replay is an important strategy in long-term classroom projects.

Project Work

A third powerful strategy for strengthening creative growth is project work. According to Katz and Chard (2000) and Allison (2004), a **project** is a focused study of something worth learning about undertaken by one or more children for as long as they remain interested. Projects offer children opportunities to apply skills, choose what topic to study, investigate questions that are personally meaningful, and revisit theories. These four characteristics support children's ability to think creatively.

Projects are an important teaching strategy because they foster meaningful learning, demand collaboration, require a range of skills, and can be as long or as short as children wish. In the following description of project activities related to construction, think about the possibilities for children's engagement in learning (Hartman & Eckerty, 1995).

All of the children were at the window watching the construction workers and equipment. They had many questions: "Why do they dig a hole first?" "What happens next?" "How do they know what to do?" In response to their questions and interest and her belief that her children were capable of pursuing extended project activities, Ms. Hartman developed a project on construction that led to the following scenario.

Ms. Hartman located several picture books that illustrated basic building principles, including Byron Barton's *Building a House* (1981) and Gail Gibbons's *Tool Book* (1982). The class looked at a real blueprint, took a walking tour of the community to look for different building styles, and interviewed an architect. Ms. Hartman also brought in picture postcards of famous buildings and lavishly illustrated books from the library. It turned out that one of the teachers had built a house the previous year and had a set of photographs that documented each building stage.

In this scenario, Ms. Hartman initiated the construction project in response to children's interest and questions. She began with a class discussion about what the children already knew about construction and what they were interested in finding out. Through their investigation of books, their examination of postcards and real materials such as the blueprint, and a walking tour of the community the children developed their own construction site to build a "class house" from blocks and boxes. Through their project, the children used their math and science skills (measuring space for the rooms in the house), literacy skills (making lists of materials needed to build the house), and social studies skills (exploring the interdependent roles of the architect, builder, and construction worker). They also developed clearer concepts of the complexities of building a house.

Project work can heighten creative thought and expression by doing the following:

- Fostering children's independent, creative thinking and involvement at different levels.
- Providing diverse cognitive challenges so that all children can experience success.
- Utilizing academic skills in relevant, highly motivating contexts.
- Encouraging cooperation to ensure successful completion of the project.
- Providing opportunities to increase knowledge and understandings and interpretations (Allison, 2004; Katz & Chard, 2000).

Strategies such as project work, investigative play, and inquiry- and problem-based learning are appropriate for all children. They take a holistic approach to teaching and learning and make learning meaningful by enabling children to actually carry out long-term projects, investigate real-world problems, and relate what they need to learn to what they already know. Keeping children engaged in learning makes further learning possible. In the next section, we present some ways to meet standards while promoting creative growth.

MEETING STANDARDS

Fostering Creative Thought and Expression

Fostering children's creative thought and expression are essential aspects of the curriculum. Perhaps more than anything else, all children want to be competent learners. We therefore must find ways to provide all children with opportunities for discovering unique solutions to problems, thinking divergently, experiencing investigative activities, learning self-control, and demonstrating prosocial behavior.

What follows are snapshots of units of study at the preschool/kindergarten, first/second-grade, and third/fourth-grade levels followed by a chart containing selected examples of possible activities that foster creative thought and expression in that thematic unit. Each activity is aligned with the appropriate content, arts, and teacher education standards.

Preschool–Kindergarten

A group of kindergartners is learning about plants and other living things through some of their activities. In the dramatic-play center, the teachers have added farmer and chef clothes and props (such as fruits and vegetables, a cash register, materials for making signs) and related books such as *The Giant Carrot* (Peck, 1998) and the children are creating their own market and acting out stories. In the block center, some children are using pots, empty seed packets, and rulers to design their own gardens. In the kitchen center, the children use pretend fruits and vegetables, seeds, and recipe cards to make applesauce, roasted pumpkin seeds, vegetable stew, and fruit salad. In the art center, children paint signs of fruits and vegetables for the fruit and vegetable market and make pictures of their own gardens using seeds and glue. In the music center, children invent a dance to make their plants grow and pop out of the ground (just as Little Isabelle does in *The Giant Carrot*) and sing and move to various recorded songs about planting and growing seeds. In the math center, children estimate how many seeds are in apples and peapods and weigh and classify seeds. In the science center, children follow instructions (for example, use 1 cup of soil for every two seeds) on how to plant their own seeds in clear plastic cups so that they can observe and record the seeds' growth throughout the unit.

At all centers, an ample supply of paper and pencils encourages children to record measurements, map out their own gardens, create recipes, take orders, and write receipts. The culminating activity for the unit invites children to replant their plants at home with their family. The students will also work together to make a class fruit salad to enjoy during snack time. The following tables show the content, arts, and teacher education standards that are embedded within the array of activities. Standards are abbreviated as follows:

Student Content-Area Standards:

Mathematics: National Council of Teachers of Mathematics (NCTM)

Social Studies: National Council for the Social Studies (NCSS)

Science: National Science Teachers Association (NSTA)

Literacy: National Council of Teachers of English (NCTE)

Student Arts Education Standards

National Standards for Arts Education

Teacher Education Standards:

National Association for the Education of Young Children (NAEYC)

Interstate New Teacher Assessment and Support Consortium (INTASC)

National Board for Professional Teaching Standards (NBPTS)

Preschool/Kindergarten: Unit on "Plants Are Living Things"			
Activity	**Student Content Standards**	**Student Arts Education Standards**	**Teacher Education Standards**
Science: *Planting seeds* Music and movement: *Singing and dancing*	NSTA A: Ability to do scientific inquiry; Understanding about scientific inquiry NSTA C: Characteristics of organisms; Life cycles of organisms; Organisms and environments	M1: K–4 Singing, alone and with others; a varied repertoire of music M8: K–4 Understanding relationships between music, the other arts, and disciplines outside the arts	NAEYC 4b: Using developmentally effective approaches NAEYC 4c: Understanding content knowledge in early childhood education INTASC Prin. 1: Content pedagogy; Prin. 4: Multiple instructional strategies; Prin. 5: Motivation and management
Math: *Estimating, weighing, and classifying seeds*	NCTM 5: Estimation NCTM 6: Number Sense and Numeration NCTM 10: Measurement	D2: K–4 Understanding choreographic principles, processes, and structures D7: K–4 Making connections between dance and other disciplines	NBPTS Prop. 2: Making learning accessible; Prop 4: Managing and monitoring student learning
Dramatic play: *Designing a fruit and vegetable market*	NCTM 4: Mathematical Connections NCTM 6: Number Sense and Numeration	VA1: K–4 Understanding and applying media, techniques and processes	See above *(Continued)*

Activity	Student Content Standards	Student Arts Education Standards	Teacher Education Standards
Acting out The Giant Carrot	NSTA B: Properties of objects and materials	VA3: K–4 Choosing and evaluating a range of subject matter, symbols, and ideas	
Kitchen: *Making and creating recipes with pretend food*	NCSS 7: Production, distribution, and consumption	VA6: K–4 Making connections between visual arts and other disciplines	
	NCTE 2: Read a range of literature from many periods in many genres to build understanding of the many dimensions of human experience	T1: K–4 Acting by assuming roles and interacting in improvisations	
Art: *Making seed pictures and signs for the play center*	NCTE 4: Use spoken, written, and visual language to communicate effectively with a variety of audiences and for different purposes	T3: K–4 Designing by visualizing and arranging environments for classroom dramatizations	
Blocks: *Designing and building block gardens*	NCTE 12: Use spoken, written, and visual language to accomplish their own purposes		

Note: D = dance; M = music; T = theatre; VA = visual arts.

First Grade–Second Grade

As part of their social studies unit, second-grade children become pioneers and plan their own expedition out west. They assign roles for all participants (such as husbands, wives, and children) and occupations (such as pioneers). The teacher provides each "pioneer" a budget and facilitates discussion on the items needed for their journey (such as an axle, wheels, and axe), travel to their destination, and factors that might affect their trip. Through a variety of explorations, investigations, and conversations, the pioneers work together to design and create a map of the West, decide how to spend their money, overcome each obstacle, and safely arrive at their new western home. During the unit, the children also sing pioneer music (such as "Home Sweet Home," "Oh Susanna," "Skip to my Lou," and "Buffalo Gals") and use the songs to inspire their pioneer letters home to family and friends. During each daily reenactment, the "pioneers" enact factors similar to those faced by early pioneers (such as cholera, weather, poor sanitation, accidental gunshots, and broken wagon axles) and each pioneer makes reflective entries in his or her diary that eventually will be part of a culminating assessment.

The following table shows the content, arts, and teacher education standards for each activity.

First Grade–Second Grade: Unit on "Pioneers"

Activity	Student Content Standards	Student Arts Education Standards	Teacher Education Standards
What do we need for our trip? Budget activity and simple machine review	NCTM 1: Mathematics as Problem Solving NCTM 4: Mathematical Connections NCTM 7: Computation and Estimation NSTA B: Physical Science—Properties of objects and materials; Position and motion of objects NSTA E: Science and Technology—Abilities to distinguish between natural objects and objects made by humans NCSS 7: Production, distribution, and consumption	T5: K–4 Researching by finding information to support classroom dramatizations	NAEYC 4b: Using developmentally effective approaches NAEYC 4c: Understanding content knowledge in early childhood education INTASC Prin. 1: Content pedagogy; Prin. 4: Multiple instructional strategies; Prin. 5: Motivation and management NBPTS Prop. 2: Making learning accessible; Prop. 4: Managing and monitoring student learning
What factors did early pioneers face that may affect the journey?	NCSS 2: Time, continuity, and change NCSS 3: People, places, and environments NCSS 5: Individuals, groups, and institutions AAHE 1: Comprehend concepts related to health promotion and disease prevention AAHE 6: Demonstrate the ability to use goal-setting and decision-making skills to enhance health	T1: K–4 Script writing by planning and recording improvisations T2: K–4 Acting by assuming roles and interacting in improvisations T3: K–4 Designing by visualizing and arranging environments for classroom dramatizations	See above

(Continued)

First Grade–Second Grade: Unit on "Pioneers" *(Continued)*

Activity	Student Content Standards	Student Arts Education Standards	Teacher Education Standards
Oregon Trail reenactment; pioneer diary	NSTA F: Science in Personal and Social Perspectives—Personal health		
	NCTE 5: Employ a wide range of writing strategies and use different writing process elements to communicate with different audiences for a variety of purposes		
How do we get to our destination? (pioneer maps)	NCSS 3: People, places, and environments	VA1: K–4 Understanding and applying media, techniques, and processes	See above
		VA3: K–4 Choosing and evaluating subject matter, symbols, and ideas	
		VA6: K–4 Making connections between visual arts and other disciplines	

Third Grade–Fourth Grade

Mr. Gore's fourth-grade class is involved in a literature unit based on the Newbery Medal–winning book *Holes* (Sachar, 1998). In math, children are creating word problems for the character Zero, based on situations he faced in the story (for example, if a round hole is 5 feet in diameter and 5 feet deep, then what is the volume of the hole?). In science, children are exploring the different layers of Earth (crust, mantle, inner core, outer core) by cutting a peach in half. The children use the peaches and other spices authentically to practice fractions while making their own recipes for the character Kate Barlow's spiced peaches. For their recipe, children design their food label including nutritional information for their cans of spiced peaches and investigate how canned peaches can be preserved. In the book *Holes*, Stanley's father is an inventor seeking the solution for foot odor. The children use the Internet to find out about the writing portion of the unit, create their own inventions using everyday found objects, and dramatize a commercial for their invention or write a jingle about it. An ongoing theme in the book and throughout the unit is power. The children also explore the topic by acting out scenes in the book and in daily life that show appropriate and/or unjust use of power.

The following table shows the content, arts, and teacher education standards for several unit activities.

Third Grade–Fourth Grade: Literature Unit on "Holes"			
Activity	**Student Content Standards**	**Student Arts Education Standards**	**Teacher Education Standards**
Find out about the layers of Earth Recipes for spiced peaches Inventions	NCTM 1: Mathematics as Problem Solving NCTM 4: Mathematical Connections NCTM 7: Computation and Estimation NCTM 13: Measurement NSTA D: Earth and Space Science—Structure of the earth system NSTA F: Science in Personal and Social Perspectives—Personal health	VA1: K–4 Understanding and applying media, techniques, and processes VA6: K–4 Making connections between visual arts and other disciplines	NAEYC 4b: Using developmentally effective approaches NAEYC 4c: Understanding content knowledge in early childhood education INTASC Prin. 1: Content pedagogy; Prin. 4: Multiple instructional strategies; Prin. 5: Motivation and management NBPTS Prop. 2: Making learning accessible; Prop. 4: Managing and monitoring student learning
Inventions	NCSS 3: People, places, and environments NCSS 4: Individual development and identity NCSS 8: Science, technology, and environment NCTE 2: Read a range of literature from many periods in many genres to build understanding of the	T1: K–4 Script writing by planning and recording improvisations T2: K–4 Acting by assuming roles and interacting in improvisations M1: K–4 Singing alone and with others	See above

(Continued)

Third Grade–Fourth Grade: Literature Unit on "Holes" *(Continued)*

Activity	Student Content Standards	Student Arts Education Standards	Teacher Education Standards
	many dimensions of human experience NCTE 4: Use spoken, written, and visual language to communicate effectively with a variety of audiences and for different purposes NCTE 5: Employ a wide range of writing strategies to communicate with different audiences for varied purposes NCTE 12: Use spoken, written, and visual language to accomplish their own purposes	VA1: K–4 Understanding and applying media, techniques, and processes VA3: K–4 Choosing and evaluating a range of subject matter, symbols, and ideas VA6: K–4 Making connections between visual arts and other disciplines	
What do I know about power? Compare/contrast situations in the book and in daily life that show appropriate and/or unjust use of power. Subjects addressed: Social Studies Drama	NCSS 1: Culture NCSS 2: Time, Continuity, and Change NCSS 4: Individual Development and Identity NCSS 6: Power, Authority and Governance NCSS 10: Civic Ideals and Practices	T1: K–4 Script writing by planning and recording improvisations based on personal experience and heritage, imagination, literature, and history T2: K–4 Acting by assuming roles and interacting in improvisations	

Frequently Asked Questions About Fostering Creative Thought and Expression

How do I foster creative thinking with children from diverse backgrounds?

All children will be better able to think creatively when learning experiences respect others. The arts and play provide children opportunities to express their cultural uniqueness, share cultural traditions, and discover their own personal identities before they can extend that learning to other cultures. A recent report (Stevenson, 2004) reveals that teachers who bring the arts into their classroom describe positive changes in their instructional practice for children from diverse backgrounds. Curricular modifications that strengthen self-expression in culturally sensitive ways include opportunities for children to build new understandings about accepting others, responsibility, and their own personal identities. Appropriate literature includes *Family Pictures* (Garza, 1990), which describes growing up in a Mexican-American community in Texas, and bilingual picture books that honor cultural and language differences for children with various heritages, such as the Kenyan tale *Bringing the Rain to Kapiti Plain* (Aardema, 1981) or *Abuela's Weave* (Castaneda, 1996), the story of how a Guatemalan girl learns of her family traditions from her grandmother (Diamond & Moore, 1995).

Other curricular modifications include the following:

- Role-play different problematic behaviors illustrated through a collection of pictures depicting problem situations (two children arguing over a toy, a child locked out of the house, a group of children teasing an Islamic girl wearing a headscarf or a Jewish boy wearing a kipa). Have children generate solutions to the problems, role-play some of them, and discuss why some solutions would be more appropriate than others.
- Adapt existing games such as lotto, bingo, and Memory to use words, numbers, or significant pictures representing the cultural backgrounds of the children in your class. Invite children and their families to supply materials to adapt classroom games.

- Engage in dramatic play with props and clothing from different cultures represented in your room, such as overnight bags for children to take pretend trips to a variety of places or travel folders and posters (Deiner, 2005).
- Express cultural and ethnic differences and share family traditions through music, which can increase children's first- and second-language usage (Ray, 1997). Figure 8.3 suggests additional resources for obtaining information about culturally diverse groups.

How do I foster creative thought and behavior with children with exceptionalities?

Inclusive classrooms benefit all children. However, children with disabilities in these settings require appropriate support to be able to participate meaningfully with their peers who do not have disabilities. According to *The Arts and Special Student Populations* (Arts Education Partnership, 2004c), "Students marginalized though self-imposed or induced withdrawal to the periphery of the classroom may increase their involvement, perhaps because they enjoy or feel competent enough to participate in arts activities. If, as a result, special populations gain self-concept through the arts, their classmates and teachers may perceive them in a new and more positive light, and a more reciprocal, inclusive social atmosphere in the classroom could enhance instructional effectiveness for all students" (p. 25). The goal of curricular and environmental adaptation is to ensure the participation and success of children at all levels. Students with exceptionalities need opportunities for decision making on projects, for being members of a classroom community that focuses on social acceptance, for using a variety of art materials, and for participating in experiences that address multiple intelligences (Bredekamp & Copple, 1997; Deiner, 2005; Erwin & Schreiber, 1999).

Everyone tells me that I have to meet the needs of individual students. How do I do that and still foster their creative growth?

In classrooms designed for children to succeed, all children participate in learning experiences that address the same curricular areas but at different levels of difficulty. When children and teachers are clear about the concepts to be learned, then teaching and learning with a focus on creative thought can occur for all children. According to *The Arts and Group Learning* (Arts Education Partnership, 2004b), "The arts are . . . a venue for exploring specific elements of collaborative learning environments such as scheduling, the nature of group work assignments, enlisting and managing subgroups or teams for various purposes, and the potential roles of the expert (whether teacher or mentor) in the group learning process" (p. 23). In one example, third- and fourth-graders studying ancient Greece work collaboratively in planning, researching, designing, and participating in their own class Olympics. Children have the opportunity to choose from activities that represent various cognitive and artistic ability levels and multiple-intelligence strength(s). Another example refers to a construction project in the community in which children with exceptionalities and children who are high achievers become city planners who evaluate community needs, such as a recycling center or a traveling library, and create possible ways to meet those needs. Children who are lower achieving might select and build the necessary buildings, make signs for the community areas, illustrate the types of buildings and equipment needed, or plan a playground. Each of these examples meets the needs of individual learners in a group setting that has the potential to unlock children's creative thought.

CHAPTER SUMMARY

1. Teachers use three fundamental theoretical perspectives to foster children's creative thought: constructivism, humanism, and behavioral/social learning. Constructivists view children as active agents in their own development. Humanists assume that people are capable of controlling their own lives. Behavioral/social-learning theorists view individuals as products of their environment.

2. There are three basic styles of adult-child interactions—autocratic, permissive, and democratic. Each refers to how demanding or responsive teachers are with children. Each also cultivates typical behaviors and approaches to problem solving.

3. Guiding children's creative growth includes facilitating the development of prosocial, cooperative, and helping behaviors. Democratic teachers use developmentally appropriate guidance techniques that help children become more caring and self-responsible.

4. Children's conflicts are a natural part of their lives. Most conflicts among toddlers involve possessions; most preschoolers' disputes are over role playing and play materials; and many elementary-grade children's disagreements with peers are over rules, social interactions, resources, and preferences.

The following resources provide *free* information for classroom teachers. Be sure to mention why you need these materials and how you will use them in your classroom.

African-American Institute
School Services Division
833 United Nations Plaza
New York, NY 10017

Afro-American Publishing Co.
1727 S. Indiana Ave.
Chicago, IL 60616

Asian-American Studies Center
3232 Campbell Hall
University of California
Los Angeles, CA 90024

Canadian International
Development Agency (CIDA)
200 Promenade du Portage
Hull Gatineau, Quebec K1A 0G4

(provides free poster kits of children in both urban and rural settings)

Hispanic-American Institute
100 East 21st St.
Austin, TX 78705

Multiculturalism National Office
11th floor
15 Eddy Street
Hull, Quebec K1A 0M5

(provides resources for educators on multiculturalism in play)

National Information Center for
Children and Youth with Disabilities
(NICHCY)
P.O. Box 1492
Washington, DC 20013

Office for Civil Rights
U.S. Department of Education
550 12th St. SW
Washington, DC 20202

(provides free pamphlets on multiculturalism)

Figure 8.3
Additional Teaching/Learning Resources for Diverse Groups

Note: Artwork and artifacts of children, families, and colleagues provide a free and ready source of relevant resources. Moreover, many embassies and consulates provide pamphlets, maps, and posters from their countries without charge.

5. Helping children learn to resolve their own conflicts peaceably encourages their ability to solve problems, take another person's perspective, and enhance social skills.

6. Three culturally relevant strategies to help children become better thinkers are inquiry- and problem-based learning groups, investigative play, and project work.

Discuss: Perspectives on Fostering Creative Thought and Expression

1. Refer to the opening scenario in which Ms. Manning intervenes in David and Ahmad's play. Think about the consequences of her actions. Suppose she had said, "Boys, stop that fighting right now!" What difference would that have made in their future ability to negotiate or to express feelings?

2. Imagine that you are responsible for making a presentation on parents' night that explains the importance of fostering creative thought. How would you show parents how this meets standards?

3. Brainstorm some curriculum projects that would be appropriate for inquiry- and problem-based learning. Select one project and figure out ways to identify the common goal, find the problem, test hypotheses, and provide feedback.

4. Refer to the chapter opening quote by Elliot Eisner. After reading and discussing the material in this chapter, present your views on why "we need to embrace a broader view of mind." Give some examples from your own experience.

Chapter 9

Assessing the Creative Processes and Products of Children

*Mary Renck Jalongo
and Marilyn J. Narey*

Children "are open to joy, curiosity, wonder, intuition, experimentation, and exploration . . . But somehow, for most of us and for our children, those things fade into the background as the years pass. School and life become hard, filled with drudgery, repetition, and 'have-to's.' Joy, curiosity, wonder, intuition, experimentation, and exploration are shunted aside as the educational process moves forward. We are told that that is the way the process is meant to work: Our children must leave behind childish things like play, performance, invention, and wonder and redirect their attention toward organization, detail, and conformity to archaic concepts of work and the workplace. This is a pronouncement that comes from deep in our culture's past, from a historically distant moment that did not appreciate the boundless potential that all our children represent . . ."

Karen Gallas, 2003, p. 169

CLASSROOM PERSPECTIVES
ON ASSESSMENT OF CREATIVE WORK

Preschool–Kindergarten

The state academic standards and science curricula in many states and countries include the study of life cycles. Ms. Conway and six other kindergarten teachers have planned an integrated unit on plants and butterflies that incorporates the arts and creative expression. Experiences for the children include planting the seeds to watch them grow and observing the metamorphosis of a chrysalis into a butterfly. The children's creative expression is fostered by activities in the arts, including drawing their observations, acting out the life cycles, creating music to describe the life cycles, reading and discussing stories such as *The Tiny Seed* (Carle, 2001) and *One Little Seed* (Greenstein, 2004), and making their own picture books about life cycles. The children also participate in a sociodramatic play center representing a plant nursery complete with cash register, plastic pots and plants, and materials for making signs and writing receipts. To assess student understanding of life cycles, the teachers engage the children in discussions about their observational drawings, dramatizations, songs, and other activities. These discussions consistently focus on meaning, the information contained, and ways of communicating ideas and feelings to others.

First Grade–Second Grade

Most teachers are familiar with pages from the sketchbooks of famous people, such as Leonardo da Vinci, that were used to record thinking, imaginings, plans, and inventions. The naturalist Charles Darwin produced dozens of sketchbooks to record scientific observations, and Queen Victoria created a watercolor memoir of her children. The child's play with ideas on the pages of a sketchbook results in a personal visual journal of creative explorations over time. In one school, the teachers of first graders have decided to introduce small, blank spiral-bound notebooks that their students will use as sketchbooks over the course of the school year. They begin by looking at examples in children's books such as Janet Stevens's *From Pictures to Words: A Book about Making a Book* (1996). Then the teachers provide a regular time each day for children to work in the sketchbooks. The time is not an absolute quiet, individual seatwork time, but rather an opportunity for the first graders to work in their preferred ways. Three students settle near a window, choosing to work near one another and initiate a dialogue; one is seated on the floor next to the aquarium to study the fish. During this sketchbook time the teachers respond to the child's work when asked (Thompson, 1995b). The teachers do not write on the students' actual drawings because it might suggest to the children that words are more important than their visual expression (Anning, 1999). Periodically, the teachers meet with one student or groups of students as they share their work and make notes about each student artist's comments. These children's daily entries, collected over several months and combined with the teachers' written notes, make each child's thought processes visible and are shared with families at conference time.

Third Grade–Fourth Grade

The teachers who work with third graders in a school have collaborated with the music teacher on a yearlong project. Their goal is for each third grader to finish the year with a record of his or her musical explorations. The project begins when the teachers and the children bring in favorite tapes, CDs, or music videos. After listening to the various examples over a period of a week or two, the teachers introduce the project to the students. Each child is responsible for experimenting with music and sounds resulting in a personal CD, an audiotaped album, or a music video. Every day, time is set aside so that children can work with instruments (such as keyboards and recorders), construct and play handmade instruments, or compose melodies and/or lyrics. Their teachers work with the community to involve local musicians and make additional instruments, books, photographs, and recordings available. An array of picture books about music and composers—such as the song picture book *The Train They Call the City of New Orleans* (Goodman & McCurdy, 2003) as well as books about people who craft musical instruments, such as *Made in Mexico* (Laufer, 2000) and *Pictures at an Exhibition* (Celenza, 2003)—are shared. The students also get inspiration from videotapes that focus on music and musicians such as *Duke Ellington: The Piano Prince and His Orchestra* (Weston Woods, 2000) and *This Land Is Your Land* (Weston Woods, 2000), a video about the songs of Woody Guthrie. Arrangements are made for students to attend concerts performed by the high school students, go on a field trip to see an orchestra play at a nearby university, and work with the artists-in-residence program. Each third grader's audiotape is stored in an envelope and labeled with the student's name. Periodically, quiet spaces and appointments are set for recording developed pieces on audiotape, CD, or video. The final musical CDs are shared and discussed by the student with peers and teacher in terms of the student's goals for the personal CD.

In each of these cases, teachers are assessing children's creative growth and artistic expression.

✿ ASSESSMENT CHALLENGES IN CREATIVITY AND THE ARTS

Assessment "involves identification of goals and purposes, selection of procedures, methods, and measures, coordination of timing, analysis of data, interpretation of results, and formulation of responses to the results" (Dorn, Madeja, & Sabol, 2004, p. 22). Contemporary assessment of creative processes and products poses some unique assessment challenges. First of all, *creative processes and products are multidimensional and complex.* Therefore, assessments of children's creative growth benefit from an interdisciplinary perspective, focusing on creative qualities demonstrated under a variety of circumstances and across subject areas. This also

Assessment involves identification of the child's goals and purposes.

means that teachers seeking to document creative thinking and arts-based learning need to model creative behaviors and actively engage children in problem-solving, divergent, critical, creative, and reflective types of thinking, hypothesizing, and inquiry (Beattie, 2000). Many educators are unaware of measures used in creativity in the arts such as personality inventories, self-report instruments, and ratings by observers. A wide variety of instruments measure cognitive processes, motivations, and interests as well as products, presentations, and performances resulting from the creative process (Baer, 1994; Feldhusen & Goh, 1995).

Second, *creative thinking and children's art are poorly understood by teachers.* Most teachers equate the arts with creativity. But creativity is not limited to the arts. It is inherent in and relevant to many other areas of the child's life and education. A child who figures out the answer to a challenging math problem is thinking creatively but is not engaged in art. Additionally, although the arts depend on creative processes, development in the arts can be assessed in areas other than creativity. For example, when a child is playing a musical instrument, technical expertise is part of the assessment. Unfortunately, many teachers restrict their definitions to activities that involve traditional materials and processes, mistakenly believing that the use of art materials makes an activity art. Such misconceptions about the arts and creativity are common among teachers and frequently are perpetuated, particularly when teachers decide to teach as they were taught.

A third assessment challenge is that *creative thought and art works are not adequately assessed by standardized tests.* Most assessment tools for children are paper-and-pencil tasks that focus on basic academic skills. The purpose of a standardized test is the comparative ranking of students, another practice that is at odds with creative processes and products (Eisner, 1994). Even tests that are designed to assess creativity sometimes rely rather heavily on a single creative behavior (such as artistic ability) or tend to assess problem solving under very restrictive conditions. Suppose that a researcher is assessing creativity during block play and provides the child with a small set of wooden blocks, then observes the child's block play during a short time period. The researcher may conclude that the child exhibits little originality. But the child may be accustomed to incorporating other miniature toys in her block play, may work exceptionally well with other children in creating large unit block structures, or may be extraordinarily imaginative with construction toys at home. The test, however, could not tap the full range of the child's play processes.

A fourth assessment hurdle is that *creative thinking and art work require real-life contexts to be valid.* A high score on a test of creativity does not provide an authentic, everyday indication of the child's creative thought and expression, such as the ability to construct an imaginative diorama based on a favorite story. The more removed from direct, hands-on, actual experience a task becomes, the less likely that it will be a good predictor of exceptional "real-world" performance. Beattie (1997) identified 12 criteria for establishing validity of performance-based assessments: relevance, content fidelity and integrity, exhaustiveness, cognitive complexity, equity, meaningfulness, straightforwardness, cohesiveness, consequences, directness, cost and efficiency, and generalizability (Dorn, Madeja, & Sabol, 2004, p. 15). Figure 9.1 provides an overview of appropriate assessment tasks, tools, and outcomes by three different groups: (1) the teacher, (2) the child, and (3) parents, families, and the community at large.

The idea that creativity and the arts require diagnostic assessment of the child's level of learning is sometimes surprising to teachers (Gilbert, 1996). Teachers—both the regular classroom teacher and teachers with specialized training in art and music—should assess and evaluate children's creative products based upon the lesson objectives. If a first-grade lesson focuses on learning to mix paint colors to match the colors observed in fall leaves, then the child's ability to mix a variety of colors is what should be evaluated. Criteria such as neatness, creativity, attitude, or behavior have no place in this assessment. If the first-grade lesson objective is for children to represent themselves through drawing with theme "I am raking the fall leaves," then instruction should involve visualizing and acting out raking leaves.

Appropriate Assessment Tasks

- Are opportunities for learning
- Enable every child to succeed at some level
- Are embedded in the curriculum
- Connect content, process, and work habits
- Acknowledge children's accomplishments
- Give children opportunities to demonstrate what they have learned
- Provide clear expectations and standards of excellence

Appropriate Assessment Tools

- Emphasize dialogue and self-reflection
- Are part of a comprehensive assessment plan
- Show the child's rate of progress
- Identify skills that still need to be developed
- Provide direction to teachers as they plan
- Suggest ways that parents and families might support play, creative expression, and the arts at home and in the community

Appropriate Assessment Outcomes

- Document not only what children are learning (content, skills) but also how they are learning it (processes)
- Engage educators, other professionals, families, and communities in rich and meaningful dialogue about the value of assessment in the arts, creativity, and play
- Convince parents, families, and communities of the contributions of creative expression, play, and the arts to children's lives

---

Figure 9.1
Appropriate Assessment Tasks, Tools, and Outcomes
Note. Adapted from Brown (1995), Educators in Connecticut's Pomperaug Regional School District 15 (1996), and Isenberg & Farley (1990).

Discussion of such things as how both hands are used to hold the rake, demonstrations of the adjustments made if the rake is taller than the child, observation of how arms have to bend, and visualization of how big the pile of leaves might be in proportion to the child all would take place. Assessment would be directly linked to the objectives of the instruction—for example, on how the child has drawn the figure and attempted to portray the action of raking leaves.

Teachers' approaches to assessment of children's creativity and artistic expression frequently conflict with theory, research, and expert opinion. According to one large study, 51 percent of teachers with specialized training in the arts often considered their knowledge of assessment methods insufficient (Dorn, Madeja, & Sabol, 2004, p. 19). Such misgivings are even more prevalent among teachers without specialized training, who avoid any assessment of children's creative or artistic endeavors. Yet if teachers leave creative products and the arts out of the assessment loop, these pursuits will be eclipsed by other areas of the curriculum that *are* tied to standards and testing. Another common mistake is making snap judgments about whether a child's work is "advanced." Performing a task earlier does not necessarily mean it has been performed better. For example, a child who draws a stick person of a ballet dancer before most of his or her peers is producing a stereotype. Imitating stereotypes has nothing to do with creativity and the arts even if it does appear ahead of most peers. On the other hand, a child who uses rudimentary lines yet captures the fluid motion of ballet deserves a positive evaluation even if the drawing does not "look like" a ballet dancer all that much.

THEORETICAL AND RESEARCH BASE: IDENTIFICATION OF TALENT AND GIFTEDNESS

Talent refers to "general, pervasive, relatively natural abilities as well as learned skills that guide and facilitate human behavior in practical and career-related domains of human activity" (Feldhusen, 2001, p. 5). The U.S. Department of Education (1993) explains that children with outstanding talent and gifts are those who show potential for performing at remarkably high levels of accomplishment when compared with others of their age, experience, and environment. Many educators are puzzled about how to respond appropriately when a child who differs dramatically from peers arrives in the classroom. There are several reasons for this reaction. The first has to do with the mismatch between the child and the planned curriculum. Teachers may fear that the child will be uninterested and may resent a child if the entire first-grade language arts curriculum is based on learning to read and the child arrives at school reading at a fourth-grade level. Another explanation for educators' mixed emotions concerning extraordinarily talented children is that U.S. society has not come to terms with reconciling excellence and equity. In fact, a little more than half of the states have no systematic gifted education plan. This disregard is a reflection of U.S. society's streak of anti-intellectualism that tends to treat high cognitive functioning as weird or highbrow. It also reflects educators' reluctance to "single out" children as talented, fearing that it might hurt other children's feelings. A third influence on attitudes toward gifted students is the availability of resources. When resources are scarce, there is a tendency to concentrate on children with learning problems whose needs seem more pressing. These influences, singly or in combination, often lead people to the erroneous conclusion that gifted children will do fine on their own. Yet, as Davidson and Davidson (2004) argue:

> True social justice means providing an education that challenges all students to the extent of their abilities—gifted children included. Blessed with brilliant minds and enormous skill, these highly intelligent students may not seem to warrant much help, but they have special needs, too. They deserve far more attention than America's education system currently offers them. The nation's future depends on their energies and talents, and wasting their childhoods because of inertia, ignorance, or ideology is as shortsighted as writing off children because of religion or race. (p. 23)

How can educators counteract this tendency to overlook talent in ways that diminish children as individuals, cause them to question why they don't "fit in," or force them to endure the frustration of having powers that they cannot put to use? The following practices support gifted and talented students:

- Value intellectual discovery as a school culture and treat learning as a joy.
- Encourage collaboration among adults (parents, families, administrators, teachers, community members) to pursue the goal of challenging children to the extent of their abilities.

Valuing intellectual discovery is one way of supporting gifted and talented children.

- Group students by competency in each subject, not by age.
- Do not define gifted programs as "enrichment" that fails to focus on advanced academic work.
- Adapt the curriculum to fit the gifted child with the same level of commitment that is made for children with learning disabilities and difficulties.
- Do not force children to study material they have mastered.
- Use a variety of flexible strategies as appropriate to meet learning goals (such as distance learning, independent study, mentoring, subject-matter acceleration, and grade skipping).
- Offer competitions and talent searches so students can get a sense of their knowledge and skill in comparison with others.
- Do not make participation in gifted programs a hardship (as by pulling children out of class, forcing them to miss important material).
- Celebrate high achievers' accomplishments.
- Recognize the special needs of gifted students (such as career planning and counseling needs and opportunities to pursue favorite subjects in depth).
- Provide ongoing professional development for teachers so that they can nurture talent, including their own, and continue their own education to make sure they meet the needs of all special learners and know the gifted education policies of the nation and the state (see http://www.geniusdenied.com).
- Teach children to accept, encourage, and admire remarkable achievements in other children rather than feel threatened by them (adapted from Davidson & Davidson, 2004).

Nathan is a first grader whose teacher is presenting a lesson on units of measure. She tells the children to look at several objects to be measured on a workbook page and asks, "What are some different ways that we could tell someone how long the line is without using a ruler?" Children make a variety of suggestions, such as using paper clips, erasers, or finger widths. Then the teacher calls on Nathan, who says, "You could ask an ant to walk across the line and tell you how many steps he took." One teacher might say Nathan's response is imaginative; another might say it is flippant. Because imagination, creativity, fantasy, and play are difficult to define and assess, they are often misinterpreted and discouraged. Sadly, Nathan's teacher replied, "And I know a little boy who is going to be walking right down to the principal's office if he doesn't behave." His teacher could not see that Nathan's family would have been amused by his reply and regarded it as original, spontaneous, and indicative of a good sense of humor. Nathan was mortified by his teacher's harsh criticism and virtually stopped participating in class. From that day forward, even when he was called on to speak, he responded by parroting back one-word or short answers that the teacher expected.

As Nathan's bad experience illustrates, a major challenge to assessment of children's creative expression and arts-based learning often is the teacher's misguided notions. Even though teachers claim to support creativity in schools, "in actual classroom practice they often frown upon traits associated with creativity or even actively dislike characteristics such as boldness, desire for novelty or originality. From almost the beginning of relevant research . . . it has been shown that teachers prefer courteousness, punctuality, obedience and receptiveness to other people's (the teacher's) ideas. In the area of thinking, high skill in memorization and accurate recall are often preferred to critical thinking or independent decision making" (Cropley, 2001, p. 137). Evidently, teachers throughout the world regard creativity as a disruptive force, based on research conducted in countries as diverse as Turkey, Australia, Nigeria, and the United States (Cropley, 2001; Scott, 1999).

Additionally, teachers' concepts of creative and artistic characteristics in children are often at odds with research findings. While the research indicates attributes such as "nonconformity," "impulsiveness," and "tries to do what others think is impossible" as indicators of creativity, teachers identified instead traits such as "sincere" and "responsible" (Westby & Dawson, 1995). Overall, teachers tend to approve of the well-mannered "briefcase" children and recommend them for gifted programs, yet fail to recognize the abilities of or even express dislike for nonconformist, creative, "bohemian" children (Dawson, 1997). In another study of the criteria that teachers used when nominating students to gifted programs (Hunsacker, 1994), the teachers said that creativity was the main criterion; however, on further investigation, teachers actually were focused on students' overall classroom performance. "Although some creative children are clearly capable of excelling in a traditional classroom, some of the most creative students may remain unrecognized or may even be punished" (Westby & Dawson, 1995, p. 9).

Even when everyone agrees that a child possesses gifts and talents, the response to that ability is often inappropriate. A common misconception is that talented children do not need to work that hard; however, as Piirto (2001) observes, "The world is full of talented people, but fully creative people do a lot of hard work" (p. 64). Too often, talented children are "overly praised and rewarded just for possessing the talent," but are not given special help by the school. They are instead thrown in with far less talented students in art, music, math, and science. This would never happen in athletics, where talented students are permitted to advance according to their abilities, competing with people of their own levels of expertise. Accurate and qualified feedback is important in the development of talent, and the child should have access to people who have some expertise. Thus, mentoring is important" (Piirto, 2001, p. 63). When such mentorship is provided, the results are impressive. Artist-in-residence programs in schools throughout the United States give children an opportunity to work alongside artists, musicians, and writers as well as gain keen insights into their personal inclinations in and capacities for creative and artistic expression. Talent is not enough because a high ability does not necessarily lead to high levels of performance. For all of these reasons—teachers' failure to understand creativity, misconceptions about children's creative and artistic behavior, and the school systems' apparent inability to provide the amount and kind of support necessary to develop talents and gifts in children—many of the most brilliant minds throughout history have been labeled as troublemakers and misfits during their school careers. Keep this in mind as you meet children who defy your expectations, challenge your authority, and prompt you to rethink the curriculum.

TEACHERS' REFLECTIONS ON ASSESSMENT

Preservice Teachers

"I'm student teaching in second grade. We have a terrific art program with real artists who visit the children and work with them. The children's artwork is amazing! Now our art teacher is leaving to work with a museum program and I wonder what will happen. When I talked with the art teacher about his decision to leave, he said that he enjoyed working with the children but did not feel that his efforts were valued all that much because administrators are so focused on test scores in reading and math and, every time the budget was cut, there was talk of eliminating his position."

Inservice Teachers

"According to our state's academic standards, all kindergarten students must be tested to determine their 'reading readiness.' As a result, the kindergarten curriculum has become like boot camp for first grade. Everything else, it seems, has been overshadowed by preparation for reading readiness tests. The test scores are used as much as a way to control teachers as they are to evaluate the children's achievement. The average school and district scores are posted on a website and teachers' reputations rise or fall based on how well their kids did during a particular year. The entire district has gone test crazy because our funding is based on demonstrating continuous improvement in test scores across the grade levels."

Your Reflections

- How do these teachers think about assessment?

- What problems have they identified concerning support for creative expression and the arts?

- What issues have they raised about assessment?

ASSESSMENT: WHY, WHAT, AND HOW

The term *student assessment* may conjure up visions of tests, checklists, gold stars, report cards, and program evaluations. Essentially, *assessment* can denote each of these, and more. As a general concept in education, assessment is the process of discovering children's knowledge, abilities, and interests (Popham, 2001); it is the "continual process of observing and recording and otherwise documenting the work that children do and how they do it, as a basis for a variety of educational decisions that affect the child" (Bredekamp, 1991, p. 21). Assessment of creative processes or products—or in any of the traditional academic subjects, for that matter—involves much more than testing for the purpose of providing grades. Teachers must realize the wealth of information that can be obtained through assessment of the creative processes and products of children and should not limit themselves to the narrow view of assessment as ascertaining a grade or percentage to label the child's work.

Therefore, it is critical to understand the why, what, and how of assessment. Teachers and others involved in the process must consider why they will conduct the assessment, or its purpose; what they will assess that will provide the desired information, or the focus; and how they will go about gathering that information or the means. Attention to the why, what, and how helps ensure that the assessment process will be appropriate and the results will be worthwhile.

Why Assess: Identifying the Purpose

The National Association for the Education of Young Children (NAEYC) and the National Association of Early Childhood Specialists in State Departments of Education (NAECSSDE) call on teachers to thoughtfully consider the real purposes of assessment. There are three general reasons for conducting an assessment:

- To make instructional decisions that benefit the child
- To identify the needs of individual children
- To improve educational programs
  (http://www.naeyc.org/about/positions/pdf/standlcurrass.pdf).

There are at least four reasons for assessing children's creative processes and products (Dacey, 1989):

1. *To develop deeper insight into creative growth.* When educators learn to observe each child's growth in creative expression and the arts carefully, they develop a new appreciation for and understanding of children's abilities. Part of that appreciation involves setting new criteria. Far too often, teachers use what they can do personally or what other adults can do as the standard against which children's work is measured.

2. *To evaluate program effectiveness.* A second major purpose of assessment is to determine the impact of an educational program on young children's growth in creative expression and the arts. Take, for instance, the teacher who creates individual folders that contain representative samples of each child's drawings and writings throughout the academic year. By combining her own insights about the child's progress with the samples, this teacher is both assessing the child's divergent thinking and judging the success of the program.

3. *To identify talents, provide enrichment, and develop potential through special programs.* A good teacher notices children's responses to and interests in music, such as the child who dances spontaneously to a lively tune or inquires about a classical piece being played at the start of the school day. Authentic assessment always expands, rather than limits, children's options. It further develops the creative and artistic potential of all children and simultaneously supports children who have extraordinary strengths.

4. *To decide whether, when, or how to intervene.* Programs for children often have a scheduled time when children can choose from among several activities. In

these situations, the teacher customarily keeps on the sidelines and facilitates rather than directly intervening. However, if a teacher sees a child wandering about aimlessly without completing any activity, the teacher can become more directive and escort a child to an activity or supervise the child during an activity to make the most of the learning opportunities provided. Observing children provides information not only about the child's cognitive functioning but also about interests, work habits, physical development, and socioemotional growth.

What to Assess: Finding a Focus

After identifying the purpose of the assessment, the teacher must clarify what will be assessed: Content knowledge? Children's understanding of processes and procedures? Evidence of effort and progress? Performance skills and techniques? The quality of the product?

Appraisals of children's work usually rely on one or more of six criteria: speed, correctness, attainment of standards, evidence of creativity, aesthetic appeal, and practical workability (Potter, 1985). The two criteria that schools use most often are the least applicable to creative expression and arts-based learning: speed and correctness. Speed should be a criterion only when time is essential. Usually, speed is important with simple tasks and procedures, such as assembling materials and putting them away after using them. Speed is not necessarily a virtue. Just as a repairperson can finish quickly without resolving the problem, a child can produce a painting at the easel in a matter of seconds without attaining the goal for the lesson.

Correctness is important with highly structured problems that have one right answer. The most important challenges in life, however, are mostly ill-structured problems. In other words, it is not possible to make a simple list and arrive at the right decision if advantages outnumber the disadvantages. Take, for example, the decision to become a teacher. Many sacrifices are involved in earning a teaching certificate; however, for many people, it is well worth it. If someone asks, "Can I become an effective teacher?" the question cannot be answered by speed (how quickly they complete the program) nor even by correctness (test scores alone). Other variables, such as commitment to children and families or an appreciation for diversity, may prove to be equally, if not more, important. And so it is with children's creative processes and products. Speed and correctness are not the sole criteria for evaluation. Potter's (1985) other four criteria—attainment of standards, evidence of creativity, aesthetic appeal, and practical workability—are important.

How to Assess: Selecting the Approach

Short-answer standardized tests promote a view of the human mind as "efficient, encyclopedic, and untroubled by ambiguities" (Wolf & Pistone, 1995, p. 61). Educators who believe in this kind of assessment have a narrow, fact-driven conception of learning and knowledge that is contradictory to true intellectual pursuit. This approach will not work for assessment of children's strengths, progress, and needs in creativity and the arts, because creative processes and products involve higher-order thinking skills that are not tapped by such approaches. Intellectual qualities such as the ability to consider varied viewpoints, employ critical judgment, engage in risk taking, form hypotheses, and develop interpretation must be part of assessment in creativity and the arts (Eisner, 1994).

One approach to assessment that is often overlooked is formative assessment. Formative assessment occurs "along the way" to adjust to learners' needs. Examples of formative assessment are notes from a class discussion, small-group interactions, journal entries, skill inventories, homework assignments, or pretests (Tomlinson, 1999). Consider the case of Lyla, a 5-year-old who tells her teacher that she wants to make a doll. After her teacher offers crayons, paints, and paper, Lyla responds, "No, I need things to make it squooshier"—in other words, this young child sought to make a doll out of fabric that would be stitched and stuffed. Through formative assessment, her teacher was able to offer the kind and amount of support Lyla needed to accomplish her goal—fabric, buttons, yarn, scissors, paper to make a pattern, and an adult with a sewing machine to stitch the edges of the two pieces of the cloth together so that Lyla could turn it right side out and stuff it with polyester fiberfill like a pillow. During formative assessment teachers also recognize the need for changes in the physical environment (materials, equipment, room arrangement) as well as pedagogical approaches (ways of giving instructions, demonstration of techniques, composition of groups, reorganization of content).

The other main category of assessment, summative assessment, occurs after the learning has taken place. Examples of summative assessments are musical performances, displays of children's artwork, presentations by a child to a panel of experts, and, of course, tests. Teachers should allow their students to demonstrate learning in a variety of modes (Gardner, 1993b). This practice should be a regular opportunity in the classroom that is given the same weight as traditional methods of evaluation. Often teachers provide opportunities for students to make posters, brochures, skits, and so on to demonstrate learning in place of a written test or report, but send the message that these products don't count for much by weighing them less when grading. Figure 9.2 summarizes assessment methods used by teachers, children, and families and communities.

TEACHERS' ROLES AND RESPONSIBILITIES

Teachers have three basic roles in assessing children's creative processes and products: observer, interactor, and evaluator.

The Role of Observer

In the role of observer, teachers observe what children do while remaining on the sidelines. Observation includes the informal impressions teachers form while watching children engaged in an activity. As Wassermann (1989) points out, "One of the most valuable yet rarely acknowledged assessment tools in educational practice is the

Prepared by the Teacher

General Guidelines: Observing young children's play, creative expression, and artworks is intended to provide a more holistic view of what children know and can do with their creative-thinking processes. Teachers need to invent a system for gathering observations regularly. All observations should be dated, keyed to program goals, and filed systematically in student work portfolios to facilitate charting children's progress over time.

- **Anecdotal records** highlight student attitudes, preferences, judgments, and participation. The teacher can make notes for younger students; older students can write their own. These notes should be dated and collected over time to demonstrate patterns of growth.
- **Checklists, developmental profiles, or logs** compare one child's progress with that of the typically developing child.
- **Conference notes** from discussions with individual children or groups of children about the content and process of their creative work demonstrate what was accomplished during major projects.
- **Interviews** with children demonstrate their emerging understanding of creativity and the arts.
- **Documentation panels** provide evidence of the learning that was achieved through the course of a major project. These large displays that chronicle the life cycle of a project are commercial-artist-quality documentation of children's accomplishments (Carter & Curtis, 1995; Chard, 1998; Jalongo & Stamp, 1997b).

Produced and Assessed by the Child

General Guidelines: In order to teach children the skills of self-evaluation, they should bear responsibility for identifying their best work and providing a rationale for its inclusion in their portfolios.

- **Self-selected work samples** may include one-dimensional works (e.g., paintings, drawings, writing) as well as photographs, sketches, and videotapes or audiotapes of works or displays.
- **Rating scales or checklists** encourage children to bring their artistic decision making to a conscious level as they are working on a project, evaluate their group's performance, or assess the overall quality of a culminating activity.
- **Child-led conferences** enable the child to present his or her work to parents and families.

Assessed by the Family/Community

General Guidelines: Parents, families, and community members need to be involved in assessing children's growth.

- **Conferences with parents and families** provide them with the opportunity to review the child's work over time.
- **Review of live or taped individual or group performances** enable parents, families, and community members to see the child's/children's conceptualization, presentation, quality, personalization, and cooperation.
- **Responses to portfolios of children's work** give families an opportunity to provide written feedback on the child's work.

Figure 9.2
Overview of Assessment Methods Used by the Teacher, the Child, and Families/Communities

As this child learns to read, the teacher is observing, interacting, and analyzing both the product and the process at various times.

sustained, thoughtful day-to-day observation of student behavior by a competent, professional teacher" (p. 368). Appropriate observations of children do the following:

- Use direct observational data and avoid high-inference, value-laden terminology.
- Accurately record the observable behavior of the child, both verbal and nonverbal.
- Describe the context in which the behavior occurred—the time, setting, circumstances, and behaviors of other children or adults related to the episode.
- Become the basis for planning a high-quality program.

How does observation support children's learning? A third-grade teacher has involved his gifted and talented students in a unit on inventions. He shares some examples from *Toys! Amazing Stories Behind Some Great Inventions* (Wulffson, 2000), *Accidents May Happen* (Jones & O'Brien, 1997), *The Kid Who Invented the Popsicle* (Wulffson, 1999), *The Kids' Invention Book* (Erbach, 1997), *Brainstorm: The Stories of Twenty American Kid Inventors* (Tucker, 1995), and *Girls Think of Everything: Stories of Ingenious Inventions by Women* (Thimmesh, 2000) with the students. The third graders' first assignment is to apply their emerging research skills in locating authoritative print and electronic sources that describe inventions and inventors of an item found in their household or classroom. As the children work at the library, their teacher places a baseball cap backward on his head as a signal to the students that he is writing down what he sees and should not be disturbed unless it is an emergency (Strachota, 1996). Over the next 15 minutes, he records episodes of student behavior on his laptop along with the date, the activity, and the child's initials. At the end of the month, he will sort the lists using the child's initials and generate a report to place in each child's file and refer to during parent/teacher conferences. During the library session the teacher noticed that some of the children were unfocused at first and decided that his instructions were not sufficiently clear. A few were seeking information about inventions they had heard about previously (such as the telephone and the steam engine) instead of focusing on the stipulation that it had to be a contemporary invention that they could bring to school and demonstrate during their presentation. As this brief description illustrates, there are three main purposes for anecdotal records: (1) to document individual student growth, (2) to demonstrate students' progress toward program goals, and (3) to assess the value of the learning activity. Figure 9.3 is a sample anecdotal record from the third graders' project on modern inventors and inventions.

Three additional observational tools are checklists, rating scales, and rubrics. *Checklists* are used to indicate the presence or absence of a behavior (Does your child play a musical instrument? Yes/No). *Rating scales* are used when it is important to know to what degree something occurs (In a typical week, how many times do you and your child read and discuss a children's book? 0, 1–2, 3–5, 6–7, 8 or more). There are many commercially available checklists and rating scales that teachers and caregivers can use as is or adapt to suit their needs (Seely, 1994). A *rubric* is a particular type of rating scale that specifies the level of performance and links it to a grade. During the invention theme, the culminating activity was for each child to create and videotape a short, evening news–type story about the invention that he or she had selected. Figure 9.4 is an example of the scoring rubric that the teacher developed to assess the quality of the third graders' presentations.

Audio and video recording are mechanical means of observing that become the teacher's eyes and ears while he or she continues to engage in classroom activities.

Student: C. J.   Observer: M. T.
Date: 9/24/05   Time: 2:45
Location: School library   Activity: Researching inventors

Ch. are deciding on an inventor. C. J.: "I'm going to do the Wright Bros. and airplanes." J. J.: "I think we have to be able to show the thing they invented when we talk about it. How are you going to show a plane?" C. J. comes over and asks, "Is it okay if my report is on the Wright Brothers? J. J. said we have to show whatever it is when we talk about it." I remind him of the instructions and criteria for evaluation and he says, "What about this book about kids who invented things? I can bring a Popsicle to school."

Figure 9.3
Example of an Anecdotal Record

Accuracy of Information

3	2	1
Information is accurate and well-documented	Most information is accurate and well-documented	Information contains errors of fact and is not supported by sources

Content of Assignment

3	2	1
Invention and inventor are contemporary	Invention and inventor are modern	Invention and inventor are from a historical era

Sources Used

3	2	1
Multiple authoritative sources were consulted	At least one authoritative source was consulted	Few or none of the sources consulted were authoritative

Use of Example

3	2	1
Student provides a actual example of an everyday item	Student provides an image of the item	Student does not provide an example or image

Structure of Presentation

3	2	1
Very clear and well organized	Moderately clear and well-organized	Not clear and/or well organized

News Story Format

3	2	1
Is concise and in the format of a news story	Is reasonably concise and in the format of a news story	Is not concise and/or in the format of a news story

Effectiveness of Presentational Style

3	2	1
Very effective use of voice and gesture during presentation	Moderately effective use of voice and gesture during presentation	Ineffective use of voice and/or gesture presentation

Figure 9.4

Scoring Rubric for a News Story About an Invention

Video recording can also be an excellent means of involving the child in self-evaluation. Movement, dance, and drama experiences viewed by both teacher and child often provoke spontaneous self-critique by the child: "Oh, you can't see my puppet's face!" or "I like the way I made my streamers move like the wind during the weather dance." Students learn to become more thoughtful observers of their own work when teachers emphasize important aspects of the process and product. Children's early experiences with self-evaluation build a foundation for self-critique and assessment that is valuable throughout life.

The Role of Interactor

Interaction includes the teacher's daily face-to-face exchanges with students as well as more structured and planned types of interaction, such as conducting a conference or interview with a child and recording the results. In the role of interactor, teachers determine the students' current level of performance as well as pose new challenges at the right level of difficulty. In contrast to observation, where the teacher remains out of the action, the role of interactor gets teachers involved in dialogue with the child about his or her creative/artistic processes and products. A kindergarten teacher, for example, meets with each of her students about their writing for 10 minutes, once a week. Usually these meetings begin with a brief review of the child's writing portfolio and discussion aimed at getting a sense of the child's goals and progress toward those goals. In preparation for conferences, the teacher also interviews each child on the topic of writing. When she asks Caleb the first question on the interview, "Tell me about your writing," he responds with the writing sample and explanation found in Figure 9.5.

Audio and video recording methods represent significant advantages where interaction is concerned. It often is not possible for a teacher to interact with a child and make notes at the same time, so mechanical means offer an opportunity to analyze the quality of the interactions. Ms. Maloney, a student teacher, set up a pet store in conjunction with a unit on economics. Through the use of videotape, Ms. Maloney is able to "step back" from her teaching and analyze the interaction between her and Lori, the second-grade girl who invited her into the role of customer.

> **Lori:**   This is my pet store. May I help you today, miss? Are you looking for anything in particular?
> **Teacher:**   Yes, I would like to buy my nephew an unusual gift. He is going to be 10 years old on Monday.
> **Lori:**   Well, isn't that just special! I hope that he is a nice boy. What kinds of animals does he like?
> **Teacher:**   He likes dinosaurs and wild animals.
> **Lori:**   Well, we are out of dinosaurs. I just sold the last one yesterday and I did not order any more. The animals are just too large for my store. We do have some parakeets and fish.
> **Teacher:**   Do you have any parrots? They are a wild animal.
> **Lori:**   Yes, I just happen to have one, beautiful colors on it.
> **Teacher:**   I'll take it. He is just beautiful. Can he be taught to talk? I heard that some of them can learn to talk, is that true?

Caleb: This says "cat" and "dog" and that's a big "G" and one hundred and one. That's just my name and . . . yeah, my name, Caleb. And one hundred and ten and . . . uh . . . nine and six. And this is a five and a four and a fancy four and a thirteen. See? I made this pretend word and then I can find words in it. I have to underline the letters so I don't forget . . . Watch this! D-o-d—that spells dad! And m-o-m spells mom. Wait. Oh, wait. D-*a*-d spells dad! Here's a "u" and an "o." Wait, here's a fancy "u" and this is a fancy "o." Watch! This is a little "t" and this here is a littler "t" and now they're connected together!

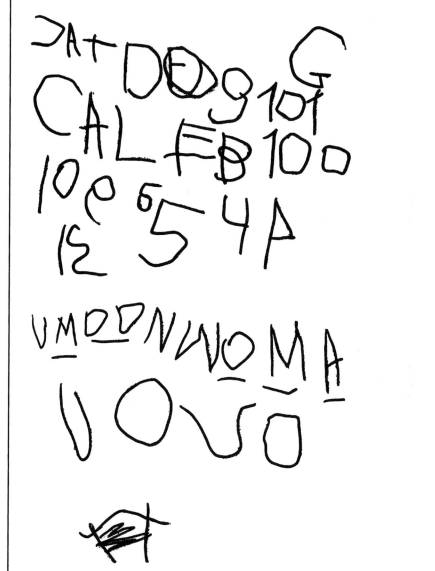

Figure 9.5
Caleb's Writing

Lori: First of all, before you get too confused, this is a she. This particular type of bird can be taught to talk, but it takes a lot of time.
Teacher: What else do I need?
Lori: You'll need a cage, food, and some items for the bird to play with.
Teacher: Well, how much do I owe you for the bird, cage, food, and two toys?
Lori: The total price is $125.33.
Teacher: Do you take Mastercard?
Lori: Yes.

By recording and analyzing this interaction, Ms. Maloney has a clearer sense of Lori's ability to take on a role, to "think on her feet," to understand basic concepts about economics as well as pet care (the topic of a previous unit), and ability to communicate. It also offers a more holistic evaluation of Lori's emerging understanding of economic principles, business ethics, and customer relations.

Part of becoming effective in the role of interactor is noticing what children do. If a preschool teacher notices that a particular child has never ventured into the block area, she could invite him into the area. If children's interest in the block center wanes, the teacher might supply additional items, such as small wooden people, animals, vehicles, and road signs to rekindle enthusiasm.

Another key to fulfilling the role of interactor is to ask good questions that generate interest and stimulate thinking. One simple way to improve questions is to include thinking words in the questions that you ask, as illustrated in Figure 9.6.

In a hands-on science activity on sinking and floating, Ms. Zezel used the following guidelines (Raths, Wassermann, Jonas, & Rothstein, 1986) to probe her third graders' thinking:

1. *Encourage children to look carefully and use what they see to support their ideas.* After equipping the children with pans of water and various objects (cork, paper clip, pencil, coin, Popsicle stick, tennis ball, feather, piece of nylon net), Ms. Zezel asked, "If the goal is to find out whether objects sink or float, how will you proceed? How could we keep track of our observations?"

2. *Invite children to compare and classify.* After the children had completed their experiments and recorded their observations, Ms. Zezel invited them to compare and classify ("Is there anything similar about the objects that floated? The objects that sank? What differences exist between the objects that floated and sank?") and to relate new information or ideas to what they already knew ("Carl thinks that big objects sink; Kim says that light objects float. What other objects might you try to test this idea? Think about all of the things that you have seen floating in water. How would you explain the fact that they float?").

3. *Have children summarize and interpret.* The teacher asked the children to "recap" what they had learned so far and to explain things from their points of view. ("What ideas do we now have about the properties of objects that sink? Objects that float?")

4. *Ask children to identify assumptions and suggest hypotheses.* Ms. Zezel asked the children to articulate their assumptions in a low-risk environment where they felt comfortable making educated guesses. ("We now have several ideas. Some

For the Teacher: A Guide to Asking Better Questions

Some simple changes in our ways of posing questions can encourage children to think more critically. As children hear cognitive terms in everyday use and practice the thinking skills that accompany these labels, they will begin to internalize these words and incorporate them into their own vocabularies.

Instead of saying . . .
"Let's look at these two pictures."

Say:
"Let's *compare* these two pictures."

Instead of asking . . .
"What do you think will happen when . . ."

Ask:
"What do you *predict* will happen when . . . ?"

Instead of asking . . .
"What did you think of the story?"

Ask:
"What *conclusions* can you draw about this story?"

Instead of asking . . .
"How do you know that's true?"

Ask:
"What *evidence* do you have to support . . . ?"

A Framework for the Child's Self-Questions about Problem Solving

Circle the strategy or strategies that you used to solve the problem.

?   I guessed.

   I looked for a pattern.

   I made a list.

   I drew a picture.

   I made a web or diagram.

   I solved a simpler problem.

   I worked backward.

   I made a table.

✓   I experimented with several different strategies.

   I asked somebody for clues.

   I collaborated with a group.

Figure 9.6
Questions That Encourage Creative Problem Solving
Note. Adapted from British Ministry of Education and Costa (1993).

When materials are unfamiliar to children, teachers should intervene and demonstrate how those materials can be used.

people feel that floating has something to do with air inside the object. Some people have concluded that objects float or sink depending on how heavy they are and on the size of the body of water. We will use the scales now to weigh each object. Refer back to your original experiment to find out if the heaviest objects always sink and the lightest objects always float.")

  5. *Encourage children to imagine and create.* Ms. Zezel urged the children to use visualization and create mental images to help them solve the problem. ("If it is true that air has something to do with floating, how does a battleship float? Imagine that your house was suddenly surrounded by deep water. What materials would you use to build something that would take you across? Why?")

  Improving the quality of learning experiences for children really demands teachers and caregivers who will allow children to take the lead, who will do less telling and more asking, and who will talk less and listen more.

The Role of Evaluator

In this role, the teacher collects samples of students' work at various stages, arranges them to highlight growth, and analyzes them to make instructional decisions. Evaluation of processes and products may be incidental or planned, use teacher-developed materials or commercially available materials, and use different methods of recording (written, oral, or mechanically recorded). Evaluating what children have learned is aligned with curriculum and instruction. Assessment is not an "afterthought," but rather an integral component of the original plan.

When an artist is seeking employment, it is customary to present a portfolio of work. These work samples, rather than a score on a test of artistic talent, are used to demonstrate competence. Creative processes and products lend themselves to performance assessment. Performance assessment "requires students to create evidence through performance that will enable assessors to make valid judgments about 'what they know and can do' in situations that matter" (Eisner, 1999, p. 659). In performance assessment, the proof that children have acquired an understanding or skill is assessed by competence (singing at a prescribed pitch), or knowing how to do something, rather than merely knowing about something (recognizing musical notation). Consider the many ways that a young child might demonstrate an understanding of some basic musical concepts (Alper, 1999; Lewis, 1983). To demonstrate an understanding of tempo (fast/slow), the child might bounce a ball

Portfolio assessment is immediately understandable to parents, and encourages children's involvement and self-evaluation.

rapidly in response to a lively tune and slowly in response to a lullaby; to demonstrate the concept of dynamics (loud/soft), a group of children might play the game Radio, in which they make their voices softer or louder in response to an oversized cardboard dial that represents the volume control on a radio; to demonstrate the concept of rhythm ("with the beat"), children might respond to cue cards (of clapping hands, snapping fingers, or stomping feet) that depict ways of moving their bodies "in time" with different musical selections. Likewise, older children might demonstrate their understanding of pitch and melody by doing the following:

- Gesturing with hands to illustrate the pitch of notes (up or down on the scale).
- Playing a pattern on a melody instrument, such as a xylophone.
- Marking on the chalkboard each time they hear a pattern of musical notes.
- Representing notes on the scale as stair steps and moving up or down.

All of these examples illustrate performance assessment because they allow the child to demonstrate understanding. Some of the defining characteristics of performance assessment are as follows:

- The tasks performed by children are relevant and interesting.
- Both the products and the processes used to achieve them are evaluated.
- Students develop skills in self-evaluation as they take greater responsibility for selecting their best work.
- Students' attitudes and feelings are considered as well as knowledge and skills.
- Results of the assessment are used to optimize children's learning.
- Assessment data are used to improve classroom practice and make informed instructional decisions.
- Results of the assessment produce a holistic picture of student performance.

Performance assessment can also be summative—that is, conducted at the conclusion of a learning process. Some examples of summative performance assessment in creativity and the arts include portfolios of artwork (see Figures 9.7 and 9.8), creative-writing journals, musical performances, debates or panel discussions in social studies, an exhibit of scale models constructed by the children, demonstrations of a craft that the child has mastered, videos of a play, and technology-based presentations that combine images, music, and dance. Advances in technology and digital imaging make it possible to store and retrieve permanent records of the students' work as visual images rather than retain the child's original work (Dorn, Madeja, & Sabol, 2004).

Teachers might also consider more unusual formats such as student-designed board games, illustrated books and comic books, and musical scores and lyrics. A third-grade teacher has shared the picture books *Talking Walls* (Knight & O'Brien, 1995), *Murals: Walls that Sing* (Ancona, 2003), and *Talking Walls: The Stories Continue* (Knight & O'Brien, 1997) with her students as part of an integrated unit on social studies and art. The culminating activity is for small groups of children to produce murals that will be displayed in a glass case in the lobby of the school. Each group has to agree upon a style and purpose for the mural. The evaluation rubric for this project was shared with the students prior to beginning the murals and is used by

What Is a Portfolio?

A portfolio is a carefully selected collection of student work samples that highlight individual effort, progress, and learning. Just as professional artists' portfolios are used in interviews to highlight what they can do, children's portfolios are a way of documenting learning.

Why Use Portfolios to Assess Creative Thought and Expression?

- Portfolios reveal and document children's learning in many different modes, on real-world tasks, over a period of time.
- Portfolios encourage self-evaluation in students.
- Portfolios help teachers make instructional decisions.
- Portfolios document student growth and progress in a way that parents/families can understand.

How Are Portfolios Used?

Armstrong (1994) recommends "the 5 Cs of portfolio development":

1. *Celebration.* Use portfolios to acknowledge and validate children's products and accomplishments during the year.
2. *Cognition.* Use portfolios to encourage students to reflect on their own work.
3. *Communication.* Use portfolios to inform families, administrators, and colleagues about children's growth and progress.
4. *Cooperation.* Use portfolios as a way for groups of children to collectively produce and evaluate their own work.
5. *Competency.* Use portfolios to establish a set of standards by which one child's work can be compared with other children's performance or with a benchmark established by the teacher.

What Is Included in a Portfolio?

Children's portfolios should not be cartons filled with every imaginable item ever produced by the child during the course of the year. Rather, they should be focused and organized by learning goals. If a teacher has the language arts goal that children read and respond to a variety of picture books, for instance, the file might contain a log of the books read by the child and stories or artwork inspired by children's books. If exploring different media is a curriculum goal in art, one of the folders might contain a sample of paintings, chalk drawings, batik, and a photograph of sculptures the child constructed out of clay, wood, and paper. To demonstrate the child's attainment of another art program goal, the refinement of a form, a folder might contain sketches of the work at successive stages and the finished product.

How Should Portfolios Be Stored and Maintained?

An expandable file with accordion-folded sides is a good portfolio. Individual folders that are keyed or color-coded to program goals can be placed inside the expandable file to organize the child's work. Include a table of contents so that teachers, administrators, parents, and children can use it.

Figure 9.7
Using Portfolios to Assess Creative Thinking and Arts-Based Learning

The child was sitting on his mom's lap at the kitchen table as she was writing out some bills. The child was imitating actions made by Mom: moving the pen over the paper.

1. Daniel's first marks—12 months: random scribbling

At this stage of development it is not appropriate to ask the child to "tell you about" his or her drawing. Instead, provide feedback such as "I like the lines that you made," or if you have observed the child working quickly, say, "those lines look really fast," or if the child has seemed to be interested in trying out various colors of crayons or markers, say, "I like all of those colors you drew."

2. Daniel's marks—14 months

3a and b. Daniel's marks—19 months: circular scribble

Figure 9.8
Portfolio of a Child's Growth Over Time

After the child created the scribbled lines, it reminded him of a pirate ship he had recently watched on a television cartoon show, and he made the major developmental step in his visual language development by naming his scribble.

4. Daniel's marks become a visual representation—24 months: naming the scribble

The child drew this with some prompting. Talking about grandma coming for a visit: "You can make a picture of Gram while we are waiting. Draw Grandma's head. Where are Grandma's eyes? Her mouth? Do you think she went to the beauty shop to get her hair fixed this morning? Does she have long arms to hug you when she comes? What kind of shoes will she wear?"

5. Daniel's first drawing of a human figure—26 months: beginning of preschematic stage

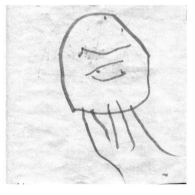

6a and b. Daniel's drawings of Mommy and Daddy—27 months: preschematic stage

(continued)

377

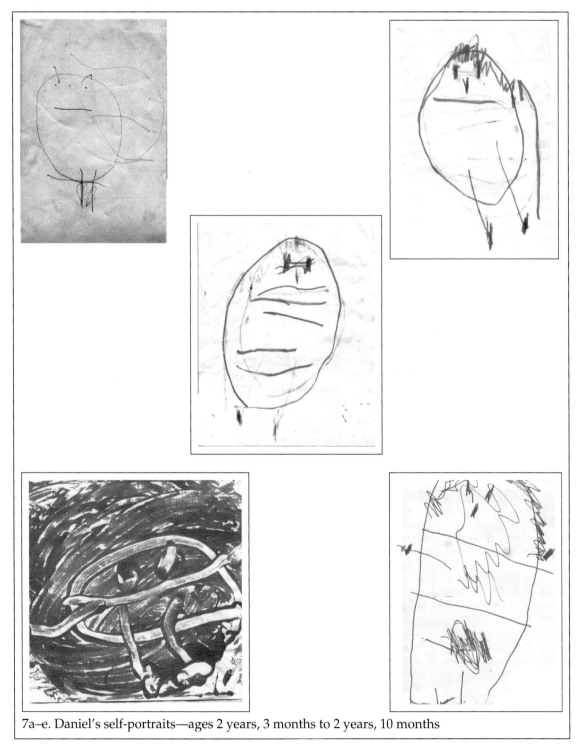

7a–e. Daniel's self-portraits—ages 2 years, 3 months to 2 years, 10 months

Figure 9.8 *Continued*

Daniel drew this portrait of Dad, perhaps concentrating on body "divisions" of neck, waist, etc. When the drawing was complete, he observed, "Daddy looks like a zebra." In this preschematic drawing the child is moving back and forth between drawing with intent (the symbol for his father) and interpreting his marks (the lines look like stripes on a zebra).

8. "Daddy looks like a zebra"—2 years, 8 months

Drawing need not be a formal process. Materials can be made available for any time a child wants to use them. This drawing was done at the pool during a break from swimming.

9. "At the Pool"—2 years, 9 months

At age 4, Daniel is moving from the preschematic stage to the schematic stage as he demonstrates great control in his ability to draw a descriptive schema for himself, the four candles on the birthday cake and the letters spelling out "Happy Birthday." Note how he has drawn the table in a fold-over fashion: he "knows" that each table leg is connected to a corner. His visual representation is an attempt to explain this knowledge.

10. "I Am Cutting My Birthday Cake"—age 4 years

(*continued*)

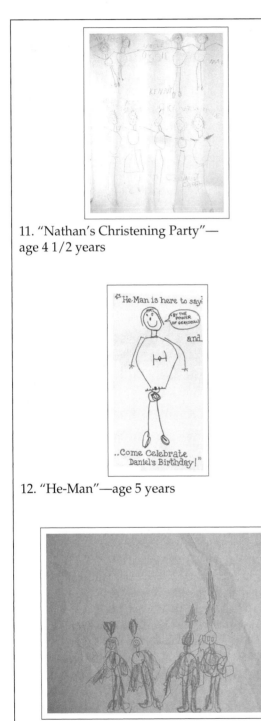

Daniel drew a special mural of all of the family members who would be attending his new brother Nathan's christening party. This is a portion of the larger drawing. Note the repetition of geometric shapes to represent various body parts. Occasionally glasses or skirts are added.

11. "Nathan's Christening Party"— age 4 1/2 years

This drawing on his fifth birthday party invitation shows further development in his schema for a person as Daniel represents his favorite action hero, He-Man. Note the similarities and differences in this example and in example 10.

12. "He-Man"—age 5 years

Daniel continues to develop his schema for people, which are often characters from adventure shows or books. During this time he is also creating props, costumes, and sets for make-believe play with his action figure characters. Note that the legs are now drawn as shapes, rather than lines.

13. "Knights in Armor"—age 5 years

Figure 9.8 *Continued*

14. "A Picture of the Person Sitting Across from Me, Charbel"—age 5 years

Daniel drew his table partner in kindergarten after his teacher instructed the class to carefully observe what the other child was wearing, what color of eyes and hair they had, etc. Although clothing is not usually included in the schema, the teacher's prompt to carefully observe what their partner was wearing resulted in a detailed drawing of the other child's sailor-type outfit with an anchor and other nautical symbols.

15. Detail from "Things I Did Over the Warm Spring Weekend"—age 5

Following the teacher's prompt, Daniel drew this picture of himself and Dad playing ball. Note the detail of five fingers and the stripes on his new shirt. He illustrates how the ball is thrown and then hit with the bat by making multiple images of the ball. This time relationship is common at this stage as the child attempts to communicate meaning. The intent is not to say that there are multiple balls, but to explain that the ball is moving through time and space.

16. "My Favorite Day in Kindergarten"—age 5 3/4 years

Daniel drew this during the last week of kindergarten. At the end of the school year the kindergarten class was finally allowed to use the gym, since the older grades were having Phys. Ed. classes outdoors. The large space with its shiny wooden floor was the setting for a favorite game, "Duck, Duck, Goose." The uniqueness of the experience made Daniel choose it in response to his teacher's request to draw their favorite day in kindergarten. He carefully drew to explain the game: classmates sitting in a circle on the wooden floor with one walking around the circle.

(*continued*)

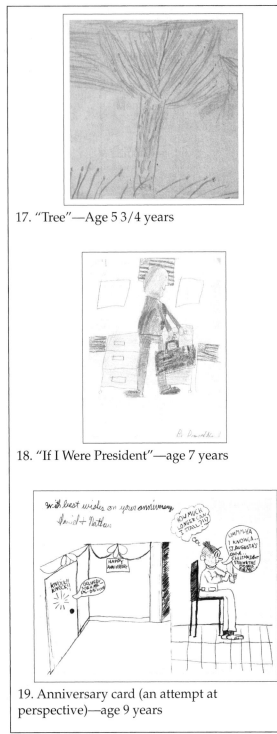

17. "Tree"—Age 5 3/4 years

At the schematic stage, children usually draw a baseline and a skyline, which indicates a means of ordering their spatial relationships and a means of connecting themselves to their environment. Usually there is no three-dimensional quality in their spatial concept. Daniel's frequent drawing and thoughtful observation, however, probably inspired the overlapping in this drawing. The sky, although not drawn all the way down to the ground, is seen through the branches of the tree, an untypical use of three-dimensionality for this age.

18. "If I Were President"—age 7 years

Here Daniel's drawing shows characteristics of what Lowenfeld termed the stage of dawning realism. Use of overlapping, the profile view, and the attention to detail, such as the shoe laces, are signs that Daniel is moving out of the schematic stage.

19. Anniversary card (an attempt at perspective)—age 9 years

Here Daniel uses a classic comic strip character (copying comic strip characters is common during this stage) to create an anniversary card for his parents. He attempts and almost accurately achieves perspective on the door wall, but still draws the floor tiles under Dagwood from an overhead view. At this stage, and not before, the child may formally be taught perspective and figure drawing techniques. For most children, this will occur by around age 11, although some, like Daniel, will show ability earlier and others, who have not had much opportunity to draw, will not be ready for this conceptual understanding until much later.

Figure 9.8 *Continued*

Daniel is clearly interested in portraying subject matter in a realistic manner. Here he uses shading to achieve a more three-dimensional quality, and his proportion when drawing people is more lifelike, based upon what his eyes see, rather than what his brain knows.

20a. "A Friend"—age 11 years

20b. "The Owl"—age 11 years

Daniel continues to attempt to portray visual reality in painting as well as drawing.

21. "Woodpecker"—age 11 1/2

the teacher, the individual children, and the class to evaluate the various murals on completion. Additionally, visitors to the building are asked to sign a guest book and comment on the children's work. After each group's mural is completed and on display, the small group explains the style that they selected and their purpose for the particular mural. One group, for example, chose to produce a mural with the characteristics of cave paintings discovered in France. They worked together to meet the challenge of simulating the rough-hewn texture of a cave wall and decided to wrinkle tan craft paper and staple it over some crumpled recycled paper. They also deliberated on ways to produce muted colors that might have been produced using natural sources. Their stated purpose for the mural was to use the style of cave art to depict a story. Discussion with their peers highlighted creative processes ("How did you get it to look old?") and products ("Which walls did you use to get the ideas for the animals?"). Figure 9.9 summarizes the types of environments, materials and climates that foster creativity.

Note that the evaluation of this project was not approached as a contest. That is because an overreliance on competitions linked with tangible rewards can undermine creativity (Fawson & Moore, 1999). This is thought to occur in two major ways: partly by constraining the response (as when the child chooses a less innovative response to avoid rejection and please the teacher) and partly by diverting attention from the intrinsic rewards of the task (as when the child becomes preoccupied with hurrying to win the prize instead of a slow and careful process) (Joussement & Koestner, 1999). Contests and tangible rewards, while commonplace, need to be used judiciously. Extrinsic rewards often are not the most effective form of summative assessment.

It is also necessary to build children's skills in evaluation. Some comments and questions to help children grow in self-evaluation include the following:

- Tell me about how you worked in your group today.
- Describe some of the things you liked about your work.
- Which things did not work well for you?
- What are some things you could do for yourself? What did you need help with?
- What did you do to help others?
- When you had some trouble, explain how you solved the problem.
- What were some of the new ideas that you had?
- What did you do the best of all?
- Were there things that you didn't try? How did you feel about that?
- Is there a particular piece of work that you feel proud of? Tell me about it.
- Tell me what you did when . . . (adapted from Wassermann, 1990, pp. 223–224).

Communication with families, the community, and your colleagues about your approaches is a key element in teaching creatively. If you fail to help others understand why you approach teaching as you do, you are likely to be met with resistance because your ways of working with students differ from the more traditional approaches. When you begin a unit of study, be certain to let others know

Classroom Environment, Materials, and Climate

Creative teachers:

- Create organizational and structural conditions that allow open and flexible distribution of roles, themes, problems, and activities.
- Provide challenging and stimulating learning materials.
- Offer opportunities to work with varied materials under different conditions.
- Establish a classroom climate that permits alternative solutions.

Professional Attitudes and Values

Creative teachers:

- Provide support and positive feedback for problem finding, not just problem solving.
- Serve as a model of creative thought.
- Tolerate ambiguity and accept alternative solutions.
- Expect and accept humor and playfulness from children.

Social Support for Creativity

Creative teachers:

- Have a cooperative, socially integrative style of teaching.
- Make it possible for children to participate in joint projects with self-selected partners.
- Surprise students with recognition for creative processes and products.
- Extend mastery of factual knowledge through collaboration.

Recognition and Respect for Children's Creativity

Creative teachers:

- Enable self-directed work that allows for a high degree of initiative, spontaneity, and experimentation.
- Encourage and accept constructive nonconformist behavior.
- Take children's questions seriously and tolerate "sensible," bold errors.
- Help students learn to cope with frustration and failure.
- Reward courage as much as being right.
- Actively teach creative strategies.
- Foster intense concentration and task commitment through high motivation and interest in self-selected topics.
- Increase autonomy in learning by recognition and self-evaluation of progress.

Figure 9.9

What Do Creativity-Fostering Teachers Do?

Note. Adapted from Clark (1996), Cropley (2001), and Urban (1995, 1996).

what you are doing, and why. Letters from teachers to families are a simple yet effective way of explaining creative approaches to teaching. Figure 9.10 is a sample letter to families that introduces a new teaching theme. Note that it has several key features. First, it keeps educational jargon to a minimum and is written in clear, simple language that is supported with concrete examples. Second, it explains what children are learning and how parents and families can help. Third, it has a positive tone so that families get a sense of your enthusiasm for teaching and efforts to motivate their child to learn. You may want to try writing a similar letter to accompany a thematic unit that you are planning.

Dear Parents and Families of Kindergartners:

Understanding patterns is an important skill for young children.

Recognizing patterns is essential for learning to read and write, to create works of art, to appreciate music, to participate in dance, and to listen to stories. Next week, we will begin our study of patterns. Children will be learning that:

Patterns are repetitions. Printed fabric is a pictorial pattern, a picket fence is an architectural pattern, a jump-rope rhyme is a pattern of sound, words are patterns of letters, and so forth.

Patterns can be found everywhere. There are social patterns, such as please and thank you; there are visual patterns, such as wallpaper; there are auditory patterns, such as clapping to the beat of music, and so forth.

Patterns occur in nature. The change of seasons is a pattern, a spider's web is a pattern, tracks in the snow are patterns.

Children can make patterns. A child can draw a border around a picture, invent motions to go with a song, or use the computer to generate patterns.

Patterns are found in different cultures. African Kente cloth is a pattern, Chinese characters form patterns, Navajo pottery is decorated with patterns, and company logos are patterns.

You will see your child bringing home geometric patterns that were produced on the computer, word search pages where the child highlights patterns of words, and patterns produced with a stamp pad and various stamps. Please display your child's work and invite him or her to talk with you about patterns.

Around your home and in the community, consider playing a "Pattern Hunt" game. For instance, while setting the table, you might say, "See if you can make a pattern of bowl, spoon, glass for everyone in the family." Stopped at a traffic light, you might say, "I spy a pattern—red, yellow, green. Do you see the pattern?"

Thank you for helping your child to understand patterns.

Sincerely,

Figure 9.10
Sample Letter to Parents and Families

Published Scales

Over the years, many experts have attempted to quantify creativity and predict potential in the arts. Nevertheless, measurement tools frequently fall short when we try to reduce complex processes to numerical ratings. Even if we do succeed in assigning a numerical value to creative processes or products, we are left with the task of interpreting those numbers. As Wassermann (1989) points out, numbers themselves do not have meaning. It takes human intelligence to make sense out of them. The results of published scales should always be viewed as one indicator in a comprehensive form of assessment rather than the "final word" on a child's play, creativity, or talent.

RETHINKING ASSESSMENT IN CREATIVITY AND THE ARTS

Teachers often are left on their own when it comes to evaluating children's creative growth and art products (Johnson, 2003). As a result, teachers are often at a loss when they must assign a grade or generate a report concerning a child's creative ability or development in the arts. Under these circumstances, teachers tend to err at one of two extremes (Bresler, 1993). At one end of the spectrum is the little-intervention approach (Gilbert, 1996), characterized by little evaluation or, for that matter, instruction ("Go ahead and make anything you want"). Teachers defend the little-intervention approach by arguing that any hint of structure or challenge will inhibit the child's creativity. They may argue that to do otherwise will damage the child's self-esteem (Thompson, 1997). Yet primary teachers actually do make judgments about children's creative processes and art products all the time (Hargreaves, Galton, & Robinson, 1996). They separate the day's works into ones good enough for display or ones to be sent home; they single out certain students as the class artists, giving them the special assignments of creating room decorations for the holidays; or they select students for various roles in a dramatic performance. These evaluations are intuitive and usually not publicly acknowledged. Often, they are based upon the teacher's preconceived notions of how child art should look or what characteristics are desirable for a child performance. Thus, in many not-so-subtle ways, the actions of teachers who argue for the little-intervention approach often contradict their own philosophical stance, and the absence of thoughtful teacher monitoring or evaluation results in programs of little substance.

At the opposite end of the spectrum is the production-oriented approach, in which cookie-cutter-type products are the norm. In the production-oriented approach, evaluation is not based on originality; rather, it is based on how closely the end product resembles the model provided by the teacher for children to copy. The problem here is that the resulting products fail to stimulate children's intellects or to engage them effectively in the arts.

A third way of abdicating responsibility for creativity and arts-based learning is by "leaving all that to the specialists," teachers who have specialized training in art and music. There are several problems here. The first and most obvious is that not every school has a music or art teacher and, even if they do, most of these teachers are itinerant without their own classroom space and are expected to teach hundreds of children of various ages for short periods of time (usually 20 or 30 minutes) once a week (Olson, 2002). To further complicate matters, many arts specialists have had little preservice instruction in assessment methods (Colwell, 1998). Therefore, even if these teachers can meet the challenge of the conditions under which they teach, they must educate themselves or rely on their own educational experiences as a student, which usually based assessment on criteria such as attendance, attitude, and cooperation rather than attainment of any arts objectives (Colwell, 1998).

What, then, is the solution? We recommend the guided exploration approach. Unlike the little-intervention or production-oriented approaches, guided exploration is teaching intensive. It allows room for improvisation, choice, and spontaneity, but it is brought to a conscious level through evaluation and feedback. It also addresses the what, why, and how of assessment.

MEETING STANDARDS

Assessment of Creative Works

In today's schools student work that is not linked to standards and assessed in some systematic way is treated as less important and less vital to educational purposes. If work is not assessed, it can be expected to be on the endangered list when resources are in short supply. Fortunately, several national organizations have generated standards and guidelines that can provide a framework for assessment in the arts, such as the National Advisory Committee on Creative and Cultural Education (1999) in the United Kingdom and the publication of the Consortium of National Arts Education Associations (1994), *National Standards for Arts Education: What Every Young American Should Know and Be Able to Do in the Arts.*

Appropriate assessment of creative works:

- Is founded on expanded definitions of intelligence and creativity.
- Is fair (gives all students an equal opportunity to participate) and adapted to special needs of individual students.
- Is oriented toward students but planned and monitored by teachers who can clearly state the purpose of the assessment, identify the domain to be assessed, understand the assessment strategy or task, prepare the actual task or exercise, devise a scoring plan, and make a plan for reporting out the results.
- Is integrated with the curriculum (supports instruction and course objectives).
- Is committed to evaluating creative work at multiple levels and from multiple perspectives.
- Is continuous and focuses on providing ongoing feedback.

- Focuses on "real-world" tasks and considers the particulars of the context in which creative works are generated.
- Includes both informal and formal assessment strategies.
- Considers not only the products but also the processes.
- Provides opportunities for students to revisit the work, refine, and revise.
- Is responsive to knowledge of disciplinary content, skills, and processes of a discipline, requisite motor skills in a discipline, appropriate procedures in particular contexts, self-appraisal of strengths and weaknesses in a discipline, and insight into the dispositions and values associated with achievement in a domain.
- Is concerned with determining students' preconceptions and changing their misconceptions.
- Is linked to standards and referenced to criteria.
- Is supportive of collaborative and cooperative learning (adapted from Beattie, 1997).

The next section describes several classroom projects that meet these standards.

Assessment in Music and Movement

Preschool

What: Child's movement/dance performance

Why: Assessment of child's understanding of movement in personal space and large muscle motor skills

How: Following explorations of walking, hopping, and other simple movements (in place) in personal space and as locomotor movements across a large defined space, children will demonstrate their ability to understand the difference among the various ways of moving their bodies.

Primary

What: Student's movement performance

Why: Assessment of student's understanding of the aesthetic quality of "texture" in visual art, music, and movement

How: Following explorations of the quality of "texture" in a variety of media, students will demonstrate understanding of texture by responding with appropriate movement to visual and musical prompts (e.g., a march versus a waltz).

Assessment of Creative Growth

Preschool

What: Child's attitudes, actions (verbal, visual, and kinesthetic), responses, communicated observations regarding encounters with his or her environment, and interactions with people, animals, and objects.

Why: Documentation of child's creative growth

How: At this level, assessment can be the responsibility of the teacher through a portfolio collection of narratives of teacher observations of the child along with photographs and artifacts of creative responses, including but not limited to those appropriately classified as art. The teacher should date entries and periodically review each child's development for the purposes of developing instruction, creating appropriate environments and opportunities, and sharing with parents and other caregivers.

Primary

What: Student's individual creative investigations, solutions, and responses

Why: Documentation of student's creative growth

How: Student's personal creativity journal. At the beginning of the school year, engage students in discussion of creative people, soliciting their perceptions and prior knowledge. Read stories of diverse creative lives and involve students in locating stories about others. Implement the yearlong production of a personal creativity journal. Suggest that the journal include reflections about attributes of creative people that students admire from their reading and from personal acquaintance, their personal assessments of their own areas of creativity, documentations of their creative responses and endeavors, and investigations that they wish to pursue that involve creativity along with their explorations and processes in pursuit of the solutions. Periodically schedule the sharing of the journals in class or small-group discussion, asking questions about development in individual perceptions of what creativity is, how the student demonstrated creativity, and how the student has demonstrated growth in creativity as evidenced by thought processes, responses, products, and so on.

Performance-Based Assessment of Integrated Learning Experiences

Preschool

What: Child's ability to visually represent and dramatically communicate the story *The Very Hungry Caterpillar* by Eric Carle (1969)

Why: Assessment of child's reading comprehension

How: Model making/dramatic play. An important aspect of literacy instruction is comprehension. In order to assess children's understanding of a story, the teacher can encourage them to create visual representations in the form of models to communicate ideas. After drawing and cutting out shapes of a caterpillar, various food, and other necessary props, the children can animate them to dramatize and retell the story. Models can provide children who are not so articulate in the classroom an opportunity to express their understandings (Pahl, 1999).

It is probably not necessary to provide instruction for model making, only materials and opportunity. Many children engage in this form of creative production quite naturally. Daniel, for instance, at age 4 and 5 would often create elaborate props to incorporate in dramatic play with the He-Man character toy figures: creating a small three-dimensional paper picnic basket and paper food for He-Man and Tela to take on a trip, or shoebox elevators to take the popular television cartoon heroes to the top floor (via an attached string pulled through the stair railing) of an office building. Researchers have observed children's creation of various modes of meaning making and translation of one symbol- or sign-making activity into another in the course of creating narratives (Dyson, 1993; Kress, 1997).

Primary

What: The student's ability to create and communicate an accurate representation of a selected science concept through movement/dance performance

Why: Assessment of the student's understanding of science concepts

How: In lieu of a traditional end-of-unit or semester assessment of the students' understanding of various science concepts, the teacher could incorporate the medium of dance. Dance is a kinetic art form, a physical language that speaks the integrated response from the mind and the body (Ross, 1994). Assessments should include the engagement of all of the cultural and semiotic tools as meaning-making resources (Johnson, 2003). By using the medium of movement/dance as a means of communicating understanding, not only will the teacher address those often-neglected students with kinesthetic intelligence, but cause all of the students to think in a new way, to translate what they know into a different language. The teacher should begin by modeling—using movement/dance to explain a concept in the course of instruction, such as the revolution of the planets around the sun. The teacher can "choreograph" and provide directions to students to perform the roles of the various planets, asking them to consider speed of rotation, tilt, moons, and so on.

Following this lesson, the teacher can explain the anticipated alternative assessment for the unit: Each student will select (or be provided by lottery) a unit science concept for which they will choreograph a movement/dance piece that effectively explains the concept. They may work individually or in a small group as dictated by the needs of their concept. Facilitated by the teacher's guiding questions, they can critically analyze video or live performances to examine how dancers portray size and space relationships, power, subtleties of movement, and so on, then experiment and apply them to their own performance development. The final assessment will be of each student's effective communication through the movement/dance piece his or her understanding of the science concept.

Frequently Asked Questions About Assessment

It seems that there really isn't much time for creative activities. Don't creative pursuits take time away from serious learning?

Creative and artistic pursuits *are* serious learning because they deal with complex thought processes as children are asked to compare, classify, deduce, investigate, inquire, invent, analyze errors, construct support, deal with abstractions, appreciate multiple perspectives, make decisions, solve problems, and evaluate products (Beattie, 1997; Marzano, Pickering, & McTighe, 1993).

It is easy to appreciate the contributions of inventions that save time or make money. But what actually determines the value of a creative product?

Creative thought is not inherently "good." Creative processes and products also can be put to destructive ends. Therefore, it makes sense to guide children in examining the underlying values of creative work. In fact, many of the activities that are used to teach media literacy take this approach (Semali & Watts Pailliotet, 1999). An advertiser might spend hundreds of thousands of dollars on a creative idea for promoting a product. But whose interests are being served? Who is most likely to be taken in by the appealing advertisement? What are the consequences for society at large if questionable claims and business practices are allowed to proliferate? Society is inundated with unstructured problems like this one, not the neat, predictable, and orderly kinds of questions too often presented in school. If we seek to prepare children for the future, we must devote attention to the thoughtful critique of creative products in society. We also must think beyond what is customary, orthodox, and conventional if the genuinely important potential of creativity—the ways in which it is used to capture the very essence of its culture—is to be realized.

What really gets in the way of creative expression?

It is no mistake that Amabile's (1986) "creativity killers" include such things as inflexible schedules, intense competition, reliance on extrinsic rewards, and lack of free time. In order to function at full creative capacity, children need the freedom to pursue questions that captivate them and work in learning environments that offer a blend of high support and high expectations (Rea, 2001).

Which is better in supporting creativity and the arts: extrinsic or intrinsic rewards?

Several researchers have argued for greater emphasis on intrinsic (within the person) rewards (Amabile, 1986; Joussement & Koestner, 1999). The difficulty with external rewards is that they can discourage the sort of innovative thought and risk taking that lead to greater originality; children may take the safer route, try to please, and become preoccupied with winning. Extrinsic motivation designed to get students to comply with learning standards sometimes decreases the pleasure children associate with learning (Levin & Greenwald, 2001). External rewards may be effective, however, when instead of being linked with some vague competition, the reward is linked to clearly defined and specified creative behaviors (Eisenberger & Armeli, 1997).

How reliable is assessment by a panel of judges or published rating scales?

Educators throughout the world are grappling with ways of designing curriculum and assessing it in ways that promote creativity. In their book on evaluating creativity, Sefton-Green and Sinker (2000) contend that evaluation is the crux of the matter. Increasingly, there is an emphasis on the contribution of the creative product or response as judged by an appropriate group of observers; in other words, a consensual process is used to assess creativity (Amabile, 2001; Priest, 2001). Alternative assessment provides numerous examples of a consensual process used to evaluate creative products, such as a team of elementary school teachers evaluating children's writing portfolios or a panel of secondary educators scoring a student's senior project. It is critical that creative processes and products be part of the overall assessment plan in the curriculum. Surprisingly, even untrained undergraduates demonstrate reasonably high levels of agreement about the creativity of products (Hennessey, 1994). Additionally, there are formal scales for assessing creative products, such as the Creative Product Inventory (Taylor, 1975) and the Creative Product Semantic Scale (Besemer & O'Quin, 1999). For more on formal measures of creativity, see Cropley (2001); Fishkin and Johnson (1998).

CONCLUSION

In an interview, E. Paul Torrance (quoted in Cramond, 2001), one of the pioneers in creativity research, talked about his 30-year study of "beyonders," individuals from various countries and walks of life whose creative achievement was remarkable in their chosen domain (Torrance, 1993). The characteristics that these individuals shared were a delight in deep thinking, a tolerance of mistakes, a passion for their work, a clear sense of purpose and mission, an acceptance of being different, a level of comfort with being a minority of one, and a relative lack of concern about being "well rounded." Based on this research, Torrance and his colleagues (Henderson, Presbury, & Torrance, 1983) advised children to pursue their interests with intensity, work to their strengths, learn to self-evaluate, seek out mentors and teachers, ignore admonitions about being well-rounded, and learn to be interdependent. Such advice, based on studies of those who excelled in their chosen fields and functioned at very high levels of creativity, are suggestive of the type of changes that need to be made in schools and programs.

As you think about assessment of creative growth and in the arts, keep in mind that effective assessment enables teachers "to diagnose student strengths and weaknesses early on and on a regular basis, to monitor student progress, to improve and adapt instructional methods in response to assessment data, and to use information about students individually and as a group to manage the classroom more effectively" (Beattie, 1997, p. 2). Teachers must examine their understandings of the role of creativity in their own lives, in their classroom, and in society. How is it exhibited, how is it valued and what end does it serve? They must teach children to critically examine creativity in their work, school, and society. Perhaps the most important role of the teacher in child-centered assessment is to view children as informants about their own growth and as partners in the assessment process.

CHAPTER SUMMARY

1. Assessment is a highly controversial issue; many inappropriate practices are commonplace. As a result, major professional organizations are urging teachers to use a wide range of observational methods as an alternative to overreliance on standardized tests.
2. Assessment is an ongoing process rather than a single paper-and-pencil test. It should include information on the child's performance of meaningful tasks over an extended period of time and should look at the learner's attitudes, processes, and effort as well as the products of learning.
3. In general, the purposes for assessing creativity are to gain insight about creativity, evaluate progress, identify talents, provide enrichment, and optimize each child's growth in creative expression and play.
4. More child-centered alternatives to standardized tests include observations, interactions, and the analysis of products or processes. One key role for teachers is the thoughtful, day-to-day observation of children. Specific techniques include interviews, conferences, portfolios, checklists, and rating scales.
5. The standards set forth by various organizations and published observation tools can be used to guide teachers' assessment efforts.

Discuss: Assessment Issues in Creative Expression and Art

1. A parent visits your classroom and comments, "I expected my child to really learn something, but it looks like she's just playing. She can do that at home." How would you respond to these objections? Support your position with your readings from this textbook.
2. Recall some occasions when you were asked to evaluate your own performance. How did that make you feel? Was your self-assessment accurate? Useful? How did your self-evaluation compare with other people's assessments of your performance?
3. When a large city school district announced that it would identify elementary schools for the study of music, dance, and languages, urban parents got in line the night before and literally camped out to get their children enrolled in a particular school. What does this behavior tell you about parental interest in traditionally "nonacademic" subjects? What will you do to change the curriculum and assessment practices that often exclude children, particularly poor and minority children, from participating in the most inviting educational programs?

Chapter 10

Developing an Appreciation
for Children's Creative Work
in Diverse Families and Communities

*The common language of creativity transcends race, country,
culture, and economic level.*

Karen Meador, 1999, p. 324

CLASSROOM PERSPECTIVES ON CULTURE, FAMILY, AND THE ARTS

Preschool–Kindergarten

Ms. Ochoa teaches kindergarten in an economically depressed rural area where some of the children live in trailer courts. She overhears two children who are building a house with blocks as they discuss their concept of a home:

Bradley: No, you can't live in a trailer; you've got to live in a house.
Carol Ann: But I do live in a trailer.
Bradley: A trailer is for camping. You've gotta live in a house, or maybe an apartment.

In response to this conflict, Ms. Ochoa initiates a "Where do they live?" bulletin board/collage. Her pictures come from local real estate advertising booklets as well as copies of magazines such as *National Geographic* and *Old House Journal*. She also finds UNICEF cards and calendars that contain photographs and children's drawings of homes from around the world. The children use these materials as resources to create their own impressive display of different homes for human beings. To extend the project even further, Ms. Ochoa invites a Habitat for Humanity volunteer to speak with the children about her work and to share photos of the homes that she has helped to renovate, including her own. As a result of Ms. Ochoa's efforts, every child's concept of what a home can be or become is expanded.

First Grade–Second Grade

The state academic standards for language arts require students to understand different points of view in a story and to produce compositions that demonstrate that ability. In a class for gifted and talented second graders, their teacher decides to use "fractured fairy tales" as a way of developing the students' perspective-taking abilities. She plans a four-day unit using the following concepts, books, and activities.

Monday

Question: How can a change in setting affect point of view in a story?

Children's Literature: The Cowboy and the Black-Eyed Pea (Johnston, 1996)—a Texas version of the fairy tale "The Princess and the Pea"; two regional variants of "The Three Little Pigs": *The Three Little Javelinas* (Lowell, 1992) and *The Three Little Pigs and the Fox: An Appalachian Tale* (Hooks, 1997).

Activity: Have students work in small groups to select a new setting for a familiar folk or fairy tale, retell it, then complete a chart that compares/contrasts the two.

Tuesday

Question: How does telling a tale from a different character's point of view change the plot?

Children's Literature: The True Story of the Three Little Pigs! (Scieszka, 1989); *The Wolf Who Cried Boy* (Hartman, 2004).

Activity: Use the book *Mufaro's Beautiful Daughters* (Steptoe, 1987) with the group to invent a script in which the story is told from the mean sister's point of view. Then distribute copies of familiar fairy tales, such as "Rapunzel," "Sleeping Beauty," and "Rumplestiltskin," and have children work with a partner to create a script for a scene depicting a different character's perspective.

Wednesday

Question: How might characters with different points of view communicate with one another through writing?

Children's Literature: The Jolly Postman, or, Other People's Letters (Ahlberg & Ahlberg, 1986); *Three Days on a River in a Red Canoe* (Williams, 1981); *Stringbean's Trip to the Shining Sea* (Williams, 1988); *Mailing May* (Tunnell, 2000); *Nettie's Trip South* (Turner, 1987).

Activity: Create a letter, postcard, greeting card, or e-mail message from one story character to another.

Thursday

Question: What can a prequel reveal about a character's reasons or motives for interpreting events in a particular way?

Children's Literature: Discuss books and movies in a series such as *Star Wars, Lord of the Rings,* and *Harry Potter.* Provide examples of storyboarding (a sequential set of drawings that depict the action in a film). Use Janet Stevens's *Tops and Bottoms* (1995), which attributes Hare's financial problems to a bet he made and lost with Tortoise.

Activity: Work in small groups to create a storyboard of the fable "The Tortoise and the Hare," which predates the story of *Tops and Bottoms.* Encourage the students to emphasize the characters' motives and then discuss how these events might have influenced Hare's behavior.

Third Grade–Fourth Grade

The national literacy standards for 9- and 10-year-old children in many countries throughout the world include teaching them to locate, interpret, and apply factual information effectively. In the refutational approach, students are supplied with a written document that includes some deliberate errors of fact (Lynch & Harris, 2000).

The students then work individually, in pairs, or in small groups and use their reference skills and tools, including the Internet, to locate authoritative information that can support or refute key statements made the text. Ms. Peterson's fourth graders, for example, are studying Australian animals and she has distributed a brief text that includes both accurate and inaccurate information. It states that a platypus has a poisonous stinger and that koalas are outgoing and kept as pets. (The first statement is true—a platypus does have a stinger to protect itself—and the second is false; koalas are wild animals that are not kept as pets.) She leads students in investigating various topics and invites them to create maps, diagrams, and a field guide that address common misconceptions. At the conclusion of the project, each student writes a paragraph summarizing the gaps that were filled in and the errors that were corrected.

DEFINING CULTURAL PERSPECTIVES ON CREATIVITY AND THE ARTS

Consider the following descriptions of how three different countries responded to the need for creative thinking in their populations.

* After Canada was ranked 15th internationally in research and development, the government issued a report in 2003 that challenged the citizenry to foster a "culture of creativity," to make sweeping changes in the educational system, and to move into the top five. Canadians are being urged to become more inventive, entrepreneurial, and technologically advanced. Now the pressure is on Canadian citizens, particularly teachers, to "think outside the box" and to address a national sense of inferiority in creative thought and participation in the arts.

* In the early 2000s, the U.K. government was anxious to raise standards and set targets in numeracy and literacy, an approach that tended to overshadow the arts. The government legislated that all language arts programs for young children would include "The Literacy Hour" (a program similar to what U.S. teachers would refer to as balanced reading, with time for reading aloud, writing, discussion, and so forth). Gradually, "expected outcomes" were specified for art as well. Yet as Barnes (2002) points out, art galleries throughout the world are filled with unexpected outcomes, not legislated ones!

* In China, where 178 million children attend elementary and secondary school, the official purpose of art in "the national curriculum is to foster patriotism, morality, and socialism"; however, the teachers recognize their responsibility to enlarge the children's vision and allow them to create according to their imaginations (Perry, 1998). Traditional art instruction in China emphasizes direct instruction in technique and imitation of the masters. Nevertheless, Chinese educators are beginning to question

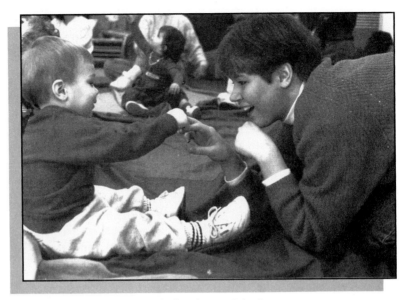

How do families encourage chidlren's creativity?

educational policies that appear to be at odds with providing more opportunities for children to think creatively (Rong & Shi, 2001).

As these snapshots of three diverse countries have illustrated, the way that nations envision the future of the children in their society influences the school curriculum. It also affects the quality of life for children and teachers in classrooms. In cultural contexts where basic needs are met, there is often greater emphasis on innovation and creative problem solving. Many wealthy nations regard technological advancement as the key to their continued economic superiority; these nations seek a highly literate populace capable of functioning more autonomously and generating innovations. Wealthy nations frequently pride themselves on their formal systems of education and the higher levels of education attained by their citizenry. In contrast, less wealthy nations often have a large supply of less educated workers who have little choice about working on farms, in factories, or in mines for low wages in order to survive:

> In technologically less developed countries where both physical survival and survival of the national identity are more important than world dominance, creativity is often seen as the key to rapid economic and social development, especially modernization and its hoped-for benefits of improved education, nutrition, and health care, tolerance of minorities, democracy and political stability. (Cropley, 2001, p. 5)

Even though there is considerable variation among cultures and countries, most children throughout the world have two things in common. First, the social and cultural contexts in which children grow up are likely to be quite different from

*The changing composition of students will influence
how teachers teach in the future.*

those that their parents experienced as children. Second, in our rapidly changing world, life for contemporary children is likely to be very different by the time they reach adulthood. Global awareness, technological advances, and different family structures are just a few of the most obvious differences (Howe, 1993; Papert, 1993). Although it is difficult to make any definite predictions about what the future will be like, one thing is certain: There will be a demand for sensitive, creative, flexible problem solvers. "One way to understand the history of human civilization is via its inventions and discoveries. All human cultural development builds on the amazing technological, scientific, educational, and moral achievements of the human mind. People of exceptionally high ability thus remain an extremely important source of cultural innovation and renewal" (Shavinina & Ferrari, 2004, p. 3).

There is little doubt that the international community needs resourceful, imaginative, inventive, and ethical problem solvers who will make a significant contribution, not only to the Information Age in which we currently live but well beyond to ages that we can barely envision.

According to many experts and leaders in the field, contemporary society needs the following:

1. Students who possess "resilience and flexibility, a creative and integrative way of thinking, and a certain psychological sturdiness in the way they face new circumstances in the company of other people" (Minuchin, 1987, p. 254).

2. A school curriculum that encourages "experimentation, risk-taking, flexibility, autonomy" and children who have acquired "a mode of learning that places responsibility on them and that allows them the freedom to try, to test, to innovate, and to be creative" (Tetenbaum & Mulkeen, 1986, p. 99).

3. A workforce that is responsible and self-disciplined and can move from one challenge to another, adapt quickly to change, produce innovative solutions to problems, and acquire expertise in more than one area (Research and Policy Committee, 1985; Tetenbaum & Mulkeen, 1986). Tomorrow's workers must be able to "figure out what they need to know, where to get it, and how to make meaning of it" (Task Force on Teaching as a Profession, 1986, p. 20).

4. A citizenry capable of reading, writing, and computing at high levels; analyzing and interpreting data, drawing conclusions, and making decisions; and functioning as part of a community (Boyer, 1995; Etzioni, 1993). As Cohen and Gainer (1995) contend: "Creativity is one of the most precious qualities human beings possess, and so is intelligence. These two qualities are needed by society to help us deal with the enormously complicated problems we constantly face" (p. 195).

Despite all of these societal demands, developmental studies suggest that human creativity is eroded, rather than strengthened, as children mature and gain additional experience in schools (Runco & Pritzker, 1999). Yet as Jonathan Kozol (1997) points out:

> Children are not simply "embryonic workers." They have value in themselves for who they are already. Children are not just "preparatory grown-ups." They are alive right now and must be valued, blessed, and treasured for the multitude of gifts they bring to us as a society, not for the added value they may bring to IBM. . . . Business needs team players who are not resistant or iconoclastic and do not waste precious time with metaphors or ethics. But society needs prophets, poets, troublemakers, saints and rebels, beautiful dreamers, glorious eccentrics. (p. 6)

Many parents and families would be uncomfortable with what Kozol proposes here. Some are more interested in seeing their child "fit in" and may urge their child to follow in family footsteps. Conversely, other parents and families may insist that their child break away from much of what their family represents and dream of the day when a child's stunning talent or advanced education enables him or her to rise above current financial circumstances. The aspirations of parents for a child can range all of the way from wishing for complete conformity to dreaming of trailblazing—and everywhere in between. The common denominator of this continuum is that whatever parents' and families' hopes for children might be, the family's influence on children is undeniably powerful.

The Influence of Parents and Families on Talent

The first and foremost social group that exerts an influence on children's creative growth and artistic expression is the family. In Greenspan, Solomon, and Gardner's (2004) review of research on talent development, they found that parents shaped children's talent in several significant ways, including modeling perseverance and industriousness, offering advice or giving explicit instruction, instilling a desire or expectation in children to participate in an activity, setting high standards and encouraging self-evaluation, offering moral support and keeping children motivated, proposing new challenges, and reorganizing their lives to permit their children's abilities to flourish. "When the child's abilities are truly prodigious, parental and social investments need to be prodigious as well" (Csikszentmihalyi, Rathunde, & Whalent, 1993, p. 26). Figure 10.1 describes what parents and families can do to support children's talent, growth, and development in creativity and the arts.

Another reason for parents and families to support children's creative endeavors and arts-based learning is that such activities often occur outside the school setting, often at home or in other out-of-school contexts. Children practice musical instruments at home. They may collaborate with neighborhood children to perform a puppet play; start a club to pursue a particular interest, such as creative writing; or they may work with other family and community members to master a craft. Interestingly, a large survey found that most elementary students reported engaging in art-making at home (80 percent). Their top three reasons for doing so were to have fun (82 percent), to relax (60 percent) or to express their ideas (56 percent). Their criteria for evaluating artwork made at home were (1) use of the artistic elements, (2) skill with art materials, (3) details in their work, (4) neatness of the product, and (5) personal satisfaction with the outcomes of their efforts (Dorn, Madeja, & Sabol, 2004, p. 30). Whether it is creative writing, making an invention, learning to play a musical instrument, learning to dance, or participating in drama, much of the training, practice, support, and performance occurs at home and therefore depends on parents and families.

The Influence of Peer Culture on Talent

There is little question that significant others exert a powerful influence on children's talents. Children "must be surrounded by individuals who support and nurture their talents. Families, peers, and instructors have all been widely noted in the literature for the important role they play in the development of expertise" (Greenspan, Solomon, & Gardner, 2004, p. 121). In a society characterized by rapid change, children may find it difficult to relate to adults whose cultural experiences have differed so dramatically from their own. Under these circumstances, children tend to form a strong peer culture. In fact, as Harris (1998) points out, most of the advice children receive is from other children. Contrary to the commonly held view that extraordinarily talented children are rejected by peers, Greenspan, Solomon, and Gardner (2004) concluded, following their study of 43 children who were exceptionally talented in various domains, that "Children developed

Tolerance. Accept that a child's creative ideas do not always work out to adults' satisfaction or even to the child's personal satisfaction. Children should not be punished and humiliated when ideas fail. In fact, one of the defining characteristics of geniuses is the ability to generate many different ideas and to know which ones are worth pursuing.

Space. Provide children with a private, relatively undisturbed, space in which their creative work can be done. Lois Ehlert, the well-known children's book author and illustrator who is famous for her collages, attributes her growth as an artist to the fact that her parents allowed her to have a large, old table of her own in the basement where she could collect bits and scraps and objects and use them to invent. She was not required to clean it up or put it away and it was always available for her use.

Materials. Children need at least some tools that will support and inspire creative exploration—scissors, crayons, paste, simple musical instruments, picture books. The chief architect of the arts and crafts movement, Frank Lloyd Wright, attributed his interest in architecture to a set of wooden blocks he received as a child.

Support. Children need adults who recognize and support their efforts. A passion for creative problem solving and the arts begins with enjoyment as children enter into these pursuits with curiosity and interest. When hockey great Mario Lemieux was a child, his parents created an indoor place for him and his brother to practice skating by putting water in the foyer and allowing it to freeze.

Role Models. Children need to see adults enjoying and participating in the arts and creative thinking. Something as simple as thinking out loud to demonstrate how you arrive at a creative solution can reap surprising benefits. The parent who repairs a household item and shares the problem-solving strategy with the child is teaching him or her to imagine different possibilities and persist until a satisfactory solution is found. It is also important for parents and families to make children aware of the true stories behind the great contributors of their era and previous eras so children can see that the path is not clear and easy.

Figure 10.1

How Parents and Families Can Nurture Creativity in Children

Note. Based on Baldwin (2001) and Piirto (1992).

strong relationships with their domain-related peers and provided moral and technical support to one another. Peers who did not participate in children's activities played an equally important role by sympathizing with the lengthy hours children were required to devote to their activities and by demonstrating enthusiasm for their involvement . . . the children in our study successfully navigated and utilized both groups of friends in the development of their talent" (p. 132). Even if a child's talents in a domain are not stunning and at the genius level, peers often are a source of feedback that is sometimes helpful and sometimes hurtful.

In consideration of peer and parent/family influences, it is essential for educators to shore up any deficiencies that might exist so that every child will have an opportunity to experience the satisfactions of creative thought processes and products. As a starting point, reflect on one fundamental question concerning the role of creative thinking and the arts in children's futures: What kind of human beings do we hope that children will become? Figure 10.2 presents a list of human characteristics that adults might consider to be important for children to develop. Look through the list and reflect on the top five traits that you hope to nurture in your students. How does your list of five compare with the lists that classmates produce? More often than not, a group of early childhood and elementary teachers will arrive at some consensus on the essential characteristics. As you review your college class's top five, consider this question: Which of these traits, based on what you have read in this book, could be enhanced and extended through creative thinking and the arts? Usually, the answer is "All of them."

The importance of a combination of characteristics that transcend the cognitive is far from new. The Chinese have a concept they refer to as *zuoren,* which refers to the process of becoming a human being in the fullest sense. Li (2004) lists seven categories of meanings of *zuoren:*

1. Pursuing fulfillment of life
2. Self-strengthening without ever stopping
3. Developing high moral/virtuous character
4. Seeking knowledge
5. Maintaining harmonious social relations
6. Striving for a successful career
7. Contributing to society

As the next section describes, the social context exerts a major influence on the development of talent.

THEORETICAL AND RESEARCH BASE: SOCIAL CAPITAL THEORY

Social capital is a general term that refers to a range of resources that are intellectual, economic, cultural, and institutional in nature (McLaughlin, 2001). These resources are differentially distributed and allocated to human beings, depending on an individual's circumstances in society, access to resources, and ability to elicit appropriate support.

Creativity and art depend on social capital to exist and to flourish. Creativity and art are not independent of culture and values; all human achievements are influenced by and produced in a cultural context that defines high ability and excellence and determines its relative value in society. As Li (2004) contends, "although high ability and excellence assume universal foundations, culture also has a role to play in how these human qualities are conceptualized and developed . . . Scholars generally agree that the social environment does play an important role in providing the opportunity for high ability and excellence to flourish" (pp. 188, 190). Each individual's

What kind of adult do you hope children will become? Read through the list and put a star next to the characteristics that teachers ought to encourage the most. Then go back through the list and circle the traits that you think your parents and family would have valued the most in a child. Compare/contrast the two lists. Then compare your lists with those of classmates.

_____ Adventurous	_____ Negativistic
_____ Affectionate	_____ Never bored
_____ A good guesser	_____ Obedient
_____ Altruistic	_____ Persistent
_____ Always asking questions	_____ Physically attractive
_____ A self-starter	_____ Physically strong
_____ Athletic	_____ Proud
_____ Attempts difficult jobs	_____ Quiet
_____ Becomes preoccupied with tasks	_____ Rebellious
_____ Careful	_____ Receptive to ideas of others
_____ Cautious	_____ Refined
_____ Competitive	_____ Regresses occasionally (playful, childish)
_____ Completes work on time	_____ Remembers well
_____ Conforming	_____ Self-assertive
_____ Considerate of others	_____ Self-confident
_____ Cooperative	_____ Self-satisfied
_____ Courageous	_____ Self-sufficient
_____ Creative	_____ Sense of beauty
_____ Critical of others	_____ Sense of humor
_____ Curious	_____ Sensitive
_____ Desires to excel	_____ Sincere
_____ Determined	_____ Socially well adjusted
_____ Domineering	_____ Spirited in disagreement
_____ Emotional	_____ Strives for distant goals
_____ Energetic	_____ Stubborn
_____ Fault finding	_____ Talkative
_____ Fearful	_____ Thorough
_____ Gets good grades	_____ Timid
_____ Healthy	_____ Unwilling to accept things on others' say-so
_____ Independent in judgment	_____ Versatile
_____ Industrious	_____ Visionary
_____ Intelligent	_____ Willing to accept judgments of authorities
_____ Intuitive	_____ Willing to take risks
_____ Likes school	
_____ Likes to work alone	

Figure 10.2
What Traits Do You Hope to Foster in Children?

experiences with aesthetic objects also shape the cultural meanings of those objects and experiences (Dorn, Madeja, & Sabol, 2004, p. 81).

From this perspective, works of art and creative thought are a resource. According to human capital theory, all individuals and groups are capable of making contributions to society and people need to be developed and preserved. In other words, human potential merits the same development as a country's natural resources or financial resources. In a review of the effects of environment on creativity, Simonton (1997) concluded that these effects are not only specific (they affect the individual's creative processes and products) but also general (they influence the creative processes and products of the society as a whole).

Creative thought and arts-based learning have both individual and social significance; therefore, in order to fully understand creative expression, we need to gain a multicultural and global perspective on the concept of creativity. Part of becoming enlightened about creative thought involves broadening our viewpoint beyond the immediate context and adopting an expansive perspective that embraces creative endeavors at different times, in other places, and within various cultures. In order to achieve this, we need to abandon what Jerome Bruner (1996) refers to as the "computational" view of thought in which the mind merely processes (inscribes, stores, sorts, retrieves, manages) information and replace it with a cultural view in which the mind itself is a cultural artifact. From the computational view, the development of mind is an inside-out operation; from the cultural view, the development of mind is an outside-in operation (Roeper & Davis, 2000) as individuals share symbol systems, modes of discourse, and ways of being in the world with their respective communities.

Bringing creative thought to fruition, contrary to popular opinion, requires more than personal ability or even individual determination; it requires social support (Gruber & Wallace, 1999; Zimmerman & Zimmerman, 2000). As Ferrari (2004) explains, "impressive artistic and creative achievements result when students' ideals correspond with what is valued in a culture and when they have the means (e.g., social upbringing, practice, and innate ability) that enable them to excel" (p. 226). Cultural capital "is a product of individual social history but is often misrecognized as inborn talent . . . we should not underestimate the extent to which dedicated training and masterful teaching contribute to producing 'stars' in a particular cultural field" (Ferrari, 2004, p. 233). Thus, whether the work in question is a technological breakthrough, a paradigm-shifting scientific theory, an aspiring singer's first CD, or an elementary school child's drawing and story, successful innovation requires some access to social capital.

By definition, a creative product, no matter how cutting-edge, consists of recombining elements of what already exists in unique ways; it bears the markings of what was invented previously and is not entirely new. For this, if for no other reason, we need to replace the metaphor that characterizes creativity as a bolt out of the blue and replace it with something completely different, such as the metaphor of a circuit board. The circuit board metaphor would characterize creative processes and tasks as a network of interconnected elements bound together by a shared background, which would represent, to extend the analogy, the cultural backdrop against which creative ideas, tasks, and products are played out. We need only to look around to see that our actions reflect a belief in social networks capable of stimulating creative thought and a conviction that some environments are more conducive to innovation than others. For example, students leave home to attend college, corporations invest millions in think tanks, and scientists work together in laboratory settings, all based on the assumption that particular environments and forms of interaction yield more creative outcomes. Rather than urging children to be creative in quiet solitude, we need to look at how creativity is nourished outside schools. Educators need to abandon the misconception that creativity flourishes only at the margins of society. "Many geniuses had to depend to a marked extent upon social skills and capabilities as well as on intellectual ones. Geniuses are often seen as essentially solitary individuals, but that depiction is not generally correct" (Howe, 2004, p. 116). Indeed, from a sociological perspective, intellectual innovations are not properties of individuals or ideas, but of dynamic networks and organizations (Collins, 1998).

TEACHERS' REFLECTIONS ON CREATIVITY, FAMILIES, AND COMMUNITIES

Preservice Teachers

"I completed a field experience in teaching during my sophomore year and again my junior year. One of the schools was in a low-income rural area and the parents and families were really in support of technology and they turned out in large numbers for any musical performances by the children. At the other school, most kids had better computers at home than at school and the parents and families were already thinking about how their kids would get into a good college. These parents seemed to associate the arts with being cultured rather than as a career path for their children. The differences in the two schools were really striking."

Inservice Teachers

"After reading an article about the educational uses of virtual reality (Cyranek, 2002), I have begun to think about it as a tool for learning rather than just an arcade game. It has possibilities as a more visual and interactive way of developing understanding and motivating students to apply what they have learned."

Your Reflections

- How are perspectives about creative thought and artistic expression affected by the individual child and family?

- Why is it important for teachers to evaluate their personal beliefs, classroom practices, and potential biases about creative expression and the arts?

- How can teachers persuade others that creative thought and the expressive arts make essential contributions to society?

Brain Research and Creative Thinking

Historically speaking, many deeply rooted dichotomies have dominated Western philosophy. Most people still believe, for example, that the following pairs of words are opposites: reason/imagination, science/art, and cognition/emotion. Even contemporary thinking contributes its own potential set of dichotomies by oversimplifying the results of brain research and treating the left side of the brain as analytical and practical and the right side as intuitive and holistic. This sort of either/or thinking has adverse consequences for creativity and innovation (Bruer, 1997; Lindsey, 1998/1999; Shore, 1997). As a society, we need to put these fragments back together again and recognize that the same brain that thinks also feels, and that the same brain that stores factual information also imagines what is not yet possible.

Complete this sentence: "The brain is like _____." If you are like most of your contemporaries, you said "a computer." If the same sentence-completion task had been posed in the 1950s, most people would have responded with "a machine." Examining the symbols or metaphors that we use to describe the human brain provides a glimpse into society's depth of understanding about the brain and its functioning. Now that we have increasingly sophisticated research about the brain, neither of these comparisons is adequate; a machine is too simple and a computer too linear. Countries that are advanced technologically often regard human creativity as the dividing line between human capacity and the capacity of computers. Donna Jo Napoli's (2001) discussion of whether computers ever can be expected to converse in ways that are indistinguishable from human interaction illustrates this point. The computer A.L.I.C.E. (http://www.alicebot.org), for example, responds to any question or statement with a preprogrammed statement or question from her database. Daisy, another computer, (http://www.leedberg.com/glsoft) is not preprogrammed; she tries to "learn" from the human. But whether programmed or not, these sophisticated pieces of equipment are not fluent conversational partners because they cannot respond to nuance and "fill in the blanks." To illustrate, Napoli (2001) offers the following question: "Why won't you go into that room?" and asks the reader to reflect on what a computer would do with the following answers: "Spiders." "Superstition." "No shoes." "No windows." "No reason." "I won't tell you." "Guess." (p. 107). As this example with supercomputers suggests, it is often nonlinear problem solving that is required in daily interactions as well as works of genius.

The human mind is conceived as an incredibly powerful parallel processor, always doing many things at once (Caine & Caine, 1991, 1997). Consider an ordinary task such as signing your name. Exactly what did you do when producing your signature? Analyze every detail of what is involved—the knowledge and skills that you needed, the experiences you had previously, every step involved in the task. If you brainstorm a list of everything involved, such as holding the pen, positioning the paper, forming each letter of the alphabet, making your signature distinctive, and knowing where to sign, you could probably come up with dozens of facts, subskills, actions, beliefs, values, and attitudes. Yet you probably did not think about any of those abilities in isolation or consciously analyze what you were doing (Neve, Hart, & Thomas, 1986). Your brain handled all of the necessary steps for you (Kline, 1995). While you were signing, your brain was helping you think about other things as well, such as the fact that you need to do some laundry, that it's raining outside, and that your chair is uncomfortable—in other words, your brain is not only running multiple chains of thought at the same time (Neve, Hart, & Thomas, 1986), but is also combining, editing, and readjusting them as they run. In fact, your brain could assemble a new pattern instantly if you were called on to sign 30 cover letters for job applications, versus signing a thank-you note to a friend, versus signing your name on a marriage license. From this point of view, (1) the brain's primary drive is to relate things to the real world, (2) the human brain is exceptionally effective at perceiving and processing patterns, and (3) learning is actually the acquisition of useful patterns of thought (Carnine, 1990; Kline, 1995).

Therefore, teaching in a way that is consistent with how the human brain works is compatible with everything that you have learned from this book thus far about creative expression and play. Figure 10.3 is an overview of the environmental, mental, emotional, and developmental conditions that foster creativity and respect the brain's natural way of functioning.

How Basic Is Creative Thinking?

A teacher held up a piece of purple construction paper and said, "What color is this?" Cris, a 5-year-old, thought for a moment and then answered, "graple." The teacher who is thinking inflexibly moves on, saying, "Can somebody help Cris?" But the teacher who really listens and respects children thinks about Cris's answer. It makes perfect sense. Cris has noticed—perhaps through direct experiences with

Teaching in a way that is consistent with the way the brain works supports developmentally appropriate practice.

- There are more than 15 million American children under age 4 (Kantrowitz, 1997).
- Researchers report that approximately half of the child's critical brain development occurs before kindergarten (Simmons & Sheehan, 1997).
- According to a study conducted by the National Goals Panel, the major risk factors for children under age 3 are inadequate prenatal care, isolated parents, substandard child care, poverty, and insufficient attention (Carnegie Corporation, 1994).
- A child is born with 100 billion neurons, which make over 50 trillion connections, called synapses. During the first 3 years of life, many more neural connections are made, literally trillions more than the brain can possibly use. Over time, those that are rarely or never used are eliminated, a process called "pruning" (Begley, 1997; Nash, 1997).
- The way in which the child is raised affects how the child's brain is wired; in other words, the early years are "when we create the promise of a child's future" (Simmons & Sheehan, 1997).
- A young child's brain development suffers if the child is not permitted to live in a healthy, safe, and stimulating environment. Researchers at Baylor College of Medicine found that children who don't play much or who are rarely touched develop brains 20 to 30 percent smaller than normal for their age (Nash, 1997).
- Research on the human brain suggests that three things contribute significantly to a child's well-being: (1) good prenatal care, (2) warm and loving attachments between young children and adults, and (3) positive, age-appropriate stimulation from the time of birth (Newberger, 1997).
- The connection between early experience and later experience is so strong that it led researchers to conclude that "early social and emotional experiences are the seeds of human intelligence" (Hancock & Wingert, 1997, p. 36).
- Neuroscientists have identified "windows of opportunity," particular time periods when the brain's circuitry matures. Different regions of the brain actively develop and mature according to certain timetables. During these periods, there is heightened sensitivity to environmental influences (Puckett, Marshall, & Davis, 1999).

Figure 10.3
Facts and Figures about Brain Research

Lollipops or beverages—that grape is the flavor associated with the color purple and has invented a word to make sense out of this observation. A good teacher might marvel out loud, saying with a tone of pleasure and surprise in her voice, "Grape-flavored things are usually purple, aren't they?" Cris's response falls somewhere between the historical dichotomies: between reason and feeling, between logic and imagination, between "left brain" and "right brain." That largely uncharted territory between what are incorrectly regarded as bipolar opposites is where genius lies. Every child—not just the compliant, the economically advantaged, or the gifted and talented—has creative potential just waiting to be set free by a great teacher. Figure 10.4 identifies the 12 qualities of genius that children possess.

1. **Curiosity:** A full-scale, active exploration of the world and ideas driven by the urge to make meaning and gain understanding.

Children have active imaginations and natural curiosity.

2. **Playfulness:** Experimenting with things and ideas in a spontaneous, intrinsically motivated way that is not bound by others' rules.

Children, even in the desperate circumstances of a war-torn country or natural disaster, manage to make playthings from the rubble.

3. **Creativity:** The ability to look at things differently, make surprising connections, and generate useful products.

Children are particularly adept at connecting the seemingly unconnected and creating interesting juxtapositions.

4. **Wonder:** Being awestruck by the world and astonished by what others might take for granted.

Children experience the world afresh and are amazed by what they encounter even when it seems commonplace to adults.

5. **Imagination:** Producing rich and varied images, even of things that do not exist.

Children's eidetic imagery—the richness of their mental images—is so strong that a frightening picture comes alive and nightmares seem real.

6. **Wisdom:** Delving beneath the surface to get to the heart of the matter.

Children have a fresh way of looking at things that often escapes their elders, who rely on years of experience.

7. **Inventiveness:** Producing surprising results from "hands-on" creativity.

Children are discoverers. They put the simplest materials to funny and sometimes bizarre uses. They play with the wrappings while the expensive gift sits idly by.

8. **Vitality:** Being awake to sensory input, responding to it fully, and actively engaged in experiences.

Children are noted for their energy levels and the passion with which they pursue their interests.

9. **Sensitivity:** Responding vividly to stimuli, thereby enriching what is experienced.

Children have a deep, yet naïve response to music, literature, and art.

10. **Flexibility:** Capitalizing on the plasticity of the mind.

Children move easily between fantasy and reality, between the inner world and outer world.

11. **Humor:** Breaking out of routine and leaving behind seriousness.

The child's sense of humor is at first slapstick, then incongruity, then word play.

12. **Joy:** Something that emanates from within when new connections, insights, feats, or skills are made.

The child finds delight in simple accomplishments.

Figure 10.4

Twelve Qualities of Genius in Every Child: Implications for Early Education

Note. Based on Armstrong (1998).

Educators overlook the genius of childhood if they allow rationality and logic to overshadow the child's natural affinity for nonliteral thinking (Egan, 1988). Rollo May (1975) poses a question that every educator should take to heart: "In our day of dedication to facts and hardheaded objectivity, we have disparaged imagination. . . . What if imagination and art are not frosting at all, but the fountainhead of human experience?" (pp. 149–150). Perhaps we have had it backward. Skills mastery is not the price of admission to creativity, as often is reflected in teachers' behavior. Students who are experiencing difficulties in mathematics or reading, for instance, may be assigned only low-level drill on the computer while classmates who are mastering these subjects are given opportunities to use the computer to design original materials, such as Web sites. Children who are in the gifted program may have mentors out in the community while others do not. Clearly, all children can benefit from using technology in creative ways and from good mentors. Yet schools often penalize children with an "eat your vegetables first" mentality about creative and artistic development. Often it is the opportunity for joyful creative expression that inspires learners to refine their skills.

Consider, for example, two children from different families who are learning to play the piano. Svetlana is an 8-year-old whose family immigrated to the United States from Russia. She has been taking lessons since she was 5, and has several talented musicians in her ancestry. Nevertheless, she says in complete candor to a visitor: "Please, just don't ask me to play the piano. I hate it." Zhu, the second child, first became interested in the piano as a toddler because she liked to sit on her grandfather's lap and experiment with the sounds made by the different keys. Sometimes they would sing songs together. Svetlana's parents believe that early, intensive drill on the technical skills will enable their child to realize her potential and surpass even the impressive achievements of her family members. There is little question that both children can play the piano at an advanced level; however, Svetlana's motivation and interest have been compromised by incessant drill and pressure. Which child is more likely to use music to enrich life? And who is more likely to develop the individual, interpretive style that is the hallmark of a great pianist? Teachers and parents must remember that although mastery of techniques is important, it should not be developed at the expense of creativity (Hope, 1990).

This describes the human resources we need in the future, but what can teachers expect from their teaching careers in the future? The next section describes some of the most recent predictions about the characteristics of tomorrow's children and classrooms.

TEACHERS' ROLES AND RESPONSIBILITIES

Educators have been criticized for decades for failing to foster creative thinking and artistic expression in their students. In 1950, J. P. Guilford, who was noted for his research into the structure of the intellect, became the president of the American Psychological Association. In his address, he asked "Why is there so little apparent correlation between education and creative productiveness?" (Fasko, 2001).

Environmental	Room arrangement that facilitates hands-on learning Independent access to materials Variety of media and resource materials
Mental	Flexible and stimulating environment Challenging (but not overwhelming) tasks Activities adapted to children's special needs
Emotional	Respect for children's contributions Support to take risks with new ideas and activities Honest, individualized praise
Developmental	Children's rates and styles of growth expected to vary Individual differences prized; cultural differences celebrated

Figure 10.5
Conditions That Support Creativity
Note. Adapted from Shallcross (1981).

In 1970, Charles Silberman noted that it was impossible to spend any prolonged period visiting public school classrooms without being appalled by the destruction of spontaneity, the joy of learning, the pleasure of creating, and self-esteem. What has been done to change this situation during the last three decades? Some would argue that very little progress has been made because the conditions that support creativity still have not been met (see Figure 10.5).

The place for novice and experienced teachers to begin is with reflective practice. First, *appreciate the family and cultural influences that shaped your self-image as a creative thinker.* What makes some teachers confident that they are creative thinkers? Why does the performance of some teachers improve with experience while the performance of others declines over the years? Figure 10.6 highlights the major influences on teachers' creativity.

It is interesting to reflect on the characteristics that are associated with creative teaching and how to develop them in yourself, something that Figure 10.7 guides you to do.

Second, *recognize the impediments to creative thought and expression.* Imagine that you are assigned to write a lesson plan and urged to "be creative." Think about all of the influences that might inhibit you from doing your best. Usually, our insecurities about thinking more creatively are affected by the following:

- *Fear of taking a risk.* Often, college students do not feel sufficiently safe and secure to "break out" and take the risks associated with being different. External pressures such as grades, peer ridicule, or the censure of the instructor might make us overly fearful of making a mistake. Internal feelings, such as not wanting to appear foolish or not wanting to be noticed, also inhibit creativity.
- *Premature criticism.* Teachers sometimes reject ideas almost immediately. A student teacher might write a lesson plan and keep deleting what was written, struggling to make the plan perfect from the very start rather than

→ **Education**

Teachers without specific training in creativity are not well equipped to serve as models of creativity for their students.

Conversely, teachers who are well informed about creative thinking processes can exert a powerful influence on their students' work.

→ **Expectations**

When teachers feel pressured to teach only the material that is tested, used to rank schools, or used to decide who is a "good" teacher, this inhibits their willingness to try new things.

Conversely, when teachers work in settings that expect and support new and interesting things from them, they are more likely to attempt new things and approach challenges positively.

→ **Resources**

When materials are in very scarce supply, it can interfere with planning for instruction and providing opportunities to be creative.

Conversely, when inviting materials are readily available, teachers are more likely to put them to use in their classrooms.

→ **Recognition**

When teachers' efforts to do more than follow the book and cover the material are disregarded, they sometimes give up and fall into the well-traveled ruts of marginal or "burned-out" teachers.

Conversely, when teachers gain the respect of their peers and leaders for daring to be different, they are more likely to continue to grow and develop as creative practitioners.

→ **Hope**

When teachers feel oppressed by lack of freedom, they feel disrespected and become apathetic and disaffected.

Conversely, when teachers are given choices, challenges, and support, they are more likely to rise to the occasion.

→ **Opportunities**

When teachers are deprived of opportunities for professional development in the area of creativity, they tend to teach the same things in the same ways, year after year.

Conversely, when teachers have opportunities to learn about and try out creative teaching strategies, they are more likely to expand their teaching repertoires beyond the ordinary.

→ **Rewards**

When teachers struggle to do more than what is minimally required and do not receive intrinsic or extrinsic rewards, their motivation to teach creatively is diminished.

Conversely, when teachers enjoy the satisfaction of a job well done and the admiration of others, they feel validated, encouraged, and energized to continue teaching creatively.

Figure 10.6

Influences on Teachers' Creativity

Note. Based on Csikszentmihalyi (1996), Piirto (1992), and Rodd (1999).

Nonconformist—Do I tend to behave, act, and think in unique ways? Am I capable of departing from routines, rules, and conventions? Am I committed to supporting children's creativity in spite of difficulties or other people's lack of support?

Inventor—When confronted with a daunting task, do I have the ability to generate a positive outcome through my resourcefulness and nonstereotypic thinking?

Self-Starter—Am I curious? Do I pursue my interests? Am I interested in knowing all that I can about something? Do I continue striving for a certain goal, not quitting until it is reached? Do I get involved in many different projects simultaneously?

Energizer—Am I willing to invest energy above and beyond what is required? Can I persuade others to join in?

Player—Do I create, understand, and take part in unexpected ideas and take pleasure in humor? Do I use humor effectively to deal with embarrassing or difficult situations?

Observer—Do I notice and remember details?

Spontaneous—Do I have the capacity to respond quickly and appropriately to unfamiliar situations?

Figure 10.7
Will You Become a Creative Teacher? A Self-Assessment
Note. Based on Csikszentmihalyi (1996) and Dinca (1999).

playing with ideas. Only after many possibilities are generated should teachers begin to exercise their more judgmental side.

- *Need for control.* If educators follow the safe, predictable path, they feel more in control of the situation. Writing a plan that is dry and ordinary, yet meets the minimal requirements, is a way of exercising control over uncertainty.

Third, *realize your power to affect children's perceptions of themselves as creative thinkers and artists.* Just about everyone who goes into teaching starts out intending to exert a positive influence on children's lives. Yet some teachers drift away from their original intentions and sink into indifference. One way to counteract stale or destructive teaching is to give yourself many opportunities to grow and learn and become a more creative human being.

As Raywid (1995) points out, teachers are powerful in their abilities to do the following:

- Establish and control the social dynamics of the classroom.
- Exert an emotional influence over children's self-appraisals.
- Exercise power over the content of a child's mind.
- Arbitrate the meaning of dialogue in educational settings for children.
- Function as a role model of habits of mind and work.

With this power comes enormous moral responsibility for the lives of children.

Fourth, *understand creative teaching.* Ask a group of teachers what it means to teach creatively and many of them will describe clever activities or visual aids that are used in the classroom. But teaching creatively is actually very different than this. It is the process of facilitating children's creative expression rather than something a teacher makes or does *for* the students. In other words, fostering creativity is an inside-out operation, not only for students but also for teachers themselves.

Fifth, *recognize creative processes and products.* The hallmark of the creative teacher is the high-quality work that his or her students produce. Creative products are:

- Novel, meaning that they are unusual and original.
- Appropriate, meaning that they are consistent with the goals of the person who created them.
- Meaningful, meaning that they are significant rather than trivial.
- Satisfying, meaning that the person who created them takes pleasure from having done so.
- Parsimonious, meaning that they are elegant in their simplicity (Amabile, 1989).

Children's creative processes and products shut down when they are forced to rigidly follow someone else's plan every step of the way. This is not to say that students will necessarily object to such direction. Actually, they may grow accustomed to it, even request it, because it requires little from them. However, just as college students might prefer a boring lecture that they can tune out over a class

Children's creative processes and products shut down when they are forced to rigidly follow someone else's plan every step of the way.

that requires active participation and demands preparation, children in the regimented curriculum are losing, not learning.

Sixth, *function as a leader in promoting creativity and the arts.* Teachers also bear responsibility for functioning as advocates, and Figure 10.8 provides guidelines for demonstrating your leadership in supporting creativity and the arts.

MEETING STANDARDS

Multicultural Education and the Arts

As Charles Silberman (1970) argued 30 years ago, "Education should prepare people not just to earn a living but to live a life—a creative, humane, and sensitive life" (p. 114). Take, for example, concerns about violence in schools and society. How might opportunities for creative expression support violence prevention efforts? The word *violence* originates in a word meaning "life force"; it has the same root word as *vital*. Originally, the word *violence* did not have the host of negative meanings that we attribute to it today. If we begin to think about violence as an outburst of life, we begin to see connections between creativity, or the life force put to good use, and the contemporary understanding of violence, or the life force put to destructive purposes. The goal of education never should be to cause children to become emotionally "flat." Rather, it should channel their interests, passions, and curiosities into socially acceptable and productive outlets. As Charles Fowler (quoted in O'Neil, 1994) contends, "We are creatures of feeling as well as thought, and schools that recognize that basic fact and address it are better schools. . . . Our spirit needs as much nurturing as any other part of our mind. Schools that ignore it are cold and desolate places. Remember: If we fail to touch the humanity of students, we have not really touched them at all" (p. 4).

Figure 10.9 illustrates the humanizing influence that creative expression and the arts can have on children.

Multicultural education is an important part of that humanizing process. According to James Banks (1996), a leading authority on multicultural education, the three major goals of multicultural education are (1) to know, (2) to care, and (3) to act. Additionally, Banks (1996) has identified four levels at which the three multicultural goals are achieved. The sections that follow examine how creative thinking and learning in the arts support each goal and level.

Level 1—Contributions

At this level, contributions are noticed and mentioned. Students might learn about an artist they have not heard of previously or learn to identify the work of a particular artist by his or her style; however, the curriculum is relatively unchanged. A teacher can begin working at the contributions level by providing students with many examples of art from different time periods and cultures in their immediate classroom environment. If there is access to the Internet and a color printer, many images can be printed and laminated for display from Web sites such as

Leadership Through Advocacy

- Learn to articulate your beliefs about the value of creative expression and play, even to those who are skeptical or nonsupportive.
- Take action to defend children's right to safe and healthy opportunities for play by engaging in activities such as cleaning up and painting an urban playground.
- Band together with respected colleagues to propose programs and policies that support children's creativity and play.

Administrative Leadership

- Join a task force, committee, or service organization that focuses on children's creative expression and play.
- Revamp the curriculum to infuse more opportunities for children to express themselves creatively and have time to play.
- Lead a group of colleagues in taking action to make your center or school an environment more conducive to children's and teachers' creativity.

Community Leadership

- Work with the community to develop an attractive display of children's work at the mall, in the local bank, or at a festival or fair.
- Join a discussion group on the Internet and share what you have learned about children's creative expression and play with parents and families.
- Seek sources of funding support for arts projects, including business sponsorship, grants, and other means of financial backing for the arts.

Conceptual Leadership

- Write a position paper on some area of children's creative expression, have it reviewed carefully by experts, then post it on the Web.
- Develop an informative bulletin board, newsletter, flyer, or other means of communication that can be shared with the general public.
- Join a group of classmates and a faculty member in making a professional conference presentation on children's creative expression and play.

Leadership Through Career Development

- Join a professional organization that supports children's creative expression and play, such as the National Association for the Education of Young Children, the Association for Childhood Education International, or the Reggio Emilia network.
- Scan the professional journals, such as *Early Childhood Education Journal, Childhood Education,* and *Young Children,* and surf the Net regularly for new information from organizations such as the Council for Exceptional Children, Americans for the Arts, and Music Educators National Conference.
- Further your education by volunteering to offer arts experiences for children, participating in conference sessions on creativity and play, and pursuing an advanced degree.

Figure 10.8

Leadership Activities to Support Children's Creativity and the Arts

Note. Based on Kagan & Bowman (1997).

Encouraging students to share their cultural backgrounds and beliefs helps promote understanding of diversity in the classroom.

Artcyclopedia.com. After the reproductions are hung where children can easily view them, teachers can engage the children in closely examining different categories of works of visual art (such as photographs, sculpture, textile art, and architecture) as well as styles and periods of art (such as commercial art, modern art, and folk art) and concepts of art (craftspersonship, art and technology, decoration, art and nature). It is important to give children multicultural experiences with art history and art criticism. Introduce them to artists and works of art from different cultural, ethnic, religious, and social class backgrounds. It is also important to show respect for works of art by avoiding disparaging terminology such as "primitive" in reference to tribal cultures' art.

Level 2—Additive

At this level, something is added to the curriculum without altering the rest of the program. Several examples of an additive approach would be a schoolwide project to recognize the contributions of African Americans, a study of regional crafts and craftspersons by all of the elementary art students, or a teacher's integrated unit on the contributions of women in science and math. In every case, the study is tacked onto the existing curriculum rather than subjected to substantial revision. Because these curriculum projects are not an "official" part of the curriculum, they might be abandoned when personnel changes occur.

From	To

Fear and Chaos → **Joy and Control**
Example: A child may resist using finger paints because they are "messy" and the child has been told to stay neat, yet with protective clothing, encouragement, and experimentation, that same child can relish the opportunity to make a finger painting.

Boredom and Routine → **Engagement and Surprise**
Example: Children are immersed in cartoon-style art at discount stores, as holiday decorations, at fast-food restaurants, and in the media, yet when they are given real works of art to examine closely and discuss, they break away from the ordinary and develop an aesthetic response to what is extraordinary and highly valued in society.

Frustration and Low Self-Esteem → **Mastery and Pride in Attainment**
Example: When first learning a simple folk dance, children may find it confusing or awkward, yet when they have supportive guidance and opportunities to practice, they experience the joy of mastering the dance and performing it gracefully.

Other Directedness and External Evaluation → **Self-Directedness and Self-Evaluation**
Example: Many of the questions and tasks that children encounter in school have one correct answer. Opportunities for creative expression give children greater responsibility for selecting tasks, pursuing them at their own pace, and evaluating both processes and products in terms of their personal satisfaction and sense of completeness.

Isolation and Exclusion → **Belonging and Community**
Example: Many creative children are cast in the role of outsiders in a society that values conformity and compliance, yet with opportunities to creatively address problems, to pursue a passion in the arts, or to participate in dramatic play, the strengths and talents of students who do not fit someone else's mold can be revealed and appreciated.

Figure 10.9
The Humanizing Influence of Opportunities for Creative Expression

Level 3—Transformation

At this level, a school infuses an array of cultural perspectives throughout the program and the basic curriculum changes. Instead of examining oil paintings of white European artists, for example, the study of art would give equal time to tribal masks designed by African artists or regalia designed by Native American tribes. Even more important, it would look at those works from multiple perspectives in ways that enrich and enlarge students' understandings of how creative thought and the arts shape a complex society. After children become aware of the contributions of artists and this is added to the curriculum, teachers can lead children to inquire about the artworks. Teachers can tell a bit of information about the artist or the time period and provide children's books about artists. Through open-ended questions—"What is going on in this picture?" "What more can you find?" "What do you see in this work that makes you say that?"—teachers build their students' strengths as beginning viewers (Yenawine, 1998).

Level 4—Decision Making and Social Action

The goal of Level 4 is social justice and positive changes to society. At Level 4, the school curriculum includes all of the previous levels and encourages students to make decisions and act on the concepts, issues, or problems they have identified. For instance, a group of students from rural Appalachia might select expanding social recognition of folk art as their goal. After students view a selection (teacher-selected slides or reproductions) of folk art portraits (Levels 1 and 2) they can represent themselves through some traditional folk art form, such as a quilt, a carving, a toy, or a doll (Level 3). Finally, students teach a student in a lower grade level how to produce the folk art form they selected. They also learn more about the crafts in their region and participate in community projects that gain more recognition for local artists, such as designing posters for a folk art festival and working with the media.

To summarize, the visual arts support multicultural education by helping children understand (1) the relevance and significance of art in human experience, (2) the perspectives posed by people of various backgrounds, (3) the commonality and diversity of humankind, and (4) the child's personal power as a creator of and responder to art, as well as the responsibilities that come with that power (Delacruz, 1995b).

CONCLUSION

Richards (2001) contends that society needs a general shift toward greater creative openness and growth, not only because it is an important form of adaptation in a complex, chaotic society but also because it offers advantages for physical and psychological health to the individual. The "personal inclinations required by the arts" are well suited to the demands of a rapidly changing society. These include play with images, ideas, and feelings; recognizing and constructing the multiple meanings of events; looking at things from different perspectives; and functioning as risk takers (Eisner, 1976). Highly creative individuals tend to seek challenges and be attracted to more multidimensional, unstructured problems—the very type that we are likely to confront in contemporary society. Thus, learning to think creatively and express oneself artistically are life skills; they are important ways to prepare children for whatever lies ahead.

In the past, in the present, and in the future, our most enlightened educational visions will be connected by the common thread of imagination, creative thought, and enhanced opportunities for artistic expression. As we look ahead, it will no doubt be possible to trace society's greatest innovations and achievements back to an abiding respect for creative thought processes during childhood. For when we value creative thinking and creative expression in society, it becomes part of our social consciousness and social capital. Society then protects its reserves of creativity by fashioning networks of support that are that are capable of instilling confidence, promoting resilience, and multiplying ways of being intelligent in every person that commence in childhood and continue throughout life.

Effective and ethical educators in a culturally pluralistic and democratic society have a responsibility to make a commitment to all children and to respect all the cultural groups and communities that those children represent. Without that

Frequently Asked Questions About Creativity, Diverse Families, and Communities

Do creative children usually become creative adults?

Based on extensive study of the early life of geniuses, Howe (2004) concluded that their patterns of development as children did not differ drastically from those who matured into unexceptional adults. Predictions about which children will become highly creative and productive as adults are notoriously inaccurate because creative gifts and contributions develop over time and are influenced by purpose, play, and chance (Gruber & Davis, 1988). Creative capacities can be underdeveloped, diminished, and ruined. Creativity is a complex developmental system that is shaped by at least seven influences: (1) cognitive processes; (2) social and emotional processes; (3) family aspects, both while growing up and current; (4) education and preparation, both informal and formal; (5) characteristics of the domain and field; (6) sociocultural contextual aspects; and (7) historical forces, events, and trends (Feldman, 1999, pp. 171–172).

What is a genius?

Defining genius is difficult because although it is used to label a person, it actually refers to the person's major creative achievements; "it is an accolade rather than a description" (Howe, 2004, p. 106). "Geniuses are, to say the least, an extremely diverse group. Some think predominantly in words, others contemplate images; some geniuses are highly intuitive, others are sharply analytical in their reasoning. But where character and temperament are concerned, shared attributes are more common . . . terms such as *curious, determined* and *diligent* apply to almost all highly creative achievers whose early lives I have explored . . . it is hard to think of any geniuses who have not relished hard work, or who have not been dogged in pursuit of their aims" (Howe, 2004, pp. 105, 110).

It seems that creativity is mainly innate, that some people are creative while others simply are not. Do you agree?

Creativity is a potential. Other traits such as interest, motivation, planning, attention, persistence, leadership, self-confidence, and self-esteem affect creativity (Amabile, 2001; Naglieri, 2001; Robinson & Clinkenbeard, 1998; Ryan & Deci, 2000). Stunning creative thought does not simply appear. Rather, it is the product of years of learning, thought, and preparation (Weisberg, 1993), and it is common to refer to the "3/10 rule"—at least 3 hours of practice per day for 10 years in order to become an expert in a field (Sternberg, 2004). Creative thought is domain specific and affected by the particulars of the situation (Han & Marvin, 2002). A person who is highly creative in one domain and environment—such as preparing a meal in a well-equipped kitchen—may appear to lack creativity in another situation—such as leading a meeting of investment bankers in a corporate boardroom. Therefore, children need to experience a wide range of interesting activities in order to discover their creative assets.

What can we learn from geniuses?

Perhaps the most important lesson is that being smart is not enough. "The lives and experiences of geniuses provide numerous demonstrations of the necessity for human qualities that go beyond the narrowly cognitive . . . little of enormous significance is achieved in the absence of diligence and the capacity for sustained hard work" (Howe, 2004, p. 117). Evidently, it is not a single, stunning talent that explains the lives of world-class geniuses, prodigies, and innovators; rather, it is a repertoire of strengths and a confluence of cultural circumstances that allow expression of remarkable achievements (Howe, 2004). Any understanding of true genius, then, must abandon the myth of the lone genius and regard genius as multifaceted (Shavinina & Ferrari, 2004). Several popular authors, notably Tony Buzan and Michael Gelb (http://www.michaelgelb.com), have written several books about what we can learn from geniuses and how to maximize creative potential.

Are there ways to make yourself more creative?

Few people possess "Big C Creativity," or the eminent creativity of celebrated geniuses, while many possess "little c creativity," or problem-solving ability that is more widely distributed among people (Craft, 2000;

Nakamura & Csikszentmihalyi, 2001; Ripple, 1989; Runco, 1996). Yet the contributions of everyday problem solving are so widespread and numerous that they may be just as valuable as the single, brilliant breakthrough. In Runco's (2004) review of the research, he identifies three general tactics that enable people to think more creatively: (1) change of perspective (taking time away from a task, incubating, traveling, or working backward); (2) use of analogies (developing productive mental models that lead to new insights, such as Eli Whitney inventing the cotton gin after watching a cat trying to catch a chicken through a fence); and (3) approaches that adapt or borrow (incorporating the approaches from another field, such as Jean Piaget drawing from his studies of biology to arrive at cognitive developmental theory).

commitment and respect, educators are incapable of addressing the needs of the diverse groups of students entrusted to their care. As educators, we need to bear in mind that, as Albert Einstein observed, "All the valuable things, material, spiritual, and moral, which we receive from society can be traced back through countless generations to certain creative individuals" (quoted in Gelb, 2002, p. 17).

CHAPTER SUMMARY

1. Creative expression and the arts are influenced by the social context in which they occur. The culture not only defines but also determines what "counts" as high ability, achievement, creativity, and art.
2. The technological era requires individuals who can think critically and independently. Education should foster the development of these traits in order for children to participate fully in society, both now and in the future.
3. Talent is important, but it is not enough. Even the most gifted individuals need systems of social support in order to realize their potential. Intelligence as it is commonly defined is not sufficient to result in high achievement either. Many "extracognitive" variables—those that rely on other talents—contribute to achievement and genius.
4. Parents, families, peers, instructors, and other significant others exert a powerful influence on the child's creative growth and artistic development.
5. There is a need to teach children in ways consistent with what we know about the functioning of the human brain. Research suggests that young children learn in a natural and integrative manner. Play, social interaction,

and psychological safety and freedom all contribute to children's learning and creative expression.

6. Fostering creativity in children and in ourselves as teachers is crucial as we confront the rapid-paced and challenging times ahead. Teaching is a moral craft because a teacher's power over children's lives in classrooms makes educators ethically and morally responsible for maximizing every child's talents and potential.

 Discuss: Contributions of Creativity and the Arts to Society

1. "It has become increasingly clear that millions of contemporary adults . . . have grown up with little or no grounding in the arts, and do not even consider participating in an artistic discipline or attending an arts event when choosing among their leisure and entertainment options" (McDaniel & Thorn, 1997, p. 6). Would you classify yourself among these adults? Why or why not? What might the implications of rejecting the arts be for your values and attitudes as a teacher?

2. President Franklin Delano Roosevelt once said, "Inequality may linger in the world of material things, but great music, great literature, great art, and the wonders of science are, and should be, open to all." Describe some practical ways that you could use your influence as a teacher to promote equity and openness in access to the wonders of the arts. How might you inform and encourage families regarding the resources and opportunities within the community that would promote children's creativity and experiences in the arts?

3. Culturally speaking, the purpose of the arts is "to destabilize fixed ideas and existing identities; to help us find a new way of seeing, of hearing, of thinking, of feeling . . . And to find from those experiences new ways of experiencing our communities, our neighbors, our society" (Nolan, quoted in Jones et al., 1996, p. 48). Suppose that you were teaching in a school with students who had recently emigrated from another country. How could you use the arts as a way to build respect for these newcomers?

4. At what point does parental challenge and support cross the line and become an instance of a parent "living through" a child? What is the difference between the "stage mom or dad" and a supportive parent? What goals need to be balanced to prevent children from being exploited? What would you do or say to help a child if it was obvious that the child's parent or family had become obsessed with making their child a star, to the detriment of the child?

Appendix A

Dance Prop Box

THEME: DANCE/MOVEMENT

GOALS FOR CENTER

- To provide opportunities to move from thinking and feeling to the physical expression of thought and emotion.
- To provide opportunities for role-playing experiences such as aerobics instructor, ballet dancer, or square dancer.
- To encourage oral language expression in describing different kinds of dances and feelings about dancing.
- To provide opportunities for talking about health, fitness, and relaxation.

MATERIALS IN PROP BOX

Mats	Hats	Mats
Feathers	Headdress	Assorted dance shoes
Tiaras	Gloves	Leotards
Boas	Balloons	Tights
Bandannas	Tutus	Dance recital costumes
Ribbons	Pompoms	Tambourines
Long skirts	Baton	Masks
Balls	Vests	

SUGGESTED SUPPLEMENTS AND MATERIALS

Book or story about dance	Hand mirror	Record player
Records or tapes for dance	Full-length mirror	Cubes
Posters of dancers	Tape player	Ballet bar

VOCABULARY

Aerobics	Circle right	Modern dance
Arabesque	Folk dancing	Plié
Ballerina	Jazz	Positions of the feet
Ballet	Jumping jacks	Recital
Choreographer	March	Rhythm
Circle left	Mask	Square dance

CHILD-MADE MATERIALS

Tambourines

Signs about the dance

Masks or headdresses

RESOURCE PEOPLE AND FIELD TRIPS

Fathers, mothers, and friends of students who are dancers could come to class and tell what they do during a day of work. The class could visit a local dance studio or children's dance theater, watch a video, or attend a film or a ballet.

INTRODUCTION OF CENTER

"Welcome to the Dance Center"

Discuss what the children know about dance and about why people dance.

Explain different types of dance (e.g., ballet, folk, modern, jazz, and square dancing).

Ask the students how many have seen or participated in a dance.

Discuss the different roles they can play at the dance center: ballerina, modern dancer, tap dancer, ballroom dancer, aerobics teacher, or choreographer.

Set a limit of four children in the center. As space becomes available, children may choose to join the dancers.

Model different dance forms to introduce some of the vocabulary, if appropriate.

ACTIVITIES

Inform the families of the new center and invite them to share dance experiences with their children.

Encourage children to try out all roles in the dance center.

Use photographs of children dancing to add to the dance book.

Visit an aerobics studio or watch a videotape of dance performances. Encourage children to imagine themselves as dancers, draw pictures, or write a story about themselves as dancers.

Ask children to choreograph their own dance. Read "I Like Me!" "I Dance in My Red Pajamas," and "The Camel Dances" from Arnold Lobel's *Fables*.

ADDITIONAL IDEAS FOR PROP BOXES

Doctor's Office
Telephone, appointment book, tongue depressors, prescription pads and empty bottles, cotton balls, stethoscope, pencils, examination mat, dolls, doll bed, bandages

Space
Sleeping bag, Ziploc bags for food, telescope, steering wheel, control panel, space suit, helmet

Birthday Party
Candles, streamers, markers, paper, cake pans, wrapping paper, boxes, invitations

Library
Children's books with pockets made from cut envelopes, videotapes, library cards, pencils, signs for story hours, cards for book pockets, date stamp and ink pad, cash register, money, book-return box

Restaurant
Aprons, chef's hat, menus, tray, pitcher, silverware, dishes, stove top (bottom of box), play money, cash register, pencils and order pads

Gas Station
Spray bottles and paper towels, used and cleaned motor parts, hammer, oil funnel, flashlight, old rags, keys, automobile supply catalogues, hoses

PROP BOXES FOR FAIRY TALES

Little Red Riding Hood
Tape recording and book of the story, red sweater or cape, basket for red apron, bow, spoon for mother, ball cap with ears for wolf, axe and hat for woodcutter, bonnet for grandmother

The Three Bears
Tape recording and book of the story, three different-sized bowls, spoons, blankets, three different hats for bears, hat or collar for Goldilocks, three stuffed bears

The Elves and the Shoemaker
Tape recording and book of the story, a few pairs of old shoes, shawl for old woman, apron for old man, doll clothes for elves, piece of brown or black felt representing leather

Cinderella
Tape recording and book of the story, apron for Cinderella, high-heeled shoe for slipper, hats for stepaunts, crown for prince

Hansel and Gretel
Tape recording and book of the story, hat and axe for father, scarf for stepmother, bonnet for Gretel, hat for Hansel, witch hat for the witch, dog bone (block)

Snow White and Rose Red
Tape recording and book of the story, apron for mother, white and red plastic flowers, scissors from classroom, bags or boxes of beads for jewels, pixie hat for gnome, brown garbage bag for bear, crown for prince, red and white collars

Source: Courtesy of Dorothy Nadeau.

Appendix B

Published Rating Scales to Evaluate Preschool Settings

Frost, J. L. (1986). Playground rating system: Ages 3–8. In J. S. McKee (Ed.), *Play: Working partner of growth* (pp. 66–67). Wheaton, MD: Association for Childhood Education International.

The rating system contains 39 items to evaluate three different areas of playground quality. It evaluates what the playground should contain, the condition and safety of the equipment, and the degree and quality of challenge and learning opportunities for children. Each item is rated on a scale from 0 ("Does Not Exist") to 5 ("Excellent; All Elements"). A score may be obtained for each individual area, as well as a total playground rating score.

Harms, T., & Clifford, R. M. (1989). *Family day care rating scale*. New York: Teachers College Press. 39 pages.

This scale defines family day care comprehensively and can be used for evaluating family day care settings. It provides ratings for space, materials, and learning activities among the six categories addressed to ensure that the environment is developmentally appropriate for young children. Each item is described in four levels of quality ranging from "Inadequate" (does not meet custodial needs) to "Excellent" (high-quality care).

Harms, T., & Clifford, R. M. (1995). *School-age care environment rating scale*. New York: Teachers College Press.

The SACERS provides a resource for identifying high-quality environments offered by schools and other organizations. The scale contains 49 items; organized within seven categories that include Space and Furnishings, Health and Safety, Activities, Interactions, Program Structure, and Staff Development.

Harms, T., Clifford, R. M., & Cryer, D. (1998). *Early childhood environment rating scale* (Rev. ed.). New York: Teachers College Press. 44 pages.
This rating scale provides guidelines for assessing the quality of the physical and social environments for young children in seven areas. Detailed guidelines are provided for room arrangement, furnishings, and displays, as well as for creative activities.

Harms, T., Cryer, D., & Clifford, R. M. (1990). *Infant/toddler environment rating scale.* New York: Teachers College Press. 48 pages.
This rating scale contains assessment criteria for children in group care up to 30 months of age. Criteria for furnishings and displays for children, space, learning activities, and program structure are among the seven categories rated from "Inadequate" (not meeting custodial care needs) to "Excellent" (describing high-quality care).

Jones, E. (1977). *Dimensions of teaching-learning environments.* Pasadena, CA: Pacific Oaks.
This rating scale describes the physical setting and the teacher's behavior along four dimensions: soft/hard, simple/complex, intrusion/seclusion, and high mobility/low mobility. It views these dimensions along a continuum and explores the possibilities of arranging environments within them.

National Association for the Education of Young Children. (1998). *Accreditation criteria and procedures of the National Association for the Education of Young Children.* Washington, DC: Author.
Contains standards for early childhood programs set by the profession. A portion of these standards describes nine aspects of the physical environment. The scale focuses on the arrangement of the environment, selection of materials, and interactions between adults and children.

Appendix C

Noncompetitive Games for Children

BALL GAMES
Preschoolers/Kindergartners
Call Ball
Form a circle with one child in the center who tosses the ball while calling another child's name. This child tries to catch the ball after the first bounce. The child continues with other children.

Basket Ball
Children stand before a plastic basket and toss the ball into the basket. The game may be played individually, in pairs, or in groups. Emphasis is on trying to hit the mark rather than keeping score, so move the basket closer or farther away to adjust the challenge level.

School-Age Children
Letter or Number Ball
As players pass a small ball around a circle, have them say a letter or a number. Players may count or say the alphabet in unison if they go in order.

Tennis
Make "rackets" out of a nylon stocking stretched over a coat hanger. Children can bat a ping-pong ball back and forth using the racket.

Lap Ball
Players form a circle and sit close to one another, with shoulders touching. They try to pass a ball around the circle from lap to lap without using their hands.

431

QUIET GAMES
Preschoolers/Kindergartners
Nursery Rhymes
Say the rhyme and follow up with action. For example: "Jack and Jill went up (children reach up high) the hill. Jack falls down (children touch the ground)." Other favorite nursery rhymes include "Humpty Dumpty," "Mary Had a Little Lamb," and "Baa Baa Black Sheep."

Toyshop
Have children pretend they are toys. When called on, each child imitates the sound and action of the toy and continues until someone guesses the name of the toy.

Clap and Tap Names
In this game, say a child's name and have the group repeat it several times, establishing a rhythm for the name. Then have the children clap the rhythm of the name while they say it. Ask them to use their feet while saying the name and, last, to move forward on that rhythm.

School-Age Children
On My Way to School . . .
Form a circle with one child in the center who says, "On my way to school this morning, I saw . . . " and then imitates what he or she saw. Others guess the imitation. The one guessing correctly goes into the center, and the game begins again.

Buzz
Players take turns counting one number at a time. Whenever they have to say a number with seven in it, they say buzz instead. If a player accidentally says *seven* (or *seventeen*, or *twenty-seven*), then the game begins again at number one.

SINGING GAMES
Preschoolers/Kindergartners
Charlie over the Water
Players join hands in a circle. One player, Charlie, is in the center. The circle moves to the left while chanting:

> *Charlie over the water,*
> *Charlie over the sea,*
> *Charlie caught a blackbird*
> *But he can't catch me.*

On the word *me* the players quickly squat. Charlie tries to tag a player before he or she gets into the squat position. The tagged child then becomes "Charlie."

Round and Round Went the Gallant Ship

In this game, children dance around in a circle with clasped hands, reciting the following verse and "bobbing" down quickly as the ship goes to the bottom of the sea:

Three times round went our gallant ship,
And three times round went she;
Three times round went our gallant ship,
Then she sank to the bottom of the sea.

A tumble as the ship goes down adds much to the spirit of the play.

Did You Ever See a Lassie?

One child is in the middle of a circle. Other children grasp hands and circle around the child in the center while singing the first two lines. During lines three and four, the children drop hands and imitate the child in the middle, who thinks up some special way to hop.

Did you ever see a lassie (laddie), a lassie, a lassie,
Did you ever see a lassie, do this way and that?
Do this way and that way, and this way and that way,
Did you ever see a lassie do this way and that?

School-Age Children

Riggety Jig

The children form a standing circle. One child begins to skip inside the circle to the following tune:

As I was going down the street
Down the street, down the street
As I was going down the street
Hi Ho, Hi Ho, Hi Ho.
A handsome fellow (pretty girl) I chanced to meet
Chanced to meet, chanced to meet
A handsome fellow (pretty girl) I chanced to meet
Hi Ho, Hi Ho, Hi Ho.

With the chosen partner, both children skip around the circle to the following tune:

Riggety jig, jig, and away we go
Away we go, away we go
Riggety jig, jig, and away we go
Hi Ho, Hi Ho, Hi Ho.

Others clap the tune.

Singing Syllables
After one player leaves the room, the rest of the group decides on a word to sing. If the word is *November*, for example, some players will sing "No No No," some will sing "vem vem vem," and the rest will sing "ber ber ber," all at the same time.

Now the player who left the room returns and tries to figure out what the word is. Everyone gets a turn to be the guesser, with, of course, a new word sung each time.

RUNNING GAMES
Preschoolers/Kindergartners
Squirrel and Nut
The children sit in a circle with heads down and hands open. One child, the squirrel, drops the "nut" (a piece of chalk or crayon) into the hands of any other child. That child immediately gets up and tries to catch the squirrel, who is safe by reaching the place of the second child. If not caught, the other child becomes the squirrel.

Cat and Mice
The cat hides behind something. Four of five "mice" creep up to the cat's hiding place and start scratching on the floor. Their scratching is the signal for the cat to start chasing them, and they are safe only on reaching their holes (places). Any mouse who is tapped becomes the cat. Other mice are then chosen, and the game begins again.

Drop the Handkerchief
One child runs around the circle and drops a handkerchief behind another player. That player picks up the handkerchief and runs around the circle in the direction opposite to that of the first player. The one who reaches the vacant place left in the circle becomes "it." Then the game is repeated.

Musical Chairs
One version of musical chairs is to play music and have children find a chair *or* a lap when the music stops. A chair is removed each time, but everyone finds a seat (by sitting on a lap).

School-Age Children
Numbers Change
Players stand in a large circle and are numbered consecutively. One player, in the center, calls two numbers (not his or her own). The center player tries to secure one of their places. The one who is left without a place now becomes the center player.

In the classroom, the number caller (who also has a number) stands in front of the room and calls two numbers. While players change places, the caller tries to take a seat vacated by one of the runners whose number was called.

Kitty in the Corner

The children form a circle on the floor. Four chairs are placed in four corners of a square. A fifth child is in the middle. When the teacher calls "Kitty in the corner," the children in the chairs change places while the child in the center seeks to get into one of the chairs. The displaced child then chooses someone to take his or her place until all have had a turn.

Squirrels in Trees

The group is divided and numbered in threes. Numbers 1 and 2 join hands to represent the tree. Number 3 is the squirrel and stands in the circle formed by the other two. There should be one or more odd squirrels without trees. The groups of threes are scattered over the play space. At a signal from a leader or the teacher, the squirrels attempt to get into trees. Only one squirrel is allowed in one tree at the same time. Someone is always left without a tree. As soon as all trees are full, the game is repeated.

PARTNER GAMES

Preschoolers/Kindergartners

Repeat

One player says a word that the other player repeats. Continue repeating the same word until one player wants to stop, which is the tricky part.

Finish My Action

One player begins an imaginary action, such as brushing teeth or raking leaves. When that player stops, the partner finishes the action. Then the partners switch roles.

School-Age Children

Copycat

With a partner, decide who will be the mirror and who will be the copycat. Players must face each other as they stay together mirroring actions.

Puppeteers

One player is the puppet on the ground, unable to move. Along comes the puppeteer, who brings the puppet to life with pretend strings. The puppeteer pulls the strings, and the puppet responds to every tug. Allow everyone a chance to be the puppeteer as well as to be the puppet.

Ali Baba and the Forty Thieves

Two players stand facing each other a few feet apart. One of the players sings the words "Ali Baba and the forty thieves" to any made-up tune, at the same time doing a hand movement, such as clapping. When the singer is finished, the second player repeats the song and the motions exactly; at the same time, the first player sings the phrase again and does something different with his or her hands—hitting one arm with the opposite hand, for example.

For the next round, the second player must copy this second set of movements, along with continuing to sing, and so on, with both players singing "Ali Baba and the forty thieves" over and over, each doing a different hand movement. The activity continues until one of the players forgets the line.

REFERENCES

Gregson, B. (1984). *The outrageous outdoor games book.* Carthage, IL: Fearon.

Kamii, C., & DeVries, R. (1980). *Group games in early education: Implications for Piaget's theory.* Washington, DC: National Association for the Education of Young Children.

Orlick, T. (1978, 1982). *The cooperative sports and games book* and *The second cooperative sports and games book.* New York: Pantheon.

Rowe, S., & Humphries, S. (1994). *Playing around: Activities and excursions for social and cooperative learning.* London: Forbes.

Sobel, J. (1983). *Everybody wins: Non-competitive games for young children.* New York: Walker.

Appendix D

Observations of Medical Play

APRIL 8: GETTING STARTED

Nick (doctor):   Come in, come in! (Puts stethoscope around neck.) Where's your heart?
Allen: Right here.
Nick: Nurse, get me the blood pressure kit.
Amanda: Where's my hat? A nurse can wear a hat, but I don't have one. Well, I'll put this nice new pretend hat on. There! How do I look?
Teacher: Amanda, you look just like the nurse at my doctor's office.

APRIL 15: DRAWING ON PRIOR EXPERIENCE

Teacher (mother):   It won't hurt my baby? Are you sure?
Markus (doctor):   Hold on to him, Mommy. Where do you think he should get his shot at?
Teacher: How about his arm?
Markus: How about his foot? I got a shot in my foot one time for stepping on a nail. A tennis shot.
Teacher: Do you mean a tetanus shot?
Markus: Yeah, that's it.

APRIL 22: BUILDING VOCABULARY

Mallory: What's that? I can't remember, and I need to use it.
Teacher: That's a thermometer. It tells you the temperature of your body.
Mallory: Oh, yeah, I remember.
Jeremy: Where's the heart thing? I want to listen to someone's heart.
Teacher: Here's the stethoscope.

437

APRIL 27: REALITY TESTING

Allen: My leg hurts, Doc.

Nick: I'll put this on. (Puts an Ace bandage on for a few seconds.) Now it's time to take it off and see if your leg is better. (Allen begins removing the bandage.)

Teacher: Allen, would the patient take off his own bandage?

Allen: Whoops. Hey, Doc, take off my bandage!

Nick: Your leg's all better, but I have to give you a shot. Now lay down. Now I'm gonna give you a shot, but I'm gonna put these cotton balls in your mouth first. (Giggles and starts to move toward Allen's mouth.)

Teacher: Nick, when you go to the doctor, how does he really use the cotton ball?

Nick: (Begins to rub Allen's arm with the cotton ball.)

APRIL 29: INTRODUCING NEW MATERIALS AND CONCEPTS

Teacher: I am a blood pressure kit salesperson. I would like to demonstrate how to use our new and improved blood pressure kit. First, you have the patient hold out her arm. Then you carefully put the arm cuff on like this. Next, you put the end of the stethoscope right under the cuff and hold it. Then you pump it up only three times and watch the needle. That's how you use this new kit. If you have any questions, just call me.

MAY 4: THE HIGH PRICE OF MEDICAL CARE

Today the theme of medical costs was introduced by Markus, who was playing the doctor and charged exorbitant rates. When the patient paid him, he said, "I'm rich! I'm rich!"

Teacher: How much do I owe for today's visit?

Kara: You owe me $235. Pay me now. (Holds out hand.)

Teacher: Here you go.

MAY 6: NEGOTIATION

Kara and Michelle started to argue about who will play the doctor and who will be the nurse.

Michelle: Okay, you can look at his throat and ears, and I'll do the eye chart and see how tall he is.

Kara: And you can do the blood pressure, and I'll give him a shot and listen to his body.

Michelle: Allen, stand against the wall here. (She puts her hand just above his head and looks at the chart.) Allen, move away. You are four feet one inch.

Later, Kara was the patient.

Allen: Okay, Kara, cover your eye and say those letters.

Kara: Those are small letters. Ready? (Reads all the letters.) There, I did it! (Big smile.) And I didn't even miss one. (Checks the chart with both eyes uncovered.)

MAY 9: INCORPORATING NEW VOCABULARY

Greg was the nurse. He said that he had a telephone call and needed to go to the scene of an accident. I asked him if nurses usually did that. He wasn't sure. I explained that the people who go to accidents in an ambulance are called *paramedics*. Later, Greg got another accident call and said, "I'm sorry, I can't come. You need the paramedics. I'll call 911 and get an ambulance with paramedics on it. They'll save 'em."

(Notepads, an appointment book, and a ballpoint pen were added to the center.) Michelle is playing the role of doctor and asks, "Why do I have paper?"

The teacher answered: "Did you ever see doctors write a prescription? The doctor writes down what kind of medicine you should take."

(Later) Michelle: I got my paper to write stuff out. Who needs a prescription? Who needs a bill?
Melanie: What do you do with a prescription?
Michelle: You take it to a drugstore and they give you the medicine you need from what's written on the paper.

MAY 13: CONNECTING WITH LIFE

Letha has been in and out of the hospital because she was diagnosed as having cancer (now in remission). When she returned to school, I changed the center to a veterinarian's office during our pets theme. Throughout the children's play, I heard her refer to her hospital experiences. Some examples of statements she made were "Is this like a people hospital? I was in a people hospital a long time."

When Brandon tried to give her a shot, she said, "Not me! I had enough shots already in the hospital. I got blood taken lots of times. The thing they used looked just like this, except longer." Their conversation continued:

Brandon: I never had that done. I'll take some blood from the dog to examine.
Letha: I'll show you how, okay? You need to put on your mask like real doctors do.
Brandon: What is the mask for?
Kurt: My bear broke his head. He was standing on his chair and fell off.
Brandon: I'll x-ray his head. But I gotta put my mask on first.
Kurt: Why?
Brandon: So I don't spit my gum on him. No. To keep out the germs.
Maryjane: Germs? Did I hear someone say germs? This is a hospital. There should not be germs. Get out, get out.
Markus: Guys, I got a . . . I got a . . . I need something. I got a sick fox here.
Brandon: Wait, I'm taking care of this one.
Amanda: I had a pet rabbit one time, I mean, a long time ago at home. His name was Henny. He was really sick, and he died a long time ago. My mom thought he would die, and he did.
Melanie: I had a gerbil, and my mom thought he was gonna die because we forgot to feed him.

MAY 16: SYMBOLIC PLAY

Shawn: I'm the doctor today.

Scott: No, I am.

Shawn: We both are. It's a big petpital.

Scott: What's a petpital?

Shawn: It's a hospital for pets.

Allen: When my brother went to the doctor's, they found out how much he weighed and how tall he got.

Teacher: Maybe we could do that for one of our animals.

Jeremy: Yeah. Let's see. I'll use this block for the uh, what's that thing called?

Letha: A scale.

Jeremy: (Brings over a toy duck.) We need to weight him.

Shayna: I'm the nurse. Put your duck on the scale, and I'll measure him.

Letha: My duck is a girl.

Shayna: Sorry. She weights, uumm . . .

Jeremy: Twenty-five million pounds!

Letha: She does not. Your scale must be broke.

Jeremy: Okay, 13 pounds.

Shayna: She's 1 foot tall, too.

MAY 18: SEX ROLE STEREOTYPES

Dee: Can I play?

Scott: No, we have two doctors and nurses. That's enough.

Teacher: I think we can find something for Dee to do.

Dee: I could be the ambulance driver.

Scott: No, you cannot.

Dee: Why?

Scott: Because! You're a girl, and girls can't be ambulance drivers.

Amanda: They can too!

Shawn: Can not.

Teacher: Scott and Shawn, why do you think that girls can't be ambulance drivers?

Scott: Because men drive better.

Shawn: Yeah.

Amanda: No, they do not.

Maryjane: Men drive lousy.

Teacher: Girls can be ambulance drivers just like boys. Girls can be doctors and boys can be nurses. My doctor is a woman.

Dee: I'm gonna find something to use for my—*my* ambulance. Whoo, whoo, ambulance comin' through. Hey, there's a sick fox over here. What kind of hospital is this anyway? I said I got a sick fox over here!

Maryjane: Oh! Hey, we need a doctor over here. We have a patient.

Shawn: I'm coming. Hold your pants on. (Children from the camping play center come over.) I wish these guys would stop coming and bugging me and my patient. This is a hospital, not a picnic. Geez.

Appendix E

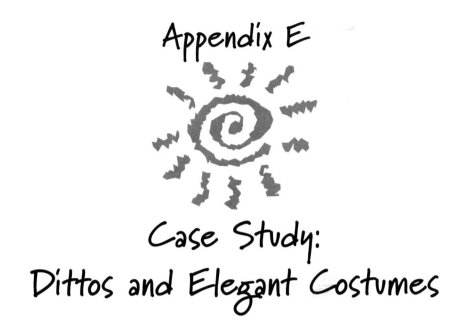

Case Study:
Dittos and Elegant Costumes

Case methodology is a form of problem-based instruction for adults. Cases help learners experience situations that they are *likely to experience* in their professional settings. Use this case to help you analyze problems of communicating about play to parents and colleagues, to set goals about play for your own professional setting, and to share your ideas about appropriate ways to respond to parental concerns about too much play in the classroom.

DITTOS AND ELEGANT COSTUMES

"What do you think of this, Clara?" asked her principal, setting a three-page single-spaced letter from a parent in front of Clara just a few minutes before school began one morning. Clara, her assistant, and her student teacher were busy preparing the room for the students' arrival, and the contents of the letter came as a complete surprise to her. As she read she felt her anger rise and a flush move from her neck up to her cheek then to her forehead as she tried to hold on to some sense of composure.

"We want Lauren moved from Miss Sparks' kindergarten class immediately," the letter began. "There is no comparison between the two classes. All Lauren does is play, play, play. She is not learning a thing. The class never does anything. The children in Mrs. Wolfe's class put on a play just last week with elegant costumes. Each child had memorized long parts and lots of songs. Our neighbor's child is in Mrs. Wolfe's class, and his pictures come home looking like they are supposed to. And the ditto sheets that they do are really helping him learn."

There was more, but Clara looked up at the principal with hurt in her eyes. "Lauren's parents just don't understand. They don't want to understand that there are other ways of teaching young children besides elaborate productions and ditto sheets—perhaps even better ways. What shall we do?"

"I don't know, Clara. I need to think about it for awhile. But I know that I will need to talk with Lauren's parents soon."

"I have talked with them so many times myself," said Clara, "but somehow it just doesn't do any good. I hate it, being put on the defensive this way."

The principal left, leaving Clara to try to salvage what remained of her morning. Soon the children arrived, and she became swept up in the momentum of the day's activities. She had no time to reflect on her own teaching philosophy and style until much later, during free choice activity time. She looked out over her class busily engaged in learning activities of their own choosing: on the floor, at tables, standing up, sitting down, moving around, quiet and chatty.

Her eyes caught Jenny. Jenny was up to her elbows in soapsuds, her face intent, her eyes sparkling. There was a daub of white at the end of her nose. "A, B, C, D, E," Jenny sang to herself as she wrote letters in the soap on the table's surface.

Clara walked over to Tommy. His eyebrows were puckered, and his whole countenance concentrated on his task. Tommy was hammering a nail at the woodworking table.

"Look, Miss Sparks! With one nail, the pieces wiggle. Two nails hold it steady," he exclaimed.

Sally and Louise then approached Clara, their heads covered with scarves, each carrying a basket.

"We're on our way to Grandma's house, Miss Sparks," said Louise. "Would you like a cookie?"

"Only if you'll be careful never to talk with strangers," replied Clara.

"Oh, we won't. We never do," the girls answered, moving on again around the room, the path invisible to all but their own eyes.

Clara continued to watch the children, jotting down a note here and there for her anecdotal records, involving herself where necessary to keep the flow of learning strong and creative. As she worked, she felt her confidence return, and at the end of the free choice time she continued her day with renewed vigor. She liked what she was doing. She was convinced that her child-centered approach to teaching was right for children.

On the way home that afternoon Clara gathered her anecdotal records about Lauren. She needed to touch base with the principal before leaving the building to clarify her own role in the matter and to find out what the principal planned to do next.

She walked out past the other kindergarten room with its displays of children's work on the walls, each one a carbon copy of the next.

"Good night," Clara called to her colleague, Mrs. Wolfe, still in her classroom.

"Oh, Clara, could we talk a minute?" Mrs. Wolfe answered. Clara stopped and went in.

"I don't know how to say this, Clara, so I'll just say it," Mrs. Wolfe began. "Lauren's mother stopped in to see me today and told me that she asked to have Lauren moved to my room. She said that many of her neighbors feel the same way about you, and that the discussions about kindergarten in the neighborhood are angry ones. They're out to get you, Clara, and I thought you'd want to know."

Clara looked at her colleague, stunned. . . .

Study Questions

Think about the above case and write down your thoughts about these questions. Be prepared to use your responses to share with your group at another class meeting.

1.   What is the problem here? Why? Explain what you mean.
2.   What are the issues in this case? Explain. Give an example from the case to illustrate each one.
3.   How powerful is the neighborhood gossip mill? What are some appropriate ways to deal with it?
4.   To what and to whom is Clara responsible? Explain.
5.   What is the role of the principal? Why?
6.   If you were Clara, what would you do and why?

Source: Courtesy of George Mason University Case Writing Team.

Appendix F

Resources for Play Materials

SELECTING AND USING SAFE PLAY MATERIALS

Bronson, M. (1995). *The right stuff for children birth to age 8*. Washington, DC: National Association for the Education of Young Children.
Provides a detailed list of age appropriate materials that are organized by different types of play.

Moyer, J. (Ed.). (1995). *Selecting educational equipment and materials for school and home*. Wheaton, MD: Association for Childhood Education International.
Contains lists of materials and equipment for classrooms for children ages birth through age 10 as well as a listing of developmentally appropriate materials that promote each type of play.

U.S. Consumer Product Safety Commission (1993, 1994). *Which toy for which child? A consumer's guide for selecting suitable toys: Ages birth through five* and *Which toy for which child? A consumer's guide for selecting suitable toys: Ages six through twelve.*
List basic safety guidelines and age-appropriate toys and materials. For additional information, write to: U.S. Consumer Product Safety Commission, Washington, DC 20207.

FREE CLASSROOM PLAY MATERIALS

For 120 decks of cards and 100 sets of dice to use as number cards for math and that are free of charge, write a letter stating you are a teacher and would like to have the cards and dice for use in your classroom. Include your name and address and send to:

Sands Hotel-Casino
136 S. Kentucky Ave.
Atlantic City, NJ 08401 (Allow 4 months for processing your request.)

FOLKLIFE AND CULTURAL ARTIFACTS

For advisory information on folklife resources and cultural artifacts, contact the following national, regional, or local agencies.

National Agencies

American Folklife Center
Library of Congress
101 Independence Ave. S.E.
Washington, DC 20540-4610
(202) 707-5510
New York Center for Urban Folk Culture
72 E. 1st St.
New York, NY 10003
(212) 529-1955

Regional Agencies

Southern Arts Federation
1401 Peachtree St. N.E., Suite 460
Atlanta, GA 30309
(404) 874-7244
Western Folklife Center
P.O. Box 1570
Elko, NV 89803
(775) 738-7508

State and Community-Based Agencies

Most states and local communities support a Council on the Arts that should be able to assist you with materials and other useful resources for classroom applications. Be sure you tell the contact person you are an early childhood educator.

Company That Produces Multicultural Materials

Mastercommunications/Asia for Kids, (800) 765-5885

References

Allison, J. (2004). Ask the expert: Jeannette Allison on the project approach. In M. Jalongo & J. Isenberg, *Exploring your role: A practitioner's introduction to early childhood education* (2nd ed.). Upper Saddle River, NJ: Merrill/Prentice Hall.

Alper, C. D. (1999). Early childhood music education. In C. Seefeldt (Ed.), *The early childhood curriculum* (pp. 237–263). New York: Teachers College Press.

Amabile, T. M. (1983). *The social psychology of creativity.* New York: Springer-Verlag.

Amabile, T. M. (1986). The personality of creativity. *Creative Living, 15*(3), 12–16.

Amabile, T. M. (1989). *Growing up creative.* New York: Crown.

Amabile, T. M. (2001). Beyond talent: John Irving and the passionate craft of creativity. *American Psychologist, 56,* 333–336.

Amann, J. (1993). *Theme teaching with great visual resources: How to involve and educate students using large, high-quality, low-cost art reproductions.* Rosemont, NJ: Modern Learning Press.

Andress, B. (1998). *Music for young children.* Fort Worth, TX: Harcourt Brace College.

Annarella, L. A. (1999). *Using Creative Drama in the Writing Process.* (ERIC Document Reproduction Service No. ED434379).

Anning, A. (1999). Learning to draw and drawing to learn. *International Journal of Art & Design Education, 18*(2), 163–172.

Armstrong, T. (1987). *In their own way.* New York: St. Martin's Press.

Armstrong, T. (1994). *Multiple intelligences in the classroom.* Alexandria, VA: Association for Supervision and Curriculum Development.

Armstrong, T. (1998). *Awakening genius in the classroom.* Alexandria, VA: Association for Supervision and Curriculum Development.

Arts Education Partnership (2004b). *The arts and group learning.* Retrieved July 25, 2004, from http://www.aep-arts.org/PDF%20Files/OpportunitiesResearch.pdf.

Arts Education Partnership (2004c). *The arts and special student populations.* Retrieved July 25, 2004, from http://www.aep-arts.org/PDF%20Files/OpportunitiesResearch.pdf

Bae, J. (2004). Learning to teach the visual arts in an early childhood classroom: The teacher's role as guide. *Early Childhood Education Journal, 31*(4), 247–253.

Baer, J. (1994). Why you still should not trust creativity tests. *Educational Leadership, 52*(2), 71–73.

Baldwin, A. Y. (2001). Understanding the challenge of creativity among African Americans. *Journal of Secondary Gifted Education, 12*(3), 121–125.

Banks, J. (Ed.). (1996). *Education, transformative knowledge, and action: Historical and contemporary perspectives.* New York: Teachers College Press.

Banks, J. A. (2001). *Cultural diversity and education: Foundations, curriculum, and teaching.* Boston: Allyn & Bacon.

Barab, S. A., & Landa, A. (1997). Designing effective interdisciplinary anchors. *Educational Leadership, 54*(6), 52–55.

Barasch, D. S. (1997, November). Creativity. *Family Life,* 54–59.

Barbour, A., & Desjean-Perrotta, B. (2002). *Prop box play: 50 themes to inspire dramatic play.* Beltsville, MD: Gryphon House.

Barbour, A. C. (1999). The impact of playground design on the play behaviors of children with differing levels of physical competence. *Early Childhood Research Quarterly, 14*(1), 75–98.

Barbour, N., Drosdeck, S., & Webster, T. (1987). Sand: A resource for the language arts. *Young Children, 42*(2), 20–25.

Barnes, R. (2002). *Teaching art to young children, 4–9* (2nd ed.). London: Routledge Falmer.

Barnhart, C. L., & Barnhart, R. K. (1983). *The world book dictionary.* Chicago: Thorndike-Barnhart.

Barrett, T. (1997). *Talking about student art.* Worcester, MA: Davis.

Baumrind, D. (1967). Child care practices anteceding three patterns of preschool behavior. *Genetic Psychology Monographs, 75,* 43–88.

Baumrind, D. (1993). The average expectable environment is not good enough: A response to Scarr. *Child Development, 64*(5), 1299–1317.

Bayless, K. M., & Ramsey, M. E. (1990). *Music: A way of life for the young child.* Upper Saddle River, NJ: Merrill/Prentice Hall.

Beattie, D. K. (1997). *Assessment in art education.* Worcester, MA: Davis.

Beattie, D. K. (2000). Creativity in art: The feasibility of assessing current conceptions in the school context. *Assessment in Education: Principles, Policy & Practice, 2*(7), 175–202.

Beeghly, D. G., & Prudhoe, C. M. (2002). *Litlinks: Activities for connected learning in elementary classrooms.* Boston: McGraw-Hill.

Begley, S. (1997, Spring-Summer). How to build a baby's brain. [Special issue]. *Newsweek, 129,* 28–32.

Bennett, N., Wood, L., & Rogers, S. (1997). *Teaching through play: Teachers' thinking and classroom practice.* Buckingham, England: Open University Press.

Bergen, D. (2002). Finding humor in children's play. In J. L. Roopnarine (Ed.), *Conceptual, social-cognitive, and contextual issues in the fields of play* (Vol. 4, pp. 209–220). Westport, CT: Ablex.

Bergen, D., & Coscia, J. (2000). *Brain research and childhood education*. Olney, MD: Association for Childhood Education International.

Berk, L. (2005). *Infants, children, and adolescents* (5th ed.). Boston: Allyn & Bacon.

Bernstein, P. (1990). On breaking 100 in music. In F. Wilson & F. Roehmann (Eds.), *Music and child development: Proceedings of the 1987 Denver Conference* (pp. 400–419). St. Louis, MO: Mosby.

Besemer, S. P., & O'Quin, K. (1999). Confirming the three-factor creative product analysis matrix model in an American sample. *Creativity Research Journal, 12,* 287–296.

Bisgaier, C. S., & Samaras, T., with Russo, M. (2004). Using wood, glue, and words to enhance learning. *Young Children, 59*(4), 22–29.

Blizzard, J. (1999). Quoted in L. Mann, Dance education: The ultimate sport. *ASCD Education Update, 41*(5), 1, 3, 8.

Bloom, B. (1964). *Stability and change in human characteristics.* New York: Wiley.

Bolton, G. (1985). Changes in thinking about drama in the classroom. *Theory into Practice, 24*(3), 151–157.

Boyd, A. E. (1989, July–August). *Music in early childhood.* Paper presented at the 21st International Conference on Early Education and Development, Hong Kong. (ERIC Document Reproduction Service No. ED310863)

Boyer, E. L. (1995). *The basic school: A community for learning.* Princeton, NJ: Carnegie Foundation for the Advancement of Teaching.

Bredekamp, S. (Ed.). (1991). Guidelines for appropriate curriculum content and assessment in programs serving children 3 through 8. *Young Children, 46*(3), 21–38.

Bredekamp, S., & Copple, C. (Eds.). (1997). *Developmentally appropriate practice in early childhood programs* (Rev. ed.). Washington, DC: National Association for the Education of Young Children.

Bresler, L. (1993). Three orientations to arts in the primary grades: Implications for curriculum reform. *Arts Education Policy Review, 94*(6), 29–35.

Brickman, N. A. (1999). *Creative representation: High/Scope preschool key experiences.* Ypsilanti, MI: High/Scope Educational Research Foundation.

Bromley, K. (1998). *Language arts: Exploring connections* (3rd ed.). Boston: Allyn & Bacon.

Bronson, M. (1995). *The right stuff for children birth to 8: Selecting play materials to support development.* Washington, DC: National Association for the Education of Young Children.

Bruer, J. (1997). Education and the brain: A bridge too far. *Educational Researcher, 26*(8), 4–16.

Bruner, J. (1968). *Toward a theory of instruction.* New York: Norton.

Bruner, J. S. (1966). What we have learned about early learning. *European Early Education Research Journal, 4*(1), 5–16.

Burke, A. F., & O'Sullivan, J. C. (2002). *A handbook for using drama in the second language classroom.* Portsmouth, NH: Heinemann.

Burns, M. T. (2002). Musical creativity. *Teaching Music, 9*(2), 40–45.

Burton, J. M. (2001). Lowenfeld: An(other) look. *Art Education, 54*(6), 33–42.

Caine, G., & Caine, R. N. (1997). *Education at the edge of possibility.* Alexandria, VA: Association for Supervision and Curriculum Development.

Caine, R. N., & Caine, G. (1991). *Teaching and the human brain.* Alexandria, VA: Association for Supervision and Curriculum Development.

Carnegie Corporation. (1994). *Starting points: Meeting the needs of our youngest children.* Retrieved January 28, 2005, from http://www.carnegie.org/starting-points/startpt1.html

Carnine, D. (1990). New research on the brain: Implications for instruction. *Phi Delta Kappan, 71*(5), 372–377.

Carter, M., & Curtis, D. (1995). *Training teachers: A harvest of theory and practice.* St. Paul, MN: Redleaf Press.

Castellano, J. A. (2003). *Special populations in gifted education: Working with diverse gifted learners.* Boston: Allyn & Bacon.

Castle, K. (1998). Children's rule knowledge in invented games. *Journal of Research in Childhood Education, 12*(2), 197–209.

Caulfield, R. (1999). Mozart effect: Sound beginnings? *Early Childhood Education Journal, 27*(2), 119–122.

Cecil, N. L., & Lauritzen, P. (1994). *Literacy and the arts for the integrated classroom: Alternative ways of knowing.* New York: Longman.

Chard, S. (1998). *The project approach: Managing successful projects (Book 2).* New York: Scholastic.

Charney, R. S. (2002). *Teaching children to care: Classroom management for ethical and academic growth, K–8.* Greenfield, MA: Northeast Foundation for Children.

Checkley, K. (1997). The first seven . . . and the eighth. *Educational Leadership, 55*(1), 8–15.

Chenfeld, M. B. (2002). *Creative experiences for young children* (3rd ed.). Portsmouth, NH: Heinemann.

Christie, J. (2001). Play as a learning medium—revisited. In S. Reifel (Ed.), *Theory in context and out* (Vol. 3, pp. 357–366). Westport, CT: Ablex.

Christie, J. F., Enz, B., & Vukelich, C. (2003). *Teaching language and literacy: Preschool through the elementary grades* (2nd ed.). Boston: Allyn & Bacon.

Christie, J. F., & Johnson, E. P. (1983). The role of play in social-intellectual development. *Review of Educational Research, 53*(1), 93–115.

Clark, B. (1988). *Growing up gifted* (3rd ed.). Upper Saddle River, NJ: Prentice Hall/Merrill.

Clark, C. (1996). Working with able learners in regular classrooms. *Gifted and Talented International, 11,* 34–38.

Clasen, D., Middleton, J., & Connell, T. (1994). Assessing artistic and problem-solving performance in minority and nonminority students using a nontraditional multidimensional approach. *Gifted Child Quarterly, 38,* 27–32.

Clawson, M. (2002). Play of language minority children in an early childhood setting. In J. L. Roopnarine (Ed.),

Conceptual, social-cognitive, and contextual issues in the fields of play (Vol. 4, pp. 99–116). Westport, CT: Ablex.

Clayton, M. K. (2001). *Classroom spaces that work*. Greenfield, MA: Northeast Foundation for Children.

Clemens, S. G. (1991). Art in the classroom: Making every day special. *Young Children, 46*(2), 4–11.

Cobb, E. (1977). *The ecology of imagination in childhood*. New York: Columbia University Press.

Cohen, E. P., & Gainer, R. S. (1995). *Art: Another language for learning* (3rd ed.). Portsmouth, NH: Heinemann.

Collins, R. (1998). *The sociology of philosophies: A global theory of intellectual change*. Cambridge, MA: Harvard University Press.

Colwell, R. (1998). Preparing student teachers in assessment. *Arts Education Policy Review, 99*(4), 29–36.

Consortium of National Arts Education Associations. (1994). *National standards for arts education: Dance, music, theater, and visual arts: What every young American should know and be able to do in the arts*. Reston, VA: Music Educators National Conference.

Consortium of National Arts Education Associations. (2002). *Authentic connections*. Reston, VA: Author.

Corbey-Scullen, L., & Howell, J. (1997). Out of the housekeeping corner and onto the stage: Extending dramatic play. *Young Children, 52*(6), 82–88.

Cox, M. V., & Ralph, M. L. (1996). Young children's ability to adapt their drawings of the human figure. *Educational Psychology, 16*(3), 245–256.

Craft, A. (1999). *Teaching creativity: Philosophy and practice*. London: Routledge.

Craft, A. (2000). *Creativity across the primary curriculum: Framing and developing practice*. London: Routledge.

Cramond, B. (2001). Interview with Paul E. Torrance on creativity in the last and next millennia. *Journal of Secondary Gifted Education, 12*(3), 116–120.

Creasey, G., Jarvis, P., & Berk, L. (1998). Play and social competence. In O. Saracho and B. Spodek (Eds.), *Multiple perspectives on play in early childhood education* (pp. 116–143). Albany: State University of New York Press.

Cropley, A. (1997). Fostering creativity in the classroom. In M. Runco (Ed.), *The creativity research handbook* (pp. 83–113). Cresskill, NJ: Hampton Press.

Cropley, A. (1999). Definitions of creativity. In M. Runco & S. Pritzker (Eds.), *Encyclopedia of creativity* (Vol. 11, pp. 511–524). San Diego: Academic Press.

Cropley, A. J. (2001). *Creativity in education and learning: A guide for teachers and educators*. London: Kogan Page.

Crumpler, T., & Schneider, J. (2002). Writing with their whole being: A cross study analysis of children's writing from five classrooms using process drama. *Research in Drama Education, 7*(1), 75–78.

Csikszentmihalyi, M. (1996). The creative personality. *Psychology Today, 29*(4), 36–40.

Csikszentmihalyi, M., Rathunde, K., & Whalent, S. (1993). *Talented teenagers*. New York: Cambridge University Press.

Cummings, P. (1992). *Talking with artists*. New York: Bradbury.

Cummings, P. (1993). *Talking with artists II*. New York: Bradbury.

Custodero, L. A., & Johnson-Green, E. A. (2003). Passing the cultural torch: Musical experience and musical parenting of infants. *Journal of Research in Music Education, 51*(2), 102–114.

Cyranek, G. (2002). Social implications of virtual worlds. *Digital Creativity, 13*(1), 1–2.

D'Amboise, J. (1991). Quoted in Music Educators National Conference, *Growing up complete: The imperative for music education* (p. 5). Reston, VA: Author.

Dacey, J. S. (1989). *Fundamentals of creative thinking*. Lexington, MA: Heath.

Dacey, J. S., & Lennon, K. H. (1998). *Understanding creativity: The interplay of biological, psychological, and social factors*. San Francisco: Jossey-Bass.

Danko-McGhee, K., & Slutsky, R. (2003). Preparing early childhood teachers to use art in the classroom. *Art Education, 56*(4), 12–18.

Dansky, J. L. (1980). Make-believe: A mediator of the relationship between play and associative fluency. *Child Development, 51*, 576–579.

Dansky, J. L., & Silverman, I. W. (1973). Effects of play on associative fluency in preschool children. *Developmental Psychology, 9*, 38–43.

Darrow, A., & Loomis, D. M. (1999). Music and deaf culture: Images from the media and their interpretation by deaf and hearing students. *Journal of Music Therapy, 26*(2), 88–107.

Darrow, A. A. (1985). Music for the deaf. *Music Educators Journal, 71*(6), 33–35.

Davidson, J., & Davidson, B. (2004). *Genius denied: How to stop wasting our brightest young minds*. New York: Simon & Schuster.

Davila, D. E., & Koenig, S. M. (1998). Bringing the Reggio concept to American educators. *Art Education, 51*(4), 18–24.

Davis, G., & Rimm, S. (1994). *Education of the gifted and talented* (3rd ed.). Needham Heights, MA: Allyn & Bacon.

Davis, J., & Gardner, H. (1992). The cognitive revolution: Consequences for the understanding and education of the child as artist. In B. Reimer & R. A. Smith (Eds.), *The arts, education, and aesthetic knowing* (pp. 92–123). Chicago: University of Chicago Press.

Dawson, V. L. (1997). In search of the wild Bohemian: Challenges in the identification of the creatively gifted. *Roeper Review, 19*(3), 148–152.

de Bono, E. (1971). *New think*. New York: Avon.

de Bono, E. (1992). *Teach your child how to think*. New York: Viking.

de León, A. G. (2002, Fall). Moving beyond storybooks: Teaching our children to read and learn. *Carnegie Reporter, 3*–11.

Debord, K., Hestenes, L. L., Moore, R. C., Cosco, N., & McGinnis, J. R. (2002). Paying attention to the outdoor environment is as important as preparing the indoor environment. *Young Children, 57*(3), 32–35.

Deiner, P. L. (2005). *Resources for educating children with diverse abilities* (4th ed.). Albany, NY: Thomson Delmar Learning.

DeVries, R. (1998). Games with rules. In D. P. Fromberg & D. M. Bergen (Eds.), *Play from birth to twelve and beyond: Contexts, perspectives, and meanings* (pp. 409–415). New York: Garland.

Dewey, J. (1916). *Democracy and education.* New York: Macmillan.

Dewey, J. (1938). *Experience and education.* New York: Macmillan.

Diamond, B. J., & Moore, M. A. (1995). *Multicultural literacy: Mirroring the reality of the classroom.* White Plains, NY: Longman.

Dinca, M. (1999). Creative children in Romanian society. *Childhood Education, 75*(6), 355–358.

Dodge, D. T., Colker, L. J., & Heroman, C. (2002). *The creative curriculum for preschool* (4th ed.). Washington DC: Teaching Strategies.

Drew, W. F., & Rankin, B. (2004). Promoting creativity for life using open-ended materials. *Young Children, 59*(4), 38–45.

DuCharme, C. C. (1991, April). *The role of drawing in the writing processes of primary grade children.* Paper presented at the Association for Childhood Education International Study Conference, San Diego, CA.

Duffy, B. (1998). *Supporting creativity and imagination in the early years.* Buckingham, England: Open University Press.

DuPont, S. (1992). The effectiveness of creative drama as an instructional strategy to enhance the reading comprehension skills of fifth-grade remedial readers. *Reading Research and Instruction, 31*(3), 41–52.

Dyson, A. H. (1993). *Social worlds of children learning how to write.* New York: Teachers College Press.

Ebbeck, M. (1996). Children constructing their own knowledge. *International Journal of Early Years Education, 4*(2), 5–27.

Educators in Connecticut's Pomperaug Regional School District 15. (1996). *A teacher's guide to performance-based learning and assessment.* Alexandria, VA: Association for Supervision and Curriculum Development.

Edwards, C., Gandini, L., & Forman, G. (Eds.). (1993). *The hundred languages of children: The Reggio Emilia approach to early childhood education.* Norwood, NJ: Ablex. (ERIC Document Reproduction Service No. ED355034)

Edwards, C. P., Gandini, L., & Forman, G. E. (Eds.). (1999). *The hundred languages of children: The Reggio Emilia approach to early childhood education—advanced reflections.* Greenwich, CT: Ablex.

Edwards, L. C. (2002). *The creative arts: A process approach for teachers and children* (3rd ed.). Upper Saddle River, NJ: Merrill/Prentice Hall.

Egan, K. (1988). The origins of imagination. In K. Egan and D. Nadaner (Eds.), *Imagination and education* (pp. 91–127). New York: Teachers College Press.

Egan, K., & Nadaner, D. (Eds.). (1988). *Imagination and education.* New York: Teachers College Press.

Eisenberger, R., & Armeli, S. (1997). Can salient reward increase creative performance without reducing intrinsic creative interest? *Journal of Personality and Social Psychology, 72,* 652–663.

Eisner, E. (1976). *The arts, human development and education.* Berkeley, CA: McCuthen.

Eisner, E. (1990). Who decides what schools teach? *Phi Delta Kappan, 71,* 523–525.

Eisner, E. (1999). The uses and limits of performance assessment. *Phi Delta Kappan, 80*(9), 658–660.

Eisner, E. W. (1994). *Cognition and curriculum reconsidered* (2nd ed.). New York: Teachers College Press.

Eisner, E. W. (1998). *The kind of schools we need: Personal essays.* Portsmouth, NH: Heinemann.

Eisner, E. W. (2003). Preparing for today and tomorrow. *Educational Leadership, 61*(4), 6–10.

Elgas, P. M., Prendeville, J., Moomaw, S., & Kretchmer, R. R. (2002). Early childhood classroom setup. *Child Care Information Exchange, 143,* 17–20.

Elias, C. L., & Berk, L. E. (2002). Self-regulation in young children: Is there a role for sociodramatic play? *Early Childhood Research Quarterly, 17*(2), 216–238.

Ellis, M. J. (1973). *Why people play.* Upper Saddle River, NJ: Prentice Hall.

Epstein, A. S. (2001). Thinking about art: Encouraging art appreciation in early childhood settings. *Young Children, 56*(3), 38–43.

Ericsson, K. A., & Charness, N. (1994). Expert performance: Its structure and acquisition. *American Psychologist, 49*(8), 725–747.

Erikson, E. (1950). *Childhood and society.* New York: Norton.

Erikson, E. H. (1963). *Childhood and society.* New York: Norton.

Erwin, E., & Schreiber, R. (1999). Creating supports for young children with disabilities in natural environments. *Early Childhood Education Journal, 26*(3), 167–171.

Etzioni, A. (1993). *The spirit of community: Rights, responsibilities, and the communitarian agenda.* New York: Crown.

Fasko, D. (2001). Education and creativity. *Creativity Research Journal, 13*(3/4), 317–327.

Fawson, P. C., & Moore, S. A. (1999). Reading incentive programs: Beliefs and practices. *Reading Psychology, 20,* 325–340.

Feeney, S., Christensen, D., & Moravcik, E. (Eds.). (1991). *Who am I in the lives of children?* Upper Saddle River, NJ: Merrill/Prentice Hall.

Feldhusen, J. F. (1995). Creativity: Knowledge base, metacognitive skills, and personality factors. *Journal of Creative Behavior, 29*(4), 255–268.

Feldhusen, J. F. (2001). Multiple options as a model for teaching the creatively gifted child. In M. D. Lynch & C. R. Harris, (Eds.), *Fostering creativity in children, K–8* (pp. 3–13). Needham Heights, MA: Allyn & Bacon.

Feldhusen, J. F., & Goh, B. E. (1995). Assessing and accessing creativity: An integrative review of theory, research, and development. *Creativity Research Journal, 8*(3), 231–247.

Feldman, D. H. (1999). The development of creativity. In R. J. Sternberg (Ed.), *Handbook of creativity* (pp. 169–186). New York: Cambridge University Press.

Felton, H., & Stoessiger, R. (1987, September). Quality learning: The role of process in art and mathematics. *National Association for Drama in Education,* 14–21.

Fennessey, S. (1995). Living history through drama and literature. *The Reading Teacher, 49*(3), 16–19.

Fennessey, S. (2000). *History in the spotlight: Creative drama and theatre practices for the social studies classroom*. Portsmouth, NH: Heinemann.

Ferrari, M. (2004). Educating selves to be creative and wise. In L. V. Shavinina & M. Ferrari (Eds.), *Beyond knowledge: Extracognitive aspects of high ability* (pp. 136–168). Mahwah, NJ: Erlbaum.

Fishkin, A. S., Crammond, B., & Olszewski-Kubilius, P. (1999). Issues in studying creativity in youth. In A. S. Fishkin, B. Crammond, & P. Olszewski-Kubilius (Eds.), *Investigating creativity in youth: Research and methods*. Cresskill, NJ: Hampton Press.

Flohr, J. W., Miller, D. C., & Debeus, R. (2000). EEG studies with young children. *Music Educators Journal, 87*(2), 28–33.

Flynn, L. L., & Kieff, J. (2002). Including everyone in outdoor play. *Young Children, 57*(3), 20–26.

Flynn, R. M. (2000). *From story to stage: Dramatizing literature using creative problem solving* [Pamphlet]. Washington, DC: John F. Kennedy Center for the Performing Arts.

Forman, G. (1998). Constructive play. In D. P. Fromberg & D. M. Bergen (Eds.), *Play from birth to twelve and beyond: Contexts, perspectives, and meanings* (pp. 392–400). New York: Garland.

Forsythe, S. J. (1995). It worked! Readers theater in second grade. *The Reading Teacher, 49*(3), 264–265.

Fox, D. B. (1989). MusicTIME and music times two: The Eastman infant-toddler music program. In B. Andress (Ed.), *Promising practices in prekindergarten music* (pp. 13–24). Reston, VA: Music Educators National Conference.

Fox, D. B. (1991). Music, development, and the young child. *Music Educators Journal, 77*(5), 42–46.

Freire, P. (1973). *Pedagogy of the oppressed*. New York: Seabury.

Freud, S. (1958). *On creativity and the unconscious* (I. F. Grant Doff, Trans.). New York: Harper & Row. (Original work published 1928)

Fritz, A. (2002). Keynote address for IDATER '98—Creativity: From philosophy to practice. Retrieved January 28, 2005, from http://www.21learn.org/arch/articles/fritz.html

Fromberg, D. P. (1998). Play issues in early childhood education. In C. Seefeldt & A. Galper (Eds.), *Continuing issues in early childhood education* (2nd ed.; pp. 190–212). New York: Teachers College Press.

Fromberg, D. P. (1999). A review of research on play. In C. Seefeldt (Ed.), *The early childhood curriculum: Current findings in theory and practice* (3rd ed., pp. 27–53). New York: Teachers College Press.

Fromberg, D. P. (2002). *Play and meaning in early childhood education*. Boston: Allyn & Bacon.

Fromberg, D. P., & Bergen, D. M. (Eds.). (1998). *Play from birth to twelve and beyond: Contexts, perspectives, and meanings*. New York: Garland.

Frost, J. L. (2004). Common issues and concerns about outdoor play environments. In M. Jalongo & J. Isenberg, *Exploring your role: A practitioner's introduction in early childhood education* (p. 175). Upper Saddle River, NJ: Merrill/Prentice Hall.

Frost, J. L., Shinn, D., & Jacobs, P. (1998). Physical environments and children's play. In O. Saracho & B. Spodek (Eds.), *Multiple perspectives on play in early childhood education* (pp. 255–294). Albany, NY: State University of New York Press.

Frost, J. L., & Woods, I. C. (1998). Perspectives on play in playgrounds. In D. P. Fromberg & D. M. Bergen (Eds.), *Play from birth to twelve and beyond: Context, perspectives, and meanings* (pp. 232–240). New York: Garland.

Frost, J. L., Wortham, S. C., & Reifel, S. (2001). *Play and child development*. Upper Saddle River, NJ: Merrill/Prentice Hall.

Furman, L. (2000a). In support of drama in early childhood education, again. *Early Childhood Education Journal, 27*(30), 173–178.

Furman, L. (2000b) Using drama and theater to provide literacy development: Some basic classroom applications. *Research in Drama Education, 7*(1), 61–69.

Gainer, B. (1997). Marketing arts education: Parental attitudes toward arts education for children. *Journal of Arts Management, Law & Society, 26*(4), 253–268.

Gaitskell, C. D., Hurwitz, A., & Day, M. (1982). *Children and their art: Methods for the elementary school* (4th ed.). Dubuque, IA: Brown.

Gallas, K. (2003). *Imagination and literacy: A teacher's search for the heart of meaning*. New York: Teachers College Press.

Garcia, C., Garcia, L., Floyd, J., & Lawson, J. (2002). Improving public health through early childhood movement programs. *Journal of Physical Education, Recreation, and Dance, 73*(1), 27–32.

Gardner, H. (1993a). *Frames of mind: The theory of multiple intelligences* (10th anniversary ed.). New York: Basic Books.

Gardner, H. (1993b). *Multiple intelligences: The theory in practice*. New York: Basic Books.

Gardner, H. (2000). *Intelligence reframed: Multiple intelligences for the 21st century*. New York: Basic Books.

Garreau, M., & Kennedy, C. (1991). Structure time and space to promote pursuit of learning in the primary grades. *Young Children, 46*(4), 46–51.

Gelb, M. J. (2002). *Discover your genius: How to think like history's ten most revolutionary minds*. New York: Quill/HarperCollins.

Gelineau, R. P. (2004). *Integrating the arts across the elementary school curriculum*. Belmont, CA: Thomson-Wadsworth.

Gilbert, J. (1996). Developing an assessment stance in primary art education in England. *Assessment in Education: Principles, Policy & Practice, 3*(1), 55–74.

Glover, J. (1980). *Becoming a more creative person*. Upper Saddle River, NJ: Prentice Hall.

Gold, R., & Cuming, G. J. (1999). Age-appropriate dance. *Dance Magazine, 78*.

Goleman, D., & Kaufman, P. (1992). The art of creativity. *Psychology Today, 25*(2), 40–47.

Golomb, C. (2004). *The child's creation of a pictorial world*. Mahwah, NJ: Erlbaum.

Green, J. (2001). Socially constructed bodies in American dance classrooms. *Research in Dance Education, 2*(2), 155–173.

Greenberg, M. (1979). *Your children need music.* Upper Saddle River, NJ: Prentice Hall.

Greenspan, D. A., Solomon, B., & Gardner, H. (2004). The development of talent in different domains. In L. V. Shavinina & M. Ferrari (Eds.), *Beyond knowledge: Extracognitive aspects of high ability* (pp. 119–135). Mahwah, NJ: Erlbaum.

Gromko, J. E., & Poorman, A. S. (1998). The effect of music training on preschoolers' spatial-temporal task performance. *Journal of Research in Music Education, 46*(2), 173–181.

Gronlund, G. (2001). Academics in the preschool and kindergarten years—Let me tell you how. *Young Children, 56*(2), 42–43.

Gruber, H. E., & Davis, S. N. (1988). Inching our way up Mount Olympus: The evolving-systems approach to creative thinking. In R. J. Sternberg (Ed.), *The nature of creativity* (pp. 243–270). New York: Cambridge University Press.

Gruber, H. E., & Wallace, D. B. (1999). The case study method and evolving systems approach for understanding creative people at work. In R. J. Sternberg (Ed.), *The handbook of creativity* (pp. 93–115). New York: Cambridge University Press.

Guilford, J. P. (1984). Varieties of divergent production. *Journal of Creative Behavior, 18*, 1–10.

Hall, M. A. (1989). Music for children. In B. Andress (Ed.), *Promising practices in prekindergarten music* (pp. 47–57). Reston, VA: Music Educators National Conference.

Hallahan, D. P., & Kauffman, J. M. (2002). *Exceptional learners: Introduction to special education* (9th ed.). Needham Heights, MA: Allyn & Bacon.

Halliday, M. A. K. (1975). *Explorations in the functions of language.* London: Edward Arnold.

Han, K., & Marvin, C. (2002). Multiple creativities? Investigating domain-specificity of creativity in young children. *Gifted Child Quarterly, 46*, 98–109.

Han, M., Benavides, A., & Christie, J. (2001). Bilingual children's language usage. In S. Reifel (Ed.), *Theory in context* (Vol 3.) Westport, CT: Ablex.

Hancock, L., & Wingert, P. (1997, Spring-Summer). The new preschool. [Special Issue]. *Newsweek, 129*, 36–37.

Hargreaves, D. J., Galton, M. J., & Robinson, S. (1996). Teachers' assessments of primary children's classroom work in the creative arts. *Educational Research, 38*(2), 199–211.

Harris, J. R. (1998). *The nurture assumption: Why children turn out as they do.* New York: Free Press.

Harrison, A. (1984). Creativity, class and boredom: Cognitive models for intelligent activities. *Journal of Education, 166*(2), 150–169.

Harrison, C. (1999). Visual representation of the young gifted child. *Roeper Review, 21*(3), 189–195.

Hartman, J. A., & Eckerty, C. (1995). Projects in the early years. *Childhood Education, 71*(3), 141–148.

Hatch, T. (1997). Getting specific about multiple intelligences. *Educational Leadership, 54*(6), 26–29.

Haugland, S. (2001). What role should technology play in young children's learning? Part 2. Early childhood classrooms in the 21st century: Using computers to maximize learning. *Young Children, 55*(1), 12–18.

Haugland, S., & Wright, J. (1997). *Young children and technology: A world of discovery.* Boston: Allyn & Bacon.

Healy, J. (1996). How to uncover the natural creative abilities in your child. *Brown University Child and Adolescent Behavior Letter, 12*(4), 5–6.

Hearron, P., & Hildebrand, V. (2005). *Guiding young children* (7th ed.). Upper Saddle River, NJ: Merrill/Prentice Hall.

Heberholz, B. (1974). *Early childhood art.* Dubuque, IA: Brown.

Heinig, R. B. (1993). *Creative drama for the classroom teacher* (4th ed.). Upper Saddle River, NJ: Prentice Hall.

Heller, P. G. (1996). Many ways of knowing: Using drama, oral interaction, and the visual arts to enhance reading comprehension. *The Reading Teacher, 45*(8), 580–584.

Henderson, M., Presbury, J., & Torrance, E. P. (1983). *Manifesto for children.* Staunton, VA: Full Circle Counseling.

Hendrick, J. (2001). *The whole child* (7th ed.). Upper Saddle River, NJ: Merrill/Prentice Hall.

Henkes, R. (1989). The child's artistic expression. *Early Child Development and Care, 47*, 165–176.

Hennessey, B. A. (1994). The consensual assessment technique: An examination for the relationships between ratings of process and product creativity. *Creativity Research Journal, 7*, 193–208.

Hennings, D. G. (2003). *Communication in action: Teaching literature-based language arts* (8th ed.). Boston: Houghton Mifflin.

Hewitt, K., & Roomet, L. (1979). *Educational toys in America: 1800 to the present.* Burlington, VT: Robert Hall Fleming Museum/University of Vermont.

Hicks, J. (2001). How do you cure a sick horse? *Art Education, 54*(2), 6–10.

Hildebrandt, C. (1992). Creativity in music and early childhood. *Young Children, 53*(6), 68–74.

Hill, P. S. (1923). *A conduct curriculum for the kindergarten and first grade.* New York: Scribner's.

Hirsch, E. S. (1996). *The block book* (3rd ed.). Washington, DC: National Association for the Education of Young Children.

Holden, C. (1987, April). Creativity and the troubled mind. *Psychology Today, 21*(4), 9–10.

Holmes, R., & Geiger, C. (2002). The relationship between creativity and cognitive ability in preschoolers. In J. L. Rooparine (Ed.), *Conceptual, social-cognitive, and contextual issues in the fields of play* (Vol. 4, pp. 127–148), Westport, CT: Ablex.

Hope, S. (1990). Technique and arts education. *Design for Arts in Education, 91*(6), 2–14.

Hope, S. (1991). Policy making in the arts and school change. In Council of Arts Accrediting Associations, *Briefing Paper* (pp. 1–5). Reston, VA: Author.

Horibe, F. (2001). *Creating the innovation culture: Leveraging visionaries, dissenters and other useful troublemakers in your organization.* New York: Wiley.

Howe, H. (1993). *Thinking about our kids: An agenda for American action*. New York: Free Press.

Howe, M. J. A. (2004). Some insights of geniuses into the causes of exceptional achievements. In L. V. Shavinina & M. Ferrari (Eds.), *Beyond knowledge: Extracognitive aspects of high ability* (pp. 105–117). Mahwah, NJ: Erlbaum.

Howe, N., Moller, L., Chambers, B., & Petrakos, H. (1993). The ecology of dramatic play centers and children's social and cognitive play. *Early Childhood Research Quarterly, 8*(2), 235–252.

Hughes, F. P. (1999). *Children, play and development* (3rd ed.). Boston: Allyn & Bacon.

Hull, K., Goldhaber, J., & Capone., A. (2002). *Opening doors: An introduction to inclusive early childhood education*. New York: Houghton Mifflin.

Humpal, M. E., & Wolf, J. (2003). Music in the inclusive environment. *Young Children, 58*(2), 103–107.

Hunsacker, S. L. (1994). Creativity as a characteristic of giftedness: Teachers see it, then they don't. *Roeper Review, 17*(1), 11–15.

Hunt, J. M. (1961). *Intelligence and experience*. New York: Ronald Press.

Hunt, T., & Renfro, N. (1982). *Puppetry in early childhood education*. Austin, TX: Nancy Renfro Studios.

Hutinger, P. L. (1997). *The Expressive Arts Project: A final report*. Macomb, IL. (ERIC Document Reproduction Service No. ED415646)

Hyson, M. C., & Christiansen, S. L. (1997). Developmentally appropriate guidance and the integrated curriculum. In C. Hart, D. Burts, & R. Charlesworth (Eds.), *Integrated curriculum and developmentally appropriate practice* (pp. 257–284). Albany: State University of New York Press.

Isaacs, S. (1933). *Social development in young children*. London: Routledge & Kegan Paul.

Isaksen, S. G. (1992). *Nurturing creative talents: Lessons from industry about needed work-life skills*. Buffalo, NY: Creative Solving Group.

Isbell, R. (1995). *The complete learning center book*. Beltsville, MD: Gryphon House.

Isbell, R. T., & Exelby, B. (2001). *Early learning environments that work*. Beltsville, MD: Gryphon House.

Isen, A. M., Daubman, K. A., & Nowicki, G. P. (1987). Positive affect facilitates problem solving. *Journal of Personality and Social Psychology, 52*, 1121–1131.

Isenberg, J., & Farley, M. (1990). *Reading assessment program review committee*. Richmond: Virginia Department of Education.

Isenberg, J., & Quisenberry, N. (2002). Play: Essential for all children. *Childhood Education, 79*(1), 33–39.

Isenberg, J. P., & Raines, S. C. (1992). Peer conflict and conflict resolution among preschool children. In J. Gittler & L. Bowen (Eds.), *Annual review of conflict knowledge and conflict resolution* (Vol. 3, pp. 21–40). New York: Garland.

Jackson, P. W., & Messick, S. (1965). The person, the product, and the response: Conceptual problems in the assessment of creativity. *Journal of Personality, 33*, 309–329.

Jalongo, M. R. (1991). Children's play: A resource for multicultural education. In E. B. Vold (Ed.), *Multicultural education in the early childhood classroom* (pp. 52–56). Washington, DC: National Education Association.

Jalongo, M. R. (2002). *Early childhood language arts* (3rd ed.). Boston: Allyn & Bacon.

Jalongo, M. R. (2003). The child's right to creative thought and expression (International Position Paper of the Association for Childhood Education International). *Childhood Education, 79*(4), 218–228.

Jalongo, M. R. (2004). *Young children and picture books* (2nd ed.). Washington, DC: National Association for the Education of Young Children.

Jalongo, M. R., & Collins, M. (1985). Singing with young children! Folk music for nonmusicians. *Young Children, 40*, 17–22.

Jalongo, M. R., & Isenberg, J. P. (2004). *Exploring your role: A practitioner's introduction to early childhood education* (2nd ed.). Upper Saddle River, NJ: Merrill/Prentice Hall.

Jalongo, M. R., & Ribblett, D. (1997). Using song picture books to support emergent literacy. *Childhood Education, 74*(1), 15–22.

Jalongo, M. R., & Stamp, L. N. (1997). Appendix D: Picture book versions of songs, chants, fingerplays, and action rhymes. In M. R. Jalongo & L. N. Stamp, *The arts in children's lives: Aesthetic education in early childhood* (pp. 157–256). Boston: Allyn & Bacon.

Jefferson, B. (1963). *Teaching art to children: The values of creative expression*. Boston: Allyn & Bacon.

Jensen, E. (1998, Spring). Quoted in K. Rasmussen, Arts education: A cornerstone of basic education. *ASCD Curriculum Update*, 2.

Jensen, E. (2000). Moving with the brain in mind. *Education Leadership, 58*(1), 34–37.

Johnson, A. (1998). How to use creative dramatics in the classroom. *Childhood Education, 75*(1), 2.

Johnson, D. (2003). Activity theory, mediated action and literacy: Assessing how children make meaning in multiple modes. *Assessment in Education, 10*(1), 103–129.

Johnson, J. E., Christie, J. F., & Yawkey, T. D. (1999). *Play and early childhood development* (2nd ed.). New York: Longman.

Jones, D., McConnell, B., & Normie, G. (Eds.). (1996). *One world, many cultures*. Papers from the 4th International Conference on Adult Education and the Arts, Caredenden, Scotland: Fife Regional Council. (ERIC Document Reproduction Service No. ED414470).

Jones, E. (1977). *Dimensions of teaching-learning environments*. Pasadena, CA: Pacific Oaks.

Joussement, M., & Koestner, R. (1999). Effect of expected rewards on children's creativity. *Creativity Research Journal, 12*(4), 231–239.

Kagan, S. L., & Bowman, B. T. (Eds.). (1997). *Leadership in early care and education*. Washington, DC: National Association for the Education of Young Children.

Kamii, C., & DeVries, R. (1980). *Group games in early education: Implications of Piaget's theory*. Washington, DC: National Association for the Education of Young Children.

Kantrowitz, B. (1997, Spring-Summer). Off to a good start. [Special Issue]. *Newsweek, 129*, 6–9.

Katz, L. G. (1988). *Early childhood education: What research tells us*. Bloomington, IN: Phi Delta Kappa.

Katz, L. G., & Chard, S. C. (2000). *Engaging children's minds: The project approach* (2nd ed.). Norwood, NJ: Ablex.

Kauchak, D. P., & Eggen, P. D. (2003). *Learning and teaching: Research-based methods*. New York: Allyn & Bacon.

Kay, S. I., & Subotnik, R. F. (1994). Talent beyond words: Unveiling spatial, expressive, kinesthetic and musical talent in young children. *Gifted Child Quarterly, 38*(2), 70–74.

Kelley, L., & Sutton-Smith, B. (1987). A study of infant musical productivity. In J. C. Peery, I. W. Peery, & T. Draper (Eds.), *Music and child development* (pp. 35–53). New York: Springer-Verlag.

Kellogg, R. (1979). *Children's drawings/children's minds*. New York: Avon.

Kemple, K. M., Batey, J. J., & Hartle, L. C. (2004). Music play: Creativity centers for music play and exploration. *Young Children 59*(4), 30–37.

Kemple, K. M., & Nissenberg, S. A. (2000). Nurturing creativity in early childhood education: Families are part of it. *Early Childhood Education Journal, 28*(1), 67–71.

Kerka, S. (2002). *Adult learning in and through the arts*. Columbus, OH: ERIC Clearinghouse on Adult, Career, and Vocational Education. ERIC Digest Number 236. (EDO-CE-02-236)

Kerlavage, M. S. (1995). A bunch of naked ladies and a tiger: Children's responses to adult works of art. In C. M. Thompson (Ed.), *The visual arts in early childhood learning* (pp. 56–62). Reston, VA: National Art Education Association.

Kinkade, T. (2002). The child's heart in art. *American Artist, 66*(716), 12.

Kindler, A. L. (2002). *Survey of the states' limited English proficient students and available educational programs and services: 1999–2000 report*. Washington, DC: George Washington University and National Clearinghouse for English Language Acquisition and Language Instruction Educational Programs.

Kindler, A. M. (1996). Myths, habits, research, and policy: The four pillars of early childhood education. *Arts Education Policy Review, 97*(4), 24–30.

Kindler, A. M. (Ed.). (1997). *Child development in art*. Reston, VA: National Art Education Association.

Kirk, S., Gallagher, J., & Anastasiow, N. (2003). *Educating exceptional children* (10th ed.). New York: Houghton Mifflin.

Klein, M. D., Cook, R. E., & Richardson-Gibbs, A. M. (2001). *Strategies for including children with special needs in early childhood settings*. Albany, NY: Thomson Delmar Learning.

Kline, L. W. (1995). A baker's dozen: Effective instructional strategies. In R. W. Cole (Ed.), *Educating everybody's children: Diverse teaching strategies for diverse learners* (pp. 21–41). Alexandria, VA: Association for Supervision and Curriculum Development.

Koch, J. (2005). *Science stories* (3rd ed.). Boston: Houghton Mifflin.

Kohn, A. (1987, September). Art for art's sake. *Psychology Today, 21*(9), 52–57.

Kohn, A. (1993). Choices for children: Why and how to let students decide. *Phi Delta Kappan, 75*(1), 8–21.

Kohn, A. (1996). *Beyond discipline: From compliance to community*. Alexandria, VA: Association for Supervision and Curriculum Development.

Korn-Bursztyn, C. (2002). Scenes from a studio: Working with the arts in an early childhood classroom. *Early Childhood Education Journal, 30*(1), 39–46.

Kozol, J. (1997). Students' needs or corporate greed? *Education Digest, 63*(1), 3–6.

Kress, G. (1997). *Before writing: Rethinking the paths to literacy*. New York: Routledge.

Kritchevsky, S., Prescott, E., & Walling, L. (1977). *Planning environments for young children: Physical space* (Rev. ed.). Washington, DC: National Association for the Education of Young Children.

Landreth, G., & Homeyer, L. (1998). Play as the language of children's feelings. In D.P. Fromberg & D. M. Bergen (Eds.), *Play from birth to twelve and beyond: Contexts, perspectives, and meanings* (pp. 193–198). New York: Garland.

Lang, S. S. (1999). Music: Good not only for the soul, but the brain. *Human Ecology Forum, 27*(2), 24.

Latham, A. S. (1997). Research link: Quantifying MI's gains. *Educational Leadership, 55*(1), 84–85.

Levin, D. (1999, November). Rethinking children's play: Changing times, changing needs, changing responses. *National PTA Magazine*, 8–11.

Levin, J., & Greenwald, N. L. (2001). Swimming against the tide: The creative child as a late bloomer. In M. D. Lynch & C. R. Harris, (Eds.), *Fostering creativity in children, K–8* (pp. 71–77). Needham Heights, MA: Allyn & Bacon.

Lewis, A. G. (1983). *Listen, look, and sing (Grades 1, 2, and 3)*. Morristown, NJ: Silver Burdett.

Li, J. (2004). High abilities and excellence: A cultural perspective. In L. V. Shavinina & M. Ferrari (Eds.), *Beyond knowledge: Extracognitive aspects of high ability* (pp. 187–208). Mahwah, NJ: Erlbaum.

Li, R. (1996). *A theory of conceptual intelligence: Thinking, learning, creativity, and giftedness*. Westport, CT: Praeger.

Lindsey, G. (1998/99). Brain research and implications for early childhood education. *Childhood Education, 75*(2), 97–100.

Lindstrom, L. (1997). Integration, creativity, or communication? Paradigm shifts and continuity in Swedish art education. *Arts Education Policy Review, 99*(1), 17–24.

Littleton, D. (1989). Children's play: Pathways to music learning. In B. Andress (Ed.), *Promising practices: Pre-*

kindergarten music education (pp. ix–xiii). Reston, VA: Music Educators National Conference.

Lowenfeld, V., & Brittain, W. L. (1982). *Creative and mental growth* (7th ed.). New York: Macmillan.

MacKinnon, D. W. (1978). *In search of human effectiveness.* Buffalo, NY: Creative Education Foundation.

Majure, J. (1995). It's playtime. *Arthritis Today, 9*(1), 46–51.

Mantione, R. D., & Smead, S. (2003). *Weaving through words: Using the arts to teach reading comprehension strategies.* Newark, DE: International Reading Association.

Manzo, K. K. (2002). Arts programs enhance some skills, study says. *Education Week, 21*(36), 5.

March, T. (2004). Webquests: The fulcrum for systemic curriculum improvement. Retrieved January 28, 2005, from http://center.uoregon.edu/ISTE/NECC2004/ handout_files_live/KEY_160238/ webquest_fulcrum_necc.pdf

Marion, M. (2003). *Guidance of young children* (6th ed.). Upper Saddle River, NJ: Merrill/Prentice Hall.

Martindale, C. (2001). Oscillations and analogies: Thomas Young, MD, FRS, genius. *American Psychologist, 56,* 342–345.

Marzano, R. J., Pickering, D., & McTighe, J. (1993). *Assessing student outcomes: Using the Dimensions of Learning Model.* Alexandria, VA: Association for Supervision and Curriculum Development.

Maslow, A. (1970). *Motivation and personality* (2nd ed.). New York: Harper Row.

Maxim, G. (1989). *The very young: Guiding children from infancy through the early years* (3rd ed.). Upper Saddle River, NJ: Merrill/Prentice Hall.

May, R. (1975). *The courage to create.* New York: Norton.

Mayesky, M. (2002). *Creative activities for young children* (7th ed.). Albany, NY: Delmar.

McAlpine, D. (1996). Characteristics of gifted children. In D. McAlpine & R. Moltzen (Eds.), *Gifted and talented: New Zealand perspectives* (pp. 43–62). Palmerston North, NZ: Massey University ERDC Press.

McCaslin, N. (2000). *Creative drama in the classroom and beyond* (7th ed.). Boston: Allyn & Bacon.

McCune, L. N., & Zanes, M. (2001). Learning, attention, and play. In S. Golbeck (Ed.), *Psychological perspectives on early childhood education* (pp. 92–106). Mahwah, NJ: Erlbaum.

McDaniel, N., & Thorn, G. (1997). *Learning audiences: Adult arts participation and the learning consciousness.* Washington, DC: John F. Kennedy Center for the Performing Arts/Association of Performing Arts Presenters.

McGinnis, J. R. (2002). Enriching the outdoor environment. *Young Children, 57*(3), 28–30.

McLaughlin, N. (2001). Optimal marginality: Innovation and orthodoxy in Fromm's revision of psychoanalysis. *Sociological Quarterly, 42*(2), 271–287.

McLean, S. V. (1995). Creating the learning environment: Context for living and learning. In J. Moyer (Ed.), *Selecting educational equipment and materials* (pp. 5–13). Wheaton, MD: Association for Childhood Education International.

McLeod, L. (1997). Children's metacognition: Do we know what they know? And if so, what do we do about it? *Australian Journal of Early Childhood, 22*(2), 6–11.

McMaster, J. C. (1998). "Doing" literature: Using drama to build literacy. *The Reading Teacher, 51*(7), 574–675.

Meador, K. (1999). Creativity around the globe. [Special issue]. *Childhood Education, 75,* 324–325.

Mergen, B. (1982). *Play and playthings: A reference guide.* Westport, CT: Greenwood Press.

Mindes, G. (1998). Can I play too? Reflections on the issues for children with disabilities. In D. P. Fromberg & D. M. Bergen (Eds.), *Play from birth to twelve and beyond: Contexts, perspectives, and meanings* (pp. 208–214). New York: Garland.

Minuchin, P. (1987). Schools, families and the development of young children. *Early Childhood Research Quarterly, 2,* 245–254.

Mitchell, L. C. (2004). Making the most of creativity in activities for young children with disabilities. *Young Children, 59*(4), 46–49.

Monighan-Nourot, P. (1990). The legacy of play in American early childhood education. In E. Klugman & S. Smilansky (Eds.), *Children's play and learning: Perspectives and policy implications* (pp. 59–85). New York: Teachers College Press.

Moore, T. (2002). If you teach children, you can sing. *Young Children, 57*(4), 84–85.

Morado, C., Koenig, R., & Wilson, A. (1999). Miniperformances, many stars! Playing with stories. *The Reading Teacher, 53*(2), 116–123.

Morrow, L. (2001). *Literacy development in the early years: Helping children read and write* (4th ed.). Boston: Allyn & Bacon.

Moyer, J. (Ed.). (1995). *Selecting educational equipment and materials for school and home.* Wheaton, MD: Association for Childhood Education International.

Myhre, S. M. (1993). Enhancing your dramatic play area through the use of prop boxes. *Young Children, 48*(5), 6–11.

Naglieri, J. A. (2001). Understanding intelligence, giftedness and creativity using the PASS Theory. *Roeper Review, 23*(3), 151–156.

Nakamura, J., & Csikszentmihalyi, M. (2001). Catalytic creativity: The case of Linus Pauling. *American Psychologist, 56,* 337–341.

Napoli, D. J. (2003). *Language matters: A guide to everyday questions about language.* New York: Oxford University Press.

Nash, J. M. (1997, February 3). Fertile minds. *Time, 149*(5), 48–56.

National Academy of Early Childhood Programs. (2004). *Accreditation criteria and procedures of the NAEYC.* Washington, DC: National Association for the Education of Young Children.

National Advisory Committee on Creative and Cultural Education. (1999). *All our futures: Creativity, culture, and education.* London: DfEE.

National Art Education Association. (1999). *Purposes, principles, and standards for school art programs.* Reston, VA: Author.

National Association of Early Childhood Specialists in State Departments of Education. (2002). Recess and the importance of play: A position statement on young children and recess. Retrieved January 28, 2005, from http://naecs.crc.uiuc.edu/position/recessplay.html.

National Association for the Education of Young Children. (1996a). *Playgrounds: Keeping outdoor learning safe*. Release #5. Washington, DC: Author.

National Association for the Education of Young Children. (1996b). Position statement: Technology and young children—ages three through eight. *Young Children, 5*(6), 11–16.

National Association for Sport and Physical Education. (2001). *Recess in elementary schools* (Position paper). Reston, VA: Author.

National Program for Playground Safety. (1999). *Our children. National PTA Magazine, 25*(2), 17.

Neely, L. P. (2002). Practical ways to improve singing in early childhood classrooms. *Young Children, 57*(4), 80–83.

Neve, C. D., Hart, L. A., & Thomas, E. C. (1986). Huge learning jumps show potency of brain-based instruction. *Phi Delta Kappan, 68*(2), 143–148.

Newberger, J. J. (1997). New brain development research: A wonderful window of opportunity to build public support for early childhood education! *Young Children, 52*(4), 4–9.

Newman, J. (Ed.). (1990). *Finding our own way*. Portsmouth, NH: Heinemann.

Nicholson, M. W., & Moran, J. D. (1986). Teachers' judgments of preschoolers' creativity. *Perceptual and Motor Skills, 63*, 1211–1216.

Odoy, H., & Foster, S. (1997). Creating play crates for the outdoor classroom. *Young Children, 52*(6), 12–16.

Olson, J. L. (2002). Children at the center of art education. *Art Education, 56*(4), 33–42.

O'Neil, J. (1994, January). Looking at the art through new eyes: Visual arts programs pushed to reach new goals, new students. *ASCD Curriculum Update*, 1–8.

Osborn, A. (1972). *Your creative power: How to use imagination*. New York: Scribner's. (Original work published 1948).

Owocki, G. (1999). *Literacy through play*. Portsmouth, NH: Heinemann.

Pahl, K. (1999). Making models as a communicative practice: Observing meaning making in a nursery. *Reading*, 114–119.

Paley, V. (1992). *You can't say you can't play*. Cambridge, MA: Harvard University Press.

Palmer, M., & Sims, W. L. (Eds.). (1993). *Music in prekindergarten: Planning and teaching*. Reston, VA: Music Educators National Conference.

Papalia, D. E., Olds, S. W., & Feldman, R. D. (2002). *A child's world: Infancy through adolescence* (9th ed.). New York: McGraw-Hill.

Papert, S. (1993). *The children's machine: Rethinking school in the age of the computer*. New York: Basic Books.

Pappalardo, R. G. (1990). Curricular issues: The visual arts and students with disabilities. In A. L. Nyman & A. J. Jenkins (Eds.), *Issues and approaches for art students with special needs* (pp. 42–54). Reston, VA: National Art Education Association.

Parker, W. C. (2001). *Social studies in elementary education* (11th ed.). Upper Saddle River, NJ: Merrill/Prentice Hall.

Parten, M. (1932). Social participation among preschool children. *Journal of Abnormal and Social Psychology, 27*(2), 243–269.

Pearson, M. (2000). All the classroom's a stage! *Education World*. Retrieved March 18, 2004, from http://www.education-world.com/a curr/ curr226.shtml

Pepler, D., & Ross, H. S. (1981). The effects of play on convergent and divergent problem-solving. *Child Development, 52*, 1202–1210.

Peregoy, S. F. & Boyle, O. F. (2005). *Reading, writing, and learning in English as a Second Language classroom: A classroom resource for K-12 teachers* (4th ed.). Boston: Allyn & Bacon.

Perkins, D. (1984). Creativity by design. *Educational Leadership, 42*, 18–25.

Perry, P. (1998). Art in a million schools: Art education in China. *Journal of Art and Design Education, 17*(3), 311–314.

Persellin, D. (1998). Quoted in M. P. Pautz, Teaching prekindergarten music. *Teaching Music, 5*(5), 40–43.

Peterson, M. (1979). *Stay in tune* [record/cassette]. Summit, NJ: Meg Peterson Enterprises.

Peterson, R. E. (2001/2002). Establishing the creative environment in technology education. *Technology Teacher, 61*(4), 7–11.

Petrakos, H., & Howe, N. (1996). The influence of the physical design of the dramatic play center on children's play. *Early Childhood Research Quarterly, 11*(1), 63–67.

Piaget, J. (1952). *The origins of intellect*. New York: International University Press.

Piaget, J. (1962). *Play, dreams and imitation in childhood* (C. Gategno & F. M. Hodgson, Trans.). New York: Norton.

Piirto, J. (1992). *Understanding those who create*. Dayton: Ohio Psychology Press.

Piirto, J. (2001). How parents and teachers can enhance creativity in children. In M. D. Lynch & C. R. Harris (Eds.), *Fostering creativity in children, K–8* (pp. 49–67). Needham Heights, MA: Allyn & Bacon.

Pintrich, P. R., & Schunk, D. (2002). *Motivation in education: Theory, research, and applications* (2nd ed.). Upper Saddle River, NJ: Merrill/Prentice Hall.

Popham, W. J. (2001). *The truth about testing: An educator's call to action*. Alexandria, VA: Association for Supervision and Curriculum Development.

Potter, F. (1985). "Good job!" How we evaluate children's work. *Childhood Education, 61*(3), 203–206.

Prescott, E. (1984). The physical setting in day care. In J. Greenman & R. Fuqua (Eds.), *Making day care better: Training, evaluation, and the process of change* (pp. 44–65). New York: Teachers College Press.

Podlozny, A. (2000). Strengthening verbal skills through the use of classroom drama: A clear link. *Journal of Aesthetic Education, 34*(3–4), 239–276.

Priest, T. (2001). Using creativity assessment to nurture and predict compositional creativity. *Journal of Research in Music Education, 49*(3), 245–257.

Prudhoe, C. M. (2003). Picture books and the art of collage. *Childhood Education, 80*(1), 6–11.

Puckett, M., Marshall, C. S., & Davis, R. (1999). Examining the emergence of brain development research: The promises and the perils. *Childhood Education, 76*(1), 8–12.

Qualley, C. (1986). *Safety in the art room.* Worcester, MA: Davis.

Ramsey, P. (1998). Diversity and play: Influences of race, culture, class, and gender. In D. P. Fromberg & D. M. Bergen (Eds.), *Play from birth to twelve and beyond: Contexts, perspectives, and meanings* (pp. 23–34). New York: Garland.

Rankin, B. (1995, February). Displaying children's work. *Scholastic Early Childhood Today,* 34–35.

Rappaport, L., & Schulz, L. (1999). *Creative play activities for children with disabilities: A resource book for teachers and parents.* Champaign, IL: Human Kinetics.

Rasmussen, K. (1998, Spring). Arts education: A cornerstone of basic education. *ASCD Curriculum Update,* 1–3, 6–7.

Raths, L. E., Wassermann, S., Jonas, A., & Rothstein, A. (1986). *Teaching for thinking: Theory, strategies and activities for the classroom.* New York: Teachers College Press.

Ray, J. J. (1997). For the love of children: Using the power of music in "English as a Second Language" programs. (Doctoral dissertation, University of California, Los Angeles, 1997). *Dissertation Abstracts International, 58,* 07A.

Raywid, M. A. (1995). A teacher's awesome power. In W. Ayers (Ed.), *To become a teacher: Making a difference in children's lives* (pp. 78–85). New York: Teachers College Press.

Rea, D. (2001). Maximizing the motivated mind for emergent giftedness. *Roeper Review, 23*(3), 157–164.

Reifel, S. (2001). (Ed.). *Theory in context and out* (Vol. 3). Westport, CT: Ablex.

Reiff, J. C. (1997). Multiple intelligences, culture, and equitable learning. *Childhood Education, 73*(5), 301–304.

Research and Policy Committee. (1985). *Investing in children.* Washington, DC: Committee for Economic Development.

Rettig, M. (1998). Environmental influences on the play of young children with disabilities. *Education and Training in Mental Retardation and Developmental Disabilities, 33*(2), 189–194.

Richards, R. (2001). Millennium as opportunity: Chaos, creativity, and Guilford's structure of intellect model. *Creativity Research Journal, 13*(3/4), 249–265.

Ripple, R. E. (1989). Ordinary creativity. *Contemporary Educational Psychology, 14,* 189–202.

Rivkin, M. S. (1995). *The great outdoors: Restoring children's right to play outside.* Washington, DC: National Association for the Education of Young Children.

Robinson, A., & Clinkenbeard, P. R. (1998). Giftedness: An exceptionality examined. *Annual Review of Psychology, 49,* 117–139.

Robinson, K. (2001). Mind the gap: The creative conundrum. *Critical Quarterly, 43*(1), 41–45.

Rodd, J. (1999). Encouraging young children's critical and creative thinking skills: An approach in one English elementary school. *Childhood Education, 75*(6), 350–354.

Roe, B. D., Smith, S. H., & Burns, P. C. (2005). *Teaching reading in today's elementary schools* (9th ed.). New York: Houghton Mifflin.

Roebuck, E. (1999). Stravinsky's *Firebird* and young children. *Music Educators Journal, 86*(1), 34–37.

Roeper, B., & Davis, D. (2000). Howard Gardner: Knowledge, learning and development in drama and arts education. *Research in Drama Education, 5*(2), 217–233.

Rogers, C. (1961). *On becoming a person.* Boston: Houghton Mifflin.

Rogers, C. (1991). Toward a theory of creativity. In A. Rothenberg & C. Hausman (Eds.), *The creativity question* (pp. 296–305). Durham, NC: Duke University Press. (Original work published 1954)

Rong, X. L., & Shi, T. (2001). Inequality in Chinese education. *Journal of Contemporary China, 10*(26), 107–124.

Ross, J. (1994). The right moves: Challenges of dance assessment. *Arts Education Policy Review, 96*(1), 11–17.

Rotigel, J. (2003). Understanding the young gifted child: Guidelines for parents, families, and educators. *Early Childhood Education Journal, 30*(4), 209–214.

Rowe, G. (1987). *Guiding young artists: Curriculum ideas for teachers.* Portsmouth, NH: Heinemann.

Rubin, K. H., Fein, G. S., & Vandenberg, B. (1983). Play. In E. M. Hetherington and P. H. Mussen (Eds.), *Handbook of child psychology: Vol. 4. Socialization, personality and development* (pp. 698–774). New York: Wiley.

Runco, M. (1997). *Handbook of creativity* (Vol. 1). Cresskill, NJ: Hampton Press.

Runco, M. A. (1986). Predicting children's creative performance. *Psychological Reports, 59,* 1247–1252.

Runco, M. A. (1996). *Eminent creativity: Everyday creativity and health.* Norwood, NJ: Ablex.

Runco, M. A. (2004). Creativity as an extracognitive phenomenon. In L. V. Shavinina & M. Ferrari (Eds.). *Beyond knowledge: Extracognitive aspects of high ability* (pp. 17–37). Mahwah, NJ: Erlbaum.

Runco, M. A. (Ed.). (1994). *Problem finding, problem solving, and creativity.* Norwood, NJ: Ablex.

Runco, M. A., & Pritzker, S. (1999). *Encyclopedia of creativity.* San Diego, CA: Academic Press.

Ryan, R. L., & Deci, E. L. (2000). Self-determination theory and the facilitation of intrinsic motivation, social development, and well-being. *American Psychologist, 55,* 68–78.

Rybczynski, M., & Troy, A. (1995). Literacy-enriched play centers: Trying them out in "the real world." *Childhood Education, 72*(1), 7–12.

Sanoff, H. (1995). *Creating environments for young children.* Mansfield, OH: BookMasters.

Santrock, J. W. (2003). *Children* (7th ed.). Boston: McGraw-Hill.

Sapon-Shevin, M., Dobbelgere, A., Carrigan, C., Goodman, K., & Mastin, M. (1998). Everyone here can play. *Educational Leadership, 56*(1), 42–45.

Schiller, M. (1995). Reggio Emilia: A focus on emergent curriculum and art. *Art Education, 48*(3), 45–50.

Schirrmacher, R. (1988). *Art and creative development for young children.* Albany, NY: Delmar.

Scott, C. L. (1999). Teachers' biases toward creative children. *Creativity Research Journal, 12,* 321–328.

Seely, A. E. (1994). *Professional's guide: Portfolio assessment.* Westminster, CA: Teacher Created Materials.

Sefton-Green, J., & Sinker, R. (Eds.). (2000). *Evaluating creativity: Making and learning by young people.* London: Routledge.

Semali, L. M., & Watts Pailliotet, A. (Eds.). (1999). *Intermediality: The teachers' handbook of critical media literacy.* Boulder, CO: Westview Press.

Shaftel, F. R., & Shaftel, G. (1982). *Role playing in the curriculum* (2nd ed.). Upper Saddle River, NJ: Prentice Hall.

Shallcross, D. (1981). *Teaching creative behavior.* Upper Saddle River, NJ: Prentice Hall.

Shavinina, L. V., & Ferrari, M. (2004). Extracognitive facets of developing high ability: Introduction to some important issues. In L. V. Shavinina & M. Ferrari (Eds.), *Beyond knowledge: Extracognitive aspects of high ability* (pp. 3–13). Mahwah, NJ: Erlbaum.

Sheldon, K. M. (1995). Creativity and self-determination in personality. *Creativity Research Journal, 8*(1), 25–36.

Shore, R. (1997). *Rethinking the brain: New insights into early development.* New York: Families and Work Institute.

Silberman, C. E. (1970). *Crisis in the classroom: The remaking of American education.* New York: Random House.

Simonton, D. K. (1996). *Selected papers in genius and creativity.* Norwood, NJ: Ablex.

Simonton, D. K. (1997). Historiometric studies of creative genius. In M. A. Runco (Ed.), *The creativity research handbook* (Vol. 1, pp. 3–28). Cresskill, NJ: Hampton Press.

Singer, D. G., & Singer, J. L. (1998). Fantasy and imagination. In D. P. Fromberg & D. M. Bergen (Eds.), *Play from birth to twelve and beyond: Contexts, perspectives, and meanings* (pp. 313–318). New York: Garland.

Singer, J. L. (1973). *The child's world of make-believe.* New York: Wiley.

Singer, J. L., & Singer, D. G. (1985). *Make believe: Games and activities to foster imaginative play in young children.* Glenview, IL: Scott Foresman.

Sloane, M. (1999). Learning resource centers: Engaging primary students. *Childhood Education, 75*(2), 76–82.

Smilansky, S. (1968). *The effects of sociodramatic play on disadvantaged preschool children.* New York: Wiley.

Smilansky, S., & Shefatya, L. (1990). *Facilitating play: A medium for promoting cognitive, socio-emotional and academic development in young children.* Gaithersburg, MD: Psychosocial and Educational Publications.

Smith, F. (1992). Learning to read: The great debate. *Phi Delta Kappan, 73*(6), 423–435, 438–441.

Smith, N., & The Drawing Study Group (1998). *Observation drawing with children.* New York: Teachers College Press.

Smith, N. R. (1982). The visual arts in early childhood education: Development and the creation of meaning. In B. Spodek (Ed.), *Handbook of research in early childhood education* (pp. 87–106). New York: Free Press.

Smith, P. K., & Connolly, K. J. (1980). *The ecology of preschool behavior.* Cambridge, England: Cambridge University Press.

Snyder, S. (1995). *Share the music, K–6.* New York: Macmillan/McGraw-Hill.

Spodek, B., & Saracho, O. N. (Eds.). (1998). *Multiple perspectives on play in early childhood education.* Albany: State University of New York Press.

Stankiewicz, M. A. (2000). Discipline and the future of art education. *Studies in Art Education, 41*(4), 301–313.

Starko, A. J. (2001). *Creativity in the classroom: Schools of curious delight.* Mahwah, NJ: Erlbaum.

State of Florida Department of State. (1990). *Children and the arts: A sourcebook of experiences for Florida's pre-kindergarten early intervention program.* Gainesville, FL: Author. (ERIC Document Reproduction Service No. ED330454)

Stephenson, A. (2002). What George taught me about toddlers and water. *Young Children,* 10–14.

Sternberg, R. J. (1998). Principles of teaching for successful intelligence. *Educational Psychologist, 33*(2/3), 65–72.

Sternberg, R. J. (2004). Wisdom and giftedness. In L. V. Shavinina & M. Ferrari (Eds.), *Beyond knowledge: Extracognitive aspects of high ability* (pp. 169–186). Mahwah, NJ: Erlbaum.

Sternberg, R. J., & Lubart, T. I. (1996). Investing in creativity. *American Psychologist, 51*(7), 677–688.

Stevenson, L. (2004). *The arts and school change.* Washington, DC: Arts Education Partnership.

Stinson, S. W. (1990). Dance for education in early childhood. *Design for Arts in Education, 91,* 34–41.

Stooke, R. (1998). Teaching through play. *Research in Drama Education, 3*(2), 272–277.

Strachota, B. (1996). *On their side: Helping children take charge of their learning.* Greenfield, MA: Northeast Foundation for Children.

Stremmel, A. (1997). Diversity and the multicultural perspective. In C. H. Hart, D. C. Burts, & R. C. Charlesworth (Eds.), *Integrated curriculum and developmentally appropriate practices: Birth to age eight* (pp. 363–388). Albany: State University of New York Press.

Surbeck, E., & Glover, M. (1992). Seal revenge: Ecology games invented by children. *Childhood Education, 69*(3), 275–280.

Sutterby, J. A., & Frost, J. L. (2002). Making playgrounds fit for children and children fit for playgrounds. *Young Children, 57*(3), 36–42.

Sutton-Smith, B. (1986). The spirit of play. In G. Fein & M. Rivkin (Eds.), *The young child at play: Reviews of research* (Vol. 4, pp. 3–16). Washington, DC: National Association for the Education of Young Children.

Swaminathan, S., & Wright, J. (2003). Educational technology in the early childhood and primary years. In J. P. Isenberg & M. R. Jalongo (Eds.), *Major trends and issues in early childhood education: Challenges, controversies, and insights* (pp. 136–149). New York: Teachers College Press.

Szekely, G. (1996). Preparation for a new art world. *Art Education, 49*(4), 6–13.

Szyba, C. M. (1999). Why do some teachers resist offering appropriate, open-ended art activities for young children? *Young Children, 54*(1), 14–20.

Taggart, C. C. (2000). Developing musicianship through musical play. In National Association for Music Education [MENC], *Spotlight on early childhood music education* (pp. 23–36). Reston, VA: MENC.

Tarnowski, S. (1999). Musical play and young children. *Music Educators Journal, 86*(1), 26–29.

Task Force on Teaching as a Profession. (1986). *A nation prepared: Teachers for the 21st century.* Washington, DC: Carnegie Forum on Education and the Economy.

Taylor, B. (1999). *A child goes forth: A curriculum guide for preschool children.* Upper Saddle River, NJ: Merrill/ Prentice Hall.

Taylor, I. A. (1975). An emerging view of creative actions. In I. A. Taylor and J. W. Getzels (Eds.), *Perspectives in creativity* (pp. 297–325). Chicago: Aldine.

Tegano, D. W., Moran, J. D., III, DeLong, A. J., Brickey, J., & Ramassini, K. K. (1996). Designing classroom spaces: Making the most of time. *Early Childhood Education Journal, 23*(3), 135–141.

Tegano, D. W., Sawyers, J. K., & Moran, J. D. (1989). Problem-finding and solving in play: The teacher's role. *Childhood Education, 66*(2), 92–97.

Tennent, L., & Berthelsen, D. (1997). Creativity: What does it mean in the family context? *Journal of Australian Research in Early Childhood Education, 1*, 91–103.

Tetenbaum, T. J., & Mulkeen, T. A. (1986). Computers as an agent for educational change. *Computers in the Schools, 2*(4), 91–103.

Thomason, C., & Thrash, D. (1999). Play it safe: A pre-installation checklist that could mean an injury and liability free playground. *Children and Families, 8*(1), 40–46.

Thompson, C. M. (1997). Teaching art in elementary schools: Shared responsibilities and distinctive roles. *Arts Education Policy Review, 99*(2), 15–22.

Thompson, D., Hudson, S., & Mack, M. (2000, March/April). The "ins and outs" of designing play areas for early childhood settings. *Early Childhood News, 6–13.*

Thompson, P., & Randall, R. (2001). Can e-learning spur creativity, innovation, and entrepreneurship? *Educational Media International, 38*(4), 289–293.

Tiedt, P., & Tiedt, I. (2000). *Multicultural teaching: A handbook of activities, information, and resources* (6th ed.). Boston: Allyn & Bacon.

Tomlinson, C. (1999). *The differentiated classroom: Responding to the needs of all learners.* Alexandria, VA: Association for Supervision and Curriculum Development.

Tompkins, G. E. (2002). *Literacy for the 21st century* (3rd ed.). Upper Saddle River, NJ: Merrill/Prentice Hall.

Torff, B. (2000). Encouraging the creative voice of the child. *NAMTA Journal, 25*(1), 195–214.

Torrance, E. P. (1993). The beyonders in a thirty-year study of creative achievement. *Roeper Review, 15,* 131–134.

Torrance, E. P. (1995). *Why fly? A philosophy of creativity.* Norwood, NJ: Ablex.

Trawick-Smith, J. (1998). Why play training works: An integrated model for play intervention. *Journal of Research in Childhood Education, 12*(2), 117–129.

Tudge, J., & Caruso, D. (1988). Cooperative problem-solving in the classroom: Enhancing young children's cognitive development. *Young Children, 44*(1), 46–57.

Turner, M. E. (1999). Child-centered learning and music programs. *Music Educators Journal, 86*(1), 30–35.

Upitis, R. (1990). *This too is music.* Portsmouth, NH: Heinemann.

Ulbricht, J., (1998). Interdisciplinary art education reconsidered. *Art Education, 51*(4), 13–17.

Urban, K. K. (1996). Encouraging and nurturing creativity in school and workplace. In U. Munander & C. Semiawan (Eds.), *Human Resource Development* (pp. 78–97). Jakarta: University of Indonesia Press.

U.S. Consumer Product Safety Commission. (2002). *A handbook for public safety.* Washington, DC: U.S. Government Printing Office.

U.S. Department of Education, Office of Educational Research and Improvement (1993). *National excellence: A case for developing America's talent.* Washington, DC: U.S. Government Printing Office.

Van Hoorn, J. J., Monighan-Nourot, P., Scales, B., & Alward, K. (2003). *Play at the center of the curriculum* (3rd ed.). Upper Saddle River, NJ: Merrill/Prentice Hall.

Varnon, D. (1997). Enriching remedial programs with the arts. *Reading and Writing Quarterly, 13*(4), 325–332.

Vergeront, J. (1996). *Places and spaces for preschool and primary (indoors).* Washington, DC: National Association for the Education of Young Children.

Verriour, P. (1994). *In role: Teaching and learning dramatically.* Markham, Canada: Pippin.

Vukelich, C., Christie, J., & Enz, B. (2002). *Helping young children learn language and literacy.* Boston: Allyn & Bacon.

Vygotsky, L. (1925). *The psychology of art.* Cambridge, MA: MIT Press.

Vygotsky, L. (1986). *Thought and language.* Cambridge, MA: MIT Press.

Vygotsky, L. S. (1933). The role of play in development. In M. Cole, V. John-Steiner, S. Scribner, & E. Souberman (Eds.), *Mind in society* (pp. 92–104). Cambridge, MA: Harvard University Press.

Vygotsky, L. S. (1967). Play and its role in the mental development of the child. *Soviet Psychology, 12,* 62–76.

Vygotsky, L. S. (1978). *Mind in society: The development of higher psychological processes.* Boston: Harvard University Press.

Walker, B. (2004). *Diagnostic teaching of reading: Techniques for instruction and assessment* (2nd ed.). Upper Saddle River, NJ: Prentice Hall.

Wallas, G. (1926). *The art of thought.* New York: Harcourt Brace.

Walling, D. R. (2001). Rethinking visual arts education: A convergence of influences. *Phi Delta Kappan, 82*(7), 626–631.

Walsh, D. J. (1993). Art as socially constructed narrative: Implications for early childhood education. *Arts Education Policy Review, 94*(6), 18–24.

Warnock, M. (1977). *Schools of thought.* London: Faber & Faber.

Wassermann, S. (1989). Reflections on measuring thinking, while listening to Mozart's *Jupiter Symphony*. *Phi Delta Kappan, 70*(5), 365–370.

Wassermann, S. (1990). *Serious players in the classroom: Empowering children through active learning experiences*. New York: Teachers College Press.

Wassermann, S. (2000). *Serious players in the primary classroom* (2nd ed.). New York: Teachers College Press.

Webster, P. R. (1990). Creativity as creative thinking. *Music Educators Journal, 76*(9), 22–28.

Weinberger, N. M. (1998). The music in our minds. *Educational Leadership, 56*(3), 36–40.

Weininger, O. (1988). "What if" and "as if": Imagination and pretend play in early childhood. In K. Egan & D. Nadaner (Eds.), *Imagination and education* (pp. 141–149). New York: Teachers College Press.

Weinstein, R. (1995). Quoted in R. W. Cole (Ed.), *Educating everybody's children: Diverse teaching strategies for diverse learners* (p. 18). Alexandria, VA: Association for Supervision and Curriculum Development.

Weisberg, R. W. (1993). *Creativity: Beyond the myth of genius.* New York: Freeman.

Wellhousen, K. (2002). *Outdoor play everyday: Innovative play concepts for early childhood.* Albany, NY: Delmar.

Werner, P., Timms, S., & Almond, L. (1996). Health stops: Practical ideas for health-related exercise in preschool and primary classrooms. *Young Children, 51*(6), 48–55.

Westby, E. L., & Dawson, V. L. (1995). Creativity: Asset or burden in the classroom? *Creativity Research Journal, 8*(1), 1–10.

Wheeler, E. J. (2004). *Conflict resolution in early childhood.* Upper Saddle River, NJ: Merrill/Prentice Hall.

Wilcox, E. (1994). Unlock the joy of music. *Teaching Music, 2,* 34–35, 46.

Wilcox, E. (2000). Music, brain research, and better behavior. *Education Digest, 65*(6), 10–15.

Wilhelm, J. D., & Edmiston, B. (Eds.). (1998). *Imagining to learn: Inquiry, ethics, and integration through drama.* Portsmouth, NH: Heinemann.

Williams, W. M., Brigockas, M. G., & Sternberg, R. J. (1997). *Creative intelligence for school.* New York: HarperCollins.

Wilson, F., & Roehmann, F. (Eds.). (1990). *Music and child development: Proceedings of the 1987 Denver Conference.* St. Louis, MO: MM3 Music.

Wilt, J., & Watson, T. (1977). *Listen!* Waco, TX: Creative Resources.

Wiltz, N. W., & Fein, G. (1996). Evolution of a narrative curriculum: The contributions of Vivian Gussey Paley. *Young Children, 51*(3), 61–68.

Wing, L. (1995). Play is not the work of the child: Young children's perceptions of work and play. *Early Childhood Research Quarterly, 10*(2), 223–247.

Wohlschlaeger, A., & Wohlschlaeger, A. (1998). Mental and manual rotation. *Journal of Experimental Psychology: Human Perception and Performance, 24*(2), 387–412.

Wolf, D. P., & Pistone, N. (1995). *Taking full measure: Rethinking assessment through the arts.* New York: College Entrance Examination Board.

Wood, C. (2001). *Yardsticks: Children in the classroom ages 4–14.* Greenfield, MA: Northeast Foundation for Children.

Woodward, C. (1985). Guidelines for facilitating sociodramatic play. In J. Frost & S. Sunderlin (Eds.), *When children play* (pp. 291–295). Wheaton, MD: Association for Childhood Education International.

Woolfolk, A. (2005). *Educational psychology.* Boston: Allyn & Bacon.

Wootton, K. (2004). Community this and community that. In L. Smyth & L. Stevenson, *You want to be part of everything: The arts, community, and learning.* Washington, DC: Arts Education Partnership.

Wright, F. L. (1932). *An autobiography.* New York: Longman.

Wright, S. (1997). Learning how to learn: The arts as core in an emergent curriculum. *Childhood Education, 73*(6), 361–365.

Yelland, N. (1999). Technology as play. *Early Childhood Education Journal, 26*(4), 217–220.

Yenawine, P. (1998). Visual art and student-centered discussions. *Theory into Practice, 37*(4), 314–322.

Yinger, J., & Blaszka, S. (1995). A year of journaling—A year of building with young children. *Young Children, 51*(1), 15–20.

Youngquist, J., & Pataray-Ching, J. (2004). Revisiting "play": Analyzing and articulating acts of inquiry. *Early Childhood Education Journal, 31*(3), 171–178.

Zimmerman, E., & Zimmerman, L. (2000). Art education and early childhood education: The young child as creator and meaning maker within a community context. *Young Children, 55*(6), 87–92.

Children's Books, Recordings, and Software

Books and Recordings

Aardema, V. (1981). *Bringing the rain to Kapiti Plain.* New York: Scholastic.

Ackerman, D. (1988). *Song and dance man.* New York: Knopf.

Ahlberg, J., & Ahlberg, J. (1986). *The jolly postman, or, Other people's letters.* New York: Little, Brown.

Aliki. (2002). *Ah, music!* New York: HarperCollins.

Ancona, G. (2003). *Murals: Walls that sing.* S. Tarrytown, NY: Cavendish Children's Books.

Andersen, H. C., & Locker, T. (1987). *The ugly duckling.* New York: Macmillan.

Anderson, M. T. (2002). *Handel, who knew what he liked.* Cambridge, MA: Candlewick Press.

Anderson, M. T. (2003). *Strange Mr. Satie.* New York: Viking.

Andreae, G. (2001). *Giraffes can't dance.* New York: Orchard/Scholastic.

Baker, A. (1995). *White rabbit's color book.* New York: Kingfisher.

Barracca, D., & Barracca, S. (1990). *The adventures of Taxi Dog.* New York: Trumpet.

Barton, B. (1981). *Building a house.* New York: Greenwillow.

Bayes, L. (1983). Bear hunt. On *Circle around* [audio recording]. Seattle, WA: Tickle Tune Typhoon.

Baylor, B., & Parnall, P. (1975). *The desert is theirs.* New York: Simon & Schuster.

Beaumont, K. (2004). *Baby danced the polka.* New York: Dial.

Belton, S. (1993). *From Miss Ida's porch.* New York: Simon & Schuster.

Brenner, B. (2003). *The boy who loved to draw: Benjamin West.* Boston: Houghton Mifflin.

Briggs, R. (1978). *The snowman.* New York: Random House.

Brown, L. K., & Brown, M. (1990). *Visiting the art museum.* New York: Puffin.

Brown, M. (1975). *Stone soup.* New York: Scribner's.

Brown, M. (1985). *Hand rhymes.* New York: Dutton.

Buchanan, K. (1994). *It rained on the desert today.* Flagstaff, AZ: Northland.

Bunting, E. (1990). *How many days to America: A Thanksgiving story.* Boston: Houghton Mifflin.

Cameron, P. (1961). *"I can't," said the ant.* New York: Coward.

Cannon, J. (1993). *Stellaluna.* San Diego, CA: Harcourt Brace Jovanovich.

Carle, E. (1969). *The very hungry caterpillar.* New York: HarperCollins/World.

Carle, E. (1984). *The mixed-up chameleon.* New York: HarperCollins.

Carle, E. (1993). *Today is Monday.* New York: Putnam.

Carle, E. (2001). *The tiny seed* (Reprinted). New York: Aladdin.

Carter, D. A. (2001). *If you're happy and you know it, clap your hands.* New York: Cartwheel/Scholastic.

Carter, D. A. (2001). *Old MacDonald had a farm.* New York: Cartwheel/Scholastic.

Castañeda, O. (1996). *Abuela's weave.* New York: Lee & Low.

Catalanotto, P. (2001). *Emily's art.* New York: Simon & Schuster.

Celenza, A. H. (2003). *Pictures at an exhibition.* Watertown, MA: Charlesbridge.

Chin, C. (1997). *China's bravest girl.* Emeryville, CA: Children's Book Press.

Chocolate, D. (1996). *Kente colors.* New York: Walker.

Cleary, B. (1975). *Ramona the brave.* New York: Morrow.

Cocca-Leffler, M. (2001). *Edgar Degas: Paintings that dance.* New York: Putnam.

Cockburn, V., & Steinbergh, J. (1991). *Where I come from! Poems and songs from many cultures.* Chestnut Hill, MA: Talking Stone Press.

Coleman, E. (2000). *To be a drum.* Morton, IL: Albert Whitman.

Cooper, E. (2001). *Dance!* New York: Greenwillow.

Creech, S. (1995). *Walk two moons.* New York: HarperCollins.

Crews, D. (1978). *Freight train.* New York: Greenwillow.

Degen, B. (1983). *Jamberry.* New York: Harper & Row.

Delibes, L. (1986). Coppelia. In M. Greaves, *Petrushka (A little box of ballet stories).* New York: Dial.

Dewey, A. (1995). *Naming colors.* New York: HarperCollins.

Dillon, L., & Dillon, D. (1983). *Why mosquitoes buzz in people's ears: A West African tale.* New York: Puffin.

Dillon, L., & Dillon, D. (2002). *Here's Bojangles: Think of that!* New York: Scholastic.

Dorros, A. (1991). *Abuela.* New York: Dutton.

Erbach, A. (1997). *The kids' invention book.* Minneapolis, MN: Lerner.

Esbensen, B. (1995). *Dance with me.* New York: HarperCollins.

Flack, M. (1932). *Ask Mr. Bear.* New York: Macmillan.

Flournoy, V. (1985). *The patchwork quilt.* New York: Dial.

Fogelin, A. (2000). *Crossing Jordan.* Atlanta, GA: Peachtree.

Gackenbach, D. (1977). *Harry and the terrible whatzit.* New York: Seabury.

Galdone, P. (1968). *Henny Penny.* New York: Seabury.

Garza, C. (1990). *Family pictures/Cuadros de familia.* San Francisco: Children's Book Press.

Gauch, P. L. (1999). *Presenting Tanya, the ugly duckling.* New York: Putnam/Philomel.

Gelsanliter, W., & Christian, F. (1993). *Dancin' in the kitchen.* New York: Putnam.

Gerstein, M. (2002). *What Charlie heard.* New York: Frances Foster.

Gibbons, G. (1982). *Tool book.* New York: Holiday House.

Glazer, T. (1982). *On top of spaghetti.* New York: Doubleday.

Gollub, M. (2000). *The jazz fly.* Summerland Key, FL: Tortuga Press.

Goodman, S., & McCurdy, M. (2003). *The train they call the City of New Orleans.* New York: Putnam.

Gray, L. M. (1996). *My mama had a dancing heart.* New York: Orchard.

Gray, N. (1988). *A country far away.* New York: Orchard.

Greenberg, J., & Jordan, S. (2002). *Action Jackson.* Brookfield, CT: Roaring Brook Press.

Greenstein, E. (2004). *One little seed.* New York: Viking.

Greigo, M. (1980). *Tortillitas para mama.* New York: Holt, Rinehart & Winston.

Grifalconi, A. (1986). *The village of round and square houses.* New York: Little, Brown.

Grifalconi, A. (1987). *Darkness and the butterfly.* New York: Little, Brown.

Gulbis, S. (2001). *I know an old lady who swallowed a fly.* New York: Cartwheel/Scholastic.

Gwynne, F. (1970). *The king who rained.* New York: Simon & Schuster.

Haley, G. E. (1988). *A story, a story.* New York: Simon & Schuster.

Hall, D., & Cooney, B. (1984). *Ox-cart man.* New York: Live Oak Media.

Hartman, B. (2004). *The wolf who cried boy.* New York: Puffin.

Hawkins, C., & Hawkins, J. (1984). *Boo! Who?* New York: Holt.

Hayes, A., & Thompson, K. (1995). *Meet the orchestra.* Stillwater, MN: Voyager Books.

Hendershot, J. (1987). *In coal country.* New York: Knopf.

Henderson, K. (1999). *The baby dances.* Boston: Candlewick Press.

Henkes, K. (1985). *Bailey goes camping.* New York: Greenwillow.

Highwater, J. (1981). *Moonsong lullaby.* New York: Lothrop, Lee & Shepard.

Hines, A. G. (2001). *Whose shoes?* New York: Harcourt Brace.

Hoban, T. (1985). *A children's zoo.* New York: Greenwillow.

Hoban, T. (1997). *Colors everywhere.* New York: Greenwillow.

Hoffman, M. (1991). *Amazing Grace.* New York: Dial.

Hogrogrian, N. (1971). *One fine day.* New York: Macmillan.

Hooks, W. G. (1997). *The three little pigs and the fox: An Appalachian tale.* New York: Aladdin.

Hubbard, P. (1996). *My crayons talk.* New York: Holt.

Hutchins, P. (1985). *The very worst monster.* New York: Greenwillow.

Hutchins, P. (1986). *The doorbell rang.* New York: Greenwillow.

Jave, J. (2002). *Horace and Morris join the chorus (But what about Dolores?)* New York: Atheneum/Simon & Schuster.

Jeschke, S. (1985). *Perfect the pig.* New York: Holt.

Johnson, A., & Huliska-Beith, L. (2004). *Violet's music.* New York: Dial.

Johnston, R. (1996). *The cowboy and the black-eyed pea.* New York: Putnam.

Johnston, T. (1984). *The quilt story.* New York: Putnam.

Jonas, A. (1989a). *Color dance.* New York: Greenwillow.

Jonas, A. (1989b). *The quilt.* New York: Greenwillow.

Jones, C. F., & O'Brien, J. (1997). *Accidents may happen.* New York: Delacorte.

Juster, N. (1988). *The phantom tollbooth.* New York: Random House.

Keats, E. J. (1962). *The snowy day.* New York: Viking.

Keats, E. J. (1971). *Over in the meadow.* New York: Four Winds Press.

Keats, E. J. (1972). *Pet show.* New York: Macmillan.

Kellogg, S. (1981). *A rose for Pinkerton.* New York: Dial.

Kelley, T. (2001). *Claude Monet: Sunshine and water lilies.* New York: Putnam.

Kennedy, J. (1983). *Teddy bear's picnic.* La Jolla, CA: Green Tiger Press.

Kimmelman, L. (2000). *Dance, sing, remember: A celebration of Jewish holidays.* New York: HarperCollins.

Knight, M. B., & O'Brien, A. S. (1995). *Talking walls.* Gardiner, ME: Tilbury House.

Knight, M. B., & O'Brien, A. S. (1997). *Talking walls: The stories continue.* Gardiner, ME: Tilbury House.

Koscielniak, B. (2000). *The story of the incredible orchestra: An introduction to musical instruments and the symphony orchestra.* Boston: Houghton Mifflin.

Krull, K. (1993). *Lives of the musicians: Good times, bad times (and what the neighbors thought).* San Diego, CA: Harcourt Children's Books.

Kuskin, K. (1982). *The Philharmonic gets dressed.* New York: HarperCollins.

Ladysmith Black Mambazo. (1994). There come our mothers. On *Gift of the tortoise* [CD]. Redway, CA: Music for Little People.

Laufer, P. (2000). *Made in Mexico.* Washington, DC: National Geographic Society.

Lester, J. (1990). *How many spots does a leopard have?* New York: Scholastic.

Levine, E. (1990). *I hate English!* New York: Scholastic.

Lithgow, J. (2003). *I'm a Manatee* [book and CD]. New York: Simon & Schuster Children's Publishing.

Lobel, A. (1970). *Frog and Toad are friends.* New York: Harper & Row.

Lobel, A. (1980). *Fables.* New York: Harper & Row.

London, J. (1996). *Hip Cat.* San Francisco: Chronicle Books.

Lowell, S. (1992). *The three little javelinas.* Hong Kong: Northland.

Mahy, M., & MacCarthy, P. (1993). *Seventeen kings and forty-two elephants*. New York: Dutton.

Manning, M. J. (2003). *The ants go marching*. Honesdale, PA: Boyds Mills Press.

Marcus, L. S. (2001). *Side by side: Five favorite picture-book teams go to work*. New York: Walker.

Martin, B. (1995). *Brown bear, brown bear, what do you see?* New York: Holt.

Martin, B., & Archambault, J. (1987). *Knots on a counting rope*. New York: Holt.

Martin, B., & Archambault, J. (1989). *Chicka chicka boom boom*. New York: Simon & Schuster.

Mayer, M. (1968). *There's a nightmare in my closet*. New York: Dial.

Mayer, M. (1977). *Frog goes to dinner*. New York: Dial.

McDermott, G. (1972). *Anansi the Spider*. New York: Holt, Rinehart, and Winston.

McPhail, D. (1999). *Mole music*. New York: Holt.

McPhail, D. (2000). *Drawing lessons from a bear*. New York: Little, Brown.

Medina-Serafin, M. (1998). Fiesta musical. On *A child's celebration of the world* [CD]. Redway, CA: Music for Little People.

Mendez, P. (1989). *The black snowman*. New York: Scholastic.

Merz, J. J. (2004). *That dancin' dolly*. New York: Viking.

Meyrick, K. (1990). *The musical life of Gustav Mole*. New York: Child's Play.

Mills, L. (1991). *The rag coat*. Boston: Little, Brown.

Mitchell, B. (1992). *Raggin': A story about Scott Joplin*. Minneapolis, MN: Carolrhoda.

Moore, C., & Young, M. (2002). *The daring escape of Ellen Craft*. Minneapolis, MN: Lerner.

Moss, L. (2001). *Our marching band*. New York: Putnam.

Moss, L., & Petit-Roulet, P. (2003). *Music is*. New York: Putnam.

Moss, L., & Priceman, M. (1995). *Zin! Zin! Zin!: A violin*. New York: Simon & Schuster.

Naylor, P. R. (1991). *Shiloh*. New York: Pearson Scott Foresman.

Oneyefulu, I. (1997). *A is for Africa*. New York: Puffin.

Oppenheim, J., & Reid, B. (1988). *Have you seen birds?* New York: Scholastic.

Orgill, R. (1997). *If only I had a horn: Young Louis Armstrong*. Boston: Houghton Mifflin.

Orozco, J. (2004). *Fiestas: A year of Latin American songs of celebration*. New York: Puffin.

Paul, A. W. (2000). *The seasons sewn: A year in patchwork*. San Diego, CA: Voyager.

Peck, J. (1998). *The giant carrot*. East Rutherford, NJ: Penguin-Putnam.

Pilkey, D. (1993). *Dogzilla*. San Diego, CA: Harcourt Brace Jovanovich.

Pinkney, A. D. (1998). *Duke Ellington: The Piano Prince and his orchestra*. New York: Jump Sun.

Pinkney, A. D. (2002). *Ella Fitzgerald: The tale of a vocal virtuosa*. New York: Jump Sun.

Pinkney, B. (1994). *Max found two sticks*. New York: Simon & Schuster.

Pinkney, J. (2003). *God bless the child*. New York: HarperCollins.

Polacco, P. (1988a). *Rechenka's eggs*. New York: Philomel.

Polacco, P. (1988b). *The keeping quilt*. New York: Simon & Schuster.

Polacco, P. (1990). *Chicken Sunday*. New York: Simon & Schuster.

Raffi. (1984). *A young children's concert with Raffi* [video recording]. Hollywood, CA: Shoreline/Troubadour.

Raschka, C. (1997). *Charlie Parker played be bop*. New York: Orchard.

Raschka, C. (2002). *John Coltrane's giant steps*. New York: Atheneum/Simon & Schuster.

Ray, D. K. (2001). *Hokusai: The man who painted a mountain*. New York: Farrar, Straus & Giroux.

Reid, B. (1993). *Two by two*. New York: Scholastic.

Reynolds, P. H. (2003). *The dot*. Cambridge, MA: Candlewick Press.

Ringgold, F. (1991). *Tar beach*. New York: Scholastic.

Roth, S. L. (2003). *Hanukkah, oh Hanukkah*. New York: Dial.

Sachar, L. (1998). *Holes*. New York: Random House.

Say, A. (1993). *Grandfather's journey*. Boston: Houghton Mifflin.

Say, A. (2003a). *Emma's rug*. Boston: Houghton Mifflin.

Say, A. (2003b). *Snow music*. New York: Greenwillow.

Say, A. (2004). *Music for Alice*. Boston: Houghton Mifflin.

Schotter, R., & Sewall, M. (1988). *Captain Snap and the children of Vinegar Lane*. New York: Orchard.

Schroeder, A. (1989). *Ragtime tumpie*. Boston: Little, Brown.

Scieszka, J. (1989). *The true story of the three little pigs!* New York: Penguin.

Seeger, P. (1986). *Abiyoyo*. New York: Macmillan.

Sendak, M. (1963). *Where the wild things are*. New York: Harper.

Serfozo, M. (1992). *Who said red?* New York: Aladdin.

Seuss, Dr. (1949). *Bartholomew and the oobleck*. New York: Random House.

Seuss, Dr. (1957). *The cat in the hat*. New York: Random House.

Shafer, A. C. (2003). *The fantastic journey of Pieter Bruegel*. New York: Dutton.

Shulevitz, U. (1988). *Dawn*. New York: Farrar, Straus & Giroux.

Shulman, S. (2004). *Old MacDonald had a woodshop*. New York: Puffin.

Slobodkina, E. (1947). *Caps for sale*. New York: Scott.

Smith, S. F. (2004). *My country 'tis of thee*. New York: Cartwheel/Scholastic.

Snape, J., & Snape, C. (1991). *Frog odyssey*. New York: MacRae.

Snyder, S. (1988). *The boy of the three-year nap*. New York: Scholastic.

Soto, G. (1992). *Neighborhood odes*. New York: Harcourt Brace.

Soto, G. (1997). *Chato's kitchen*. East Rutherford, NJ: Putnam.

Sounds of Blackness (1991). *The evolution of gospel* [audio recording]. New York: Polygram Records.

Spier, P. (1961). *The fox went out on a chilly night*. New York: Doubleday.

Spier, P. (1997). *Peter Spier's Rain.* New York: Doubleday Books for Young Readers.

Stanley, D. (1996). *Leonardo da Vinci.* New York: HarperCollins.

Steig, W. (1969). *Sylvester and the magic pebble.* New York: Prentice Hall.

Steig, W. (1982). *Doctor De Soto.* New York: Farrar, Straus & Giroux.

Steptoe, J. (1987). *Mufaro's beautiful daughters.* New York: Lothrop, Lee & Shepard.

Stevens, J. (1987). *The city mouse and the country mouse.* New York: Holiday House.

Stevens, J. (1995). *Tops and bottoms.* San Diego, CA: Harcourt Brace Jovanovich.

Stevens, J. (1996). *From pictures to words: A book about making a book.* New York: Holiday House.

Sweet Honey in the Rock (1989). *All for freedom* [audio recording]. Redmond, CA: Music for Little People.

Taback, S. (1997). *There was an old lady who swallowed a fly.* New York: Penguin Books.

Tafuri, N. (1988). *Junglewalk.* New York: Greenwillow.

Taylor, M. (2002). *Roll of thunder, hear my cry.* New York: Puffin.

Thimmesh, C. (2000). *Girls think of everything: Stories of ingenious inventions by women.* Boston: Houghton Mifflin.

Tucker, T. (1995). *Brainstorm: The stories of twenty American kid inventors.* New York: Farrar, Straus & Giroux.

Tunnell, M. O. (2000). *Mailing May.* New York: HarperCollins.

Turner, A. (1987). *Nettie's trip south.* New York: Simon & Schuster.

Udry, J. (2002). *The moon jumpers.* New York: HarperCollins.

Van Allsburg, C. (1988). *Two bad ants.* Boston: Houghton Mifflin.

Venezia, M. (1995). *Aaron Copland (Getting to know the world's most famous composers).* San Francisco: Children's Press.

Venezia, M. (1999). *John Philip Sousa.* San Francisco: Children's Press.

Walter, M. P. (1987). *Ty's one-man band.* New York: Simon & Schuster.

Warhola, J. (2003). *Uncle Andy's: A faabbbulous visit with Andy Warhol.* New York: Putnam.

Waters, K., & Slovenz-Low, M. (1990). *Lion Dancer: Ernie Wan's Chinese New Year.* New York: Scholastic.

Weiss, N. (1987). *If you're happy and you know it.* New York: Greenwillow.

Weitzman, J. P., & Glasser, R. P. (2002). *You can't take a balloon into the Museum of Fine Arts.* New York: Dial.

Wellington, M. (2002). *Squeaking of art.* New York: Dutton.

Wescott, N. B. (1987). *Peanut butter and jelly.* New York: Dutton.

Weston Woods. (2000a). *Duke Ellington: The Piano Prince and his orchestra* [video cassette]. New York: Top Dog Media.

Weston Woods. (2000b). *This Land Is Your Land* [video cassette]. New York: Top Dog Media.

White, E. B. (1952). *Charlotte's web.* New York: Harper & Row.

Williams, K. L. (1990). *Galimoto.* New York: Lothrop, Lee & Shepard.

Williams, K. L. (1994). *When Africa was home.* New York: Orchard.

Williams, S. (1992). *I went walking.* San Diego, CA: Harcourt Brace Jovanovich.

Williams, V. B. (1981). *Three days on a river in a red canoe.* New York: Greenwillow.

Williams, V. B. (1986). *Cherries and cherry pits.* New York: Greenwillow.

Williams, V. (1988). *Stringbean's trip to the shining sea.* New York: HarperCollins.

Winter, J. (1988). *Follow the drinking gourd.* New York: Knopf.

Wolff, A. (1984). *A year of birds.* New York: Dodd.

Wulffson, D. (2000). *Toys! Amazing stories behind some great inventions.* New York: Holt.

Wulffson, D. L. (1999). *The kid who invented the popsicle.* New York: Puffin.

Young, E. (1992). *Seven blind mice.* New York: Putnam.

Zelinsky, P. (1990). *The wheels on the bus.* New York: Dutton.

Zelinsky, P. O. (1986). *Rumpelstiltskin.* New York: Dutton.

Zelinsky, P. O. (1992). *Knick-knack paddy whack!* New York: Dutton.

Software

Bailey's Book House. (1993). Redmond, WA: Edmark.

Color Me. (1988). Northbrook, IL: Mindscape.

Crayola Make a Masterpiece. (2002). San Francisco: Selectsoft Publishing, 1999, Wisconsin Rapids, WI.

Cubby Magic: Folktales Around the World. (1999). Wisconsin Rapids, WI: Humanities Software.

Delta Draw. (1988). Cambridge, MA: Spinnaker.

Facemaker. (1986). Cambridge, MA: Spinnaker.

Fantastic Animals: Mix-Up Puzzler. (1990). New York: Bantam 500.

I Can Be a Dinosaur Finder. (1999). Carson, CA: Educational Insights.

I Spy. (1997). New York: Scholastic New Media.

Kid Desk! Internet Safe. (1999). Redmond, WA: Edmark.

Kid Pix 2. (1994). Novato: CA: Broderbund.

Kid Works 2. (1992). Torrance, CA: Davidson & Associates.

Millie and Bailey Preschool. (1997). Redmond, WA: Edmark.

Millie's Math House. (1993). Redmond, WA: Edmark.

Reader Rabbit. (1989). Fremont, CA: The Learning Company.

Richard Scarry's How Things Work in Busytown. (1990). Menlo Park, CA: Paramount.

SimCity 2000. (1994). Walnut Creek, CA: Maxis.

Storybook Weaver. (1992). Minneapolis, MN: MECC.

Thinkin' Things. (1993). Redmond, WA: Edmark.

Wiggins in Storyland. (1994). Fremont, CA: Media Vision.

Blue's Clues 1 2 3 Time Activities. (1999). Woodinville, WA: Humongous Entertainment.

Glossary

Note to the student: A glossary should be used to help you remember terms with which you are familiar. For a deeper understanding of any of these terms, we encourage you to reread the chapter sections in which those terms appear. The chapter reference is in parentheses.

active learning Concrete experiences that are "hands-on," challenging, and relevant to the learner. (Chapter 2)

adventure or "junk" playgrounds Collections of tools and materials that allow children to build, create, and pretend using these items outdoors. (Chapter 6)

aesthetic Having to do with feelings, ideas, and perceptions about beauty. (Chapter 4)

affective Describes feelings or emotional responses. (Chapter 4)

autocratic Demanding obedience, following specific rules, and imposing inflexible standards on behavior. (Chapter 8)

behaviorism The view that a person's environment is the most important variable in shaping his or her development. (Chapter 8)

brainstorming Generating as many ideas as possible without evaluating them in order to enhance creativity. (Chapter 5)

center-based classroom A classroom arranged into various areas each containing interesting and accessible materials that offer children choices and support their independence. (Chapter 6)

child-centered Describes activities and programs that base decisions and policies on the needs of the children and place concerns about the learners first. (Chapter 6)

classical theories Theories about play that sought to explain the causes and purposes of play from the nineteenth century through World War I. (Chapter 2)

climate The feeling created by a learning environment. (Chapter 6)

cognitive Having to do with knowledge, understanding, and intellectual growth. (Chapter 4)

cognitive-development theory Jean Piaget's view of how children's intellectual abilities develop and progress through a series of stages. (Chapter 2)

complex units Units with subparts made of two totally different elements for children to manipulate or invent. (Chapter 6)

conflict resolution A problem-solving process enabling children to understand and resolve their disputes or disagreements peacefully. (Chapter 8)

construction materials Varied materials that children can combine and recombine to build something. (Chapter 7)

constructive play Creating or engaging in problem-solving behavior according to a preconceived plan. (Chapter 2)

constructivism The belief that children are more than passive recipients of information and actively build their own understandings. Based on Piaget's cognitive-developmental theory. (Chapter 8)

controlled scribbles Scribbles with a definite shape that are produced when the child has better control over the writing implement. (Chapter 3)

convergent Describes materials or experiences that lead children to think about a single answer or one right way of arriving at a solution. (Chapter 7)

cooperative learning Working collaboratively in a group to achieve a common goal. (Chapter 8)

creative/contemporary playgrounds Superstructures with movable parts that are action-oriented, provide safe underneath surfaces, and promote all forms of play. (Chapter 6)

creative teachers Educators who are committed to supporting children's play and facilitating children's creative expression. (Chapter 8)

creativity A thinking and responding process that involves connecting with our previous experience, responding to stimuli, and generating at least one unique combination. (Chapter 1)

democratic Having high expectations, understanding child development, showing and expecting respect, allowing decision making, and setting reasonable limits for behavior and practices. (Chapter 8)

developmentally appropriate materials Materials, experiences, and activities that are carefully matched to the children's developmental levels. (Chapter 7)

divergent Describes materials and experiences designed to elicit many different student responses that promote exploration, experimentation, and problem-solving. (Chapter 7)

dramatic play The child's use of props, plot, and roles to symbolize real or imaginary experiences. Also referred to as pretend, fantasy, make-believe, or symbolic play. Dramatic play is typical of 2- to 7-year-olds. (Chapter 2)

enactive stage The developmental stage during which physical activity and music are intertwined. (Chapter 4)

enactment Adopting actions, feelings, thoughts, and behaviors of people in particular situations. This ability typically begins at age 3. (Chapter 5)

formal or scripted drama The most structured dramatic form, which includes a prepared script used in a practiced production and is viewed by an audience. (Chapter 5)

functional play Simple, pleasurable, repeated movements with objects, people, and language to learn new skills or to gain mastery of a physical or mental skill. Also referred to as sensorimotor, practice, or exercise play and typical of infants and toddlers. (Chapter 2)

game A form of play in which children follow a set of predetermined rules and procedures and assign players specific roles. (Chapter 7)

gross motor materials Materials designed to foster large muscle activity and coordination. (Chapter 7)

hands-on materials Manipulatives that children can use to enhance their understanding and learning; promote learning by doing. (Chapter 5)

hollow blocks Large wooden blocks with an opening for carrying. (Chapter 7)

humanism The belief that people are capable of controlling their lives through choice, creativity, and self-realization. (Chapter 8)

iconic stage The developmental stage during which children use pictures and real objects to represent ideas and experiences. (Chapter 4)

imagination The ability to form rich and varied mental images or concepts of people, places, things, and situations that are not present. (Chapter 1)

indirect guidance Child-centered strategies that teachers use to plan, arrange, and manage people and classroom space, materials, and schedules. (Chapter 8)

informal drama Spontaneous enactments that include dramatic and sociodramatic play, pantomime, and movement activities. (Chapter 5)

investigative play Actively exploring and experimenting during play. (Chapter 8)

learner-centered art Allowing children to direct their own work, valuing the process as much as the product, and fostering originality rather than conformity. (Chapter 3)

manipulative materials Concrete materials that aid small muscle activity in the fingers and hands, basic concepts, and eye-hand coordination. (Chapter 7)

medium The means or channel through which the artist conveys a message. (Chapter 3)

modern theories Theories of play, prominent after World War I, that emphasize the consequences of play for children. (Chapter 2)

multicultural education Learning that respects and celebrates children's diversity (ethnic, racial, religious). (Chapter 5)

naming of scribbling Children's verbal labeling of a scribble they have produced. (Chapter 3)

natural and everyday materials Materials with specific nonplay purposes—such as rocks, leaves, sand, buttons, and pots and pans—that children can use to employ imaginative and divergent thinking and to imitate and model adult roles. (Chapter 7)

nonrepresentational drawing A stage in children's drawing in which drawings do not resemble the items being represented. (Chapter 3)

one-way communication A focus on messages from the school to the family. (Chapter 8)

permissive Having a disinterested attitude that results in an inconsistent environment and fails to promote children's self-control. (Chapter 8)

play-debrief-replay Wassermann's three-step model for organizing instruction and challenging primary-grade children's divergent thinking. (Chapter 8)

practice theory A theory that proposes that play prepares children for the future roles and responsibilities needed to survive in their culture. (Chapter 2)

preschematic Describes children's drawings that are just beginning to represent the object being depicted, yet are difficult for adults to interpret without the child's explanation. (Chapter 3)

process An emphasis on the way something (such as a piece of artwork) is produced, including the problem-solving strategies used and the originality or inventiveness exhibited. (Chapter 3)

project An in-depth study that is usually initiated, planned, and evaluated by the children. (Chapter 8)

prop boxes or dramatic play kits Collections of real items or props that have a relation to one another. For example, a chef's hat, apron, cookware, and plastic food could be in a prop box for a restaurant center. (Chapter 5)

psychoanalytic theory A theory that perceives play as an important outlet for emotional release and for developing self-esteem as children learn to control their thoughts, bodies, objects, and social behaviors. (Chapter 2)

random scribbling Random marks that are produced by toddlers when the writing implement happens to make contact with the writing surface. (Chapter 3)

readers' theater A form of interpretive drama during which readers assume a role, read, and orally interpret the parts of the story that relate to their role. (Chapter 5)

recapitulation theory A theory that proposes that play enables children to revisit activities of their ancestors and shed any negative behaviors in order to prepare them for living in today's world. (Chapter 2)

recreation/relaxation theory A theory that suggests that play replenishes or "re-creates" energy used in work. (Chapter 2)

referent An object or symbol that stands for something else. (Chapter 3)

repeated shapes A stage in children's drawing where scribbling is well controlled and small geometric shapes are repeated, almost like designs. (Chapter 3)

representational art A stage in children's drawing in which the drawings begin to resemble the items being depicted. (Chapter 3)

representational use Children's intentionally planning and acting on ideas and ways familiar to their world. (Chapter 7)

room arrangement The way space is organized for children's learning and movement. (Chapter 6)

schematic A category of children's drawings in which the child's work clearly resembles the objects drawn. (Chapter 3)

self-expressive materials Resources that encourage children to experiment with various roles, feelings, and behaviors and express them through drama, music, and art. (Chapter 7)

simple units Play materials that have no apparent use with no subparts for children to manipulate or create. (Chapter 6)

skill and concept materials Materials that are prescriptive and product-oriented. (Chapter 7)

sociocultural theory A view that learning occurs in a social context and is fundamentally social in nature. The major vehicle for learning is interaction with an emulation of role models. (Chapter 2)

sociodramatic play Symbolic play that involves two or more children who communicate verbally about the play episode and enact social roles. (Chapter 2)

space The degree to which the physical environment is arranged to develop active, creative thinkers. (Chapter 6)

story or interpretive drama Interpretive drama creating a rendition or reenactment of someone else's ideas and words, often based on children's literature. (Chapter 5)

story play or story dictation Guided drama using children's original stories as the content for enactment. (Chapter 5)

supercomplex units Play materials having three or more subparts that children can juxtapose. (Chapter 6)

surplus-energy theory A view that human beings have certain amounts of energy to be used for survival, and the excess energy not spent forms a surplus that is expended through play. (Chapter 2)

symbolic play The child's use of props, plot, and roles to symbolize real or imaginary experiences. Also referred to as pretend, dramatic or sociodramatic, fantasy, or make-believe play. Symbolic play is typical of 2- to 7-year-olds. (Chapter 2)

symbolic stage The developmental stage during which a child uses abstract symbols, especially language, to represent ideas and experiences. (Chapter 4)

table blocks A variety of small, colored cubed blocks used alone or in pairs on a table or hard surface. (Chapter 7)

three-way communication Collaborating among the home, school, and community to support children's creative expression. (Chapter 8)

time A feature of creative environments that conveys a clear message about the importance of an activity or experience. (Chapter 6)

toys Materials specifically designed for children's play and learning. Toys and playthings reflect their society, politics, and cultural issues. (Chapter 7)

traditional playgrounds Playgrounds containing large, steel, immovable equipment designed for physical exercise outdoors. (Chapter 6)

two-way communication A dialogue between schools and families that encourages and respects families' contributions to the interaction. (Chapter 8)

unit blocks A set of large, smooth hardwood blocks in a wide array of shapes used for constructive play and large building projects on the floor. (Chapter 7)

water table A raised frame that holds a large container of water so that several children can stand next to it and engage in water play with toys, various types of plastic containers, or tubing. (Chapter 7)

Index

Note: Page numbers followed by letters *f* and *t* indicate figures and tables, respectively.